A

POPULATION AND CULTURE

Culture

and

Human Fertility

A Study of the Relation
of Cultural Conditions to
Fertility in Non-industrial and
Transitional Societies

by

FRANK LORIMER

With special contributions by
Meyer Fortes, K. A. Busia, Audrey I. Richards
Priscilla Reining and Giorgio Mortara
Foreword by Frank W. Notestein

Under the auspices of the International Union
for the Scientific Study of Population
(Committee on Population Problems of Countries in
Process of Industrialization)
in co-operation with the United Nations
Educational, Scientific and Cultural Organization

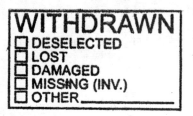

GREENWOOD PRESS, PUBLISHERS
NEW YORK

Preface

by
FRANK W. NOTESTEIN

In 1951 the International Union for the Scientific Study of Population established a Committee on Population Problems of Countries in Process of Industrialization. In view of the limited financial resources of the union, it was expected that the committee would do little more than represent the union in matters touching its field of competence as opportunity arose.

The first such opportunity came when the United Nations Educational, Scientific and Cultural Organization offered to underwrite the costs of a study of social and cultural conditions affecting fertility in non-industrial societies to be carried out under the auspices of the committee. The survey was undertaken as part of Unesco's programme for promoting cross-national, cross-disciplinary understanding of population problems, and was regarded as a very significant contribution toward that goal. In this project the committee's active members have been Professor Raymond Firth, Dr. Alberto Arca Parró and the undersigned as chairman. In view of the wide separation and heavy commitments of the members it seemed quite impossible for the committee to become an efficient operating body. It was, therefore, decided to ask Professor Frank Lorimer of the American University to undertake the assignment for the committee.

It gives us great pleasure to present the results of Professor Lorimer's work. Part One deals with problems of general theory, the remaining parts present the results of a number of special studies undertaken by scholars collaborating with him for the purpose of this investigation upon whose work he has drawn heavily in developing his general theory. We hope other students of population will derive as much interest and stimulus as we have in reviewing the work of Professor Lorimer and his colleagues.

The study attempts to develop coherent interpretations of a large mass of diverse demographic, anthropological and other scientific evidence. The committee believes these formulations have value, especially as presenting hypotheses for research and revealing points at which more precise information is needed. Professor Firth, as an anthropologist, and I, as a demographer, have reservations with respect to some of the interpretations. Other scholars who have seen the manuscript support interpretations with which we would disagree. Professor Lorimer himself has indicated that his inferences at many

points are tentative formulations. The committee, like the author, presents the study to the public, not as a definitive formulation of the many complex aspects of this subject, but as a significant and valuable, though necessarily subjective, interpretation. The committee shares the author's hope that the publication of this work will lead to more intensive scientific investigations and more definitive knowledge in the future. We believe that Professor Lorimer's work, because it is his own untrammeled product, will accomplish more, both constructively and provocatively, than could be expected at this stage from a study that achieved unanimous agreement by an emasculating compromise.

Finally, we wish to express our deep gratitude to Professor Lorimer for the energy, imagination and scholarly dedication with which he has approached his arduous task.

CONTENTS

PART ONE

General Theory

by
FRANK LORIMER

Levels of fertility in non-industrial societies generally loom high as against modern European experience. There has, therefore, been a tendency to treat information on the fertility of any non-industrial society as merely another illustration of this general antithesis. Relatively little effort has been spent on investigating the influence of particular cultural conditions on fertility in different primitive and agrarian societies, or on the study of ways in which these conditions may influence future trends of fertility.[1]

A mass of incidental, though generally inconclusive, evidence on this subject is available in historical, anthropological, sociological and demographic studies. The present study explores some of this information in a search for clues to specific relationships between culture and fertility. Information from various sources is brought into focus in the hope that a synoptic view may reveal some general relationships. The material presented below is purposely selected from a wide preliminary search. Such an eclectic treatment is necessarily subject to bias, and cannot provide definite conclusions. It may, however, yield evidence that will enable us to reject some hypotheses, and to formulate alternative hypotheses that can be tested in intensive studies.

Several general theories in this field have been advanced by modern scholars. A brief critical review of these theories leads to the statement of a different approach that will be emphasized in the present enquiry.

The classic statement of one current theory of the relation of culture to fertility in non-industrial societies was formulated by Carr-Saunders in 1922.[2] After an extensive review of anthropological literature on societies at different technical levels in all parts of the world, he concluded that the evolution of human culture brought a universal tendency toward the

---

[1] The paucity of information on this subject is indicated in the chapter, 'Social and Economic Conditions Affecting Fertility' in *The Determinants and Consequences of Population Trends: A Summary of the Relationships between Population Changes and Economic and Social Conditions*, United Nations, 1954.

[2] A. M. Carr-Saunders. *The Population Problem. A Study in Human Evolution.* Oxford, 1922.

maintenance of an 'optimum population' appropriate to the resources of each area and the economic technology of its occupants. The author noted certain practices which 'incidentally' limit the increase of population. He listed under this head pre-puberty sexual intercourse, prolonged lactation, war, and negligence in the care of children. Such factors were assumed to contribute to the reduction of the margin of natural increase above an 'optimum' trend. In addition to such practices, there was assumed to be an almost universal resort to explicit measures for the control of population.

'There is another class of factors the primary and not the incidental function of which is either to reduce fertility or to cause elimination. These factors are prolonged abstention from intercourse, abortion, and infanticide. The view put forward here is that normally in every primitive race one or more of these customs are in use, and that the degree to which they are practised is such that there is an approach to the "optimum" number.'[1]

A review of information on abortion, infanticide, and abandonment of infirm or aged persons under stress of necessity (especially in Australia, the Arctic, and some Pacific areas), and of the abstention from sex relations with a woman who is nursing an infant (widely prevalent in Africa) is followed by a theory of the origin and maintenance of these customs.

'It is now clear how these factors originate. Among more or less nomadic peoples[2] abortion and infanticide are practised because of the difficulty of transporting and of suckling more than one child at a time. Abstention from intercourse arises as a taboo. The problem we have to face is how these practices could come to be of the necessary intensity. Now men and groups of men are naturally selected on account of the customs they practise. . . . Few customs could be more advantageous than those which limit the number of a group to the desirable number, and . . . once any of these three customs had originated—it would by a process of natural selection come to be so practised that it would produce an approximation to the desirable number. . . . To all members of such a group, confined as they are within the knowledge of them all to a limited area, the disadvantages of too many mouths must be obvious. Therefore even among the more primitive races there may be some semi-conscious adjustment of numbers by means of one of these methods. However . . . even if there is no semi-conscious deliberation among the lower groups, there is to some extent an automatic adjustment to the needs of the moment.'[3]

A contrary theory (formulated chiefly with reference to Asiatic agrarian societies) has been advanced by several American demographers in

[1] ibid., p. 214.
[2] The author refers here to primitive nomadism with a hunting and gathering economy, not to the advanced nomadism of pastoral societies.
[3] ibid., pp. 222–3.

16

recent years. This theory has been concisely stated by Notestein as follows:

'Any society having to face the heavy mortality characteristic of the premodern era must have high fertility to survive. All such societies are therefore ingeniously arranged to obtain the required births. Their religious doctrines, moral codes, laws, education, community customs, marriage habits, and family organization are all focused toward maintaining high fertility.'[1]

A somewhat modified statement of this thesis, referring to birth rates in pre-modern Europe, is presented by the same author in a later article, as follows:

'Although they [birth rates in Europe] were lower than in Colonial America, or in the Orient today, they were high by present standards. Indeed, they had to be high. We may take it for granted that all populations surviving to the modern period in the face of inevitably high mortality had both the physiological capacity and the social organizations necessary to produce high birth rates.'[2]

A somewhat intermediate position with respect to the control of fertility in primitive societies has been formulated on the basis of a survey of information in the files of the 'Cross-Cultural Survey' at the Institute of Human Relations, Yale University.

'Human reproduction is effected by biological processes assisted by learned behaviour. The customs which are thus in adjustment to the imperfections of the human biological processes of reproduction arise from a desire to bear children. This wish for offspring is not an innate component of human nature; it is not a basic drive. On the contrary, it is an acquired motive which is constantly being reinforced by social rewards and punishments. Promises of security, approval, and prestige support the desire for children; threats of insecurity, punishment and ridicule block incipient wishes to escape the pains and cares of childbirth and parenthood. . . .

'Conflicting with the desire for children are other motives. Paramount among these is the wish to avoid pain and suffering. Childbirth is an unpleasant experience. The woman who becomes pregnant finds herself increasingly handicapped and frustrated. . . . She fears that her labour will be painful, that her child may be deformed or stillborn, and that she may die in childbirth. She knows that after her baby is born she must spend the greater proportion of her time attending to its wants. From such frustration and fears as these comes the wish to avoid conception and its sequels of pregnancy and birth. . . . If people are to

---

[1] F. Notestein. 'Population—the Long View', *Food for the World*, T. Schulz, Editor, Chicago, 1945, p. 39.
[2] F. Notestein. 'Economic Problems of Population Change.' Mimeographed copy of address to Eighth International Conference of Agricultural Economists, Michigan State College, 15–22 August 1952.

reproduce, social life must offer enough rewards for bearing children to more than outweigh the punishments involved in reproduction.'[1]
In another publication the same author offers certain generalizations concerning the control of conception 'obtained by examining data on 200 societies from all over the world'.

'*Attempts to Induce Conception.* A particularly striking fact emerging from this survey is the universal concern over the inability of an adult woman to conceive. In nearly every one of these societies, the barren woman is either an object of pity or scorn. . . . Practices designed to promote fertility are completed by prescriptions on the diet and sexual behavior of pregnant women . . . notably abstention from sexual intercourse during the entire period, or at least the last few months of pregnancy. These prescriptions are accompanied by miscellaneous rules. Considering also the extreme pressures against childlessness, they express in eloquent fashion society's interest in reproduction, as viewed in cross-cultural perspective.

'*Attempts to Prevent Conception.* . . . Viewed in cross-cultural perspective, both abortion and infanticide are universally known. In nearly every society, they are practiced at least occasionally. At the same time, it is also clear that strong social pressures are brought to bear against any excessive indulgence in abortion and infanticide. . . . Contraceptive attempts are not . . . viewed as sinful or criminal in most societies, and some sort of device to prevent conception is available to the members of practically all the societies in our sample. These techniques designed to prevent conception vary markedly in their probable effectiveness. Some are so clearly magical that they may be dismissed at once as having no practical effect. Others, just as clearly, are relatively effective. . . .

'Emerging from this brief survey of the control of conception in cross-cultural perspective is the impression of a *delicate balance* between pressures toward bearing children and tendencies to avoid birth.'[2] [Italics added.]

Each of the positions described above is based on substantial evidence, and each is at least partially valid. Yet, in the judgment of the present writer, none gives adequate recognition to the diversity of cultural conditions influencing fertility in different societies, with proper attention to their basic social structures and major characteristics.

We will find that some stable cultures do tend to promote a very high level of fertility, with almost complete absence of restraining factors. On the other hand, practices tending toward the restriction of fertility are

---

[1] Clellan Stearns Ford. *A Comparative Study of Human Reproduction.* Yale University Publications in Anthropology, No. 3, 1945, pp. 86–7.

[2] Ford. 'Control of Conception in Cross-cultural Perspective' in 'World Population Problems and Birth Control', Conference Chairman, C. G. Hartmann, *Annals of the New York Academy of Sciences*, Vol. 54, Article 5, 1952, pp. 763–76.

strongly emphasized in some other societies. In still other societies, cultural conditions may be characterized as ambivalent or neutral with respect to the reinforcement or restraint of biological factors conducive to reproduction. This may be attributed to a 'delicate balance' within such a culture between contrary forces, or simply to its 'indifference' with respect to reproduction. One of these interpretations may be more appropriate in some cases, and the other in other cases.

It is obvious that our proto-human ancestors, prior to the rise of culture, achieved effective reproduction. Presumably they did so with essentially the same biological equipment and basic psychological impulses as modern man, and without institutional sanctions. We may, to be sure, assume that proto-human females were not deeply moved by sentiments arising from consideration of the pains and deprivations of maternity. But the force of such sentiments in most primitive societies is also subject to doubt. Little girls have mothers. They grow up expecting to become mothers, with some awareness that this experience will bring both hardships and satisfactions. Little boys similarly expect to follow the roles of their fathers. Their associates naturally assume that these expectations will be fulfilled. Biological impulses motivate appropriate response. This basic pattern tending toward the replacement of generations requires no ingenious interpretation in terms of cunning design or the differential survival of beneficent innovations, though the basic pattern may be profoundly modified in different cultures.

The rise of culture brought stable social relations and complex motivations. Conceivably this was associated with some decline in capacity for procreation, but there is absolutely no evidence to support such a supposition. On the other hand, the rise of culture may or may not have increased the probabilities of conception, but it must have increased the chances of successful gestation and parturition, and the chances of survival from infancy to maturity. The maintenance of effective reproduction would, therefore, appear to require only that new motivations toward the suppression of reproduction be balanced, at least in part, by new positive motivations. We may properly affirm that any surviving culture must be compatible with effective reproduction, but this is different from saying that it must provide powerful sanctions for reproduction.

Again, the available evidence, as interpreted by the present writer, does not support the hypothesis that cultural forces tend universally to promote a nice adjustment of population to resources within constant areas. The living space of most primitive societies is frequently contracted or expanded with the waxing and waning in relative power of competing societies on its margins. And the record of famines, wars and migrations points toward recurrent maladjustment in the relations of people and resources, rather than toward the maintenance of an 'optimum' population in each tribal territory. The motivation for achieving such adjustment may be more compulsive for some island populations, but even relatively small islands are frequently occupied by several distinct and antagonistic societies.

All of the theories mentioned above, in spite of their partial validity, appear to suffer from a common limitation. In each case, the reproductive practices of particular societies are treated apart from the total social structures within which these practices are operative. Practices in this sphere of human behaviour are then interpreted directly with reference to some universal economic or demographic needs or universal psychological motivations. Such universal needs and motivations must be constantly kept in mind and given proper emphasis. But progress made along other lines in recent decades in the study of culture suggests the utility of a different approach.

Attempts to describe the evolution of social institutions, stimulated by the success achieved in studies of organic evolution, have generally led to conflicting and inconclusive theories. Limited insights into the conditions of prehistoric human society are provided by painstaking paleontological and archeological investigations, by studies of human biology, and by the analysis of diverse contemporary societies. But it is widely recognized today that the present institutions of all societies have emerged from such tangled webs of interacting tradition and experience that it is impossible to unravel the lines of their origin and early development.

The attempt to relate human behaviour to biological needs, environmental conditions, and changes in economic technology has also proved less promising than it appeared to be a few decades ago. Such an approach does offer some significant contributions to an understanding of the growth and distribution of the world's population. It also contributes to an understanding of the common basis of all familial and kinship systems, and reveals some specific conditions that have influenced all social life. But it offers a very inadequate approach to the investigation of the many subtle and complex forces that determine the patterns of human culture.

Modern anthropologists usually place major emphasis on the interpretation of particular social institutions through the examination of their 'functions', in association with other factors, in the whole life of any society. This approach is based on the thesis that the various elements of the culture of any society must interact to provide an adequate basis for some degree of social stability. The efficacy of this thesis as an instrument of analysis has been demonstrated in many studies. But here too we must be cautious. Even in the organic world some phenomena, say a chickadee's black cap or the rhythm of his song, cannot readily be interpreted in functional terms. And no human society is so completely integrated as a biological organism. Even in cases where it is possible to define the 'core values' of a particular society, the same values may be served by a variety of alternative institutions. Furthermore, any living society must tolerate a wide range of individual deviations, and it may include incongruous elements, adopted from other cultures and only partially assimilated.

20

These problems are, of course, recognized by anthropologists who stress a functional approach; they point to the importance of studying relations between traditional social patterns and deviant behaviour, modifications of institutions 'borrowed' from another society to perform new functions in the society that adopts them, and modification of the indigenous institutions of a society under new conditions.

There has recently been a new emphasis on the attempt to test by precise statistical enquiries some of the critical inferences drawn from such studies. This is illustrated in the work of Barnes, Mitchell, and their associates on the relation of stability of marriage to type of kinship structure.[1] This approach suggests that a closer integration of cultural and demographic studies may result in important contributions to our understanding of human affairs. Unfortunately in the present study we can merely suggest some of these possibilities in very general terms.

The purpose of this study may then be restated as an examination of cultural conditions affecting fertility in different non-industrial societies in the context of their social organization and cultural values—especially with respect to the organization of the family and kinship relations and, at a later stage, with respect to degrees of social mobility. Owing to the scope of the undertaking and the author's limitations, this purpose can be carried out only in a tentative and exploratory way.

[1] See, for example, J. A. Barnes, 'Measures of Divorce Frequency', *Royal Anthropology Institute of Great Britain and Ireland*, Vol. 89, Nos. 1 and 2, 1949.

CHAPTER I

Capacity for Procreation
and Levels of Natality

THE NATURE OF THE PROBLEM

It is important, in considering the extent to which the tendency to have children is released or repressed in different societies, to have some idea of the potential capacity of human stocks for the production of living offspring. What level of natality would be attained in a population in which all social factors were conducive to the maximum expression of fecundity?[1]

No precise answer to this question, even for a particular population, can be given at present. It is obvious that there are wide individual variations in procreative capacity. Some couples are incapable of a single live birth; other couples have more than twenty children. It is therefore possible that average procreative capacity may vary appreciably among different racial stocks and among different strains within the same stock. Here, as in most questions relating to possible variations in genetic capacities in man, we have no scientific basis for any general assertion or denial. Again, capacity for procreation is influenced by environmental conditions affecting physical development, such as nutrition, mode of living, climate, etc.[2] The whole subject of human fecundity is extremely complex and has not yet received adequate attention in medical, biological, and demographic research. The only positive assertions that can be made with assurance are that there are important variations in fecundity among people living in different conditions, but that in general variations among human populations in natality are more powerfully influenced by social and psychological factors.

[1] In present English demographic usage 'fecundity' refers to *capacity* to produce living offspring; 'fertility' refers to actual performance. In French demographic literature the cognate terms have the opposite meaning: 'fertilité' refers to capacity; 'fécondité' refers to performance. The term 'reproduction' is usually understood to refer to the net effect of procreative tendency and the tendency to survive from birth to procreative ages. The terms 'procreative capacity' and 'natality' appear free from ambiguity, but have not been widely used in English literature. The term 'fertility' is, therefore, generally used in this text to mean 'natality', except where such use might lead to confusion. More explicit terminology is used here to avoid ambiguity.

[2] Recognition of this general principle does not, in itself, give any support to extravagant assertions about the role of any particular factor without efficient control of other factors. See, for example, the recent book by Josue de Castro, *The Geography of Hunger* (Boston, 1952), and the review of this book by Kingsley Davis in *The American Sociological Review*, Vol. 17, No. 4, August 1952.

The fecundity of individuals is affected by many physiological factors. Either males or females may be absolutely sterile. In some cases, the union of a particular male and a particular female may be sterile although each may be fecund in other unions.[1] It is, therefore, possible that the mean fecundity of populations in which non-fecund marriages are likely to be dissolved and in which the separate persons promptly take other spouses, or in which there is considerable promiscuity, under conditions not conducive to disease or acute social conflict, might be raised by such practices. On the other hand, tolerance of promiscuity, especially prior to puberty, may lower final fecundity, even in isolated societies not exposed to venereal diseases. There is little or no reliable evidence on this subject. We will, therefore, generally limit our attention merely to the capacity to produce viable offspring under the usual conditions of marriage prevailing in any society.

Promiscuity is clearly conducive to low fecundity in a population in which it becomes associated with a high frequency of venereal diseases. Low natality in such populations, though due indirectly to cultural conditions, may be mainly the result of an increase in sterility. The relation between culture and natality in this case is real, but indirect; it may also coincide with the spread of anti-natal practices in the culture of the same society. We will return to this topic at a later point (Chapter III).

Another area on the borderline between cultural and physiological conditions affecting fertility involves the frequency of coitus. Apart from specific timing with reference to knowledge about ovulation, the chance of conception in any given period rises to a hypothetical point with increased frequency of coitus; beyond this point the chances of conception are reduced, through decrease in number of active spermatozoa released in each sexual union and in other ways. But, again, the possible influence on natality of variations in patterns of sexual behaviour must for the most part be ignored here. We should, however, bear in mind the possible influence on fertility in different societies of decline of sexual activity with advance in age prior to the complete eclipse of procreative capacity.

Many of the problems mentioned above are resolved by limiting our attention, as already suggested, to 'the capacity to produce viable offspring under the usual conditions of marriage and sexual behaviour prevailing in any society'. But this leads directly to a new difficulty which complicates the interpretation of much of the information at our disposal—namely, the possible selectivity of marriage in many societies with respect to fecundity. This problem is negligible in a society, such as the Hindu, in which marriage is almost universal and is arranged at a very early age, often prior to puberty. It is also negligible in a population in which it can be assumed that all mature individuals are exposed to frequent risk of

[1] Edward Reynolds and Donald Macomber. *Fertility and Sterility in Human Marriages.* Philadelphia, 1924.

pregnancy without respect to marital condition. But in most societies neither of these extreme conditions prevails. In Western European society marriage is usually delayed until long after puberty; but sexual relations are frequently established between men and women who contemplate marriage but who have not made precise and irrevocable arrangements for marriage. Under such circumstances the decision to marry at a particular time may be influenced by the advent of pregnancy. Therefore in many countries those who marry at an unconventionally early age tend to be 'selected', or differentiated, from the rest of the population with respect to their fecundity.[1]

Even apart from the question of selectivity, the occurrence of premarital conceptions complicates the interpretation of information on nuptial fertility. Thus in some European countries there are about 500 legitimate births per year per 1000 married women under 20 years of age. Such a high rate is never found in a population in which most women are married at very early ages. Moreover, most of the married women under 20 years of age in European countries at any given moment are within one or two years of their twentieth birthday. If a rate obtained in this way is treated as an average rate over a five-year period, and used in computing total nuptial maternity ratio, the resultant estimate is seriously distorted.

The possibility of selective differentiation among 'cohorts' of couples married at different ages seriously complicates the interpretation of information on the frequency of childlessness, and on levels of completed fertility.[2] This is one among several major pitfalls in the way of our present undertaking. The problem is encountered not only in European societies, but also in some Oriental societies and, perhaps most acutely, in societies with many informal or 'consensual unions'.

---

[1] The frequency of premarital conception in Europe is indicated by a ratio of 144 births during the first year after marriage (resulting from conceptions prior to marriage or during the first few months thereafter) per 100 births during the second year, in nine European countries for which precise data for the year 1939 are presented in the United Nations *Demographic Yearbook, 1949–50*, whereas the expected ratio without premarital conceptions would be in the vicinity of one-half this figure. Countries where duration of marriage is calculated by calendar years are excluded in this computation. For discussion of such indices, see W. A. B. Hopkins and J. Hajnal, 'Analysis of Births in England and Wales, 1939, by Father's Occupation, Part 1', *Population Studies*, September, 1947; also J. Bourgeois-Pichat, *Mesure de la fécondité des populations*, Paris, 1950. Premarital pregnancies were admitted by 23 per cent of the British wives married before 1925 and by 17 per cent of those married thereafter in the sample described by E. Lewis-Faning, *Report on Family Limitation and its Influence on Human Fertility during the Past Fifty Years* (Papers of the Royal Commission on Population, Volume I) London, 1949, Table 68, p. 94.

[2] The term 'cohort' is used in demography (originally in studies of mortality) to refer to a class of individuals or couples whose behaviour is observed during a time-sequence, with analogy to the experience of a military cohort which retains its identity although progressively depleted in successive engagements.

OBSERVED LEVELS OF FERTILITY IN POPULATIONS RELATIVELY FREE FROM ANTI-NATAL PRACTICES[1]

After these initial warnings, we will review some information on observed rates in societies characterized by high fertility, and will then proceed to a more analytical approach. A series of age-specific rates that can be accepted as representative of the highest reasonably reliable rates of this sort now available is given in Table 1. Evidence on still higher levels of fertility in some populations for which age-specific rates are not available will be examined shortly.

There are obvious irregularities in the age-specific rates shown in Table 2. In many cases these may be due to errors in reports concerning the ages of persons in the populations, or the ages of mothers when giving birth. In some cases all rates for an area may be deflated by under-registration of births. However the Japanese data and the Brazilian data are obtained from census reports, and the former have been found to be quite free from serious errors. Again, the fertility rates for married women at ages 15–19 years and at ages 20–24 in most countries tend to be inflated by the selective factors noted above. The Chinese data and the Indian data are derived from special surveys, under conditions designed to increase accuracy, but in the face of appreciable difficulties. The fertility rate for married women in the Yangtze area at ages 15–19 years (0.204) is not far above that (0.177) for Indian women in the Mysore area, where bias due to selective factors at marriage might be assumed to be at a minimum. The rates for Chinese women in Malaya (regardless of marital condition) are estimated rates, derived by Smith from a combined series of data adjusted to eliminate assumed errors.

The extreme deviations in each age class in this series (unsupported by equally high rates reported for another area) are especially suspect. If we select the highest reported marital fertility rate for Indian women at ages 15–19 years (which is assumed to be especially significant in view of their early marriages), and then arbitrarily select the *second* to the top rates at all other ages, we obtain the series shown in Table 2. The summation of these rates (multiplied by five) gives 7.45 births per woman during the childbearing period as a hypothetical total maternity ratio. Little im-

---

[1] Indices of fertility used in this text are defined and the interrelations among these indices are examined in a supplement, to be published separately: Frank Lorimer, *Measures of Fertility*, The American University Bureau of Social Science Research, 1954.

The terms 'maternity rates' and 'maternity ratios' are used in this text to express relations between frequencies of live births and numbers of women at specified ages in a population. The term 'rate' is limited to measures involving frequencies of events within a specified period of time (e.g. one year). The average number of live births per woman is referred to as a 'maternity ratio'. A 'total maternity ratio' gives the average number of live births per woman of completed fertility. One type of maternity ratio is obtained by cumulating age-specific maternity rates. A different type of 'retrospective' maternity ratio is obtained from census data on numbers of previous live births reported by women at any age, e.g. at ages beyond the completion of the childbearing period.

TABLE 1. Age-specific Annual Maternity Rates and Total Maternity Ratios for Selected Populations with High Fertility.[1]

Population	Ages in years and rate	
	15–19	20–24
Bulgaria, 1901–05 [2]	0.024	0.289
Japan, 1925 [3]	0.049	0.239
Same. All births per married woman	0.322	0.338
Northern rural area, 1930	0.061	0.284
Aomori Prefecture, 1930	0.127	0.309
China		
Yangtze area, 1931–35 [4]	0.078	0.325
Same. All births per married woman	0.204	0.349
Yunnan area, 1942 [5]	0.053	0.162
Same. All births per married woman	0.120	0.173
Chinese in Malaya, 1946–48 [6]	0.108	0.333
Brazil, 1940 [7]	0.082	0.256
Mexico, 1929–31 [8]	0.117	0.229
Puerto Rico, 1944–48 [9]	0.088	0.266
India		
Ramanagaram District, Mysore, 1950: Births per married woman [10]	0.177	0.314
Bengali areas, 1945–46 Singur (rural; Hindu): Births per married woman	0.118	0.323
Park Circus (Calcutta; Muslim): Births per married woman	0.129	0.276

[1] Rates at extreme ages: births to women under 20 years per woman aged 15–19 years; births to women 45 years or over per woman 45–49 years. Additional decimals were generally used in obtaining total maternity ratios.

[2] R. R. Kuczynski. *Balance of Births and Deaths, II*. New York, 1928, p. 152.

[3] Rates for Japan, 1925. Adjusted from Table 5, Irene B. Taeuber and Frank W. Notestein, 'The Changing Fertility of the Japanese', *Population Studies*, 1 (1), pp. 2–28, June 1947—assuming 1,048 males per females at birth. Other Japanese rates from unpublished data by Irene B. Taeuber, 'Northern Rural Area'; Hokkaido, Aomori, Akita, and Iwate, except places with 10,000 or more inhabitants.

C. M. Chiao, Warren S. Thompson, D. T. Chen. *An Experiment in the Registration of Vital Statistics in China*. Oxford, Ohio, 1938, p. 45. Hsiao Chi, Kiangyin, Kiangsu (Mean age at first marriage: 18.8 years).

Ages in years and rate					Total maternity ratio (5 × sum of age-specific ratio)
25–29	30–34	35–39	40–44	45–49	
0.312	0.309	0.204	0.121	0.056	6.57
0.269	0.237	0.182	0.079	0.013	5.34
0.296	0.252	0.195	0.088	0.016	7.53
0.318	0.282	0.220	0.100	0.014	6.39
0.301	0.257	0.190	0.078	0.010	6.36
0.322	0.260	0.207	0.083	0.005	6.40
0.335	0.272	0.226	0.096	0.006	7.44
0.171	0.154	0.130	0.070	0.021	3.80
0.181	0.158	0.145	0.087	0.027	4.45
0.353	0.286	0.208	0.088	0.011	6.94
0.308	0.271	0.207	0.127	0.041	6.45
0.243	0.217	0.156	0.083	0.005	5.25
0.267	0.243	0.162	0.044	0.012	5.41
0.264	0.201	0.146	0.024	0.001	5.64
0.288	0.282	0.212	0.100	0.033	6.78
0.268	0.225	0.143	0.044	0.010	5.48

[5] Ta Chen. *Population in Modern China*. Chicago, 1945, p. 92. Cheng Kung, Yunnan. Data for year 1942 only, when registration was assumed most complete.

[6] T. E. Smith. *Population Growth in Malaya*. London, 1952. Revised estimates, p. 73.

[7] Giorgio Mortara. *Determinação da fecundidade feminina segundo a idade conforme o censo de 1940, e aplicações ao cálculo da taxa de natalidade, da tábua de fecundidade e do coeficiente de reprodução, para a população do Brasil*. Rio de Janeiro, 1948, p. 24; rate at ages 15–19 adjusted to include births to women under 15 years.

[8] Mortara, op. cit., p. 25.

[9] J. W. Combs Jr., Kingsley Davis. 'The Pattern of Puerto Rican Fertility', *Population Studies* 4, p. 376, March 1951. Means of 5 rates, with sums of 2 rates in extreme age classes.

[o] Unpublished data from small sample surveys, from C. Chandrasekaran. (See Table 3.)

portance can be attached to figures obtained by such a procedure, except that they provide a first crude approximation to an estimate of the highest fertility values to be expected under any actual conditions.

TABLE 2.   Hypothetical Age-Specific Maternity Rates and Total Maternity Ratio.[1]

Age in years	15–19	20–24	25–29	30–34	35–39	40–44	45–49
Rate	0.18	0.34	0.34	0.29	0.21	0.10	0.03

Corresponding total maternity ratio   7.45

In any case, the hypothetical total maternity ratio (about 7.5 births per woman living through the childbearing period) shown in Table 1 is not unrealistic. It is exceeded in some populations in two respects. First, the reported average number of births in a cohort of women who begin child-bearing in their early teens and live through the childbearing period often reaches or exceeds the vicinity of nine births per woman. We must, how-ever, recognize that such 'selected' cohorts of women married at unusually early ages may include an unusually high proportion of especially fecund women. Secondly, more conclusive evidence that the level of fecundity indicated in Table 1 is not excessive comes from findings that the levels of natality maintained in some total populations imply, as we shall see, an average of about eight births per woman living through the childbearing period.

We will first take account of the first type of findings referred to in the previous paragraph, and consider related evidence of the frequency of childlessness in relation to age at marriage. Data from the Census of England and Wales, 1911, and the Census of Canada, 1941, are given in Table 3. Low frequencies of sterility among couples married at early ages appear in these figures and in comparable figures for many other countries.[2] These figures are undoubtedly influenced by marital selection to some extent, but the degree of this influence is unknown. Kuczynski, after a critical examination of such evidence, concluded that: 'Involuntary sterility is rare; it is much rarer than generally believed.'[3] He based this conclusion chiefly on low frequencies of childlessness among marriages with wife under 25 years of age in various European populations in the late nineteenth and early twentieth centuries. He also gave special attention to the finding that only 4.0 per cent of all ever-married women (all ages

[1] The figures, which have no precise value, have been rounded to two decimals.
[2] R. R. Kuczynski. 'Childless Marriages', *Sociological Review*, 30 (2), pp. 120–44, April 1938; 30 (3), pp. 213–35, July 1938; 30 (4), pp. 346–64, October 1938. Kuczynski empha-sizes the selectivity of surviving couples in 1911 from marriages of earlier periods. How-ever, Italian data presented in this article show even lower frequencies of childlessness at given ages at first marriages among wives aged 45–54 than among wives aged 55–64 or 65 and over, and a similar relationship is often found in other census reports.
[3] ibid., 30 (4), p. 357.

TABLE 3. Percentage Distributions by Number of Children Ever-born: Marriages (Selected Classes) England and Wales, 1911; Ever-married Women (Under 20 Years at Marriage), Rural Quebec, 1941.

Number of children ever-born	England and Wales, 1911 [1] Couples married, 1861–71				Rural Quebec, 1941 [2] Ever-married women aged 45 years or over, age at marriage under 20 years
	Wife's age at marriage in years				
	15–19	20–24	25–29	30–34	
	%	%	%	%	%
0	3.5	5.8	9.8	15.8	4.0
1	2.6	3.3	5.0	7.5	2.4
2	3.3	4.2	6.8	10.7	2.8
3	3.9	5.4	8.1	13.1	3.1
4	4.8	6.7	9.8	14.5	3.5
5	5.6	7.6	11.0	13.5	4.2
6	6.3	8.9	12.2	10.7	4.7
7	7.4	9.7	11.6	6.8	5.1
8	8.8	10.8	9.9	3.6	6.0
9	9.9	10.7	7.0	1.8	6.5
10	11.0	9.7	4.3	1.0	7.8
11	9.7	6.7	2.2	0.4	7.7
12	8.8	5.0	1.3	0.3	9.4
13	6.1	2.8	0.6	0.2	8.3
14	3.8	1.5	0.2	0.1	7.6
15	2.0	0.7	0.1	0.0	6.0
16	1.2	0.4	0.1	0.0	4.5
17	0.6	0.2	0.0	0.0	2.6
18	0.3	0.1	0.0	0.0	2.0
19	0.1	0.0	0.0	0.0	1.0
20 or more	0.1	0.0	0.0	0.0	1.2
Average number of births	8.4	7.0	5.3	3.7	9.9

[1] The English data refer to present marriages, husbands and wives enumerated on same schedule, both living in 1911, without reference to possible previous marriages. The data for marriages, wives aged over 35 years at marriage, are omitted; 29.9 per cent of these marriages were childless, but in some cases the husband or wife may have had children by a previous marriage. To a lesser extent, this possibility may affect results at other ages. Great Britain, General Register Office, *Census of England and Wales,.1911, Vol. 13, Fertility of Marriage*, Part 2, London, 1923, Table XVI; average number of births from data in Table XVIIA.

Data from Census of Canada, 1941. Among women of same age at census but married at all ages, 9.9 were childless, but there were on the average 7.5 children ever-born per-ever-married woman; 27 per cent were married under 20 years of age. All values for this population may have been somewhat affected by selective out-migration.

at marriage) born in French Canada and living in Massachusetts in 1885 were childless. The rising frequency of childlessness in marriages at later ages might be somewhat influenced in a negative way by any previous selection of especially fecund women in early marriages, but one would not expect a large effect from such indirect selection in this population. Moreover, it is unlikely that many English couples in this period practised contraception at the beginning of their married life (see discussion below of findings by Lewis-Faning). These and comparable findings for other countries suggest that each postponement of marriage to a successively later age significantly increases the chances of sterility.

Sample studies of the population of India where early marriage is conventional, and therefore free from selection with respect to fecundity, have particular interest. Unfortunately we are limited here to the results of relatively small field studies (see Table 4). The weighted average of the proportions of childless wives in the three samples of Hindu population in Bengali is 5.3 per cent. The proportion is much higher in the sample from a Muslim district of Calcutta, but it appears to be even lower in the large sample of Lucknow and Kanpur households, predominantly Hindu. It may also be noted that only 4 per cent of the Ashanti women aged 35 or over in the district study by Meyer Fortes were reported as never pregnant.[1] Practically all of these women had been married under 20 years of age, and the modal age at first marriage was 17 years. Fortes, however, raises the possibility that some childless couples may have succeeded in concealing their disability in this respect. This possibility must also be taken into account in the information from samples of women in India.

The question requires further investigation, but tends clearly to indicate lower frequency of sterility in some populations with a very early conventional age for marriage than in most European populations with a much higher conventional age for marriage—in spite of health conditions that might be supposed to be less favourable to high fecundity. (There is, of course, a high frequency of sterility in some impoverished populations, but this can generally be attributed to the influence of infections, or other inhibiting factors.)

Valuable information on the total performance of cohorts of mothers classified with respect to age at the time when the first child was born, from the 1940 Census of Brazil, is given in Table 5. These figures describe the experience of mothers throughout the childbearing period without regard to variations and changes in marital status. The information for women reporting first births at 12–14 years must be accepted with caution, due to the possibility of gross distortion due to errors in the reports. The table as a whole, however, clearly shows a positive association between early age at initiation of maternity and total number of births. Data from Scotland, 1911, on total maternity ratios of married couples with completed

[1] Meyer Fortes. 'A Demographic Study in Ashanti'. See this present report, Part Two.

fertility show a rise from about 8.5 births to wives married under 16 years of age to a maximum of about 9.5 births to wives at 17 years, but a marked decline thereafter.[1]

There is no evidence, so far as the present writer is aware, that the fertility of any whole population ever reaches such a high level as that of some of the selected cohorts, described above. We do, however, have positive evidence that the fertility of several whole populations has attained a level of fertility sufficient to give about 8 live births per woman living through the childbearing years.

In Soviet Armenia, 1926–27, there were about 55 births per year per 1,000 population.[2] Taking account of the actual sex and age composition

TABLE 4. Frequency of Childless Wives in Samples of Indian Population.

Area and notes	Number of wives	Proportion childless
Bengali areas[1] (wives aged 40 years or over)		%
Singur (rural, Hindu), no contraception	166	4.8
Baniatola (Calcutta, Hindu), medium economic class; slight contraception	164	6.7
Ballygunge (Calcutta, Hindu), upper economic class; some contraception	214	4.7
Park Circus (Calcutta, Muslim), no contraception	152	10.5
Lucknow and Kanpur[2] (wives all ages, in unbroken marriages)	769	4.4
Mysore areas[3] (wives aged 45 years and over; uninterrupted wedlock to 45 years of age)		
Bangalore city	1 164	5.4
Towns	263	3.8
Rural areas	873	5.4

[1] Unpublished data provided by C. Chandrasekaran. As the data refer to women who never became pregnant, the proportion childless would be somewhat higher than that indicated here. Except for Park Circus area, the number of women married more than once was negligible.

[2] J. N. Sinha, 'Fertility and Age at Marriage'. Document P 43/Nov. 16, International Statistical Institute, New Delhi Session, 1951. These data and related findings are described more fully by Sinha in an unpublished doctoral dissertation, Department of Sociology. Lucknow University.

[3] Unpublished data from United Nations-Government of India Population Survey. Combined data for 5 areas of Bangalore City, 15 towns (10,000 to 25,000 population), and 3 rural areas.

---

[1] Values read from chart by Bourgeois-Pichat, op. cit., p. 46.

[2] Reported rates, 1926: 53.6; 1927: 56.1. F. Lorimer, *Population of the Soviet Union*, Geneva, 1946, p. 83. The mean of these figures, 54.85, is used in computing estimated total maternity ratios.

TABLE 5. Brazil, 1940. Mothers by Age at Birth of First Child and Total Number of Children Born Alive.[1]

Age in years at birth of first child	Number of women	Average number of live births per woman
12–14	27 634	8.98
15–19	464 309	8.83
20–24	602 520	7.62
25–29	257 669	6.28
30–34	113 234	5.08
35–39	45 554	4.14
40–44	17 582	3.67
45–49	—[2]	—[2]
50 and over	—[2]	—[2]

[1] Instituto Brasileiro de Geograpfia e Estatística Estudos de Estatística Teórica E Aplicada, Estatística Demografica, No. 6: *A prolificidade da mulher, segundo a idade inicial da atividade reprodutora, no Brasil*, Rio de Janeiro, 1949, p. 13.
[2] The data for women reporting first births at ages over 45 years, as noted by Mortara, are obviously distorted by mistakes in statement of age or other errors. The numbers so reporting and average numbers of births tabulated per woman at these ages were: 45–49: 5,486: 4.19; 50 and over: 879: 4.87.

of the population and applying the fertility schedule for Brazil 1940 (or that for the Ukraine 1926–27) to obtain substitute total maternity ratios, we estimate that the Armenian women at this time were tending to have about 7.9 births per woman living to the end of the childbearing period. A comparable female gross reproduction ratio (3.89 female births per woman living to the end of the childbearing period) had previously been obtained by using data on number of children aged 2 years in 1926 and life-table values for 1926–27.[1] The corresponding net reproduction ratio obtained in this way was 2.53, implying an intrinsic rate of natural increase in the vicinity of 32 per thousand per year. There was an actual increase of 45.5 per cent in the population of the republic between 1926 and 1939, indicating an average increase of 31 per thousand per year. This must have been largely due to natural increase, although there was some in-movement from outside the U.S.S.R. during the inter-census period. These independent inferences are, therefore, quite consistent and show an extraordinarily high level of fertility.[2]

The settled Muslims of Palestine are reported to be a people with

[1] Lorimer, op. cit., p. 92.
[2] The corresponding general maternity rates per thousand population are:
$$G_{15-49}: 238 \qquad G_{15-44}: 259$$
The estimated total maternity ratio by short-cut method (30 G_{15-44}) is 7.8 births per woman.

unusually high fertility. The reported birth rate of Muslims at the time of the 1931 census of Palestine was 53.65 births per 1,000 population.[1] Age-specific maternity rates relative to the estimated population were officially calculated in 1938 and later years, and the 1938–42 rates were used to obtain substitute total maternity ratios for earlier years. Estimated total maternity ratios obtained in this way were 6.72 in 1931, 7.50 in 1938, and moved upward irregularly thereafter to the extraordinary figure of 9.81 in 1945. However, as shown by Loftus, this procedure was subject to gross distortion, due to errors in age reporting at the time of the 1931 census and later errors of estimate for this unstable population. Therefore he applied a short-cut method, similar to that reviewed in a supplement to this report, to obtain revised total maternity ratios. Working at first with general maternity rates at ages 15–49 years and multiplying these by 35 he obtained total maternity ratios of 7.85 in 1931 and 7.67 in 1938. In the light of our discussion of this procedure to appear in the supplement, we can assume that these ratios are somewhat too high. However, he also adjusted the available data to obtain estimated general maternity rates at ages 15–44, and multiplied these rates by 30 to give a second (and more accurate) series of ratios. On this basis the estimated total maternity ratio for 1938 is 7.33 births per woman; it falls irregularly to 6.85 in 1942, but rises to 8.28 in 1945. All the data involved in these calculations are subject to errors, but Loftus gives reasons for supposing that such errors cause only moderate distortion of the results. We may conclude that the fertility of this population fluctuates from year to year around a high level, tending toward an average somewhere between seven and eight births per woman living through the childbearing period.

The population of New France, later the Province of Quebec, appears to have had the highest recorded fertility of any whole population. The original data of the early census reports of 1666, 1667, and 1681 were used by Sabagh to obtain detailed classification by sex, age, and marital status as a basis of the calculation of substitute indices of fertility (i.e., indices obtained by application of another age-specific schedule of fertility, with adjustment of results to give the observed total number of births.[2] The information on births was obtained from ecclesiastical records of baptisms. Unfortunately Sabagh used an inappropriate schedule of fertility (Sweden 1776–85), with quite low rates at early ages. The resulting distortion was fairly large in this case, due to the peculiar and rapidly changing sex and age structure of the colony at this time. The magnitude of this distortion is indicated, and further insight into the actual situation is obtained, by using alternative schedules of fertility (see Table 6). The results shown here indicate an apparent level of fertility tending to result

[1] All data on this topic are from the following article: P. J. Loftus, 'Features of the Demography of Palestine', *Population Studies*, 2 (1), pp. 92–114, June 1948.
[2] Georges Sabagh, 'The Fertility of French-Canadians During the Seventeenth Century', *The American Journal of Sociology*, 47 (5), pp. 680–9, March 1942.

in an average of about nine births per woman living through the child-bearing period. This conclusion must be received with caution due to peculiar circumstances affecting this population, and the impossibility at present of complete investigation of all relevant conditions.

TABLE 6. Population and Estimated Total Maternity Ratios, French Canada, 1666, 1667, 1681.

Date	Total population[1]	Females relative to total[1]	Wives relative to all females[1] 15–49 years	Substitute total maternity ratios, with application of specified schedules of fertility		
				Sweden[1] 1776–85	Brazil[2] 1940	Bulgaria[2] 1901–05
		%	%	%	%	%
1666	3,215	36.7	88.6	12.01	9.05	8.79
1667	3,918	38.5	85.0	10.68	9.00	8.90
1681	9,677	44.5	76.7	9.67	8.88	9.08

[1] From Sabagh, op. cit. He placed greater reliance on the use of age-specific nuptial fertility rates, but these involve another sort of bias, as already noted.

[2] Using schedules reported elsewhere in this chapter, a crude birth rate of 50 per thousand, following Sabagh, is used in these calculations for the years 1666 and 1667. The crude birth rate in 1681 is assumed to be 47 per thousand, the mean between the average rates for 1668–80 and 1681–90, according to Kuczynski, *Birth Registration and Birth Statistics in Canada*, Washington, 1930, p. 199.

A very high level of fertility continued to characterize the population of Quebec during the middle decades of the nineteenth century, after the cessation of immigration and the stabilization of the population structure.[1] The crude birth rate around the time of the 1851 census, which provides complete information on the age and sex composition of the population, was about 50 per thousand. Vincent and Henry used a fertility schedule 1930–32, to obtain a substitute total maternity ratio for 1851. The resultant estimate is 7.96 births per woman living through the childbearing period; similar figures would be obtained in this case by application of other reasonable schedules, due to the relative stability of the population structure at this time. They note that the total maternity of married women would have been even higher.

It is interesting to note that Vincent and Henry were concerned in this article with estimating the possible rate of increase of a stable population characterized by complete release of potential capacity for procreation and

[1] Paul Vincent and Louis Henry, 'Rythme maximum d'accroissement d'une population stable', *Population*, 2 (4) 1947, pp. 663–80.

by such low mortality as that of the white population of New Zealand, 1934–38. They estimate that these conditions would give a net reproduction ratio of 3.6 (implying a rate of increase over 40 per thousand per year), sufficient to double the population in 16 to 17 years. At this rate, a population of one million persons would increase to 64 million persons in 100 years.

The data on the age distribution of the population of the United States at the beginning of the nineteenth century, and its actual increase during successive inter-census periods indicate that seven to eight children were born per woman living through the childbearing years. The available information, however, does not provide an adequate basis for a precise estimate.

An ingenuous method of analysing fertility by computing probabilities of further increase of family for wives at various ages and parities, developed by Henry, has been applied to census data for populations only slightly affected by anti-natal practices.[1] His study provides estimates of the proportions of newly married wives at any age, or of mothers at first, second, or any subsequent maternity at any age, expected to bear one or more additional infants. The study includes an analysis of data from the 1911 census of England and Wales, including marriages of 1851–60 and 1861–70; the 1920 census of Norway, including marriages prior to 1888; and the 1941 census of Canada, including married women in rural Quebec born prior to 1876. The results in each case are subject to some bias, but the distortions by bias are not large, and the results are surprisingly consistent.

One of the interesting results of this investigation, bearing on relations of fecundity to age and to previous childbearing experience, will be discussed below in this chapter. We merely note at this point that the results of this intensive investigation appear consistent with an assumption that the fertility of marriages in the groups listed above was slightly, but only slightly, affected by voluntary control; expressed fertility appears to have approached closely to biological capacity. Also, the material is consistent with the thesis that there was some selectivity with respect to fecundity among couples married at various ages, but indicates that the effect of such selectivity on the completed fertility of marriages at various ages can not have been very great.

The interesting question arises as to whether or not populations with unusually high fertility differ in biological capacity from the common lot of mankind, or whether their apparent high achievement in this respect *merely* reflects an unusually positive response to social conditions conducive to maximum fertility. This question can not be answered with any certainty. Obviously, fairly favourable health conditions are required, though all populations lived under rather primitive conditions. Obviously, too, social

---

[1] Louis Henry. *Fécondité des mariages: nouvelle méthode de mesure.* Paris, Institut National d'Etudes Démographiques, 1953. His method involves a special application of the general method of 'cohort analysis'.

conditions were favourable to high fertility. But the possibility of unusual genetic characteristics is also present. Selective migration is a possibility in the case of the French Canadian population, if recruited mainly from sons and daughters in large families which found it difficult to obtain necessary land or other resources for livelihood in France. In any case, constant negative selection against the out-cropping of genetic factors inducing sterility must be most powerful in populations where the average size of family is very large. Conversely, the absence of such powerful selection over successive generations in populations where the average size of family is small might be conducive to the gradual accumulation of genetic factors tending to induce sterility. In any case we have no basis for an assumption that all human populations have approximately the same genetic capacity for reproduction.

PREGNANCY RATES DURING NON-CONTRACEPTIVE EXPERIENCE

Another approach to the estimation of fecundity is provided by intensive studies of the frequency of conception and maternity in the experience of contemporary populations, classified with respect to anti-natal practices. Unfortunately, we encounter other pitfalls here—comparable to and perhaps even more serious than that encountered in the interpretation of fertility in relation to age at marriage—namely (a) the selectivity of contraceptive practice with respect to fecundity and (b) the necessity of reliance on personal reports on previous behaviour and motives. After this initial warning, we will describe briefly two major studies in this field, and review some of their findings.

The Indianapolis Study. This concerns a random sample of native white, Protestant couples, married once only in 1927–29, and living in Indianapolis, Indiana, U.S.A., April 1941–January 1942—both spouses having urban background, having completed elementary schooling, wife under 30 years and husband under 40 at marriage, marriages uninterrupted by death or divorce. Interviews were completed with 1,080 couples, randomly selected within specified strata; data for random series in various strata were then duplicated to provide information on a hypothetical random sample of 1,977 couples, representing the specified 'universe'. The universe was purposely limited to a population assumed to be familiar with contraception and regarding it as readily available in accordance with personal preferences. It was, in fact, found that some contraceptive practices had been adopted by practically all the 'relatively fecund' couples in the sample (99.6 per cent if all practices are included; 98.4 per cent excluding practices assumed to be contraceptive in effect, but alleged to have been followed for other reasons, p. 213). The average interval between marriage and time of the interview was 13.1 years (p. 355). The median age of wives at the apparent beginning of 'conjugal experience' was 21.0 years.[1] The results of this investigation are described in a series of reports (not yet complete): P. K. Whelpton, Clyde V. Kiser and others, *Social and Psychological Factors Affecting Fertility*, Reprints from *Milbank Memorial Fund Quarterly*, New York, 1943 ff. (Vol. I. Articles I–V, pp. 1–138; Vol. II. Articles VI–IX, pp. 139–466—especially Article VIII: 'The Comparative Influences on Fertility of Contraception and Impairments of Fecundity', by Whelpton and Kiser, pp. 303–58; Vol. III. Articles XI–XVII, pp. 467–799).

The British Hospital Study. This treats a sample of British couples of all ages in uninterrupted first marriages, represented by wives receiving selected types of hospital service in various localities in England and Scotland, August 1946–June 1947. The analysis of factors relating to fertility and fecundity relates to a series of 3,281 cases, excluding wives receiving maternity and pre-natal service and excluding, in the case of the older women, marriages interrupted by death or divorce before the wife was 45 years old (p. 4). The sample was designed to yield an approximately random sample of all couples under the specific conditions; but it was found that couples of high social status were under-represented, and the sample was somewhat over-weighted with wives of higher than average fertility. The mean age at marriage among wives in this sample who were married before 1940 was 24.3 years, about a year less than the average for comparable cohorts of the general population (data from pp. 40, 65).[2] The population treated in this survey is one in which birth control had been much less generally practised than in the selected Indianapolis population; the proportion reporting such practices ranged from 15 per cent among wives married before 1910 to 66 per cent among those married 1935–39. The results of this investigation are given in the following publication: *Papers of the Royal Commission on Population*, Volume I: *Report on An Inquiry into Family Limitation and Its Influence on Human Fertility During the Past Fifty Years*, by E. Lewis-Faning, London: 1949, 202 p.

Whelpton and Kiser, using data of the Indianapolis study, estimate that if there had been no anti-natal practices, there would have been on the average 5.2 pregnancies per couple during the period covered by the study (average interval, 13.1 years).[3] Taking account of miscarriages, stillbirths, and multiple births gives an expectation of 4.6 live births.[4] This would

---

[1] Unpublished information provided by Clyde V. Kiser. The term 'conjugal experience' as used by the present writer includes premarital exposure to conception as reported or inferred.

[2] 'Marriage' in this context apparently refers to formal marriage, although premarital exposure to conception was taken into account at other points in this report.

[3] The precise figure obtained by one method is 5.265 (p. 319); that obtained by a different procedure is 5.188. Whelpton and Kiser, op. cit., p. 356.

[4] The precise ratios of live births to pregnancies are 0.8726 (p. 319), and 0.8824 (ibid., p. 356).

indicate a general rate of 0.35 births per woman per year. The basic procedure followed in this study was the estimation of (a) proportions of couples able to have a first, a second, and each successive pregancy, and (b) periods of time required for each successive pregancy among those able to conceive. These procedures will be discussed shortly in more detail.

Among the couples in the Indianapolis sample, 27 per cent were classified as 'relatively sterile'. This term as used here has a special meaning. All couples with no pregnancy during a three-year period without contraception (except in the case of a few couples who nevertheless had four or more live births) or during a two-year period in the case of never-pregnant couples, as well as any for whom there was clinical evidence of incapacity to produce living offspring, were classed as 'relatively sterile' (pp. 164–5). Dividing the sample on this basis, it was estimated that if there had been no anti-natal practices, each of the 'relatively fecund' couples would have had on the average 5.86 live births, and each of the 'relatively sterile' couples would have had on the average 1.10 live births during the period (13.1 years on the average) covered by the study (p. 356).

Lewis-Faning estimates that each couple in the British hospital sample, in the absence of any anti-natal practices, would have about 5.0 live births between marriage and the end of the childbearing period (p. 14). The basic procedure followed in this study was the calculation of pregnancy rates under specified conditions with respect to contraceptive practice during successive five-year 'segments' of married life. The pregnancy rates obtained in this way for each type of contraceptive practice relate frequency of conception to years of exposure (including the experience of couples who did not become pregnant during the period under consideration, but excluding periods of pregnancy and post-partum sterility). The selectivity as regards fecundity of the various groups classified with respect to contraceptive practice is shown by the different rates thus obtained within each segment (see Table 7).

Numbers of pregnancies expected in the British hospital sample during a 20-year period under changing conditions as regards contraceptive practice were obtained by applying such rates—taking into account the time required for each pregnancy and a brief subsequent time during which conception is unlikely, summing the figures thus obtained in successive segments, and extending the estimate to cover the fourth, relatively unimportant, five-year period of conjugal life by adding one-half the values obtained for the third five-year segment. Cumulative numbers of expected pregnancies under specified conditions, obtained in this way, are as follows (p. 14): (a) no control at any time—3.6 pregnancies; (b) no control within particular 'inter-pregnancy' intervals, but attempted control during other 'inter-pregnancy' periods in same segment—6.0 pregnancies; (c) no control at some times, but attempted control during other parts of same 'inter-pregnancy' period—8.3 pregnancies.

The mean (7.15) of the last two figures is then taken, for reasons stated in the text, as an estimate of the average capacity for pregnancies of couples who practise contraception intermittently throughout marriage, thus indicating that they consider themselves fecund through all segments of married life. Assuming a ratio of 87 live births per 100 pregnancies, it is estimated that on the average the couples who practised contraception could have had 6.2 live births between marriage and the end of the child-bearing period (if they have not practised contraception or abortion). The expected total capacity for live births of the couples who never practised contraception would appear to be about 87 per cent of 3.6, or about 3.1 live births between marriage and the end of the childbearing period; but this figure is replaced by other values in the final estimate. The average capacity of total marriage cohorts in the general population is estimated by holding constant the estimate (6.2 births) for couples practising contraception, and combining this figure with the actual numbers of births reported by wives who never attempted to control childbearing—using the percentages of couples who reported no such attempts to obtain weighted averages. The proportions of wives reporting no attempt to control fertility, among those married at various dates prior to 1930, were as follows: before 1910, 85 per cent; 1910–19, 60 per cent; 1920–24, 42 per cent; 1925–29, 39 per cent. The average numbers of births in these cohorts per couple were respectively: 4.9, 4.0, 3.2, and 3.1 live births. The decline over time in the last series gives further evidence

TABLE 7. Pregnancy Rates per Year of Non-contraceptive Practice (Excluding Pregnancy Periods), by Duration of Conjugal Experience and with Reference to Contraceptive Practice at Other Times, British Hospital Sample.[1]

Conditions	Segments of conjugal experience		
	First 5 years	Second 5 years	Third 5 years
No control at any time	0.45	0.23	0.17
Attempted control during other inter-pregnancy periods in same 'segment'	1.29	0.50	0.24
Attempted control during other part of same 'inter-pregnancy' period	1.42	1.14	0.52

[1] Adapted from Lewis-Faning, op. cit., p. 13. Some of the terms used here differ from those in the original text. 'Conjugal experience' here includes reported pre-nuptial intervals after initiation of regular sex relations. 'Inter-pregnancy period' here includes the interval between initiation of 'conjugal experience' and first pregnancy. All later inter-pregnancy periods exclude a three-month interval after delivery, or a one-month interval after a miscarriage, in view of evidence indicating that these are usually intervals of relative sterility (pp. 119–22).

of the increasing selectivity of couples deficient in fecundity among those not practising contraception or abortion. The estimated average capacity of successive marriage cohorts in the whole population (combining decreasing proportions of progressively less fertile couples with the constant figure for couples practising contraception) was nearly constant over time—varying only between 5.1 and 4.9 live births. This yields the over-all average figure mentioned above (5.0 live births) as the estimated *total* childbearing capacity of British couples married at the ages observed in this series. This is only slightly above the estimated average capacity (4.6 live births) of the couples in the Indianapolis sample during the first 13.1 years of married life.

The expected number of live births, in the absence of contraceptive practice, among couples in the British hospital sample during the first 13.1 years of their married life has been estimated by the present writer from Lewis-Faning's material. The estimated figure is 4.2 live births, as compared with the expected 4.6 live births under similar conditions in the Indianapolis study. The corresponding rates per person per year are 0.32 and 0.35 live births, respectively. The estimated capacity of the 'relatively fecund' couples in the Indianapolis sample was 0.45 live births per year. Henry, using American hospital data by Pearl on women interviewed near time of maternity, estimated median rates of live births per year among women of continuing fertility who reported no contraceptive practice. These rates show only moderate variations. They range from 0.44 live births per year at ages 20–24 to 0.38 live births per year at ages 35–39 as reported by fertile women aged 40 years or over. But lower rates at ages 20–24 years, 0.43, 0.42, and 0.41 live births per year were obtained from reports by fertile women aged 35–39 years, 30–34 years, and 25–29 years, respectively.[1]

The analysis of previous English, Norwegian, and French Canadian experience by Henry (cited above) shows marked declines with advancing age in the probabilities of increase of family. In the case of women at first maternity these probabilities run as follows:

	25 years	30 years	35 years	40 years
England and Wales, 1911 census, marriages 1861–70	0.964	0.942	0.903	0.792
Norway, 1920 census, marriages to 1888	0.970	0.954	0.914	0.770
Rural Quebec, 1941 census, married women, born to 1875	0.960	0.932	0.868	—

[1] Henry, op. cit., p. 96. On the relative constancy of pregnancy rates in non-contraceptive experience among women of continuing fertility, see also: Regine K. Stix and Frank W. Notestein, *Controlled Fertility*, Baltimore, 1940.

On the other hand, at any given age the prospects of further increase of family, though generally higher for mothers than for newly married wives, were relatively independent, among mothers, of the number of infants already borne. For example, at age 30 years, the probabilities of further increase of families run as follows:

	Newly married	Number of previous births				
		1	2	3	4	5
England and Wales, 1911 census, marriages 1861–70	0.896	0.942	0.938	0.937	0.936	—
Norway, 1920 census, marriages to 1888	0.924	0.954	0.951	0.947	0.940	—
Rural Quebec, 1941 census, married women, born to 1875	0.886	0.932	0.942	0.942	0.948	0.953

The somewhat lower prospect for fertility of brides at a relatively advanced age, as compared to mothers at the same age, suggests some negative selection in the former case with respect to fecundity. The finding for mothers of different parity at a given age is surprising, because pregnancy and parturition sometimes cause later sterility. It may be, however, that this tendency is balanced by a cumulative selection of relatively fecund women in each successive maternity.

ESTIMATES OF STERILITY FROM STUDIES OF NON-CONTRACEPTIVE EXPERIENCE

An estimate of the extent of sterility in the British hospital sample is relatively simple. In this sample, 6.9 per cent of the wives were childless and also reported that they had never made any effort to prevent births. Only 8.2 per cent of all wives were childless (pp. 17–18). The proportion of absolutely sterile couples in this sample must, therefore, have been between these 7 and 8 per cent. We remember that this sample included wives married at all ages.

Estimation of the extent of sterility in the Indianapolis sample involves much greater difficulties. Among the couples classified as 'relatively fecund', 69.5 per cent reported contraceptive practice prior to the first pregnancy, and 49.2 per cent of those classed as 'relatively sterile' did so. Taking into account 'douching for cleanliness only', the proportions rise to 74.2 per cent and 54.6 per cent respectively (pp. 212, 216). Furthermore, among the 'relatively fecund' couples, 37.6 per cent of all first pregnancies occurred while contraception was practised, and the proportions of such 'accidental pregnancies' among 'relatively fecund' couples rise to over

41

50 per cent of all second pregnancies, nearly two-thirds of all third pregnancies, and almost three-fourths of all fourth pregnancies, and over three-fourths of all later pregnancies (p. 222). As the authors note, those who did not resort to contraception prior to the first pregnancy may have included a disproportionate number of couples who doubted their capacity to have as many children as wanted and who for this reason were eager to have a first pregnancy as soon as possible:

Only 4.6 per cent of all couples in the Indianapolis sample had neither practised contraception at any time nor ever been pregnant; this figure is raised to 5.2 per cent by including some couples who after having used contraception for a time were told by a physician that they had always been sterile. Another 6.0 per cent had always used contraception with apparent 'success', in that no pregnancy had ever occurred, and this figure is raised to 6.4 per cent by including some couples who discontinued contraception only after an operation that made future conception impossible. Finally, 4.7 per cent used contraception part of the time, but not during other long periods of married life. Thus no pregnancy had occurred to 16.3 per cent of all couples. Considering the several categories separately, Whelpton and Kiser estimate that 9.8 per cent of all couples had been unable to conceive (pp. 345–6). Taking pregnancy wastage into account, 19.3 per cent of all wives in the Indianapolis sample were actually childless, and Whelpton and Kiser estimate that about 10.2 per cent of all couples could never have had a live birth (pp. 338–9). A comparable estimate, from data by Kiser on a random sample of childless native white wives in New York City, married 10 years or more and under 50 years at time of interview, was that 8.0 to 9.0 per cent of all wives in this population were involuntarily sterile (cited p. 339). The estimate of absolute sterility in the Indianapolis sample is surprisingly high—especially in view of the low average age at marriage, and the exclusion of all wives married after their thirtieth birthday. But in the light of all the evidence this estimate appears to be conservative, because it is evident that a considerable proportion of those who practised contraception with apparent 'success' during all or the early part of their married life must really have been sterile. The apparent evidence that sterility is appreciably higher in the urban population of the United States than in many countries raises a question that cannot be easily answered.

Estimates are also presented on the time required for each conception, in the absence of contraception, among those able to have pregnancies of various orders. The authors estimate that the average time required (exclusive of one month allowed for the puerperium, i.e. temporary sterility, after each delivery) declines from 13.9 months during the first inter-pregnancy period (i.e. before the second conception), to 11.4 months during the second inter-pregnancy period, 9.7 months before the third, and so on to about 7.0 months in the seventh and each subsequent inter-pregnancy period. This indication of rising frequency of conception in

42

successive inter-pregnancy intervals is surprising. It may, of course, be due wholly to the increasing selectivity of non-contraceptive experience with advance in length of married life. However, these estimates, especially those for second, third, and later inter-pregnancy intervals are necessarily dependent in large part on reported information concerning the length of time between cessation of contraceptive practice and conception among those who said that they ceased practising contraception in order to conceive. These reported intervals were frequently very brief. It must be noted that reports on this subject are peculiarly subject to bias because they involve the question as to whether children who are now beloved members of the family were 'accidentally' conceived or 'planned'.

It appears to the present writer that lower estimates of increase in sterility subsequent to each successive pregnancy, and higher estimates of the time required for successive conceptions would be more in line with the indirect evidence of other studies. If the estimates were modified in these two ways the resultant final estimate of procreative capacity might be lowered, or raised, or might remain unchanged.

No critical investigation of the relation of age at the beginning of 'conjugal experience' to fecundity is yet available from either of the studies reviewed here. Some indirect evidence on this subject from the Indianapolis study is presented in Tables 8 and 9. In Table 8 the absence or possible reversal, at ages under 18 years, of the apparent relation at later ages is interesting, but may be a chance finding. The increased frequency of childless couples within each theoretical fecundity class, as shown in Table 9, is also apparently significant. However, it must be emphsized that the results given in this table reflect social and psychological conditions as well as differences in fecundity. No firm conclusions can be

TABLE 8.   Wives Classified by Age at Marriage. Percentages of 'Relatively Sterile' Couples. Indianapolis Study.[1]

Age of wife at marriage, or inferred age at beginning of conjugal experience	Number of couples, inflated sample	Percentage of couples, classified as 'relatively sterile'
Total	*1 977*	*27.0*
25–29 years	277	38.3
22–24 years	426	29.3
20–21 years	475	27.4
18–19 years	497	21.5
Under 18 years	352	23.9

[1] Unpublished data provided by Clyde V. Kiser. See text for definition of terms.

drawn from this material without more intensive analysis of the basic data with respect to these problems.

Table 9. Wives in Various Fertility Classes. Percentage Distribution by Age at Interview. Indianapolis Study.[1]

Fertility classes	Age in years at interview			All ages	
	Under 35	35–39	40 +		
	Estimated age at marriage [2]			Number [3]	Percentage
	Under 22	22–26	27–29		
Couples classified as 'relatively fecund'	%	%	%		
No live birth	54.1	35.5	10.8	93	100
One live birth	66.5	30.7	2.7	182	100
Two live births	71.8	25.5	2.1	236	100
Three live births	72.8	22.7	4.1	199	100
Four live births	83.7	16.0	0.7	—[4]	100
Couples classified as 'relatively sterile'					
No live birth	48.3	41.3	11.3	80	100
One live birth	58.0	36.9	3.9	76	100

[1] Data from Whelpton and Kiser, op. cit., p. 194; number of cases, p. 186. The percentages shown here at ages 35–39 are sums of three figures; the percentage 'under 35 years' at interview is obtained by subtraction.
[2] Estimated ages at marriage are not given in the original publication and are mere approximations.
[3] Numbers prior to inflation of sample.
[4] Number not reported; four or more live births: 150 cases.

PREGNANCY WASTAGE

The Indianapolis study and the British hospital study provide estimates of pregnancy wastage through miscarriages and stillbirths. Lewis-Faning, in the British study, concluded that an average wastage of about 13 per cent must be assumed in all pregnancies under the conditions represented in his sample (p. 14). He does not appear to have taken the frequency of multiple births into account at this point. In the United Kingdom, 1929–37, 1.247 per cent of all births were multiple births.[1] One may therefore assume that the additional infants in multiple births (exclusive of the first infant

[1] Institut International de Statistique, *Aperçu de la démographie des divers pays du monde, 1929–1936.* The Hague, 1939, p. 263.

in each delivery) would raise the estimated ratio of live births to pregnancies in the British sample from about 87.0 per cent to about 87.6 per cent. In the Indianapolis study two estimates were made of the expected average ratio of live births to pregnancies over a 13-year period, combining information on spontaneous abortions, therapeutic abortions, and stillbirths, and making allowance for multiple births. The values thus obtained were 87.3 per cent and 88.2 per cent (pp. 319, 356). The approximate agreement in the over-all estimates of pregnancy wastage provided by the British study and the Indianapolis study may be in part spurious. The proportion of reported miscarriages in the Indianapolis material rises from 6.7 per cent of the first pregnancies and 8.4 per cent of the second pregnancies to 14.1, 13.2, and 15.9 per cent of the third, fourth and fifth or later pregnancies—excluding from the computation in each case pregnancies reported to have been terminated by induced abortion. If some of the events reported as miscarriages, especially in the higher pregnancy orders, had really been induced abortions the over-all figure for involuntary pregnancy wastage would be lower.

Miscarriages are generally much more frequent than stillbirths. These losses must vary widely under different conditions. Unfortunately reasonably reliable information for large populations is available only with respect to stillbirths, and only for a few countries. The average ratio of reported stillbirths to reported births in nine European countries that provide reasonably comparable and reliable information declined from 2.9 per cent in 1935 to 2.05 per cent in 1949.[1] The downward trend during this period, which is confirmed by other information, suggests that frequency of stillbirths is positively associated with the general level of mortality. Unfortunately, information on this subject for countries where health conditions are unfavourable is generally quite unreliable. Ratios of over 10 reported stillbirths per 100 reported live births appear in United Nations series only in the case of two African territories (Cape Verde Islands, and São Tome and Principe), and in both cases there is warning that the data are 'affected by incomplete or irregular registration'. It is possible that some post-natal deaths are classified as stillbirths in these statistics. It may, however, be assumed that in large populations the ratio of stillbirths to live births now varies from a minimum in the vicinity of 1.5 per cent to much higher figures. There is no reliable information on the frequency of miscarriages in large populations.

Total pregnancy wastage may be well below 12.5 per cent under favourable health conditions, but must be far higher in some unhealthy situations. For the present we may arbitrarily assume an average ratio of about 87.5 live births per 100 pregnancies. A frequency of 32 to 35 live births per 100

[1] Unweighted averages of values for Austria, Belgium, Czechoslovakia, Denmark, Finland, Italy, Norway, Switzerland, and England and Wales from data in United Nations *Demographic Yearbook 1951*. In some of these countries, the minimum period of gestation required in definition of a stillbirth is 28 weeks, in others 26 weeks or six months.

woman-years would then correspond to a frequency of 36.6 to 40 pregnancies per 100 woman-years.[1]

ADOLESCENT STERILITY

The theory of 'adolescent sterility' may at first appear inconsistent with the theory of increasing sterility with advance in age; but the two theories are not inherently contradictory. Indian data presented by Sinha indicate longer intervals between effective marriage and first conception among those married before 19 years than at later ages, although the highest total fertility is attained by women married at 16–18 years. The fertility of wives married at still earlier ages appears to be reduced slightly by pregnancies prior to full maturity, and this effect is intensified as regards the production of children who survive the perilous years of childhood in India (see Table 10). The numbers in this sample are small, but the results are internally consistent and congruous with other information.

The thesis of 'adolescent sterility' has been emphasized by some anthropologists to account for the relative infrequency of early pregnancies in some societies in which there is widespread juvenile promiscuity.[2] As stated by Ford:

'There is considerable evidence that even in those societies where adolescent sexual intercourse is promiscuous and unrestrained, childbirth among the unmarried is relatively infrequent. As has been pointed out this may be the consequence of practices of contraception, abortion infanticide, or enforced marriage. Nevertheless, the evidence suggests that social techniques are not so extensively employed as to account entirely for the rather surprising infrequence of childbearing by adolescent girls. It seems likely that, in addition to these social factors, the first few years after the menses appear as a period of relative sterility. A considerable amount of data in substantiation of this possibility have been collected by physiologists and anthropologists. The explanation for this period of relative sterility is not known, but it is believed that fecundity depends upon a general physical maturation process which is incomplete at menarche.'[3]

[1] The time required for gestation and recovery of procreative capacity after termination of pregnancies is taken into account in these values. The corresponding frequency of pregnancy per 1,000 years of exposure to risk of pregnancy (such as the rates shown above in Table 6) would, of course, be higher. One may assume about nine months as average full-term pregnancy and, following Lewis-Faning, a three-month recovery interval after each delivery of a living child, and, more arbitrarily, averages of 4.5 months of pregnancy and a one-month recovery in all other pregnancies. The corresponding frequencies of conception relative to exposure to risk would be 560 to 638 per 1,000 years, or 47 to 53 per 1,000 months.

[2] See Ashley-Montagu. 'Adolescent Sterility', Quarterly Review of Biology, 14, pp. 13–34, 192–219, 1939.

[3] Clellan S. Ford, A Comparative Study of Human Reproduction (Yale University Publications in Anthropology No. 32). New Haven, 1945, p. 22.

The same theory had previously been advanced by Duncan on the basis of his investigations of demographic data for Scotland near the middle of the nineteenth century.[1] The phrase 'adolescent sterility', though convenient, has been properly criticized by Beebe as misleading because the evidence does not indicate complete sterility during a definite period but, rather, sub-fecundity resulting in low pregnancy rates or long intervals of exposure to risk prior to conception. Although the achievement of full

TABLE 10.   Data Relating to Fertility of Marriages by Age at Marriage. Study by J. N. Sinha in Lucknow and Kanpur.[1]

Age at gauna[2]	All durations of marriage		Duration of marriage 21–30 years		Duration of marriage 31 years +		
	Number of wives	Mean interval between gauna and first live birth in years	Number of wives	Mean number of births	Number of wives	Mean number of births	Mean number of living children
Under 13, or 'prior to puberty'	128	5.0	26	6.6	58	7.8	4.4
13–15	273	3.2	79	7.2	71	8.1	5.2
16–18	305	2.5	76	7.4	33	8.4	5.6
19–21	166	1.7	43	6.2	15	7.5	5.0
22–24	57	1.7	18	6.0	—	—	—

[1] J. N. Sinha, 'Fertility and Age at Marriage'. Document P 43/Nov. 16, International Statistical Institute, New Delhi Session, 1951.
[2] 'Gauna' refers to consummation of marriage, assumed to establish actual conjugal relations.

capacity to produce living offspring may have no fixed relation to age at menarche (first menstruation), it should be noted that the average age at menarche may be considerably higher in some populations living under primitive conditions, as in parts of Africa and Melanesia, than in modern Europe or in India.[2] In any case, full capacity for the bearing and nursing of infants involves many complex biological processes which are not perfectly synchronized with the beginning of ovulation and menstruation.

Intensive and carefully controlled interview data reported by Beebe from a study in a southern mountain region of the United States, where early marriage is common and where there is little contraceptive practice,

[1] J. M. Duncan, *Fecundity, Fertility, and Sterility.* Edinburgh, 1866.
[2] See article by Fortes in this report; also, Raymond Pearl, *The Natural History of Population,* London, 1939.

have direct bearing on this problem. The data relate to women married at early ages, excluding those pregnant at time of marriage. The material shows that the interval between puberty and first pregnancy is highly variable, and is not systematically related to age of menarche. But the average time required for conception declines sharply in this series as age at beginning of conjugal experience advances, up to about 20 years, as follows: [1]

Age at marriage	13	14	15	16	17	18	19	20–21	22 +
Interval, in months, between marriage and first conception (smoothed values)	7.5	6.4	4.6	3.6	3.2	3.1	2.7	2.5	2.5

Presumably the decline in fecundity due to the accumulation of impairments begins at, or before, the achievement of fully mature capacity for procreation. New pathological conditions are also sometimes brought about by the process of gestation, whether interrupted by miscarriage or completed by a full-term delivery. It is conceivable that maternity under normal conditions may sometimes increase the chances of conception in later years, but the writer does not know of any evidence that relates directly to this question, whereas impairment of future fecundity during parturition is sometimes obvious. Again, increase in impairments of fecundity with advancing age may be caused by infections (gonorrhea, syphilis, or other diseases) or by accidents. It is probable, however, that even apart from such external causes, some aspects of the linked processes of maturation and senescence that eventually lead to the menopause induce reduction or cessation of fecundity long before that event. A decline in the average weight of ovaries during the thirties may have some significance in this respect.[2]

The emergence and decline of fecundity in women are not identical with the onset and cessation of menstruation, but they are obviously related phenomena. We should, therefore, include an account of Pearl's compilation of reported mean ages of women at menarche and at menopause.[3] The mean values found in 142 series of data on the menarche range from 13.2 years to 17.0 years; the mean of these means is 15.2 years (somewhat inflated by the frequent practice of reporting findings by complete years of age). The mean ages at menopause in 20 series range from 44.0 years to 49.4 years; the mean of these means is 46.4 years. Thus Pearl's data indicate an average continuation of menstruation over a span of about 31 years.

[1] Gilbert W. Beebe, *Contraception and Fertility in the Southern Appalachians.* Baltimore, 1942, p. 70.

[2] Jean Oliver, 'Structural Aspects of the Process of Aging', *The Social and Biological Challenge of Our Aging Population*; Eastern States Health Conference, 31 March–1 April 1949. New York, 1950.

[3] Raymond Pearl, op. cit., pp. 46–58, and Appendix.

Questions relating to the maturation and decline of fertility have been discussed here solely with reference to women. Comparable processes take place in the lives of men, but over a much longer span. In any case, advance in the age of one spouse is linked with that of the other. If we recognize that apparent decline of fecundity in women with advancing age may be in part a function of declining fecundity in men, or in the conjugal relations of spouses, we can ignore these aspects in order to simplify the analysis.

HYPOTHETICAL FECUNDITY OF A MODEL POPULATION

We will review at this point some of the major factors in the fecundity of human populations, with attention to their possible nature and magnitude under relatively favourable physical conditions. However, in doing so, we must bear in mind that the form of each of these functions may vary in different populations, and that any suggested magnitude may be exceeded in some populations but may be far above its true value in other populations.

The maturation of procreative capacity in females sometimes occurs at very early ages, in rare instances before 10 years of age.[1] A curve representing the proportion of women who would become able to bear living offspring at various ages, if free from any impairments to fecundity, must rise slowly at first, with gradual acceleration to some point of inflexion, beyond which it begins to level off. Its upper limit, subject to the reservation about impairments to fecundity, can be taken as 100 per cent. In other words, all women can be assumed to achieve 'maturity' in reproductive capacity, though some may remain sterile. It is not unreasonable to assume that this function could be represented by a symmetrical curve, having its point of inflexion at the age at which one-half of all women would have a first child if fully exposed to risk of conception and free from impairments to fecundity. In the light of the evidence reviewed in connexion with the theory of 'adolescent sterility', it seems likely that the inflexion point of such a curve may be well beyond the average age at menarche. The age 18.0 would appear to be an appropriate figure for general use, though its actual location in different populations must vary widely.

The following arbitrary formula for the maturation of procreative capacity (A) conforms to the conditions stated above, and gives values that are reasonably consistent with empirical observations:

$$A = \frac{1}{1 + e^{1.2(18.0-a)}}$$

In this and the following formulae, the initial letter (in this case: A)

[1] ibid., p. 57.

denotes the particular function in question; *a* denotes precise age in years; *e* denotes the base of the Naperian system of logarithms. It should be noted that 'age' here refers to time of delivery of a mature foetus, not to age at conception.

Values obtained on this formula rise from 0.01 per cent at age 10.5 years to about 5 per cent at age 15.5 years, 14 per cent at 16.5 years, 35 per cent at 17.5 years, 65 per cent at 18.5 years, 86 per cent at 19.5 years, and level off above 99 per cent after 22.0 years.

B. The extent to which fecundity is initially free from impairments, and the accumulation of such impairments with advancing age, involves more complicated issues. A formulation in terms of age similar to that given for the maturation of procreative capacity must ignore the relative influence of abstention from maternity or of successive pregnancies on this function, or must be stated with reference to some specified frequency of pregnancies. In view of the ambiguity of present evidence on this subject, this consideration is ignored in the formula suggested below. The arbitrary assumption used here is that 96 per cent of all women are initially capable of procreation, subject to the limitations of maturation and senescence. It is then assumed that this proportion is gradually reduced after 16.5 years at a gradually accelerated rate due to the accumulation of impairments to fecundity so that only about 90 per cent of all women remain fecund at age 27.5 years, only about 70 per cent at age 40.5 years, and none at age 55 years. The influence of concomitant variations in the procreative capacity of males is assumed to be taken into account in this formulation. The following formula conforms (at values of *a* above 16.5 years) to these assumptions: unity minus 0.01 times *e* to the power $(a—16.5) / 12$ plus 1.3863.[1] Otherwise stated:

$$B = 1 — 0.01 \ e \ [(a—16.5) / 12] + 1.3863$$

C. Although the final cessation of ovulation (associated with the menopause) is presumably induced by some of the factors involved in the earlier impairments of fecundity, the cessation of ovulation must be recognized as an independent factor. It is here assumed that the proportion of otherwise fecund women who retain at various ages the capacity to bear living offspring, as modified by processes associated with the menopause, can be represented by a symmetrical curve analogous to that used to represent the maturation of fecundity. It is, however, assumed that the change with age of this function in any population is somewhat more gradual—in view of Pearl's finding (in the publication previously cited) that the standard deviation of ages at menopause is greater than that of ages at menarche, and the information on maternity rates. The inflexion point of this curve

[1] The constant 1.3863 is exponent of *e* which gives the B = 0.96 when *a* = 16.5.

is placed at 46.5 years. The following arbitrary formula meets these conditions:

$$C = 1 - \frac{1}{1 + e^{\cdot \, 8(46.5-a)}}$$

According to this formula, less than 1 per cent of all women who are otherwise fecund, lose the capacity to bear living offspring due to processes directly associated with the menopause prior to 40.5 years, but the combined effect of factors B and C reduces the proportion of women assumed to remain fecund at this age to 69 per cent. The proportion represented as fecund, taking both of these factors into account, declines in successive years to 60 per cent at 42.5 years, 52 per cent at 43.5 years, 40 per cent at 44.5 years, 28 per cent at 45.6 years, 16 per cent at 46.5 years, and becomes less than 1 per cent at about 50 years of age.

Finally it is assumed that, if exposed to risk of conception in conjugal unions, the proportion of women who are capable of bearing live offspring at successive ages (P) is represented by the product of these three functions:

$$P = A \times B \times C$$

This formulation provides a hypothetical model, or schema, of fecundity which may have some useful applications. It could obviously be improved by a more accurate formulation of its component functions on the basis of more precise information.

On any assumption about the frequency of live births per year to women at various ages in fecund unions the schema can be used to provide a series of expected age-specific maternity rates per woman in the general population, including .women not in fecund unions—if all women experienced conjugal life throughout the childbearing years and if no antinatal practices were adopted.

In the absence of any clear evidence to the contrary, we tentatively assume that the frequency of live births per fecund woman per year remains constant at all ages. We experiment here with the hypothesis of 0.36 live births per year per woman in a fecund conjugal union. The resultant values are shown in Table 11. We also show, in the same table, an empirical series of age-specific maternity rates derived by Mortara from 1940 Brazilian census data. The values derived by Mortara were smoothed to eliminate variations assumed to result from errors in the reporting of ages, and were adjusted to give appropriate rates in successive units of time. A slight upward adjustment was also made on the assumption that some post-natal deaths were reported as stillbirths. The Brazilian rates presented here represent, even more accurately by virtue of these adjustments, the actual experience of a particular population. It should also be emphasized that the validity and theoretical significance of the results is enhanced by the accidental circumstance that the general level of fertility appears to have remained practically constant during the preceding 20 years, and probably during the last half century.

TABLE 11. Age-specific Maternity Rates (f_x) and Maternity Ratios($\bar{c}_x$). Observed Values, Brazil, 1940, and Hypothetical Fecundity Model.[1]

Age	Brazil, 1940			Hypothetical model			
	$100 f_x$ Age x to age x−1	$100 \bar{c}_x$ Exact age x	Per cent of total maternity. Exact age x	Capable of procreation. Per cent of all women	$100 f_x$ Age x to age x−1	$100 \bar{c}_x$ Exact age x	Per cent of total maternity. Exact age x
14	0.6	0.0	0.0	1.4	0.5	0.2	0.0
15	1.2	0.6	0.1	4.6	1.7	0.7	0.1
16	3.5	1.8	0.3	13.6	4.9	2.4	0.3
17	7.4	5.3	0.8	33.9	12.2	7.3	0.9
18	12.8	12.7	2.0	61.5	22.1	19.5	2.3
19	16.9	25.5	4.0	81.4	29.3	41.6	5.0
20	20.5	42.4	6.6	89.9	32.4	70.9	8.5
21	23.6	62.9	9.8	92.5	33.3	103.3	12.4
22	26.2	86.5	13.4	93.0	33.5	136.6	16.4
23	28.3	112.7	17.5	92.7	33.4	170.1	20.4
24	29.9	141.0	21.9	92.2	33.2	203.5	24.5
25	31.0	170.9	26.5	91.5	32.9	236.7	28.5
26	31.6	201.9	31.3	90.8	32.7	269.6	32.4
27	31.1	233.5	36.2	90.0	32.4	302.3	36.3
28	30.5	264.6	41.0	89.1	32.1	334.7	40.2
29	29.8	295.1	45.7	88.2	31.8	366.8	44.1
30	29.0	324.9	50.4	87.2	31.4	398.6	47.9
31	28.1	353.9	54.9	86.0	31.0	430.0	51.7
32	27.1	382.0	59.2	84.8	30.5	461.0	55.4
33	26.0	409.1	63.4	83.5	30.1	491.5	59.1
34	24.8	435.1	67.4	82.1	29.6	521.6	62.7

35	23.5	459.9	71.3	80.5	29.0	551.2	66.3
36	22.1	483.4	74.9	78.8	28.4	580.2	69.8
37	20.6	505.5	78.4	77.0	27.7	608.6	73.2
38	19.1	526.1	81.6	74.8	26.9	636.3	76.5
39	17.5	545.2	84.5	72.5	26.1	663.2	79.7
40	15.9	562.7	87.2	69.9	25.2	689.3	82.9
41	14.3	578.6	89.7	66.7	24.0	714.5	85.9
42	12.6	592.9	91.9	62.5	22.5	738.5	88.8
43	10.9	605.5	93.9	56.9	20.5	761.0	91.5
44	9.2	616.4	95.6	48.9	17.6	781.5	94.0
45	7.5	625.6	97.0	38.1	13.7	799.1	96.1
46	5.7	633.1	98.1	25.6	9.2	812.8	97.7
47	3.9	638.8	99.0	14.6	5.3	822.0	98.8
48	2.1	642.7	99.6	7.1	2.6	827.3	99.5
49	0.3	644.8	99.9	3.1	1.1	829.9	99.8
50	—	645.1	100.0	1.2	0.4	831.0	99.9
51	—	645.1	100.0	0.5	0.2	831.4	99.96
52	—	—	—	0.2	0.1	831.6	99.99
53	—	—	—	0.01	0.0	831.7	100.0
Total Maternity Ratio		6.45				8.32	

[1] See text for description of procedures. The values of the factors used in the estimates of proportions of women capable of procreation are given in Appendix A. The observed values, Brazil, 1940, are from the following study: Giorgio Mortara, *Determinação da Fecundidade Feminina Segundo a Idade Conforme O Censo de 1940, e Aplicações ao Cálculo da Taxa de Natalidade, da Tábua de Fecundidade e do Coeficiente de Reprodução, Para a População do Brasil*, Table III, col. e, and Table III, col. f. See also pp. 15, 25. Rio de Janeiro, 1948.

The level of fertility is higher at every point in the model population than in the Brazilian series. The maximum rate of births per 100 women per year in the latter series is 31.6 whereas the maximum in the model is 33.5. More important in effect on total fertility, the Brazilian series reaches its maximum at a later age, 26.5 years, in contrast to 22.5 years in the model, and falls away from the maximum more rapidly in subsequent years. Departures along these lines from absolute procreative capacity at various ages would be expected in the actual behaviour of any population. Some women do not enter conjugal life until the middle twenties; all women do not share in conjugal life even when the proportion doing so is highest; and at later ages an increasing proportion is removed from conjugal life by death of spouse, separation, or estrangement. There is, moreover, some reduction of births in Brazil by contraception and abortion, though these practices are not widespread. Finally, it is possible that the accumulation of impairments to fecundity may mount more rapidly with age in Brazil than in some other populations. The hypothetical rates of the model are imaginary. Presumably they do not precisely represent the procreative capacity of any actual population. Certainly they could not be expected to fit precisely the biological conditions of any particular population selected at random. Nevertheless, the two series are quite consistent except for differences that are capable of rational interpretation. Some further observations on the relations between those series will be made in the following section.

LEVELS OF NATALITY IN RELATION TO PROCREATIVE CAPACITY

Even if, by chance, the model of fecundity presented in Table 11 truly represented the 'absolute biological capacity for procreation' of any population, this would not give a wholly realistic estimate of the level of fertility to be expected under cultural conditions most conducive to high fertility. Unlimited expression of procreative capacity at very early ages is repugnant to the ideals of most societies, as detrimental to health and welfare. Moreover, although our evidence indicates that this might slightly increase total fertility, it is probable that it would decrease net reproduction, due to the increased mortality of girls who become mothers at very early ages and the high mortality of their infants. This is shown in the Indian study by Sinha, cited above. Even in societies generally characterized by very early marriages, such as China (see surveys cited above in Table 1) and Soviet Armenia (official data for 1924), the median age of brides at first marriage is usually a little over 18.0 years. Births at about age 18.5 years are, of course, the result of conceptions between 17.5 and 18.0 years. Some births, however, do occur at very early ages in all societies with high fertility. With these considerations in mind, it seems most realistic to assume a frequency of births prior to 19.0 years similar to that found in

Brazil (say 0.250 births per woman) in place of that found in the model population (0.416 births per woman). This reduces the total number expected per woman living through the childbearing period to 8.15 births. We shall still refer to this adjusted estimate as representing hypothetical rates in a population 'with very early marriage'.

We can now obtain some idea of the influence of postponement of marriage, with avoidance of pregnancy prior to marriage, to successive ages on fertility—comparing results obtained from the Brazilian series and from the model population (with the slight adjustments described in the preceding paragraph). We will arbitrarily use the term 'average age at marriage' with the implication that all births prior to nine months thereafter are precisely balanced by reductions due to delays in marriage beyond this time. We must also ignore the influence of delay in initial maternity on fertility at later ages. There is probably some influence of this sort, but the information reviewed above suggests that in a population with no attempt to control fertility this influence is not very great. On this basis, the estimated proportions of total reproductive capacity eliminated by postponement of marriages from 'very early ages' to successively later ages are as follows:

Average age at marriage	Fertility eliminated	
	Brazil	Model
	%	%
'Very early ages'	0	0
20.25 years	9.8	10.6
24.25 years	26.5	28.2
28.25 years	45.7	44.2

It may at first appear surprising that the results obtained in these two series are so similar. This is partly the result of our arbitrary adjustment of births at ages under 19.0 years in the model population to the observed level in Brazil. Otherwise, to the degree that the model population truly represents potential procreative capacity, the agreement can be interpreted as follows. In Brazil the reduction of fertility through avoidance of births outside of regular conjugal relations (supplemented to some extent by abortion, contraception and the effects of disease) is apparently about as intense at later ages, due to widowhood, separations, estrangements and inhibitions, as that at earlier ages due to postponement of initial exposure to conception.

Conditions tending to reduce fertility throughout the childbearing period, especially at later ages, similar to those in force in Brazil, are operative in varying degrees in all societies. Nowhere do all women enter new conjugal unions immediately after the death of a spouse. Everywhere there are conflicts in personal relations, with resultant overt separations or covert estrangements and inhibitions. And everywhere conjugal partners are separated occasionally by economic necessity, ceremonial obligations, responsibilities to absent kin, or other circumstances. Such considerations account in the main for our earlier finding that even in societies with early marriage and strong emphasis on children, the actual level of fertility rarely rises above an average of 6.0 to 6.6 live births per woman living through the childbearing period. According to the information given in the supplement, the lower of these figures would normally correspond to crude rates between 40 and 50 births per 1,000 population per year; the latter figure corresponds to crude rates of 44 to 55 births per year. Higher levels are found in exceptional circumstances. But the figures just cited represent the levels that can ordinarily be expected where cultural conditions are most conducive to high fertility.

Widespread sterility can, of course, cut down the level of fertility drastically, apart from the direct, psychological influence of cultural conditions on reproductive behaviour.

On the other hand, a general postponement of marriages until women are 24 or 25 years of age (reinforced by strong emphasis on avoidance of childbearing prior to marriage) tends to reduce the level of fertility by 25 per cent, more or less, below that expected in a population characterized by very early marriages. The average number of births per woman would then drop to about 4.0 to 4.9 with no greater control over fertility in other respects similar to that now prevailing in Brazil. The expected crude birth rates would then be between 30 and 40 per 1,000 population per year. Powerful cultural forces, however, are required to sustain any general acceptance of such a long interval between puberty and the beginning of conjugal life.

It is clear from our investigation of information bearing on this subject that the capacity for procreation of some populations is well above observed rates in many populations in which fertility is relatively free from any conscious control—as illustrated by rates presented above in Table 1. It is probable that some of the rates shown in Table 1 are grossly deficient. For example, the very low rates reported by Ta Chen from an experimental census inquiry in Yunnan Province (giving only 3.80 births per woman of completed fertility, or 4.45 births as a cumulated nuptial maternity ratio) are peculiarly open to suspicion, on this ground, or they must reflect abnormal conditions.

But the evidence from many studies of total maternity ratios in the vicinity of about 6 live births per woman of completed fertility in populations with traditional modes of life conducive to high fertility, including almost universal marriage of women at early ages, can not be set aside in this way. In some of these populations the evidence on fertility is confirmed by complementary studies of mortality and rates of natural increase.

56

We must, therefore, accept the finding that, among relatively stable populations in which there is no recognized social condition tending to lower fertility, the average number of births per woman of completed fertility varies in different populations from about 6 to about 8 live births—with levels more frequently near the lower than the upper limit of this normal range. In view of the complexity of the reproductive process, it is quite possible that variations in fecundity among different populations may be affected by variations in genetic factors. Levels of fecundity may also be depressed in many populations by malnutrition, and by the prevalence of various diseases such as malaria, influenza, leprosy, yaws, etc.—even apart from the more specific possible effects on fertility of some venereal diseases. Finally, we must give attention to the possible subtle influence on fertility of many cultural factors, such as estrangement or temporary separation of spouses, within societies in which social institutions are generally favourable to high fertility.

CHAPTER II

The Relation of Kinship Systems to Fertility

KINSHIP AS A FACTOR IN SOCIAL ORGANIZATION

The interests and behaviour of individuals vary within each society, and ways of living change with time. But continuity of life is sustained through accepted patterns of social relations and common beliefs, goals, and rules of behaviour.

The basic social structure and values of many societies are anchored in a system of kinship relations. The degree of emphasis on family and kinship, as well as the nature of these relations, varies widely among societies at all technical levels. But family and kin are important everywhere, and they form the basic structure of social organization in many non-European societies. An examination of the relation of kinship systems to fertility opens an avenue to the central issues of this inquiry.

We will need to distinguish between societies with widely different techniques. Terms commonly used for this purpose, such as 'primitive', 'agrarian', and 'industrial' may suggest false implications. It is impossible to characterize the social organization of one society as more 'primitive' than that of another. Yet a significant distinction can be made with respect to techniques. The techniques of some societies, however elaborate or ingenious they may be, are 'primitive', in the sense that no use is made of some important inventions, such as draft animals in agriculture or written records. These technical limitations do affect social organization; they imply relative isolation from the cultural forces released by such inventions; and they tend to be associated with a predominance of face-to-face relations in social life. The term 'primitive society' should, therefore, always be understood to mean simply 'a society with primitive techniques'.

The term 'agrarian society' or 'agrarian civilization' is used here to denote the social life of a population mainly dependent on non-mechanized agriculture, but with written records and a political system organized on a territorial basis. Agrarian societies maintain trade between villages and town and city centres. They have middle-men, government officials, and a priesthood; but these classes form only a small part of the total population. Some 'pastoral societies', as in Central Asia, are similar in some aspects of their social organization to 'primitive societies' and in other respects to 'agrarian societies'. All of these classifications, though useful, are somewhat arbitrary because the distinctions to which they refer are present in varying degrees in different societies.

Finally, the characterization of modern society within the sphere of western European influence as 'industrial' is also open to misinterpretation. This society is distinguished by a series of related technical, economic and social inventions. Mechanized industry is only one aspect of its institutional structure, and this aspect can easily be over-emphasized. This false emphasis is, in fact, sometimes responsible for errors in programmes of economic development.

The greatest diversity in social organization is found among primitive societies. For example, family relations are highly permissive and equalitarian in some primitive societies but rigid and authoritarian in others. However, primitive and agrarian societies are often alike in emphasis on well-defined rights and obligations among specific groups and in their respect for traditionally recognized roles and status. A basis principle of social organization in many such societies is described in the following quotation. 'The principle is not precisely that of the old slogan, "From each according to his ability, to each according to his needs". It is crossed by another, "From each according to his status obligations in the social system, to each according to his rights in that system".'[1] The basic social structure of the complex Japanese empire has been described as that of a 'web society';[2] and the term might appropriately be applied to many small, isolated societies.

Kinship provides the most pervasive fabric of the social structure of many primitive and agrarian societies. Kinship systems are themselves rooted in elementary biological and social needs through the operation of the primary family relationships: parents–children, husband–wife, and siblings. But in many societies kinship systems, though rooted in these primary human relations, become autonomous institutions. As the carriers of a wide range of values they may exercise dominance over the personal relations of individuals within nuclear families. In such societies it is often the clan or the lineage that is vested with sacred prerogatives. Thus in many societies it is an extended kinship group, rather than two spouses united in marriage, that 'God hath joined together' as being 'one flesh'. Marriage is then conceived as essentially an arrangement between two kinship groups, to be formed or dissolved only on their authority and in accordance with established rules and regulations. A whole kinship structure comes to have a major interest in individual families as modes of renewing its life and extending its power and prestige.

The primary family relations have their own roots in basic human needs. The nature of human reproduction poses certain problems to which every enduring society must offer some solution. One of the most obvious, though

---

[1] Raymond Firth. *Elements of Social Organization*. London, 1951, p. 142.
[2] Frank Gibney. *Five Gentlemen of Japan*. New York, 1953.

perhaps not the most important, of these problems is that of sexual competition. Promiscuous sexual relations among children and youth, under the restraining influence of a stable adult community, may be compatible with effective co-operation in economic activity and defence. Accordingly, many preliterate societies permit juvenile promiscuity. On the contrary, unregulated sexual competition among the adult members of a society tends to disrupt orderly social life. Adult sexual relations are institutionalized to some degree in all societies. The institutionalization may be imperfect; but it provides a norm supported by community sentiment in the adjustment of personal relations. Marriage establishes legally sanctioned sexual relations between one man and one woman (monogamy) or between one man and several women (polygyny) or, in a few societies, between one woman and several men (polyandry).

Similarly, the prohibition of sexual relations among persons in certain kinship categories appears to be, in principle, one of the few universal social restrictions on human behaviour. This principle has infinite variety in mythical justification and in types and degrees of extension; but almost always it excludes competitive sexual relations between parents and their children and between brothers and sisters within the immediate family. This institution may have been motivated in part by instinctive attitudes, but it appears to have been socially reinforced as an essential condition of orderly social life. It can, in other words, be interpreted in terms of its 'functional' value in social organization.

Social provisions for the protection and nurture of the young answer to needs that are critical for the maintenance of any society. The physical need, which is wholly met by instinctive motives among other mammals, is particularly acute in man because of the prolonged helplessness of human infants. This prolongation of immaturity in man is, in turn, associated with the submergence of specific instincts in the emergence of higher intelligence and greater capacity for learning. Moreover, in addition to the physical needs of a child for protection and nurture, there is the social need of each new member of a community to acquire some assured status and some definition of his role in relation to other members of the community. These needs are met by the social institutions of parenthood.

The parturition and nursing of infants by mothers provides a biological foundation, with instinctive support and immediate satisfaction, for maternity as a social principle. 'Social maternity' thus merely reinforces and extends the biological principle of maternity.

On the other hand paternity, as a force beyond the mere act of impregnation, has no firm basis in man's biological nature. 'Among our structurally closest analogues—the primates—the male does not feed the female. Heavy with young, making her way laboriously along, she fends for herself. He may fight to protect her or to possess her, but he does not nurture her.'[1]

[1] Margaret Mead. *Male and Female.* New York, 1949, p. 189. Reference to Solly Zuckerman, *Functional Affinities of Man, Monkeys, and Apes.*

The economic need of mothers and children demands the fixation of specific responsibility for their nurture. Moreover, the relation of children to a 'father' provides a pivot in fixing the roles, rights, and privileges of different individuals in an orderly society. Accordingly, all primitive societies give explicit recognition to paternity as a social principle. 'Social paternity' may be based, in part, on some apprehension of the nature of biological paternity. But in many cultures the definition of a 'father' does not require biological paternity as an essential condition, and the paternal relation as socially determined is given priority over biological paternity in the regulation of community life. Social paternity is usually determined by marriage. In fact, marriage might be most accurately defined, with regard to its function in many societies, as a social institution whereby a particular man acquires rights and assumes obligations with respect to the children borne by a particular woman, at least to those born while the marriage is in force, and sometimes to those born before this period or conceived thereafter. In some societies if no children are born within a reasonable time the marriage becomes void, or the woman's kin are held responsible for amending it by providing a sister or other woman to produce the children that were the primary objective of the marriage. However, marriage always involves other rights and obligations in sexual and economic relations. The social principle of paternity, defining the role of the husband-father, is the keystone in the social structure of the primary family.

The sense of unity among brothers and sisters is a product of spontaneous childhood responses. Parents also have a natural interest in fostering among their children sense of membership in a common group. But the unity of the sibling group is also institutionally reinforced by social arrangements and expectations. This is important because such 'unity' is often marred by rivalry and conflict, which may outweigh the motivations toward affection and common interests. The great stress placed on 'the harmony of brothers' in Confucian precepts often merely holds an intense rivalry among the sons of a Chinese father within the bounds of proper decorum.[1] There is emphasis on the sibling group in all societies, though in many societies this group is sharply differentiated, not only with respect to sex, but also with respect to order of birth. And within polygynous households a mother and her children, usually living in a separate house, form a nuclear subgroup within the nuclear family. All the boys in such a household may accept one another as brothers, but they are conscious of the distinction between full brothers and half brothers. If, as is frequently the case, biological conception is thought to originate in a woman (though it may be understood that the unformed child is 'nourished' by male secretions) full brothers regard one another as blood brothers, whereas other boys in the household are merely brothers by common kinship status.

The social institutions of maternity, marriage, paternity, and fraternity,

[1] Francis Hsu. *Under the Ancestor's Shadow.* New York, 1948, p. 244.

61

reinforced by the prohibition of incest, are rooted in the nature of the reproductive process and in the universal human need for orderly social life. All these institutions converge in the family. Primary family relations also generate more extensive kinship relations, which are organized in very different ways in different societies. And the form and functions of the primary family are defined in most societies in the context of these more extensive kinship systems.

TYPES OF KINSHIP SYSTEMS[1]

Each primary 'nuclear family' is mortal. It is formed, and it passes away. Moreover, each individual will normally be a member of two nuclear families successively, as a son and then as a husband-father, or as a daughter and as a wife-mother. No two members of a nuclear family enter directly into the other nuclear families of its other members—except in the case of two sisters marrying one husband in a polygynous household. Again, no two individuals, except siblings, have the same circle of persons related by common biological descent.

A further consideration is even more critical. The circle of kin, as defined by an individual with reference to descendance through mother and father, and through their mothers and fathers, et cetera, is not, and cannot be, a cohesive kinship group. It includes individuals on maternal and paternal sides, at each ascending and descending juncture, who may not be related to one another, and according to the rules of many societies must not be related to one another. I may feel myself to be related to the children and grandchildren of my paternal grandfather's brothers and sisters, and to those of my paternal grandmother, my maternal grandfather, and my maternal grandmother; but these four sets of relatives have no necessary relationship to one another.

A system of kinship that is reckoned by each individual with reference to ascendance and descendance, without distinction between male and female lines, is called a *cognatic system* by some authors. 'Persons are cognatic kin or cognates when they are descended from a common ancestor or ancestress counting descent through males and females.'[2] It is, however, important to emphasize, as already noted, that in such a system an indi-

---

[1] The following exposition is heavily dependent on the treatment of kinship systems in the symposium: A. R. Radcliffe-Brown and Daryll Forde, *African Systems of Kinship and Marriage*, London, 1950, 399 pp. This dependence applies both to the theoretical exposition by Radcliffe-Brown in the 'Introduction' and to the treatment of particular kinship systems by various contributors. It must, however, be emphasized that we shall use extraneous material and develop implications which are foreign to the intent of the authors of this symposium and which might not be acceptable to them. In particular, so far as the present writer can perceive, the theoretical treatment by Radcliffe-Brown is free from the taint of any interest in the possible relation of kinship systems to human fertility.
[2] Radcliffe-Brown, 'Introduction' in Radcliffe-Brown and Forde, op. cit., p. 4.

vidual includes among his cognates persons who are not cognates to one another. The circles of kinship are formed and reformed in each successive generation.

In a cognatic system, as defined above, the emphasis in kinship relations rests on the nuclear family. A society with such a kinship system will not have a rigid social structure, or the major elements of its social structure will be formed in other ways, for example, through emphasis on sex and age associations, or the political organization of village and territorial activities.

Contrary to some earlier speculative theories, cognatic kinship systems with emphasis on the nuclear family, are widely prevalent among societies with the most primitive techniques. The 'clan' system, involving a radically different unilateral principle, appears most commonly at a higher technical level.

'The clan is a widespread but far from universal phenomenon and is absent from some of the rudest marginal peoples, such as the Andamenese pygmies, the Ona and Yaghan of southernmost America, the unequivocally simple people of the Mackenzie area, of Washington, Oregon, Nevada, and Utah. . . . In the large and culturally diverse area, such as America north of Mexico, the rudest people lack clans; unilateral systems are generally associated with farming tribes and exceptionally complex societies of hunters, such as the Tinglet of northern British Columbia. In Siberia equivalent findings appear; the simple Chukchi and Koryak are clanless and have kinship terminologies which in no way suggest a pristine unilateralism; but the Yakut and other Turkic peoples, the feltmaking, iron-smelting pastoral nomads of the area, are organized into rigid patrilineal clans and phratries.'[1]

Clans are, however, found in some populations with very primitive technology. In some Australian tribes there is both a complicated kinship system involving clans and an emphasis on age-grading. The latter system 'divides, first, the men from the women . . . on the basis of those who are initiated into the mysteries and those who are not, and then redivides the men on an age-graded scale based primarily on the place a man achieves within the rest of his social organization through *rites de passage*'.[2] The participation of a Murngin in the age-grading structure revolves around his position in the immediate family structure and his place in ceremonial mysteries. However, the whole social structure is built on the kinship pattern.

'The very complex kinship structure with its seven lines of descent and five generations in each line is but an elaboration of the immediate family of orientation and that of procreation, that is, of the family into which he is born and that which he creates at marriage. The underlying mechanism controlling the relations of these two families is that of asym-

[1] Robert H. Lowie. 'Social Organization', *Encyclopedia of the Social Sciences*.
[2] W. Lloyd Warner. *A Black Civilization*. New York, 1937, p. 5.

63

metrical cross-cousin marriage, which here means that a man marries his maternal uncle's daughter but not his father's sister's daughter . . . the result of this asymmetry has been to give a tremendous lateral spread to the kinship structure instead of keeping it narrowed to the two lines of descent where symmetrical cross-cousin marriage takes place.'[1]

A cohesive and continuing kinship structure can be formed either by emphasis on patrilineal descent or by emphasis on matrilineal descent. In either way the unity of the sibling group is preserved—especially as regards those who by virtue of their sex are part of a continuing lineage. A group of brothers, or a group of sisters, acquire hereditary rights and transmit them to their descendants of the same sex. Such a group usually maintains rights and obligations with respect to their siblings of the opposite sex throughout their lives, but the children of these other siblings are assimilated into other lineages. This does not imply an absence of affectionate relations between individuals and their nephews and nieces with whom they have no legal bonds. In fact, the emphasis in affectionate relations is frequently found to lie outside of, and sometimes in antithesis to, lines of control and of legal rights and obligations. A large group of kindred bound by descent from a common ancestor (in the case of patrilineal lineages) or ancestress (in the case of matrilineal lineages) is referred to by anthropologists as a *clan*. A 'patrilineal clan' is sometimes called a *gens* (plural *gentes*), after the usage of the Romans; but this distinction in language seems to be going out of style. A patrilineal system is often called an *agnatic* system, again in accordance with Latin terminology. The term 'lineage' is commonly used to denote a functionally distinct unilateral group of kin within a clan, if this smaller group is distinguished as a social entity.

The traditional terms patriarchy or 'father-right' and matriarchy or 'mother-right' emphasize lines of authority or legal rights affecting personal relations and the transmission of property, as contrasted with mere recognition of lineage. They are useful terms, although used with false implications in some early theories. They imply strong emphasis on matrilineal or patrilineal descent, plus an emphasis on the rights of men or on the rights of women in social organization and in the definition of social obligations.

Emphasis on patrilineal descent and father-right, or on matrilineal descent and mother-right is increased as clans, or lineages, acquire status through the control of property or the possession of exclusive religious privileges, such as the possession of an ancestral shrine or rituals. In this way a clan becomes a corporate group, and the interests of its members are oriented toward the enhancement of its prestige and the perpetuation of its power. This identification of interests is intensified by emotional response to the clan as the source of the life of its members and as the vehicle of their immortality. The sense of kinship within the clan is

[1] Warner, op. cit., p. 7.

commonly emphasized by a prohibition against marriage among its members. A corporate clan provides and controls in high degree the means of sustenance and the destiny of its members. Therefore in societies where father-right or mother-right is strongly emphasized, the clan becomes the focus of all those sentiments of loyalty which a western European divides between his immediate family, his church and his nation.[1]

It must not be assumed that every primitive society can be easily classified as 'cognatic' or 'patrilineal' or 'matrilineal'. Actually patrilineal and matrilineal inheritance are matters of degree; they may be expressed in many different forms; and most societies give some recognition to both principles. Conflicting interests lead to all sorts of compromises in social structure between emphasis on matrilineal and patrilineal relations. There may even be a 'full and simultaneous development of both patrilineal and matrilineal kin groups', with both groups corporately organized. Among the Yakö of the Cross River region in Nigeria, both patriclans and matriclans have distinct economic and religious organization. Residence is patrilocal, and there is a high incidence of polygyny, with frequent increase of household by capture or purchase of children from other tribes. But matrilineal groups have powerful religious sanctions, control marriage arrangements and burials and, according to traditional laws, now widely challenged, regulated the transmission of accumulated wealth in livestock or currency (brass rods or modern coins).[2]

More commonly, simultaneous emphasis on matrilineal and patrilineal interests tends to check the full development of either principle. Various compromises between these principles among some societies in Central Africa are described by Richards.[3] For example, among the Bemba of the north-eastern plateau of Northern Rhodesia, descent and inheritance are matrilineal but 'positional'. 'The social status and kinship possessions of each dead person, man or woman, is passed on to a selected heir or heiress' within the matrilineage. This refers chiefly to the transfer of a person's

---

[1] The term 'corporate group', as used here, includes the principle of indefinite continuity through time, or 'perpetuity'. This is in accordance with its use by Maine, who applied the term 'corporation' to the continuing family in early Roman society, which was legally unaffected by the succession of one *pater familias* by another. 'Succession in corporations is necessarily universal, and the family was a corporation.' (Sir Henry Maine, *Ancient Society*, 1861; Everyman Edition, London, 1917, p. 109.)

This principle is not stressed in Weber's conception of a corporate group (Verband). He defines it as a closed group, or one that limits the admission of outsiders by rules, with 'a formalized system of authority'. (Max Weber, *The Theory of Social and Economic Organization*, translated by A. M. Henderson and Talcott Parsons, New York, 1947, pp. 145–6.)

As used in this report, the term implies all of these principles: indefinite continuity, closed or formal membership, a formal system of authority, as well as some major function, or functions, in social life.

[2] Daryll Forde. 'Double Descent Among the Yakö', in Radcliffe-Brown and Forde, op. cit., pp. 285–332. See also S. F. Nadel, 'Dual Descent in the Nuba Hills', ibid., pp. 333–59.

[3] Audrey I. Richards. 'Some Types of Family Structure Amongst the Central Bantu', in Radcliffe-Brown and Forde, op. cit., pp. 207–51.

guardian spirit, intimate personal possessions and the social status, because the Bemba have little material property. Girls are nominally married before puberty. A man gives small gifts to his father-in-law, and works for him during an indefinite period. He thus earns the right to be accepted, in a formal ceremony (sometime after the puberty of his wife) as a member of his wife's clan, and is released from taboos to which he was previously subject in his relations with his wife's kin. Thereafter he may settle permanently in his wife's village; but he is free for the first time to remove his wife and children to his own village. But this is a 'male dominant society'. The husband has a right to the labour of his wife; she rarely has a separate granary; and the husband exercises control over his wife even while he remains in her father's village. Authority over children is divided between the father and the mother's brother, and is strongly influenced by the relative personal power of each. Finally, an older man acquires increased authority within the extended family of father, daughters, and their husbands and offspring. Richards makes the following comment which has special significance for our purposes:

'Note that among the Mayombe, with their corporate matrilineages, it is thought to be the duty of all women to produce as many children as possible for their brothers, whereas the insistence is only strong in the case of the royal women among the Bemba, and it is only the ruling dynasty that can be reckoned as a corporate matrilineage in any sense of the word.'[1]

It is important to take account of the fact that the Bemba of the plateau region and many of the tribes in river and swamp districts of Northern Rhodesia are forced, by the infertility of the soil or the need to seek new forest clearings, to shift their residence frequently. Such shifting of residence tends to promote 'shallow' kinship systems.

Emphasis on the mother-right is more pronounced among the Yao of Nyasaland, also described by Richards. Villages here are more stable, and there is more real property. A group of sisters and their children, or a woman and her children, with their eldest brother, as head, with his wife and children, form the principal operational unit in Yao society. Inheritance is matrilineal, and the matriclans seem to have a corporate character. In spite of some conflicts and strains in the social structure of the Yao, which are discussed by Richards, the emphasis on matrilineal relations seems to be clearly predominant in the organization of this society.

The situation among the Kongo and Mayombe in districts between the interior Congo Basin and the Atlantic has been complicated, especially in the case of the former, by wealth acquired through trade in contact with Europeans over several generations and a high incidence of slavery. There are large marriage payments in these societies, and the husband acquires immediate right to bring his wife to his village, but children are returned

---

[1] ibid., p. 223, note 1.

to the wife's brother at puberty, and descent and succession are matrilineal.

The situation among the Ila in the Kague River basin of Northern Rhodesia is equally, or even more, complex. There is some evidence here of double descent groups, with exogamous matrilineal and patrilineal kinship groups. Inheritance is shared in a wide group in which both sides of the family are represented.

In ancient Hawaiian and some other Polynesian societies, the principle of bilateral descent is associated with an emphasis on the differentiation of generations. The pattern of primary family relations then differs from that of the nuclear family in a society with a simple cognatic system.

Among the New Zealand Maori, descent is traced through both paternal and maternal lines, though with some emphasis on paternal descent. Nevertheless, there are continuous groups of an essentially corporate character (except that membership is not rigorously defined) in Maori society which in function resemble corporate lineages formed on a unilineal principle. The continuity of the Maori descent groups is achieved by emphasizing the accepted lineage of the group with which spouses establish their residence, usually the husband's kindred, but occasionally the wife's kindred. In either case the children are entitled to claim rights in the descent group from which a parent or grandparent had separated, as regards residence, at marriage. But these collateral relations are usually not emphasized, and unless re-established, they tend to be ignored—leaving descent groups, each of which traces its origin from a single ancestor. The lines between the living members of a group and its ancestor may include one or more female links. Kinship relations are also complicated by frequent adoptions, even of children whose parents are living; but these transfers occur only among near kin.[1]

The smallest functionally important group in traditional Maori society is the *whanau*, the family group that shares a hut—typically an extended family. Nuclear families within this group are recognized in personal and in some economic relations; but the *whanau* functions as a unit in most social and economic affairs. A more inclusive descent group (analogous to a corporate lineage) is called a *hapu*. The members of a *hapu* are bound by common descent from the same ancestor. But intermarriage among them is not prohibited, and was in fact encouraged. Similarly a tribe (*iwi*), the largest kinship group, comprises a number of *hapu*. Each tribe assumes derivation from one member of a company of ancestors who established themselves in New Zealand at some earlier time, coming in a fleet of canoes. Groups of tribes are loosely associated by the tradition that their ancestors were members of the same canoe. But this association did not, in the past,

---

[1] The treatment here is based on the exposition by Raymond Firth, *Primitive Economics of the New Zealand Maori*, London, 1929—with some rephrasing by the present writer to bring out comparisons and contrasts with other material in this study.

67

prevent frequent wars between tribes associated with the same ancestral canoe.

Formerly, the legal title of a kinship group to its lands was frequently menaced by the conflicting claims of another group. Conflicts among *hapu* within the same tribe were usually settled by adjudication; and all the *hapu* of a tribe rallied to defend their tribal lands against outside forces. Rank and authority within each kinship group was determined primarily by descent and order of birth. However, an incompetent tribal chief might be displaced by another, who would assume this authority in all matters except certain religious functions. The scope of a *hapu* corresponds roughly to that of a village community, though a *hapu* might have branches in several villages, and a village might contain members of several *hapu* (resident in separate quarters within the village).

Maori society has a strong artistic emphasis, which found expression in community workshops, with skilled carvings, etc. There is keen competition among kinship groups in artistic achievements and in dispays of hospitality, as well as in military and economic affairs. According to a supplementary communication from Professor Firth, the members of a Maori *hapu* take pride in its size, as compared with other *hapu*, and welcome births in any of its member families with joy.

Information on the Maori is particularly interesting as showing how functions that are frequently characteristic of unilineal kinship systems in other societies are performed in this society by groups that are organized on a different system of kinship relations.

We have drawn attention to some of these variant patterns in order to emphasize the dangers of unwarranted simplification in the treatment of kinship systems. The classification of kinships by major types is useful, and essential to our purposes, but we must bear in mind the abstract nature of any such classification. In Weber's sense they are 'ideal types'. The correspondence between the social structure of any actual society and one of these ideal types is a matter of varying degree and emphasis.

Four major categories of kinship systems may now be listed as follows:
1. Simple cognatic systems, without emphasis on distinction between matrilineal and patrilineal descent. In such societies, emphasis in kinship relations tends to be focused on the nuclear family.
2. Patrilineal systems, with emphasis on father-right.
3. Matrilineal systems, with emphasis on mother-right.
4. A residual category of intermediate and complex kinship systems that deviate significantly from any of the three theoretically simpler types.

The implications for fertility of some intermediate or complex kinship systems may approach those of a society with strong emphasis on patrilineal or matrilineal relations.

The unilateral systems (types 2 and 3 above) are parallel and, in some ways, similar systems. They tend to have quite different implications with respect to relations between husband and wife. But in many other respects, including emphasis on values relating to reproduction, they may have similar implications. The extent to which these systems have a common character is emphasized in the following passage:

'While in one sense mother-right and father-right are opposite types of system, there is another sense in which they are only contrasting varieties of a single type. What they have in common is the extreme emphasis on the lineage, matrilineal or patrilineal, and they both contrast strongly with systems based mainly on cognatic kinship; in both, the jural relations in kinship are rigidly confined to one lineage and clan. Possessive rights over the children belong entirely to the lineage, and inversely it is within the lineage that the individual has his most important duties and also his most significant rights, such as the right of support and rights of inheritance over property. In religion also . . . it is the lineage or clan ancestors to whom one owes religious duties, and from whom one may ask for succour. The institutional complex of which mother-right and father-right are contrasting forms is thus one that can hardly make its appearance except at a relatively high stage of social development, where property and its transmission have become important, and where social continuity has come to be based on lineage.'[1]

THE DEMOGRAPHIC IMPLICATIONS OF EMPHASIS ON MOTHER-RIGHT

The Ashanti are selected for special consideration because emphasis on matrilineal relations is a basic principle of their social organization and because we have especially rich information on their culture and demography.[2] There are now more than a half-million Ashanti[3] most of whom live in a fertile region of the Gold Coast between the coastal Colony and the interior Northern Territories. (The word 'Ashanti' is used to refer to a political division, or to the principal ethnic group in this division.) They speak an Akan language, and their ancestors seem to have lived in this general region over many generations. They had a relatively advanced native agriculture before contact with Europeans, and remained independent until their subjugation by the British a half-century ago. Their economy has been changed by the introduction of cocoa as a commercial

---

[1] Radcliffe-Brown, in Radcliffe-Brown and Forde, op. cit., pp. 76–7.

[2] Meyer Fortes, 'Kinship and Marriage among the Ashanti', in Radcliffe-Brown and Forde, op. cit., pp. 252–84; also, Fortes: 'A Demographic Field Study in Ashanti', this report, Part Two. K. A. Busia: 'Some Aspects of the Relation of Social Conditions to Fertility in the Gold Coast', this report, Part Three The Gold Coast: *Census of Population 1948, Report and Tables*, p. 422, London, 1950.

[3] According to the 1948 census there are 580,000 Ashanti in the Gold Coast of whom 505,000 are in Ashanti. There are 139,000 Brong, of whom 136,000 are in Ashanti. The total population of Ashanti is 818,944 persons, of whom 816,673 are Africans.

crop on farms owned and operated by Ashanti, external and internal trade, and the use of industrial products, including textiles, kerosene, and corrugated iron for roofing. There has been rather large migration into the region during the last quarter century.[1] Roads, schools and hospitals have been built. A small minority has acquired the rudiments of formal education and a few individuals have achieved high professional status. A considerably larger number, perhaps one in every eight persons, is affiliated with Christian churches; but most of the Christians adhere in varying degrees to their ancient traditions. The social organization of the Ashanti, though modified and subject to new strains, has remained remarkably stable during the economic transition of recent decades.

The Ashanti nation emerged during the eighteenth century as a powerful confederation of semi-autonomous chiefdoms grouped round a kingship. They fought six wars against the British, prior to their final subjugation; there were also wars between the king and rebellious chiefs. Alien elements have been introduced into all chiefdoms, by the capture or purchase of slaves in former times and by voluntary migration. Political offices have both a fixed territorial position and a sacred status in the kinship system. The kingship, chiefships, and lineage headships are symbolized by sacred ancestral 'stools', which belong to particular matrilineal lineages.

Along with the matrilineal kinship structure, there is a bond of affection between fathers and children. Patrilineal descent is recognized as a spiritual principle. A spirit (*ntoro*) is transmitted through fathers to children, and the father has the responsibility of naming his children. 'Ashanti say that a man wants children so that he can pass on the names of his forebears. It is a very important filial duty as well as a source of pride.'[2] No disgrace is attached to a birth prior to marriage, if the child is conceived after the woman's nubility ceremony and if the child is acknowledged and named by the father. If not so acknowledged, the child still has legitimate status in his mother's lineage, but those involved in the event suffer disgrace. Each individual belongs to a *ntoro* group, receives special protection from its god, and must observe its rituals. A woman must also observe the *ntoro* taboos of the father of her child during pregnancy and nursing, to avoid injury to the child. According to Fortes, 'the *ntoro* concept emphasizes in particular the bonds between father and son which give continuity to the male side of family and kinship relations. Adherents to the same *ntoro* in any locality do not meet for ritual or social purposes and do not constitute an organized group analogous to the lineage ... there is no corporate organization based on the father's line, nor are there jural or

---

[1] Among Africans living in Ashanti in 1948, 104,000 persons were born in districts of Ashanti other than those in which they were enumerated. An additional 142,000 persons were born outside Ashanti, comprising 70,000 born in the Northern Territories, 40,000 in the Colony, 6,000 in British Togoland, and 26,000 born elsewhere. Only 37,000 persons born in Ashanti were enumerated elsewhere in the Gold Coast.

[2] Fortes, 'Kinship and Marriage' etc., p. 266.

political rights (such as rights of inheritance) or duties derived from paternal descent.'[1]

Various kinds of matrilineal groups are distinguished by Fortes. The principal corporate group in political, legal and ritual affairs is the 'lineage' (*abusua*)—sometimes referred to as a 'maximal lineage' in distinction to component branches or 'segments'. The male head of a lineage is elected by the consensus of its members of both sexes. He receives custody of the male ancestral 'stools' of the lineage, the symbol and sanction of his legal power. Every person of free matrilineal descent is by birth a member of his mother's lineage, and citizen of the chiefdom in which the lineage is legally domiciled. The senior woman of a lineage has heavy moral responsibilities, especially over its female members. She supervises nubility ceremonies, and is concerned with the maintenance of peaceful family relations. The senior woman of a chiefdom, the 'queen mother', is custodian of its sacred female ancestral stools, and performs rites of worship analogous to those of her brother the chief.

Every long-established Ashanti village was formerly divided into 'wards', each of which was occupied mainly by members of a single lineage. This might be a maximal lineage, tracing descent over ten or twelve generations, or it might be a major segment of a lineage which had its principal location elsewhere. Such a segment might eventually establish itself as a separate lineage. The descendants of a woman from another locality, whether an Ashanti or a foreign slave, may be incorporated into a local lineage as an attached segment, but if of authentic Ashanti descent they also may retain rights in their original lineage. Each maximal lineage acts as a unit in political and religious affairs, but the distinction between those of common descent and other affiliated segments, especially between persons of authentic and those of alien origin, is preserved over many generations. Dispersed members of a lineage, living in other localities, can be elected to an office in the lineage or can establish claims to property of the lineage; but to exercise these rights they must return to its seat.

Ownership of land and other economic property is vested in a 'lineage segment'. In theory, any of a lineage is eligible for selection as the heir of a deceased member, if qualified by his personal relation; but in practice inheritance of property and provisions for the remarriage of widows are restricted within the segment. Such a segment, sometimes described as 'the children of one womb', is united by common descent to a grandmother, great-grandmother, or other near ancestress. It has a recognized leader, but is informally organized.

Each lineage is, in theory, a branch of a widespread matrilineal clan (also called *abusua*). There are eight such clans among the Ashanti. All members of a clan regard each other as relatives, are expected to extend

---

[1] ibid., p. 267. The only exceptions noted by Fortes are certain palace functionaries in the service of the king.

hospitality to one another, and must avoid marriage within the clan. All clans are usually represented in each chiefdom. These clans exercise an important unifying force in Ashanti political life and culture.

Personal relations in Ashanti are charged with the values implicit in the kinship system. The household, occupying an independent dwelling, may have a female or a male head. In the former case, it may comprise the head, her sons and daughters, her sister or sisters, and their sons and daughters, and perhaps the children of their daughters. If a man is the head, it will usually include his wife or wives and their children, but may also include one or more sisters and their children. 'In a relatively stable Ashanti community between 40 and 50 per cent of the population lived in matrilineal households under female heads, and only a third of all married women reside with their husbands, the remainder living chiefly with matrilineal kin.'[1] Both men and women may hold property. In either case inheritance is confined to the matrilineage, but men take precedence over women in the inheritance of a man's property.

The members of a lineage have a sense of identity in origin and destiny. 'A death is felt as a shock and a loss by all members of a lineage wherever they may be.'[2] All members gather to take part in a funeral, contribute to its expenses, and observe prolonged mourning taboos. Formerly, the members of a lineage were always buried in its own sacred burying ground.

A birth increases the life of the household, the lineage, and the clan. It brings added strength and prestige to its members. As already noted, it also brings pride and joy to the father. All these values are focused in the woman's role as mother.

'The Ashanti regard the bond between mother and child as the keystone of all social relations. Childlessness is felt by both men and women as the greatest of all personal tragedies and humiliations. Prolific childbearing is honoured. A mother of ten boasts of her achievement and is given a public ceremony of congratulation. As intercourse between husband and wife is prohibited only during the seclusion and convalescent period of 80 days after delivery, children often follow rapidly after one another. By custom, still generally observed outside the big towns, birth must take place in the mother's natal home. . . . Maternal grandmothers *(nanā)* play a great part in child-rearing. Indeed they can sometimes be very autocratic in this regard, arguing that a grandchild *(nāna)* belongs more to the lineage *(abusua)* than to its parents and therefore comes most appropriately under its grandmother's care.

'But the critical feature, Ashanti say, is the bond between mother and child. They look upon it as an absolutely binding moral relationship. An Ashanti woman stints no labour or self-sacrifice for the good of her children. . . . To show disrespect towards one's mother is tantamount

[1] Fortes, 'Kinship and Marriage' etc., p. 262.
[2] ibid., p. 256.

72

to sacrilege. Ashanti say that throughout her life a woman's foremost attachment is to her mother who will always protect and help her. A woman grows up in daily and unbroken intimacy with her mother, learns all feminine skills from her, and above all derives her character from her. This often leads to differences between husband and wife and so to divorce. For a man, his mother is his most trusted confidant, especially in intimate personal matters. A man's first ambition is to gain enough money to be able to build a house for his mother if she does not own one. To be mistress of her own home, with her children and daughter's children round her, is the highest dignity an ordinary woman aspires to.'[1]

As pointed out in the foregoing statement, the emphasis on matrilineal rights and the tendency for women to remain within maternal households make husband-wife relations tenuous. The strongest and most enduring bonds of an Ashanti woman, those with her mother, her brothers and sisters, and her children, are not destroyed by breaking her marital relation with one man and uniting with another. But to do so she must obtain the approval of the male head of her lineage. A man also has a first loyalty to his own lineage. High frequency of divorce is characteristic of Ashanti society. Apparently this has always been the case, and it seems to be a general characteristic of societies with major emphasis on mother-right.[2] This tendency is quite consistent with firm adherence to the central moral values of Ashanti society. It was also consistent with its powerful sanctions for high fertility—though it may somewhat partially modify their effect to the extent that women remain unmarried at times.

The legal principles of Ashanti society are now being subjected to severe strain with the increase of wealth, the growing power of men and women to direct their own affairs and promote the interests of their own children, and the influence of European culture.[3]

Christianity provides no support for the role of corporate kinship groups, but throws its emphasis on primary family relations—thus tending to induce intense but 'shallow' kinship relations.

'Missionary teaching lays special emphasis on the bonds of marriage and parenthood; and modern opportunities for accumulating private means and holding fixed property, such as cocoa farms and buildings, work in favor of ties between parents and children. As a result the solidarity of the maximal lineage has declined in matters of a personal or domestic nature; but the strength of matrilineal kinship within the constellation of kinship ties crystallized in the domestic groups remains unimpaired.'[4]

---

[1] ibid., pp. 262–3.
[2] Other evidence on this point will be noted below.
[3] See comment on this point in Busia, 'Some Aspects of the Relation of Social Conditions to Human Fertility in the Gold Coast', this report, Part Three.
[4] Fortes, 'Kinship and Marriage' etc., p. 261.

It appears to the present writer from the information at his disposal that there is considerable similarity between Ashanti culture and that of other major societies in well settled districts of the southern Gold Coast. Some societies with major emphasis on patrilineal descent also have political structures rooted in kinship systems and symbolized by sacred 'stools'. It also seems that Christianity finds a common motive with these traditional cultures in its emphasis on values of parenthood (though these are differently phrased), whereas it conflicts sharply with their norms of marital relations.

The demographic information at our disposal shows that a uniformly high level of fertility is maintained throughout the stable residential districts of Ashanti and the Colony. Natality may be somewhat lower in some of the less stable communities of the Northern Territories; but the census information on the population in this region is less reliable. In any case there is greater variation among districts in cultural conditions in the north.

A brief description of the sources of our demographic information follows:

The 1948 Census. This gives information on the whole population of the Gold Coast, with distinction in all cases between major divisions (Colony, Ashanti, Northern Territories) and much information by districts. Inquiry was made in a random sample of area units on the number of children ever born to each woman and number living. These data are tabulated by political division and by age of woman. Enumerators were instructed to obtain such information from all adult women, but the figures show that many younger women were omitted. The census officials found that the women omitted were in many cases unmarried and childless. The resulting bias is particularly serious at younger ages among Accra women (unpublished data provided by the Statistical Department, shown here in Table 12). On the other hand, the high ratio of living children to births reported by older women in Accra suggests a downward bias, due to omissions of children dying in infancy. A different bias may possibly arise from the inclusion of adopted children. The practice of adoption is especially widespread among the Ashanti, and Ashanti women often refuse to distinguish between own and adopted children. It is likely that the second of these biases is generally the more powerful, and that the average number of children shown for older Ashanti women (especially those over 60 years of age in the census returns) has an upward bias on this account.

An intensive demographic field study in Agogo, capital of a chiefdom in southern Ashanti, by Professor Meyer Fortes (presented in this report, Part Two) was very carefully controlled. The enumerators were students at a local teacher-training school, and they were closely supervised by a mature professional worker with intimate and prolonged association with

74

the people of this community. The specific objectives of the inquiry included the following items: (a) complete coverage of the resident households; (b) the greatest possible accuracy in the information on ages; (c) complete pregnancy records, with information on the approximate ages of women at each vital event, outcome of each pregnancy, and the ages at death of any children deceased before the time of thè survey; (d) related physiological and social information; (e) elimination of cases of adopted children from the maternity records of each woman.

The reporting of miscarriages and stillbirths appears to have been incomplete, for reasons stated by the author. But the intensive inquiry into pregnancy histories undoubtedly fortified the information on numbers of live births.

A sampling investigation of variations in fertility and related attitudes in various parts of Ashanti and the Colony by students of the University College of the Gold Coast, under the direction of Professor K. A. Busia. Attention in this study, carried out by students during their Easter vacation, was focused on social conditions and attitudes. It is possible that in some cases there were departures from the sampling design.

This study, which is also presented here, in Part Three, makes an important contribution to our knowledge of social conditions and attitudes. The collection of demographic data was incidental to this objective, and Professor Busia does not regard these results as authoritative. In any case, it must be emphasized that the data on fertility from this study refer to total pregnancies (including miscarriages and stillbirths) as reported by married women only.

Information on fertility among the Tallensi, from a previous study by Professor Fortes.[1] The Tallensi are one of the more stable tribal groups in the Northern Territories. They are also mainly an agricultural population, but chiefly engaged in subsistence production.

The Tallensi kinship system is partrilineal. There is strong emphasis on kinship, and the political structure is rooted in the kinship structure. The Tallensi also are eager to have children. The gross reproduction ratio obtained by Fortes in this study is 3.1 daughters per woman, indicating a total maternity ratio of about 6 live births per woman.

Information on fertility from the sources listed above, except that for the Tallensi, is presented in Table 12. The average number of children ever born, 6.22 live births, as reported by Agogo women aged 45–59 years probably provides the most reliable index, though a distinctly conservative estimate, of the general level of fertility among the Ashanti during recent decades. A figure in this vicinity is supported by other evidence presented below by Fortes (Part Two of this report).

[1] Meyer Fortes. 'A Note on Fertility among the Tallensi of the Gold Coast', *Sociological Review*, 35 (4–5), July–October 1943.

TABLE 12. Children Ever Born per Woman at Specified Ages in Years. Samples of Gold Coast Population.

	Children ever born per woman at specified ages: Ages of women in years								Ratio: $\bar{c}_{25-34}$ to $\bar{c}_{45-59}$	Ratio: living children to births (mothers 45–59 years)
	15–19	20–24	25–29	30–34	35–39	40–44	45–59	60+		
Fortes[1]										
Agogo	0.50	1.58	2.36	3.58	4.75	5.46	6.22	6.09	0.48	0.65
Census[2]										
Gold Coast (Total)	0.59	1.59	2.60	3.70	4.68	5.36	6.29	6.62	0.50	0.54
Ashanti	0.54	1.53	2.83	3.89	5.00	5.69	6.78	7.94	0.47	0.58
Colony	0.55	1.61	2.56	3.65	4.52	5.38	6.20	6.51	0.48	0.58
Northern Territories	0.71	1.62	2.55	3.69	4.77	5.21	6.22	5.88	0.50	0.46
Accra	1.13	1.85	2.60	3.41	3.92	4.85	5.36	5.24	0.56	0.68

	Pregnancies to married women at specified ages: Ages of women in years						Ratio: $\bar{c}_{25-34}$ to $\bar{c}_{45-59}$
	18–24	25–29	30–34	35–39	40–47	48–50	
Busia[3]							
Rural	1.9	2.9	4.3	5.7	6.7	7.3	0.49
Small towns	1.8	2.9	4.3	5.7	6.7	7.2	0.49
Urban	1.5	2.7	4.1	5.4	6.5	7.2	0.47

[1] Data from Fortes, 'A Demographic Field Study' etc., Tables 22, 24, 25.
[2] The Gold Coast, Census of Population, 1948, Report and Tables. (Tables 30, 31, p. 396.) Unpublished data for Accra provided by Statistics Department, Government of the Gold Coast; returns from 1,162 women aged 15 years and over.
[3] Data from K. A. Busia, 'Some Aspects' etc., Table J.

There is no clear evidence of any important recent change in level of fertility in Gold Coast regions if we are warranted in assuming that the census figures for women over 60 years of age in Ashanti and, to a lesser extent, in the Colony, are inflated by adoptions reported as births. The numbers of children reported by women aged 25–29 and 30–34 years indicate a sustained high level of fertility. There is, however, some evidence from the field study of an increase in sterility among younger women in Agogo—the proportion of those childless being 6 per cent among women aged 30–34 years in contrast to an extremely low apparent frequency (4 per cent) among the older women. Fortes suggests that this change, if such change has really occurred, may have been influenced by introduction of new infections after the opening of the road connecting Agogo with other communities.

The information on possible rural-urban differences in fertility in the Gold Coast is ambiguous. The apparently high figures for younger Accra women shown by the census survey certainly have an upward bias, due to omissions of single women; at the higher ages there may possibly be some downward bias, due to the omissions of some children dying in infancy. The information obtained from the field study reported by Busia indicates no rural-urban difference at older ages but slightly lower fertility at younger ages in the large town, which Busia suggests might be attributed to some delay in marriage. One would also expect a somewhat higher frequency of sterility and perhaps some furtive practice of abortion in the large towns.

The fertility of Ashanti women at Agogo is sustained at a high level, as would be expected from the information on their social structure and culture, similar to that commonly found in Asiatic peasant populations. It is, however, presumably well below the maximum procreative capacity of this population. This, too, would be expected from our information on the instability of marriage relations in this community. As shown by the demographic field study, about one-sixth of the total experience of Ashanti women between first marriage and the end of the childbearing period is passed during periods of separation from spouses. Although it cannot be assumed that exposure to risk of pregnancy is completely eliminated during such periods of separation, the frequency of pregnancy must be appreciably reduced.

There is also some delay after puberty in the formation of conjugal unions, which must in any case be postponed until after the formal nubility ceremony. Attitudes recorded in the survey reported by Busia show a rising interest in education (though this is less marked with respect to girls), quite definite interest in gainful activity by women (corresponding to fairly large opportunity for participation in trade), and a definite tendency toward some postponement of marriage. These tendencies can be expected to lead to a gradual slight decrease in fertility; but there is no present indication that the level of fertility (now sufficient to bring a doubling of the population in each generation) is likely to be lowered to any marked degree in the near future.

The evidence reviewed above leads to the following conclusions. First, the social organization of the Ashanti, with corporate unilineal kinship groups and strong emphasis on mother rights, provides powerful motivations and support for high fertility. Secondly, cultural conditions tending to induce high fertility among the Ashanti, though modified through social changes now in process, continue to enforce a high actual level of fertility. Thirdly, somewhat similar trends appear to be present in other societies in the Gold Coast with traditional patrilineal kinship systems.

We will now review briefly a few references to other societies with strong emphasis on mother-rights.

An intensive demographic study has been carried out in one other African society with such emphasis: the Yao of southern Nyasaland. Here, too, the investigator, J. C. Mitchell, found strong support for high fertility.[1] The major corporate groups in this society are matrilineal kinship groups. Marriage is early and predominantly matrilocal. At the time of a girl's first pregnancy there is a special ceremony attended only by women who have already borne children. A woman thereby acquires a new status, and is referred to by a different term. Another term will later be used to denote her status as a mother, and still another will be used when she becomes the mother of three or more children. Finally, a distinctive term is used for a woman who is no longer capable of bearing children.

There is little ceremony at marriage, and divorce is frequent. A birth is attended by the female relatives of both spouses. Sex relations are resumed after four or five months, following ritual intercourse whereby a taboo, previously in effect since the birth, is lifted. But the next pregnancy, it is felt, should be delayed until after the nursing baby is weaned; it is possible that *coitus interruptus* is used for this limited time. Various estimates indicate a total maternity ratio of 5.5 to 6 or more live births per woman living through the childbearing period.

The Yao were formerly great traders in active contact with Arab slave merchants. They adopted the Islamic religion, but retain to a high degree traditional kinship system and marital relations.

The American culture with greatest emphasis on mother rights is that of the pueblo-dwelling people in the south-western United States: the Zuni, the Hopi, and with some extraneous elements, the pueblos at Taos. These societies have been studied intensively by Cushing, Stevenson, Kroeber and others. Their culture has been eloquently interpreted by Benedict as 'Apollonian'—characterized by emphasis on order, co-operation, ritual, self-restraint and courtesy.[2] Social organization here is rooted in the matri-

[1] J. Clyde Mitchell. 'An Estimate of Fertility in Some Yao Hamlets in Luwanda District of Southern Nyasaland', *Africa*, 19 (4): 293–308, 1949.
[2] Ruth Benedict. *Patterns of Culture*. New York, 1934, Chapter IV, 'The Pueblos of New Mexico'.

lineal kinship system. Marriage is matrilocal. Marriages are formed with little ceremony and are dissolved at the will of either spouse. Houses and land are owned by matrilineal groups. A husband must labour to help replenish the granary of his wife and her sisters. But men have equal dignity, and even greater responsibility for religious ceremonies and of course, in former times, for war. Men as well as women have private material and ritual possessions. The central motives of pueblo ceremonies are the presence of the gods, the coming of rain, health, the fertility of the fields, and the fertility of women.

No intensive demographic study of pueblo societies has come to the attention of the writer, except a special investigation of the frequency of pregnancies among Taonan women.[1] For this purpose data obtained in interviews were checked against parish registers. Reports that were judged to contain serious errors, as tested by the parish registers, were omitted. Also, 'some small families of one or two children' and childless women (said to be 'very few') were omitted. Aberle comments that 'the older women were eager for the younger women to have as many children as possible. The younger women seem to want offspring and take great pride in their babies'. Among 45 women aged 40 years or over in this series there were on the average 9.4 pregnancies per woman; but as already noted a biased sample with respect to fertility was purposely selected for this investigation. The average age of the mother at the birth of a first child was 17.8 years. Among women of completed fertility the average age of the mother at the birth of her last child was 35.8 years. The modal interval between the termination of one pregnancy and the next conception was estimated to be 15 months. Among 686 reported pregnancies there were 32 miscarriages (4.7 per cent) and 10 stillbirths (1.5 per cent). All informants agreed that there were no contraceptive practices in this society.

The latest detailed census data on the demographic characteristics of Indian tribes in the United States come from the 1930 census. At that time, 680 children aged 0–4 years were reported per 100 Indian women aged 15–44 years. This ratio is over 50 per cent above that in the white population at this time; but the corresponding ratio (making allowance for difference in age classification) in the white population in 1800 was some 30 per cent, more or less, above the Indian figure in 1930. The child-woman ratios (0–4 / 15–44) of the pueblo stocks in 1930 were as follows: Taonan, 634; Hopi, 711; Zuni, 708.[2] Much higher ratios for the total Indian population and for these pueblo stocks, though not for all tribes, were given in 1910. Unfortunately the census data for the American Indian population, both in 1910 and 1930, are very erratic and apparently quite unreliable.

It is certain that the fertility of the pueblo Indians has remained high,

[1] Sophia B. Aberle, 'Frequency of Pregnancies and Birth Interval among Pueblo Indians', *American Journal of Physical Anthropology*, 16 (1); 68–80, July–Sept. 1931.
[2] United States Bureau of the Census. *Indian Population of the United States and Alaska, 1930.*

but there may or may not have been an appreciable decline during recent decades. The pueblo stocks, in spite of instability of marriage and rather close contact with Europeans over a long period, have remained relatively free from white admixture. Their traditional cultures, though modified, have remained intact to an unusual degree among North American Indian societies. This may be due in part to continued residence in their ancient locale. In part it must be attributed to the vitality of their culture.

The relations of matrilineal kinship systems to fertility in some Melanesian societies are obscure to this writer. Apparently some of these societies have suffered depopulation; but the writer is not familiar with a clear exposition of the traditional culture and circumstances leading to such a trend in a society with a strong emphasis on mother-rights.

Many aspects of the culture of the Trobriand Islanders have been expounded with brilliance by Malinowski.[1] But the precise implications of their social organization for fertility remain somewhat ambiguous; and no specific demographic information is at hand. Most of the Trobriand Islanders belong to totemic, exogamous, matrilineal clans. Inheritance, hereditary offices, and magical formulas are normally transmitted from a man to his sister's children. Only matrilineal kin are entitled to share in mortuary rites and mourning behaviour. But objects of economic importance, such as garden land and pigs are owned by men. Canoes are owned by individual chiefs, hereditary heads of clans, or sub-clans, though such ownership involves definite social obligations.[2] The society provides much opportunity for the acquisition of personal prestige. A young man and woman who have already enjoyed sexual relations in the bachelor's house begin their married life in the home of the man's parents. Later they establish a separate house. Food is contributed annually by the wife's kin. A woman's kin retain legal authority over her and her children, and may later reclaim the children.

Malinowski was convinced that the Trobiranders have no understanding of the relation between coitus and pregnancy, and he was intrigued by the question as to why premarital births are unusual in spite of the usual premarital sex relations. He discusses the possibility of anti-natal measures chiefly in this connexion. He assumes no contraception; he was informed that abortions are sometimes induced, but rarely.[3] Fertility in marriage is welcome, and is said primarily to be a matter of great importance to a woman's kinsmen. 'The kinsmen rejoice, for their bodies become stronger when one of their sisters or nieces has plenty of children.'[4] Trobriand fathers also have a warm affectionate interest in children. Owing to certain inhibitions affecting the relation of kinsmen to anything connected with

[1] Brolislaw Malinowski. *The Sexual Life of Savages in Northwestern Melanesia.* London, 1929; and other publications.
[2] Malinowski. *Argonauts of the Western Pacific.* London, 1922, pp. 116–20.
[3] Malinowski. *The Sexual Life* etc., p. 168.
[4] Quotation from a native informant, ibid., p. 170.

the sexual life of their clan sisters, a girl's father has the chief responsibility for approving or disapproving a proposed marriage. On the whole, Malinowskis material is consistent with the thesis that emphasis on matrilineal kinship tends to promote high fertility; but the emphasis on kinship is crossed by rather free personal interests; and the implications of social organization for fertility are not specific.

THE RELATION OF PATRIARCHAL SOCIAL ORGANIZATION TO FERTILITY

In general, the evidence reviewed in the previous section tends to support the thesis that emphasis on corporate, continuing kinship groups provides powerful motivation for high fertility. We have also noted that such corporate kinship groups tend to be formed in societies with strong emphasis on a principle of unilineal descent. This thesis was formulated with reference to matrilineal systems; but its logic is equally appropriate to patrilineal or agnatic systems. In societies with emphasis on unilineal descent and corporate kinship groups, numerous children are valued as fortifying the position of a continuing lineage, in which the security and prestige of its members are rooted, increasing its economic and military power, enriching its life, projecting this life into the future. Interest in fertility in such societies is, in large measure, an expression of the internally collective, externally competitive, ethnocentrism of such kinship units. Similar motivation is generated within the lesser kinship segments and household units formed on the same principles within the larger lineage and clan structures.

This interest is reinforced by the mystical association of human fertility with the fertility of fields and flocks. This association seems to have been expressed in some of the earliest known objects of human representative art: female figurines with exaggerated mammalian organs, found in Upper Paleolithic deposits in Europe. 'The shape of the carvings of women makes it as good as certain that these served as fertility fetishes.'[1] The same motive is expressed in the rituals of many primitive societies.

Societies with strong emphasis on agnatic lineage are generally also patriarchal. We avoided the word 'matriarchal' in the previous section because males exercise a measure of dominance in all human societies. Therefore, strong emphasis on mother rights establishes a balance between men and women in dominance. But where there is strong emphasis on patrilineal lineage and father-rights, this balance is lost—though, of course, women, children, commoners and slaves influence the decisions of the elite in all societies, even if only subtly and indirectly.

---

[1] A. L. Kroeber. *Anthropology*. New York, 1948, p. 640. Interest in fertility is also reinforced in all societies by the spontaneous interest of adults in children, response to their affection and gaiety, sympathy with their woes, and personal satisfaction in meeting their needs and moulding their lives.

Gluckman presents an exposition of the kinship system of the Zulu and its social implications, in contrast to that of the Lozi.[1] The latter have a 'shallow' collateral kinship system. Gluckman also draws attention to many parallels between the social organization of the Zulu (a Bantu people in southern Africa) and that of the Nuer (a Nilotic people in the Sudan). We will also have occasion to note some interesting parallels between both these societies and the Masai (also a Nilotic people, living in Kenya). The Zulu, the Nuer, and the Masai are all warriors. They also have wealth in cattle. Some aspects of their culture imply a mystical association between human lineages and cattle. The drinking of milk together among some of these people is a symbol of kinship. Among the Zulu a wife (who necessarily comes from a different lineage) is not at first permitted to drink the milk of the cattle of her husband's lineage, but must bring a heifer provided by her kinsmen to meet her personal needs. After she has borne children to her husband's lineage, she becomes in a sense assimilated to such an extent that this and other tabus in relation to her husband's kin are relaxed. In all those societies marriage payments by a man and his kin to the kin of a woman taken as a wife always involve the transfer of cattle. Such transfer has a symbolic significance in the establishment of mutual obligations between two groups of kindred, as well as important economic value.

The Zulu have patrilineal, exogamous clans that are widely dispersed. These comprise lineages, which comprise segments, which comprise households—all formed on genealogical principles but involving increasing specificity of location in the lesser units. In this respect, their social structure may be regarded for our purposes as similar to that previously described in the case of the Ashanti—though for other purposes (e.g., analysis of political systems) the distinctions in structural relations may be quite important. All members of a clan recognize each other as kinsmen, may drink milk together, are prohibited from marrying one another's sisters or daughters, have common religious bonds with the same ancestors, have a common sacred song, and owe loyalty to a common political head. But the sense of kinship within lesser lineages and segments of lineages becomes increasingly intense.

Marriage is essentially an arrangement between groups of kindred of different clans. It is validated by a transfer of cattle to the family of a woman who goes to serve a man of different lineage as his wife and to bear children for him and his lineage. There are also elaborate marriage ceremonies, spread over many days. 'The ceremonial chiefly expresses the hostility and conciliation of the two lineages concerned.'[2] Once the transfer of the marriage-cattle is made, but not until then, a woman becomes the proper wife, or one of the proper wives, of a man. Henceforth, he is her husband and the 'father' of children that she may bear, regardless of who

[1] Max Gluckman, 'Kinship and Marriage among the Lozi of Northern Rhodesia and the Zulu of Natal', in Radcliffe-Brown and Forde, op. cit., pp. 166–206.
[2] ibid., p. 190.

may be their genitors. Ordinarily, of course, the husband is the genitor of the children born to him while he is living. Adultery and desertion are strictly suppressed, but in the event that a woman deserts her husband to live with another man, the children born from this union are still recognized as her husband's children. 'The Zulu say "cattle beget children". The purpose of the cattle is to procure children, and the Zulu say that in the past they began to pay cattle only when a child had been born.'[1]

If a man dies without having achieved adequate paternity, it is the responsibility of a loyal kinsman to engender children on his behalf. Formerly a widow was assigned in a special conjugal relation to a kinsman of her husband. She was not to marry a man outside the kinship group of her deceased husband. She is now permitted to do so by government regulations which forbid the assignment of a woman in conjugal relations against her will. But in this case her second husband must return the marriage payment to the heirs of the dead husband, less one beast for each child born to him.

'If a woman dies before bearing children she has not fulfilled the purpose for which the marriage-cattle were given, even though she has worked and given sexual services, and her family must replace her with a younger sister or else they must replace the marriage payment. A younger woman should also be sent to bear children for a barren woman, or her parents must return the cattle.'[2]

Sons are wanted by a man because they enhance his prestige and that of his lineage, bring added military power, and contribute to the increase of wealth. Daughters are equally welcome because, when they become marriageable, they bring cattle that can be used to obtain additional wives for a father or wives for his sons. For a woman, the bearing of children is the essential key to a position of some dignity. And, of course, Zulu like all other people love and enjoy their children.

The chastity of women is highly valued among the Zulu. This was formerly upheld with strong sanctions. Incomplete sexual intercourse (*inter crura*) was allowed between unmarried warriors and young girls. But if an unmarried girl became pregnant by a young warrior both they and their families were liable to be killed; but such disaster could be avoided by hastily arranging marriage with an older man. Adultery too was severely punished, with death, or flogging with thorny branches, or cacti were thrust into the woman's vagina.[3] A separate beast (not part of the essential marriage payment) is given by a groom to his bride's mother as a payment for the virginity of her daughter. Similarly a man who seduces a virgin becomes liable to pay compensation to her mother.[4] These payments to a mother are recognition of her responsibility in this matter.

[1] ibid., p. 184.
[2] ibid., p. 185.
[3] ibid., p. 181.
[4] ibid., p. 194.

Polygyny is highly developed among the Zulus, as in many African societies. We noted above that is. is found even in matrilineal societies in Africa, though it would seem anomalous in such societies. It is more extensive and has larger significance in patriarchal societies.

A Zulu man provides a separate house, and allots land and cattle to each of his wives. This 'house property' in inherited by the sons of that wife in preference to their half-brothers by other mothers. But in Zulu society the wives are graded, and the son of the principle wife becomes the chief heir to his father's property, though other sons also receive some inheritance.

Gluckman states that he has observed no important differences between the Zulu and the Lozi in the psychological relations of husbands and wives, in spite of radical differences in structural relations between marriage and kinship systems in these societies.

'Zulu and Lozi marriages do not generally spring from romantic attachments, and their concept of love between the sexes is on the whole restrained, though sexual attraction between men and women may make them brave severe sanctions. In both societies there is only a limited field in which men and women can associate.'[1]

There is no reason for doubting this observation, and Gluckman is concerned with the point that difference between the Zulu and Lozi in the stability of marriages does not arise from immediate personal relations in these societies, but from their social structures. But surely he does not intend to imply that social structure does not influence personal relations. The present writer would suppose that, in general, a cognatic system with emphasis on nuclear families would remove one barrier between husbands and wives (the sense of original membership in sharply differentiated lineages), and would tend to increase the 'field' of common activities and interests that are shared by husbands and wives. For this reason, he would expect such social structure, 'other things being equal', to promote intensity of common interests and affection between husbands and wives. Similarly, though for a different reason, he would expect emphasis on mother rights to be generally more conducive to affectionate relations between spouses, in view of the larger degree of equality between men and women in responsibilities and privileges that tends to exist in this case, in contrast with patriarchal social organization. This question will not be pursued further at this point, but it has some relevance to formation of parental attitudes to children and interests associated with fertility.

Gluckman develops his analysis of the contrasting social structures of Zulu and Lozi societies with special attention to factors affecting the stability of marriages. He distinguishes between the legal stability of marriage and stability of personal relations and household units. He finds that, among the Zulu, 'The outstanding fact is the extreme endurance of the

[1] ibid., p. 179.

husband's rights and their passing on his death to his agnatic heirs. Legal marriage and the domestic unit it establishes are thus very stable, though there may be frequent adultery.'[1] Among the Nuer, another society with strong emphasis on patrilineal kinship (as among the Zulus, and in contrast to the Lozi) the legal emphasis in marriage is the same as with the Zulu, even though they have frequent changes in the constitution of households. 'Marriage is stable in that wherever the woman is her husband accompanies her, even after his death, to be pater of her children, for whoever the genitors are, they belong to the man or group who gave cattle for them.'[2] Among the Zulu and the Nuer, this is associated with the emphasis on unilateral agnatic groups. Among the Lozi, on the other hand, there is a quite different emphasis, attributed largely to their ecological situation.

'For them it is not important to fix an individual's relationship to a single line, but to emphasize his links with many lines; therefore marriage does not tie a woman's procreative power to one line. She produces for many lines. Among the Zulu economic and other interests coincide with the pull of agnatic ties; among the Lozi, with their limited resources centered in restricted dwelling-mounds, economic interests may pull a man to settle with his mother's kindred, in either of her lines of descent. As a woman's productive capacity is not tied to a single lineage group, the child goes to its genitor, not to the legal husband of the woman. This removes the main buttress of marriage; since the children can shift their allegiance and emphasize that relationship which most pleases or profits them, the family as a whole is an unstable association. . . . Adulterers can claim their children, and adultery is incessant. Men divorce their wives easily and at personal will; women are always straining to be released. Marriage, as well as domestic association, is unstable.'[3]

At one point, Gluckman states: 'In many tribes the family is unstable; in some (e.g. Nuer) as a domestic unit, despite strong marriage ties, while in others the marriage tie also is fragile. Stability inheres in the extended kinship groupings and relationships which form the structure of the society.'[4] At other points he examines the possible effects on marriage of permanence of residence, the moral code of military age-sets among Zulu, and presence of wealth available for large marriage payments. Later on he makes the following observation:

'However, I have not had space to examine whether a kindred group becomes stable about a fixed piece of land, or herds of cattle, and whether this and the rights of the children to the property, are not what stabilize marriage, rather than agnatic descent and father-right themselves. It appears to me that property in this form is by itself insufficient, since

[1] ibid., p. 201.
[2] loc. cit.
[3] ibid., pp. 201-2.
[4] ibid., p. 190.

we have many records of peoples with matrilineal succession to valuable lands or herds among whom marriage is very unstable.'[1]

One point to be considered in this connexion is the difference in implications, for fertility and the reproduction of lineages, of stability of marriage in matrilineal and in patrilineal societies. In the former the lineage retains its offspring regardless of the stability of domestic arrangements between spouses or the nature of legal marriage ties. Assuming the availability of consorts, the formation, dissolution, and reformation of conjugal relations does not greatly affect the natural increase of the extended kinship group. Lack of rigidity in marital relations is not, therefore, essential in a matrilineal society to the interest of the lineage in the production and retention of offspring. On the other hand, there is always an intimate bond between mothers and children. To maintain procreation and identification with the children who are growing up, an agnatic lineage must maintain firm control over the women who are obtained to procreate children for the lineage. An agnatic society may, therefore, tend to develop strong sanctions for the maintenance of such permanent control over the lives of the wives of its members.

The cultural conditions that tend to promote 'stability' of particular marriages do not, of course, necessarily tend to promote the 'stability' through time of the social institutions that determine marriage relations. It is possible that under some conditions relatively free marital relations may be more amenable to gradual modification toward a pattern of stable monogamous families, during a process of cultural transition, than rigid regulations for maintaining the stability of patriarchal (often polygynous) families. This may or may not be so. In any case, it is important to note that the phrase 'stability of marriage' is sometimes used to denote two radically different matters, which must be clearly distinguished.

If, as Gluckman suggests, corporate agnatic lineages tend to enforce permanence of marital relations, this factor in itself would probably tend slightly to raise the expected level of fertility in patriarchal societies as compared with societies placing strong emphasis on mother rights. For we have already noted that among the Ashanti the instability of conjugal relations must reduce somewhat their level of fertility. However, other differences between these contrasting types of unilateral kinship system may exert more powerful influence in the opposite direction.

Two culturally prescribed modes of the control of fertility are widespread among patriarchal societies in Africa. The first of these modes, which is common to many different types of society in Africa and in some other world regions, is the cultural prohibition on inducing pregnancy in a nursing mother. The second, which follows a particular pattern in some patriarchal societies in Africa, is postponement of the marriage of young men, associated with special provisions for incomplete sexual intercourse. We will consider each of these modes separately.

[1] ibid., p. 205.

86

Prescription against sexual intercourse with the mother of a nursing infant or, in some societies, a modification of sexual practices to avoid causing pregnancy in such circumstances, can be given a simple interpretation which seems quite adequate. We know that under the conditions prevailing until very recently in most primitive societies a fourth or more of all babies usually die within the first few years after they are born. Even if the milk of cattle, treated without knowledge of sanitation, is freely available, the transition from nourishment at the mother's breast to exclusive dependence on any other nourishment is a dangerous affair. Abrupt weaning must often have been followed by the sickness and death of the child. Such association of events must have been a matter of common observation. If one has a preference for modernistic interpretations, he can phrase this experience as causing feelings of guilt in the parents which are referred to the sexual behaviour which resulted in pregnancy and the forced weaning of the present infant. But this is unnecessary. Motivation for fertility in all societies is toward children, not toward live births as statistical data. A baby at the breast is worth more than one in the womb and ,one lying neglected on the ground. Of course, the inferences of people with meagre symbolic apparatus and a strong sense of the presence of unknown agents are not formulated in syllogisms, but are blended with many irrelevant associations. The common observation referred to above would be differently interpreted in various cultures, and the inference that the pregnancy of a nursing mother should be avoided would be phrased in different ways. We may refer to such avoidances for convenience as the 'lactation taboo', but the avoidance does not always have the force of a taboo.

The question immediately arises, on the interpretation suggested above, as to why no such taboo was found in Ashanti society, which has a strong emphasis on the nurture of living offspring. No definite answer can be given. This omission in Ashanti culture may have been the 'chance' result of unknown factors. The taboo is not found in the other African matrilineal society, the Yao, with similar emphasis, which was reviewed more hastily in the previous section. We may note, however, that the problem of pregnancy for a nursing mother is mitigated if she is living in a household with sisters who share a common interest in her children.

There appears to be an association between polygyny and the lactation taboo, though the association is imperfect. Polygyny facilitates the avoidance of sexual intercourse with a nursing mother, and it is highly probable that the lactation taboo gains currency most easily in a society where the cultural leaders are polygynous. Polygynous husbands in Africa commonly avoid sexual intercourse with a wife who is nursing a child, but continue sexual relations with other wives. In some African societies a monogamous husband is permitted extra-marital sex relations at this time; in other societies this is not so. Again in some societies there is cultural provision for some sort of incomplete intercourse at such times; in other societies this is not so.

Missionaries have generally opposed the whole idea, as conducive to polygyny or immorality, and have judged that the length of the lactation period could be safely reduced. Progress in sanitation has reduced its importance. In any case, the weakening of traditional culture has led to the modification of many ancient rules. There are many reports of reduction of the lactation period in recent years in various localities.

Among the Baganda, a wife lived apart from her husband for three years while nursing his baby; but if she was his only wife 'she joined her husband and continued to nurse the baby'. After the child was weaned, the husband jumped over his wife to break the spell.[1] The Bantu child in South Africa is usually not weaned until he is two or three years old. If the mother becomes pregnant before this she 'cuts the road' of the nursing child. If sexual intercourse is resumed before this, magic is practised to insure the child against harm.[2] Among the Arapesh of New Guinea, to cite an interesting variation, while the mother is pregnant, the husband engages in active intercourse to 'nourish' the foetus. After the birth the father neglects his work and sleeps beside the mother and child, but, even if plurally married, he must refrain from sexual intercourse with his other wife.[3] There are many variants in such practices, but these need not be elaborated.

The following generalizations seem to be warranted:

1. Cultural prohibition against inducing pregnancy in a nursing mother is not necessarily founded in motivation for control of size of family or reduction in growth of population.
2. It is not chiefly an expression of individual preference, but a culturally prescribed regulation.
3. It does tend to cause some reduction in gross fertility; it may or may not cause slight reduction in net reproduction.
4. There is a tendency for this practice to be associated with polygyny, and any influence toward reduction of actual fertility is likely to be most pronounced in polygynous households.
5. This practice is entirely congruous with strong cultural emphasis on high fertility.

Postponement of the marriage of young men among the Zulu was dictated by the emphasis on military power in this society, and the official organization of age-sets of young men and of young women. 'Regiments could only begin to marry when the king gave them permission as a set to marry a younger age-set of girls, who by this time would be well in their twenties. A man in an older regiment could marry a girl whose set had not yet had

[1] Rev. John Roscoe. *The Baganda*. New York, 1911, pp. 55–6, 74.
[2] Eileen J. Krige. 'Individual Development', in I. Schapera, *The Bantu-Speaking Tribes of South Africa*. London, 1937.
[3] Margaret Mead. 'The Arapesh', in Mead, Editor, *Cooperation and Competition Among Primitive Peoples*. New York, 1937.

its mates indicated.'[1] As noted above, incomplete sexual intercourse was permitted between young warriors and young girls, but pregnancy was prohibited with extreme sanctions. Such sanctions have now been banned by the government, but according to Gluckman, Zulu girls in Natal still do not usually marry until their early twenties. Similar practices were prevalent among other Bantu tribes in southern Africa with emphasis on military power and the initiation of boys and girls into age sets.

A similar pattern is highly developed among the Masai, a Nilotic people in East Africa, with strong emphasis on patriarchal and military virtues. Boys were initiated into age regiments once every seven years, thus involving considerable delay for some individuals. They were obligated to seven years of preparatory military service as bachelors. Prior to initiation boys were under strict sanctions to avoid any sexual association with girls. The initiated bachelors, however, who lived apart in groups, were permitted to invite young girls, who had not yet been initiated into a marriageable age set, to spend the night in the bachelor's house. During these years impregnation was strictly taboo, and only incomplete intercourse was permissible. The presence of other girls and men in the house was assumed to provide each girl with some assurance and protection. After this preliminary service, the bachelors gained status as full warriors. Marriage was now permitted with nubile girls in an appropriate age class. Among the Masai girls attain this status during their teens, so that the fertility of women is not appreciably reduced by this arrangement. The social structure of the Masai is maintained among dispersed branches without major reliance on the personal authority of a particular official.[2]

Another minor, culturally sanctioned check on fertility needs only brief mention. Among the Tallensi it is considered improper for parents to continue to bear children after a son has taken a wife.[3] A similar cultural motive in force in a town in south-west China is reported by Hsu.[4]

We have not been able to obtain much specific information on actual levels of fertility in various patrilineal societies in Africa. Some relevant data are available from the 1911 and 1936 censuses of the Union of South Africa. The ratio of children aged 0–4 years per 1,000 women aged 15–44 years in the Bantu population of the Union as a whole, was 673 in 1911 and 657 in 1936. These values are only slightly below that stated above for the American Indian population of the United States in 1930, but are far below the extremely high ratio (872) obtained for the East Indian population of the Union of South Africa in 1930. In 1911 the corresponding ratio (511) for the Bantu population of Natal (including large Zulu elements) was definitely below that of all Bantu in the Union, but in 1936 the Natal Bantu ratio (622) was nearer to the all-Union Bantu ratio (657).

[1] Gluckman, op. cit. p. 181.
[2] Based on an account by Leaky.
[3] Information provided by Professor Meyer Fortes.
[4] Francis Hsu. *Under the Ancestors' Shadow.* New York, 1948.

The low 1911 figure may have been due to faulty enumeration, or to very high child mortality. Using similar data, and assuming constant mortality rates for the Bantu population in all areas, Badenhorst estimates female net reproduction ratios among Bantus in South Africa in 1936 as follows: Union, 1.52; Zululand, 1.46; rest of Natal, 1.55.[1] The figures suggest that fertility among the Zulu is rather high, but perhaps somewhat below that of the Bantu population of the Union as a whole.

Presumably specific information was obtained on the fertility in the Masai District of Uganda in the 1948 Census on East Africa. But unfortunately the detailed information obtained in this inquiry has not yet been published. Current opinion in this region assumes that the fertility of the Masai is moderately high; but we have no reliable evidence on the subject.

The evidence reviewed above, chiefly from Africa, is inadequate to establish any firm general conclusion. But it gives some indication of a general principle which can now be given explicit formulation, subject to confirmation, rejection, or modification through later investigations. Corporate unilateral kinship groups and the related emphasis on mother rights or father rights in social organization tend to generate strong motivations for high fertility. These motivations spring from the ethnocentric character of the interests formed in lineage relations. These may be crossed by other motives that are culturally compatible with the emphasis on high fertility, but which nevertheless somewhat modify its actual expression—such as emphasis on avoiding pregnancies that would interfere with the nourishment of a living child or emphasis on the maintenance of efficient military organization. However, these counter forces have no essential relation to cultural conditions that in some other societies with different social organization create strong motivations for the limitation of fertility.

Our formulation may be too restricted in its limitation to societies with unilateral kinship systems. In so far as corporate kinship groups, as previously defined in the chapter, are formed on different principles, they might be expected to have somewhat similar influence on fertility. But there is frequent association between corporate kinship groups and emphasis on patrilineal or matrilineal descent, and in the material that we have reviewed the force of corporate kinship systems usually has a generic relation to the principle of unilineal descent.

The hypothesis does not, of course, imply that high fertility is not to be expected in societies without corporate kinship groups. We shall, in fact, review other evidence contrary to any such implication. Our tentative affirmation is simply that corporate kinship groups generate strong motives for high fertility, and that this particular sort of motivation is specific to societies in which such groups play a significant role.

---

[1] L. T. Badenhorst. 'Territorial Differentials in Fertility in the Union of South Africa, 1911–1936', *Population Studies*, 5 (2): 134–62, Nov. 1952.

CHAPTER III

Environment, Culture and Fertility

INTER-SOCIETAL COMPETITION, KINSHIP STRUCTURE AND RE-PRODUCTION

Competition, as a biological process, may or may not involve combat. Species of grass 'compete' with one another for the occupation of a plain, as do non-combative animals that obtain nourishment from the grass. In part, the competition among groups of men for the occupation of resources in different parts of the world, which has been going on during several hundred thousand years, is of this sort. A group that develops techniques appropriate to the use of certain resources can establish itself in a region which other groups, though unmolested, might be unable to occupy. But most primitive tribes have economic techniques that would enable them to use more ample resources than they possess, and their own resources are exposed to occupation by surrounding tribes that could use them to good advantage. Under such conditions biological competition among primitive societies tends to find expression in war.

Among societies at similar levels of technical skill, the ability of any society aggressively to extend the area under its control or defensively to resist conquest by others is mainly determined by its social structure and culture. The critical need of a people in an area of vigorous inter-societal competition is effective social organization. One important consideration is the extent to which a common culture tends to unite a relatively large population through adherence to traditional goals, and promotes ethno-centric loyalty to this society and hostility to any forces that threaten its interests. Increase in the number of individuals in a society accentuates the need for orderly arrangement of affairs. The importance of joint actions on a large scale in war requires an accepted social structure. Such a structure is also needed for an efficient allocation of the economic resources within the control of any society to use by its component groups.

A unilineal system of descent, tending to promote the formation of co-ordinated corporate groups, is appropriate to these needs. Every individual has a definite place in the system. Lines of control are maintained through successive generations. And these lines of control can be differentiated indefinitely by division of clans into lineages, branches, and sub-branches, or consolidated by the fusion of groups.

Broad areas with resources appropriate to the support of various tribal

91

societies and more restricted regions with highly prized resources have been the scene of shifting occupancy by successively dominant groups. The dominant tribal societies at any particular time in many areas exposed to intense inter-societal competition can be shown to have established themselves in their observed positions within a few centuries.

The formation of agrarian civilizations, with political systems organized on a territorial basis, permitted the growth of large stable populations in some regions, notably in the Mediterranean basin, southern and eastern Asia, and middle America. These populations were able to resist tribal invasions so long as their political systems remained effective. Even when overrun by invading hordes, the established civilizations might assimilate the invaders, as in China. Even a civilization shattered in conquest usually passed on improved lands and other resources, and its institutions often influenced later civilizations formed in its place. The margins of established civilizations set restrictive, though variable, limits to the zones remaining open to competition among tribal societies.

In other cases, the topographic or climatic margins of regions of most intense inter-tribal competition are occupied by less powerful peoples who have taken their refuge in mountains, forests, swamps, or deserts. And outside these realms lie the barren Arctic, Australia, New Zealand, and the smaller islands of the Pacific.

Corporate clans and lineages (with closed membership, a system of authority, and continuity through successive generations) are widely prevalent among the dominant tribal societies in areas of intense competition for resources among tribal societies. They are a common, though not universal, characteristic of societies in such situations. These forms of social organization are not found with equal frequency among people with more primitive techniques in regions of refuge. And they are not found, at least with the same force, in well-established agrarian civilizations.[1] The situation in the most isolated regions of the world is more varied and ambiguous.

An initial tendency to emphasize a unilineal principle of descent may have come about in various ways—influenced by a tendency for spouses to reside with the kin of the husband or with the kin of the bride, or by increase of property to be transmitted in accord with some fixed principle, et cetera. The critical question about social institutions is not that of origins, but that of functions in the continued life of a society.

The foregoing observation about the distribution of corporate kinship groups suggests that their contribution to effective social organization may be especially important to tribal societies in situations of actual or potential conflict with other tribal societies, and that they may have promoted the ascendancy of peoples with such organizations. This suggestion, even if valid, should not be pressed too far. The function of corporate kinship

[1] See Chapter V.

groups in primitive societies is not limited to situations of actual or potential conflict. They promote orderly adjustment of peaceful economic activities. And they stimulate healthy emulation among groups in valour, the production and display of economic goods and objects of art, in dances and ceremonies. They enhance the sense of unity within each group through recognition of its unique origin and, frequently, its unique spiritual heritage and obligations.

Corporate kinship groups, according to the thesis defined in the previous chapter, also tend to induce strong motivation for high fertility. Under normal conditions the level of fertility characteristic of societies with such groups is likely to be well above that required for mere replacement of population, bringing increase of population. Under the conditions of inter-tribal competition for resources, increase of population in any society does not necessarily depress its level of subsistence. It may, on the contrary, increase its power to retain its present resources or to enlarge these resources through the occupation of adjacent lands. If our analysis is correct, the primary 'intent' of corporate groups or the major need to which they are a response, is not increase of population. But this effect is compatible with the ecological situation of societies in which such groups receive greatest emphasis.

The general theory here presented as an hypothesis is (a) that there is some functional relation between corporate kinship structure and inter-societal competition for resources; (b) that there is a secondary relationship between corporate kinship structures and high fertility, and (c) that these relations are conducive to the survival and ascendancy of peoples with these characteristics in areas where the occupation of resources by any people is largely determined by its competitive relations with other peoples.

Africa south of the Sahara remained into the modern era a region of tribal migrations. Incidentally, it may be that some African tribal nations were on the point of achieving sedentary civilization at this time—for example, the Baganda, the Ashanti, or the Yoruba—taking account of their trends in agriculture and political organization. But the Baganda, like most of the Bantu nations in east and south Africa, were relatively recent occupants of their present positions. There is a wide prevalence of corporate kinship systems among the dominant African societies. They frequently have a clan organization, and co-ordinated corporate lineages within the clan structure. The structure of families conforms to the principle of descent recognized in the lineage system. These characteristics promoted the expansion of the peoples that achieved dominance in this area.

There is a striking absence of culturally sanctioned measures for the restriction of procreation among the major tribal groups in Africa—although such measures do appear to be prevalent among some primitive societies. In this statement we obviously exclude practices described in the previous chapter relating to sexual intercourse with mothers of nursing children, and the temporary control of fertility by junior age classes, as among the Zulu and the Masai. We assume that these practices are not directed toward restricting the number of children in a group, for reasons already stated. We also exclude occasional resort to anti-natal measures in exceptional circumstances, as for example, to avoid embarrassment from a pregnancy resulting from adultery, or other deviant behaviour by individuals. Such practices occur in all societies, though there is variation in the degree to which they may be repressed by strong sanctions or condoned as merely regretable lapses from correct behaviour. The significant consideration is the extent to which a society gives approval to, or tolerates a frequent occurrence of, infanticide or abortion or traditional practices (whether or not effective) that are alleged to prevent conception. Killing or abandonment of aged persons, though not directly concerned with fertility, might also be viewed as symptomatic of a similar concern. None of these tendencies, so far as we have been able to learn, are found in African societies south of the Sahara—except in the Kalahari region, under conditions that will be described later in this chapter.

The Turkic and Mongolian pastoral societies of central Asia adhere rigidly to a principle of unilineal descent—always patrilineal in these societies—and they have corporate kinship groups. This is clearly shown in a recent comprehensive study by Krader.[1] Four Mongolian societies within Russian or Chinese spheres of influence at present and the large Turkic society of the Russian Asiatic steppes, the Kazakhs, are examined in detail. Incidental attention is also given to other societies in the same broad zone. A general pattern of kinship relations is widely prevalent. Some of the variations of this pattern are peculiar to particular cultural contexts. But many of its most important variations have a systematic relation to such conditions as transition to agricultural practice and sedentary life, or the impact of Russian or Chinese administrative systems. The nomadic Turks are nominally Muhammadan; the Mongols are generally, in varying degree, Buddhist. But, except in the case of some of the Buddhist societies, these affiliations have had little influence on their social life.

The Kazakhs increased in number during recent centuries to such a degree that they may have become the largest cohesive tribal nation in the world. About 4 million Kazakhs were enumerated in the 1926 census of the Soviet Union. Their original political structure, based on patrilineal principles, was unstable. It was possible for a Khan to establish hegemony, as a Great Khan, over all three major divisions, the Great Horde, the Middle Horde, and the Lesser Horde. These rankings, as all others, were stated in terms of order of generations or the birth order of brothers among mythical ancestors. The hordes comprised component patrilineal clans.

[1] Lawrence Krader. *Kinship Systems of the Altaic-Speaking Peoples of the Asiatic Steppes.* Harvard University, 1953 (unpublished doctoral dissertation).

The relative uniformity of the vast region in which they became dominant favoured the growth of a large population with common culture. But it may well be that the extent of this domain and the size of the population strained the capacity of a tribal political structure to maintain orderly relations. There was constant rivalry among the Khans and frequent shifting of allegiance by clan heads so that the horde divisions became confused. Leaders with great personal capacity organized effective resistence to the extension of exterior authority, and extended their own control into some agrarian districts to the south, east of the Aral Sea. But any consolidation of power tended to be ephemeral. Khanates and hordes had, in form, a highly corporate character; but in practice they were unstable.

Clans are divided into lineages on the principle of affiliation through descent, and the lineages are likewise divided into *auls*, i.e., patrilineal-kin-villages.[1] Each *aul* has fixed winter quarters and organized long seasonal migrations from this base. The members of each clan worship its mythical ancestor. The members of each lineage worship the ancestor of the lineage, who may also be mythical. Each clan, or in some pastoral societies, only each lineage, is exogamous. Each descent group has a closed membership, determined by birth or by the formal adoption of males from other groups. Clans and lineages own pasture rights, and these are assigned by each lineage among its component *auls*.

A close group of agnatic kinsmen (related by a common male ancestor) and their extended families comprise an *aul*. There are usually 10 to 15 extended families in an *aul*. The extended family typically includes all the living sons of the head and their wives and sons, if any, and the unmarried daughters of the head or of his sons. A payment, *kalym*, is made by the kinsmen of the groom to the kinsmen of the bride; the latter give her a dowry, but this is usually much less than the *kalym*. Authority is strongly patriarchal. Wives never become full members of their husband's family in the steppe societies, but they bow to his hearth at marriage and feed the fire with bits of fat—interpreted both as freeing the woman from the influence of her ancestral spirits, inimical to her husband's clan, and as a rite to insure her fertility.[2] A woman's status advances with fulfilment of her role as child-bearer. For example, a childless widow is assigned to an appropriate kinsman of her husband. But a widowed mother is free to exercise personal choice in this matter.

Extended families, *auls*, and clans have traditionally fixed heads. In the families and in the *auls* this is by seniority of generation and order of birth; in the clan it is by hereditary lineage. The lineage group, on the other hand, has no formal leadership pattern. Krader notes that in this respect the lineage lacks one of the criteria of a true corporate group. Again, the

[1] The description given here, unless otherwise indicated, has specific reference to the Kazakhs—prior to the changes in their society under Soviet administration during the 1930's.

[2] Krader, op. cit., p. 578.

95

clan has proved highly vulnerable to administrative interference by imperial authority. And in sedentary populations, the clan withers. It survives only in a vestigial institution, the patronymic sib. The strongest corporate group of Kazakh society, and among the steppe societies in general, appears to be the patrilineal-kin-village. This might be interpreted as the localized branch, or sub-branch, of a lineage.

Krader also makes the interesting observation that the extended family in steppe societies is essentially a corporate group—although some of the sons may withdraw from this 'corporation' at the time of their father's death and may establish separate 'corporations', of which they become the heads. An extended family, and also the paternal authority within this family, is perpetual—though at the death of the person exercising this authority, his eldest son succeeds him in this position. This observation is in line with Sir Henry Maine's original ascription of corporate character to the *patria potestas* in early Roman society. 'The Family, in fact, was a Corporation.' Passages from the oldest engraved codes, fifth century B.C., 'indicate that what passed from the Testator to the Heir was the *Family*, that is, the aggregate of rights and duties contained in the *patria potestas* and growing out of it'.[1] It should be noted that, according to Maine, the original testament in Roman law was not the exercise of an option but the confirmation of a relation determined by the sacred principles of the society. The extended family appears to have greater corporate force, as compared with the lineage, among Asiatic steppe societies than in Africa. And this also seems to have been the case in Roman society in the period of the early republic. But these apparent differences may be due, in part, to differences in interpretation.

There is no evidence of any appreciable practice of anti-natal measures among any of the steppe societies. In the case of the Kazakhs, the barren nature of their terrain, their acquired skill in meeting the problems of this terrain, and their rapid increase in number brought a large measure of security with respect to other nations—prior to the operation of Russian agents and the intrusion of Russian colonists. Prior to that time, and to a large extent under the Empire, the competition of which they were most conscious was competition among kinsmen for the ownership of herds and among groups of kinsmen for pasturage rights, and the struggle of each family against nature to obtain nourishment for its animals. It might have been supposed that these considerations would have induced anxiety about a large increase of the members of the family. But all the evidence is to the contrary. It should perhaps be noted that the Kazakh social organization had been formed in a much smaller population, which increased rapidly during the eighteenth and nineteenth centuries.

The levirate, bigamy or concubinage, and other devices to assure continuity of lineage are culturally sanctioned. Motherhood advances the

[1] Sir Henry Maine. *Ancient Law.* London, 1861; Everyman Edition, 1917, pp. 108, 112.

status of women. However, positive anxiety for offspring in the steppe societies seems to be limited to the need for a surviving son. The tragedy of failure in this respect can be only partially remedied by adopting the younger son of a close kinsman—keeping as close as possible to one's own line, rather than adopting a son-in-law as might be done in China or Japan. But girls, for whom the father will receive *kalym* when they are given in marriage, seem to be accepted without question.

Buddhism among Mongols where lamasaries are numerous does provide a cultural mechanism that must tend to check the increase of population. Younger sons are frequently assigned to lamasaries well before puberty. They thereby become incapable of legal paternity, and their actual contribution to natural increase is probably greatly reduced. The situation is obscure, at least to the present writer. It would be of interest to explore the social and demographic significance of this institution.

Estimated gross reproduction ratios by regions, derived from the 1926 census of the Soviet Union, are uniformly high for the three major geographical divisions of the Kazakh Republic. If accepted at face value, they indicate averages of 7.3 to 8.0 births per woman living through the childbearing period in each division of the Republic, with the highest ratio in the Eastern division. These estimates must be viewed with great caution, because they are dependent on the reported numbers of children aged 2 years in the census, and on subsitute life table values. The high mortality rates of the life table for the Vyatka district in the Volga valley were used in estimates for all steppe groups. The estimates of fertility in this series were also very high for the Tadzhik republic, occupied chiefly by an Iranian mountain population, and for the Kalmyk and Turkmen regions in the vicinity of the Caspian. These are ratios for entire districts, but the Russian population of Siberia as a whole appears on these estimates to have a level of fertility similar to the average level of the steppe ethnic districts. The estimates are somewhat lower, indicating about six children per woman, for settled Uzbekistan, and for Buryat Mongolia. Ratios of children under 5 years to women (rather than estimated reproduction rates) suggest somewhat lower levels of fertility in some of the steppe groups, with a distinctly low value for Buryat Mongols; but these ratios are thought to be even less reliable.[1] High fertility among the Kazakhs from about 1830 to 1930 is proved by the increase of this population which doubled, approximately, during the century—in spite of undoubtedly high mortality.

The culturally more advanced ethnic groups of the Caucasus mountains, the Iranian plateau, and the inter-mountain Transcaucasus region are generally characterized by firm social control and by extremely high fertility. As noted in Chapter I, reliable indices of fertility among the Armenians

---

[1] The data on children under 5 years of age at the end of 1926 are affected both by under-enumeration of infants (a characteristic of many census enumerations) and by violent conditions during the early 1920's which tended to reduce numbers of children at ages 3–4 years.

within the Soviet Union indicate an average of about eight births per woman living through the childbearing period. The culture of the Armenians is far removed from that of a primitive society; but they retain a strong emphasis on patrilineal descent and patriarchal authority. Marriage occurs at an early age, and is practically universal. Extremely high fertility is also characteristic of the Turkic Azerbaidzhans in the Transcaucasus—a population that intruded into this region from Iran. Fertility, as of 1926, is also high among Georgians, though not so high as among Armenians and Azerbaidzhans. Maximum levels of fertility are also indicated for several of the smaller nationalities in districts of the Caucasus mountains. This whole region has, of course, long been an area of intense inter-societal competition, strong ethnocentric loyalties, and strong social discipline.[1]

The questions considered in this section throw light on the demographic significance of polygyny. Polygyny as a principle is a widespread institution. Like corporate kinship groups, it seemes to be more generally present among relatively advanced primitive societies in zones of intense competition than among those with simpler techniques in marginal areas. It is widely present, frequently to a high degree, in Africa. It also occurs in central Asia, although there most men have only one wife, and almost none except great chiefs and princes have more than two, whereas in some African tribes even moderately wealthy men have several wives.

There has been considerable attention to the influence of polygyny on the fertility of women. The Culwicks found no relation between polygyny and fertility in their study; neither does Fortes in his study published in this report.[2] On the other hand, official reports on population and vital statistics derived from 'sampling' investigations in the Belgian Congo show large differences in apparent fertility in most regions between wives in polygynous households and wives in monogamous households[3]. Most statistics on this subject, however, have not been well controlled, and the empirical evidence is ambiguous. On *a priori* grounds it would seem probable, in view of what we now know about the ovulation cycle and the chances of conception, that even a moderate dispersion of the husband's sexual acts would be likely to cause some reduction of the fertility of married women. The effects of favouritism and avoidance could be even greater. And the frequent association of polygyny and the lactation taboo would also need to be taken into account.

Another aspect of the subject is suggested by an early demographic field study by Charles and Forde.[4] The study was made in a southern Nigerian

[1] Frank Lorimer. *Population of the Soviet Union*. Geneva, 1946, pp. 87–98.
[2] A. T. and G. M. Culwick, 'A Study of Population in Ulanga, Tanganyika Territory', *Sociological Review*, 30 (4), 1938, and 31 (1), 1939; Fortes, op. cit.
[3] Congo Belge, Services des A.I.M.O. du Gouvernement Général. *Démographie Congolaise 1950*. Leopoldsville, 1951 (mimeographed).
[4] Enid Charles and C. Daryll Forde. 'Notes on Some Population Data from a Southern Nigerian Village', *Sociological Review*, 30 (2): 1–16, April 1938. The data relate to the large semi-Bantu village of Umor east of the lower Cross river.

village, composed of residential groups of patrilineal kinsmen, their wives and children, a few unrelated adherents and a few adopted children. Among adults estimated to be 18 years old or over in the neighbourhood studies, there were 112 men (including three unmarried men, and four men living elsewhere whose wives and children are not taken into account) and 193 women, giving the ratio: 172 women per 100 men. It appeared, in the first place, that there were a considerable number of foreign women among the wives in this neighbourhood and in other neighbourhoods in the same village, Umor, whereas fewer of the women born in Umor had married men in other villages.

'Secondly, Umor, in common with other Cross river villages which have grown wealthy with the development of river trade in palm oil, has received a considerable accession of population by purchase of foreign children, and most of these have been females. These children have been brought to Umor by traffickers who obtained them by theft or purchase in the densely populated and impoverished Ibo country west of the Cross river.'[1]

The distribution of men by number of wives is as follows: unmarried, 3; one wife, 50; two wives, 36; three wives, 16; four or five wives, 4. No accurate determination of fertility was made, but it was estimated that on the average each male living through the childbearing period may have had more than seven children born alive.[2] It is easy to see that if the fertility of the woman in this neighbourhood had been close to that of women in the Gold Coast the average number of births per man would have been very high. It can, of course, be assumed that all children born in patrilineal, polygynous households are assimilated into the community of their fathers.

The major demographic significance of polygyny may be its role as an instrument of demographic expansion and cultural assimilation. In the illustration cited above, the demographic expansion of the patrilineal society was achieved by the purchasing power and charm of its members. In the case of military conquest of other populations by a patrilineal society practising polygyny such demographic expansion can be achieved more directly.

The remarkable expansion of the Arabs after the time of Muhammad in the early seventh century from a relatively small ethnic group to congeries of nations, and the continued expansion of successive Muslim societies, was expedited by this practice.[3] Such expansion was not incompatible with the Koranic limitation to four wives for each man.

The social structure and mythology of tribal societies that establish themselves in some fruitful land where they build a new civilization, or conquer and reshape an old civilization, might exert lasting influence on

[1] ibid., p. 13.
[2] The fertility indicated is said to recall 'that of the Ukraine, 1896–97, when the gross reproduction rate was 3.63', ibid., p. 11.
[3] Franz Boas. *Mind of Primitive Man.* New York, 1911, p. 15.

its later culture. The original institutions, ideals and moral principles of these in-migrant populations may have been formed in the relatively plastic experience of primary personal relations and oral traditions. These institutions and principles may then become fixed in written codes, preserved and interpreted by conservative scribes, and in sacred books cherished by priests and scholars. An agrarian society resident in stable villages tends to be a conservative society. But old institutions tend to lose their original function and force under altered circumstances, and old traditions are reinterpreted and applied in different ways.

The formation of a political system on a territorial basis impinges on the role of kinship systems in social organization. There is evidence of a weakening in this way of the earlier patrilineal clan structure among the Baganda, before they were appreciably affected by European influences.

'By the middle of the nineteenth century, Buganda was a kingdom acknowledging one king rather than a series of multiple kingdoms, and the authority of the king and the chiefs appointed by him came to be stronger than that of the clan heads. . . . The king acquired the power to give out land to his faithful subjects and these strips of land might be far away from the clan centre.'[1]

Polygyny on a wide scale, as well as a rigid kinship structure, are incompatible with the conditions of a stable population. Assuming approximate equality in numbers of males and females, the relative availability of men and women as spouses is influenced mainly by age patterns in marriage. Difference in age at marriage, if men marry later than women, may bring some excess of potential wives. For example, if all men became eligible for marriage at 22 years but all women at 16 years of age, in a population in which at each age the number of men was the same as the number of women, and one-fourth of all persons aged 16 years and over were under 22 years of age, there would be four marriageable women for each three marriageable men. Such a surplus might, however, be absorbed by remarriage of widowers if most widows did not remarry. In any case, the extent of polygyny cannot be very great in a stable population if all men are able to marry. In fact, polygyny does tend to disappear or to be reduced in scope in agrarian civilizations.

The preferred family pattern of agrarian civilizations in Asia tends to be an agnatic group-family; in medieval Europe it was a nuclear family (husband, wife and children). In both situations the family, or a group of families in association or in the service of a landowner, tends to be the principal economic unit. And the family, as a unit, is emphasized as the focus of social affairs. Interest in kin, though still important, tends to be subordinated to interest in family.

The extended or joint family, or any close-knit group of families, provides strong economic and social support for parenthood. But the moti-

[1] Richards and Reining, Part Four.

vations for childbearing in agrarian societies may be less compulsive than in primitive societies with large corporate kinship groups. Some of the cultural motives for fertility operative in agrarian countries may be derived from principles that were formulated in a previous context. Other motives with similar direction may emerge as responses to prevailing conditions of life. These topics must be reserved for later consideration.

'MARGINAL' SOCIETIES IN ISOLATED AND 'MARGINAL' AREAS

The ambiguous word 'marginal' is used in the title of this section to suggest the obscure nature of the relation between various conditions that must here be taken into account. We are concerned with possible associations among (a) certain types of economy; (b) certain types of social life, and (c) certain physical conditions.

A 'marginal' society can be defined as one with economic, social and military characteristics that barely assure, or fail to assure, its survival. A 'marginal' area, in an ecological sense, can be defined as a relatively unattractive area adjacent to a region characterized by more intense competition for occupancy.

Some relatively barren regions, notably those occupied by Eskimos and by Australians, cannot well be described as 'marginal' in the ecological sense, as defined above, in view of their extent and isolation. The North American arctic is a vast barren region, and the dispersed Eskimo bands occupying this realm have been long isolated from competition with societies of a different type. Similarly, Australia, though rich in resources for a society with advanced technology, provided meagre resources for the support of people with primitive techniques. And this, too, is a vast, isolated area.

Contrasts in culture between these particular societies could hardly be more extreme. The Eskimo have elaborate and skilfully designed economic equipment, highly valued as private property. The Australians use only very simple equipment, and have little property of any sort. Eskimo social life has little formal structure; their culture has, in fact, been characterized as 'individualistic'.[1] Australian social life has a very complex, formal structure, as indicated above in the quotation from Warner.[2]

Yet both of these peoples are subject to severe restrictions due to the limitations of their environment. Populations must be dispersed in relatively small groups. The search for sustenance requires long seasonal migrations. Aged and infirm persons must sometimes be abandoned. The consensus of observers describing conditions in various localities indicates a fairly wide prevalence of culturally sanctioned anti-natal measures,

[1] Margaret Mead. *Co-operation and Competition in Primitive Societies.*
[2] W. Lloyd Warner, cited in Chapter II.

including infanticide, in both societies.[1] It seems reasonable in these cases to attribute such practices quite directly to the recognition of basic human needs and the precarious nature of the resources available for meeting these needs.

The interrelations of environment, culture, and fertility seem much more complex and illusive with respect to 'marginal' societies in 'marginal' areas. Lowie listed the Andamese Islanders, the Ona and Yaghan of southernmost America, the tribes in the mountainous Mackenzie area in the north-west United States, and the Chukchi and Koryak of north-west Siberia, as among 'the rudest marginal peoples', and noted that such societies often lack clans organized on a principle of unilateral descent.[2] The names of some of these and other 'marginal' societies appear in lists of societies tolerating abortion or infanticide, compiled by Carr-Saunders and by Ford—but some of the societies, for which the evidence that we have reviewed leads us to doubt the significance of similar reports, also appear in these lists.[3] We have not been able to review these reports in detail; we are, therefore, unable to make any general statement on this subject.

Only one Bantu society is mentioned in the symposium, *African Systems of Kinship and Marriage*, as tracing descent through simple cognatic relations. The Lozi, as described by Gluckman, live in small villages on mounds in the flood plain of the upper Zambesi river. Each of these scattered and rather isolated villages is limited by its resources to a few families, with usually about six to ten adult males. The development of this tribe's kinship structure, unusual in Africa, has been attributed to the peculiarity of its situation.[4] Gluckman comments on the subject, in the light of more comprehensive information, as follows: 'Shallow kinship systems ramifying in all lines, short-lived villages of varied constitutions, and slash-and-burn shifting cultivation form a single coherent complex'.[5] Unfortunately, we have no specific information on attitude or practices relating to fertility among the Lozi.

The arid region in south-west Africa centred in the Kalahari Desert is now mainly occupied by Bushmen and Hottentots. The situation of the Bushmen is the more precarious. Apparently, they were progressively pressed back into their present restricted area by the advance of more powerful nations, including the Hottentots. Later both Bushmen and Hottentots were hard-pressed by the expanding, southward-moving Bantu tribes. The Bushmen, who are primitive nomads, hunters, and collectors of wild food, have suffered severe depopulation, so that there are now only

[1] Specific evidence on this subject with respect to the Australians is reviewed by Warner.
[2] Robert H. Lowie, quoted in Chapter II.
[3] References in the introduction to this part.
[4] Max Gluckman. 'Kinship and Marriage among the Lozi of Northern Rhodesia and the Zulu of Natal', in Radcliffe-Brown and Forde, *African Systems of Kinship and Marriage*, pp. 167–8.
[5] ibid., p. 167.

about 7,000 of them, dispersed in various small tribes. The Hottentots, who are a pastoral people, formerly owning large herds of cattle, have been less severely restricted.[1]

There is some evidence that these people, especially the Bushmen, have developed cultural devices that tend to check the growth of population. Both sometimes permit the abandonment of aged persons, in case of economic necessity, upon the decision of a son with approval of his kinsmen.[2] This is similar to the practice of some Eskimo tribes, and seems likely to be associated with similar provision for infanticide. Nevertheless, children, especially sons, are highly valued in both societies, and the culture of the Hottentots gives definite recognition to the interest in fertility, perhaps a survival from more prosperous times. Unfortunately our information on these matters is rather obscure, in part because the original social structure of both groups has been largely disrupted in the process of retreats, in part because there has not been much intensive study of these societies. The available information is reviewed by Schapera.

Both societies permit infanticide under some conditions, but there is no clear indication that these conditions have any particular relation to economic factors. Twins are regarded as unlucky in both societies. In the Hottentot tribe on which there is the best information, formerly one twin was put out of the way, though this is not done today.[3] Practice in this matter seems to vary among the Bushmen tribes, different groups allowing both infants, one only, or neither to live.[4] Both societies formerly prescribed infanticide in some other situations of ill-omen, such as the birth of a deformed child. Such practices are not necessarily inconsistent with a positive emphasis on fertility; but they suggest a relatively low intensity in this emphasis.

Hottentot women occasionally resort to abortion, and this is becoming more prevalent. But such an act makes the woman and those assisting her traditionally liable to punishment, and punishment was probably more rigorously enforced in former times.[5]

The northern Bushmen, recognizing that mothers must nurse their infants for three years or more in view of the lack of any other appropriate food, but having no provisions for preventing conception by a nursing mother, usually destroy a new infant born to a woman with another babe at the breast. This is done reluctantly, to preserve the life of the older child, sometimes against the protest of the father.[6]

The nuclear family of a husband, his wife or wives, and their children is the basic unit of economic and social life among the Bushmen. Families

---

[1] I. Schapera. *The Khoisan Peoples of South Africa*. London, 1930.
[2] ibid., p. 359.
[3] ibid., p. 266.
[4] ibid., p. 114.
[5] ibid., p. 260.
[6] ibid., pp. 115–16.

are associated in small autonomous bands, probably groups of male relatives.[1] There is no formal recognition of unilateral kinship relations. Marriages are arranged on the initiative of the prospective husband with little formality, though he is expected to live with his wife's parents during the first year after marriage and to provide them with game. They do not involve any precise obligations between the kin of the husband and the kin of the wife. However, a marriage is not legally established until a child is born, and the sterility of a woman is recognized as a reason for divorce.[2]

Hottentot society had originally a firm kinship structure, with patrilinial exogamous clans. Children belong to the clan of the father, which regulates descent and inheritance and functions as a political unit with an hereditary chief. The clans are grouped in tribes. Nowadays, marriage is initiated by the man and, except for the provision of cattle for the wedding feast by a man's kin, the only exchange of cattle is the gift of a cow by each spouse to the mother of the other. Schapera suggests that these practices may be the vestiges of a previous bride-price transfer.[3] But if no son is borne by a wife, the husband temporarily takes a concubine (who may later marry another man) to achieve this aim.[4] There were formerly strong sanctions against adultery, except with the consent of the husband. There is a preference for male infants, and a deformed child, if it is a female is especially likely to be buried.[5] Siblings have status within the family with respect to their seniority. The elaborate puberty ceremonies of girls include portents of future fertility. All property except land is privately owned. The eldest son is usually the chief heir, though there may be equal division.[6] Thus the present social organization of Hottentot society, when it is most intact, seems to include elements of compromise between the interests of the patrilineal clan and the more immediate interests of the nuclear family.

Some characteristics of both Bushman and Hottentot social life do in effect tend to reduce fertility, and these characteristics seem appropriate to and may have been influenced by economic needs and limitation of resources. But the connexion between cultural conditions influencing fertility and environmental conditions is obscure.

The fragmentary material reviewed in this section suggests that limitation of resources may often lead, directly or indirectly, to practices restricting procreation among isolated societies in barren areas—along the lines defined in more general terms by Carr-Saunders.[7] Apparently such societies also frequently lack corporate kinship groups.

[1] ibid., pp. 75–85.
[2] ibid., pp. 105–9.
[3] ibid., pp. 247–8.
[4] ibid., p. 252.
[5] ibid., p. 266.
[6] ibid., pp. 319–26.
[7] See the introduction to this part.

Relatively small islands or groups of islands often support mutually hostile populations. Even so, the limited opportunity for expansion may be a significant factor among the objective conditions of cultural evolution, as contrasted with conscious psychological interests. Moreover, some of the larger Pacific Islands are broken by rugged terrain into relatively isolated districts. Although societies isolated by water or by mountain ranges can engage in raids or in migratory invasions, relative isolation provides some limitation of resources and some degree of security, and there is less opportunity for the consolidation of large expansive societies.

Did the relative isolation of primitive societies in the Pacific afford opportunity for the development of cultural institutions that include specific motives and means for the adjustment of population to resources ? Even where this was not so, did island population tend to develop types of social organization with less emphasis on high fertility than those of the dominant African and Asiatic societies ? There is some evidence in support of an affirmative reply to these questions.

Tikopia: Rational Control of Fertility in a Primitive Society

Tikopia is a small island north of the New Hebrides and east of the Solomons. It has now about 1,750 inhabitants. It is now politically part of the British Solomon Islands Protectorate. There are no permanent white residents on the island. The Tikopians are classed as Polynesians, though living on the fringe of Melanesia. Their traditional culture remains relatively intact, though modified by European influences. They are still engaged in a subsistence economy, but this is now supplemented by some movement to other areas for work on plantations.[1]

A group of families of common patrilineal descent form a 'house' (*paito*), and are part of a patrilineal clan (*kainanga*) which traces its ultimate origin to an individual family circle. The status of an individual in the society is mainly determined by his *paito*, whose members accept common responsibility for guardianship of the children, regulate the assignment of land, grant a house-site and an associated name to each nuclear family, and co-operate in economic and ceremonial activities. However, according to Firth, 'the nuclear social group in Tikopia is the family of parents and children'. Polygyny is an approved pattern, and the existence of some polygynous households complicates family relationships, but does not alter 'their essentially personal nature'. A separate family name is given to each polygynous wife; she and her children are regarded as a family

---

[1] Raymond Firth. *We, the Tikopia*, London, 1936; also *The Work of the Gods in Tikopia*, London, 1940.

entity. Each child is cared for in life and death by his own mother's relatives.[1]

Sons usually separate from the parental family at marriage, each building a house near that of his father, or on his father's land in another village or elsewhere in the same village. However, the youngest son may stay in the parental house and accept the responsibility of providing food for his parents, working his father's immediate orchards for this purpose.[2]

There is close and intimate association between husband and wife in the economic sphere and in the care of their children, though each has specific duties.

'They commonly go out to their orchards together in the morning to plant, and to gather materials for the midday meal, and they usually combine in the preparation and cooking of the food. On the other hand, the husband makes all the nets for the household—or gets them made by some other man—even the *kuti* which his wife uses; he fells the trees for her to make the bark-clothes for them both, cuts the coconut fronds from which she makes baskets and floor-mats, and catches fish in the open sea for the common meal. All manner of woodwork, too, is in his care, as well as such tasks as the building or re-thatching of their dwelling. She is responsible for sweeping the house out and keeping it in order . . . for plaiting the floor-mats and bed-mats and beating and dyeing the bark-cloth of the family, and airing this property from time to time to stop it from being mildewed; she goes out each day with the hand-net on the reef and obtains a most valuable contribution to the larder therewith. She is also primarily responsible for seeing that the family water-bottles are kept filled and that there is food in the kit on the hook to dispense hospitality to any visitors who may drop in. . . . Close co-operation also takes place between the married pair on any occasion when ritual which affects either of them is performed.'[3]

The limited resources of the little island are intensively utilized, and ownership is strictly defined. Gardens are made up the mountain side. Even patches of apparently wild forest are filled with trees, shrubs, and plants, each of which is likely to be utilized in one way or another.[4] The whole territory is held in strict ownership. Each married son will be assigned the use of part of his father's orchards. When the father dies, the orchards are generally distributed among his sons, or the ground in each orchard is divided between them. When a woman marries she usually receives an allotment of land from her father to be used for the benefit of her children, but she does not acquire permanent title to this land; it reverts to her father or his heirs when she dies.[5]

[1] ibid., pp. 131–8, 345–6.
[2] ibid., p. 179.
[3] ibid., pp. 136–7.
[4] ibid., p. 375.
[5] ibid., pp. 390–3.

106

There is hereditary social stratification. But in spite of intense concern about the control of resources, there is little emphasis on wealth as a basis for prestige. In considering the selection of a spouse, discussion centres on family relations and personal characteristics, not on wealth in coconut trees and orchards.

The traditional pattern of personal and social relations, centred in the nuclear family, and the obvious limitation of available resources for the sustenance of life, emphasized by recurrent droughts and famines, have led to the formation of attitudes and practices tending to restrict the number of families and size of each family. The older men of the *paito*, who have responsibility for the regulation of inheritance and the allocation of land, recognize a responsiblity for influencing the number of families among whom the land must be divided.[1] This recognition is explicit. It is stated by one Tikopian as follows:

'Families by Tikopia custom are made corresponding to orchards in the woods. If children are produced in plenty, then they go and steal because their orchards are few. So families in our land are not made large in truth; they are made small. If the family groups are large and they go and steal, they eat from the orchards, and if this goes on they kill each other.'[2]

Tikopian culture provides a series of devices that tend in effect to check the growth of population. These are listed as follows:

Celibacy. The younger sons of a family were sometimes enjoined to remain single. The head of the house might require them to refrain from marriage if the offspring of the elder brother occupied all the food resources available to his line. The sons required to remain celibate were permitted to have sexual relations, but were expected to avoid having children.[3]

Prevention of conception. The recognized method of avoiding unwanted pregnancies is *coitus interruptus*. This is used by both married and un-married couples. Married couples do so when they do not desire to enlarge their families. In olden times there was a ritual called *fono*, in which the heads of families 'were exhorted to limit the number of their children by *coitus interruptus*, and the reason given was the prevention of theft and other social disorder'. Young unmarried men employed it because they did not wish to make a girl pregnant and so be forced to marry when marriage was not desired, either by them or their families. The topic is not freely discussed, but young men are enlightened by their companions when they start indulging in sex practices.[4]

Abortion. Abortion is not prevalent, but it is sometimes used by both the married and unmarried women. Married women resort to it 'when the children are many and the land not plentiful'. If an unmarried girl becomes

[1] ibid., p. 414.
[2] ibid., p. 491.
[3] ibid., p. 414.
[4] ibid., pp. 490–1.

pregnant, the society expects marriage to take place before the birth of the child. In that case, no stigma is attached to either the child or the mother. But if marriage for some reason cannot be arranged, the girl may attempt abortion. This may be done at any stage of gestation, and sometimes results in death of the mother.[1]

Infanticide. A husband may decide that a child borne by his wife should not be allowed to live. This may be due to lack of resources, or to resentment if he believes that another man was the genitor. In either case the decision is made within the family circle, without outside sanction. Occasionally an older mother may order an unmarried daughter to destroy her baby. The method in any case is the same: the face of the child is turned down at birth and it is allowed to smother.[2]

The toleration or encouragement of 'sea voyaging'. A desire for adventure sometimes calls young men to set out in their canoes and never come back.[3] The sea may claim other victims too. A hint is given, for example, in a discussion of the unmarried mother. If her lover doesn't want to marry her, and the society does not force him to accept his responsibility, 'she may go to another man who went to her; or she may go to death in the ocean; or she may dwell in the unmarried state'.[4]

Inhibition against conception by the mother of a married son. This principle, already noted in some other societies, is presumably of minor importance. Its rationale among the Tikopia, as interpreted by Firth, is very interesting:

'Their son, if he saw his mother pregnant, would be ashamed in the presence of people. The central idea is that the external evidences of sexual behaviour should not be present in both generations at the same time. In view of the taboo between parents and children, the arrival of the new baby which forces on the young man the realization of his parents' intercourse is a source of embarrassment.'[5]

The first four practices listed above, if applied at all rigorously, would result in very effective control of fertility. But this has not always been the case, and in recent decades their force has been lessened by the influence of Christianity. There was, therefore, during the 1930's, some active consideration of the application of a final drastic procedure that seems to have been actually put into operation by the Tikopia at two previous times. This is as follows:

Expulsion of part of the population. Two different modes of selection are recognized: (a) other clans might join in driving from the island all members of one clan or district; (b) the families of superior social status might join in driving out those with the lowest status.[6]

[1] ibid., p. 528. This statement describes an earlier situation. Abortion, particularly by unmarried girls, is now more prevalent.
[2] ibid., p. 529.
[3] ibid., p. 415.
[4] ibid., p. 526.
[5] ibid., p. 492.
[6] ibid., p. 415.

So far as the writer is aware, Firth's account of the Tikopia is not matched by any similar account of graded devices for the control of the growth of population in a primitive society. We must remember that there have been few, if any, equally intensive investigations of an equally undisturbed Polynesian culture. Neverthelesss, such a system, as consciously rationalized by the Tikopia, is certainly very unusual, if not unique.

Ambiguity of the Relations of Culture to Fertility in some Societies

There appear to be conflicting tendencies in the relation of traditional culture patterns to fertility in many Pacific Island societies. The region as a whole has also been characterized by extraordinary shifts in demographic trends.

Buin. Hilde Thurnwald, who has worked both in Africa and in Oceania, emphasizes the contrast between relative lack of interest in maternity among women in Buin society (a Melanesian island society, off Bougainville, in the north-west Solomons) and that characteristic of some Bantu tribes in East Africa.[1] She was also impressed, in collecting genealogical records in this area, to find that there were many women with no children or very few children in generations living before European influences were felt. According to the combined records of four generations including the present, slightly over one-third of 530 women were reported as childless, with an apparent average of about three children per mother, or about two children per woman.[2]

The Buin claim that sexual morals were much stricter in former times. This claim in itself carries little weight; but they support it with specific details. The wives of a chief were formerly respected with great fear. His wives and those of other powerful persons were jealously secluded. Severe sanctions, death or heavy fines, were used to check adultery. Today youths who return with money from labour on plantations have little respect for the old proprieties, and exercise a strong personal attraction. On the other hand, a traditional practice of female entertainment provided by chiefs in the men's hall has been suppressed.

The Buin believes that a woman can render herself permanently sterile by eating the powdered bark of certain trees, mixed with clay, a medicine called *uale.*[3] Some women take this medicine even before marriage, and many are alleged to do so after one or two children are born. Magic is also invoked by other women or by their husbands to induce pregnancy. A childless woman is called *uale*, but this is said to carry no stigma. Barrenness is not a cause for divorce. The woman who takes *uale* does so secretly, but is not punished if she is discovered. Men generally want children, but are not eager for a large number because of the expenses required for ceremonies connected with birth and childhood. (This is the only suggestion

[1] Hilde Thurnwald. 'Woman's Status in Buin Society', *Oceania* 5 (2), 1934, p. 161.
[2] ibid., p. 164.
[3] ibid., p. 162. (No evidence is given as to whether or not this has any actual effect.)

in the account of economic motivation for restricting fertility, and it is not emphasized.)

Both abortion and infanticide are tolerated. Infanticide is culturally prescribed in the case of an infant born to a woman dying in childbirth. At present abortion and infanticide are practised to prevent or destroy fatherless children, or children assumed to have been conceived in adultery. The frequency of infanticide is said to have been checked in recent years by the influence of missionaries and the threat of government action.[1] Interestingly enough, this society has no taboo against sexual intercourse with a nursing mother, after the short period of seclusion following delivery—perhaps because of its relatively weak interest in progeny.

Some features of the foregoing account could be interpreted as showing not merely the lack of strong cultural emphasis on fertility, but also a definite concern for its control, and this could have been influenced in its origin by economic conditions. If so, the measures and attitudes thus developed have been distorted through the forces of social disorganization into means of avoiding social responsibilities. The fluid, amorphous character of Buin society could lead to rapid natural decrease or, with accommodation to present conditions, to rapid natural increase.

Lesu. Powdermaker reports that in Lesu, a Melanesian village on the east coast of New Ireland, children are received with love and given great attention. This is a patrilineal society with totemic clans and 'moities'. The clan exercises important economic functions; the 'moity' is mainly a religious institution, responsible for ceremonies connected with birth, circumcision, marriage, pregnancy, and death. The elders of the clan are the real governing force. Residence is usually matrilocal, with formation of extended families. A husband may have several wives, and a wife may have two husbands.[2]

Powdermaker has presented vital statistics from genealogical records obtained from Lesu women. Difficulties inherent in such statistics are discussed in the supplement; the results must be used with caution. Exclusive of women in the most recent generation (presumably of uncompleted fertility), 35 of 295 women were recorded as childless (12 per cent). There was an apparent average of 2.9 births per mother, or 2.6 births per woman. Only 10 per cent of all women were reported as having had more than four children.[3] Girls in Lesu marry soon after puberty, usually to somewhat older men. There was no adult woman in the community who had never married. There is a strong taboo against coitus during the period of lactation. This is extended to require abstinence from sex relations by the owner of a sow during the month after she has borne a litter.[4]

[1] ibid., pp. 148, 166.
[2] Hortense Powdermaker. *Life in Lesu.* New York, 1933, pp. 39–44, 226–7.
[3] Powdermaker. 'Vital Statistics of New Ireland as Revealed in Genealogies', *Human Biology* 3 (3), pp. 351–75, 1931.
[4] Powdermaker. *Life in Lesu,* p. 79.

There is no indication of infanticide. Extra-marital sex relations are now quite common. But there is no evidence of extensive resort to abortion, and this is not socially approved. There is, however, an ancient lore about 'sterility leaves', and an appreciable minority of the women attempt to prevent future pregnancies in this way. Although the majority of the women questioned by Powdermaker said that they wanted more children, some stated definitely that they did not. Reasons given for not wanting children, or more children, were: fear of childbirth, desire to avoid its pains, interference with dancing, and interference with sex life, though the last was mentioned only in describing reasons why other women did not want children.[1] Although Powdermaker says that this is a strong and conservative society, there seem to be elements of conflict or ambivalence both in its general social organization and in behaviour and attitudes relating to fertility.

Arapesh. The traditional culture of the mountain Arapesh (a Papuan-speaking people in north-west New Guinea) combines intense interest in fertility with definite provision for checking excessive increase of population. These are a timorous, gentle people dependent for their livelihood on gardens in a rather barren country. Mead has described the eagerness with which the Arapesh father 'nourishes' the expected infant that is being formed in his wife's womb by repeated copulations. He ceases to do so when the condition of the woman shows that the child is fully formed, and he refrains from any sex act, even with another wife if he is polygynous, until the child is weaned (usually about three years after birth).[2] It is considered desirable that the next child should not follow too closely, so that the infant can gradually learn to eat more and more solid food. But if the mother does become pregnant, her present baby is weaned more abruptly. A little baby is never left alone, but is constantly nurtured with great tenderness and anxiety by both father and mother. According to the usual pattern, a boy of 12 to 14 begins to feed and cherish his betrothed young wife, 'himself playing the role that his mother has played to him'.[3]

Nevertheless, as soon as an infant is delivered, the midwife calls to the father who has been waiting outside, telling him the sex of the child and awaiting his word: 'wash it', or 'don't wash it'. The latter is a euphemistic commend to let the child die. This command is rare, but there is a definite preference for boys and if there are already several girls and no son, a girl baby may be put away. In view of the lactation taboo, any other procedure would greatly delay the chance of having a boy. However, Mead also states that an infant may not be kept 'when food is scarce, or if there are several children, or if the father is dead'.[4] The extension of the lactation taboo to

[1] ibid., pp. 242–3.
[2] Margaret Mead. *Sex and Temperament in Three Primitive Societies.* Reprinted in *From the South Seas*, New York, 1939, pp. 31, 36–8.
[3] Margaret Mead. *Male and Female.* New York, 1949, p. 66.
[4] Mead. *Sex and Temperament in Three Primitive Societies.* Reprinted in *From the South Seas*, pp. 32–3.

a second wife may, of course, be due to 'sympathetic' extension of the original practice. This seems particularly plausible, in view of the men's anxiety about sex as shown by their belief that they expose themselves to witchcraft by giving semen to a foreign or aggressive woman. It might, on the other hand, be interpreted as indication of a lack of eagerness to have many children, which is, of course, perfectly compatible with an intense eagerness to have some children.

Mundugumor. Another New Guinea mountain society described by Mead, the Mundugumor, also has an ambivalent attitude toward fertility, but for entirely different reasons. The Mundugumors are a ferocious people with an abundance of resources, inherited from the labour of their ancestors and augmented by trading, chicanery, and predatory raids on the weaker people around them. Until very recently they were cannibals and head-hunters. They numbered about 1,000 persons in 1932.[1] They were formerly more numerous (like the Arapesh in this respect, though in no other way). The men engage in war, alliances, trade, and highly artistic carving. Other work is done by women and young boys. The wealthier men supplement their marriages within the tribe by acquiring additional wives, sometimes seven or eight, from other weaker tribes.

Their traditional kinship system is highly complex. Inheritance (except with respect to rights to land, which in view of its abundance is not a matter of great concern) follows a *rope*: 'A rope is composed of a man, his daughters, his daughters' sons, his daughters' sons' daughters; or if the count is begun from a woman, her sons, her sons' daughters, her sons' daughters' sons, and so on'.[2] All property, with the exception of land, passes from father to daughter. Sons are bound to their mother's rope, and receive no important property from their father. The system leads to rivalry between brothers, halfbrothers, sons and fathers and, likewise, between daughters and mothers, co-wives, brothers and sisters. Fathers protect their daughters; mothers protect their sons. Against this pattern exists the custom of a brother exchanging his sister for a wife for himself. Girl must be exchanged for girl. This is theoretically the only way a wife may be obtained, but in practice sons without sisters get wives by elopement and fighting, and then payment of a highly-valued, ornamented flute. But, even with enough sisters to provide a wife for each son, hostility is present because of the acceptability of polygyny. Older sons try to exchange their sisters, rather than save any for their younger brothers. The father, too, may claim the right to exchange his daughter for an additional wife:

'. . . Instead of permitting his son to use his sister to obtain a wife, the father can use her himself; he can trade his adolescent daughter for a young wife. The father has already a strong sense of possession in his daughter. She belongs to his rope, not to her brother's rope. She gardens

[1] ibid., p. 169.
[2] ibid., p. 176.

with her father, works in the bush with her father, uses kinship terms calculated through her father when she talks, bears the name of one of her father's female ancestors. Her father has the closest supervisory rights over her; he may sleep in the same sleeping basket with her until she marries, and accompany her if she gets up in the night. He comes to regard her as his property, of which he can dispose as he wishes.'[1]

Pregnancy, birth and nursing are said to be hated by the women, and are avoided if possible, and the husband's reaction to his wife's pregnancy or the birth of a male child is equally negative:

'When a Mundugumor woman tells her husband that she is pregnant, he is not pleased. It makes him a marked man. When he goes among a group of men who are carving a slit gong, they will officiously and with broad grins brush up the chips lest he tread upon any of them, which would be bad for the child, whom he does not want, and for the slit gong, from the manufacture of which he is thus publicly excluded. If he fences a garden, someone else will insert the posts; if he gathers ratan in the bush, some impudent boy will warn him to pluck only the green ratan or the child will stick fast in his wife's womb. These taboos, which might unite him to his wife in care for the child if having a child were something to look forward to among the Mundugumor, are used by his associates to aggravate his annoyance with his wife. He abuses her for having become pregnant so quickly, and curses his anti-pregnancy magic that he had set in motion in vain. . . .

'. . . the pregnant woman associates her pregnancy with sexual deprivation, her husband's anger and repudiation and the continual risk that he will take another wife and temporarily desert her. . . . The first highly charged days of marriage in which an active interest in sex held them both together have given place to anger, hostility, and very often to charges of infidelity, as the husband refuses to believe that he is responsible for this unwelcome event. . . .

'This attitude towards children is congruent with the ruthless individualism, the aggressive specific sexuality, the intrasex hostility, of the Mundugumor. A system that made a son valuable to a man as an heir, as an extension of his own personality, might combine the Mundugumor personality type with an interest in parenthood, but under the Mundugumor rope and marriage system a man has no heirs, only sons who are hostile rivals by definition, and daughters who, defend them as he will, will eventually be torn from him. . . .

'Before the child is born there is much discussion as to whether it shall be saved or not, the argument being partly based upon the sex of the child, the father preferring to keep a girl, the mother a boy. The argument is weighted against the mother, however, because her father and brother also prefer a girl. . . . Once a son is born it is absolutely

[1] ibid., p. 179.

necessary that he should have a sister to exchange for his wife. . . . A girl-child, therefore, has a better chance of survival than a boy; she is an advantage to her father, to her brothers, and also to the entire kin-group on both sides, who, if she is not requisitioned at home, may use her to compensate for one of her cousin's wives.'[1]

Adoption is a common occurrence. Children who might otherwise have been killed by their parents are sometimes taken in this way. One of any pair of twins is always available for adoption. In fact, Mead suggests that both men and women often prefer to adopt children, rather than to endure the difficulties and privations of pregnancy and delivery. The preference in adoption is usually for a girl.[2]

The conflicts and resentments within Mundugumor society that Mead reports had been intensified by the bitter experience of subjugation to governmental authority only a few years before her stay there. Its culture seemed already 'broken', with many men away for work and ceremonies neglected. This could easily bring about, in various ways, a sharp decline in fertility.

Obviously, Mundugumor social organization had supported a continuing society. And its population had been maintained, prior to a recent period of decrease, though in part this may have been done at the expense of other populations through the acquisition of additional wives. But major elements of conflict and instability were inherent in the traditional culture.

Interpretation. In the four societies mentioned above, Buin, Lesu, Arapesh, and Mundugumor, there seem always to have been some cultural factors that tended partially to check or offset factors making for high fertility. *Some conflicting institutional factors or ambivalence in attitudes toward fertility appear to have been present in many Pacific Island cultures.* It should, however, be noted that Samoan culture, to which we will refer in the following chapter, appears to deviate from this general pattern; this also appears to have been so among the Maori of New Zealand; and there are probably many other exceptions.

The Pacific 'region' is utterly heterogeneous in every respect except one: the absence of close association with a continental land mass. Nevertheless, our partial evidence seems to support a thesis with respect to this 'region' similar to that advanced by Ford, but given more general application by him, that there is often a 'delicate balance' between tendencies toward having children and tendencies toward an avoidance of childbearing.[3] The influence of new culture contacts on demographic trends in the Pacific will be treated in Chapter VI.

[1] ibid., pp. 189–92.
[2] ibid., pp. 193–4.
[3] See Introduction.

114

CHAPTER IV

Culturally Uncontrolled Trends in Fertility

INTRODUCTION

In the preceding chapters we have investigated some ways in which social structure and culture may be related to levels of fertility in primitive societies. In some cases the relation seems to be fairly definite; in other cases it is ambiguous. In the last part of the preceding chapter we were drawn toward a conclusion that the culture of some societies may be essentially indifferent to the frequency of births, in effect as well as in intent. The discovery of positive evidence of the influence of social factors on fertility in some situations gives no reason for assuming that all variations in fertility among populations reflect differences in cultural conditions. Animals procreate without benefit of cultural sanctions. A recent whimsical essay deals with the problem, 'Why is a Yak?' Various possible teleological interpretations, such as uses of a Yak's tail as a fly-swatter, and the convenience of its name in anagrams, are examined. But the final solution of the problem is as follows: 'Once there was a mama Yak, and a papa Yak. That is why there is a Yak.'

As noted in the introduction to this report, our proto-human ancestors, without the support of kinship structures or social ideals conducive to high fertility, must have maintained a level of fertility like that found in many non-industrial societies today. We may, therefore, expect to find high levels of fertility in societies where cultural conditions are merely permissive to the natural procreative tendency of human populations. In such situations, natural increase may be largely determined by biological factors, with only slight modification of reproductive behaviour in the interest of orderly social relations. Some restraint of aberrant behaviour, excesses, and conflicts might, in net effect, induce levels of fertility slightly above, or slightly below, but not very different from those resulting from similar biological factors in a proto-human population prior to the rise of culture.

Variations in biological factors, in conjunction with conditions affecting food supply, the frequency of accidents, and diseases, obviously affect both mortality and fertility. Apart from the direct influence of cultural conditions on fertility, natural increase tends to rise with physical conditions favourable to the parturition of embryos and to the survival of infants

115

from birth to maturity. It tends to fall with starvation, malnutrition, or disease. Variations in genetic constitution among populations must influence both fecundity and vitality; but we have little knowledge, as yet, about the nature and possible importance of such factors in human populations. Some diseases, such as malaria and influenza, both raise mortality and lower fecundity. Diseases affecting the reproductive organs impair fecundity and frequently cause absolute sterility.

Thomas Malthus, in the first edition of his *Essay on the Principle of Population*, proceeded on the assumption that the 'principle of population' conformed almost universally, as a 'natural law', to the sort of conditions mentioned above. He assumed that a high level of fertility is generally a simple consequence of 'the passion between the sexes', except as checked by 'misery' (war, starvation, disease) or 'vice' (disease due to socially disapproved conduct, abortion, infanticide). He modified this position in later editions by recognizing the possible role of 'moral restraint' as a 'preventive check' in an enlightened population. He assumed, however, that any widespread and effective exercise of such 'moral restraint' was a relatively rare social achievement. The increase of population was conceived as largely a 'natural' phenomenon, determined by biological factors. Thus, according to Malthusian theory, culture is irrelevant to fertility—except in so far as it may be conducive to 'vice' or, in rare circumstances, severe restraint of sexual activity. There is clearly some contradiction between the basic assumption on which we have been proceeding and the basic assumption of Malthusian theory. This contradiction can, however, be narrowed by more precise attention to the interaction of biological and cultural factors in the determination of fertility.

The rise of culture brings greater sensitivity to suffering, and attention to means for promoting desirable events and avoiding unpleasant ones. But observation of many aspects of life in primitive societies, including the behaviour of those conducting and of those undergoing initiation ceremonies, suggests the prevalence in primitive societies of a certain indifference both to the suffering of others and to personal discomfort. An old man who had participated in a mass burial of living wives at the death of his chief was asked by the anthropologist, to whom he recounted this event, 'But didn't they scream?' His reply was significant of attitudes that are by no means uncommon even in more advanced civilizations: 'Oh, no. We filled their mouths with mud, and they died quietly enough.' Sympathy and the desire to avoid pain and hardship are universal. But these tendencies are balanced by powerful trends toward accepting usual events as 'natural' and inevitable, and toward behaving as others with whom one is associated have behaved and expect one to behave. The expectations generated in any society by the biological forces of reproduction tend to perpetuate the relatively free operation of these forces—except in so far as these tendencies are modified by overriding cultural motives.

Actually, the social organization of any stable, intact society usually exerts a positive influence on fertility—either reinforcing conditions favorable to procreation, sometimes with strong social sanctions, or inducing tendencies toward the restraint of fertility. But in some situations these influences may be so conflicting or ambivalent as to be neutral in net effect. In particular, processes of social conflict and cultural shock may disrupt the fabric of social relations and destroy the values that give human life coherence and force, leaving in their wake a chaos of conflicting interests, or an apathetic accommodation to circumstances. Under such conditions trends in fertility tend to be determined by dissociated motives, inconsistent with orderly social life, or by elemental human impulses— along with physical factors affecting health and disease, fecundity and sterility.

New forces, to which a traditional society cannot adjust through tolerable modifications of its ways of living, may disrupt the whole basis of orderly social life, creating a condition of 'cultural shock'. This may come as a result of conquest, or enslavement, or merely through new contacts and opportunities that stimulate responses incongruous with previous' ways of living and former values. The motivations released in such a situation may be mutually inconsistent, bringing about conflict and confusion. The behaviour of individuals no longer provides patterns to which other individuals can relate their interests and activities with some sense of security. This is the process of social disorganization.

The conflicts and frustration characteristic of acute social disorganization may lead to sharp declines of fertility. Lack of social support for personal needs and new opportunities for profit or pleasure may result in widespread avoidance of parental responsibilities. Another condition, distinct from social disorganization, is frequently associated with it: an increased prevalence of diseases, including diseases tending to cause sterility.

Human beings cannot long endure a situation of acute conflict. Conflict tends to be followed by acquiescence and accommodation. Orderly social relations of some sort begin to emerge, and new routines are established. Men and women in sexual relations take account of the satisfactions and security of more or less stable conjugal unions. The process of accommodation may, nevertheless, leave a residue of frustration, apathy, and irresponsibility to social obligations. Such a situation does not generate the aspirations or self-confidence required for sustained action toward the achievement of accepted goals. The role of cultural values in the determination of behaviour becomes relatively weak.

The pattern of social accommodation thus tends to release elemental drives in reproductive behaviour, but channels these drives along conventional lines, consistent with orderly social relations. In such situations biological factors, in association with cultural indifference to the frequency of births, may induce high fertility.

The Nkundo

Demographic statistics in the Belgian Congo are derived from selected samples of tribal registers. The tribal registration system, though enforced as a means of political control, is imperfect; and samples have in the past been selected without scientific design. The figures for any particular district obtained in this way are, therefore, subject to large error.

Nevertheless, significant differences in vital trends among some large regions are clearly established by fairly consistent findings in various districts within these regions, and are supported by a consensus of opinion among administrative officials and scientists familiar with local conditions. Similarly wide variations are shown by census findings in territories under British administration east of the mountain divide.

One broad area of apparently low fertility is found in the river and forest region in the central part of the Belgian Congo south of the great bend of the Congo and east of Lake Leopold II—notably in the Equateur and Tshuapa districts, and the adjacent Sankuru and Maniema districts to the south. A second area of low fertility is found in the Uele district in the northern savanna. These five districts are classified by Belgian officials as 'regressive' in population type. Four districts with conspicuously high fertility are Bas-Congo (extreme west), Kwango (south-west), and Haut-Katanga (extreme south-east), and Kivu (extreme east); these are classed as 'progressive' in population type. The other 10 districts of the Congo

TABLE 13.

District (and number of sample groups)	Children as percent of total population	Annual rates per 1,000 population		Annual births per 1,000 women aged 15–45 years
		Births	Deaths	
'Progressive' Type				
Kasai (5)	37.5	38	22	148
Kwango (14)	41.9	42	26	179
Haut-Katanga (14)	43.3	48	24	216
Kivu (29)	43.7	43	27	180
Bas-Congo (10)	43.9	40	17	170
'Regressive' Type				
Tshuapa (21)	25.4	18	25	66
Uele (12)	26.0	19	20	70
Equateur (12)	29.2	26	17	97
Maniema (16)	30.2	22	19	88
Sankuru (10)	31.8	24	23	102

are classified as 'intermediate' in population type. The majority of the districts classed as 'intermediate' verge toward the 'progressive' type, with rapid natural increase. This is notably so with respect to the Kasai district, which is contiguous to Kwango and the Haut-Katanga and forms part of the same general region.

Mean values on several indices for the sample groups of the rural tribal population in each of the 10 districts listed above, as found in 1950, run as given in Table 13.[1]

In general, the upland savannas (except in the Uele district) and the highlands tend to have higher fertility than the interior forest region. The predominantly matrilineal tribes in the Bas-Congo, Kwango, Kasai and Haut-Katanga districts are also generally characterized by high fertility; but so are the patrilineal tribes in the Kivu district. Bantu peoples are predominant in most of the districts of all types listed above (but the dominant Uele groups are Sudanese). There are scattered pygmoid groups (Batswa and others) in the central forest zone; they seem generally to have somewhat higher fertility than the dominant Bantu in the same vicinity. Although broad differentiations with respect to ecology or traditional kinship structure may have some significance, attention must be given to the influence of specific conditions in particular areas.

The Tshuapa River region Nkundo, or Mongo, are selected for special attention because, in addition to the population statistics collected in 1950, we have an authoritative account of cultural conditions influencing family life in this population, by an author who combines scientific objectivity with sympathetic imagination, who has observed Nkundo life through long and intimate association, and who has a precise knowledge of 'their rich and subtle language'.[2]

The Nkundo are a Bantu group with a million or more members in various tribes with similar culture. They were formerly a 'master race' who established their position in their present situation by military migrations from the north. It seems likely that at first the intruding population was much smaller, and that the intrusion was followed by rapid natural increase in the new situation; but this is mere conjecture. The Nkundo drove out many of the previous inhabitants of the region, and subordinated the remainder as slaves or retainers. The transfer of a slave was formerly one of the key elements in the complex series of exchanges involved in marriage. These people are mainly agricultural, with secondary interest in trapping and fishing. The Nkundo were in a position to extract large profits from the slave trade in its heyday.

---

[1] Congo Belge: Service des AIMO du gouvernement général: *Démographie Congolaise: 1950* (mimeographed report). In this report, which deals only with non-urban tribal population, no demographic information is presented for one of the 20 administrative districts of the Congo.

[2] Le Révérend Père G. Hulstaert. 'Le mariage des Nkundo'. *Institut Royal Colonial Belgique, Section des sciences morales et politiques. Memoirs.* 520 pp., 1938.

The Nkundo were conquered and subjected to external authority near the end of the nineteenth century. In their case the agents of the conquest were black troops from other regions. The humiliation of conquest and the disruption of traditional lines of control tended toward social disorganization. So did the increase of wealth through commerce in the hands of individual household heads, bringing new opportunities for enhanced prestige by display of wealth.

Palm oil and related products are the most important articles of commerce today. With the increase of commerce, many Nkundo have found employment in Coquilhatville, the large city nearest to their forest homes, but some have gone as far as Leopoldville or Stanleyville, or have found work on the Congo freighters. The demographic survey of 1950 shows that almost 10 per cent of the total population in the Nkundo samples covered moved out in the year of the survey. The report describes the outmigration from the entire Tshuapa district as an 'exodus to European centres and developments'. Women as well as men often go from the villages to the towns to engage in trade.

The traditional kinship structure of the Nkundo is patriarchal, but Hulstaert does not give a detailed exposition of its structure. It appears to have been modified and weakened by social changes during the last century. The indigenous political structure at present is characterized as a rather loose 'democratic-oligarchic' regime.[1] Women are active in trade, but do not hold property.[2] Authority is centred in the patriarchal head of the household; households form the basis of economic and social organization. Patrimony is collective.[3] Household heads have religious and social obligations to the patrilineal clans of which they are members. The principle of clan exogamy is maintained.

The Nkundo are, of course, polygynous. In former times adultery, especially a continued affair, rendered a woman liable to severe punishment, and in theory this is still true. Sanctions are applied directly by the husband. However, unless stirred to wrath by flagrant provocation, he is expected to show proof that his rights have been violated to the elders of his lineage and to obtain their authorization.[4] Though a husband has the right to kill an adulterous wife, this rarely occurs, and might lead to a clan war. He may, however, beat her or, stripping her naked, expose her to ridicule, or put her neck in a forked stick (as is done in transporting slaves); an incorrigible wife might, in fact, be sold as a slave. The woman has no redress, but her kin may beg or buy her release from continued punishment. If aroused to jealousy by flagrant acts of her husband, a wife may assault the woman involved or withhold favours from her husband; but she has no recognized rights in this connexion.

[1] ibid., p. 12.
[2] ibid., VI: II.
[3] ibid., p. 25.
[4] ibid., p. 315.

The sanctions for maintaining the fidelity of women to their marital obligations seen similar to those among the Zulu and other strongly patriarchal societies; but somehow among the Nkundo these sanctions have largely lost their force. There was never a strong injunction among the Nkundo against pre-marital sexual relations; an illegitimate child belongs to the mother and is recognized and supported by her family, though if the mother later marries the child may be transferred to the authority of her husband. Divorce was permissible, and might be initiated by the woman. Even adultery, in spite of strong sanctions to the contrary, seems always to have been fairly frequent. Under present conditions, pre-marital promiscuity has become practically universal, and both adultery and divorce are widespread. In a series of 112 marriages recorded at a mission station, only 37 of the brides were marrying for the first time; 18 were widows; 7 were accepting traditional obligations as 'inherited widows' or 'replacements' for a sister; but 50 had been previously divorced, if we include three cases of girls who had withdrawn from pre-puberty unions. About two-thirds of the divorced women who were remarrying had formerly been members of polygynous households.[1] Do moral sentiments associated with a strong clan structure exert a more powerful influence in Zulu society? Or does the high degree to which the marital fidelity of wives in patriarchal, polygynous societies is an obligation maintained by force render it everywhere vulnerable to collapse under the impact of new associations and greater freedom? Would Zulu morality prove equally susceptible to corruption under similar conditions? The profound novel by Alan Paton, *Cry the Beloved Country*, suggests that this may be so.

The strongest affectional bonds in Nkundo society, according to Hulstaert, are those between parents and children, between brothers and sisters, and between friends of the same sex. The members of the family have constant need of one another. 'A man isolated from his parents is a pariah.'[2] Though a father has great affection for his children, he may severely punish a child who has wronged the honour of his family. The mother, who is not a part of the same lineage, is likely to take the side of the child. The need of preserving family solidarity commonly leads to indulgence of children. The love of sons and daughters for their parents, especially the mother, tends to be sincere and deep. There is also a strong affectional bond between brothers and sisters, and this is maintained even after the sister's marriage. Paternal uncles and aunts are classed as 'fathers', maternal uncles and aunts as 'mothers'.[3]

Boys and girls at puberty commonly separate from their parents, each joining a group with others of the same sex and similar age. Boys are circumcised. There has recently been a trend toward preference for the

[1] ibid., p. 112.
[2] ibid., p. 25.
[3] ibid., p. 30.

increased freedom of an individual hut.[1] There are frequent and sincere friendships among companions of the same age and sex. These are sometimes formalized in friendship pacts, which are especially frequent between women; these pacts may endure for a long time, but they are sometimes broken. Men occasionally loan wives to friends who are their companions of age.[2]

There has always been some homosexual practice. Among men this was most common among those who were unable for a long time to obtain wives; but this tendency has been reduced by the greater freedom of heterosexual relations. Among women, homosexual practice was especially common among co-wives in polygynous households.[3]

An approach to marriage is now usually initiated by the young persons themselves, leading to intimate affairs and small gifts. There may then be an initial arrangement by a man and his father with the girl's father.[4] Further arrangements are mediated by a *ndonga*, or chief, who acts as a neutral to guarantee the legality of the payments and the obligations incurred by those involved in the marriage. He receives presents in payment from both families. A small conventional payment is presented by the *ndonga* on behalf of the man to the girl's family. If this is lifted from the ground by the girl and accepted by her father, the man may take the girl to his village as *bompaka* (wife); but this by no means establishes the full legality of the marriage or the husband's rights to the children that she may bear. Formerly the man and his wife usually remained for a time in the father's household; but this is becoming less common.[5] The man is expected to give presents to his wife, some of which she usually sends to her family. Also the man and his family, in accepting presents of food from the wife's family, deepen their obligations. The man, often after a considerable period, must then make a larger, conventionally prescribed, payment to the woman's father, and send other gifts to her mother and other relations. The copper rings and forged objects delivered at this time may have been received by his family as marriage payments for a female member, or the man may acquire these goods by labour or prowess. The *bompaka* now becomes a *wali* (a legally recognized wife).[6] The man and his family again receive gifts from the wife's family; occasionally, though rarely, these gifts may surpass in value the payments received by them from the man— thus displaying the wealth of the wife's family, and enhancing her status. In former times, a wealthy father sometimes gave his son-in-law the means of procuring a second wife immediately, so that the daughter might at once become a *nkita* (chief wife).[7] Eventually, a final payment must be made by

[1] ibid., pp. 509–10.
[2] ibid., p. 56.
[3] ibid., pp. 95–6.
[4] ibid., p. 103.
[5] ibid., pp. 117–18.
[6] ibid., pp. 129–38.
[7] ibid., p. 153.

the husband to his wife's father—even though in the meanwhile she may have died or have been divorced—to establish his legal rights over her children. This payment was formerly a slave, usually a female slave, or other object of comparable value. Hence the Nkundo saying, 'the marriage bond is fixed by the slave'—analogous to the eastern and southern Bantu saying, 'cattle make the marriage'.[1]

As a matter of preference by their parents, girls were sometimes retained to an unusually advanced age at marriage. An unusual institution, the *bolumbu*, was known in ancient times though necessarily limited to very wealthy families. A wealthy man might dedicate a favourite little girl as *bolumbu*. She was dressed in rare furs, honoured in a public ceremony, and for a time withdrawn from ordinary associations. After emerging from seclusion she enjoyed a special prestige, was released for life from all labour; was retained for a longer than usual time by her parents, and eventually married with great ceremony a man of wealth and distinction.[2]

Marriage, though providing the labour service of females and essential to a man as a means of obtaining sons and daughters, is motivated in large part by personal attraction. There is usually a rise of affection between husbands and wives. In spite of jealousies within a polygynous household, the return of the husband from a journey is likely to be greeted by a great demonstration of spontaneous affection.[3] But the attachment between married people is less strong than that of sons and daughters for their parents. Rarely will a wife remain with a husband who has an incurable malady, is impotent, or becomes impoverished.[4]

The Nkundo greatly desire children, and have no general preference for either boys or girls.[5] Twins are especially welcome.[6] A birth is celebrated with joy by the whole village. All who have seen the infant (usually all those in the village) must religiously abstain from any enterprise until the umbilical cord is detached. Labour in the fields in violation of this principle would make the fields barren. The mother maintains seclusion during a period of several weeks. Any sex act on her part, even with her husband, during this period would cause the death of the infant—except that the night after the cord has dropped the spouses have ritualistic coitus (usually incomplete) to break the pregnancy spell (*bokoka*). If this rite is neglected, ordinary sex intercourse must be avoided until the child is weaned.[7] Previously, several months before the expected delivery, the pregnancy spell had been established by a ceremonial anointing of the pregnant woman by her mother and ritualistic sex intercourse between the woman

[1] ibid., p. 161. As stated by Hulstaert: 'La force du mariage se trouve dans l'esclave.'
[2] ibid., pp. 30 ff.
[3] ibid., p. 43.
[4] ibid., pp. 37–8.
[5] ibid., pp. 464–7.
[6] ibid., p. 501.
[7] ibid., p. 488.

and her husband (or the child's father if the woman was unmarried) 'to fix the life of the child'. There must be scrupulous avoidance of adultery by both spouses (but not of sex relations between a husband and his other wives) while the *bokoka* is in force. After the delivery a mother must keep a nursing child with her at all times, especially during sexual relations, to preserve its life. The child is named by the father, often with the name of a disembodied spirit. There is much rivalry among spirits for this honour; measures of protection must often be taken against offended spirits.

Abortion has always been known; but it was formerly practised only in exceptional circumstances, usually against the wishes of the husband. It might be motivated by a woman's antipathy to her husband, or exhaustion after bearing many children, or, very rarely, by the desire of a famous dancer to preserve her grace after the birth of a few children. Pregnancy in an unmarried woman involved no disgrace and was not a cause for abortion. In more recent years abortion has become quite frequent, and is sometimes practised to maintain the pleasures or gains of illicit sex relations.[1]

Sex has always been treated naturally and under normal conditions carries no suggestion of shame. Mothers assist little girls in modeling their sexual organs to facilitate later sexual acts. Sexual motifs are present in many dances. The tatooing of girls emphasizes sexual characteristics. There was also an ancient custom of douching after coitus, using gourds; but there is no indication that this was regarded as a contraceptive practice. *Coitus interruptus*, except in the ritualistic relations of spouses mentioned above, was never practised. Infanticide was unknown.[2]

There has always been a certain individualistic strain in competition for prestige in Nkundo society.

It is not difficult to see that in a population with this cultural background, the rise of the European slave trade, the shock of conquest, the increase of opportunities for commerce, and new cultural contacts might give rise to social disorganization, especially in the sphere of personal and sexual relations. First in the towns and later in the villages, many young men began to avoid the responsibilities of marriage. And many young women, at first accepting gifts in occasional sexual relations, drifted toward prostitution in varying degrees. Approximately one in nine of natives, perhaps one in three of all adult native women, in Coquilhatville is an unmarried woman living apart from any legal relatives.[3] According to ancient Nkundo law, a husband might collect payment for damages from a man known to have had adulterous relations with one of his wives. In recent years, some husbands have exploited this institution as a semi-commercial practice. The very fact that the Nkundo are physically attrac-

---

[1] ibid., pp. 466–7.

[2] ibid., pp. 64–7, 92, 97. The information on douching was obtained by the present writer from a reliable authority.

[3] ibid., p. 77.

tive and highly intelligent has intensified rather than moderated these tendencies. Such conditions necessarily tend toward delay of marriage, increase of anti-natal practices, and the spread of venereal diseases. This demographic effect may also be increased by other unhealthy conditions in this tropical forest zone. According to Belgian authorities, leprosy as well as venereal disease is common in this region.[1]

We have described this situation in some detail because it represents a trend that has been repeated in varying degrees and in various ways in many countries and at many times. Though such a situation may persist for a long time it is often a relatively transient condition. It may, therefore, be designated as acute social disorganization. It represents one type of response to cultural shock—involving both physiological and cultural factors tending to induce low fertility. The reduction in fertility is in part motivated by personal preferences, but these preferences are largely deviations from current, as well as traditional, social norms.

Baganda and Bahaya

The contribution by Richards and Reining (presented in Part IV of this Report) describes social conditions affecting fertility in two African populations in the vicinity of Lake Victoria, and presents the preliminary results of surveys in this region, together with comparable data from the 1948 East African Census.

The economic situation of the Baganda is in some respects comparable to that of the African population of the Gold Coast Colony or the Ashanti. They have settled residence in agricultural villages and have developed commercial crops (in this case chiefly cotton), along with continued production of native food crops (in this case chiefly bananas). Buganda (the country of the Baganda) has for some time been an area of net in-migration. But in contrast to the Gold Coast, it is a region of relatively low fertility. According to the 1948 census, there had been on the average only 3.7 live births per woman of completed fertility, owing largely to a high frequency of childlessness (24 per cent). In the Mengo district around Kampala, there had been, on the average, only 3.2 live births per woman of completed fertility. The intensive study by Richards and Reining in three agricultural villages in this district lead to a similar finding: 3.1 live births per woman of completed fertility, with 32 per cent of these women, all of whom had some conjugal experience, childless. Most women had married before they were 20 years old. About half of the marriages conformed to customs. The remainder were divided, in order of numerical importances between Christian marriages, unions by consensual agreement, and Muslim marriages.

There is indubitable, though indirect, evidence that all Baganda want

---

[1] Congo Belge: Service des AIMO, op. cit.

children (except perhaps a few atypical persons in large towns). It is almost equally certain that no type of contraception is practised to any appreciable extent (again, with the exception of a few atypical persons in large towns)—except the traditional avoidance of sexual intercourse with a mother who has a nursing baby. There is now less emphasis on this principle than in former times and there is a tendency to shorten the time before a baby is weaned. There are occasional induced abortions, but these seem to be rather rare. There is widespread, and quite intense, anxiety about sterility.

Fertility is somewhat higher, on the average, among the Bahaya on the southern shore of Lake Victoria, in northern Tanganyika; but here, too, the average is below that generally expected in African populations. According to the 1948 census there were 4.3 live births per woman of completed fertility in the Bukoba district; but in the villages within this district selected for intensive study by Richards and Reining the observed average was 3.7 live births. Only 7 per cent of 71 women aged 60 years or over were childless, but 18 per cent of an equal number of women between 45 and 59 years of age had never borne a living child, and 21 per cent of those aged 35–44 years. There is, therefore, a suggestion of a fairly recent increase in the frequency of childlessness in this population although, in view of the small size of the sample, the finding must be accepted with caution. If so, this contrasts with the situation in Uganda where the incidence of childlessness seems to have been about as high among women who attained puberty forty or fifty years ago as among the younger women. The specific evidence from the sample on this point is slender, but the conclusion is supported by the census data on childlessness among all women aged 45 years or over as a class. The statements made above, with respect to the Baganda, about a general tendency toward early and universal marriage of women and about the general desire for children also fit the Bahaya (except that marriages here are more commonly of the customary type, with few Christian marriages and almost no Moslem marriages).

The Bahaya also have developed a cash crop, coffee. But their contacts with the outside world have been more limited, and tribal traditions are somewhat stronger here than in Buganda. There has been more out-migration of Bahaya, and less in-movement of other elements, than among the Baganda.

The cultural backgrounds of the Baganda and the Bahaya are rather similar. Both are Bantu people, and there has long been considerable interchange of ideas among the Bantu in the vicinity of Lake Victoria. Both have traditional patrilineal kinship systems, but circumstances have led in both cases to a shift of emphasis from kinship groups to immediate families. In neither case do clans or lineages, at least under present conditions, have a definitely corporate character.

The political system of the Baganda, prior to the establishment of the British protectorate near the end of the nineteenth century, was perhaps the most highly centralized empire in Africa south of the Sahara. A

126

relatively brief period of intense conflict, during which the British acquired supreme authority, had been preceded by a period of active trade both with the Arabs and with the British under the last absolute sovereign, Mtesa, 1860–84. The authority of the original kinship system was apparently weakened by the centralized imperial system and later by controversy between Protestants, Catholics, and Muslims, and by the development of new legal and commercial institutions. The present system of land tenure has some feudalistic aspects, but the land (except some estates acquired in an early period) remains in the hands of Baganda. The Baganda enjoy a considerable measure of local autonomy, and have responded positively to increasing opportunities for education. Baganda society, superficially at least, seems to have acquired many of the characteristics of a stable peasant society. It seems to be the sort of society in which demographers generally expect to find very high fertility; and, apparently, this would be so if a realization of the strong personal interest of the Baganda in children were not thwarted by a high incidence of physiological sterility.[1]

The present interest of the Baganda in children is different from that of people within a social organization oriented to traditional kinship values. The interest in children among the Baganda is only part of a diffuse system of values. Marriages tend to be formed increasingly by personal choice, and romantic attachment may lead to shifting interests. Nuclear families and individuals exercise a considerable degree of independence. No strong kinship group exercises constant guardianship over the reproductive powers of women in order to promote its ideals and interests. Moreover, married couples are expected to establish separate households, and economic difficulties often force men to delay marriage. No joint family system provides security and promotes the stability of family relations.

If there are no strong motivations for limitation of offspring, as apparently there are not in Baganda society, 'the attraction between the sexes' and a diffuse interest in children can lead to very high fertility. They permit the free release of natural procreative capacity. But among the Baganda, and to a lesser extent among the Bahaya, procreative capacity itself appears to be severely limited. Why? Perhaps there is some deficiency in the Baganda diet, of which *matoke* (cooked banana) is a major part. But there is little specific evidence in support of this hypothesis. Moreover, it can be fairly assumed that the Baganda, who only a few centuries ago gained control of the region they now occupy, were an expanding population during the eighteenth and nineteenth centuries. On this hypothesis it would be necessary to assume a serious deterioration in diet during the last century. This may have happened, but it seems unlikely. Perhaps

[1] An educated young man of Baganda family in Kampala told the present writer that because of his interest in making provision for higher education for his children he planned to have only four children; but he stated that he did not know any others who entertained such ideas of family limitation.

cultural changes have induced psychological disturbances that hamper reproduction. But there is no evidence to this effect.

The most plausible suggestion seems to be that fecundity has been reduced by diseases, especially venereal diseases. Medical authorities in the region know that both syphilis and gonorrhea are prevalent, but there seems to be no precise evidence on the degree of their prevalence. Richards and Reining received positive responses to a direct question, 'have you ever had a venereal disease?' from 29 per cent of the women interviewed in the Buganda sample; but they point out that this information is unreliable because minor diseases are frequently interpreted by native women as syphilis. They found that this question aroused no resentment. Venereal diseases appear to be accepted with unusual equanimity in this population; this would seem to suggest an absence of any great anxiety to avoid exposure to risk of infection. This writer knows of no information on the extent to which these people are aware of the relationship between these diseases and sterility. Baganda tell the story that the councillors of a former monarch, having learned that the monarch had contracted gonorrhea, composed and popularized a song deprecating all who had not achieved this distinction. Presumably few persons deliberately sought to enhance their prestige by such achievement, but it may have provided a convenient rationalization for indifference.

Richards and Reining doubt that the high frequency of sterility among the Baganda can be attributed mainly to venereal diseases. The evidence on the subject is certainly inconclusive, and we are forced to suspend judgment. We simply add the further comment that the apparently more recent increase of sterility among the relatively isolated Bahaya would be consistent with this hypothesis—especially in view of the known movement of some Bahaya women as prostitutes to and fro between the Bukoba district in Tanganyika and larger towns in Uganda.

Finally, it is interesting to explore the possible relations between culture and fertility on this hypothesis. We can do this, in theory, without assuming that the hypothesis is valid. These relations might be as follows: The decline of patrilineal kinship structure as an organizing principle in Baganda society, with the relaxation of cultural compulsions for high fertility, occurred in a society where the marital rights of men were traditionally interpreted as property rights—to the point that it was considered proper to bury alive many of a monarch's wives at the time of his death. With decline of royal authority, respect for the property rights of other polygynous husbands also declined. There may well have been a common failure on the part of both men and women immediately to give an idealistic interpretation to rights and obligations that had previously been maintained by force. Women who for many generations had been treated mainly as economic and reproductive instruments might, in the course of cultural shock, still retain their value as economic contributors and as objects of sexual desire. But deep respect for women as persons requires a more profound re-creation of cultural motives. This is not easily achieved in a few decades.

Moreover, even a moderate decrease in the cultural demand for numerous progeny may have tended to relax the urgency of early marriage and strict adherence to traditional family relations. Cultural conditions tending to decrease the intensity of interest in procreation, though not leading to anti-natal measures, may have led to a relaxation of marital obligations and so, indirectly to an actual, though unintentional, decline of fertility.

The transition among the Bahaya toward less rigid family relations was, it seems, facilitated by the interpretation given in their culture to ritualistic coitus, following delivery of a baby, described above as present with different cultural significance among the Nkundo. The *bisisi* (cleansing a woman after childbearing and defining the legal paternity of her next child) was gradually developed in a way that contributed to instability of marital relations.

The information at our disposal on the demography of the Baganda and the Bahaya is still inconclusive. It is quite certain that the relatively low present level of fertility among the Baganda and the Bahaya must be attributed mainly to physiological factors, but the nature of these factors is unknown. A second possible inference is more speculative. In spite of the relatively successful economic adjustment of these people to changed conditions and their positive response to new opportunities, the radical transition through which they have passed may, temporarily, have created great confusion in some aspects of this social life and this, in turn, may have contributed indirectly to an unwanted reduction of procreative capacity.

Ruanda-Urundi

Both in the Belgian Congo and in British East Africa, fertility tends generally to rise with the transition from large lake and river basins to the more isolated central mountain districts. A similar relationship in the Congo was noted above in the section on the Nkundo. The positive associations between altitude and fertility in Tanganyika are being investigated in studies, as yet unpublished, by H. A. Fosbrooke, senior sociologist, Arusha, Tanganyika.

The demographic situation in Ruanda-Urundi, a plateau area between Uganda, Tanganyika and the Congo, is characterized by an unusually high level of fertility and rapid natural increase. The first scientific investigation of this situation has recently been conducted by Gourou, chiefly through a critical development of registration data.[1]

The terrain of Ruanda-Urundi, now controlled by the Belgian Govern-

---

[1] Pierre Gourou. *La densité de la population au Ruanda-Urundi*. Institut Royal Colonial Belge, 1953.

ment, as a trustee of the United Nations, is very diversified, with a consequent diversity of population density; but about half its total population is in districts with 100 to 200 persons per square kilometre. Within these districts, clusters of rural population in relatively favourable situations range from 200 to 400 persons per square kilometre. Even within Ruanda-Urundi, high density tends to be associated with high altitude. Gourou notes several reasons for this, but places major emphasis on the fact that high altitude is favourable to the health of cattle, and this has provided a basis for a remarkable organization of pastoral society in this region. This cohesive society was able to resist the devastations of the slave trade, and has remained relatively immune to foreign influences.[1]

The society of Ruanda-Urundi is, however, a composite of diverse cultures. The politically and economically dominant group are the Hamitic Batutsi—tall, elegant fellows, formerly renowned in war, and now famous for their skilful dances, who are the great cattle owners. But numerically they·are a relatively small element in the total population. The bulk of the population is made up by Bahutu (and some Batwa) engaged in agriculture and crafts and in the care of livestock leased to them by the Batutsi.[2] They are the descendents of the original population of the region, later conquered by the Batutsi. The initial shock of conquest occurred several centuries ago, and has given way to a submissive accommodation by the indigenous population to the institutions of the dominant race. It is this vassal society that now provides the main source of rapid natural increase.

Most of the population of Ruanda-Urundi now suffers from extreme poverty and inadequate nutrition.[3] It continues, nevertheless, to sustain a rapid natural increase. 'Apart from an accident such as the famine of 1942 the population of Ruanda-Urundi is in good demographic health.'[4] Conservative estimates of vital rates derived from the probably incomplete official statistics are: death rate 25 per 1,000, birth rate 40 per 1,000, natural increase 15 per 1,000 per year.[5] The approximate validity of this finding, as regards the rate of natural increase, is confirmed by examination of ratios of children (all ages under about 15 years) to women (all ages over about 15 years). Both mortality and fertility may be actually higher than indicated by the official statistics, but increased control of tropical disease is certain to result in an acceleration of natural increase.[6] Gourou concludes his treatment with a penetrating discussion of the implications of this demographic situation for economic planning.[7]

We have not attempted to explore anthropological literature for intensive

[1] ibid., pp. 31–4. See also Chapter IV, pp. 63–77.
[2] Also, some Batwa.
[3] ibid., Chapter VI, pp. 109–34.
[4] ibid., p. 143.
[5] loc. cit.
[6] ibid., p. 149.
[7] ibid., 'Conclusion', pp. 150–94.

studies of cultural conditions in this region. We would expect to find strong support for high fertility in the social organization of the Batutsi. We would not expect to find similar cultural sanctions for high fertility in the modified culture of the Bahutu today, but rather a generally indifferent and permissive attitude toward uncontrolled reproduction—resulting in equally high, or perhaps even higher fertility. This sort of trend is, in any case, clearly evidenced in many parts of the Pacific and in some regions in the Americas—as will be shown in the later sections of this chapter.

The Tswana of Bechuanaland

The situation of the Tswana, a branch of the Bantu-speaking Sotho, in eastern Bechuanaland has been affected by migration from the region they originally occupied, and by pressure of population upon resources in their present situation. Extensive cultural information and some demographic data about these people come from investigations by Schapera.[1] Their retreat to a relatively unfavourable situation was a fairly recent event (1869), caused by advancing European (Boer) settlement. Their original social organization is still reasonably intact, but is being powerfully affected by missionary activity, schools, trade contacts with Europeans, British political control, and above all, by extensive labour migrations. Their fertility has been declining but in the mid 1930's it was higher than that of the Baganda and Bahaya for whom we have comparable statistics for 1952.

The original social organization of the Tswana was conducive to high fertility. It is true that their traditional culture provided for infanticide in some circumstances, namely, to avoid the evil consequences of an ill-omened birth in the case of an infant born feet first.[2] Also *coitus interruptus* was practised as a means of permitting sex relations but avoiding pregnancy by a nursing mother. Both of these devices (but the first very rarely) are now sometimes used in connexion with prenuptial sex relations. The chastity of girls prior to marriage, or at least prior to initiation into marriageable age sets, was formerly enforced by strong sanctions, but this injunction is now widely ignored.[3] There was also, apparently, occasional resort to secret abortion in embarrassing circumstances, but such behaviour, if discovered, was severly punished. All of these practices, in their original cultural context, were consistent with a strong emphasis on high fertility, motivated by the interests and ideals of patrilineal lineages, to which individuals were definitely subordinate. Interest in high fertility as a motive force in the original social organization of the Tswana is indicated by many

[1] I. Schapera, *Married Life in an African Tribe*, London, 1940; *Migrant Labour and Tribal Life*, London, 1947; and 'Cultural Changes in Family Life', in I. Schapera, Editor, *The Bantu-Speaking Tribes of South Africa*, London, 1937, pp. 357–87.
[2] Schapera, *Married Life in an African Tribe*, pp. 224–5.
[3] ibid., pp. 43–4.

specific provisions relating to marriage, similar in many cases to those present among the Zulu, and by the persistence of strong desire for many children even under present conditions. To the Kgatta (a branch of the Tswana studied intensively by Schapera), 'it is inconceivable that a married couple should for economic or personal reasons deliberately seek to restrict the number of their offspring'.[1] An average of 5.4 children had been borne by 184 wives in monogamous marriages of completed fertility. Only 4 per cent of these women had never borne a child.[2]

We shall not attempt to review specific features of Tswana social organization, or the account of how various practices have been modified under the impact of changed conditions—though Schapera's whole treatment of these topics is highly relevant to our problem. The general implications of this material appear similar to inferences already drawn from other material. We shall merely note a few items that may suggest some modification of these inferences.

Marriage among the Tswana was formerly somewhat delayed by the requirement of prior initiation into age sets which neither boys nor girls usually entered until their late 'teens—in spite of a tradition of infant bethrothals. Modern conditions have tended to cause further delay in marriage, so that the modal age at marriage is now within the range 21–25 years for women, and 26–30 years for men.[3] The abandonment of polygyny, increase of labour migrations, and other conditions leave some unmarried young women in the villages; and the failure of women to marry at all is now less exceptional than was formerly the case. Such delay of marriage may exert an appreciable influence on the level of fertility of the Tswana.

The major factor tending toward social disorganization among the Tswana seems to be the large-scale migration to outside areas for wage-work for several months at a time, with men sometimes remaining away for several years. In 1937, 44 per cent of 3,933 registered tax-payers among the Kgatta worked outside the reservation for all or part of the year—usually leaving their wives behind in the reservation villages.[4]

Relaxation of sexual morals, especially among unmarried men and women, has inevitably brought increase in anti-natal practices and some increase in disease.[5] There is some evidence that gonorrhea (but not syphilis) may have been a disease known in ancient times for which there were traditional medical practices in this society; but the evidence is not precise.[6] However, in the sample of Kgatta wives from whom data on fertility were obtained, the frequency of childlessness among the older women was very low (4 per cent). It was also low (10 per cent) in the sample

[1] ibid., p. 213.
[2] ibid., p. 220.
[3] ibid., p. 71.
[4] ibid., p. 142.
[5] ibid., pp. 43–4.
[6] ibid., pp. 194–7.

as a whole, if we assume that many of the younger childless women in the sample were still able to bear living children.

The general effect of 'cultural shock' sustained by the Tswana appears to have been in the direction of a reduction of fertility. Such reduction seems as yet to have been rather moderate in scope, but we lack precise information on this point. In the future this trend may, of course, be intensified or reversed, or intensified for a time and then reversed.

Conclusion

The disorganization of traditional social structures and related value systems, under the impact of outside forces, has resulted in some African societies in behaviour leading to frequent avoidance of childbearing, or sterility, or both—causing declines in fertility dissociated from any positive cultural motives in the direction of small families or the control of fertility.

In the case of the Buhutu of Ruanda-Urundi, accommodation to domination by a master race, the Batutsi, seems to have resulted in rapid natural increase and rising pressure of population on land resources. We have advanced the hypothesis that this trend is essentially a biological phenomenon, released by cultural indifference to fertility; this hypothesis is not supported in this case by any specific information on Bahutu culture, but is consistent with evidence concerning similar demographic trends in other regions.

It seems reasonable to conclude that in the continent of Africa as a whole there will be a general weakening of the traditional kinship structures that formerly provided the major framework of social organization. High evaluation of large families and related attitudes toward reproduction seem to be more persistent than the social structures that previously provided special support and motivation for these attitudes. The major contrasting trends of fertility in the immediate future, in various African societies, are likely to be either (a) declines resulting from acute social disorganization and/or disease or (b) constant levels or inclines resulting from the dominance of biological forces released by permissive attitudes and cultural indifference to fertility along with accommodation to foreign economic and political control.

The emergence of a positive small-family ideal seems as yet to be hardly above the horizon, even among African societies that are most advanced in the autonomous development of modern economic, cultural, and political techniques.

DEPOPULATION AND POPULATION GROWTH IN MICRONESIA

Rivers, in the early 1920's, attracted the attention of the scientific world to the problem of depopulation in primitive societies, giving special attention to Melanesia, but also taking account of parallel trends in other areas.[1] He recognized increases in mortality due to violent conflicts and the introduction of new diseases as a major cause of the depletion of previously isolated societies under the impact of European political, economic, and cultural forces. But he also, with good reason, gave attention to declines in fertility as an important aspect of these trends. He particularly emphasized the effects of European influences, including missionary activities, on the indigenous societies. He maintained that these influences 'disrupted the whole institutional organization of these lives'. He asserted that the resultant 'loss of interest in life' had adversely affected both mortality and fertility. He expressed the judgment that, as regards fertility, increase of sterility had been far less important than increase of preventive measures through the expansion of primitive anti-natal practices that had previously been used only in unusual circumstances. He went on to suggest that this was, in large part, a deliberate expression of strong resentment. 'The people say, "Why should we bring children into the world only to work for the white man?"'[2] His psychological interpretations appear over-simplified in the light of more recent anthropological and psychological studies. But his basic analysis of the problem still merits serious attention.

There is as yet little reliable evidence on the possible role of various specific mechanisms whereby acute social disorganization may be translated into actual decrease in the frequency of births. Some of the possible mechanisms can be listed as follows:

1. Increase of sterility due to spread of new diseases through contact with foreign persons, and possibly intensified by increase in the frequency of extramarital sex relations.
2. Increase in extra-marital sex relations involving resort to anti-natal practices (especially abortion)—along with increased avoidance of marriage or separation of spouses, with substitution of types of sexual activity less likely to result in the production of live births.
3. Low frequency of coitus within marriage, owing to estrangements between spouses, ill-health, or psychological depression or apathy.
4. Anti-natal practices by spouses.

Information on population trends in Micronesia has been reviewed, with an extensive bibliography, by Taeuber and Han as a 'Current Item' in *Population Index*.[3]

The Chamorro

Pitt-Rivers cited the Chamorro, 'a strong, bold, well-made people', as one

---

[1] W. H. R. Rivers. 'The Psychological Factor', in Rivers, Editor, *Essays on the Depopulation of Melanesia*. Cambridge, 1922.
[2] ibid., pp. 103–4.
[3] Irene B. Taeuber and Chungnim C. Han. 'Micronesian Islands under United States Trusteeship', *Population Index* 16 (2): 93–115, April 1950.

134

of the conspicuous illustrations of a population passing rapidly toward extinction.[1] This appeared to be so in the early 1920's, but there is a sequel to the story. The nominal survivors of the Chamorro, the biological stock having been modified by foreign admixture, and their original culture having been replaced by modes of behaviour appropriate to their present situation, are now tending toward rapid natural increase, both on Guam and on the Pacific islands formerly mandated to Japan. Taeuber and Han summarize this transformation as follows:

'It was almost a century and a half after Fernando Magellan's ships had secured provisions at Guam that Jesuits arrived in the Marianas to establish the sovereignty of the Spanish Crown and convert the natives to the true faith. Spanish, Dutch, and English explorers and traders had already visited the islands and brought epidemics that decimated a population variously estimated to have numbered 50,000 to 150,000, but there had been no permanent occupation. In 1668 the Mission Fathers started a campaign of rapid conversion that led to rebellion and massacre in 1670, then 30 years of sporadic war between the native Chamorros and the soldiers of Spain. Famine, cholera, and smallpox reinforced the guns of the West in so weakening the natives that the Spanish could concentrate all surviving peoples under military control in Guam. Further famines and epidemics were the inevitable consequence of this concentration of people who lived by subsistence activities. A count made in 1710 indicated that some 4,000 natives in Guam and Rota were the sole surviving aborigines of the once populous Marianas. Decline continued for half a century more, until in 1764 Chamorros and mestizos combined numbered less than 1,800. The Spanish encouraged or forced movements in from the Philippines, particularly movements of Tagalogs from Luzon, and the soldiers of Spain mingled with the native women. And thus in the nineteenth century numbers began to increase, haltingly at first, then more rapidly.

'The numbers that have been cited here are only crude approximations of the demographic decline and recrudescence of the native peoples of the Marianas. But whatever the numbers, the broad outlines of the story are clear. Western contact meant disease, epidemics, a more deadly form of war, and forced transplantation under conditions that brought famines and greater vulnerability to alien disease. The indigenous peoples survived technically through a biological intermixture that involved native women and alien men. Culturally the survivors of the concentration on Guam and their descendants were subjected to a fairly uniform indoctrination of Spanish culture and Jesuit Catholicism for over two hundred years. From this came an integrated culture, an accommodation to the pecuniary economy of the alien West, a family system and reproductive values in the primitive Catholic tradition, and rates of population increase

---

[1] Rivers, op. cit., p. 100. The Chamorro are a group of mixed Spanish and indigenous stocks. The other indigenous people of this area are called Kanakas.

that today accord with the Malthusian interpretation rather than with that of the necessary depopulation of the Pacific areas.'[1]

The importance of some of the cultural factors mentioned in the preceding paragraph may be questioned. Although the cultural and demographic changes described here took place under Roman Catholic influence, a very similar set of changes occurred under Protestant influence among the New Zealand Maori—formerly a declining population, but now increasing rapidly with about 50 births per 1,000 population per year. Moreover, the present writer questions the degree to which the present levels of fertility in this population, or that of the Maori, can be truly attributed to the 'family system and reproductive values' of any positive cultural tradition.

While the trend of the Chamorro population turned upward, the Kanakas were barely maintaining their numbers during the inter-war period. In contrast to the Chamorro, who increased by 32 per cent from 2,824 persons in 1920 to 3,720 persons in 1935, the Kanaka population increased by only 3 per cent, from 45,681 to 46,853. In some districts, most conspicuously in Yap, the native population was declining sharply.[2] Interestingly enough, rates of population change among native populations in the Micronesian Islands were positively associated with expansion of Japanese economic activities and the assimilation of native workers into these activities.[3]

The contrast in reproductive trend among the groups mentioned above and in different islands is indicated roughly by the ratios of children to women. These run as follows:[4]

TABLE 14.

District or people	Children 0–4 per 1,000 women 15–45	
	1930	1935
Total Natives		
Total	588	557
Chamorro	834	822
Kanaka	523	536
Saipan	755	798
Chamorro	810	812
Kanaka	617	755
Kanakas		
Yap	285	346
Palau	607	618
Truk	603	570
Ponape	801	700
Jaluit	537	402

[1] Taeuber and Han, op. cit., pp. 95–6.
[2] ibid., p. 103.
[3] loc. cit.
[4] Abstracted from Table 3, Taeuber and Han, op. cit., p. 104.

During the 1930's the League of Nations addressed inquiries to the Japanese Government concerning the severe and protracted depopulation of Yap.[1] As a result, a Japanese physician (Fujii) carried out medical examinations of 89 per cent of the islanders, including attempts to diagnose gonorrhea by microscopic examinations of smears and urethral secretions. He found that 24.8 per cent of the men in his series seemed to have gonorrhea, and 42.8 per cent of the women. Almost no syphilis or chancroids could be discovered. Fujii treated the gonococcal infections in 11.2 per cent of the supposedly infected individuals. Apart from this measure, no intensive programme of treating this disease has ever been attempted in Yap.

Within the age range of 26 to 50 years, Fujii found that 30.8 per cent of the women reported that they had never conceived, and only 3.0 conceptions were reported per ever-pregnant woman aged 41 years or over.

The crude birth rate from 1917 to 1929, under the Japanese, was 14.4 and the crude death rate 38.8 per thousand. The unabated spead of depopulation from 1930 to 1946 indicates that these rates probably did not change much until after World War II.

With the arrival of the American administration in 1945, new public health measures were introduced. Within a few months, the practically universal lesions of yaws had been eradicated by mass injections of arsenicals. No other mass therapy, however, has so far been attempted.

Fertility and mortality in recent years appear to be quite different than in the 1930's. From 1946 to 1951, the crude birth rates have varied from 27.1 to 36.1, and the death rates from 22.6 to 17.3 per 1,000. In general, the birth rates are twice as high as during the Japanese regime, and the death rates have been halved. Nevertheless, in 1948, the percentage of never-pregnant women aged 26 to 50 years was even higher than Fujii reported, namely, 34.4 per cent, but it is possible that some of the younger women in this series may yet conceive.

An American medical survey of the Yapese was carried out by the staff of the hospital ship U.S.S. *Whidbey* in 1949. This survey disclosed, on the basis of chest X-rays and tuberculin tests, that arrested cases of pulmonary tuberculosis are rampant in Yap. Several other surveys also corroborate the findings of the *Whidbey* study to the effect that intestinal parasites are practically universal. Genital examinations of some men were carried out, including microscopic examinations of urethral secretions in cases of urethritis. This study disclosed practically no gonorrhea. The reasons for

[1] The description of this population is based on material presented in Edward E. Hunt, Nathaniel R. Kidder, David Schneider, and William D. Stevens, *The Micronesians of Yap and Their Depopulation.* Report of the Peabody Museum (of Harvard) Expedition to Yap Island, Micronesia, 1947–48. Washington, 1949, iii, 198 pp., p. 43. Supplemented by information received in correspondence from Dr. Edward E. Hunt, Harvard University.

this marked discrepancy with Fujii's findings are unknown, but perhaps unrecognized chronic gonorrhea is still prevalent.

On purely medical grounds, the improved health and well-being of the Yapese in recent years, particularly the virtual eradication of yaws, may have raised their morale. In addition, specifically cultural factors seem to have been operative, both in the depopulation, and in the present increase. The rate of increase in the last year for which data are available was about 2 per cent per year. It is not assumed that this rate will be sustained, but continued increase seems probable.

In 1947–48, under the auspices of Harvard University, an anthropological expedition went to Yap to study the depopulation, and found considerable cultural evidence relevant to the problem.

The low birth rate under the Japanese seems not to be explained by temporary absences of men from Yap. Although most Yap men have spent years as labourers in other parts of Micronesia, the men absent for more than five years had as many recognized progeny in Yap as those absent for a shorter period. Since the absentees seldom stayed continuously abroad, they seem to have fathered at least some of the children attributed to them during their visits at home.

The individual life cycle of the Yapese points up many of the traditional cultural limitations on fertility. A child is born and brought up in a dwelling inhabited by a nuclear family, set apart from neighbours. Adolescents are not expected to perform serious work; they carry on premarital sexual play in secluded parts of the village, including types of incomplete sexual intercourse. The male may ejaculate either within or outside of the vagina.

Marriage is defined as the settling down of partners in a separate house. Parents may attempt to arrange marriages, even of their infant children, but such attempts are not always successful. Once a pair have begun to live together, this acomplished fact is often solemnized by gift exchanges between the families.

An important extramarital relationship, which has only recently been discontinued, is the maintenance of female entertainers in the young men's clubhouses. These entertainers, or *mispil*, were often secured by a mock capture from a neighbouring village, and played an intellectual and erotic role similar to that of the Japanese *geisha*.

Married couples show little outward affection. If no children are born, almost no social pressure is exerted on them to stay married. Childless marriages are often short-lived, and the divorce rate is higher than in any Western country.

Copulation is subject to numerous regulations. Yap men are volubly fearful of 'too much' copulation; that is, more than two or three times a month. A man who seems weak or unable to work is ridiculed as having 'copulated too much'. The actual coital frequency may be low. In the case of 16 young adults who responded to questioning on their sexual activities, only four admitted to coitus within the preceding two weeks. Sexual intercourse is theoretically forbidden when a man is fishing or constructing a canoe, house or road. If he becomes an important religious specialist, he is expected to remain continent for life. Continence is also enjoined on participants in sea voyages, ceremonials, and those mourning for the dead. A woman should not copulate during menstruation, pregnancy, nor during the period from her confinement until her child can walk and speak.

In the culture of Yap, rank and prestige are greatly emphasized, so that men and women eat apart, and individuals of widely different ages also eat separate food. This separation occurs even within the family. The inconvenience of this kind of housekeeping leads many women to hope for only a few children. During the Japanese period, the difficulty of raising a family when the husband was often away may also have minimized the desire for children, and at that time, pregnancies may often have been terminated by abortions with sticks, leaves or salt water douches. Menstrual hygiene was also unsanitary; spongy plant fibres were typically used as tampons or pads.

In recent years, health has improved, mortality decreased, and several social and cultural changes have helped to raise the birth rate. Few young men are now away from their home villages, so that they probably have more uninterrupted sexual access to young Yap women than in the past. Coital taboos are probably being relaxed. More family members are eating together than previously, so that housekeeping is easier, and the mothers' desire for children is correspondingly increasing. Fewer abortions, and the adoption of American habits of menstrual hygiene, are probably enhancing female fertility. As more children are born, marriages are becoming more stable, so that the likelihood of additional childbearing increases. With improved health and sanitation, the population may show increase in the future, in accordance with the apparent trend at present—in striking contrast to its previous trend toward depopulation.

The trend toward depopulation in Yap seems to have involved three conditions. First, the original social structure and culture were conducive to moderately low fertility, compatible with an ecological situation where mere maintenance rather than increase of population was advantageous. Secondly, life in Yap underwent acute social disorganization under foreign domination, resulting in social and psychological disturbances. Thirdly, this social change was associated with a spread of diseases tending to increase the frequency of sterility. Improvement in health, along with a tendency toward more orderly and regular living, appear to have brought a new trend toward increase of population.

139

The population of Samoa is selected for special attention because, in spite of superficial resemblance to the shift toward high fertility in the process of accommodation among the Chamorro, the Maori, or the Amerindian population of the United States, there is some evidence of a subtle but significant difference in the nature of the factors influencing fertility in Samoa.

Recent annual average rates of total population increase, including the effects of migration, are as follows: Western Samoa (New Zealand administration), 1921–26, 2.2 per cent; 1926–36, 3.1 per cent; 1936–45, 2.25 per cent, to a total population of 68,000; American Samoa, 1930–40, 2.5 per cent; 1940–50, 3.7 per cent, to a total of 18,600 persons.[1] The increase in American Samoa, 1940–50, was appreciably affected by increase of U.S. military personnel and in-movement of workers from Western Samoa and elsewhere. There has never been a large number of Europeans in Western Samoa; though contract labourers from China and elsewhere were brought in relatively small numbers from 1870 to 1936 to work on the coconut plantations. According to the census classification, there were 62,000 Samoans, 5,000 persons of mixed blood, and 1,300 others (including 630 other Pacific Islanders) in Western Samoa in 1945.[2] The classifications are inaccurate, but give an approximate picture of the trend. Census data for 1906 had shown only 33,500 Samoans, less than 1,000 persons of mixed blood, and about 3,000 others (including 1,347 other Pacific Islanders).

The United Nations, in its report on Western Samoa, notes:

'It is probable that the birth rate of the Samoans was in the range of 45 to 55, or even higher, throughout the period 1906 to 1945 (except perhaps in the period 1918–19). Such a birth rate is consistent with the rapid population growth indicated by the census figures for 1921 to 1945. It is the birth rate of a people reproducing near the limit of physiological capacity.'[3]

This remarkably high birth rate has been associated with a remarkable reduction of mortality which can be credited largely to the success of the public health programme carried out during the last few decades by the New Zealand Government. The estimated average annual death rate was reduced from about 50 per 1,000 in the middle of the nineteenth century to about 21 per 1,000 from 1926 to 1945.[4]

The Samoan population apparently decreased prior to about the middle of the nineteenth century and then remained fairly constant to the end of

---

[1] United Nations, *Demographic Yearbook 1949–50*, p. 95.
[2] United Nations (Population Division), *The Population of Western Samoa*. Reports on the Population of Trust Territories, No. 1, Lake Success, 1948. (Prepared by John D. Durand with the assistance of Chia-lin Pan), pp. 11–14, 45.
[3] ibid., p. 17.
[4] .bid., pp. 4, 23.

the century. Moderately reliable estimates give 40,000 to 45,000 in 1845, and about 30,000 in 1849. The population probably had been higher in the early eighteenth century than in 1845, but may never have been so high as at present. Durand believes that the decline can be attributed wholly to excess mortality, and that there is no reason to assume a general decline in fertility at any time.[1]

There seems never to have been a 'demographic crisis' associated with a 'cultural crisis' in the development of Samoa. The islands contained no easily exploitable wealth, were not of great strategic importance, and were off the main highway of Pacific traffic. The development of coconut plantations under European auspices in the late nineteenth century did not bring profound disturbance. Missionary activity was moderate in its methods. In 1836 there were only 10 missionaries, chiefly from the London Missionary Society, in what is now Western Samoa.[2]

Samoan culture also seems to have had certain characteristics that facilitated the transition to European political control, and adaptation to European cultural influences.

According to Mead:

'The Samoans have made one of the most effective adjustments to the impact of Western civilization of any known people. From the European's technology they took cloth and knives, lanterns and kerosene, soap and starch and sewing-machines, paper and pen and ink, but they have kept their bare feet, their cool sarongs, their houses built of native materials fastened together with coconut fibre cord. . . . Neither literacy, nor missions, nor modern technology have finally disturbed the evenness and flexibility with which this group of people, their culture based on diffuse but warm human relationships, has adapted to change.'[3]

Speaking of the emotional stability of the Samoan child, Mead notes that an important factor influencing this stability is the lack of pressure to make important choices. 'Children are urged to learn, urged to behave, urged to work', she says, 'but they are not urged to hasten in the choices which they make themselves. . . .' The Church adapted to this belief in the following way:

'This laissez faire attitude has been carried over into the Samoan Christian Church. The Samoan saw no reason why young unmarried people should be pressed to make momentous decisions which would spoil part of their fun in life. Time enough for such serious matters after they were married or later still, when they were quite sure of what steps they were taking and were in less danger of falling from grace every month or so. The missionary authorities, realizing the virtues of going slowly and sorely vexed to reconcile Samoan sex ethics with a Western

[1] ibid., pp. 4, 17–20.
[2] ibid., p. 4.
[3] Margaret Mead. *Male and Female*, pp. 119–20.

141

European code, saw the great disadvantages of unmarried Church members who were not locked up in Church schools. Consequently, far from urging the adolescent to think upon her soul the native pastor advises her to wait until she is older, which she is only too glad to do.'[1]

Samoan social organization was never based on a rigid kinship structure. There is a strong emphasis on group life, but the organization of activities and interests is very different from that in a clan-structured society. There is a strong emphasis on rank among the Samoans, but on acquired rank, not on position in an hereditary kinship structure.

'A Samoan village is made up of some thirty to forty households, each of which is presided over by a headman called a *matai*. These headmen hold either chiefly titles or the titles of talking chiefs, who are the official orators, spokesmen and ambassadors of chiefs. In a formal village assembly each *matai* has his place, and represents and is responsible for all the members of his household. These households include all the individuals who live for any length of time under the authority and protection of a common *matai*. Their composition varies from the biological family consisting of parents and children only, to households of fifteen and twenty people who are all related to the *matai* or to his wife by blood, marriage or adoption, but who often have no close relationship to each other. . . . No one living permanently in another village is counted as a member of the household, which is strictly a local unit. Economically, the household is also a unit, for all work upon the plantations is under the supervision of the *matai* who in turn parcels out to them food and other necessities.

'Within the household, age rather than relationship gives disciplinary authority. The *matai* exercises nominal and usually real authority over every individual under his protection, even over his father and mother. . . .'[2]

Married couples join the household of either the girl or the boy, determined not by formal kinship obligations but 'on the basis of rank or the industrial needs of the two households'. The social and economic life of the married couple is merged with that of the whole household.

'In most marriages there is no sense of setting up a new and separate establishment. The change is felt in the change of residence for either husband or wife and in the reciprocal relations which spring up between the two families. . . . But the young couple live in the main household, simply receiving a bamboo pillow, a mosquito net and a pile of mats for their bed. Only for the chief or the chief's son is a new house built. The wife works with all the women of the household and waits upon all the men. The husband shares the enterprises of the other men and boys.

[1] Margaret Mead. *Coming of Age in Samoa.* Reprinted in *From the South Seas*, New York, 1939, p. 232.
[2] ibid., pp. 39–40.

142

Neither in personal service given or received are the two marked off as a unit. . . .'[1]

The traditional 'joint household' in Samoa creates no compulsion toward high fertility, but it provides a congenial atmosphere for children, and economic and emotional support for the parents. 'After the birth of the first child', Mead says, 'the other children arrive frequently and with small remark. Old gossips count them and comment on the number living, dead or miscarried in previous births'. She adds, 'The mother of many children is rather taken for granted than praised'.[2]

Girls are taught by the time they are eight or nine to avoid older groups of boys, and consider little boys their own age as enemies. A few years later, however, it is quite acceptable for them to gain sex experience. The usual pattern is for a boy to find a confidante, a *soa*, who will approach the girl of his choice for him. Occasionally, two adolescents will 'slip away alone into the bush' without following the accepted pattern because they are fearful of ridicule if anyone should find out about their affair. More commonly, however, an older man is the first lover of a young girl. He courts the girl personally, being 'neither shy nor frightened', and not wishing to trust an intermediate. Boys also frequently have their first sex experience with an older woman.[3]

In the pattern of premarital relationships, there are many words, songs, caresses, and promises of long-lasting endearments, but in actual practice there is little fidelity. The community is not seriously concerned with such affairs. On the other hand, marriages are arranged between families, though with some attention to the wishes of the young.

'Marriage is regarded as a social and economic arrangement, in which relative wealth, rank, and skill of husband and wife, all must be taken into consideration. There are many marriages in which both individuals, especially if they are over 30, are completely faithful. But this must be attributed to the ease of sexual adjustment on the one hand, and to the ascendency of other interests, social organization for the men, children for the women, over sex interests, rather than to a passionate fixation upon the partner in the marriage. As the Samoans lack the inhibitions and the intricate specialization of sex feelings which make marriages of convenience unsatisfactory, it is possible to bulwark marital happiness with other props than temporary passionate devotion. Suitability and expediency become the deciding factors.'[3]

No reference is made to infanticide. Abortion is known and is sometimes practised; but there seem to be few incentives for its use; and it has surely been discouraged by Christian missionaries, native pastors, and doctors. According to Mead: 'When a Samoan woman does wish to avoid giving

[1] ibid., p. 188.
[2] ibid., pp. 189–90.
[3] ibid., pp. 86–8.
[4] ibid., pp. 105–6.

143

birth to a child, exceedingly violent massage. and the chewing of kava is resorted to, but this is only in very exceptional cases, as even illegitimate children are enthusiastically welcomed.'[1]

According to Keesing: 'The Samoans, like other Polynesians, had very different sexual standards from those which the western moralist of today upholds as ideal, especially regarding the conduct of unmarried girls or unattached women; while all children found a welcome place in the Samoan household, regardless of any question of their "legitimacy".'[2]

The question arises as to why the traditional Samoan culture did not lead to excessive accumulation of population and inadequacy of sustenance, with resultant influence on social institutions. The average density in Western Samoa, with an estimated population of 83,000 at the beginning of 1952, is 28 persons per square kilometre, similar to that in Hawaii.[3] It was presumably well below this level in 1800. The writer does not know how long the present society has been resident in the islands. If it is the product of fairly recent settlement, there might have been opportunity for free expansion in a land of plenty. There were, of course, frequent tribal wars here, as in Hawaii, and the surviving groups may have maintained adequacy of resources in this way. It is also possible that fertility was not so high in ancient times, and that it has risen under European influence. However, except for the occasional resort to abortion or primitive contraceptive medicines mentioned by Mead, there seems to be no trace in the present Samoan culture of any traditional restrictions on fertility which must have been far above the normal level of mortality prior to the introduction of new diseases through contact with foreign visitors.

The culture of Samoa can be characterized as 'permissive' to fertility. The whole traditional social organization provides strong support but not strong incentives, for high fertility. Samoan society has not been distorted by 'cultural shock'. Instead, its social institutions have been only gradually modified, and the force of its original culture is still vital. In the process of gradual changes, the positive motives for high fertility have been generally reinforced by modern European influences.

An objective demographer may see dangers ahead in an indefinite continuation of the present high level of fertility in Samoa. But such a problem lies outside the concern of present Samoan culture.

The break-up of traditional social organizations, in the absence of dynamic forces making for the emergence of new positive social goals, led in some Pacific areas (notably among the Chamorro of Guam and the Maori of New Zealand) to rapid depopulation followed by rapid natural increase. These demographic trends are interpreted as representing successive aspects of the process of acute social disorganization and chronic accommodation to external forces.

[1] ibid., p. 153.
[2] Felix M. Keesing. *Modern Samoa*. London, 1934, p. 451.
[3] United Nations. *Demographic Yearbook 1952*, p. 100.

By contrast, Samoa furnishes an example of the gradual modification of social institutions to new situations and the continuance of a culture which is 'permissive' as regards high fertility.

DECLINE AND RISE OF INDIAN POPULATION IN AMERICA

It can be said that, in spite of initial decreases, the number of 'Indians' in the United States today is probably larger than the number of 'Indians' in the same territory before the coming of Europeans; but the term 'Indian' has different biological as well as different cultural meanings in these two references.[1] Similar statements hold for the Americas as a whole. The ascendant groups today are in many cases the survivors of minor groups in the total population of an earlier period. In some cases, ascendant groups are of relatively pure Amerindian stock. This is the case, for example, with the Navaho, formerly a small nation, but now the largest and one of the most rapidly increasing Indian groups in the United States, and only slightly affected by admixture of non-Indian stocks. More frequently, however, the ascendant groups are racially composite.

Investigation of the processes of decline of aboriginal populations in the Americas is beset with many difficulties.[2] The most useful data are usually provided by old mission records. We shall review briefly some of the major findings derived from the use and interpretation of such records by one investigator, S. F. Cook.

'The dynamics of response to external disturbance seems to exhibit a basic pattern repeated with only local variation by all primitive peoples. With respect to both numbers and time two phases may be distinguished. One is the primary or declining, the other the secondary or recovery, phase. During the former, which begins with the initial disturbance, the population decreases, the diminution proceeding either until extinction terminates the history of the group or until a minimum is reached without extinction. In the former case there is no secondary phase. In the latter the recovery phase follows with a tendency toward increase in numbers and generally with qualitative alteration in the race.

'In the initial phase the reduction in net population is usually due

[1] Frank Lorimer. 'Observations on the Trend of the Indian Population in the United States', in Oliver La Farge, Editor, *The Changing Indian*. Norman, Oklahoma, 1942, pp. 11–18. See also, H. L. Shapiro, 'The Mixed Blood Indian', op. cit., pp. 19–27.
[2] See Nathan L. Whetten. *Rural Mexico*. Chicago, 1948. For example, Whetten cites various estimates of the population of what is now Central Mexico at the time of the arrival of the Spaniards in 1516 as varying from 7 million to 30 million (pp. 21 ff.). Whetten accepts the lower estimate of 7 million in 1516, and observes that this population had declined to about 5 million after the conquest; he admits, however, that what proportion of this reduction was due to factors other than wars and massacres is not known. Thereafter, he notes a gradual increase in population. Various estimates of the population of Mexico from 1521 to 1940 are presented by Whetten in Table I, p. 23.

145

to a marked increase in death rate. There may or may not be a simultaneous falling off in birth rate. In specific instances which have been investigated with some care there is frequently wide divergence of opinion concerning the content or even the presence of this trend. Adequate censuses are uniformly lacking and casual observation by untrained, albeit interested, observers is untrustworthy. On the other hand, widespread mortality is unmistakable although its magnitude in the past has often been seriously exaggerated.'[1]

In an intensive study of·one Mexican community, Teotlalpan, Cook found that the downward trend of the population which had continued through many generations was arrested around the year 1800, and then gave way to a steady increase which has continued to the present time. This seems to have been fairly typical of the changing trend of the Indian population in Mexico as a whole. Cook was impressed with the fact that the upward trend. 'has been primarily due to prolific reproduction by the mestizo, rather than by the racially pure Indian'[2]. He attributes this to biological characteristics of the hybrid population:

'Regardless of the individual characteristics the final outcome of the interbreeding process is inevitably a new genetic strain, the most striking feature of which is a capacity to adapt itself favourably to the precise environmental changes which were deleterious to the indigenous primitive population. Indeed, such hybrid strains are frequently better fitted for survival than either of the parent stocks. Associated with the ecological improvement is usually an increased virility from the reproductive standpoint. Whether for external somatic or internal genetic causes, the birth rate of such groups tends to increase significantly, although the death rate may remain at a high level.'[3]

The assumption that any rise in fertility involved in the shift from natural decrease to natural increase was due largely to changes in physique has a strong basis—though changes in cultural conditions from conflict and acute frustration to acquiescence and accommodation must always be taken into account. But the suggestion that genetic factors may have been important in this change is purely hypothetical. As such it merits careful investigation. But there is no conclusive evidence that racial admixture was an essential aspect of the process. The rapid increase of the relatively pure-blood Navaho in the south-western United States, mentioned above, is evidence to the contrary. Again, in some relatively undeveloped regions in Mexico today, natural increase is much more rapid among racially pure Indian stocks in some isolated mountain districts than among the more hybrid

[1] S. F. Cook. 'Demographic Consequences of European Contact with Primitive Peoples', *The Annals of The American Academy of Political and Social Science*, Vol. 237, January 1945, p. 108.

[2] Cook. *The Historical Demography and Ecology of the Teotlalpan*, in *Ibero-Americana*, No. 33. University of California Press, 1949, p. 16.

[3] Cook, 'Demographic Consequences', etc., p. 110.

stocks in the humid lowlands.[1] It is entirely possible that hybridization was chiefly significant as a sympton of cultural assimilation, accommodation, and the adoption of more sanitary practices rather than as a process affecting genetic constitution of surviving stocks.

In Baja California (the peninsula separated from the rest of Mexico by the Gulf of California), where the decline of the principal indigenous ethnic groups proceeded toward extinction, the introduction and spread of venereal diseases seems to have been a major force. The earliest extant records for this area refer to the period 1760–72, with the single exception of those of Purisima Conceptión which began in 1730. The difference in dates is important because European control was rapidly extended here during this period. The data on family composition indicate that an earlier decline was intensified during the mid-eighteenth century.[2] In contrast to the mainland of Mexico opposite Baja California, where there does not seem to have been widespread infection of this kind, syphilis became 'well-nigh universal' in some parts of the peninsula, particularly in the south. 'That all the Indians at Todos Santos, that all the surviving Pericues were infected gives the appearance of a completeness seldom observed.'[3] This was perhaps only one factor in the decline, but in this case it may well have been the critical factor. On the other hand, in many other situations initial decreases of Indian population were mainly due to violent deaths in the process of conquest and to the later spread of smallpox, tuberculosis, and other infectious diseases causing high mortality.

With the re-establishment of permanent village locations, agricultural practices that provided subsistence, and orderly patterns in personal relations, with less frequent exposure to, or greater resistance to, deadly infections, the biological forces promoting procreation again became effective. In association with declining mortality, this brought a rising rate of natural increase.

But this is not the whole story. It would be fallacious to assume that stable conditions of living merely release natural procreative tendencies; though for some situations this interpretation is approximately, if not precisely, sufficient. The life of successive generations of neighbours in small villages under fairly constant conditions tends to generate positive motivations for high fertility. Many of the Indian and mestizo villages in Mexico and the south-western United States have held ten or more generations of descendants, with few in-migrants and little cultural stimulus from the outside world. Such villages have fostered a strong sense of mutual dependence and common interests and attitudes. Frequent maternities are expected, and in fulfilling community expectations parents feel themselves

[1] Roxana Arce Ybara, 'Problemas Demograficos de la Cuenca del Papaloapan', *Memoria del Congreso Científico Mexicano*, XII, Ciencias Sociales, 1951, 383–9.
[2] Cook, *The Extent and Significance of Disease among the Indians of Baja California, 1697–1773*, Ibero-Americana, No. 12, 1937, p. 3.
[3] ibid., pp. 32–3.

more firmly established as 'normal' members of the community. Ancient practices and new religious values may be woven into these patterns of village life.

The positive aspect of the relation of culture to fertility in stable agricultural villages is nicely illustrated in the study by George M. Foster of Tzintzuntzan, a Mexican community on the site of the capital town of the ancient Tarascan empire.[1] It is situated on the shore of Lake Patzcuaro in Michoacan. Old temples still stand on a hill above the village; the bones of many persons sacrificed in ancient rituals lie below the cliff. The ancient town had a large population, but no exact estimate is possible. The empire over which it presided maintained its position as a rival of the Aztecs until the Spanish conquest.

The census records of the village show, in spite of rapid natural increase, a fairly constant population over the last half-century, owing to steady loss through out-migration. Some migrants have returned, including some who had travelled as seasonal labourers into the United States. A few persons have come from other villages. Most of the villagers are the descendants of ancient Tarascans and their Spanish conquerors; it is not a homogeneous mestizo community. A special census in connexion with Foster's study gave 1,231 persons as the total population in 1945. It draws support from farming, fishing, and crafts—with some piecework on contract and some travel for wage-work outside the village. Some of the women are skilful potters. Work proceeds at a leisurely pace: 'Here we work three or four hours, then we rest.'[2] Men do not engage in pottery, which is regarded as 'dirty work'. A good road now passes through the village, which became a *municipio* in 1931. It has a school and a community centre. The fine old church was damaged some years ago by fire, and a simpler building is now used. The people are entirely Catholic.

A careful check of vital statistics showed that since 1931 (when the village became a *municipio*) the registration of live births was accurate within 2 to 5 per cent. The proportion of women 16 through 45 years old in the total population in 1945 (21.4 per cent) is somewhat low, due to a slight excess of females in the adult population. The data indicate an average annual birth rate, 1935–44, in the vicinity of 48 per 1,000, with an average death rate of about 30 per 1,000.[3] Abortions are sometimes sought by unmarried girls, and occasionally by married women who already have large families. There is a professional abortionist in the village. But large families are expected and are nurtured with great affection. The disposal of the afterbirth, following an old Tarascan custom, and related attitudes provide a key to positive cultural values that help to sustain high fertility.

[1] George M. Foster, assisted by Gabriel Ospina. *Empire's Children: The People of Tzintzuntzan*. Smithsonian Institute of Social Anthropology, Washington. Printed in Mexico.
[2] ibid., p. 129.
[3] Figures on proportion of women and rates computed from data presented by Foster, ibid., pp. 28–30, 224.

It is usually buried under the hearth stones. 'In a sense it represents a link that emotionally binds the individual to his home and his land. A house becomes a home to a new wife when the first placenta is buried, and as others follow the bond grows stronger and stronger. Dona Andrea reminisces . . . "Why, the placentas of all my children are buried in that very spot".'[1]

Life in Tzintzuntzan over the last three centuries has given rise to some positive forces toward social cohesion and to some cultural motives for high fertility, in spite of some contrary tendencies. This is true, in varying degrees, of many old Mexican villages both south and north of the present border between Mexico and the United States. In other villages and among many who have been from villages into cities but have found only a precarious basis for their lives, there is much evidence of frustration and maladjustment.

The culture of Indians living on reservations in the United States ranges from that of societies with intact social organizations to extremely disorganized groups, held together chiefly by common participation in certain privileges. We cannot attempt here to deal with the complex problems that would be encountered in any attempt to go beyond this simple generalization.

Average levels of fertility in recent decades among Mexicans and Indians in the United States have been quite similar, and also resemble the average level in the total population of Mexico. These averages are all well above those of both whites and Negroes in the United States. Data relating to Mexicans in the United States are available from only one census, in 1930. Ratios of children under 5 years of age to women 20–44 years from that census, and from the Mexican census of 1931 and 1940 give a rough indication of these relations: United States, 1930: Mexicans, 906; Indians, 928; Whites, 481; Negroes, 497. Mexico, 1930: 796; 1940: 814.

It is at least apparent that any initial trends toward depopulation in the Indian population of North America have given way to quite different trends—involving other factors and creating other problems.

We should really deal in this chapter with the possible effects on fertility of the distortions of social life caused by slavery in the Americas. We must avoid this task for the reason that we have avoided discussion of demographic trends in particular Indian tribes, i.e. its terrific complexity. Moreover, demographic trends among American Negroes, especially in the United States, as well as among whites, have been greatly influenced by modern technical processes. Some observations relating to this subject will be made in the following chapter, especially in taking account of information on Puerto Rico and Brazil.

[1] ibid., p. 226.

The experience of the Indian population in North America conforms in some respects to changes in African and Oceanic societies affected by conquest or the impact of powerful outside forces in other ways. Here, too, acute social disorganizations led to declines of population which, in some cases at least, involved declines of fertility. This was also true in many parts of South America.

In the Americas, and especially in the areas of early Spanish conquest, the processes of accommodation led long ago to upward trends in natural increase and high fertility among Indians. Later experience has fostered more positive cultural values, though the blight of ancient conflicts and frustrations still exerts a baneful influence. In many isolated rural areas, both frustration and the positive cultural values of cohesive group life, in varying degrees of relative importance, tend to perpetuate high levels of fertility.

CHAPTER V

Cultural Conditions and Fertility in Stable Agrarian Civilizations

EARLY BACKGROUNDS OF ASIATIC AND WEST EUROPEAN SOCIETIES

Many of the great agricultural civilizations rose through gradual transitions from tribal societies with patrilineal descent and corporate clans and lineage groups. This is true, for example, of Chinese and Roman civilizations, and both the early Aryan and the later Muslim military migrations into India brought social structures of this sort.

We drew attention in Chapter III to the way in which a centralized political system, organized on a territorial basis, tends to impinge on the functions of kinship systems formed in tribal societies. Patterns of stable village organization and the formation of specialized classes, including literate administrative and priestly classes, have a similar effect.

Institutional forms often persist in developing societies with changed significance, and sometimes with attenuated functions. Also the functional principles of a plastic society with oral traditions may be formalized in a later conservative society in sacred books and precepts and in legal codes.

The practice of 'clan' exogamy in China is relevant to this hypothesis. The *tsu* of Chinese society, translated as 'clan' by some ethnographers and as 'sib' by others, usually includes a large number of persons scattered through various localities, all of whom carry the same surname. Marriage between any two persons having the same surname is taboo in classical Chinese culture. In some parts of China this has little or no more functional significance than a taboo in America on the marriage of two persons named 'Smith' would have. Members of a *tsu* cannot trace common descent, and in so far as there is any worship of *tsu* ancestors it is only worship of a 'cloud' of ancestors without even clear mythical notions of their distinct personalities. In some regions of south China there are *tsu* villages, and here the *tsu* tradition has more force—analogous to the sense of kinship among people bearing the same name in particular localities in the southern Appalachian mountains, though the latter have no inhibition against marriage among persons with the same surname. But in most parts of China this is not so.

Again, the pattern of *tsu exogamy* is crossed in Chinese culture by preferences and inhibitions of an entirely different character, which could hardly have arisen except in a society that included literati who had made systematic observation of the skies. Each individual believes himself affected throughout his life by his position in the zodiac at birth. This is assumed to have deep significance for his character and destiny. Two individuals with the same birth year in the zodiac calendar have a sense of affinity that may be more profound than that created by the knowledge that they have the same surname. The investigation by soothsayers of the horoscopes of two possible spouses is considered quite as important as attention to their 'clan' affiliation. And it has far more complex and subtle implications that can only be divined and manipulated by persons versed in sacred wisdom.

The only cogent interpretation of the functionless patronymic taboo in Chinese society is that it is the survival of an ancient institution that had functional value when corporate patrilineal clans were vital elements in the structure of an earlier tribal society.

An intermediate pattern that can reasonably be interpreted as representing a late stage in the transition of the functional clans of a tribal society to the mere patronymic sibs of a sedentary civilization is present among the Monguor of Kansu.[1] These are a Mongolian people; they are now dependent on agriculture but presumably are descended from pastoral nomads. They speak an Altaic language, with some admixture of Chinese. Their 'clans' have little more function than the 'clans' of northern and central Chinese society, except that they have a somewhat stronger religious character and usually bury their dead in separate 'clan' cemeteries. The Monguor have been influenced by Chinese culture, and their patronymic sibs might be interpreted as an institution influenced by Chinese culture. This is possible. In any case, the two lines of interpretation suggested here are not mutually exclusive.

The possible influences of earlier tribal kinship systems on family structure and religious ideology in classical Chinese society are more elusive than its influence on the pattern of exogamy, but may have deeper and more far-reaching significance. The social life of agrarian societies tends to be focused in the families rather than in clans and lineages. But in many Asian societies, as in early republican Rome, the family has a more or less corporate character.

There is strong emphasis on the continuity of the agnatic lineage, involving worship of founder-ancestors as a spiritual community and of particular ancestors enshrined in mortal memory as individual spirits. This involves father-son identification, unity of brothers, and obligations to expected descendants.

The family is, at least ideally, extended to include all the living male offspring of a living man, or of a deceased father, and their wives and unmarried daughters. The ideal family is a patrilineal, or agnatic, group-family.

[1] Krader, op. cit., Chapter IV.

The family[1] usually has a recognized seat of authority in the senior male member, though he may be expected in some matters to consult with close kinsmen, or decisions may be referred to a council of family members. The father (patriarch, pater familias) or the elder brother exercising this authority is assumed to act in the interest of the whole family, with piety to his ancestors and fidelity to his descendants, and he feels deep responsibility for these obligations.

There is some clearly formulated principle of succession for transfer of the authority and property of the family through successive generations.

Marriages of members of a family are formal acts, and are conceived and arranged in the interest of the group-family, not primarily in the interest of the individuals immediately concerned. The same principle applies to adoptions, or other changes in the legal status of individuals.

A village, or a nation, is usually conceived as a collectivity of families, rather than as a collectivity of individuals. Also, membership in social classes or castes and political traditions governing the transmission of supreme authority in the state usually conform to principles of descent similar to those recognized in family relations. However, the state and the village have primarily a territorial rather than a kinship structure. Administrative officials are appointed as individuals and, in China, may be selected through an examination system. Also, a village collectivity is an open membership group, which can be entered informally by families that are not related to its present members. The village is not a corporate entity.

Traditional family organization is supported by the whole cultural context, and by specific moral and religious sanctions—such as the emphasis on filial piety in Chinese religious dogma. The welfare of the spirit of deceased persons is, at least in part, dependent on pious acts by their descendants.

The soul of a Hindu can depart in peace from its body only if the skull is opened by a son, who at the same time succeeds him as heir to the authority and obligations of his father. In China and in Japan, the continued piety and ceremonial acts of descendants affect the spiritual welfare of the ancestors, and these ancestors in turn oversee the fortunes of their living descendants. In the evolution of classical Japanese culture, especially in its later imperial phase, political and military loyalties were given supreme emphasis; but communion with his ancestors remains one of the

---

[1] A group-family is sometimes, in form and character, an extension of the agnatic core of a father and his sons—retaining a sense of continuity with his ancestral lineage. Or the group-family may be a joint family of brothers, or other close agnatic male kin of co-ordinate rank, with their wives and children; and such a joint family may have an established pattern of leadership as, for example, recognition of the senior brother. These two types are not sharply differentiated in practice, and one is frequently associated with the other. The terms 'extended family' and 'joint family' are used without distinction by some authors, with a preference for one or the other term. We are, therefore, using the term 'group-family' where convenient to avoid the ambiguity; but we shall not adhere rigorously to this usage, especially citing material from various sources.

most solemn responsibilities of the Japanese Emperor. Religious principles associated with family and kinship relations are present in all Asiatic societies; but these are crossed by, and harmonized with, obligations to the spirits of places, and to the gods of nations or of great religious movements.

These characteristics have been stated in broad, general terms. There are, of course, infinite variations in patterns of social organization among Asiatic societies. One distinctive characteristic of Japanese culture was mentioned in the previous paragraph, but there are many others. Again, emphasis on group life in India, as contrasted with China, is more diffuse. It is divided between the autonomous village, the endogamous caste, and the extended family.[1] And within India cultural variations are immense, and some communities in south India have radically different marriage patterns. The writer omits specific treatment of the Islamic Near East, owing to his ignorance on this subject.

Two complementary hypotheses seem appropriate to the family patterns and related values of some Asiatic agrarian societies—neither of which affords a wholly adequate basis of interpretation apart from the other:[2]

1. The structure and values of the prevalent agnatic group-family relations emerged as adaptations of forms of kinship relation that had major functional value in relatively mobile tribal societies in competitive relation with other societies. They are, in part, sustained by the persistence of principles formed in this context.

2. Some stable patterns of group life are essential to the orderly life of any society and to the well-being and security of its members. The patterns of family life in agrarian societies have the function of meeting this ever-present need. They are, in part, maintained and constantly adapted as responses to this need.

Pre-industrial society in western Europe had a radically different social structure and radically different values. It was also an agrarian society with a similar need for orderly social relations. But in medieval western Europe the major functional groups on social life were the feudal estate and the nuclear family: husband, wife, and children. Within the feudal estate, the individual nuclear families were relatively distinct and mobile. There is hardly a trace of ancestor worship in this society. Why the difference? No simple answer can be given, but four possible factors merit attention.

It is possible that the tribal societies of western Europe in the pre-Roman period placed less emphasis on a unilineal principle of descent, and lacked the corporate kinship groups widely prevalent among tribal societies in the Asiatic plains. But this is uncertain.

[1] Jawaharlal Nehru, *The Rediscovery of India*. New York, 1946, pp. 242–52.
[2] There are, of course, many variations in family patterns among agrarian societies in Asia. The hypothesis, as stated, may be quite inappropriate to the populations of the Malay peninsula, except as influenced by migrations from China. For example, family relations among the Malays of Malaya tend to be informal and 'permissive'.

154

Radcliffe-Brown seems to assume that this is so, but the evidence which he cites is drawn from inheritance practices among Anglo-Saxons and Germanic nations during the medieval period.[1] Maine, on the contrary, assumes that the Germanic tribes had patrilineal kinship groups; but he apparently believed that such groups were a universal characteristic of primitive societies in one stage of social evolution. Nevertheless, he observed that this principle was somewhat 'attenuated' among the western European tribal nations encountered by the Romans. The term 'ruder' which he uses in the following passage may reflect a theoretical bias.

'The earliest modern writers on jurisprudence remark that it was only the fiercer and ruder of the conquerors of the empire, and notably the nations of Slavonic origin, which exhibited a Patria Potestas at all resembling that which was described in the Pandects and the Code. All the Germanic immigrants seem to have recognized a corporate union of the family under the *mund*, or authority of a patriarchal chief; but his powers are obviously only the relics of a decayed Patria Potestas, and fell far short of those enjoyed by the Roman father. The Franks are particularly mentioned as not having the Roman Institution, and accordingly the old French lawyers, even when most busily engaged in filling the interstices of barbarous custom with rules of Roman law, were obliged to protect themselves against the intrusion of the Potestas by the express maxim, *Puissance de père en France n'a lieu*.'[2]

It is possible that a 'rudeness' of the forest-dwelling tribal societies of western Europe led to reliance on all cognatic relations, rather than emphasis on the principle of unilineal descent. This would be in line with some suggestions already mentioned, notably Gluckman's statement on the ecological aspect of kinship systems.[3] But our suggestion here is purely speculative. The study of early documents on European tribal societies has usually led to an opposite conclusion.[4]

The present writer is not qualified to form any judgment on this subject. It seems best to proceed tentatively on the assumption that there may have been some emphasis on a principle of unilineal descent in early Celtic and Germanic societies, though the degree of such emphasis and its precise implications in their social organization is uncertain.

The structure of feudal society in medieval Europe conflicts with the persistence of corporate lineage groups or group-families as a primary element of social organization. The feudal structure of Japanese society in some periods did not obliterate the force of agnatic descent as a major principle

---

[1] Radcliffe-Brown, op. cit., Introduction.
[2] Maine, op. cit., pp. 84-5.
[3] See Chapter III, above.
[4] See Rudolf Huebner, *Grundzüge des Deutschen Privatrechts.* Leipzig (5th edition, 1930); translated with commentary by F. S. Philbrick, *A History of Germanic Private Law*, Boston, 1918.

of social organization. The difference, however, might be attributed either to the greater initial force of this principle in Japan, or to differences in the nature of feudal systems in Japan and in Europe.

Christianity was inimical to ancestor worship. It is possible, also, that in more subtle ways the emphasis of Christianity on the sanctity of marriage, the spiritual rights of the individual, and the spiritual community and authority of the Church promoted emphasis on the nuclear family as the primary unit of social organization.

The final formulations of Roman law in the late imperial period, notably under Justinian, provided a major apparatus for the definitions of rights and obligations in medieval society.

The kinship structure of primitive Roman society and the corporate nature of the family in the early republican period (as demonstrated by Maine) had been pulverized in the later commercial and political society of ancient Rome. Contracts and testaments became instruments of individual action. Women acquired the capacity to receive and to transmit property; they became fully recognized as persons in a legal sense. The legal system inherited from late Roman society and diffused throughout western Europe was a system of individual rights and obligations.

In any case, whatever the conditions that may have been responsible for this situation, western European society in the medieval period was organized on basic principles which are radically different from those generally prevalent in Asiatic societies. Inheritance was regulated on simple cognatic lines; by degree of consanguinity without distinction between maternal and paternal links in kinship relations. And the primary unit of social life was the simple nuclear family.

This contrast in social backgrounds, in spite of a similarity in the economic basis of life, between agricultural societies in Asia and in western Europe is reflected in different modes of family life, in associated cultural values and in different levels of fertility.

ASIAN PATTERNS OF FAMILY LIFE

A group-family is the ideal in the principal agricultural civilizations of Asia. In practice this ideal is more frequently compromised than completely realized. It nevertheless exerts a powerful influence on personal obligations and ideals, and tends to provide group support of individual family units that may have separate residence. The presence of the ideal in China is shown by the tendency to interpret a joint household containing several conjugal units as a sign of wealth and welfare, in contrast to the situation today in the western world where 'doubled-up' families with more than one conjugal unit are usually interpreted as an index of economic hardship. The force of the group-family as a spiritual unit appears in the *ie* family of Japan, with many of the functions of a family, although its units maintain separate residence. The extended family is also prevalent in India, perhaps with greater actual frequency there than in China.

In the following brief account we shall give attention mainly to China, because of the availability of studies on Chinese family life, with a few observations on Indian society. This treatment is obviously inadequate to the topic, but an adequate treatment in brief compass is hardly possible. We shall also give special consideration to an earlier trend of population in Japan.

Some recognition of lineages is provided in South China by *chih* groups who join in religious observance to ancestors, but these are loose groups with no formal organization. Social organization is mainly centred in the *chia* (family household). Ideally the *chia* is an agnatic group-family. Under the pressure of circumstances or conflicting interests, it is frequently divided, leaving a stem family (the head, his wife, their unmarried sons and daughters and perhaps other unmarried close relations) and branches, or merely several conjugal families.[1]

Lang classified families in some north China villages by social class and by type. She found that 54 per cent of the farm labourers' families were simple conjugal families and only 11 per cent were group-families. Among the landlords, however, the proportions were just about reversed; only 12 per cent of these families were conjugal, and 53 per cent were extended or joint-families. The proportions for the in-between classes show intermediate gradations. She summarized her findings as follows: '. . . the composition of the family is largely determined by its social and economic status . . . the proportion of joint families increases and the proportion of conjugal families decreases as one ascends the social scale.'[2] Ta Chen made a similar observation in south China: 'Nothing so much indicates the social status of a household in the Chinese countryside as its size, which is a matter of pride, more especially, when it contains a large number of males.'[3]

According to Fei, describing a village west of Shanghai in north China, 'A *chia* is essentially a family, but it includes children even when they have grown and married. Sometimes it also includes some relatively remote patrilineal kinsmen.'[4] But, in fact, only 37 families among 359 in his series included both a senior married couple and one or more married sons. There were family groups that did not include any married couples. The most common single type, with 138 cases, was a married couple with some kin

[1] D. H. Kulp. *Country Life in South China.* New York, 1925.
[2] Olga Lang. *Chinese Family and Society.* New Haven, 1946, p. 138.
[3] Ta Chen. *Emigrant Communities in South China.* New York, 1940, p. 125.
[4] Haiao-Tung Fei. *Peasant Life in China: A Field Study of Country Life in the Yangtze Valley.* London, 1946, pp. 27-9.

other than their own children but not with another married couple. He also found that 'people who are better off marry earlier than those who are poor', though age at marriage is lower among those in agriculture than among those living in urbanized areas or engaged in industrial occupations. He also affirms that the wealthy pride themselves on having more children than others.[1] The information from various studies on relation of age at marriage and number of children per marriage to social status is, however, less consistent than that relating to size of household.

Lang and Fei both stress, as the major forces making for division of households, the difficulty of maintaining the extended family on its limited hereditary land-holdings and the consequent necessity of seeking supplemental income from domestic cottage industries or work for wages.[2] Hsu, on the other hand, describes a different force making for the division of joint families in a prosperous commercial town in west China. Here the emergence of conflicting interests among brothers, held together so long as the father lives, often leads at his death to the formation of separate conjugal families as economic units, though these families may continue to live in the ancestral house and to join in displays of family prestige.[3]

But division of primary responsibility for immediate economic affairs among separate family units, where it occurs, does not destroy a strong sense of large family identification and mutual obligations. A deep sense of moral obligation, reinforced by affection and by pride, preserves the larger unity of near kin as a powerful force. No self-respecting Chinese could endure the disgrace of allowing the son or daughter of his brother to pass the proper age of marriage without achieving family status. Such cohesion of near kin is generally characteristic of Asiatic societies.

In Japan in the period immediately after World War II, few persons reported themselves as unemployed. The economy was disorganized, and many factories were in ruins or standing idle. Individuals exercised all possible initiative in meeting their immediate needs, but in doing so they were not alone but were supported by family and kin. Many returned to native rural districts to be temporarily sustained as supplemental members of farm families that were already hard pressed. Some were aided, so far as possible, by paternalistic corporations. The 'web' of Japanese life sustained its individual members.

Hsu defines father-son identification as the central value of Chinese culture, and he sees this as based on the two principles: 'patriliny' and 'generation'. The first is the principle of agnatic lineage. The second denotes an emphasis on the subordination of each generation to that from which it derives its life. '. . . the father-son identification is merely a necessary link in the great family combination, with numerous ancestors

[1] Haiao-Tung Fei. *Peasant Life in China: A Field Study of Country Life in the Yangtze Valley.* London, 1916, p. 34.
[2] Lang, loc. cit.; Fei, op. cit., p. 33.
[3] Francis Hsu. *Under the Ancestor's Shadow.* New York, 1948, p. 114.

at one end and innumerable descendants at the other. . . .'[1] Marriage is, of course, arranged by the parents and, according to Hsu, is commonly phrased as 'seeking a daughter-in-law for the father'. The father-son identification leads a well-to-do father to maintain his son in idleness, as an expression of his economic competence and of his love, just as a well-to-do European, whether or not there are young children at home, may insist that his wife eschew gainful work for similar reasons but related to the husband-wife-children identification in western European society. Prestige, though a matter of intense anxiety in Chinese life, is never phrased as personal success. House symbols of honour are ancestral emblems, or certificates of merit received by an ancestor; the dignity of the lineage cemetery is as important as the dignity of the residence; ceremonials of display are always lineage ceremonies. Any personal achievement is attributed to good fortune or the grace of one's ancestors.[2]

As Hsu insists, Chinese culture is not fatalistic. Its relation to the living past is vital, and this provides strong motivation for the vigorous pursuit of the familistic goals defined in its traditions. Competition for prestige among family groups is intense. The pursuit of these goals, however, directs striving toward the meticulous imitation of ancient examples. The father-son identification as the core of Chinese culture generates strong identifications with all agnatic kin, in varying degree according to their proximity in the lineage.

To a person nurtured in an Asiatic society large cohesive families not only appear as a source of needed prestige and of collective economic security, but are also a source of deep emotional security. A person born in a large family household grows up to cherish participation in such a family as a way of life, and will in turn want to surround himself with numerous progeny during the prime of life and in his old age.

The emphasis on group life also modifies the ownership of land by recognition of customary rights and social obligations. In China, according to Fei '. . . individual ownership is always included under the name of *chia* ownership. . . . These two types of ownership do not seem . . . mutually exclusive. Everything owned by an individual is recognized as part of the property of the *chia*. . . .'[3] Even when a division of the common holding actually does take place between a father and his sons, '. . . [a son's] right over these allotments is still not complete. His father, as long as he is living, can strongly influence his use of the land and the house. The son cannot sell them against the will of the father. . . .'[4]

Asiatic agrarian society prescribes universal marriage at early ages. The modal age of brides at first marriages in the Yunnan series presented by Ta Chen is between 17 and 18 years of age; 87 per cent were married

[1] Hsu, op. cit., pp. 236–7.
[2] ibid., pp. 260–4.
[3] Fei, op. cit., p. 57.
[4] ibid., p. 68.

before they were 20 years old, and half of the remainder during the follow-ing year.[1] Ages of brides in first marriages are slightly higher in the study reported by Chi-Ming Chiao, using data from Buck's survey of rural China. In the north China sample, 80.2 per cent were married before the twentieth birthday and 97.3 per cent before they were 25 years of age. In the south China sample, 67.5 per cent were married before 20 years; 97.6 per cent before 25 years.[2] In ancient Hindu law, a girl must be married before puberty, and in case of her husband's death becomes a widow; but the wife usually did not enter her husband's home until after puberty, and she returned thereafter for visits with her family during the first few years. This prescription has been superseded by new legislation passed by the Government of India; but this legislation was passed over strong oppo-sition. Marriages of men occur at somewhat later ages, but about half of the men aged 15–19 years are already married, as shown in samples of the Chinese population, and by official data for India. And in both countries marriage of men as well as of women is almost universal.

In China, Japan, and India, interest in fertility is commonly phrased, not as a diffuse desire for children but as a desire for sons. The birth of a female child does not bring promise of the later receipt of bride-wealth that can be used to obtain a wife for the son. On the contrary, considerable wealth must be expended by well-to-do families in marriage festivities; and this often imposes financial burdens on both parental families. Inability to make such provision creates embarrassment for poorer families; but some provision is always made to assure the attainment of marriage, which is an absolute moral necessity. Sometimes a little girl, provided by a poor family, is adopted and brought up as the prospective daughter-in-law of a humble man. Moreover, anxiety to arrange the marriage of a daughter into a family of appropriate social status leads in some countries, as in India, to the provision of a dowry. This is a sheer loss to the parents. A daughter will not have resources at her disposal to support them in their old age.

It is the sacred duty of a man in China to have a surviving son, or sons, to fulfill his obligations to his father and his father's lineage. In Hindu culture a man needs a surviving son, who alone can perform the required rituals at the time of his death. A woman's greatest need in both cultures is to satisfy the needs of her husband and the expectations of her kin; and her own life will be dignified and enriched by children.

Under conditions where about half of all infants born alive die before reaching maturity, the anxiety for sons, even for the assured survival of a single son, results in large families. In fact the limitation of interest in progeny to interest in sons has no effect on size of family, unless female infants are killed or grossly neglected. Otherwise, along with the sons, an

[1] Ta Chen. *Population in Modern China*. Chicago, 1946, p. 114.
[2] Chi-Ming Chiao, 'A Study of the Chinese Population', reprinted from *Milbank Memorial Fund Quarterly* (Vols. 1 and 2), 1933–34, p. 31.

appropriately equal number of daughters will be produced as a by-product of the interest in male heirs.[1] Once born, girls are usually accepted and nurtured with affection. Perhaps after there are two living sons, a father can have some sense of security, but in many cases one boy will have died before this happens. Therefore the father, to meet his religious and social needs, in an Asiatic society requires about five children (fewer if he is lucky with respect to their sex and survival, more if he is unlucky in this way). He often has many more.

It would be a mistake to place undue stress on religious rules and social obligations in determining interest in children in the societies we have been considering, to the neglect of more immediate personal needs. Fei makes the point that 'the child helps the development of intimate relations between husband and wife, who are little acquainted with one another before marriage'.[2] It may be added that in the restricted life of an Indian or a Chinese peasant woman, her warm relation with her children provides what may be her only source of deep personal satisfaction. Again, an Indian in conversation with a European visitor remarked: 'You bring up your children; we live with ours.'

Agrarian societies in Asia provide positive motivation for *high fertility*. On the other hand, it is almost certain that fertility in most Asiatic countries is appreciably below procreative capacity. The traditional injunction against the remarriage of widows in India, though in no wise demographic in intent, would in itself have this effect. There is also some prejudice against widow remarriage in China.

It has been widely reported that female infanticide is a recognized practice in China, especially in north China, to which poor families are sometimes compelled to resort under the stress of poverty. This, of course, is specifically intended to reduce the size of families with limited resources. A more benign method of effecting a very moderate reduction of fertility was followed in the prosperous south-west town described by Hsu. There was a general consensus that it was improper for parents to continue to bear children after a bride was brought into the family as a son's wife. The father and mother then sometimes arrange separate places for sleeping. It is reported that in other villages the pregnancy of the father's wife under such conditions is generally interrupted by an induced abortion.[3] This suggests that abortions may sometimes be induced, even before a son's marriage, after the survival of one or several heirs has been assured.

[1] The writer experimented with the notion that a desire for 'three sons' would lead to a smaller average size of completed families, assuming cessation of childbearing as soon as this goal was achieved, than a desire for 'six children'. He soon discovered that this notion involved a statistical fallacy.
[2] Fei, op. cit., p. 31.
[3] Hsu, op. cit., pp. 109–10. This principle is also found among the Tallensi of the Gold Coast northern territories.

161

The most extensive exercise of anti-natal measures in a pre-modern Asiatic society appears to have been in Japan during the later Tokugawa period. The population had, by the year 1726, increased to a high density, in relation to the resources of an isolated agrarian economy. According to the official records the population fluctuated around a constant level from that time to 1852, during a time of increasing discontent. Irene B. Taeuber in a critical review of the basic sources concludes that there was, in fact, little increase of population during this period. She concludes that the birth rate on the average must have been definitely higher than indicated by the official statistics (20 to 30 per thousand) to equal the probable death rate in normal years plus excess mortality at times of calamity. Even so, it must have been significantly below the general level most commonly found in Asiatic countries. Although the extent of infanticide and abortion was grossly exaggerated by contemporary writers, they appear to have been sufficiently widespread to have effected a very significant reduction in fertility.

Dr. Taeuber has kindly placed at our disposal unpublished material that includes her interpretation of the possible nature and motivations of the limitation of fertility within the framework of Japanese institutions and culture. This is highly pertinent to our present inquiry. Without attempting to deal with the relevant but complex structure of Japanese society, we will quote at length passages on this particular topic from her forthcoming study of the population of Japan, to be published by Princeton University Press:

'The geographic and social-class incidence of family limitation was more complex than simply an urban-rural dichotomy. Abortion was associated with the elite of this closely structured society: the Tokugawa families, the *daimyo*, the *samurai*, and the rich merchants. Infanticide was most prevalent among the peasants. Among all classes, however, there was presumed to be a religious differentiation, the majority of the Buddhist sects repudiating methods of limitation that involved the taking of life. In Shintoism, on the other hand, there were no superindividual taboos on interference with the developing foetus between conception and independent viability. Families limited their numbers in ways consistent with their values, their aversions, and their superstitions. Limitation applied to birth orders beyond the first or, more specifically, to conceptions or deliveries that occurred after the production of a son. In infanticide, where there was a choice, destruction was more likely for the girl baby than for the boy baby. The survival of the family through the male line was the pre-eminent value; other motivations entered only after this duty to the generations had been fulfilled. However, birth order and sex were not the only factors considered in the decision as between death and survival. "Elderly" couples in their late thirties or early forties felt it somewhat improper to have a child, especially if there was a daughter-in-law in the house. Moreover, parents were apt

162

to decide against the continued existence of an infant born in years of unfavourable zodiacal and calendar combinations.[1]

'It is often assumed that the goal of the familistic society is multiplicity of descendants. If this is so, then we would have in premodern Japan a familistic society whose members behaved in ways opposed to the basic values of that society. If the motivations for this behaviour were the inexorable pressures of a poverty that precluded another mouth to feed, it would be possible to reconcile the co-existence of the unlimited familistic ideal with substantial recourse to the limitation of descendants. If the motivations involved aspirations for the future as well as the pressures of the present, however, the art of reconciliation would necessitate modification of the traditional assumptions that the supremacy of the family in Far Eastern societies requires the supremacy of the values of quantity in human reproduction. Thus, the questions involved in the existence of abortion and infanticide in feudal Japan achieve a fundamental significance for the evaluation of familism itself in its relation to that abundant production of children which is so critical a problem in much of the contemporary East. . . . We shall consider the peasants first, for here the motivations have the greatest quantitative relevance to the dynamics of the population.

'Life was difficult for the peasants of feudal Japan. Land was scarce, production was limited, and feudal levies were high. Poverty was omni-present, malnutrition common, and starvation a recurrent threat. These economic pressures for the limitation of numbers impinged on a family structure that was exclusive rather than equalitarian. In general the eldest son succeeded the father as household head and thus had an assured future, but the possibilities for the futures of second, third or higher order sons were dark indeed. There was little place in this crowded rural society for the establishment of a branch household in a nearby area. An occasional son might be adopted by a family that lacked an heir. An appreciable number escaped the village through migration to the city, while still others secured temporary work on other fiefs or on imperial estates. In this situation where the land was filled and opportunities alternative to agriculture very limited, *mabiki* (infanticide) and *kakeochi* (escape) were the alternatives to a cumulation of people hazardous alike to the individual family and the village community. . . . If the focus is shifted from the larger society to the individual family, the limitation of offspring appears as a product of the familistic system itself. The pre-eminent necessity was the continuity of the family through the male line. In an ideal world the values of living and the emphasis on the continuity of life might be expected to create a milieu in which each additional child would be welcomed and many surviving offspring would mean prestige for the mother and honour for the father. In a

[1] Reference is made here to an article by Eijiro Honjo, in *Keizai ronso*, 1933.

163

real world there were conflicts between the fulfilment of the duties to the ancestors through unlimited child-rearing and the responsibilities for the present and future welfare of the children who were already born. In this situation, the young couple tried to raise their first son; all the observations of the late Tokugawa and the early Meiji eras indicate that the eldest son was subject to no hazard of willed death, that, furthermore, the first two or three children were relatively secure. When the heavy infant mortality of the period is considered, this would mean that the practical decision as to life or death for a child was not required until four, five, or even six children had been born, for a large portion of those born would die in infancy or early childhood. When one further considers the hazards to the health and life of the mother, it becomes apparent that a large proportion of the families of the feudal period would never face the necessity for a decision as to infanticide. That decision, when it was made, would be against a background of child-rearing and in a situation where father, mother, two or three surviving children, and perhaps some grandparents or other relatives were dependent for life itself on food that must often have been inadequate for health and vitality. In this situation infanticide might be a sad imperative of the familistic system for a mother whose alternatives and perhaps "natural" reaction would be the preservation of the newly born at all costs. The strength of the familistic values would determine the limitation of offspring in the interests of those already born.'

Taeuber's treatment then gives special attention to the situation among the *samurai*, the military class of glorified status but impoverished resources. They were enjoined from marriage prior to 30 years of age. The military interest of the rulers here conflicts with their interest in promoting high fertility. This is analogous to the conflict discussed in the previous chapter between military and family interests among the Zulu and the Masai, but here it is limited to a special class. Nevertheless, the *samurai* as well as the commoners in Japan adopted anti-natal measures within marriage. But we need not here trace the special motivations that actuated this class.

FAMILY AFFAIRS IN PRE-INDUSTRIAL WESTERN EUROPE

Agriculture in medieval western Europe was generally less intensive than in southern and eastern Asia; but here, too, prevailing practices brought people together in stable, self-governing village communities within the framework of a central political system.

A common feature of these peasant societies, in Asia as in Europe, is a central tendency toward family-sized land holdings, either owned outright or cultivated under some form of long-term customary lease. The distribution of landed property and, by extension, of a landowning mentality, was relatively widespread. The term 'property' must here be given broad interpretation to include various modes of possession, even feudal tenures which legally are not ownership at all. Even the unfree serf, the most lowly among the many ranks of feudal peasantry, had customary rights of tenure in his family's plot or strips of land, and occupied a socio-economic status more stable and more secure than that of a modern unskilled wage-worker.

It is true that in some parts of Europe serfs were chattels that could be bought and sold by their lord. But all feudal societies had a considerable complement of free peasants and, even more important, the typical form of purchase and sale of serfs was precisely as part of the landed property that was being transferred. In other words, as has been said, though the peasant was tied to the land, the land was also tied to the peasant. In meeting the needs of his family, the peasant was at the mercy of legal land owners, and subject to arbitrary rents and interest, and perhaps ultimate foreclosure. Nevertheless, the principle of customary tenure produced a deep-rooted sense of 'possession' of land and attachment to fields handed down from generation to generation. In this sense, the inheritance of family 'property' through successive generations provided a socio-economic basis for family life in the agrarian society of pre-industrial Europe that was essentially similar to that provided by socio-economic structures of Asiatic societies.

Western European family structure and the regulation of inheritance remained remarkably stable in their essential features over a long period of time. For example, the basic pattern of these relations seems to have been very much the same in thirteenth century England and in sixteenth century England. Moreover, these two sets of relations were linked in the very foundations of western European social history.[1] Kinship was so closely associated with the inheritance of land that 'kind' in medieval English usage denoted both a man's group of blood relatives (kin, kindred) and the right of inheritance (*habere kendam*).

The principle of primogeniture in the transmission of family holdings prevailed in many districts, but in other districts holdings were divided. It is sometimes assumed that prevalence of one or the other of these principles has an important influence on attitudes toward fertility, but this is doubtful. The fragmentation of a small family holding through its division between many sons and the cutting off of all but one of many sons from land rights are the two horns of an inescapable dilemma in a predominantly agrarian economy where property rights are held by the nuclear family and the principle of individual inheritance is respected. One of these horns tended to be accepted as the lesser of two evils in some regions, the other in another region. Preference was sometimes shifted uneasily from one to the other. The relative effect on fertility of one or the other of these choices, so long as the basic dilemma remains unsolved, is quite uncertain.

[1] George G. Homans, *English Villages of the Thirteenth Century*, p. 158.

We will here give major attention to the effects of the individual inheritance because this remained the dominant mode in England and seems to have been widespread in France and Germany, as well as in England, during the feudal period. Even within England other customs were prevalent in certain regions, e.g., Kentish *gavelkind* involved divided descent of holdings. In post-feudal times the division of family property among all children became prevalent in some parts of France, and gained increasing popular approval. The nobility, however, had generally favoured the principle of individed inheritance so long as all cultivated land was subject to feudal property relationships. So long as a feudal overlord retained some rights of co-ownership in a plot of land, divided transfer of this plot tended to involve him in increasingly complicated webs of relationships.

The most potent effect on fertility of preoccupation with problems about the control and transmission of the property of the nuclear family seems to have been a strong tendency toward postponement or avoidance of marriage.

Among medieval English villagers it was customary for the eldest son to delay marriage until the father either died, or retired and gave over his holding to him.[1] Marriage was, therefore, often postponed until far beyond the age of physical maturity. This connexion between entering upon the family's holding and acquiring a bride was so close that frequently the marriage contracts contained detailed provisions about the arrangements for support of the groom's parents as pensioners on the property. Fees and fines to the peasant's lord for permission to marry and for transfer of the holding were often assessed simultaneously. Sometimes, bethrothal agreements contained clauses specifying that the marriage ceremony should take place at such time as the groom's father surrendered management and control of the farm. Several years might then elapse between bethrothal and marriage. Not infrequently, children were conceived during this time, in which case marriage usually took place at some time before the expected birth. But this caused inconvenience and embarrassment, and betrothed couples were under constraint to avoid pregnancy.

The heir's propertyless brothers might choose one of several courses. One might marry an heiress who had title to her father's holding because she had no brothers; or she might be a widow (if she had children, title to her holding would probably pass to them rather than to her second husband and his heirs). Other brothers might remain on the family holding as hired hands, provided that they did not marry. Or they might go to work as farm labourers for other peasants who did hold land. The old English word for hired man indicates the close association between propertyless status and non-married status: the hired labourer was the 'anilepiman'—the 'only', or single, man.

[1] Homans, op. cit., p. 159. This pattern, as noted below, was given extreme emphasis in Ireland at a later time.

166

'... a man could keep himself alive by taking work as a farm labourer, but he could not keep a wife or found a family unless he had land. No land, no marriage—that is the rule which names like anilepiman and husband prove was acknowledged by countrymen.'[1]

The same held for the non-inheriting brothers in those parts of France and Germany where undivided descent of land prevailed. They were not allowed to marry as long as they stayed on the family holding. If, then, these younger brothers remain on the land, they are substantially lost to the marriage and reproductive market. The alternative open to them was to leave their homes and pursue some other calling. They might enter the Church, which in Catholic ages and countries would have a similar effect. Or, they might enter the service of some great household; but servants and retainers were also unable to marry; in some areas there were actual legal prohibitions against the marriage of domestics. The problem of the property-less younger brothers was essentially the same in the middle ages as in later times.[2]

The sons of peasants who could not expect inheritance might move into the towns. In that case they might become apprenticed to a master crafts-man belonging to one or another of the craft guilds. The apprentice was expected to put in long years of training and service in a master's shop. While the age at which he qualified as a journeyman or master himself varied widely, it was apparently felt that he should not enter upon in-dependent exercise of his skills, or upon marriage—until perhaps the age of 24. Tawney cites contemporary documents to show sporadic concern during the first two centuries of the modern era about young townsmen setting up house and founding families before they were properly equipped to do so. Parliamentary legislation was resorted to in attempts to prevent such goings-on, and craft guilds, in complaining about the prevalence of uncompleted apprenticeships, underscored the evils of 'over-hasty mar-riages and over-soon setting-up of households by the young folk of the city, be they never so young and unskillful'.[3] There is ample evidence that early marriage without an adequate financial basis offended against the customs and mores of the age. Both in town and country marriage was dependent upon adequate economic security. This means that those who took the place of fathers or craft masters in the economic scheme of things married late, while those who were not able to enter upon property tenure of some sort, or fortunate enough to accumulate property, often did not marry at all.

Far from any general encouragement of marriages in European feudal society, there were frequent regulations that a peasant must obtain the lord's permission to marry. There was also an early English custom that

[1] Homans, op. cit., p. 137.
[2] Doris May Stenton. *English Social History in the Early Middle Ages.* London, 1950, p. 155.
[3] R. H. Tawney. *The Agrarian Problem in the Sixteenth Century.* London, 1912, footnote 3, pp. 104–6.

required him to pay 'merchet' as compensation to the lord for the giving of his daughter, but it is suggested that the lord usually did not demand so much that the marriage could not take place.[1]

In the sixteenth and seventeenth century edicts were issued against the marriage of paupers in many of the German states. King Frederick of Wuerttemberg, concerned with the effects of land tenure systems on the chances of marriage of younger sons, decreed in 1807, 'that throughout our kingdom there shall be unfettered freedom to marry, save for the restrictions of canon law or of regulations relating to conscription'. But the restrictions were renewed soon thereafter. Limitations on the right to marry were finally removed, after lengthy debate, in the North German Confederation in 1868. Such restrictions, however, remained in force even longer in some German states.[2]

Mathorez found evidence of widespread and increasing celibacy in France in the eighteenth century.[3] But this information was largely drawn from selected family records, and the resultant picture probably gives an exaggerated notion of the extent of this tendency.[4]

Many of the seventeenth and eighteenth century writers quoted by Kuczynski were much concerned about the discrepancy between natural fecundity and actual fertility which, in accordance with mercantile economic theory, they considered a national misfortune.[5] They tended to attribute it to a variety of causes, but gave attention chiefly to conditions inimical to the existence of marriage. In general they assumed the existence of various classes of men who were economically unable to support families. This was not interpreted mainly as economic incapacity to support large families but, more absolutely, as inability to marry. The measures proposed for promoting more rapid increase of population were almost invariably aimed at encouraging more universal marriage, rather than with increasing fertility within marriage.

It is extremely difficult to obtain any decisive evidence of the extent of marriage or ages at marriage in medieval Europe or during early modern times. The earliest precise information refers to the Scandinavian countries. In Sweden in 1750, at ages 15–19 less than 1.0 per cent of the men and only 4.4 per cent of the women were married; at ages 20–24 years, men 16.0

---

[1] Stenton, op. cit., p. 151.

[2] Glass. 'Malthus and the Limitation of Population Growth', in *Introduction to Malthus*, ed. D. V. Glass. London, Watts & Co., 1953.

[3] J. Mathorez. *Les étrangers en France sous l'Ancien régime*. Paris, 1919, 2 vols. Vol 1, pp. 48–9. Mathorez's account of high fertility at early times in France, as background to his account of its decline in the eigthteenth century appears somewhat inconsistent with information from other sources.

[4] For a note on this topic referring to a later period see Jean Bourgeois-Pichat, 'Evolution de la population française depuis le XVIIIᵉ siècle', *Population* 6 (4): 635–62, 647. However, it is here stated that marriage in the late eighteenth century in France was a little later than it had been two centuries earlier.

[5] R. R. Kuczynski. 'British Demographers' Opinions on Fertility, 1660–1760', in Lancelot Hogben (ed.) *Political Arithmetic*. New York, 1938, pp. 283–327.

per cent, women 27.0 per cent; at ages 25–29 years, men 57.4 per cent, women 55.5 per cent. The maxima for men were during the 40's—about 91 per cent; for women only 79 per cent. It has been estimated that from 1751 to 1800, only 8 per cent of all brides were under 20 years, and only 41 per cent under 25 years at first marriage; among grooms only 24 per cent were under 25 years at first marriage. Age at marriage appears to have been rising during this period both among men and among women. Ages at marriage may, therefore, have been somewhat lower at an earlier time in Sweden. However, in Iceland in 1703 age at marriage was higher and nuptiality less prevalent than in Sweden in 1750.[1] These figures are, however, less significant with respect to fertility than would otherwise be the case, because one or several children were often born before marriage.

Russell presents certain data relating to the extent of marriage, and ages of women at marriage in England during the late medieval period; but there are many problems in connexion with their interpretation. Poll tax records of 1377 (some districts only) were used to obtain an indication of the percentages of men and of women aged 14 years and over, who were married and living with spouse at this time. Disregarding the data for 74 persons in very small hamlets the proportion of men registered as married and living with wife varies from about 60 per cent in several large towns to 71 per cent in London (part of borough only) and, near the other end of the scale of communities, 73.5 per cent of all men in places of 51 to 100 inhabitants. The proportion of women reported as married and living with husband is somewhat higher than that for men in some districts, somewhat lower in others; the range is from 56 per cent in Carlisle and Kingston on Hill to 74 per cent in places of 26 to 100 inhabitants and 76 per cent in London.[2]

With respect to age at marriage of women, Russell uses data from inquisitions (post-mortem) concerning the status of heirs subsequent to the death of a land-holder. He points out that heiresses may have been married earlier than other women to keep them out of the hands of custodians. An added difficulty is that marital status is often not explicitly stated in the records; but may be inferred from use of a surname other than that of the father, or other evidence. The proportions of married women at various ages where positive indication of marriages was found may, therefore, be somewhat less than the proportions actually married. The data are interpreted by Russell as showing that, as regards age at marriage '. . . the general average for the upper classes declined from about 24 in the time of Edward I [1272–1307] to below 20 for the period of Henry VII'. Russell offers no interpretation. In fact, he states: 'The evidence that the marriage age was being lowered in the later medieval

---

[1] Gille. 'The Demographic History of the Northern European Countries in the Eighteenth Century', *Popular Studies* 3 (1), June 1949.
[2] Josiah Cox Russell. *British Mediaeval Population*. Albuquerque, 1948, Table 7.6, p. 154.

169

period in England was hardly expected.'[1] However, the evidence does not seem to the present writer to be wholly conclusive. If we combine the scattered data on women by single years of age into five-year age classes and also combine the information for the first two periods (where the pattern is similar) we obtain the following results for the three periods (period A: time of Edward I and Edward II, 1272–1327; period B: time of Edward III, 1327–77; period C: time of Henry VII, 1485–1509).[2]

TABLE 15.

Age of heiress at time of father's death	Absolute numbers			% 'married'		
	A	B	C	A	B	C
10–14	55	58	33	5	17	18
15–19	65	79	45	35	38	69
20–24	118	72	34	51	75	79
25–29	47	46	26	85	74	96
30 plus	117	87	85	74	67	89

In the first place, the rather high proportions apparently married among girls under 15 years of age remind us that we are dealing with a special group of heiresses whose marriages may have been arranged for property considerations, and who may not be at all representative of the whole population. The increase in the proportion of married women among heiresses aged 15–19 years at time of father's death is striking, but the finding is based on a very small sample, and may be a chance effect. The apparent increase in the proportion married among heiresses who were over 30 years when their fathers died is almost equally striking and is based on a somewhat larger sample. The figures can, at best, be said to suggest either (a) a general increase in nuptiality and a lowering of the age at marriage during the fifteenth century in the English upper class with property in land or (b) some change in legal procedures with special reference to heiresses, or in the nature of entries in the inquisition. No more positive conclusion seems warranted.[3]

Tawney finds evidence of a shift toward lower age at marriage in England during the sixteenth century. He ascribes a tendency in this direction, tending to promote more rapid increase of population, to an increase in the proportion of landless persons in England in the sixteenth and seventeenth centuries:

[1] ibid., pp. 147, 158.
[2] ibid., Tables 7.8 and 7.9, pp. 157–8.
[3] Professor Russell, who is continuing his studies of medieval population, is convinced that there was a general lowering of age at marriage and an increase of fertility in Europe during and after the thirteenth century. (Letter to the writer, January 1953.)

'When a large number of agricultural and industrial workers (in the sixteenth century probably a majority) were small landholders or small masters, did the fact that they had to wait for the death of a parent to succeed to their holding or (in towns) for the permission of the guilds to set up shop (i.e., to reach their maximum earning powers), tend to defer the age of marriage? If the possibility of this being the case is conceded, ought we to connect the slow growth of population between 1377 and 1500 (on which all historians seem to be agreed) with the wide distribution of property and ought we to think of the considerable increase in the landless proletariat which took place in the sixteenth and seventeenth centuries as tending in the opposite direction?'[1]

Our search for quantitative information concerning marital conditions in western Europe in medieval and early modern times has not led to any positive results—probably owing at least in part, to our failure to make a more intensive study of the subject. We can, therefore, only fall back on the qualitative evidence that, although marriage may often have occurred at early ages, there were major economic obstacles to marriage for large elements of the population under the social conditions prevailing in agrarian western Europe.

A principle of major importance in its influence on fertility within the sphere of the Latin law is the recognition of the right of inheritance by females, at least in the absence of a male heir. As a result, a father with several daughters but no surviving son did not face the prospect that his property would be dissipated among distant kin at his death. There was, to be sure, among the upper classes a strong interest in the continuance of the 'family name'; but this interest was less imperative. The prospect of property enhanced the marriage prospects of his daughters, with whom the father's indentification in western society was hardly less than his identification with sons.

The economic obstacles to marriage in pre-industrial western Europe are postulated on a major premise, which was so universal in this society that it is commonly ignored but which is not present, at least to the same degree, in Asiatic societies—namely, that an individual man is responsible for the support of his wife and children. This principle is implicit in the emphasis on the nuclear family as the pivot of social organization. It is hardly an exaggeration to say that it is the mainspring of the limitation of fertility in western European society.

The development of demographic trends in Ireland following the potato famine in the 1840's has implications for an understanding of factors relating to the control of fertility that were implicit in western European culture. This development has a significance that is in some ways similar to the implications, already discussed, of the decline of fertility in Japan during the late Tokugawa period with respect to cultural forces implicit

[1] Tawney, op. cit., footnote 3, pp. 104–6.

171

in eastern Asiatic culture. The Irish in the mid-nineteenth century, like the Japanese in the eighteenth century, were subjected to severe and continuing economic strain. In each nation the response resulted in a reduction of fertility. But in making this response each nation used the institutional devices provided by its culture, and adhered to its distinctive modes and norms of behaviour. The Irish record is reviewed and interpreted as part of a more general exposition by Glass. The manuscript of this paper has been placed at our disposal through the courtesy of Professor Glass. Some extracts on this topic are presented below.[1]

'Everyone has heard of the great Irish famine, the culmination of the series of failures of the potato crop upon which the people had come increasingly to depend since the late eighteenth century. The potato was a bad master—both a symptom and a cause of the economic degradation of the country. Coupled with the iniquities and confusion of the system of land tenure, it encouraged a spendthrift agriculture. Because in good years the potato had a high yield, it allowed an increasing fragmentation of land holdings. And because in good years a small patch of ground was enough to support a family, marriage was easy. Families were large, and what evidence there is, suggests a rapid growth of population. It was not so high a rate of growth as in England and Wales—some 20 per cent between 1821 and 1841 as compared with over 30 per cent in the latter country—but it was one not supported by the kind of industrial developments which were taking place in England. Hence the people of Ireland were pressed closer to the threshold of famine; and they were thrust across it by potato disease in 1845.[2] Population growth came to an end. Between 1841 and 1851 the numbers of the Irish people as a whole fell by 1.6 millions, and since that time the population has not ceased to decline. In 1851 the population of the 26 counties was 5.1 millions; in 1946 it was 2.96 millions.

'Emigration has accounted for a large part of the decline. Even before the great potato blight, large numbers of Irish were migrating, from Protestant Ulster as well as from the Catholic South. The gross emigration from Ireland as a whole amounted to about 3.8 million persons in the period 1851–1900, and in 1901 over 2.5 million Irish-born persons were to be found living abroad in the United States, Canada, Australia, and Great Britain.[3] The *net* migration in the period 1851–1936 from the areas which now constitute Eire probably exceeded 3.5 million persons, a number larger than the total population of Eire in 1946.[4] After the

[1] D. V. Glass. 'Malthus and the Limitation of Population Growth'. The extensive documentation provided in this paper is omitted in these extracts.

[2] On the famine years and the toll in mortality, see G. O'Brien, *The Economic History of Ireland from the Union to the Famine*, London, 1921, Chapter 7.

[3] Eire, *Census of Population 1936*, Vol. IX, Dublin 1942, p. 20.

[4] The net emigration 1871–1936 amounted to 2.33 millions (Ireland, *Census of Population 1936*, vol. 9, Dublin 1942, p. 17). Statistics of net emigration for the preceding 20 years are not available. But the gross emigration from the areas which now constitute Eire

172

great famine, and by a largely spontaneous process which has still not been explained fully, a tighter link was forged between agriculture and the family. The dependence upon the potato was lessened, the area under hay increased and the numbers of cattle grew. The fragmentation of holdings went no further.[1] Instead, it became customary, *as it had been before the potato era* [italics added], for the farm to be passed intact to one child. A father would, during his own lifetime, arrange the marriage of the chosen son and hand the farm to him, retaining certain rights to support during old age. The dowry brought in by the bride would be used partly to compensate the father for giving up the farm, partly to satisfy the claims of other children. Other sons might receive a professional or business training. And if the sum of money brought by the bride was sufficient, the daughters might be given dowries and marry farmers in their district. The alternative was to move into town and find jobs, or to emigrate. Women often went abroad to save money for a dowry; with that, they might marry into a farm on their return home. Men also sometimes returned with their savings to re-establish themselves in their homeland.[2] But with the ending of fragmentation, and with the tieing of rural marriage to dowries in cash or land, the chances of marriage were reduced. And they were further lowered for men because of the shortage of women. . . . Indeed, slightly more women than men were lost by net emigration during the years 1871 to 1936. Hence the ratio of females to males in the population of Eire has fallen with high consistency since 1851. In 1936, there were 952 females per 1,000 males in the population, one of the lowest ratios in the Western world. Because of this total combination of demographic and social factors, Eire, with its focus on the family and its tight links between family and farm, has tended to become a nation of elderly bachelors. In 1841, 10 per cent of the men between the ages of 45 and 54 years were unmarried. By 1936 the figure had risen to 33.5 per cent, more than three times larger than the comparable figure for England and Wales in 1931. And though, with the relative shortage of women, the proportion of spinsters is smaller . . . [the percentage at ages 45–54 years rose from 11.4 per cent in 1851] to 25.1 per cent in 1936, 53 per cent higher than that in England and Wales in 1931.

'Moreover, less marriage is accompanied by later marriage. Of the married women under 45 years of age in Eire in 1936, 52.7 per cent were within the age group 35–44 years, as compared with 45.2 per cent

amounted to about 1.6 millions in 1851/70 (*Census of Ireland 1871, General Report*, pp. 434–5; *Census of Ireland 1881, General Report*, pp. 378–9). These latter figures may well underestimate the amount of net emigration. Hence the total net emigration in 1851–1936 must be over 3½ million and perhaps as much as 4 million persons.

[1] N. J. Bonn. *Modern Ireland and her Agrarian Problem*, Dublin and London, 1906, p. 46.
[2] See C. M. Arensberg and S. T. Kimball. *Family and Community in Ireland*, Cambridge, Mass., 1940, Chapters 6–8.

in England and Wales in 1931.[1] In a society in which fertility within marriage is to a substantial extent uncontrolled, the higher average age of married women may have a significant effect on the numbers of children born to a marriage. . . .

[Information bearing on the control of fertility within marriage is reviewed, including data on occupational differentials. The concluding paragraphs in this section are as follows.]

'Taking all women who married before their forty-fifth birthday, and whose marriages had lasted 30–34 years by census date, the average number of live-born children per woman in Ireland was 4.94 in 1946 as compared with 6.77 in 1911, a decline of 27 per cent, a small part of that decline being accounted for by a higher age at marriage of the women enumerated in 1946. For Great Britain the comparable average number of children for women enumerated in 1946 is 2.90, 41 per cent lower than for Eire. Hence the decline of marital fertility in Eire has been substantially smaller than that in Great Britain, and the level of completed fertility, as recorded in 1946, substantially higher than that in Great Britain. Though there is no reason to doubt that family limitation is being practised in Eire, it is not being practised to the same extent, or with so stringent a desire for the control of family size as in Britain. . . .

'In a highly familistic society, like that of rural Ireland, and one in which the farm is the focus and the transfer of the farm the basis of marriage, the pressure against extra-marital sex relations is very strong. The double standard applies there as in other Western countries. But the material collected by Arensberg shows that the social conventions punish heavily women who have illegitimate births. This agrees very well with the comparative statistics of illegitimacy in Eire, England and Wales, and Scotland.

[Information is presented on trends in the frequency of illegitimate births as per cent of all births in Eire, England and Wales, and Scotland from 1871–80 to 1931–40. The changes from the first to the last of these periods were as follows: Eire, 1.6 per cent to 3.3 per cent; England and Wales, 5.0 per cent to 4.3 per cent; Scotland, 8.8 per cent to 6.5 per cent.]

'The figures are not conclusive. They do not show, for example, the illegitimate births occurring to Irish girls who went to England or Scotland to bear their babies. And in any case it would be necessary to know, in addition, the comparative proportions of women who are pregnant when they marry—proportions which cannot be calculated from the Irish statistics. Nevertheless illegitimacy appears to be at a rather lower level in Eire than in Britain, though the upward trend

---

This is not, of course, the same as age at marriage. The annual marriage statistics for Eire do not allow direct calculations of age at marriage in the same way as is possible for England and Wales.

174

suggests that here, as in the case of marital fertility, the traditions are slowly relaxing.

'In sum, the picture of population control in Eire since 1841 fits in fairly closely with the Malthusian ideal. Though there has been mass emigration, that emigration has been supplemented by, and has not been a substitute for, control by postponement or avoidance of marriage. Within marriage itself, fertility has fallen relatively slowly from its high level in the nineteenth century, and certainly much less than in Great Britain. And the postponement of marriage has not been counter-balanced by any equivalent increase in illegitimacy. Each of these particular facts can to some extent be matched elsewhere in the Western world. Marriage rates have been very low in Sweden, but there have been very high illegitimacy rates. Fertility is high in the Netherlands, but the marriage rates are also high. It is in the combination of circum-stances that Ireland has been unique, as well as in the net result of those circumstances, a consistent decline in total population.'

It is apparent from this account that the major institutional device by which the Irish achieved control of fertility under the pressure of economic distress was by a severe control of marriages along with strong sanctions against extra-marital fertility. The degree to which the Irish enforced reduction in marriage is, perhaps, without parallel in the experience of any other nation. The trend toward low frequency of marriage among women during the first half of the childbearing period was carried forward long after famine and the threat of famine had been removed.

The percentages of single persons by sex in each five-year age class in 1941 in Ireland were as follows:[1]

TABLE 16.

Age in years	Male %	Female %
15 and over	57.1	47.9
15–19	99.8	99.0
20–24	96.8	87.6
25–29	83.0	63.5
30–34	64.2	44.5
35–39	49.9	34.9
40–44	39.8	28.5
45–49	34.1	26.0

As noted by Glass, under the stress of famine, the Irish reverted to a pattern of family relations that had been a feature of their early social organization but had been relaxed during the prosperous years of large

[1] Data from the United Nations, *Demographic Yearbook 1949–50.*

175

potato harvests. Right to livelihood from the family's land was limited to one son, and his right to marry was withheld until the father was prepared to surrender control and he and his wife were ready to make way for the son's bride by retiring to separate quarters within the house. This institution and associated cultural values have been vividly described by Arensberg and Kimball.[1]

The Irish experience illustrates the restrictive character, as regards fertility, of family structure in pre-industrial western Europe in association with sanctions against extra-marital fertility, though such restriction of marriage was not enforced with equal intensity in any other situation.

There was, of course, some restriction of fertility within marriage in medieval society. This might be achieved either by avoidance of sexual relations between spouses after several children had been born or by the practice of *coitus interruptus* or, occasionally, by abortion. Such practices were apparently present, but were certainly not widespread.

LEVELS OF FERTILITY IN ASIA AND IN PRE-INDUSTRIAL WESTERN EUROPE

Levels of fertility in agrarian western Europe for the times and places for which we have reliable information concerning the period before the industrial revolution were definitely well below the levels usually found in Asiatic agrarian societies. Our earliest precise information on fertility in Europe relates only to northern European countries where the system of parish registers has provided especially rich material for demographic analysis. Excluding Finland, where the population had a somewhat different cultural background, the apparent average birth rates during the period 1735–1800 were as follows:[2] Sweden, 33.6; Denmark, 30.8; Norway, 33.0; Iceland, 33.1.

These rates may have a slight downward bias, owing to some omission of children dying in infancy; but they may be accepted with confidence as indicating conditions close to those actually prevailing. It is safe to assume that the average crude birth rate for this period was not above 35 per thousand in any of these countries. The average birth rate in Finland during this period was 40.7 per 1,000 population. The average number of children ever born per woman living through the childbearing period in Sweden, 1776 to 1880, varied between 4.15 and 4.65 births per woman—with little or no clear secular trend during this period. The average for northern Europe in the eighteenth century seems to have been less than 5.0 live births per woman.

Near the middle of the nineteenth century when official registration

[1] C. M. Arensberg and S. T. Kimball. *Family and Community in Ireland*. Cambridge, Mass., 1940.
[2] Gille, op. cit., p. 30.

data became available for England and Wales, the crude birth rate was similar to, but slightly higher than in the northern countries. A critical review of birth registration data by Glass indicates that during the four decades prior to 1880 the crude birth rate in England, corrected for changes in the completeness of enumeration, was nearly constant at about 35 to 36 births per 1,000 population—except for a possible slight rise in the 1850's.[1] It is unlikely that fertility had been at a greatly different level in Britain during the preceding decades.

Bourgeois-Pichat, by an ingenious use of census data on age distribution and supplemental information on mortality, estimates that the female gross reproduction ratio in France during the mid-eighteenth century was about 2.50, which corresponds to a total maternity ratio of about 5.1 births per woman living through the childbearing period. He estimates that fertility was about 6 per cent below this level during the period 1771–75; declined rapidly during the revolutionary period to give a gross reproduction ratio of 2.0, 1801–05; and declined rather steadily with some short-term fluctuations to give a gross reproduction ratio below 1.5 before the end of the nineteenth century.[2] The decline of fertility in France during the last quarter of the nineteenth century appears to have been more rapid than at any other time after the last quarter of the eighteenth century.

Official vital statistics, subject to varying degrees of accuracy, became available for most western European countries near the middle of the nineteenth century. Kuczynski gives all available birth rates for Belgium, Denmark, England and Wales, Scotland, Ireland, Finland, France, Germany, Holland, Norway, Sweden and Switzerland. The only rates in this series above 38 births per 1,000 population are those for Finland prior to 1905 and Germany 1771–80 (but not previously). The apparent average birth rates in these countries, 1876–80, were as follows: Belgium, 32.0; Denmark, 32.0; England and Wales, 35.3; Scotland, 34.7; Ireland, 25.8; Finland, 36.9; France, 25.3; Germany, 39.2; Holland, 36.4; Norway, 31.6; Sweden, 30.3; Switzerland, 31.3.[3]

There is no precise evidence on fertility in western Europe during the medieval and early modern periods except for a few atypical localities. We know that the movement of total population was irregular in many countries. It is possible that fertility fluctuated around a general level not very different from that in effect near the end of the eighteenth century, rising at some times and in some regions and falling at other times. This seems to be as plausible an assumption as any other, but we really have no knowledge on the subject.

[1] D. V. Glass. 'A Note on the Under-Registration of Births in Britain in the Nineteenth Century', *Population Studies* 5 (1): 70–28, July 1951.
[2] J. Bourgeois-Pichat. 'Evolution de la population française depuis le XVIIIᵉ siècle', *Population* 6 (4): 635–662, Oct.-Dec. 1951, p. 654, graph. 6, p. 654.
[3] R. R. Kuczynski. *Balance of Births and Deaths*, I. New York, 1928, p. 6.

Significantly higher birth rates have been widely prevalent in Asia. According to estimates presented in the United Nations *Demographic Year Book*, 1949–50, average crude birth rates of the Near East, South-Central Asia, and Eastern Asia exclusive of Japan are now between 40 and 45 births per 1,000 population per year. Estimates of fertility in India by K. Davis derived from successive census reports from 1881 through 1941 give 10-year average birth rates ranging from 45 to 49 per 1,000 population per year, and total maternity ratios from 5.7 to 6.4 births per woman.[1] The series give some indication of a slight downward trend. The nature of these estimates makes precision impossible but removes the possibility of such gross errors as may result from the use of incomplete vital statistics.

The average level of fertility among East Indians in the Caribbean may be somewhat below the general average in India; but in practically all political divisions in this region it is well above that of either Negro or white groups. The Indian communities of East and South Africa maintain very high fertility. Martin reports the following average total numbers of live births per Indian woman aged 45 years or over: Kenya, 6.0; Uganda, 6.0; Tanganyika, 6.4. These are generally above those for Africans in the same region—as are East Indian indices of fertility in the Caribbean above those of Negroes or white in the same areas.[2] Net reproduction ratios were estimated by Badenhorst for different ethnic groups in magisterial districts in the Union of South Africa. The mean ratios in all districts for each ethnic group were as follows: Bantu, 1.60; coloured, 1.79; Asiatic, 2.27.[3]

The established Chinese population of Formosa (Taiwan), drawn chiefly from the southern coastal region of China, has conspicuously high fertility— as shown in a study by Barclay. Three-year average crude birth rates centred on the years 1930, 1935, 1940, after slight adjustment for under-registration, are 47.3, 46.6, and 45.3 births per 1,000 population, in spite of a sex and age structure tending somewhat to lower these rates. At the same times, the general maternity rates were 221, 225, and 217, respectively, per 1,000 women 15–44 years. The average total maternity ratio during the decade, 1930–40, is 6.83 live births per woman living through the childbearing period.[4] An estimated total maternity ratio of 6.93 births per Chinese woman living through the childbearing period in British

[1] Kingsley Davis. *Population of India and Pakistan.* Princeton, 1951, pp. 69, 87. Total maternity ratios cited above are from gross reproduction ratios presented in the text.
[2] W. F. Searle, E. J. Phillips, and C. J. Martin. 'Colonial Statistics'. *Journal of Royal Statistical Society*, A 93 (3): 284–91 (1950).
[3] L. T. Badenhorst. 'Territorial Differentials in Fertility in the Union of South Africa— 1911–1936', *Population Studies* 6 (2): 135–62, Table 12, p. 159. The standard deviation of the mean in each case was in the vicinity of 0.3. Estimates were derived from child-woman ratios. The same life table was used for all non-white groups.
[4] Information provided by George W. Barclay, from forthcoming publication: *Colonial Development and Population in Taiwan*, Princeton. The total maternity ratio is obtained from census data by procedures involving application of Japanese fertility schedule for derivation of substitute rates.

Malaya, 1946–48, was obtained by T. E. Smith—and was found to be definitely above that among the Malayans.[1]

The fertility of oversea Japanese seems to show remarkable adaptability to different situations. Numbers of live births per woman classified as 'yellow' in the 1940 census of Brazil are as follows: aged 60 years and over, 4.56; aged 50–59 years, 5.19; aged 40–49 years, 5.68.[2] These data are interpreted by Mortara as showing rising fertility among Japanese in Brazil. On the contrary, in the United States and Hawaii there has been rapid decrease of fertility among Japanese in recent decades (see Chapter VI).

As noted in Chapter IV, the fertility of Armenians, Azerbeidzhans, and some other peoples in the vicinity of the Caucasus mountains and the Iranian plateau seems to be extremely high—with seven to eight children per woman living through the childbearing period—well above the general level in southern and eastern Asia. And the settled Muslims of Palestine were found during the 1930's to be as prolific as the high-fertility nations of the Caucasus.

On the other hand, Malaysians apparently have somewhat lower average fertility than the averages usually ascribed to Indians, Chinese, Thai, or Koreans; and rural districts in British Malaya chiefly occupied by indigenous Malaysians show somewhat lower indices than Malaysians in rural districts with many in-migrants from Java. An estimate by Smith, with an upward correction of raw data from the census and registration system, indicates a probable total maternity ratio of about 5.5 births per woman living through the childbearing period.[3] A detailed study of regional differences leads him to the conclusion that 'the least fertile group consists of the descendants of the Malay rice-planters who settled in Kedah, Perlis, and Kelantan many centuries before the southern two-thirds of Malaya began to be developed'.[4] Divorce is relatively frequent in this region, but the proportion of women within the childbearing period who were actually married at the time of the census was above the general average. Less than 10 per cent of the Malay women past childbearing ages in these districts reported themselves as childless. Smith adds the comment, '. . . probably the true explanation of fertility differences is buried deep in local Malay cultures'.[5]

It is likely that if accurate data were available many significant differences in fertility would be found among various groups in complex civilizations such as those of China and India—with a tendency toward perhaps 4 or 5 births per woman in some local groups, about 6 in others, and perhaps 7 or 8 in others.

[1] See above, Chapter I, Table I; also citation to table.
[2] See contribution by Mortara, below. Part Five.
[3] Smith, op. cit., p. 48. (GRR 2.672; Sex ratio 105.6.)
[4] ibid., p. 51.
[5] ibid., p. 55.

We can safely assume, as a generally average rate, that women living through the childbearing period in the agricultural societies of Asia bear in the vicinity of 6 living children. Their sisters in western European villages in the late pre-industrial period were probably having, on the average, between 4.5 und 5 births; and it is likely that the average was somewhere in this vicinity through much of the medieval period.

We have omitted discussion of cultural conditions and fertility in eastern Europe in order to simplify the presentation. In general, fertility in the Balkans and among the Slavs of the Russian plain, prior to modern conditions, approximated the level generally prevalent in Asiatic societies. Several reasons for the contrast in this respect between western and eastern Europe are apparent. Eastern Europe was not strongly influenced by Roman traditions. The south-western Slavs, long under Ottoman control, had quite different social institutions than the western European nations. The eastern Slavs were a rapidly increasing population, able to spread out to the north, then to the south, and then to the east through a vast area sparsely occupied by less powerful societies. Slavic societies generally gave strong emphasis to patrilineal descent and patriarchal authority; and they tended to form cohesive social groups. This is conspicuously evidenced in the *zadruga* of the south-eastern Slavs—a joint household of family units, typically having 10 to 20 members, closely related by blood or adoption, which regulates the control of property, labour, and livelihood. The strength of the group principle also appears in traditional Russian life in the structure of the original Cossack (*kosaki*) agricultural-military groups and in the *mir* (formed in the period following the emancipation of the serfs). Incidentally, it may be noted that the *zadruga* became subject to strong disruptive influences during the twentieth century, and was weakened and tended to break up in many districts during the 1920's and 1930's.[1] This was also a period when birth rates were falling quite rapidly in south-western Europe. There may have been some association between these trends. The interrelation of various conditions affecting fertility in eastern Europe would repay intensive study. It is omitted here in order to focus attention on the broad, significant contrast between cultural conditions affecting fertility in agrarian western Europe and agrarian Asia.

The high fertility characteristic of stable agrarian civilizations in Asia seems to us to present a theoretical problem that merits more serious attention than it has usually received. The fertility of Asiatic agrarian societies has always been *incongruous* with their ecological situation. It tended to induce a rate of increase of these populations that could not be supported by the economic basis of their existence.

---

[1] Philip E. Mosely. 'The Peasant Family: The Zadruga, or Communal Joint Family in the Balkans, and Its Recent Evolution', in Caroline F. Ware, editor, *The Cultural Approach to History*. New York, 1940.

A similar level of fertility among the eastern Slavs was congruous with their situation. Under sanitary conditions not very different from those prevailing in Asiatic societies, the Russian population within the territory under the domain of Peter the Great grew from about 18 million persons in 1724 to 94 million persons in 1897[1]—but this increase was absorbed in an expanding base, and it made possible the extension of Russian domination throughout Central Asia and Siberia to the Pacific coast. Again, as noted in Chapter III, the population of the Kazakh pastoral nomads, whose sanitary practices were certainly not superior to those of sedentary villagers, doubled during the century ending in 1930; and it is quite probable that it had doubled during the preceding century. But this increase, prior to the time that the Kazakhs began to be hemmed in by Russian colonists, was appropriate to their situation.

But the potential of Asiatic agrarian populations for natural increase, even prior to the introduction of modern sanitary measures, led to repeated fluctuations—with eras of increasing population terminated by famines, political chaos, and epidemics. The population of China under the Han dynasty (near the time of the Birth of Christ) had apparently reached about the same magnitude as it had in the middle of the seventeenth century A.D. In the intervening interval, the tendency toward rather rapid increase of population induced by its high fertility was successively interrupted by famines, political disorders, and invasions from the steppes.[2] Thereafter, there was again a period of rapid increase continuing into the nineteenth century. In India the pattern is more complex; but here, too, there was already a very large population, similar in size to that at the beginning of British rule, at the time of Asoka in the third century B.C., and again after consolidation of Mogul power, at the end of the sixteenth century A.D.[3] By contrast, the population of central, western and northern Europe remained small throughout the medieval period, with irregular but generally upward trends. This trend was interrupted by the Black Death and the Hundred Years War, and continued thereafter at a moderate rate into the seventeenth century.

Obviously people in agrarian societies, or any other societies, do not consciously regulate reproduction in the interest of national demographic trends. But families in agrarian Europe did take their own expected resources into account in decisions relating to family affairs. And, in general, we have assumed that in the long run there is likely to be some relation between cultural patterns and ecological conditions.

This brings us to the question of the fundamental factors responsible for the dominance in Asian agrarian societies of social and cultural conditions

[1] Lorimer, op. cit., p. 10.
[2] Ta Chen. *Population in Modern China*. Chicago, 1946, Chapter I. See also A. J. Jaffe, 'A Review of the Censuses and Demographic Statistics of China', *Population Studies* 1 (3): 308–37, 1947.
[3] Kingsley Davis. *Population of India and Pakistan*. Princeton, 1951, Chapter 3.

tending to induce a level of fertility well above that adequate for the maintenance of these populations, and tending in fact to cause constant hardship and recurrent calamities.

All of the following factors must be taken into account, though their relative importance is uncertain and presumably varied widely in different situations.

The needs for security, of villages and of individuals, fostered the formation and perpetuation of cohesive groups and emphasis on the values of co-operative relations. Co-operative groups, as such, do not necessarily create motivation for high fertility. But they do inherently provide economic and personal support for individuals who adhere to generally accepted ways of living. Therefore, such groups ordinarily support their members in the bearing and nurture of children. These members, therefore, have a sense of security in venturing into marriage and parenthood.

Particular cultural principles in many Asiatic societies, notably in China and in India, promote early and universal marriage, in order to provide maximum assurance of surviving male heirs. These particular principles appear in many cases to be survivals, or culturally associated with survivals, from patrilineal lineage systems that had functional value in expanding tribal societies but do not have such functional value under the actual conditions of stable civilizations.

Restriction of reproduction in most Asiatic countries, in view of cultural compulsions for marriage in an early phase of the reproductive period (e.g., marriage of women before 18 or 20 years of age) could only be effected by difficult post-marital control of fertility. The means available for doing this have either been repugnant to spontaneous and acquired devotion to children, in the case of infanticide, or have involved hardships or serious risks, as in the practices of abortion, avoidance of sexual intercourse between spouses, or modes of incomplete sexual intercourse. An alternative practice tending to lower fertility is an injunction against remarriage of widows, as in Hindu culture; but this is motivated by other values and its effect on reproduction, though by no means negligible, is incidental to its primary purpose.

Actually, the general level of fertility in the principal Asiatic societies seems to have been reduced, perhaps ordinarily by 10 to 25 per cent or more, below their capacities for procreation by one or another of the practices listed above or by some combination of these practices. Any greater effect would have required very strong motivation—as in Tokugawa Japan, or in north China during times of famine.

The spontaneous satisfactions of parenthood in all societies foster interest in the bearing and nurture of children. The conditions of agrarian life, in Asia as in medieval Europe, minimize competing interests and needs.

It is possible that in some Asiatic situations in spite of many positive cultural motivations for personal and group achievement, the shock of prior conquests or the sheer persistence of poverty may have given rise to apathy and indifference in the conduct of personal affairs.

By contrast, the social structure of western European society emphasized one major principle that had important implications for the control of fertility: the relative independence of the nuclear family fixed responsibility with respect to marriage on the parents or the individuals immediately concerned, and fixed responsibility for the procreation and nurture of children on small family units—though these primary units were subject to the legal regulations of the larger society and the influence of its ideals. In particular, the fact that indefinite delay in marriage was culturally permissible tended to make marriage patterns in western Europe more variable, and more responsive to changes in economic conditions.

RELATION OF RELIGION TO FERTILITY

Religion, being concerned with affairs that are regarded as extraordinary and as having unique importance in life, is an intrinsic aspect of the culture of all societies. It is such an integral part of the texture of many relatively simple cultures that it is not easily isolated for separate analysis. But in complex cultures distinctively religious institutions and values have more independent existence and their influence on fertility may be more specific. It seems advisable to consider various aspects of the relation of religion to fertility, somewhat systematically, in one portion of our study—in spite of the fact that some of these aspects may have special pertinence to topics already treated, and others may be related more directly to subjects to be examined in the following chapter.

Religion in Primitive Societies

It is especially difficult here to dissociate the influence of distinctly religious factors from other cultural conditions affecting fertility. This is sometimes possible. For example, among the matrilineal Ashanti, the primary social organization places little emphasis on the relations of fathers to children. But the doctrine that a personal *ntoro* (spirit) is transmitted from paternal ancestors to infants, exclusively through males, gives men a pride and responsibility in parenthood that they would not otherwise have.

As is well known, the principle of human fertility is associated in the thinking of many people with the fertility of soils or of herds, and both are subjects of religious interest. This tendency was apparently present in the minds of the earliest men who have left objects of art for our present admiration. The same theme is emphasized in the rituals of many societies.

An important aspect of the relation of religion to fertility in many primitive societies is its intensification of personal identification with the members of one's lineage, clan or society as distinct from all others—

'Children of Abraham' or the 'True Believers', as contrasted with 'Uncircumcized Philistines' or 'Infidels'—which in its nationalistic aspects is known as ethnocentrism.

The ancestors and gods of a primitive society are its peculiar heritage. A particular society has sole responsibility for the preservation and perpetuation of this heritage, and for the goods and values associated with it. The sense of mutual responsibility for the welfare of other members of a spiritual community and the intensified competition with other societies are conducive to the maintenance of a high level of fertility. This tendency in some situations is associated with political nationalism. It is possible, for example, that the unusually high fertility of the Armenians, the Georgians, the Azerbaidzhans, and other nationalities in the vicinity of the Caucasus has been influenced by their ethnocentrism, intensified by religious differences.

Religious Communities in Composite Societies

A somewhat similar complex of factors tending to sustain high fertility is frequently found in socially distinct religious societies within a composite civilization—as for example among the Amish in Pennsylvania or the Mormons in Utah and vicinity.[1] A condition contributing to the maintenance of high fertility in sectarian minorities is the resistance created by their religious faith against the assimilation of culture patterns developed in other communities. This is emphasized in some religious societies by the distinctive clothing, hair dress, etc. Such general resistance to the assimilation of new culture patterns often tends to enforce the persistence of traditional patterns of family life conducive to high fertility in spite of changes in technical and economic conditions that might otherwise lead to lower fertility.

On the other hand, a culturally conditioned trend toward lower fertility may progress rapidly in a closely-knit religious community, under changed objective conditions, if the cultural leadership of this community participates actively in the technical advances. This is indicated by recent rapid changes in fertility in areas in the western United States chiefly occupied by Mormon communities, and by trends of fertility in Jewish communities in Europe and America during the last century. It is, also, illustrated by the case of the Parsis in India. We will summarize here an account by Chandra Sekhar of the trend of fertility in the last of these groups.[2]

[1] See, for example, Walter M. Kollmorgen. *Culture of a Contemporary Rural Community. The Old Amish of Lancaster County, Pennsylvania*, United States Department of Agriculture, Washington, 1942; Lowry Nelson, 'Some Social and Economic Features of American Folk', Brigham Young University Studies, 4, Provo, Utah, 1933. Also, N. I. Butt, *Fruits of Mormonism*, New York, 1925.

[2] C. Chandra Sekhar. 'Some Aspects of Parsi Demography', *Human Biology*, 20 (2), 1948, pp. 47–89.

184

The original Parsi community entered India after the fall of the Sassanian dynasty to Arab conquerors (A.D. 641), bringing ancient Iranian culture and the tenets of Zoroastrian doctrine. Through natural increase and continued accessions from Iran, the community had increased to 115,000 persons in 1941. They are scattered all over India; but slightly over half live in Bombay Presidency. And 89 per cent of the total community live in towns. It is a closed group that does not accept converts. It has maintained a strong social structure, and prescribes rigid norms of social and religious behaviour. The Parsi Panchayat controls large religious and charitable trusts, provides subsidized schools open to the children of all members, housing schemes, and health services. The community contains many wealthy members, but the majority are occupied in small enterprises. Among occupied males in Bombay in 1931, 9 per cent were domestic servants and 10 per cent were engaged in 'insufficiently described occupations', presumably of a very minor character. Many find themselves unable to meet the needs of the family at Parsi standards, which are higher in some respects than those of the general population. In fact, 40 per cent in the mid-1940's required some sort of assistance from the Parsi Panchayat.[1]

The Parsi population of India, living in a country with high incidence of disease, has made remarkable achievements in health and longevity. The infant mortality rate of Parsis in Bombay was reduced from over 200 per thousand in the first decade of the twentieth century to well under 100 in the 1940's, and only 68 per thousand in 1944 (the last year in the series here reported). The general death rate over the previous decade was about 15 per thousand.[2]

The general birth rate among Parsis in Bombay was low, as compared with the general average, even at the beginning of the century, but remained fairly constant within the range 24 to 30 per thousand, from 1900 to 1920. Thereafter, it declined to the vicinity of 15 per thousand in the early 1940's (reaching a low point, 14.3, in 1942 but rising to 19.4 in 1944). As a result, the balance between births and deaths in the whole community has been small and fluctuating above and below the zero point during the last half century.[3] One of the important factors in the low fertility of Parsis is late age at marriage, with a trend toward further advance in age at marriage during the first quarter of the present century—associated with an apparent tendency in some cases to refrain from marriage altogether. In 1931, in all India, only 18 per cent of the Parsi women aged 15–19 years were married—as compared with 85 per cent of the Hindu women and 85 per cent of the Muslim women in this age class. Even at ages 30–34 years only 72 per cent of the Parsi women were married (excluding 'widowed or divorced') as compared with 82 per cent of the Hindu women and 85 per cent of the Muslim women. Among Parsi men, the proportion

[1] ibid., pp. 60–1.
[2] ibid., pp. 62–3.
[3] ibid., p. 56.

married rose slowly by age, from 14 per cent at ages 20–24 to 58 per cent at ages 30–34 and 80 per cent at ages 40–44 years.[1]

Although social cohesion within the Parsi community has been weakened by urban life and interest in commercial and technical enterprises, it still has a far stronger social structure than is usually found in any urban group. The marked decline of fertility in such a group is a phenomenon of much theoretical interest. The Parsi community responded positively to opportunities for commercial and scientific advances opened by European contacts, while maintaining distinct religious traditions. An intensive analysis of the play of cultural forces in relation to the trend of fertility in this remarkable community, which has produced many illustrious scholars, financiers, scientists, and leaders in political and social affairs, would be extremely interesting.

Highly developed religions, with a sacred literature and a highly developed body of theological and ethical doctrines, even though largely limited to one society, may place less emphasis on ethnocentric values than the religions of many primitive societies. They may, to the extent that this is so, provide less compulsive motivation for very high fertility. This appears to have been true of later Hebrew religion, prior to the dispersion of the Jews after the destruction of Jerusalem, as compared with earlier Hebrew religion—though the dispersion brought a new emphasis on cohesive ethnic principles. Religious movements within vast societies, such as those of India and China, are often characterized by greater tolerance for diverse cultural traditions than is usually found either in the religions of primitive societies or in traditional inter-society religious movements. On the other hand, they usually bring strong emphasis on group life and, especially in China, on family and kinship obligations.

Islam

Mohammedanism gives strong and unequivocal emphasis to high fertility, and Mohammedan social structures universally support high fertility. This is an essential aspect of the zeal for the extension of Islam and the expansion of Mohammedan societies. The emphasis on fertility is associated with the toleration of polygyny, following the example of the Prophet and the precepts of the Koran. It should, however, be noted that all except one of the Prophet's wives had been widows. Also Mohammed did not endorse unlimited polygyny, but rather restricted the practice already present in Arab society. A specific text on this subject runs as follows:[2] 'And if you fear that you cannot act equitably towards orphans, then marry such women as seem good to you, two and three and four; but if you fear that you will not do justice (between them), then (marry) only one.'

[1] ibid., p. 59.
[2] References in this section are from an unpublished paper by M. Yasin; but the present writer is responsible for the interpretations given here.

Polygyny is, of course, practised to a much lesser extent in stable Mohammedan societies today than in association with earlier movements of ethnic expansion.

In one of the sayings attributed to the Prophet in Islamic tradition he is reported to have expressly forbidden celibacy. Other sayings, however, enjoin those who are unmarried to exercise continence. The Koran explicitly encourages marriage, even the marriage of slaves: 'And marry those among you who are single and those who are fit among your male slaves and your female slaves; if they are needy, Allah will make them free from want out of His Grace; and Allah is Ample giving, Knowing. And let those who do not find a match keep chaste until Allah makes them free from want out of His Grace.'

One of the verses of the Koran cited below is interpreted by many Muslim scholars as an injunction against any voluntary limitation of fertility; but there is not unanimous agreement on this interpretation: 'And do not slay your children for fear of poverty. We give them sustenance and yourselves too.'

The word 'children' in this text is usually interpreted to include prospective children too. There are two apparently contradictory sayings of the Prophet on record, with reference to an old form of birth control called *azal* (meaning desire by man that his wife may not have conception), one allowing *azal* and the other disallowing *azal*. According to the opinion of some Muslim scholars the two sayings relate to two different situations. When conception is expected to endanger the life of the wife and she is agreeable to the avoidance of conception, it is permissable, whereas in other cases it is forbidden. There appears, at present, to be wide divergence of opinion among Muslim religious leaders and educators on this subject.

The whole emphasis in Islamic culture on strict conformity to social obligations and the sense of the divine destiny of the followers of the Prophet as the exponents of the only true Faith are perhaps more important in promoting high fertility than any specific precepts of Islamic doctrine. Associated with these values is a strong sense of the omnipotence of Fate. Among orthodox Muslims and many humble followers of the Prophet, the circumstances of human life are not influenced by the actions of individuals. It is, in fact, impious for them to attempt to interfere in any way with the courses of nature. It is, then, not surprising that Muslim populations are generally characterized by extremely high fertility, and include some groups (Palestine Muslims and Azerbaidzhans in the U.S.S.R.) with recorded fertility at or near the maximum indicated by any moderately reliable data.

Buddhism

Buddhism in ideology and in practice appears to approximate neutrality on the issue of family planning except in societies like Japan, where it has been profoundly influenced by the inclusion of familistic motives. In so far as is known, Hinayana Buddhist leaders have proposed no doctrinaire position on the subject. The emphasis in Buddhism on relations between the individual and the universal, the importance of motive in evaluating behaviour, the tradition of the Buddha's personal rejection of previously accepted family ties, would seem, on *a priori* grounds, conducive to limited rather than unlimited fertility. It is not improbable that any reluctance of the south Asian Buddhist laity to accept principles of family limitation would rest more upon 'folk' and secular institutional grounds than upon actual religious principles and precepts. This thesis has some empirical support.[1]

The provision for periods of monasticism by the laity, as in Thailand, must exert some influence toward reduction of fertility. As noted in Chapter IV, Lamaism in inner Asia provides a rather powerful instrument for absorbing surplus male population (e.g., younger brothers) and may tend to check increase of population—but Lamaism is far removed from southern Buddhism.

Bryce Ryan has reported the results of an inquiry on attitudes toward family planning among priests of the Hinayana or Theravada Buddhists in Ceylon.[2] This branch of Buddhism, found also in Burma, Thailand and Cambodia, espouses doctrines of ahimsa (non-harming, especially non-killing) and rebirth. Ryan finds no inconsistency between either of these doctrines and contraception, and this view is supported by the expressed attitudes and interpretations of well educated Buddhist priests. Among Ceylonese priests interviewed by Ryan, the vast majority of these with high educational qualifications or scholarly attainment, found no inconsistency between Buddhist ideology and contraceptive practices. Except for a few who did not consider population growth a serious problem, nearly all of these stated that they would approve a governmentally sponsored programme of family planning. This question, however, was not generally viewed as a matter of intense religious concern.

In sharp contrast to the scholarly priests, those having a minimum of education (usually apprenticeship in village temples) were in almost complete agreement that contraception was wrong according to Buddhist teachings. Usually this position was rationalized on the grounds that 'prevention of birth is tantamount to killing'. Conviction, however, was weak and it was readily apparent that most of the priests were being pressed for a response to a question about which they had not thought and about which they had little concern. Many of them affirmed the view that such matters should receive the attention of government if population growth were a serious problem. They, themselves, wished no part in it.

[1] Bryce Ryan. 'Institutional Factors in Sinhalese Fertility', *Milkbank Memorial Fund Quarterly*, 30 (4), October 1952.
[2] 'Hinayana Buddhism and Family Planning in Ceylon', paper presented at the Milkbank Memorial Fund Conference, November 1953.

In no quarter among Buddhists in Ceylon, either among priests or the laity, is there any apparent tendency to attach spiritual value to unlimited fertility. Very few priests at any educational level believed that spiritual merit was enhanced by large numbers of offspring, although many of the least educated felt that Buddha favoured families of many children over small families.

Ryan believes, on the basis of these observations, that only a very meagre opposition to family planning would be raised by the priesthood in Ceylon. Explicit doctrinal bases for opposition are lacking, and scholarly religious leaders are well aware of this. Some indeed see positive support for family limitation in Buddhist teachings, on the grounds of 'good motivation'. While the bulk of village priests would probably have negative attitudes, their role generally would be merely one of passivity and unconcern.

Christianity

Christianity, like other inter-society religions, is characterized by great diversity of sects. It is difficult to find common elements, other than origin and the acceptance of common sacred writings and symbols, among all Christian sects. There is, however, a core of common principles within the early Christian movement, the western medieval church, and the modern Roman Catholic and major Protestant churches. But in so far as a core of European Christian principles exists, its relations to fertility are largely indirect and cannot easily be formulated.

Like other religious movements, Christianity intensifies some types of group cohesion. It exerts a moral force tending toward the stability of marriage and other social relations, and it heightens the evaluation of children as immortal souls received by parents in sacred trust. All these factors are conducive to high fertility, but they are influences common to many religions rather than characteristics peculiar to Christianity.

Emphasis on the nuclear family would seem to be one distinctive common characteristic of the early Christian movement and of Christianity in modern societies which has fairly direct relation to fertility. This emphasis has both a negative and a positive aspect.

Negatively, this emphasis implies the repudiation of compulsory kinship bonds. There was already a strong emphasis on primary family relations in Jewish society under the Roman Empire, and this was intensified in the teachings of Jesus. To the prospective disciple who suggested that he delay active participation in the promotion of the new religious movement until he had 'buried his father' (i.e., fulfilled his obligations to his aged parents), Jesus gave a reply that must sound like the height of blasphemy to a devout follower of Confucius: 'Let the dead bury the dead.'[1] The

[1] Matthew viii: 21–22.

positive assertion that husband and wife are one flesh is accompanied by the negative assertion that in entering marriage, a man 'leaves his father and his mother'.[1] The emphasis in early Christianity on the nuclear family as contrasted with extended kinship obligations, was appropriate to the social scene in late Roman society. It may have been one factor, along with many others, responsible for the lack of emphasis on kinship systems in the social structure of medieval Europe.

The importance of kinship obligations and even of primary family obligations has also been modified in Christian doctrine by emphasis on the subordination of all personal interests to a divine mission. This emphasis, in association with the influence of Platonic philosophy and personal revulsions against social patterns in late Roman society, gave rise to ascetic motives in Christianity. But the principle of primary loyalty to God was harmonized in the earliest Christian teachings with the acceptance of ordinary family relations as a normal pattern for most men and women. And the religious sanction of marriage and parenthood is emphasized in all the major institutional branches of Christianity. In contrast to Tibetan Buddhism, for example, ascetic tendencies in Christianity have never presented a serious threat to the force and stability of the nuclear family pattern.

The positive aspect of the distinct emphasis on the nuclear family in western European Christianity is more elusive and has often been neglected. The high evaluation of each person as a child of God and an immortal soul and the emphasis on love as the supreme virtue, though expressed in universal terms, lead in effect to emphasis on respect for personality and on affection in the immediate personal relations. Moreover, the absence of an assured status for the individual within a large kinship group intensifies the sense of need for security in intimate personal relations. Christians derive some assurance of security from membership in a divinely ordained community, especially within the Roman Catholic community or in small cohesive sects like the Amish. But the primary source of this security for most individuals in Western society is found in the nuclear family. This is generally assumed to be incomplete unless it includes children, as the unique expression of the creative partnership of husband and wife, as vital to a normal range of experience and interests, and as source of affectionate and, in varying degree, economic support in later life.

The intensity of the cultural compulsions toward marriage and parenthood in western European Christian society has not received adequate recognition from most social scientists. Alarmist writers, obsessed with visions of approaching catastrophe and eager to provide ammunition for recommended reforms, have gloated on 'the twilight of parenthood' and 'the decline of the West'. A different evaluation of the situation is presented by the late Ruth Benedict, a philosophical anthropologist—with direct

[1] Matthew xix, 5.

190

reference to the conditions in the United States. She comments on distinctive characteristics of the American family: free choice of spouse, freedom and privacy in separate homes, right of divorce, an unusual degree of 'potential leisure' due to modern techniques, and its non-authoritarian character. She states that '. . . often the family is made a convenient whipping boy among many peoples who disapprove of the way the world is going'.[1]

'In the United States the reason for having children is not, as it is in most of the world, the perpetuation of the family line down many generations. In most countries people have children because there must be someone to till the piece of land in the village where the family has lived for centuries, there must be an heir to inherit the *Hof*, or there must be a son to perform the ancestral rites. In our atomistic American families these motivations seldom arise. We have children, not because our parents are sitting in judgment, not because of the necessity of having an heir, but because we personally want them—whether as company in the home or to show our friends we can have them.'[2]

'The family in the United States is an institution remarkably adapted to our treasured way of life. The changes that are occurring in it do not mean that it is decaying and needs to be saved. It offers a long array of privileges. It needs more consideration in political tax-supported programs, by means of which many difficulties that beset it could be eradicated. Finally, Americans, in order to get the maximum happiness out of such a free institution as the family in the United States, need to parallel their privileges with an awakening responsibility.'[3]

The statistics on marriages and births in Europe and in the United States during the last decade (even with due allowance for effects due to changes in the timing of marriages and births) seem to support a moderately optimistic interpretation of the role of the family in contemporary Christian society. There are, to be sure, many forces in urban, industrial society that are inimical to the vitality of family relations. But there are also powerful cultural forces in Western European society that tend to endow the family with a high degree of vitality. It is reasonable to suggest that the high evaluation of marriage and parenthood in contemporary society (as contrasted for example with Hellenistic society) may be attributed in part to the influence of Christian traditions.

Another general aspect of Christianity which may have exerted an appreciable influence on fertility has come through its relation to the development of modern humanitarian principles, involving social action in the protection of children and interest in child development. The relation

[1] Ruth Benedict. 'Are Families Passé?', *Saturday Review of Literature*, 31 (52), 25 December 1948, p. 5.
[2] ibid., pp. 28–9.
[3] ibid., p. 29.

191

of these movements to fertility would seem to be two-fold. On the one hand, they have promoted interest in and high evaluation of children, and thus intensified motivation for parenthood. On the other hand, concern for children as persons, rather than as mere agents for the perpetuation of a group or the promotion of group interests, involves concern for health, opportunities for play and creative expression, and education. These cultural trends are conducive to the regulation of births in relation to economic resources. The net effect of the active development of these principles, especially within modern Christian civilization, may therefore have been to moderate rather than to elevate the trend of fertility.

The rise of Protestantism was associated with the rise of democracy, individualism, social mobility, and the enlarged role of the bourgeoisie in European society. It is apparent that the rise of the Protestant movement was associated with the emergence of forces that eventually led to widespread limitation of fertility in Western Europe and in America. This is implicit in the apparent association between Protestantism and the rise of capitalism; but the precise significance of this association is obscure.[1] The question of possible relations between the distinctive theological and moral tenets of different Protestant movements and fertility is extremely complex, and we shall not attempt to formulate any hypotheses on this subject.[2]

The significance of most data on comparative levels of fertility in Catholic and non-Catholic groups is limited unless the influence of other social factors that may be associated with denominational affiliation is controlled in some way. Such associated factors are controlled to some extent in a study by Whelpton and Kiser of native white women in one American city. It was found that in those with only elementary schooling there was little difference in fertility between Protestants and Catholics, the standardized rates for births to women of all ages being 224 and 230, respectively. Among Protestants with high school experience the rate drops to 123, and with college experience to 99. But among Catholics with high school experience the rate is 154, and with college experience it is 134.[3] Somewhat similar results were obtained by cross-tabulating religious affiliation with rental

[1] For a presentation of some theories on the relations between the 'Protestant Ethic' and the development of capitalism, see: R. H. Tawney, *Religion and the Rise of Capitalism*, New York, 1926. Also consult *From Max Weber: Essays in Sociology*, translated and edited by H. H. Gerth and C. Wright Mills, New York, 1946, Ch. XII, pp. 302–22. Weber's original contribution to this topic was entitled 'Die Protestantische Ethik und der "Geist" des Kapitalismus', *Archive für Sozialwissenschaft*, 20 and 21, Tübingen, 1904–5; later in *The Protestant Ethic and the Spirit of Capitalism*, translated by Talcott Parsons, London, 1930.

[2] We shall also fail to advance any specific hypotheses on relations between modern Judaism and fertility, for the same reason.

[3] P. K. Whelpton and Clyde V. Kiser, 'Social and Psychological Factors Affecting Fertility, 1. Differential Fertility Among 41,498 Native-White Couples in Indianapolis', *Milbank Memorial Fund Quarterly* 21 (3), July 1943, p. 261. The values cited here relate to couples both of whom had the specified characteristics.

values. The findings of this study indicate that in this urban population the high level of fertility among those with fewest advantages was relatively independent of religion, but that the influence of Catholicism tended to moderate the resort to family limitation at higher educational and income levels.

A study by Derksen of regional variations in the Netherlands shows that high fertility was associated with adherence to the Roman Catholic Church, but it was also associated to an almost equal degree with adherence to the Reformed Church (the most orthodox of the major Protestant denominations in this country). He studied the statistical relation to fertility of data on various characteristics of the population of the Netherlands, for the 11 provinces and 6 major cities. After experimentation with other variables, he found that a combination of (a) proportion of adherents to either the Roman Catholic Church or the Reformed Church (positively associated with high fertility) and (b) average of intelligence test scores by military conscripts (negatively associated with fertility) provided the best predictive index of local variations in fertility.[1] The two factors in this index were found to have fairly equal weight as statistical determinants of fertility.

A series of intensive studies, such as those cited above, in various situations would be required before one could draw any general inferences on this subject.

The nature of the decline of fertility in Ireland, mainly through delay or avoidance of marriage (with some shift in recent years toward periodic control of sex relations within marriage or other methods of regulating births) has surely been influenced by Catholic doctrine, but the degree to which the actual decline differed in effect from that expected in a population with different religious sentiments but under the same economic and social conditions cannot be measured. The fact that the earliest decline of fertility in Europe occurred in France and the recent spectacular decline of fertility in Italy show that the association between fertility and religious affiliation in Europe is less complete than has sometimes been assumed.

The problem of the relation of Catholicism to fertility in that half of the world's Catholic population that lives in countries influenced by Spanish and Portuguese conquests, and later characterized by slow development of mechanical industries, requires special attention in this study. The objectives and methods of these conquests and their subsequent influence

---

[1] Johannes D. D. Derksen. *Recent Demographic Changes in the Netherlands.* Mimeographed Paper, 1946. The formula used here is as follows: $g = 0.80\ k - 2.63\ q +$ constant:

$g =$ average number of legitimate births in 1931 per 1,000 married women under 50 years of age on 31 December 1930.

$k =$ percentage of the population belonging to the Roman Catholic Church and to the orthodox Reformed Church on 31 December 1930.

$q =$ average intelligence coefficient as given in Central Bureau of Statistics, *Intelligentieverhaudingen in Nederland*, 1935.

The multiple correlation coefficient was found to be equal to 0.935.

on economic and social development, were mainly determined by secular interests. Similarly, the relations of ecclesiastic doctrine and practice to the development of family relations and fertility in these countries require cautious consideration. The problem is carefully formulated in the following statement:

'There is another point worth noting, when it comes to discussion of sex practices in some regions where somewhat different values are set on human fertility than we are accustomed to in our milieu. Reference is made to areas where very early marriages or high fertility rates are taken for granted regardless of circumstances, or where the custom of irregular marriages or concubinage is prevalent. The full application of Christian teaching on sex would gradually modify the mores of these areas. Within the Catholic scheme of values, chastity holds high place. That means promiscuity and high illegitimacy rates will be affected where these values are accepted. Marriage will be held in greater esteem, and the practice of chaste continence when desirable or necessary, will be more readily approved. The conditions in certain so-called Catholic countries, which are well known to sociologists and students of population, do not reflect the Church's moral teaching. Rather they indicate how the weaknesses of certain cultural patterns persist despite the introduction of religious values. Genuine Christianization of peoples, then, would indirectly work toward a goal many social planners seek, namely stabilization of marriage and a sense of responsibility in making economic provision for offspring.'[1]

Informal conjugal relations, cultural indifference to fertility, and irresponsible procreation have been relatively widespread in many populations influenced by the Spanish and Portuguese conquests. As stated in the preceding quotation, these conditions are contrary to the intent of Catholic doctrine, which is directed toward the sanctity of family life and responsible parenthood. A proper treatment of this topic requires an appreciation of the essential principles of Catholic doctrine in this field.

Catholic theory regarding human fertility involves a conception of man and his place in the universe. Specifically it is based on a fundamental premise concerning the nature of marriage:

'The primary end of marriage is the procreation and education of children; the secondary end, mutual comfort and the remedy of concupiscence.'[2]

A second premise of Catholic theory is that ethical conduct involves conformity to the natural order:

'Moral obligation corresponds to the notion of an order established by creative intelligence and imposing itself upon human reason. The good,

[1] Rev. William J. Gibbons, S.J. 'The Catholic Value System in Relation to Human Fertility', in George F. Mair, editor, *Studies in Population:* Proceedings of the Annual Meeting of the Population Association of America, Princeton, 1949, p. 128.
[2] Code of Canon Law, canon 1013, No. 1. Cited by Gibbons, op. cit., footnote 13, p. 131.

for each and everything, is to be in its own place within the order. Moral good is the subordination of man's free activity to the order willed by God. . . . God, nature's Author, has created man with the nature he possesses for the purpose of having him attain happiness through the perfection of his nature. Man, by developing himself in conformity with his nature, tends at one and the same time toward perfection and happiness. Accordingly, prescribed acts are those which are necessary because they are required for man's development; permitted acts are those which are conformable to man's development but are not strictly demanded of it; and forbidden acts are those which are opposed to man's development. As St. Thomas put it, "We do not wrong God unless we wrong our own good".'[1]

It may be noted that the first of these premises is consonant with values held in many non-Catholic cultures and by many non-Catholic moralists, though most contemporary thinkers would prefer a more positive phrasing of the affectional aspects of married life and wider allowance for individual variations. The second premise is philosophical, but it, too, is consonant with the thinking of many non-Catholic philosophers.[2] The specific precepts of Catholic morality in this field, however, are not self-evident but are dependent on definitions formulated by ecclesiastic authority, which are frequently not accepted by non-Catholic thinkers and which are sometimes misinterpreted by some Catholics.

Catholic authority now recognizes the propriety under some conditions of the control of fertility within marriage by planned limitation of coitus to supposedly sterile periods in the menstrual cycle. The conditions of such practice are defined by principles of broad social significance. An initial intention at the time of marriage of one spouse 'to restrict the marriage right, not merely its use, to the sterile periods' is rejected as inconsistent with a valid marriage. Apart from this, it is deemed morally essential that the intention in observing those periods regularly be based 'on sufficient and secure moral grounds'.[3]

'The marriage contract which confers upon husband and wife the right to satisfy the inclinations of nature, sets them up in a certain state of life, the married state. But upon couples who perform the act peculiar to their state, nature and the Creator impose the function of helping the conservation of the human race. The characteristic activity which gives their state its value is the *bonum prolis*. The individual and society, the people and the state, the Church itself depend for their existence in

---

· [1] Jacques Leclercq, *Marriage and the Family*; a study in social philosophy, New York, 1945, p. 117. Cited by Gibbons, op. cit., footnote 5, pp. 130–1.
[2] Compare the criticism of the dichotomy in contemporary society between 'means' and 'ends', rendering the first degrading and the second desultory, and thus minimizing the significance of experience, in John Dewey, *Nature and Experience*.
[3] Pius XII, 'To the Italian Catholic Union of Midwives, October 29, 1951', in, *Moral Questions Affecting Married Life; Two Addresses of His Holiness Pope Pius XII* (English text). National Catholic Welfare Conference, Washington. Paragraphs 32–3.

the order established by God on fruitful marriage. Therefore, to embrace the married state, continuously to make use of the faculty proper to it and lawful in it alone, and, on the other hand, to withdraw always and deliberately with no serious reason from its primary obligation, would be a sin against the very meaning of conjugal life.

'There are serious motives, such as those often mentioned in the so-called medical, eugenic, economic, and social "indications", that can exempt for a long time, perhaps even the whole duration of the marriage, from the positive and obligatory carrying out of the act. From this it follows that observing the non-fertile periods alone can be lawful only under a moral aspect. Under the conditions mentioned it really is so. But if, according to a rational and just judgment, there are no similar grave reasons of a personal nature or deriving from external circumstances, then the determination to avoid habitually the fecundity of the union while at the same time to continue fully satisfying their sensuality, can be derived only from a false appreciation of life and from reasons having nothing to do with proper ethical laws.'[1]

The official church doctrine in these passages clearly enunciates the principle that this specific mode of behaviour must be evaluated in its full ethical context. It excludes from approval any intention to avoid the normal responsibilities of parenthood for hedonistic motives. The acceptance of responsibility for parenthood, which in Catholic theory and in the judgment of many non-Catholic moralists is a basic condition of true marriage, is here accepted as determined by the whole intent of the couple, rather than with reference to the intent of each specific act—there being obviously no intent to reproduce in specific sexual acts purposefully restricted to sterile periods.

A similar principle, involving interpretation of a specific act in terms of its whole context, is established with respect to surgical operations, but is limited in this case to considerations affecting the physical health of the individual concerned. 'Catholic theory has always recognized the lawfulness of surgical operations which might deprive the individual of some organ or limb, but which are necessary for preservation of life or proper health.'[2] But any surgical act, even at the request of the individual concerned, or any use of mechanical or chemical means to prevent conception or parturition—even though motivated by broad social considerations, comparable to those accepted as valid for the limitation of coitus to sterile periods—is rejected as a violation of the natural order:

'Every attempt on the part of the married couple during the conjugal act or during the development of its natural consequences, to deprive it of its inherent power and to hinder the procreation of a new life is immoral.'[3]

---

[1] ibid., paragraphs 35–6.
[2] Gibbons, op. cit., p. 116.
[3] From Encyclical *Casti connubii*, by Pius XI, 31 December 1930, cited by Pius XII, op. cit., paragraph 24.

The whole intent of these prescriptions is to promote ethical conduct and responsible parenthood:

'So much, then, for what concerns your apostolate [that of Catholic midwives] in winning couples for the service of motherhood not in the sense of blind slavery under the impulse of nature but of a use of the rights and duties of married people governed by the principle of reason and faith.'[1]

'La morale catholique ne répugne donc pas à une juste "rationalisation des naissances". Elle n'a jamais rejeté l'intervention de la raison, lorsque celle-ci ne prétendait pas s'affranchir de toute dépendance. Elle lui a, au contraire, toujours reconnu une haute valeur et l'a plus d'une fois défendue contre des détracteurs. Par suite même de l'importance qu'elle reconnaît à la vie sexuelle et à la diffusion de la vie, la morale chrétienne ne peut que souhaiter de les voir de moins en moins abandonnées à l'instinct, de plus en plus contrôlées par la raison, elle-même guidée par la morale et par la foi. Toute nouvelle possibilité dans cette voie doit être considérée comme heureuse.'[2]

'But human fertility, since man is a creature of reason and not mere instinct, must be a reasonable fertility. Multiplication of children as a result of license, or over-indulgence, or improvidence, implies varying degrees of moral guilt, depending on the extent to which the individual is personally responsible, and the relationship which exists between his own unrestrained sexual gratification and the future welfare of the children. The fertility that Christian tradition exalts is, therefore, rational fertility, not, as is sometimes thought, mere multiplication of offspring in itself.

'It is to be feared that on occasion, excessive concentration on the negative side of sex, and on the moral strictures which delimit its use, leads to false or deceptive conclusions. This inadequate approach, which tends to overlook the Church's positive teaching on human reproduction, is not confined to those social scientists who ignore the full range of Christian values; it also extends to some Catholics, who become excessively preoccupied with the moral prohibitions their Church makes known to them.'[3]

Objectively, Catholic doctrine has radically different effects in populations at different educational and social levels and with different religious experience. In well-disciplined, healthy, literate groups, with firm adherence to Catholic principles, it promotes a high sense of responsibility in parenthood. Sexual behaviour and fertility are controlled in high degree by

[1] Pius XII, op. cit., paragraph 42.
[2] Clement Mertens, S.J. 'Doctrine catholique et Problème de la population', *Nouvelle Revue Théologique*, December 1952, p. 1048.
[3] Gibbons, op. cit., p. 118.

cultural values. And demographic data indicate that in such groups there is opportunity for a reasonable control of fertility.

The effects of Catholic doctrine in this field tend to be quite different in populations handicapped by poverty, with meagre provisions for education, and habituated to laxity in marital relations. Here, the positive teachings of the Catholic Church concerning marital relations are widely neglected, as shown by census data and vital statistics. Nonconformity in such matters is popularly interpreted as an attribute of human frailty. On the other hand, a violation of the specific injunction against interference with the biological relation between coitus and procreation may be interpreted as a wilful defiance of divine law, involving risk of dire punishment. The specific injunction operates with a force similar to that of a taboo in primitive society. The power of the state has been directed in some countries to its enforcement. In any case, compliance with this injunction is easy in situations where the burden assumed by parents for the nurture and education of children is light. The observed tendency in such situations toward the dominance of biological factors over cultural factors is inconsistent with Catholic teaching as described in the preceding quotations. But Catholic teaching as sometimes interpreted and applied may have contributed to the persistence of this tendency.

GENERAL SURVEY OF CULTURAL CONDITIONS AFFECTING FERTILITY IN NON-INDUSTRIAL SOCIETIES

Before passing to the consideration of changes associated with the introduction of modern technology, it seems advisable to bring together various hypotheses already formulated concerning relations between culture and fertility in pre-industrial societies. We will arrange these hypotheses in schematic form, so as to consider their mutual implications, and their consistency or inconsistency. These hypotheses and some related inferences will be stated in dogmatic form. But all statements in this section are presented as hypotheses, and as providing a theoretical frame of reference for more intensive, scientific inquiries.

We have treated social structure and culturally defined values, in conjunction, as constituting the organization of a society. The term 'social structure' denotes the 'implicit constitution' of a society: its interacting, customary modes of behaviour that define personal relations and provide an accepted basis for the co-ordination of interests and activities. It includes forms of political control, household and village arrangements, modes of economic activity, religious institutions and obligations, kinship and family patterns, etc. The term 'cultural values' is understood to refer to attitudes and interests which are, in part, engendered by a particular social structure and which in turn motivate and direct the activities of the individuals who form a society.

198

Cultural Conditions and Fertility

The modes of behaviour and values implicit in the social organization of a society may tend to sustain a high level of fertility or may tend to induce, or at least to permit, restriction of procreative capacity. In either case, there is some significant relation between the particular cultural conditions and actual levels of fertility.

In other societies, especially those affected by widespread social disorganization, there may be little relationship between socially accepted values and actual levels of fertility. Under such conditions variations in fertility are largely determined by biological capacity and drives and by physiological conditions affecting fecundity, or by deviant personal interests.

The relation or lack of relation between culture and fertility, as stated in the preceding paragraphs, defines extreme types. In all actual societies there is some admixture in varying degrees of these contrasting relations.

The Relation of Ecology to Culture and Fertility

Primitive societies in more or less isolated and restricted areas, or forced by limitation of resources to move in small bands in search of sustenance, or pressed into unfavourable locations by the expansion of more powerful societies may include in their culture approved methods of restricting fertility. Or, perhaps more commonly, their cultures in the absence of strong motives for high fertility may be indifferent, ambivalent, or permissive with respect to anti-natal practices. However, there are many variations and deviations in these relations. One cannot safely draw inferences from knowledge about the environment of a people, including its relations with other people, about its cultural values with respect to fertility. For example, the Caucasus mountains might be defined as a 'refuge region'; but they support some nationalities with unusually high fertility.

Tribal societies that have established their positions in favourable situations through expansion at the expense of other peoples, or maintain such positions by effective resistance against competition with other peoples for the control of their resources, must have a strong social organization that provides efficient co-ordination of activities. Many of these societies emphasize unilineal descent, and have corporate kinship groups, such as clans and organized lineages. Such societies tend to generate strong cultural motives for high fertility. The relationships, again, are variable; but there appears to be some association between (a) a tendency toward dominance in inter-societal competition for control of resources; (b) social organization involving corporate kinship groups, and (c) cultural motivation for high fertility.

Problems arising in any such society through increase of population tend

199

to be solved through enlargement of the resource base, or the occupation of new resources. This process obviously cannot be continued indefinitely. It apparently reaches some limits, perhaps through increase in size beyond the capacity of a tribal society to maintain effective political control over its component parts, so that it becomes vulnerable in competition with other societies.

The expansion of a patrilineal society may be facilitated by polygyny which, whatever its intent, operates as a mechanism promoting the assimilation of foreign elements, and the increase of patrilineal lineages.

The social structure of tribal societies that move into areas where intensive cultivation of crops is already an established practice, and become subject to a political system organized on a territorial basis, is likely to be radically changed. The persistence in full vigour of corporate clans and lineages among the matrilineal Ashanti, now living in stable agricultural villages, raises interesting questions; but these reach beyond the scope of this study. The original social structure of a tribal society that is gradually transformed into a stable agrarian civilization may exercise a significant influence on its subsequent culture.

Corporate Kinship Groups

The apparent tendency of such groups, both to provide economic and personal support for mothers and children and to generate strong motives for high fertility has already been discussed at length in previous chapters, and was mentioned in the foregoing paragraph. Perpetual lineage groups, knit by a spiritual bond as descendants of the same ancestor and having common economic and political interests, engender strong ego-group identification. Each member has a sense of personal satisfaction in the achievements and expansion of his group and of his society. His 'ego' is enlarged by each child borne by a member of his group and suffers loss in the death of any member. The projection into the future of this ego-group identification creates a strong sense of responsibility for the bearing and nurture of progeny. It also stimulates competition for one's lineage against other lineages, and intensified competition between one's society and other societies.

Matrilineal and patrilineal lineages appear to generate equally strong motivations for high fertility, though they sometimes have radically different influences on husband-wife relations. The fertility of some matrilineal societies may be somewhat lowered by instability of conjugal unions. The control of fertility within junior age classes in some patriarchal societies with strong emphasis on military organization may also involve some reduction in births. But in both cases these tendencies are merely minor modifications of a general trend toward high fertility.

Group-families in Agrarian Civilizations

The group-family, even in its attenuated form as an ideal union of smaller family units forced by circumstances to maintain separate households, provides economic and personal support for the marriage and procreation of its members.

Group-family life as such, does not seem to have such an intrinsic tendency to provide strong motives for high fertility as do corporate lineages. But extended families are commonly associated with, and in part promoted by, traditional religious values and patterns of inter-group competition for prestige that do provide strong motivation for early marriage, and create anxiety to have surviving male heirs. The whole cultural context in which extended families tend to be idealized is likely to be conducive to high fertility.

Somewhat paradoxically, cultural provision for the adoption of children in Asiatic societies may facilitate some reduction of fertility—by permitting the substitution of a kinsman's son or a son-in-law to fill the role of true son and heir.

Cultural insistence on the marriage of women in an early phase of their childbearing period makes control of fertility within marriage the only possible means of restricting childbearing. The extent to which this may be done depends on (a) the means that are technically available; (b) cultural attitudes toward these means; and (c) the intensity of motivation for restriction of childbearing.

Emphasis on the Nuclear Family

In societies with collateral kinship systems and other aspects of informal social organization, the nuclear family may become the principal focus of social life. This principle, except for its presence in some societies with very primitive techniques, is a distinctive (almost unique) characteristic of Western European society and its derivative societies in the new world.

Emphasis on the nuclear family is sometimes confused with individualism. This confusion has vitiated much social and demographic theory. Some cultural motives are conducive to an emphasis on individual interests and self-determination. This is true of religious emphasis on personal relations between man and God, and of scientific or philosophical emphasis on critical thinking, as well as of more ordinary economic and hedonistic motives. The emphasis on individual values, which tends to be characteristic of an urban society, may be harmonized with broad cultural motives and social interests, including interest in primary family relations. But the conditions of modern urban life clearly bring increased emphasis on individual values.

On the other hand, though medieval European and early American societies were not organized mainly on a kinship structure, emphasis on the individual was subordinated to emphasis on the family, both in economic and in cultural affairs. Their cultures should be described as familistic, but with specific qualification. They were nuclear-familistic societies. Modern European and American society is still characterized by strong emphasis on nuclear family relations, but also by strong emphasis on individual values. Many of the problems of modern social life revolve around the attempt to achieve a harmonization of these distinct ideals, which are in part conflicting and in part complementary.

Any familistic society places a high valuation on children as essential to complete family life, but not necessarily on large families. Age at marriage and number of children may vary widely in societies with cultural emphasis on the nuclear family—as determined by economic and cultural conditions.

Relation of Formal Social Structure to the Control of Fertility

Stable intact societies vary in degrees of formal structure. A highly structured society which has standardized kinship relations, patterns of village organization, formal religious organization, and perhaps caste or class differentiation, age classes, etc., defines the status and roles of its constituent members, and places a high premium on conformity to social ideals. It also provides strong lines of social control.

A highly structured society will tend to enforce high fertility (a) if the objective conditions of its existence, such as wealth of resources, or opportunity for unlimited expansion through conquest, are favourable to high fertility, or (b) if its accepted religious or other cultural values prescribe high fertility.

Under different conditions, a high degree of social structure may be conducive to the restriction of fertility. This is, perhaps, best illustrated by the decline of fertility in recent years within the highly structured society of Japan. Tikopia, which provides the classic illustration of economically-motivated control of fertility in a stable primitive society, also has a highly structured social organization.

A loosely structured society may be characterized by very high or very low fertility as determined by cultural and economic conditions.

Social Disorganization

The break-up of traditional social structure and the conflict in values resulting from conquest, slavery, or other kinds of 'cultural shock' produce chaotic situations. A similar process may result from a sudden acquisition of new powers and new opportunities.

Slavery is a powerful instrument of deculturation, stripping persons of their kinsmen, gods, language, and ideals, and subjecting them to use as instruments of economic production and sexual satisfaction by their masters. The new powers and opportunities thus acquired by the masters may be almost equally disruptive of coherent social relations in their

202

affairs. The blight of slavery was evident in the late Graeco-Roman society; it still exerts a powerful influence in large areas of the Americas: the southern United States, the Caribbean, and Brazil.

Violent conquest involves similar processes of disorganization. We have already considered these effects in some African and Pacific areas. Similar effects were, of course, produced through the conquest of indigenous stocks in the Americas.

Social disorganization of a less violent character may result from sudden transitions from agricultural to commercial activities, movement from rural to urban environments, or rapid industrialization (as will be suggested in the following chapter). The degree and nature of such disorganization is determined, in part by the nature of the original society affected by new forces, in part by the conditions of the transition.

Acute social disorganization promotes conflicts and may release an undisciplined individualism. It is sometimes associated with increased spread of certain diseases. It may lead to sharp declines of fertility.

Fatalistic acceptance of circumstances is likely to emerge as a sequel to social disorganization. Such a tendency may also arise directly from processes of social disorganization in situations that do not involve personal or social conflicts. Accommodation to the need for security brings acceptance of orderly relations, and often promotes adherence to more or less stable conjugal unions. These processes tend toward the formation of an orderly society without firm attachment to cultural goals, and without strong aspirations. This involves cultural indifference to fertility. Such conditions tend to release biological impulses for reproductive behaviour, channelled within conventional limits, but otherwise modified only slightly by any cultural factors.

The maximum level of fertility in any population may require a combination of strong social support for family life, strong cultural motives for large families, good health, and perhaps a favourable genetic constitution.

Very high levels of fertility, sufficient to allow fairly rapid natural increase even under rather unfavourable conditions, are characteristic of many tribal societies and agrarian civilizations where social conditions make for early marriage, and provide strong support and some positive motivation for high fertility.

Equally high levels of fertility are found in some populations where there are no cultural prescriptions for early marriage and only weak cultural incentives to high fertility but where, on the other hand, there are no strong cultural or personal motivations for the control of reproductive behaviour. This is likely to be particularly characteristic of populations that have passed through a process of social disorganization to a more or less apathetic accommodation to the circumstances of their existence.

The relations of religion to fertility have been reviewed in the preceding section. These relations are so complex that no significant general conclusions appear that are capable of succinct formulation.

CHAPTER VI

The Relation of Cultural Conditions
to the Demographic Transition

THE NATURE OF THE DEMOGRAPHIC TRANSITION

Prior to the rise of modern technology the mere continuance of a population required, under different conditions, that each woman living through the childbearing period bear on the average some four to six or more children. It required, in other terms, the actual realization of some 50 to 75 per cent or more of the total procreative capacity of the population. A higher fertility was needed to offset unusual calamities, such as loss in war, or to provide increase in population or expansion into new territory. About half or more of the female infants died before they reached the centre of the reproductive period. Similar conditions have prevailed until recently in most non-industrial societies. But with the spread of modern sanitation— an aspect of modern technology that is capable of relatively rapid diffusion —spectacular declines in mortality are being achieved in many regions. In the technically most advanced societies less than 10 per cent of the female infants born alive now die before reaching the centre of the child-bearing period, and the loss is less than 25 per cent in many countries with low levels of living. Further advances in vitality during the next few decades are fairly inevitable.

The acceleration of the growth of population in non-industrial countries due to declines in mortality creates serious public problems. Increases in consumption needs, even at the previous levels of living, tend to absorb increases in production. The need for utilizing the labour of the increasing child population hampers the development of the skills essential for efficient use of new techniques. Therefore, per capita investment in the development of human resources, as well as in productive equipment, tends to be retarded. These relations hold even in undeveloped countries with low initial density of population. They are complicated by other grave problems in regions where the population is already large in relation to land and other natural resources. Such public problems do not immediately influence the attitudes and behaviour of most individuals. But any wide-spread introduction of new techniques does immediately change economic relations between parents and children. The new techniques require new skills for their effective operation. The required investment in the nurture and education of each child, to meet new standards and to equip youth for effective participation in a technically advanced society, rises. Conversely, the economic contribution to the parental family expected from a child before he assumes family responsibilities on his own account declines toward zero.

These changes in objective conditions eventually affect the attitudes of individuals toward size of family. The higher vitality of children eliminates one factor in the motivation for large families. The change in economic relations is probably even more powerful, as parents accept new standards for child development and education. The spread of science, commerce, and technology promotes a realistic appraisal of such objective relations. Increase in opportunities stimulates democratic aspirations and promotes confidence in the capacity of individuals to achieve desired goals. These changes tend to bring a reduction of fertility levels. The new levels, as determined by personal preferences, apparently tend to be located somewhere in the vicinity of those required for replacement of population under present conditions of mortality. Relatively few couples in contemporary societies desire to remain childless or to have only one child. The number of such couples is usually exceeded by the number of those who desire to have three or more children. Of course, the achieved levels differ from the preferred levels due to sterility on the one hand and to unwanted births on the other hand. Actual performance is powerfully influenced by changing circumstances. In any case, the average size of completed families appears, at present, to be fairly constant in the technically most advanced countries—somewhere in the vicinity of the replacement level. Fertility falls below this level in congested urban centres and in periods of depression; it rises above this level in situations more favourable to family life and in periods of prosperity. It must, however, be emphasized that the present apparent equilibrium between births and deaths in Western European societies has no foundation apart from the social structure and culture of these societies.

The shift from high mortality and high fertility to moderate mortality and moderate fertility which has taken place in many countries in association with the development of scientific and mechanical technology is frequently referred to (as in the title of this chapter) as 'the demographic transition'. This term is useful in indicating a general tendency; but it may convey a false impression of simplicity and uniformity. There is no necessary co-ordination between movements of mortality and movements of fertility, except that a decline of mortality creates one condition favourable to a decline in fertility. In the United States the decline of the crude birth rate began to exceed the decline of the crude death rate more than a hundred years ago, as shown by a continuing decline in the rate of natural increase from 1800–20 to the 1930's. In France the declines of fertility and of mortality ran fairly parallel during the nineteenth century and the early decades of the twentieth century. In most European countries the decline in fertility lagged far behind the decline in mortality. In some Asiatic and

Latin American countries there have been large declines in mortality with no indication to date of any general decline in fertility.

The analysis of ways in which cultural conditions influence trends of fertility in relation to economic and social development in non-industrial societies is a subject of critical importance. Our investigation moves in this direction. But it has seemed necessary to give primary attention in this respect to certain basic, preliminary topics: namely, the nature and limits of human procreative capacity, general relations between cultural conditions and fertility in non-industrial societies prior to the impact of modern technology, and problems of methodology.

In the present chapter we will review some information on changes in fertility, or the absence of such change, under particular cultural conditions, in relation to economic and technical developments. But this review must be even more cursory than the previous survey of general relations between cultural conditions and fertility in non-industrial societies. It is presented as an invitation to new research rather than as a summary of established findings.

THE DEMOGRAPHIC TRANSITION IN EUROPE: FRANCE AND ENGLAND

The cultural conditions favourable to a partial control of fertility in pre-modern Europe were considered in Chapter V—with major attention to the pattern of family relations, with emphasis on the nuclear family, in relation to systems of land tenure and inheritance.

The control of fertility in Europe prior to the nineteenth century was achieved in the main through social barriers to early marriage. The economic motives enforcing delay or avoidance of marriage probably led occasionally to restriction of births within marriage, by avoidance of sexual relations after several children had been born or by modes of incomplete intercourse, or by induced abortions. As evidenced by the reports of older married couples in England, obtained in a recent survey, control of pregnancies by couples married in the early decades of the twentieth century was still effected largely by 'non-appliance' methods.[1] There is indirect evidence that this was true of the early movement toward control of pregnancies within marriage in France. In Germany and in Russia, even in the twentieth century, control of fertility within marriage seems to have been effected in large part by abortion. In its later phases the trend toward family limitation in Europe was facilitated and accelerated by new contraceptive techniques. The initial movements toward limitation of families in Europe, however, were largely independent of any inventions in this field.

[1] E. Lewis-Faning. *Papers of the Royal Commission on Population*, Volume I: *Report on an Inquiry into Family Limitation and Its Influence on Human Fertility During the Past Fifty Years*, Table 38, p. 54.

It is important to bear in mind certain general conditions in the social background of early modern Europe which affected later trends in fertility: Europe at the beginning of the industrial era had a social structure favourable to the control of fertility; it had at its disposal means for supplementing the control of fertility through delay of marriage by a partial control of fertility within marriage; but the nature of these means was such that they were likely to be applied only under the stimulus of new and strong motivations.

A new stimulus toward restriction of fertility of families was provided by the development of modern technologies, as they affected vitality and economic relations. All this is common demographic knowledge. What we do not understand, but need to understand, is this: 'By what social processes did technical and economic changes in Europe induce new personal motives for family limitation, and how were these processes affected by different social and cultural conditions?' An understanding of these relations would contribute directly to a correct appraisal of the possibilities of demographic transition in other countries, and of the relation of various social conditions to possible future trends.

The nature of the problem with which we are concerned is suggested by asking two questions which appear as enigmas to anyone who assumes an automatic relation between the rise of industry and the decline of fertility. First, 'why did a general decline of fertility not begin in England in advance of similar declines as in central and northern Europe, in view of England's obvious lead in the processes of industrialization?' Secondly, 'why did a general decline of fertility in France begin some 70 to 100 years earlier than in any other European country?' We can offer no solution to these questions. We can merely cite some relevant information, and raise some specific questions. We will first note some information on social and demographic conditions in England.

According to official statistics the crude birth rate in England and Wales, 1870–74, was 35.5 per 1,000. This was somewhat above the rates indicated by official statistics for the 1850's and 1860's; but the apparent rise was due, at least in part, to improvement in the registration of births. It can, however, be asserted with confidence that there was no general trend toward lower fertility in England and Wales during the third quarter of the nineteenth century. A significant decline, though at first very gradual, began in the 1870's. The maternal gross reproduction ratio for 1880–82 was 2.8 per cent below that for 1870–72.[1] The corresponding ratios for 1890–92, 1900–02, and 1910–11 were 12.8 per cent, 23.4 per cent, and 37.3 per cent, respectively, below the 1870–72 level.[2]

The Industrial Revolution had brought about a basic transformation of English economy some 50 years before the beginning of the general

[1] D. V. Glass. 'Changes in Fertility in England and Wales, 1851 to 1931', in Lancelot Hogben, editor, *Political Arithmetic*. New York, 1938, p. 168.
[2] ibid., p. 169.

decline in fertility. New manufacturing industries had advanced rapidly during the era of the Napoleonic Wars (1796–1815). The Liverpool-Manchester railroad, linking these important industrial and transportation centres, was opened in 1830. Iron had been already introduced into ship construction, and steam-power into navigation. A population dependent on mining for its maintenance had been formed in the coal and iron districts. The condition of the new industrial proletariat was a source of unrest, and a cause of political concern. The provisions of the Poor Law for the relief of paupers and the Corn Law passed in 1815 to aid agriculture by curtailing the importation of grain were subjects of prolonged controversy. The meagre provisions of early factory acts in 1802 and 1816 were replaced by the passage in 1833, over vigorous opposition, of a new Factory Act. This prohibited the employment of children under 9 years old in textile mills; limited the employment of those 9–13 years to 48 hours per week, and of those 13–18 to 69 hours per week; required provision of schooling two hours per day for employed children under 13 years; and established a system of factory inspection.

Census data of 1911 on numbers of children borne by surviving couples (husband and wife both living in unbroken marriage) show little change in fertility between couples married 1851–61, and those married 1861–71. But couples married, 1871–81, had on the average 9 per cent fewer children in the course of their married life than those married in the previous decade. There were, however, some significant differences between occupational classes in the marital fertility of the oldest surviving couples. Among couples married 1861–71 those in the professional and administrative groups (Class I) had 12 per cent fewer children than the general average. This occupational group also led in the subsequent general decline. The skilled worker and intermediate worker groups (Classes III and IV) conformed closely, as regards marital fertility, to the general average, and changes in successive marriage cohorts proceeded at the average rate. In the special class of textile workers (Class VI), the 1861–71 cohort showed a marital fertility 6 per cent below the general average, but the subsequent rate of decline in this group (as shown by the 1871–81 and 1881–86 cohorts) ran parallel to that in the whole population. Among unskilled workers (Class V) and employed agricultural workers (Class VIII), and miners (Class VII) the initial marital fertility of the 1861–71 cohorts was above that of the general population—by 4 per cent in the first two classes, and by 13 per cent in the case of the miners. Declines in fertility in these classes also lagged behind the general trend. The numbers of children ever born to surviving couples married 1881–86, classified by occupational status of husbands in 1911, as percentages of the average numbers ever born to surviving couples of all classes married 1851–61, were as follows:[1] all classes, 82 per cent; professional and administrative (Class I), 63 per

---

[1] The miscellaneous group of retired workers (Class II) is omitted.

cent; textile workers (Class VI), 76 per cent; skilled workers (Class III), 83 per cent; intermediate workers (Class IV), 84 per cent; unskilled workers (Class V), 90 per cent; agricultural labourers (Class VIII), 94 per cent; miners (Class VII), 102 per cent.

In interpreting these data on completed marital fertility, it must be taken into account that they may have been affected by differences in the proportions of spouses who survived to 1911 and by differences in ages at marriage. The differences are, nevertheless, very interesting. The lead of the upper occupational class, with greatest opportunity for personal achievement and greatest involvement in education, is clearly significant. In the case of the textile workers, the previous decline of child labour and the continuing opportunity for employment of women were undoubtedly factors affecting the relatively low fertility of this group at the beginning of the period under observation, and its subsequent decline in step with that in the general population. The fertility of unskilled workers, most of whom must have been employed in urban occupations, was the same as that of agricultural labourers in the marriages of 1861–71, and the subsequent decline was only slightly in advance of the latter. Employment in mining tended to sustain a high level of fertility.

A different approach to the analysis of changing fertility in England and Wales in the late nineteenth century is provided by an investigation by Glass of information on political areas.[1] There was considerable variation in current levels of fertility among counties and among component districts during the third quarter of the nineteenth century. Possible declines in fertility appear in some areas from the 1860's to the 1870's, matched by apparent rises in other districts. But there is no obvious and consistent pattern in these regional variations. The trend of fertility in London at this time was not very different from that of the general population. The Welsh mining district and some areas of heavy industry in England, Durham for example, show conspicuously high fertility. Textile districts generally show low fertility. But areas of initially low and declining fertility also include some predominantly agricultural counties, such as Cardiganshire in northwestern Wales. It is interesting to find that Rochdale, famous for its impetus to workers' education and consumer co-operatives, is among the localities with initially low and declining fertility.

The systematic analysis of these variations provides some more precise findings. Correlations among registration counties in England and Wales between (a) gross reproduction ratios and (b) proportions of unmarried women among those aged 20–44 years were as follows:[2] 1850–52, 0.742 $\pm$ 0.061; 1870–72, 0.841 $\pm$ 0.040; 1890–92, 0.849 $\pm$ 0.038; 1910–12, 0.724 $\pm$ 0.064; 1930–32, 0.433 $\pm$ 0.110.

There was also a significant positive correlation (0.520 $\pm$ 0.098) between changes in gross reproduction ratios and changes in proportions of un-

[1] Glass, op. cit.
[2] ibid., p. 196.

209

married women, by counties, from 1871 to 1891. But this relation becomes insignificant (0.165 ± 0.131) during the next 20-year period. Finally, this relation was reversed during the period 1911 to 1931.[1] It seems reasonable to infer that the social forces that at first had found expression largely in severe postponement or avoidance of marriage later led to increased emphasis on methods of controlling fertility within marriage.

Employment of children was positively correlated with fertility around the middle of the nineteenth century. Employment of children under 10 years of age had largely disappeared prior to 1851; but the proportion of children aged 10–14 years who were gainfully occupied in 1851 ranged from 13 per cent in Middlesex County to 44 per cent in the West Riding of Yorkshire, with 28.3 per cent as the average for the whole country. This average declined only slightly during the next 20 years, to 26.3 per cent in 1871, but more rapidly thereafter, to 14.4 per cent in 1911. In spite of the relative constancy of child labour from 1851 to 1871, the correlation among counties between gross reproduction ratios and percentages of children 10–14 years who were occupied dropped from 0.489 ± 0.116 in 1851 to 0.291 ± 0.140 in 1871. By 1911 the correlation had become negligible and insignificant. There is a suggestion of some correlation by counties between declines in child labour and declines in fertility, but the correlation (0.145 ± 0.149) is low and not statistically significant. Child labour may have exerted a positive influence on the maintenance of fertility in England during the first half of the nineteenth century, but this influence did not appear as a major factor affecting changes in fertility during the last quarter of the century.[2]

On the other hand, there was no pronounced change in the degree of the employment of women from 1851 to 1911. The proportion of women aged 15 and over who were gainfully employed rose slightly from 38.2 per cent in 1851 to 41.1 per cent in 1871, but declined to 35.5 per cent in 1911. But the negative correlation among counties between employment of women and fertility rose from a low and dubious value in 1850–52 to a high value in 1910–12 as follows—using proportions of women who were employed, standardized with respect to the proportion of women who were aged 20–44 years:[3] 1850–52, 0.156 ± 0.149; 1870–72, 0.422 ± 0.125; 1910–12, 0.708 ± 0.067.

There was some shift over this period in types of female employment. The proportions employed in agriculture, clothing manufacture, and textiles declined; the proportions employed in commerce and distribution rose; the proportion in domestic service (about one-third) remained fairly co⌐

---

[1] In formal terms, the correlation between changes in reproduction ratios and changes in per cent unmarried in this interval (0.510 ± 0.100) is similar to that in 1871–91. Bu the proportion of unmarried women declined from 1911–1931, whereas it had risen from 1871–91.

[2] ibid., pp. 209–10.

[3] ibid., p. 205.

stant. This shift in types of employment does not seem to have been sufficiently drastic to account for the changed relation between female employment and fertility indicated by these correlations. There was also a rising correlation among counties during this period between percentages of women aged 15 years and over who were employed and percentages of women 20–44 years who were unmarried, leading to the conclusion that postponement of marriages accounts in large part for the apparent influence of the employment of women on the decline of fertility.[1]

The late origin and diffuse pattern of the decline of fertility in England suggest the influence of forces of a general character in English society, generated by advances in commerce, industry, and education, tending toward restriction of fertility, but long held in check by counterforces tending to sustain a rather high level of fertility. Before forming any hypothesis about conditions exercising indirect positive or negative influences on fertility, we will take account of some trends and conditions in France during the late eighteenth and the nineteenth century.

Fertility and mortality in France seem to have been fairly constant during the first three-fourths of the eighteenth century, as evidenced by a reconstruction of the distribution by age of the population in 1775, an analysis of the level of mortality, and incidental information. Fertility was somewhat above mortality, allowing an average natural increase of about 4 per 1,000 per year from 1700 to 1775. This would indicate a maternal gross reproduction ratio in the vicinity of 2.50 (about 5.1 live births per woman living through the childbearing period), slightly above the estimated ratio in 1771–75. Precise values cannot be provided, but the approximate accuracy of these conclusions is supported by concurrent evidence.[2]

A general decline of fertility (which continued into the twentieth century) began in France in the 1770's, about one hundred years before there is any definite evidence of a comparable trend in England. The estimated gross reproduction ratios during the period of initial decline run as follows:[3] 1771–75, 2.39; 1776–80, 2.36; 1781–85, 2.32; 1786–90, 2.24; 1791–95, 2.16; 1801–05, 2.01.

The precise values are subject to error; but the evidence that fertility was lower around the turn of the century than it had been in the 1770's is conclusive. The decline continued fairly constantly thereafter, somewhat more slowly and irregularly during the first three-fourths of the eighteenth century, and more rapidly thereafter to the time of World War I.

The estimated average age of women at marriage or remarriage around 1770 was 27 years. Their average age at first marriage was in the vicinity of 25 years. The average was perhaps slightly higher than in the twentieth

[1] loc. cit.
[2] Jean Bourgeois-Pichat. 'Evolution de la population française depuis le XVIIIᵉ siècle', *Population* 6 (4), pp. 635–62.
[3] ibid., p. 644.

century, but the difference in any case was very slight. The proportion of women marrying also remained relatively constant. The decline of fertility in France throughout its whole course was almost wholly a function of increasing control of fertility within marriage.[1]

The decline in France, as in England, was widely diffused. It moved at different rates in different departments at different times, but it is difficult to establish any general correlations between the social characteristics of various districts and rates of decline. In 1851–61, the average number of legitimate births per 1,000 married women aged 15–44 years was higher in 10 departments classed as 'most rural' than in the remainder, the rate of this group being 236. But the rate in the next most rural group (214) was not significantly different from that in the most urban group of departments (217), and the variation among the intermediate groups was small and irregular.[2] This seems to indicate that there was resistance to decline in some relatively isolated rural districts, but that degree of urbanization did not exert a major influence on the incidence of the decline. In 1801, the proportion of the total French population in cities of 100,000 or more (2.8 per cent) was lower than in the Netherlands, England, Italy, Spain, or Portugal; the corresponding percentage in 1870 (8.3 per cent) was still below that of the Netherlands or England, though above that of Italy, Spain, or Portugal.[3]

The long-time trend of fertility has led to generally low reproduction rates in the centre and south, with relatively high rates in the northern and north-western departments, including some of the principal areas of heavy industry. On the other hand, fertility has been consistently lower in Paris than in the nation as a whole.

A thesis advanced by Goldstein that fertility in the later nineteenth century was higher in 'proletarian districts' whether urban or rural (as indicated in the latter case by a high ratio of agricultural labourers to proprietors) is supported by some specific evidence. During the period 1876–96, the general maternity rate (birth per 1,000 women 15–44 years) was about one-seventh higher in the most industrial departments (as measured by per capita consumption and industrial capital) than in each of three groups of non-industrial departments. But in a group of non-industrial departments with the lowest rural level of living, the general maternity rate was nearer to that of the highly industrial group (the rate for the latter being only 6 per cent above that for the former). He also advanced the thesis that the decline of fertility during the last quarter of the nineteenth century was least rapid in the 'proletarian' districts; but Spengler presents contrary evidence on this point.[4]

[1] ibid., p. 647.
[2] Joseph J. Spengler. *France Faces Depopulation*. Durham, North Carolina, 1938, p. 87.
[3] ibid., pp. 26, 29.
[4] ibid., pp. 81–2. Reference to Goldstein, *Bevölkerungsprobleme und Berufsgliederung in Frankreich*, Berlin, 1900.

The initial decline of marital fertility in France, like the later decline in England, was not associated with any important innovations in contraception. The spread of douching as a contraceptive practice did not come until a later time.

It has sometimes been argued that increased emphasis on equal division of family property in France in the late eighteenth century and recognition of this principle in the Napoleonic Civil Code was a major factor in promoting control of fertility among French peasants. In the previous chapter we expressed doubt about the validity of this assumption on theoretical grounds. In this connexion it may be noted that Levasseur found that, contrary to common belief, family size was as great in more subdivided as in less subdivided agricultural areas of France.[1] It is, however, possible that, apart from any inherent association between one or another inheritance pattern, any interference with traditional and accepted modes of transmitting property by the promulgation of a uniform code would intensify the problem of inheritance and promote anxiety about the number of heirs among whom a family holding must be divided—or, if the code had an opposite intent, about the number of sons who would be left without property.

It may well be that the early decline of fertility in France was in some way related to social and cultural conditions leading to the Revolution or with the progress of the Revolution. One aspect of this possible association is the intellectual revolt against authority and dogma of all kinds. It could be argued that the individualistic and rationalistic attitudes thus engendered in French culture were important in making new economic incentives for family limitation effective that would otherwise have been checked by inhibitions and social disapproval. This suggestion may have some force, but it cannot be easily tested. A critical consideration is the extent to which such attitudes really affected the general population, especially in rural communities.

A somewhat similar but still more elusive thesis could be framed with reference to influence on distinctive values in French culture of the luxury centred in the royal court and the appropriation of its creations by the republic in the revolutionary movement. This thesis is subject to the same objections and difficulties as the first.

Consideration should perhaps be given to the possible effects of the spread of educational opportunities and rising interest in child development. These tendencies, though elevating the role of parents, increased the economic and psychological demands of each child on the resources of his parents. According to Mathorez, children in the upper and middle classes received little parental attention under the old regime—responsibility for their care being transferred soon after their birth to nurses, prior

---

[1] E. Levasseur. *La Population Française*. Paris, 1889–92, 3 vols. II, p. 75, III, pp. 176–8. (Citation from J. J. Spengler, *France Faces Depopulation*.)

213

to the rise of public interest during the eighteenth century in a movement for the better care of children.[1] The publication of Rousseau's *Emile* in 1762 and the work of Pestalozzi, his more painstaking contemporary Swiss compatriot, attracted attention to the subtler, personal needs of children. Aries cites literary evidence to the effect that prior to this time, authors rarely gave much attention to children but that about this time children begin to appear as interesting literary subjects.[2] But these tendencies were not confined to any particular country.

Measures for establishing public schools, introduced by Talleyrand and by Condorcet, were passed by French Assemblies in 1791 and 1792. Napoleon emphasized the importance of education, and centralized the school system under the authority of the State (Edict of 1808). However, there was no legislative provision for compulsory elementary school attendance until 1882. Only 14 per cent of all French brides had been able to sign their names, 1681–90. The proportion had risen to 27 per cent, 1786–90, but the later rise was only gradual (35 per cent, 1816–20; 53 per cent, 1854–56) until the last quarter of the century. The trend was similar, though more advanced, among husbands. 'Early French studies reveal no negative correlation between mortality or births per marriage by region and ability to sign name.'[3]

' The early development of education in England was perhaps more localized, and had stronger social class associations than in France—at least prior to the Education Bill in 1870. Parents in London were required to pay fees for enrolment of their children in elementary schools until 1891, though prior to that time they could seek remission of these fees on the ground of poverty.[4] However, the actual extension of provisions for education seems to have progressed at fairly similar tempos in France and in England.

Attention should perhaps be focused on the social aspects of economic developments in England and in France during the late eighteenth and early nineteenth centuries. The expansion of mechanical industries in England took place in a population that already included large impoverished elements who had lost their status in the earlier agricultural society. There had been increasing concentration of landed property in England during the eighteenth century—with wealth gained in part through colonial enterprises and foreign trade, and in response to the rising commercial importance of wool. The process was accelerated during the latter half of the century and was substantially completed before the end of the Napoleonic Wars. An estimated one-third of all holdings of independent farmers in 1740 were engrossed before 1788, prior to the spurt of statutory

[1] J. Mathorez. *Les étrangers en France sous l'ancien régime.* Paris, 1919, 2 vols. I, p. 22.
[2] Philippe Aries. *Histoire des populations françaises et les attitudes devant la vie depuis le XVIIIᵉ siècle.* Paris, 1948, p. 474.
[3] Spengler, op. cit., p. 74.
[4] *The New Survey of London Life and Labour.* London, 1934, pp. 102–3.

enclosures at the beginning of the nineteenth century.[1] The plight of English workers again became acute with the discharge of military personnel after 1815, and the depression that followed the end of the Napoleonic Wars. Meanwhile, great wealth, accumulated through trade and early ventures in manufacturing in the hands of a competent and enterprising mercantile class, was available for the financing of large-scale industries; and Britain's political situation assured a world market for its products. The new industrial recruits, many of them pauperized by the shift in agriculture, had to work long hours and to place their children at work for low wages. Many of them had moved from the social context of village life into crowded and unsanitary urban dwellings in socially-unstructured settlements adjacent to the mills, docks, and mines.

A depressed class—whether impoverished farm tenants or an urban proletariat—does not develop the intense motivations required for the effective control of fertility, especially when only crude and unpleasant methods are available for this purpose. A half-century passed before the progress of British economic and social changes, motivated in part by humanitarian movements and in part by the formation of workmen's associations and political agitation, provided a basis for the rising aspirations that motivated a trend toward lower fertility.

Aries suggests that the rapid formation of large-scale industries retarded the demographic transition in England.[2] But the tempo of the change may have been less important that its antecedent conditions. As Ashton insists, the rise of mechanical industries was not primarily responsible for the poverty associated with this movement.[3] It may have contributed to a trend toward social disorganization. But the basic problem had already been created by the disruption of agricultural society; the development of mechanical industries provided the. means whereby this problem was eventually overcome.

Economic development in France in the late eighteenth and early nineteenth centuries brought diverse social changes. Agricultural society remained intact, and had improved its status as it emerged from feudal conditions. As De Tocqueville showed, nearly a century ago, French cultivators had been strengthening their hold on the land over a long period; the Revolution climaxed this trend and established the legal rights of the cultivators by destroying the remaining feudal prerogatives of the aristocratic class.[4]

Meanwhile, in the absence of large concentrated wealth in the hands of great masters of commerce, new opportunities for commerce and mechanical production stimulated a multitude of small ventures. The number and diversity of these enterprises aroused new aspirations for economic achieve-

[1] P. Mantoux. *The Industrial Revolution in the Eighteenth Century.* 1928, pp. 140–6.
[2] Aries, op. cit., pp. 348–53.
[3] T. S. Ashton. *The Industrial Revolution, 1760–1830.* London, 1948.
[4] Alexis De Tocqueville. *L'ancien régime et la révolution.* Paris, 1856.

ment, which were not limited to a small class but which were widespread. In other words, the situation stimulated a vigorous social mobility.

In the *atelier*, employees were personally associated with the *patron*, and the *patron* maintained social relations with professional groups.

'Sans oublier son passé rustique, soumis aux influences de son entourage bourgeois, le monde ouvrier, grâce à la lenteur de l'industrialisation, ne parvenait pas à se constituer en société à part. . . . Chez eux subsistait toujours une place pour le calcul individuel, l'organisation méthodique de la vie. La classe existait sans doute, mais elle restait ouverte, on pouvait en sortir, et on le savait.'[1]

The basic socio-economic structure of French society, with the nuclear family as the primary unit and with strong informal kinship and community relations, remained intact, but was modified to permit greater mobility. At the same time French culture was permeated with new aspirations, greater emphasis on individual rights, and a challenge to traditional authority and values. These conditions found political expression in the Revolution, and the drama of the Revolution intensified their force. They also gave added impetus to motives for postponing or curtailing the obligations of parenthood, which had long been operative in Western European society. In the new cultural milieu, the French populace sought means of achieving this goal without sacrifice of the benefits of conjugal life.

It is significant that in France the demographic transition began before the objective conditions of life were profoundly changed by new technical processes. According to the estimates of Bourgeois-Pichat, cited above, there had been no significant change in mortality in France prior to the initial decline of fertility. Increase in the vitality of infants cannot, therefore, have exerted a significant influence on attitudes toward prolificacy, as it may have done in many other countries. It is true that increase in commerce and mechanical crafts opened new economic opportunities, but the changes in this respect were at first gradual and relatively modest. Such technical changes did become more important as the nineteenth century progressed, and these changes were associated with further declines of fertility. But they do not appear to have been operative in France in the late eighteenth century with sufficient force, in comparison with their force in other European countries, to account for the great difference in the timing of trends toward widespread limitation of fertility within marriage.

The distinction between social structure and culture may be useful here. We suggest, as an hypothesis, that the distinctive character of the demographic transition in France may be due mainly to distinctive changes in personal relations, attitudes and values, i.e., in the cultural aspects of its social life.

[1] Aries, op. cit., p. 375.

216

On the other hand, we suggest that in interpreting the persistence of high levels of fertility in England, after there had been profound changes in its economic technology, emphasis must be given to changes in social structure. Changes in the economic basis and structure of agricultural society had led to the formation of an impoverished, unskilled industrial proletariat. In the absence of advances in industry, this dispossessed farm population would have remained an impoverished rural proletariat, perhaps with equal or greater indifference to fertility. It may be that the 'brutal force' of early large-scale industrial processes, bringing families into crowded and unsanitary city slums, also exercised a depressing influence. In any case, the situation provided no real basis for widespread and confident aspiration toward improvement of the conditions of life by individual effort. On this hypothesis, processes of 'social disorganization' in England during the late eighteenth and early nineteenth centuries are viewed as the major counter-forces that checked the force of factors tending toward restriction of fertility.

The preceding discussion is grossly inadequate to the complex problems to which it has been directed. We have been unable, within the time at our disposal, to take proper account of the rich literature on the demographic transition in these two countries. And we have not ventured to review situations and trends in other European countries at all.

In any case, the record is clear on two negative points of theoretical importance: first, a trend toward increased control of fertility is not necessarily dependent on large-scale industrialization; secondly, the rapid introduction of mechanical industries into a previously non-industrial society does not automatically bring a trend toward increased control of fertility.

The formulation in proper perspective of the complex factors creating positive motives for restriction of fertility, with varying force in different situations at different times, is far more difficult.

THE RELEASE OF FERTILITY IN COLONIAL AMERICA AND ITS SUBSEQUENT DECLINE

Societies of European origin in the Americas generally had at first significantly higher fertility than the parent populations in Europe. This appears most clearly in the English and French colonies in North America, where analysis of demographic trends is not complicated by the fusion of European and indigenous populations.

The average woman living through the childbearing period in France in the eighteenth century had about 5 live births during her life. This resulted in a crude birth rate in the vicinity of 40 per 1,000. The level of fertility was then definitely lower in the northern European countries. In England it appears to have been similar to, or somewhat below that in France. The general level of fertility in both the French and English colonies in America during the eighteenth century was about 25 per cent, more or less, above the general level in France or England.

In French Canada the crude birth rate apparently rose after 1680, as the distribution by age and sex approached the normal pattern for a rapidly increasing population. The average crude rate by decades from 1691–1700 through 1731–40 ranged between 54 and 58 per 1,000.[1] After some critical review of findings on this subject, we have concluded that on the average a woman living through the childbearing period in the early French settlement apparently had about 9 births.[2] Unfortunately, there is little information on the trend of fertility in this colony from the middle of the eighteenth to the middle of the nineteenth century. In the mid-nineteenth century the crude birth rate in Quebec Province was in the vicinity of 45 per 1,000; it declined very gradually to about 40 per 1,000 at the beginning of the twentieth century, 1901–10.[3] The general maternity rate, taken as births per 1,000 women aged 15–49 years, 1859–60, was about 193 in Quebec (indicating about 6.4 births per woman living through the childbearing period) as compared with a rate around 100 in France at this time. The proportions of married women in specific age classes in Quebec Province at this time were not significantly different from those in France.[4]

Fertility in the British American colonies may have been somewhat lower in the eighteenth century than it was in French Canada, but not greatly so. The most significant contrast between British America and French America is not in their initial levels of fertility but in the striking divergence between these populations in later trends.

Thompson and Whelpton derive a crude birth rate of 55 per 1,000 from the census returns of 1800 on the age distribution of the white population in the United States.[5] Their estimated general maternity rate is 278 births per 1,000 women 15–44 years. (This would correspond to a rate in the vicinity of 220 births per thousand women 15–49 years—the type of rate used in the previous paragraph.) The estimated crude birth rate declined to 48.3 in 1840, 35.2 in 1880, and 26.1 in 1920. Similarly the general maternity rate (g 15–44) declined to 222 in 1840, 155 in 1880, and 113 in 1920. The estimates for the early nineteenth century are subject to considerable error, owing to lack of information on mortality; those prior to 1830 may also be somewhat affected by necessity of adjustments of the data on age distribution. The apparent slight decline in the estimated general maternity rate from 278 in 1800 to 274 in 1810 has no significance,

[1] R. R. Kuczynski. *Birth Registration and Birth Statistics in Canada.* Washington, 1930, p. 199.
[2] Chapter I of this part.
[3] Kuczynski, op. cit., pp. 199–201.
[4] Tentative estimates by the writer. The figures cited have only approximate accuracy.
[5] Warren S. Thompson and P. K. Whelpton. *Population Trends in the United States.* New York, 1933, p. 263.

but the further decline in this rate to 260 in 1820 is probably indicative of a real change, and the further decline to 240 in 1830 is clearly so.

Child-woman ratios in the white population classified by size of community are given for the years 1820, 1840, and 1890. These run as follows:[1]

TABLE 17.

Size of community	Children 0–4 years per 1,000 women 20–44 years		
	1820	1840	1890
500,000 and over	—	—	513
250,000–500,000	—	665	500
100,000–250,000	827	778	529
25,000–100,000	786	663	487
2,500– 25,000	906	739⎱ 1 121	731
Rural	1 286	1 138⎰	

There was clearly a marked differential in fertility by size of community at the beginning of the nineteenth century. Analysis of declines from these data is complicated by the shifting position of cities between different classes. Taking this into account, it is probable that from 1820 to 1840 the decline progressed more rapidly in cities than in rural localities. Wide differentials by size of community were apparent in 1840.

It has also been shown by Jaffe that at the beginning of the nineteenth century there were marked differences in fertility, both within rural populations and within city populations, in relation to indices of social status—with lower fertility at upper socio-economic levels.[2] These differences are not great, and could be attributed in whole or in part to differences in ages at marriage. It is clear that the growth of commerce, and industrial activities (chiefly small enterprises at this time) and residence in cities stimulated reduction in size of family in the United States even during the first quarter of the nineteenth century.

But regional differentials widened during the nineteenth century. Using child-woman ratios[3] (in this case of children under 5 years per 1,000 women

[1] ibid., p. 279. Combined ratio for places under 25,000, weighted by populations, p. 47.
[2] A. J. Jaffe, 'Fertility Differentials in the Whole Population in Early America', *Journal of Heredity* 31: 407–11, 1940. ('It is, however, important to note that at first the levels of fertility in urban communities in the United States were not appreciably different from levels that had been generally prevalent for a long time in western European countries.')
[3] The distribution of ratios is taken from a chart prepared by the Bureau of Agricultural Economics and reproduced by the United States National Resources Committee in *The Problems of a Changing Population*. The values for Rhode Island and Delaware are not clearly legible and are therefore omitted. The percentages of urban population (cities of 2,500 population or over) are from a tabulation published by the Bureau of the Census, in the 1940 report, *Population*, Vol. I.

TABLE 18.

Census	Child-woman ratios (range)	States in range	% urban
1800	600–700	Connecticut	5.1
		Massachusetts	15.4
	700–800	New Hampshire	2.9
		Maryland	7.8
	800–900	New York	12.7
		Pennsylvania	11.3
		Virginia	1.8
		New Jersey	0.0
	900–1,000	Maine	2.4
		Vermont	0.0
		North Carolina	0.0
		South Carolina	5.4
		Northwest frontier	0.0
	1,000+	Territories corresponding to:	
		Michigan	—
		Ohio	0.0
		Kentucky	0.0
		Tennessee	0.0
		Georgia	3.2
		Mississippi	0.0
1840	400–500	Massachusetts	37.9
		Connecticut	12.6
	500–600	Vermont	0.0
		New Hampshire	10.0
	600–700	Maine	7.8
		New York	19.4
		New Jersey	10.6
		Maryland	24.2
	700–800	Pennsylvania	17.9
		Virginia	5.7
		North Carolina	1.8
		Michigan	4.3
	800–900	South Carolina	5.7
		Kentucky	4.0
		Ohio	5.5
		Wisconsin	0.0
		Florida	0.0
		Louisiana	—
	900–1,000	Georgia	3.6
		Tennessee	0.8
		Illinois	2.0
		Indiana	1.6
		Northwest frontier	0.0

Census	Child-woman ratios (range)	States in range	% urban
1840	1,000+	Missouri	4.3
		Arkansas	0.0
		Mississippi	1.0
		Alabama	2.1
1860	400–500	Vermont	2.0
		New Hampshire	22.1
		Massachusetts	59.6
		Connecticut	26.5
	500–600	Maine	16.6
		New York	39.3
		New Jersey	32.7
		Maryland	34.0
	600–700	Michigan	13.3
		Pennsylvania	30.8
		Ohio	17.1
		Virginia	8.5
		North Carolina	2.5
		South Carolina	6.9
		Tennessee	4.2
		Arizona–New Mexico	5.0
		Louisiana	26.1
	700–800	Wisconsin	14.4
		Illinois	14.3
		Indiana	8.6
		Kentucky	10.4
		Missouri	17.2
		Mississippi	2.6
		Alabama	5.1
		Georgia	7.1
		Florida	4.1
		California	20.7
	800–900	Texas	4.4
		Arkansas	0.9
		Iowa	8.9
		Minnesota	9.4
	900–1,000	—	
	1,000+	Northwest frontier	0.0
1880	300–400	Maine	22.6
		New Hampshire	30.0
		Massachusetts	74.7
		Connecticut	41.9
	400–500	Vermont	10.0
		New York	56.4
		New Jersey	54.4
		Maryland	40.2
	500–600	Pennsylvania	41.6

Census	Child-woman ratios (range)	States in range	% urban
1880		Ohio	32.2
		Michigan	24.8
		Wisconsin	24.1
		Illinois	30.6
		Indiana	19.5
		California	42.9
		Colorado	31.4
		Arizona	17.3
		New Mexico	5.5
		Nevada	31.1
	600–700	Virginia	12.5
		North Carolina	3.9
		South Carolina	7.5
		Georgia	9.4
		Florida	10.0
		Alabama	5.4
		Mississippi	3.1
		Louisiana	25.5
		Kentucky	15.2
		Tennessee	7.5
		Minnesota	19.1
		Iowa	15.2
		Missouri	25.2
		Kansas	10.5
		Wyoming	29.6
		Montana	17.8
		Oregon	14.8
	700–800	West Virginia	8.7
		Arkansas	4.0
		Texas	9.2
		North Dakota	7.3
		South Dakota	7.3
		Nebraska	13.6
		Washington	9.5
	800–900	Idaho	0.0
		Utah	23.4

15–49 years) the changing pattern by states in the whole population is summarized above—the figures in the last column referring to per cent of urban population in each state at a given time.

The northern New England states (Maine, New Hampshire, and Vermont) in 1840 and thereafter have ratios that are lower than would be expected merely with reference to degree of urbanization. These were areas of early settlement, with relatively stable populations, and with strong emphasis on education.

Pennsylvania retains a ratio above expectation as regards degree of urbanization. This state had received many of the latest German and Scotch-Irish (Protestant) migrants in the colonial period.

States within areas ceded by France (Louisiana) or by Mexico (Texas, New Mexico and, at first, California) have ratios above expectation as compared with other equally rural areas.

States and territories in the expanding frontier have extremely high ratios. The high ratio in Utah in 1880, in spite of a moderate degree of urbanization, and a progressive development of commercial agriculture, can be attributed in part to the influence of Mormon culture.

It is apparent that urbanization and related economic and social conditions have exerted a powerful force toward restriction of fertility in the United States and Canada. But this force has been modified by other, more complex social and cultural conditions.

Remarkably high levels of fertility have persisted until quite recently in some areas in America. We have already referred to one such area adjacent to the United States, namely, rural Quebec. The rural population of Quebec lives in community clusters. The Catholic Church provides an accepted religious and cultural leadership. Opportunity for expansion of established communities has been limited for a long time, but opportunities for employment in other areas have been accessible for those choosing to migrate. The colonial population was unsympathetic to the revolutionary movement in France and has remained conservative in its traditions. Regional interests as well as religious differences of the people of Quebec and those in other parts of Canada have been conducive to ethnocentrism. These conditions tended to create a cohesive society that provided social support and cultural motives for high fertility.

The same principle, stated in somewhat different terms, holds true with respect to cohesive religious groups in various rural districts in the United States, including several already mentioned: the Old Order Amish in small communities in Pennsylvania; the Mormons in the great Rocky Mountain basin; and the 'Spanish-Americans' (Mexicans) in long established communities in the southwest, chiefly in New Mexico. All these societies have long provided strong motivation for high fertility, though this tendency has been greatly modified among Mormons in recent decades.

Distinct cultural patterns were also in some cases preserved by physical isolation. This has notably been the case in the Kentucky Highlands. Here the cultural traditions of eighteenth century colonists, as modified in the isolation of mountain recesses, were reinforced by strong kinship bonds and religious interests. As late as 1930, the child-woman ratio in Leslie County, in the heart of the highlands (1,255 children under 5 years per 1,000 women 20–44 years), was above the general level in colonial America.

A somewhat similar situation, due rather to cultural than to physical isolation, is found in some immigrant communities in rural districts.

In the groups described above, social organization has a positive relation to the persistence of high fertility. Large families are supported by the social structure and encouraged by specific cultural motives.

The residential distribution of the social groups described above stands out in a map prepared by the National Resources Committee showing maternal net reproduction ratios by counties in the United States in 1930, areas having net reproduction ratios above 1.50 being highly shaded.[1] The only exceptions are the Amish, whose communities are numerically outweighed by 'ordinary people' in the same counties. Rural Quebec does not of course appear in this map of the United States; but its influence is partially responsible for the high shading of the adjacent county in northern Maine.

There are other highly shaded areas in this map where the persistence of high fertility is not clearly associated with distinctive cultural patterns or close-knit or isolated social structures. These are rural districts occupied by populations with an extremely low level of living and often without strong social organization. Some of the groups discussed above have low average income, others have moderately high average income; the relation of culture to their fertility is positive and to some extent independent of economic level. But in general in the United States poverty, especially in rural districts, also seems to operate as an independent variable favourable to high fertility. A grouping of counties by level of living in 1930 showed that in each of five major regions the group with the lowest level of living had the highest net reproduction ratio.[2]

The largest impoverished rural population in the United States is that of tenants and labourers in the cotton and tobacco districts of the Old South—including both whites and Negroes—especially prior to recent economic and social changes.

We omit any special treatment of the trend of the Negro population in the United States, because this raises special problems relating to mobility and urbanization and lying, for the most part, outside the scope of this report. In general trends of natural increase among Negroes and whites within the same areas have been very similar in recent decades. The high frequency of childlessness among Negroes presents a special and very complex problem, involving both health conditions and social conditions in varying degrees in different situations. The frequency of childlessness, however, was low among older Negro women born in the South for whom data are available from the 1910 census. The problem relates directly, for the most part, to conditions since emancipation. It is a special problem on which knowledge is needed, but about which at present not much is known.

[1] United States National Resources Committee, op. cit., Figure 4, opposite p. 122.
[2] ibid., p. 136. The country was divided into six major regions, but there were no counties at the lowest level of living in the Far West.

An intensive study by Margaret Hagood in 1938 of a small sample of mothers in tenant farm families in an upland tobacco-growing district of North Carolina provides significant material on the relations of cultural conditions to fertility in this particular non-industrial population.[1] The average number of children born alive by each woman in the sample was 6.3; the figure is not presented as statistically significant for any total population but as indicating a characteristic of the group studied. The sample included some women who had passed the childbearing period, but the majority were still able to have more babies. Their attitudes toward childbearing are best summarized by the term *ambivalence*.

'Attitudes toward childbearing are the core of interest in the study of fertility, for it is the psychological reaction to external factors, such as traditional and economic pressures, which finally translates these societal forces into effects on the birth rate. These attitudes are difficult to state summarily. Undoubtedly there is ambivalence. The traditional pattern of the glory and the actual or imagined value of a large number of children pull in one direction, while the desire to avoid the suffering of childbearing, the trouble of caring for another child, and the responsibility of another mouth to be fed and body to be clothed pull in the other. An approximate balance of these forces means that the former wins out because children keep arriving when a laisser-faire policy is adopted. . . .

'The ambivalence is manifested almost universally among these mothers in the difference in attitudes toward past and future childbearing. There is pride in having borne the number they have, yet almost never is there expressed a desire for more. The most common examples of the first is the ever-present suggestion of self-esteem in both words and intonation of answers to the question of how many children the mother of a large family has—"Eleven. I done my share, didn't I?" or "Ten and all a-living". . . . The bearing, "raising", and "marrying off" of children are everywhere recognized as being a positive achievement, a contribution to the world as well as to the immediate family. The remembrance of qualms or regrets over discovering oneself pregnant fades with time as does the pain of childbirth, leaving the note of pride prevailing with regard to the past.

'On the other hand, every one of the mothers with babies of two or under, either explicitly or by inference, expressed the attitude, "I hope this is the last one". So many of them used these identical words, that the stereotyped expression may be interpreted as the verbalization of a fairly rigid and universal attitude, although in most cases the effecting of the wish was limited to "hoping".'[2]

There is now a growing trend toward the limitation of births among these women, but this has not yet had much effect. Only a few of the women

[1] Margaret Hagood. *Mothers of the South*. Chapel Hill, North Carolina, 1939.
[2] ibid., pp. 120–1.

said that they had practised any sort of birth control, but most of them approved such practice. Some expressed the hope that their daughters would do so more effectively than they had. Conversation on the subject, in spite of perfect rapport, was hindered by the lack of appropriate vocabulary and a tendency to resort to indirect statements and similies.

Neither the mothers nor their children received proper medical care: 'Lacerations, hermorrhoids, and dislocated uterus are among the most frequently reported after effects of childbearing. In most cases the doctor does not come back after the delivery if the tenant home is a long way out of town. The lack of medical attention to these ailments is almost universal, perhaps because of no money to pay the doctor, perhaps because of a reticence about examination for female troubles.'[1]

'More important is the neglect of chronic troubles from lack of money for medical treatment, or from inadequate or "quack" treatment. One mother can't pay to have "this here cross-eyed knee-baby's eyes straightened", although he has failed in school for two years and the teacher says it is mainly because he cannot see. In many of the children tonsils and adenoids were suspected from facial expression and tone of voice, and need of dental attention was quite obvious. A crippled son can stay in the hospital only so long as the money collected by the church lasts; then he has to come home and wait for more to be collected before he gets additional treatment.'[2]

The parents usually send their children to school, as required by the law. Some say this law is a good thing, but others resent it. However, children are usually kept out of school at busy times in farm work. There is much friendly visiting among neighbours, but the strongest formal social tie outside primary family relations is the relation between tenant and landlord, covering a limited period. The cultural poverty of these tenant farmers stems directly from their economic poverty, and in turn it helps to perpetuate this poverty. Yet there is increasing readiness among the children of these families to respond to new opportunities.

'Ambivalence', as defined by Hagood in this context, is psychologically different from 'indifference', as a personal characteristic. But it is the psychological correlate of the phenomenon that we have described as 'cultural indifference'. The cultural inertia characteristic of the group studied by Hagood is not representative of the main stream of American life. But it is (or was until recently) characteristic of other depressed communities outside this main stream.

Theoretically, the central problem in the interpretation of the general trend of fertility in Anglo-American society is the early rise to a level well above that in Europe, the emergence of wide differentials, and the trend

[1] ibid., p. 116.
[2] ibid., p. 131.

226

toward decline in advance of that in any European country except France. The basic social fact underlying these shifts in fertility may be found in the distinctive characteristics of the Anglo-American family, as formed in colonial and pioneer experience. With abundance of land resources and associated opportunities for gainful employment, the restraints on family life inherent in European land-tenure and guild systems were removed. The pattern of separated farm homesteads intensified both the independence of family units and mutual dependence of members on one another. Physical, social, and technical mobility reinforced the same tendencies. As stated by Calhoun, the American family form was from the start an 'entrepreneurial enterprise'.[1] Young men and women, after participating during their youth in the parental enterprise, were expected to join in forming an independent family, to build an enterprise of their own, to rear children, and to share according to their circumstances in the support of aged and dependent relatives. Anglo-American society has sometimes been described as 'individualistic', but this is fallacious—particularly as regards colonial, pioneer, and rural society. It is definitely a 'familistic society', not a society of corporate kinship groups or of joint families, but a 'democratic-nuclear-familistic' society. This emphasis is in part a continuation of the Christian-European tradition and a condition prescribed by the requirements of colonial and pioneer life.

In early American society, especially in rural communities, parental responsibilities required only procreation, physical nurture, moral discipline, affection, and tutelage as apprentices in the parental enterprise. In return, children provided not only psychic satisfaction but economic aid. They contributed actively for a time to the family farm enterprise and provided an essential basis of security in old age to their parents.

Colonial conditions were favourable to rather early marriage, although information on this point is obscure:

'If one makes allowance for the higher average ages which prevailed in Europe up until the Industrial Revolution, as already remarked upon, it becomes understandable that foreign observers would comment upon the "early" age at marriage in this country. It is unlikely that the English comedian who reported that Virginia ladies married nearly ten years earlier than in England meant that the Virginian ladies married at 14 or 15, but more likely ten years earlier than the upper classes in England—or 17–18, at least. Up until the 1800's no shift in the American marriage customs has been noted, and hence this comment on American youth by an Englishwoman in 1819 (written in New York State) is relevant: both sexes, she said, "are for the most part married ere they are two-and-twenty, and it is indeed usual to see a girl of 18 a wife and a mother". The social attitude that the bride should marry before 20,

---

[1] Arthur W. Calhoun. *A Social History of the American Family from Colonial Times to the Present* (3 vols.). Cleveland, 1919; reprinted, New York, 1945.

and the generally observed motherhood before 20 would make it probable that this age was a typical one, with the male marrying somewhat later.'[1] Almost unlimited resources were at hand for development and cultivation. Under changed circumstances, as parental responsibilities came to include a prolonged period for formal education or the provision for children of land within established communities, pressures for family limitation comparable to those in European societies came into operation—first in urban communities and then in established rural communities with high standards of living. The American family, which tended to be independent of larger group control, was peculiarly free to adapt its reproductive behaviour to its own interests—including its interest in children.

The main trend in American cultural life has been directed toward achievement in new enterprises, with the nuclear family as the focus of affection and aspirations, and emphasis on democratic social relations and the freedom of individuals. Under the conditions of pioneer life this culture promoted an extraordinarily high level of fertility. As the objective conditions changed, the same culture promoted restriction of fertility. American culture today does not prescribe size of family. But it generates attitudes that have a strong tendency both to treat parenthood as a major goal, and to restrict the size of families.

Certain counter forces have tended to resist the general decline of fertility associated with technological progress in America, and to sustain high levels of fertility in some groups. First, there has been the positive counter force of adherence to traditional values, especially within cohesive groups. Secondly, there has also been inertia, stemming from lack of effective social relations or strong motivations toward goals beyond immediate needs and interests. The relative importance of these two counter forces that have resisted the trend toward family limitation cannot be determined; but obviously neither has been dominant in American society.

THE TREND OF FERTILITY IN THE SOVIET UNION

Changes of fertility in the Soviet Union have been unusually rapid, as compared with trends in other populations with initially high fertility. These changes in fertility have been due in part to changes in governmental policy, but in large part they reflect the influence of profound and rapid changes in social life. The outstanding facts about the trend of fertility in the country as a whole and about regional differentials in the early Soviet period have been described by the present writer in a previous publication.[2] These can be summarized, with a supplemental note based on recent information.

[1] Thomas P. Monahan. *The Pattern of Age at Marriage in the United States.* Philadelphia. Stephenson-Brothers, 1951, 2 vols., I, p. 102.
[2] Frank Lorimer. *The Population of the Soviet Union.* Geneva, 1946.

The general level of fertility had been very high in Russia prior to World War I, but had been declining gradually in the western provinces and in cities. The total maternity ratio in the European part of the U.S.S.R. had declined from about 6.7 in 1894, under the imperial regime, to 5.4 (births per woman living through the childbearing period) in 1924.[1] The comparable figure for 1938 is about 4.4.

The crude birth rate, 1899–1901, according to official statistics in 39 provinces corresponding roughly to the European area of the U.S.S.R., was 50.4 per thousand.[2] This was appreciably higher than in 11 western provinces under the imperial regime which were later incorporated into the Baltic states, Poland, or Rumania. The corresponding rate in this western area was 40.3 per thousand. The crude birth rate, according to official statistics, in the European area of the U.S.S.R. was 43.5 in 1926 and 43.0 in 1927. The estimated crude birth rate, 1926–27, in the whole Soviet Union was 45.0.[3] The rate fell to about 30 births per thousand population in 1935, but moved in the following years to 33.6 in 1936, 39.6 in 1937, and 38.3 in 1938.[4]

There are no precise figures on fertility in the Soviet Union for the intervening years. It is probable, taking economic conditions into account, that the rate in 1934 was about the same as in 1935. There is evidence that there was only a slight decline from 1926 to 1928. The decline from 1928 to 1934 must, therefore, have been precipitous, from about 43.7 to about 30.1—an estimated decline of over 30 per cent in five years. On this assumption, it can be estimated that there were about 10 million fewer children under 14 years of age in the Soviet Union when it became involved in World War II than there would have been if fertility had remained at the 1926–27 level. Incidentally, the reduction in the number of dependent children must have provided an appreciable measure of relief to the strain on the Soviet economy of rapid industrialization and war during the critical years, 1934–45.

The rate of natural increase in the population of the Soviet Union has been somewhere in the vicinity of 16 per thousand in recent years.[5] The crude death rate was presumably somewhat less than 15 per thousand.

[1] ibid., p. 131. The figures in the source are maternal gross reproduction ratios. These were derived from census data of 1897 and 1926, in combination with life tables. The true reference is to the years specified above, but there was slight change from 1894 to 1897 or from 1924 to 1926. The 1938 figure is derived from the reported birth rate for that year, in combination with an estimated distribution of the population by sex and age.
[2] ibid., p. 35.
[3] ibid., pp. 81, 134.
[4] ibid., p. 134. The last of these rates was officially announced. The other rates in this series were obtained by linking official statements on relative changes for other years with the absolute figure for 1938.
[5] According to a statement by a U.S.S.R. delegate to the United Nations Assembly, 8 December 1952, 'the net increase of population of the U.S.S.R. in the past three years has been 9.5 million'.

Its crude birth rate must, therefore, have been somewhere in the vicinity of 30 per thousand—similar to the low level reached in the mid 1930's and well below the rate in 1937 or 1938 or even lower.[1]

It is apparent that the moderation of fertility in western and urban areas of the late Russian Empire was due to influences analogous to those operative in Western Europe. Similar influences are evident in regional differentials in the early Soviet period. Using substitute maternal gross reproduction ratios derived from census data, the figure for rural districts within the European part of the U.S.S.R. declined from 3.46 in 1894 to 2.87 in 1924—a decrease of about 17 per cent. That for urban districts within the same area declined from 2.13 in 1894 to 1.71 in 1924—a decrease of about 20 per cent. In view of the margins of errors in these figures, the difference in rates of decrease is not significant, but the information shows that the urban-rural differential was maintained and possibly widened in these early declines.[2]

The outstanding feature of the series of estimated regional gross reproduction ratios, 1924, is the marked urban-rural differential in every district. The lowest ratios are found in the urban parts of the Leningrad region (1.23), the Moscow region (1.37), and the Azov region, including Rostov, (1.37). These were at or below the replacement level. The highest ratios are found in the rural areas of culturally distinct or isolated regions.[3]

There is very little information on regional trends in fertility under the Soviet regime. The continued very high rate of natural increase in the Transcaucasus republics, 1926–39, shows that the initial high fertility in this region must have persisted through the 1930's with only moderate changes. On the other hand, information on ratio of abortions per 100 live births in Moscow, which rose from 19 in 1924 and 55 in 1926 to 271 in 1934 and 221 in 1935 shows that the decline in fertility in the largest city from 1924 through 1934 must have been very rapid.[4] Public provisions for abortion which had been introduced and were rapidly expanded in the early Soviet period were modified in 1935 to eliminate abortion of first pregnancies or in rapid succession. The abortion clinics were closed by government order, 27 June 1936, and all abortions were henceforth prohibited except for medical or eugenic reasons.[5] The extent of provisions for abortions in rural districts prior to 1935 is not known precisely, but clinics were established in some collective farm communities. It is probable that increased resort to abortion was most marked in areas already characterized by moderate and declining fertility.

[1] The highest death rates shown for any European countries, 1949–50, in the United Nations *Demographic Yearbook* 1952, were: Austria, 1949, 12.9; Belgium, 1949, 12.9; France, 1949, 13.9; Ireland, 1951, 14.3; Scotland, 1951, 12.9; Yugoslavia, 15.4. In Japan, the rates were 11.6 in 1949, 10.9 in 1950, and 10.0 in 1951.
[2] Lorimer, op. cit., p. 131.
[3] ibid., pp. 90–2.
[4] ibid., p. 127.
[5] ibid., p. 128.

The sharp decline of fertility in the Soviet Union during the years 1926 to 1935 and its partial recovery in the late 1930's must be attributed in part to the changes in facilities for abortion and in part to the economic crisis associated with drastic changes during the 'hard years' of the First Five-Year Plan (1928–32) and improved economic conditions in the late 1930's.

The long-time trend toward reduction of fertility, which appears to have continued into the post-war period, can be interpreted as in part an extension of the decline already apparent in the western and urban areas of Russia prior to the Revolution. The question of major interest from the standpoint of this inquiry is the degree to which this trend was accelerated by changes in social and cultural conditions under the Soviet regime. Unfortunately, it is impossible to answer this question. One can only list some of the factors that may have been operative without any attempt to weigh their possible influence: extensive shift of men and women from private farms to collective farms and to work for wages or salaries in industrial, commercial, and administrative activities; increase in school attendance and in literacy; improvements in health; increased inter-regional movements of the population; provision of public facilities for child care; family allowances (after their extension on a broad basis in 1944); ideological and legal changes affecting attitudes toward the family and patterns of family life, etc.

One can only draw the very limited conclusion that Soviet experience, to date, confirms the general thesis that a rapid introduction of new techniques with associated changes in social conditions is generally conducive to decline of fertility. One can not isolate the influence of specific factors, or distinguish between the influence of factors that are unique in Soviet experience and those of a more general nature.

DECLINE OF FERTILITY AMONG JAPANESE

Social changes in Japan during the last quarter of the nineteenth century and thereafter brought about tendencies toward postponement of marriage and the control of fertility within marriage. The growth of commerce and industry created expanding opportunities for economic activity in cities and promoted their rapid growth. Declining infant mortality in a society favouring primogeniture in inheritance resulted in an increasing supply of sons obliged to seek their livelihood outside of agriculture. The spread of education for both boys and girls facilitated their adjustment to the conditions of urban life, and intensified their aspirations toward economic and social advance. The diversity of small enterprises stimulated social mobility.

'In 1920 the national gross reproduction was 2.7. The regional distri-bution of fertility rates indicated higher levels of human reproduction in those areas where the old feudal agrarian order prevailed without much modification, lower levels in those areas where urban residence and industrial employment signalized the development of the new culture and the new economy. In 1920 and 1925 crude birth rates of 40 to 50 or even more were characteristic of the agricultural villages in the isolated areas of the northeast. In 1920 gross reproduction rates in these areas were 3.0 to 3.5, while in the cities of Tokyo, Osaka and Kyoto they were below 2.0. As intimated, relationships between fertility, urban-rural residence, occupational structure and migration patterns were definite. Much of the variation in fertility between regions was related further to differences in the age at marriage and the duration of married life. By 1925 the fertility of married women was already lower in the cities than in the rural areas, lower in the industrial provinces than in the agricultural ones. . . . At any given time fertility was higher in the rural and isolated areas, lower in or adjacent to the great cities. It was higher among the agriculturalists, lower among the professional and white-collar groups. It was higher among the uneducated or the poorly educated, lower among the more educated. But for practically all groups fertility was decreasing. Gross reproduction rates for the 47 provinces, and for the rural and urban areas of each province considered separately, moved consistently downward in the successive quinquennial periods from 1920 through 1940. Annual and cyclical variations in fertility from 1925 to 1950 were comparable to those of the nations of the West. Difficult conditions in 1938 and 1939 were accompanied by sharp declines in fertility, whereas during war-time, full employment, planned military leaves and pronatalist economic and medical assistance maintained fertility at relatively high levels. In the late war and early postwar years there was first a collapse and then a brief revival in fertility. The crude birth rate of 34.3 in 1947 was the highest in two decades, the 1947 gross reproduction rate of 2.2 was almost as high as that of 1935. Decline came quickly, however, and by 1950 the gross reproduction rate had dropped to a level only slightly above that projected on the basis of prewar trends.'[1]

The decline in fertility in Japan since 1947, as shown by changes in the birth rate, has proceeded as in Table 19.[2]

Taeuber and Balfour estimated that if 1925 age-specific maternity rates had remained unchanged the increase of women in the childbearing ages would have resulted in an increase of the total number of live births from 1.9 million in 1925 to 3.4 million in 1950. Actually there were only 2.4 million births in 1950. The latter figure was weighted more heavily by births in recent marriages than the former, due to increase of marriages in

[1] Irene B. Taeuber and Marshall C. Balfour, M.D. 'The Control of Fertility in Japan', in *Approaches to Problems of High Fertility in Agrarian Societies.* Milbank Memorial Fund, 1952, pp. 102–28, pp. 105–6.
[2] Figures for 1947 and 1948 are from *Population Index*, 17 (3), July 1951, Table 2, p. 236. Those for 1949–52 are from *Population Index*, 19 (3), July 1953, Table 2, p. 242.

TABLE 19.

Year	Births per 1,000 Population
1947	34.3
1948	33.4
1949	32.8
1950	28.2
1951	25.6
1952	26.0

the years immediately after World War II. In spite of this favourable factor, the actual number in 1950 was 31 per cent below the 'expected number'.

Three-fourths of this deficiency can be attributed to reduction in the proportions of women married in various age classes in 1950, as compared with 1925. This reduction in proportions of women married was due in part to a deficiency in the number of adult males in the population of Japan in 1950, due to the effects of the war. A similar effect had been produced in the pre-war period by out-migration. In part, however, the reduction was due to an increased tendency for women (though not for men in the post-war period) to postpone marriages to later ages.

Studies carried out in the Research Institute of Population Problems in the Japanese Welfare Ministry show that even in 1940 among married women aged 45 years or over, 15 per cent had never borne a child and 47 per cent had borne only one to three children. The proportion of childless couples was lowest, less than 4 per cent, among persons on relief, and it was relatively low among the wealthy. It was below the national average for farmers, but within the farming population the proportion of childless couples decreased quite consistently with size of holding, and increased sharply with increasing age at marriage. Childlessness was less prevalent among wives of labourers, salaried groups and business men in urban areas than among their rural counterparts.[1]

In traditional Japanese culture there was no sharp distinction between contraception and abortion:

'The character commonly used to signify birth limitation in the advertisements in the mass-circulation women's magazines includes both contraception and abortion. A carefully conducted public opinion poll on population included a specific question as to the meaning of the character for birth control or contraception, as contrasted to the character for birth limitation as a generic term, including abortion. Five per cent of the national sample of respondents gave an almost correct answer; 48 per cent said simply that they did not know; 47 per cent

[1] ibid., pp. 110–11.

gave answers indicating a vague belief that there were differences between the two.'[1]

Nevertheless, there is fairly extensive interest in, and practice of, contraception in Japan. Studies on this subject are said to provide 'suggestive rather than definitive' results.

'But the studies do indicate that a majority of the people "favor" birth control, and this majority becomes preponderant if married women with few children and those beyond the age of conception are excluded from the sample. Approximately one in five married couples admits the practice of contraception now or at some time in the past; the number sinks to one in 10, or even 20, in agricultural villages. The extent of contraceptive practice is positively correlated with urban residence, degree of education, and upper social-economic status. It appears to decline with distance from the great urban centers. The techniques employed by the married couples of postwar Japan who were practising contraception were the ones traditional in the culture. One-third to two-fifths or more used the condom; another one-fourth or more relied on periodic abstinence and one-tenth used coitus interruptus. These three methods together accounted for some three-fourths of the contraceptive experience reported.'[2]

Abortion has long been a traditional means of limiting fertility in Japan, in association at earlier times with infanticide. The Eugenic Protection Law of 1948 made legal, under definite but rather broad conditions, both sterilization and abortion. The number of legal abortions, thereafter, rose rapidly from 6,400 in January 1949 to about 56,000 in May 1951. The latter figure would suggest a total of about 600,000 per year.[3] A large proportion of these legal abortions were performed after review of applications and approval by legally established commissions. In the previous year, 1950, the number of legal abortions was about four-fifths of this number. But according to an estimate by Dr. Koya, there were also some 112,000 illegal abortions in that year, bringing the total to about 600,000 in 1950.

According to Taeuber and Balfour the increase in legal abortions in the post-war period accounts for a significant part, but hardly a major part, of the total decrease of marital fertility during this period. The frequency of reported abortions relative to the frequency of live births varied greatly in different parts of Japan in 1950, and the pattern of these variations seems to be affected by administrative procedures as well as by social factors. The relative frequency was high (over 300 reported abortions per thousand live births) in Nagoya, Kyoto, and Osaka, but appreciably lower (under 200) in Tokyo. On the other hand, the ratio was high in some rather isolated rural areas (over 300 in Toyama and Nagano prefectures)

[1] ibid., p. 111.
[2] ibid., p. 112.
[3] ibid., p. 118.

and generally high in the economically rather undeveloped districts of western Honshu, along the Sea of Japan. By age, the frequencies of reported abortions appear to have been highest among those under 20 years, including young married women, and at late ages, 40 years and over. As observed by Taeuber and Balfour, 'It is improbable that the resort to abortion could have attained its 1950 magnitude without a cultural base in which abortion was accepted and practised'.[1]

In many respects, of course, the forces making for decline of fertility in Japan are similar to those that have been operative in western Europe: growth of commercial and industrial activity, increase of interest in and opportunities for education, lowered infant mortality, increased mobility, etc. It is also possible that some kinship patterns in Japan, notably the provision for acquiring a son by adoption, allowed some relaxation of the traditional motives for high fertility.

One aspect of the relation of the recent rapid decrease of fertility in Japan to its social structure and culture may be theoretically even more significant. Japanese society has a remarkably firm and complex social organization, involving kinship relations, political and military control, and a network of formally organized neighbour associations (*tonari-gumi*), even in large cities—the latter being a traditional pattern which had been allowed to decline, but was reviewed and operated very effectively during the war. Similarly, there are few cultures in which the emphasis on the subordination of personal interests to social obligations is so intense as in Japan. It is a highly structured and a highly disciplined society. Strong lines of social control, operating through family and through economic and political relations tended to sustain high fertility in ancient Japanese society—except in a period of chronic depression and disorder. The same social characteristics, under changed technical and social conditions, appear to be enforcing a drastic reduction of fertility. This tendency is, to be sure, associated with an increased assertion of personal interests and some trend toward individualism; but this trend is still far less advanced in Japanese society than in most cultures with similar advance in technology. This suggests the thesis that intensity of social organization may be a force in the restriction of fertility under some conditions, as well as the support of fertility under other conditions.

It may be useful to take account of recent rapid declines of fertility in some overseas Japanese populations—for example, in Hawaii. Here individualistic motives may be assumed to have greater force, but they still operate within culture patterns that promote a high sense of responsibility for family and civic obligations. The fertility of Japanese women of completed fertility in Hawaii in 1950 was relatively high. The average number of children ever born per woman aged 45 years or over (taking account of the number of single women, as well as ever-married women,

[1] ibid., p. 125.

reporting on this question) is 5.26 among the Japanese; the same figure (5.26) is obtained for the combined group of Chinese (5.12), Filipino (5.45), and all others except Hawaiians and Caucasians. The comparable figure for Hawaiians and part-Hawaiians is somewhat lower (4.57) and that for Caucasians is much lower (2.99). Quite different results are indicated in an analysis by Rose Siegel of recent differentials in fertility among racial groups in Hawaii—as indicated either by child-woman ratios in 1950 or by relevant current vital statistics, 1949–50.[1] Synthetic total maternity ratios (comparable to female gross reproduction ratios, but referring to total births) for 1949–50 run as follows: Hawaiian and Part-Hawaiian, 5.57; Caucasian, 2.90; Japanese, 2.53; all other races, 4.09.

Ratios of children aged 0–4 years per thousand women aged 15–49 years run as follows: Hawaiian and Part-Hawaiian, 795; Caucasian, 442; Japanese, 429; all other races, 612 (Chinese, 449; Filipino, 813; other races, 568).

The results, as noted by Siegel, are biased by the system of racial classification in official statistics for Hawaii. No persons of mixed racial parentage are classed as 'Caucasian', but all persons of mixed descent with one Hawaiian or part-Hawaiian parent are classed in that group. Taking account of the actual patterns of intermarriage among various ethnic groups (e.g., the high frequency of Chinese-Hawaiian intermarriages as compared with relatively low frequencies of interracial marriages among the Japanese) gives some indication concerning the figures subject to most serious bias. The figures have an upward bias in the case of the Hawaiians, but a downward bias in other groups, especially the Chinese and to a lesser extent the Japanese. But even with these reservations, there is clear evidence of a rapid decline in the fertility of Japanese in Hawaii in recent decades, as compared with other racial groups—and most conspicuously so in comparison with the Filipino group. There has also been a similar sharp decline of fertility among Japanese in the United States in recent decades.[2] The social changes induced by residence in the western social milieu of the United States or in the blended Oriental-European culture of Hawaii have, of course, exercised a critical influence on these trends. But such changes are not necessarily wholly different from cultural changes that may occur within Oriental societies under new technical conditions.

THE ABSENCE OF DEMOGRAPHIC TRANSITION IN BRAZIL

A contribution by Giorgio Mortara, presented in Part Five of this report, provides an authoritative synthesis of the results of a series of intensive

[1] Rose Varon Siegel, unpublished study, 1953.
[2] George Sabagh and Dorothy S. Thomas. 'Changing Patterns of Fertility and Survival among Japanese Americans on the Pacific Coast', *American Sociological Review*, 10 (5), October 1945, 651–7. These findings refer to trends in force prior to disturbed conditions in this population during World War II.

investigations of fertility in Brazil, carried out by the Instituto Brasileiro de Geografia e Statística. These investigations have yielded precisely formulated findings on a wide range of topics. Although information is lacking at some critical points, the findings on many topics have a high degree of accuracy. This extraordinary achievement has been made, in the absence of reliable vital statistics, through skillful and painstaking analysis of data from census inquiries.

Perhaps the most extraordinary result of this inquiry, as noted by Mortara, 'is that of finding in the modern world a large country, within the sphere of western civilization, where the influence of social and economic factors on fertility is relatively limited, the predominant influence being that of the biological factor'.[1]

The crude birth rate in Brazil as reflected in 1940 census data is found to have been between 42 and 44 per 1,000 population. The corresponding death rate is 18–20, allowing a natural increase in the vicinity of 24 per 1,000 population per year. The level of fertility reflected in the 1940 census is very close to, though possibly slightly below, that represented in the 1920 census.

There are considerable variations in fertility among regions, though with respect to some regional comparisons the implications of various indices are inconsistent. Fertility is lower in cities than in rural districts. But apart from this contrast, the inter-regional variations have a small range and any systematic interpretation of the pattern of regional variations is extremely difficult. Mortara compares the experience of a scientist testing the validity of promising hypotheses on the nature of variations of fertility in Brazil with that of a traveller lost in a jungle whose despair deepens as he eagerly follows paths that end in thickets.

An appreciable proportion of births in Brazil occur outside of institutionally recognized marital relations. According to the 1940 census, 25.8 per cent of the single women aged 25–29 years are (or have been) mothers. Among single women 50 years old and over, 39.5 per cent are mothers—with an average of 5.6 live births per mother. However, the fertility of single women is much below that of married women. At ages 25–29 years, 81.5 per cent of the married women are mothers. Beyond 50 years of age, 91.5 per cent of the married women, 87.3 per cent of the separated or divorced, and 91.7 per cent of the widows are mothers—with averages of 8.2, 6.6, and 7.4 live births per mother. Among all women aged 50 years or over (regardless of marital status at the time of the census), 84.2 per cent were mothers—with an average of 7.6 children per mother.

Absence of 'marriage' has different significance in various regions. In cities it frequently means the absence of any stable conjugal union. In

---

[1] Mortara's text was prepared prior to the completion of the present writer's text. His terms may not at all points be intended to carry the implications given to these terms in the present text. Mortara's formulations have influenced our interpretations; but the former are independent of the latter.

rural districts, conjugal unions among unmarried persons often have a high degree of stability. Nevertheless, the absence of institutionally recognized formal relations reduces the responsibility of those associated in these unions, both with respect to one another and with respect to their children.

Respect for marriage as an institution, in spite of the frequency of births outside of marriage, clearly operates as a factor tending to restrain fertility. This is shown, for example, by the fact cited above that only 25.8 per cent of the single women 25–29 years old (single women being about three-tenths of all women at these ages) reported live births, as compared with 81.5 per cent of the married women. But measurement of the extent to which marriage as an institution influences fertility in Brazil is difficult for several reasons. In the first place, the passage of individuals with advancing age from the class of single persons to the class of married persons complicates the analysis. The proportion of single women in different age classes declines from 85.6 per cent at 15–19 years, to 48.1 per cent at 20–24 years, 29.1 per cent at 25–29 years, and to 14.5 per cent at 50 years and over. There is, of course, in the reports by married women on the number of previous births, no differentiation between pre-marital and post-marital births. Mortara deals with this problem in his analysis.

Mortara suggests that the institution of marriage is 'the most important social factor influencing the level of fertility in Brazil'. It is obviously an important factor. But the present writer doubts that the net effect of this institution on the actual level of fertility in Brazil is so large as he infers. Mortara estimates from the precise information at his disposal that there is an average retardation of eight years in the initiation of fertility due to avoidance of maternity prior to marriage. But in making this estimate he does not take account of the possible influence of 'adolescent sterility' (in the restricted sense in which we have used the term) as a factor tending to prolong intervals between menstruation and first pregnancy. The evidence on this subject is somewhat problematic, but we concluded that it provides substantial support of the concept.[1] If this conclusion is correct, it would lead to a downward revision of Mortara's estimate.

Another important consideration in this problem is the possible relation of absence of marriage to the incidence of sterility. If a tendency to neglect marriage as an institution is associated with behaviour tending to increase sterility, it is possible that in Brazil the influence of marriage in reducing sterility and thus indirectly tending to raise the general level of fertility is as powerful as its direct tendency to lower the general level of fertility by inhibiting extramarital fertility.

At the risk of venturing into 'the jungle' of unrewarding hypotheses to which Mortara has referred, the writer suggests that this interpretation may have some relevance to the analysis of regional and other differentials

[1] See above, Chapter I.

in fertility in Brazil. There are wide regional variations in the extent of extramarital fertility. Among women of all ages (above 12 years) who have ever borne a child, the proportion of single women varies from 30.6 per cent in Pará, 27.7 per cent in Maranhão, 23.0 per cent in Mato Grosso, 22.1 per cent in Amazonas, and 21.3 per cent in Bahia, at one extreme, to 1.7 per cent in São Paulo, 3.1 per cent in Minas Gerais, 3.6 per cent in Ceará, 3.9 per cent in Paraná, and 4.8 per cent in Santa Catarina at the other extreme. But the general maternity rate is as high or higher in the latter group as in the former:

TABLE 20.

State	Births per year per 1,000 women aged 15 years and over (standardized for age)
Pará	294
Maranhão	312
Mato Grosso	304
Amazonas	334
Bahia	322
São Paulo	329
Minas Gerais	353
Ceará	351
Paraná	354
Santa Catarina	353
All States (Brazil)	330

Mortara points out that the lack of concern about fertility outside of marriage which is prevalent in some regions and among some groups in Brazil reflects the influence of slavery, which remained in force to 1888.

The present writer suggests that the influence of slavery may also be reflected in the widespread lack of concern about the economic and social consequences of unlimited fertility, within or without marriage. The presence of an expanding frontier may also, in a more positive sense, have encouraged high fertility. According to Freyre, patterns of promiscuity were established among Portuguese active in the slave trade long before the conquest of Brazil, and again in relations between conquerors and natives in the conquest of Brazil.[1] The rise of the great sugar plantations, according to Freyre, brought a regime of uncontrolled sexual relations. New conditions have, of course, made possible the formation of new social patterns. But in Brazil, as in the United States, the blight of abolished

[1] Gilberto Freyre. *The Masters and the Slaves* (translated from fourth edition by Samuel Putnam). New York, 1946.

systems of slavery is still felt in different ways. It is significant that the regions of highest frequency of extra-marital births in Brazil are either old plantation areas or sparsely settled regions with relatively large indigenous populations.

If the hypothesis set forth above is correct, it may be that the promotion of greater respect for marriage would temporarily tend to raise the level of fertility in some regions where marriage is now most neglected. But advance along this line is an essential condition of any far-reaching rational control of fertility. Increased emphasis on restricting procreation outside of marriage signifies a movement toward recognition of social obligations in personal relations. But it does not necessarily imply a recognition of social responsibility for the consequences of procreation.

On the contrary, the evidence clearly indicates, as stated by Mortara, 'that the restraint exercised by economic and social factors is quite feeble, except as regards the influence with respect to marriage'. Among the states listed above as having a low frequency of extra-marital fertility, all except one have an apparent level of fertility above the national average. The exception is São Paulo. This is the state with the lowest relative frequency of extra-marital fertility (1.7 per cent on the index described above). Another factor seems to be at work here, which may be an extension of the recognition of economic and social factors, beyond restriction of extra-marital fertility, to some restriction of fertility within marriage. This is one of the two states in which Mortara suggests, on the basis of incidental information, that there may be an appreciable, though not extensive, practice of family limitation, the other being Rio Grande do Sul. In São Paulo the proportion of the total population living in cities (36 per cent) is higher than in any other state, and this affects the results. (We have omitted references to the Federal District, as presenting special conditions.) The information on Rio Grande do Sul does not fit neatly with the formulations outlined above. The proportion of single women among all mothers in this state (11.3 per cent) is practically the same as the average for all Brazil. But it has a low general fertility rate as defined above (307, national average being 330). However, the relative frequency of illiteracy here (39 per cent) is lower than in any other state, indicating a relatively high cultural level, in spite of the moderately high frequency of extra-marital births.

We have discussed briefly a few aspects of the information presented by Mortara that seem especially relevant to formulations developed in other contexts. It would be superfluous for us to offer a summary or review of the series of scientific findings brought together in his systematic presentation.

240

A large field study of cultural conditions affecting fertility has been made in one-non-industrial country that may be on the threshold of a demographic transition. The reference is to an investigation in Puerto Rico, 1949–50, involving intensive interviews with 13,272 adults, selected to give a representative sample of the whole population. This approach to demographic studies has not in the past received the attention that it merits. A large demographic field study is now being conducted in Mysore, India, under the auspices of the United Nations at the request of the Government of India; but findings from the latter study are not yet available. The data from the Puerto Rican study have not yet been analysed in depth to show inter-relations among social and cultural factors affecting fertility, but information on a wide range of topics with considerable cross-classification has been published.[1]

The level of fertility in Puerto Rico appears to have been fairly constant during the last half century. An apparent slight rise in marital fertility around the 1920's or early 1930's, suggested by an intensive analysis of demographic data from the study, may merely reflect more accurate reporting by younger women. A slight decline, thereafter, to the apparent earlier level may reflect mere broadening of the married population in the total population, or it may possibly indicate a slight decline. The actual change, if any, over this period was very slight.[2] On the average, 5.7 live births were reported per ever-married woman aged 49–53 years. Among all women at these ages, 95 per cent reported themselves as having married; 13 per cent of these ever-married women were childless. There had been 6.6 live births per mother.

Puerto Rican economy is still largely dependent on agriculture, and the processing of agricultural products. It had been a slave plantation area. Though slavery had been abolished, the people were poor when the island came under the control of the United States, and there was little change in general level of living thereafter, until the last few years. (The introduction of some new industries and a recent substantial rise in real income could not be reflected in the data of the survey, but the preceding decade was a period of recovery.) Coffee agriculture declined long ago in competition with rising production under more favourable conditions in other countries. The sugar industry expanded under corporation control; concentration of

[1] Paul K. Hatt. *Backgrounds of Human Fertility in Puerto Rico.* Princeton, 1952. The study was conducted under the joint auspices of the Social Science Research Centre, the University of Puerto Rico, and the Office of Population Research, Princeton University.
[2] ibid., Chapter VII. The analysis is confused by an attempt to isolate the fertility of married couples in a situation where marital status is frequently ambiguous, especially in retrospective reports on previous experience. In the records, a first marriage was rarely dated after a first birth. All births after date of the reported first marriage were elaborately classified as 'post-nuptial'.

ownership of sugar plantations was maintained until the enforcement, in the middle thirties, of limiting legislation. Among household heads giving information on occupations, 37 per cent reported themselves as dependent on agriculture (about a third of these being wage-workers in sugar production) as compared with 8 per cent dependent on manufacturing. Only 26 per cent had independent enterprises or worked on their own account, as compared with 55 per cent employed in private concerns or by the government, while 19 per cent of the household heads were reported as engaged in domestic activities or as students.[1] Over half of the adults interviewed lived in the open country. The society has a proletarian character, but is largely rural.

The population has become more mobile. Among those 30–49 years old, 61 per cent were living outside the *municipios* where they were born, as compared with 43 per cent of those aged 50 years and over. There has been a significant migration from Puerto Rico to the mainland of the United States during the last few decades, chiefly to New York City, with some movement back and forth. Schools have been extended. At ages 20–29 years, 91 per cent had some schooling and 18 per cent had some high school experience, as compared with only 42 per cent having any schooling and 3 per cent having passed beyond the elementary grades among those aged 50 years and over.[2] The people are predominantly, though not exclusively, Roman Catholic. At ages 50 and over, 20 per cent endorsed the statement, 'religion is the most important thing in my life', and 15 per cent of those aged 20–29 years did so. But 26 per cent of the older group and 32 per cent of the younger group preferred the statement, 'I am religious in my own way'. Most of the rest expressed a generally positive attitude, with less than one per cent at any age expressing active opposition to religion.[3]

There is no evidence of any general trend toward increased formalization of conjugal unions. Among all ever-married persons, the proportion of those whose last union was legalized and had continued to the time of the study or until the death of a spouse declines from 75 per cent at ages 50 years and over, to 71 per cent at ages 30–49 years, 68 per cent at ages 20–29 years, and 59 per cent at ages under 20 years.[4] But the proportion of those legally married tends to rise within each cohort as it advances in age.

In addition to such measurable characteristics, it may be important to note that the Popular Party had risen to power about a decade before the survey. It exerted a vigorous leadership tending to stimulate new aspirations.

There are significant differentials in fertility within Puerto Rico by size of community, by level of living, and by educational experience (see

[1] ibid., pp. 32–3.
[2] ibid., pp. 256–62.
[3] ibid., p. 260.
[4] ibid., p. 296.

242

Table 22). The types of situation in which fertility is relatively low (urban residence, better houses, and experience of formal education) are expanding situations. If the expansion is rapid, and if these situations maintain their influence on fertility, this must bring about a general decline of fertility.[1] Education is the variable that is expanding most rapidly, and merits special attention on this account. The expansion of education may have further importance with respect to fertility. It may be assumed that the more educated members of the community play a more active role than others in the diffusion of attitudes. A further consideration, possibly very important, is that some definite expansion of diversified economic opportunities is taking place in Puerto Rico today (along with opportunity for unlimited movement into the United States) so that those who prolong attendance at school can have confidence that this is not leading to a dead-end.

Actually, recent data since the survey was carried out give some evidence of a decline in fertility. Crude birth rates for recent years run as in Table 21.

TABLE 21.

Period	Births per 1,000 population
1936–40	38.9
1941–45	40.0
1946–50	40.5
1951	37.2
1952	36.2

It is particularly opportune that, at just this juncture, the survey gives information on a wide variety of attitudes relating, directly or indirectly, to family life and fertility in Puerto Rico. It must, of course, be recognized that many of these attitudes are unique to the Puerto Rican situation. They do, however, give some insight into a movement of values that may be associated with an incipient movement toward lowering of fertility. We shall note in brief a few outstanding items. On critical points we shall give particular attention to the attitudes of those with some high school experience on the hypothesis that they have a leading role in the formation of community attitudes. For a similar reason, we shall also give attention to differences in attitudes between older and younger members of the adult population.

The hope that children will have school privileges is universal. Somewhat

[1] The number of cases is small in some cells of our table, but the pattern is consistent. Moreover, this pattern is confirmed by partial independent tabulations shown in ibid. Tables 258, 260, and 262.

TABLE 22. Pregnancies per Woman, to Specific Ages, in Cohorts Classified by Age at Survey, Puerto Rico.[1]

Life period:	To age 34 years			To age 44 years	
Cohort by age at survey:	34–38	39–43	44–48	44–48	49–53
Residence[2]					
Open country	5.4	5.5	5.2	6.8	7.1
10,000–49,999	3.5	3.6	4.4	5.3	4.5
50,000 +	3.3	2.8	3.1	3.7	4.6
Monthly Rent (in dollars)					
Under 5.00	5.2	5.6	4.8	6.5	6.3
5.00–9.99	5.1	4.8	5.0	6.5	6.6
10.00–19.99	4.4	4.5	4.8	5.7	5.7
20.00 +	3.1	3.0	3.4	4.1	4.6
School (years completed)					
Under 4	5.2	4.9	4.9	6.2	6.6
4–8	4.2	4.4	4.5	5.7	4.5
9 +	2.7	2.3	2.1	2.5	3.2
Number of Women					
Residence					
Open country	267	306	277	277	216
10,000–49,999	120	117	113	113	62
50,000 +	142	107	111	111	87
Monthly Rent (in dollars)					
Under 5.00	230	158	137	137	95
5.00–9.99	228	155	142	142	109
10.00–19.99	191	130	146	146	102
20.00 +	129	129	119	119	81
School					
Under 4	430	313	334	334	287
4–8	284	229	173	173	88
9 +	70	56	43	43	20

[1] Derived from Hatt, op. cit., Tables 259, 261, 263.
[2] Omitting communities (not open country) with less than 10,000 persons.

surprisingly, the only data published on this subject are responses to a question relating to interest in schooling for sons. At all ages and economic levels a majority of the adults express a wish that a son should complete high school (the median number of years stated as a preference dipping only slightly below 12 years at the lowest rental level—less than $3 per month). Furthermore, statements of expectation of 'education' for sons

244

run high. The median value begins at 6 years of schooling among those living in dwelling units for which they pay less than $3 rent per month, and moves to 11 years of 'expected schooling' for sons in the class paying $10 to $20 for rent, and still higher in the upper class. These expectations will often not be realized, but there can be no question about the prevalence of the ideal.

An attitudinal preference for small families is almost equally widespread. An expressed desire for no children is extremely rare (less than one-half of one per cent), and only 2 per cent prefer one child only. The modal preference is for two children; this is accepted as the 'ideal' size of family by 46 per cent of the men and by 51 per cent of the women—the women having a slightly stronger preference for very small families than the men (though the reverse relation seems to be prevalent in the United States). Many of the adults who have followed or are following the large family pattern in practice regard a small family as the ideal—with an apparent discrepancy of at least three births in 24 per cent of the cases.[1] When the question is phrased, 'How many children would you like a daughter of yours to have?' the preference for small families is even stronger, with about 7 per cent expressing a preference for one child only. Combining stated preferences for 0, 1, and 2 children, 60 per cent of the men and 66 per cent of the women express the hope that their daughters will have such very small families. On the question about 'ideal' size of family, younger adults express the stronger preference for small families than their elders. Among those aged 50 years or over, only 37 per cent favour the two-child family, in contrast to 55 per cent among those aged 20–29 years.

Among adults classified by school attendance, stated preference for the two-child family rises regularly from 41 per cent among those who have never attended school to 57.5 per cent among those with high school experience—and the percentage recognizing very large families as the ideal (6 or more, or an indefinite number) drops from 11 per cent to 1.5 per cent. Then an interesting change occurs. With the exception of 1.5 per cent who express an extreme opinion (either for one-child families or for 6 or more children), the 467 persons with college experience who were interviewed replied by naming some definite figure ranging from 2 to 5 children; but there is a shift toward preference for a moderately large family. The percentage describing families with 3 to 5 children as the 'ideal' is higher in their case than the proportion accepting two children as the ideal. This is not so at any other educational level except among those never attending school. The idealization of the two-child family seems mainly to represent a reaction among those with a moderate degree of education against the very large families widely prevalent in Puerto Rico—and this reaction is most intense among those with some high school education.

[1] ibid., p. 57.

The medians of stated preference for age at marriage are 26.6 years for men, and 20.8 years for women—as compared with the medians in previous practice, as indicated by the survey, about 24 years for men and 18 years for women. There is general agreement among men and women and among various educational groups on this subject.

Adults were asked to choose between alternatives in answering the question, 'Would you approve of limiting the number of children in the family on the part of' (1) everyone who wishes to; (2) those who are too poor to care for children properly; (3) only those whose health is endangered by childbearing ; (4) no one. The percentage of those who selected one of the first two replies rises gradually from 62 per cent among those with no schooling to 71 per cent among those with some high school experience. It declines to 64 per cent among those who have been to college, but with them the number selecting the third reason (perhaps deemed most relevant to their own situation) is higher than at any other level. In both the high school group and the college group, only 7 per cent express absolute opposition to the principle of family limitation. Such absolute opposition is expressed by 18 per cent of those who have never been to school at all.

There has been a trend toward sterilization as a means of controlling fertility in Puerto Rico. Among 1,535 women married during the decade 1930–39 (which ended about 10 years before the study) 183, or about 12 per cent, had been sterilized. The operation was most frequently performed after 3, 4, or 5 births, with 4 as the median. It appears to have been more frequent at upper rather than at lower income levels.

About 18 per cent of all adults express the opinion that consensual union is a good life (or the best life) for a man; and there is little difference in this respect among older and younger adults. But 17 per cent of those over 50 years express indifference on the subject, whereas only 12.5 per cent of those 20–29 years and 10 per cent of those under 20 years do so. Moreover, 20 per cent of those over 50 years but only 8 per cent of those under 20 years also say that it is a good life for a woman or express indifference.

Only 12 per cent of those who have been to high school and only 6 per cent of those who have been to college state the opinion that consensual union is a good life for a man, in contrast to 20 per cent of those with no schooling. The contrast is even sharper with respect to expressions of indifference. Only one-half of one per cent of the college group say that consensual union is a good life for a woman and only 1.3 per cent express indifference. Among the high school group, 1.4 per cent take the positively favourable position, and 3.5 per cent the indifferent one. By contrast, 6.5 per cent of the unschooled adults say this type of union is good for a woman, and 16.6 per cent say it 'doesn't matter'. Nine-tenths of the high school and college group say this is 'bad' or 'very bad' for a woman. Although no evidence of any change in general practice in this respect was found, it is apparent that disapproval tends to be associated with increased education.

246

Those with more schooling are much more favourable to employment of women outside the home than those with little or no schooling.

Those with high school or college experience express a slightly higher evaluation of religion than those with little or no education, but the difference is small. However, those with education attend religious services much more frequently than those without schooling. The percentage attending weekly or more often rises from 11 per cent among the unschooled to 27 per cent at the high school level and 35 per cent at the college level. Similarly, the percentage 'never' attending religious services drops from 22 per cent at the lowest educational level to 15 per cent and 12 per cent at the upper levels.

Summarizing the items noted above, we find that advance in education in Puerto Rico is associated with interest in increased schooling, a preference for small or relatively small families, approval of formal education, approval of employment of women, support for the family as an institution, and support of religious institutions. This constellation of values stands in contrast to attitudes of submission to circumstances and indifference to goals that have stemmed from social disorganization and persistent poverty in Puerto Rico.

CONCLUSIONS

The hypotheses developed in this study suggest the operation of five major conditions as tending to induce high fertility.

1. Perpetual groups of a corporate character, with membership wholly or mainly determined by descent, and with established lines of authority usually imply emphasis on inter-group economic and cultural competition within a society, and are frequently associated with a tribal organization oriented toward military power in competition with other societies for the control of natural resources. Such groups tend to motivate and support high fertility.

2. Sacred values and religious sanctions in some cultures, though not in all cultures, motivate the procreation of large families as an ideal, or motivate early marriage as a means for assuring the perpetuation of family lines, or inhibit interference with reproductive processes.

3. Cohesive groups, such as extended families, provide strong support for their members in fulfilling expected roles and they tend to enforce conformity to norms approved by their leaders and generally by their members. They do not necessarily stimulate high fertility, if dissociated from emphasis on competitive relations or sacred values that require high fertility. But in the context of most agrarian cultures under pre-modern conditions, they have generally tended to promote high fertility. In other situations their influence might, at least in theory, be directed toward restriction of fertility—though the pattern in Tikopia provides

the only non-ambiguous concrete illustration of such an emphasis. However, the highly structured societies of Japan and the Parsi community in India have permitted spontaneous action by individual families in the control of fertility. It may even be that, in spite of the absence of official encouragement or even the presence of official opposition to these trends, the highly disciplined personal character of the members of these societies has been an important factor in the efficacy of their spontaneous responses.

4. The lack of efficient, convenient, or culturally acceptable means of controlling human fertility has tended to prevent effective restriction, especially in societies with a strong cultural preference for early marriages, except in response to very strong motivation.

Motivation for limitation of families in pre-modern Europe was sufficiently strong to cause widespread postponement of marriage but not sufficiently strong to cause any widespread resort to available anti-natal practices. The early phase of the modern movement toward family limitation in European society was due to the rise of more intense motivation for the control of fertility or a shift in cultural attitudes toward available means, or both. But in its later phases this movement has been powerfully influenced by the development of more efficacious and convenient and more culturally acceptable techniques of regulating procreation.

The future prospects of present agrarian societies with respect to the control of fertility may be affected by the wider range of measures now available and the possibilities of new developments in this field.

5. Apathetic acceptance of circumstances—especially in situations where traditional values have been weakened through processes of social disorganization, but which are relatively free from acute social conflict or a prevalence of sterility-inducing diseases—tends to promote a high level of fertility through relaxation of restraints on man's biological propensity for procreation.[1]

Conditions which, it has been suggested, may induce reduction of fertility come under two main categories.

1. Acute social disorganization may release modes of behaviour that are inherently incompatible with any stable patterns of social life, and may be associated with the spread of sterility-inducing diseases. These conditions may lead to declines of fertility that have no necessary limit short of the extinction of the society in which they prevail, or a transition toward more orderly social life and improvements in health.

2. Social and cultural adjustments to actual conditions of living tend to induce widespread restriction of fertility when such restriction is

---

[1] The influence of new access to unlimited resources available for exploitation with traditional techniques—as in colonial America—should logically be listed as a sixth major condition. It is omitted from this brief summary in view of its lack of relevance to the modern scene.

recognized, or assumed, to be favourable to the achievement of accepted goals.

The first conditions in each of the two preceding lists can be considered in the same context. The free play of tribal societies and the maintenance in full force of their traditional forms of authority and of the control and transmission of property is nearly at an end. In most parts of the world such societies where they still exist are subject to outside interference and restrictions; their social structures are either in process of dissolution or are undergoing important modifications.

Societies with traditional cultures may or may not develop the necessary adaptability to meet changed conditions without disruptive disorganization. The factors which determine whether or not this happens are very complex. The subject is one that merits and is receiving major scientific attention; it far exceeds the scope of this limited study. We will note only a few aspects, directly related to our topic.

Any transition to new modes of stable social life—involving stable conditions of economic enterprise or employment, stable patterns of family life, and improved conditions of health—will, quite inevitably, involve rapid increases of population over a very considerable period. Any concern about limitation of families as a means of improving the adjustment of population to resources is so foreign to traditional modes of thinking in most tribal societies that any suggestion along this line is likely to be immediately repudiated. It is likely, in fact, to be interpreted as a device to distract attention from claims for more ample resources against other native populations or colonists. Fortunately, tribal societies by their nature rarely make intensive use of resources, so that there is generally a relatively low ratio of population to natural resources in their situations. A period of rapid growth of population must be expected as a result of such transition— as, for example, a doubling of the native population in Africa south of the Sahara during the next forty to fifty years—except where this is checked by chaotic social conditions or disease. Eventually, as social progress is advanced, the trend toward rapid increase may be checked by a rationalistic restriction of fertility; but we noted that even in the coastal region and university circles of the Gold Coast any such tendency is, as yet, barely incipient.

Conditions that seem to be important in arresting tendencies toward acute social disorganization, or correcting such a tendency already in force, include stable economic enterprises and employment, improved health, and the emergence of new emphasis on the values of marriage and parenthood in the nuclear, monogamous family. The latter trend involves a shift from attitudes toward wives and children as possessions to be 'claimed' and exploited to attitudes of greater respect for wives and children as *persons* to be cherished and enjoyed, and to greater sense of responsibility for the nurture and education of children. This trend will, in part, emerge as a response to new opportunities for the education of children. Such conditions, which appear essential for the promotion of stable social relations, may also be required as an essential basis for an eventual orderly and rational control of fertility.

Sacred values lie outside the scope of the social scientists, except as regards the study of their objective relations, including conditions affecting their development and their role in human affairs. Such values are constantly in process of development, re-interpretation, and new application in any living society. For example, ancient religious dogmas are interpreted in application to industrial relations to which they originally had no explicit reference. Moreover, their implications, as viewed by those who cherish them most deeply, involve issues of precise interpretation and emphasis not fully appreciated by others. Only those who cherish these values sincerely are capable of developing them, in the context of changing conditions, in such ways that religious values can function as vital forces in the culture of any society.

Cohesive groups with firm lines of authority have, in the past, rarely exerted a positive influence in the direction of any restriction of fertility, as noted above. The moderate, but significant, control of fertility in pre-modern Europe, mainly through postponement of marriage, and the more drastic control of fertility through its restriction within marriage in modern European society have been brought about by the spontaneous responses of nuclear families to their actual conditions of living, in societies with a rather loose structuring of personal relations. Even in modern Japan the trends toward postponement of marriage and toward restriction of fertility within marriage have been spontaneous individual responses rather than socially directed movements—at least prior to the last few years. But this is not an inevitable relation, inherent in the nature of cohesive groups.

It is by no means impossible that socially directed movements, sometimes with government sponsorship, led by intellectual, social, and religious leaders, teachers, physicians, and councils, such as the panchayats in India, may play a far larger role in this sphere of human interests in Asia than has been the case in Europe. It is important to note in this connexion that the cultural conditions that have tended to sustain high fertility in most Asiatic societies have not explicitly required unlimited fertility. They have required early marriage, but this seems subject to modification. And, with improved conditions of child health, the deep cultural need for a surviving son can be assured with smaller families than were required in the past.

Any significant trend toward lowering of fertility must, however, in the last analysis be a 'democratic process'—in the sense that it can only be achieved by a widespread popular response in matters of sexual behaviour and family interests to actual conditions of life, as perceived and interpreted by the many individuals who form a nation. It will, therefore, be affected by two sets of background conditions:

First, ways in which objective conditions of living impinge on the affairs of individuals and primary families in towns and villages—opportunities

250

for raising real levels of living through diligence, prevention of the economic exploitation of children, possibilities of improved positions for children through their attendance at schools, opportunities for gainful employment by women, possibilities of improvement in health through greater emphasis on sanitation, nutrition, and improved methods of child care, etc.

Secondly, factors affecting the ability of individuals to understand objective relations, and to draw correct inferences about the relation of behaviour to welfare—through the acquisition of words and concepts useful in analysing these relations, and increased understanding of mechanics, agronomy, contracts, politics, physiology, etc.

Any public policy directed toward lowering fertility, to be effective, must not only provide efficient and acceptable means of controlling fertility, but must also be concerned with the development of 'background conditions' favourable to such control.

In view of the infinite complexity of the factors tending to induce a demographic transition in the context of an economic and social transition, problems of policy and administration influencing these changes can only be adequately resolved by political leaders and scholars who comprehend these problems, both in detail and in broad perspectives. In any case, recognition of the responsibility of the people of any nation and of their accepted leaders for guiding its affairs is a basic principle of international relations. Even from strictly demographic considerations, as suggested in the following paragraph, there is added reason for insistence on strict adherence to this principle.

Cultural inertia, such as that likely to result from the breakdown of social institutions and the disorganization of personal relations, tends to leave elemental impulses toward procreation relatively unrestrained, and thus to hamper any rational adjustment of reproductive patterns to objective conditions. In the opinion of the present writer, it is the most powerful obstacle in the modern world to the rational ordering of personal behaviour influencing population trends. This may be a gross exaggeration of the importance of this condition, but there can be no doubt that it is one of the major factors in perpetuating levels of fertility that now hamper real economic advance in many countries. The Charybdis of social disorganization and irresponsible procreation can be avoided in escaping the Scylla of obsolete custom only if the processes of economic, social, and demographic transition are guided by accepted and well-equipped leaders.

This leads to a final conclusion. It is important that there be in every society a core of competent scientists equipped to analyse and interpret social and demographic trends, and to discover the larger implications of actual and possible changes. The degree to which a society is able to determine its own destiny depends in part on the extent to which it participates in advancing the general fund of the world's knowledge about human affairs and on its capacity to interpret accurately the conditions affecting its own life.

PART TWO

A Demographic Field Study in Ashanti

by
MEYER FORTES

With the assistance of
T. E. Kyei, K. D. S. Baldwin,
Sheila Mallett

CHAPTER I

The Social Background

INTRODUCTION

The field study recorded here was undertaken with three main objects in view. I wanted to find out how far certain customary laws (such as the law of clan exogamy) and conventional ideals (such as that of local endogamy) which might be expected to influence demographic conditions, are actually followed. I wanted also to obtain some reliable information on the trend of fertility in a southern Ashanti community and relate it to the social and economic organization. Lastly, I wanted to try out the possibility of using a team of volunteer workers, not specifically trained for such tasks, in social enquiries of this sort. The study was one of the projects undertaken in the course of a social, geographical and economic survey of the territory of Ashanti in the Gold Coast, carried out by the Sociological Department of the West African Institute in 1945.[1] The study was carried out in the township of Agogo, Ashanti-Akim. Agogo is the capital township of a locally autonomous political sub-division of Ashanti which was one of several areas selected 'for intensive investigation. The study included a detailed enquiry into land utilization and land tenure (Steel); the systematic estimation of family incomes and expenditure in relation to occupational differences (Ady); and the collection of sociological data on family

[1] The geographical research was carried out by Mr. R. W. Steel, M.A., B.Sc., of the School of Geography, University of Oxford, who was a temporary member of the staff of the West African Institute for this purpose. The economic investigations were under the direction of Miss Peter Ady, M.A., of the Institute of Statistics, University of Oxford, who came out to the Gold Coast as a Colonial Research Fellow. As Head of the Sociological Department of the West African Institute, I was myself responsible for the sociological enquiries. We also had the assistance of a number of African field workers seconded to us by various Gold Coast Government departments, and I make grateful acknowledgment for this valuable and indispensable help. The scope and aims of the survey are briefly described in a joint paper by myself and my colleagues (M. Fortes, R. W. Steel, and P. Ady, 'The Ashanti Survey, 1945–46', *Geog. Jnl.*, 110, 4–6 1948, pp. 149–79) and my paper 'The Ashanti Social Survey: A Preliminary Report', *Rhodes-Livingstone Institute Journal*, VI, 1948. Certain features of Ashanti kinship institutions to which reference is made in the present paper are more fully described in my paper 'Kinship and Marriage among the Ashanti' in *African System of Kinship and Marriage*, edited by A. R. Radcliffe-Brown and Daryll Forde, 1950.

Bamboi
Kintampo
Prang
Attabubu
Wenchi
Techiman
Nkoranza
Kasei
Berekum
Ejura
Sunyani
Bechem
Mampong
Fwidiem
Efidusai **Agogo**
Asokore
Goaso
Kumasi
Konongo
Nkawie Kuma
Juaso
Kokei
Nyamieni
L.Bosumtwi
Bekwai
Obuasi
Prasu

10 5 0 10 20 30
MILES

Ashanti Gold Coast

Sketch map to show situation of Agogo

256

structure, political and legal institutions, and other relevant aspects of social organization (Fortes).

Agogo is in Southern Ashanti (see map), which can fairly be described as one of the most prosperous parts of the Gold Coast. At the present time cocoa growing is the basis of the economy of Southern Ashanti and Ashanti-Akim is one of the oldest cocoa growing districts of Ashanti. Our records show that cocoa was first planted in Agogo over forty years ago,[1] but food crops like the plantain, the yam, the cocoyam, maize and cassava are also grown extensively in the region. The railway and the excellent road system, the considerable development of gold mining, and the expansion of commerce following on the rapid establishment of cocoa farming, have led to the growth of a number of modern towns in Southern Ashanti, notably the capital, Kumasi (population 70,000). During the past 25 years Southern Ashanti has thus become the most densely populated part of the territory. According to the census of 1948 the total population of Ashanti[2] numbered 818,944, about two-thirds living in the southern part of the country. A fair proportion (rising to as much as 45 per cent in some of the towns) consists of immigrants from other parts of the Gold Coast. Labourers from the Northern Territories and clerical workers, artisans and traders from the Gold Coast are found in every town and village of Ashanti. The census of 1931 is known to have been far from accurate and the apparent increase of about 41 per cent in the population of Ashanti between 1931 and 1948 must not be accepted without reserve. But all the evidence points to a considerable increase during this period and this must be mainly due to natural increase among the Ashanti themselves. Adequate data for assessing this have not however hitherto been available.[3]

The economy of modern Ashanti is based on the export of cocoa, gold, timber and kola nuts, supplemented by the cultivation by traditional methods of food crops for home consumption and by other indigenous food-getting activities such as hunting and fishing. Imported goods of all kinds, especially textiles, but including also a great range of other goods such as kerosene, gunpowder, cigarettes, cement and galvanized iron for building purposes, tinned foods, tools and implements, etc., have become essential items in the Ashanti pattern of consumption. There is a vigorous internal trade in which both large oversea firms and numerous native

[1] Cocoa was first introduced into the Gold Coast in 1879 but did not become firmly established as an export crop until about 1900. As is well known, cocoa growing is almost entirely a peasant industry, cf. W. E. F. Ward, *A History of the Gold Coast*, Allen & Unwin, 1949, pp. 350–1.

[2] See *The Gold Coast Census of Population 1948, Report and Tables*, published by The Crown Agents for the Colonies, 1950, p. 42, Table 4.

[3] For a critical discussion of the general demographic situation in Ashanti see R. W. Steel, 'The Population of Ashanti: A Geographical Analysis', *Geog. Jnl.*, 112, 1948, pp. 64 ff. The 1948 census report (p. 25, Table 7), estimates an average annual percentage increase of 2.44 as having occurred in Ashanti since 1931.

petty traders play a part. Forty years of missionary and Government activity have, moreover, led to the emergence of a literate minority, the building of schools and churches, and the growth of Christian communities in almost every village. European medical services provided by the Government, missions and private practitioners are well established in the towns and the demand for them far exceeds the available facilities. The first stage on the way to a differentiated economy of a European type has already been reached in Ashanti. This is clearly seen in the contemporary social structure. There have been great changes also in the political and legal institutions of the country which have contributed to this process of structural differentiation.

These changes have gone farthest in the urban centres; in the rural areas the traditional norms and values still prevail among the majority of people. The small minority of literate people employed as clerks, teachers, and government servants are very often immigrants. Most Christians are still illiterate and live in accordance with the same standards as their pagan relatives, apart from matters of formal religion. In particular, rank and political allegiance, rights of domicile and of inheritance, the regulation of marriage and of residence, and the most important legal and moral obligations of the members of a community towards one another are determined by the rules of kinship; and in Ashanti the fundamental law of kinship is the reckoning of descent in the matrilineal line.[1] It is of great significance that the principle of matrilineal descent and the legal rules, the domestic arrangements, the affective attitudes and the customary values bound up with it retain as strong a hold among literate and Christian as among illiterate pagan Ashanti, and among the townsfolk as well as among the farmers and hunters of the villages.

Agogo is one of the largest rural townships of Southern Ashanti.[2] Its economy is typical of this part of the country. It has also been a centre of missionary work for half a century and now has a large Christian community. An excellent hospital with a European staff, famed throughout the Gold Coast, was established in the township by the Basel Mission in 1929.[3] By 1939 not only were the people of Agogo and the neighbouring villages making great use of the medical facilities offered by the hospital but patients were flocking to it from every part of the Gold Coast. Catering for this traffic was a profitable sideline of many of the local people. The

[1] cf. R. S. Rattray, *Ashanti*, 1923; and M. Fortes, 'Kinship and Marriage in Ashanti', op. cit.

[2] For further details, see M. Fortes, 'Time and Social Structure: An Ashanti Case Study', in *Social Structure:* essays presented to A. R. Radcliffe-Brown, ed. by M. Fortes, Clarendon Press, 1949.

[3] The medical staff was German and Swiss and at the outbreak of the war in 1939 the German doctor in charge was interned. The hospital was closed down and some of the buildings were requisitioned as a training centre for clerical and office staff for the armed forces. By 1945 the buildings had been returned to the mission but the hospital had not yet been re-opened.

pre-natal and infant clinics run by the hospital staff are said to have been popular with the local women.[1] Unfortunately there are no statistics available from which the influence of the hospital on the health conditions of the area can be gauged. Besides the hospital, the Basel Mission also maintained a training college for women teachers to which students from all over the Gold Coast were admitted. The village school was said to have been of rather a low standard in 1939 but was being extended to cover the whole primary course in 1945. A regular market and several petty traders' stores as well as the buying sheds of firms engaged in the export of cocoa show that Agogo is an active centre of local trade.

The social conditions of Agogo are thus representative of the economically and socially stratified society that is emerging in Southern Ashanti. It is characteristic of these conditions that traditional norms and values flourish undiminished in association with—often in opposition to—the habits and practices that have grown up as a result of the changes outlined above. Indeed in this respect Agogo is somewhat more conservative than most other townships of equal importance in Southern Ashanti. The great majority of its inhabitants are illiterate farmers. On many a Sunday morning, while the service is going on in the Christian church, a lively and vociferous crowd can be seen celebrating a native religious cult a stone's throw away. In domestic life and family relations in particular, the people of Agogo follow the customs of their fathers and grandfathers.

Several circumstances strengthen the hold of the traditional way of life in Agogo. The township is in a comparatively isolated geographical position, 18 miles from the nearest urban centre, the mining town of Konongo, and it has a road connexion only with Konongo. Though this has not prevented immigration into or emigration from the township, these movements have been less extensive than is the case in many other cocoa areas of Ashanti. Both native tradition and references by nineteenth century European travellers show that Agogo has been in existence on its present site for at least a century and probably for twice or even thrice that length of time. This stability has been due to a large extent to its geographical situation, but also to the fact that it is the capital township of a chiefdom which is fairly small and compact. Before the British conquest and the adoption of cocoa farming, the majority of the subjects of such a chiefdom would have had their homes in the capital township. Most of their farms would have been within walking distance, and those whose farms lay further afield would have had cottages on their farm land where they could stay for short periods during the planting and harvesting seasons. Yet further afield out in the forest or on the Afram plains would have been the occasional hunting camps of the men who gained their livelihood almost entirely from hunting or from fishing. This pattern of

---

[1] Owing to the closing down of the hospital, it was unfortunately not possible to get at the records and figures to substantiate these statements. I am quoting local African informants.

settlement has been very largely retained in Agogo. The total population of the chiefdom is about 4,800 (males, 2,300; females, 2,500).[1]

All these people have homes in the township, but about 20 per cent nowadays also have cottages on their farmlands where they live for two or three months at a stretch during peak periods of the agricultural year. This concentration of population in one place has been a great advantage for the present enquiry.

As in most large Ashanti settlements, there is a marked preference for local endogamy in Agogo. The great majority of the women marry men of the chiefdom or of nearby villages of adjacent chiefdoms, as we shall see, and extensive genealogies collected by Mr. T. E. Kyei show that this has been the custom for many generations. Genealogical data show that over 90 per cent of the locally born inhabitants are the children of Agogo-born parents and grandparents.

The population we are concerned with in this enquiry thus presents a very high degree of social and ethnic homogeneity. The tendency towards local inbreeding is common amongst most of the indigenous peoples of West Africa. The biological effects of this have never been investigated. It is conceivable, however, that it may be a factor in local variations in reproductive performance which may be masked in a sample taken indiscriminately over a wide geographical range even within the same tribe.[2] This source of bias is eliminated by restricting an experimental enquiry like the present one to a concentrated, homogeneous population. There is an advantage also in holding environmental variables constant by limiting such a study to one locality. Southern Ashanti and Northern Ashanti, though occupied by people of apparently common stock speaking the same language and following the same customs, differ quite markedly in climate, vegetation and other ecological conditions[3] and there are corresponding differences in the staple diet of the two areas. In the north the yam is the basic foodstuff, in the south it is the plantain and the cocoyam. The economy of the north is still almost wholly a subsistence economy, as cocoa cannot grow there and no other export crop or industry exists. Southern Ashanti, however, is so uniform in climate and environment that conclusions reached about any locality in this area are broadly applicable to the whole.

[1] On the basis of his land utilization survey, Mr. Steel estimated the population of the chiefdom at about 4,500. My own estimate based on the fertility census (see below) was approximately 5,000. A figure about halfway between these two estimates is probably as near as one can get. This excludes people not resident in the chiefdom at the time of the survey but who nevertheless regard Agogo as their home and are estimated to number not less than 600. According to the census of 1948, the total population of Agogo was 4,744 (males, 2,220; females, 2,524) and possibly more.

[2] As for instance was done by A. W. Cardinall in his analysis of the 1931 census data—see his *The Gold Coast, 1931*, Government Printer, Gold Coast, 1932. The otherwise admirable paper by Mr. and Mrs. Culwick, to which reference is made below, is open to the same criticism.

[3] cf. R. W. Steel, *Geog. Jnl.*, loc. cit.

This argument applies also to the endemic diseases found in the tropics. Malaria, which is generally held to be one of the main causes of infant mortality, is endemic throughout Ashanti; whereas sleeping sickness is said to be hyperendemic in some areas (e.g., in the vicinity of Kumasi) and relatively uncommon in other areas.[1]

Finally, it is possible that local demographic variations may be correlated with variations in sexual, marriage and kinship customs and relations. The minor local differences found in this sphere in Southern Ashanti are too small to have any influence. Thus, the widespread African custom which prohibits sex relations between the parents of an infant throughout the lactation period is not met with anywhere in Ashanti. The economic responsibilities of women, the treatment given to parturient mothers and new-born infants, the values attached to offspring, techniques of infant care and weaning, and the numerous other customary practices which might affect the health and survival of infants and children, are much the same in all rural districts of Ashanti.

To sum up, then, Agogo may be taken to be fully representative of the rural districts of Southern Ashanti, more particularly of its more prosperous and conservative areas.

FIELD TECHNIQUES AND PROBLEMS

In Ashanti, field work that demands intimate contact with the people can only be successfully carried out with the support of the chief and elders of the community. If the subject of one's investigations concerns the women, it is essential also to have the support of the queen mother, who is the supreme authority in all matters pertaining specially to women. In Agogo we were lucky enough to find an educated chief who quickly grasped the purpose of our enquiries. His help and that of his sister, the queen mother, made it possible to enlist the co-operation of the older women, who are the key persons in all family affairs.

The most difficult part of the present enquiry was the actual collection of the data. This task was under the direct supervision of my principal research assistant, Mr. T. E. Kyei, who had been seconded to the Ashanti

[1] Information from Dr. G. S. Saunders, Director of the Anti-tryponomiasis Campaign of the Gold Coast Medical Department. So little is known of health conditions in Ashanti rural areas that it is not worth speculating on their possible effects on demographic conditions. (But cf. reference to a paper by Colbourne, p. 318, below.) All medical practitioners, both official and private, with whom I have discussed this subject are, however, emphatic as to the toll taken by malaria among young children. A small investigation made at my request in a village 30 miles from Kumasi, showed that 13 per cent of a group of 196 children aged 6–13 years had enlarged spleens. Blood slides of 69 of these children showed that 50 per cent had malignant tertian parasites. I was informed on the highest authority that 70 per cent of nearly 5,000 men from Ashanti who volunteered for military service in 1942 were rejected as unfit.

Social Survey by the Gold Coast Department of Education. Mr. Kyei is a member of an important Agogo lineage and this proved to be a major contribution to the success of our investigations. His intimate knowledge of the community and his personal influence with kinsfolk and friends enabled us to check errors in the information given to us and to resolve discrepancies that might have escaped notice.

Vital statistics are of course not recorded in Agogo our anywhere else in rural Ashanti. We were obliged therefore to fall back on the census method in order to obtain the data we required. The limitations and drawbacks of data obtained in this way are obvious[1] and all they can be expected to yield is some general indications of demographic trends. The most satisfactory use of the census method would be to take a census of the entire population being studies on a given day and then to record every birth, death and marriage in the community for a calendar year thereafter. This would meet the requirement, sometimes overlooked in demographic investigations in societies without vital records,[2] and the data used should refer to a fixed period of time. We had, however, neither the time nor the staff for such a task and had to be content with a single census. To minimize errors such a census should be completed in the shortest possible time, ideally in one day. If it takes a long time, births, deaths, and marriages will take place in the meantime, and those occurring among families interviewed at the outset will be overlooked, while those which befall the families interviewed towards the end will be counted. In Ashanti there is a further reason for concentrating a census into the shortest possible time. Both men and women are in the habit of moving about a good deal. They go off to their more distant farms for a few days at a time, or pay a visit to the nearest town, or to kinsfolk in other parts of the country. Lastly, speed is advisable owing to the residential arrangements of Ashanti families. In Agogo, as was known to us from preliminary enquiries, many married pairs do not live in the same house. The wife and the young children live with her maternal kin and the husband with his.[3] But husband and wife are often found in each other's homes and double countings can easily occur. Indeed, this happened in a few cases in the present enquiry, when a woman was first recorded in her own home by one interviewer, and later in her husband's home by another interviewer. These cases were, however, detected by Mr. Kyei.

Our original intention was to make a census of a representative sample

[1] They are discussed by Enid Charles and Daryll Forde, 'Notes on Some Population Data from a Southern Nigerian Village', *Sociolog. Review*, 2, Vol. XXX, 1938 and by M. Fortes, 'A Note on Fertility among the Tallensi of the Gold Coast', *Sociolog. Review*, 3–4, Vol. XXXV, 1943.

[2] As for instance by A. T. and G. M. Culwick, 'A Study of Population in Ulanga, Tanganyika Territory', *Sociolog. Review*, 4, Vol. XXX, 1938 and 1, Vol. XXXI, 1939.

[3] Subsequent investigation showed that nearly three out of four married women in Agogo normally live with their own maternal kin. The details are given in Fortes, 'Time and Social Structure', 1949.

of Agogo families. The custom of husband and wife so often living in separate domestic groups was, however, a serious obstacle. Another difficulty was the high incidence of divorce. In the absence of statistical information about the incidence of different kinds of domestic and family groups, or the age, sex and occupational composition of the community, it was obviously not going to be possible to cast a representative sample. In view of these difficulties and since our main object was to gather data for estimating demographic trends, we decided to confine the enquiry to the women only and to include in the census the entire adult female population resident in the township during the time of the census. This meant that a considerable number of interviewers would be needed to get through the census speedily and also that they should preferably be women. For though Ashanti of both sexes take the greatest pride in their children and are always ready to talk about them, many of the details we were interested in were felt to belong essentially to the province of the women. Men and women who are not close kin do not talk about sexual and reproductive matters; and though our enquiry was not concerned with the more intimate aspects of sex and reproduction it was clear that male interviewers might cause embarrassment to many of the women.

The first practical problem thus turned out to be the recruitment of a sufficiently large group of female interviewers. This difficulty was overcome through the kindness of the Principal of the Basel Mission Training College for Women Teachers. The college stands on the outskirts of Agogo, and though all the students are boarders they are known to the people of the township. The staff, both African and European, are highly respected throughout the district. With the co-operation of the principal a team of 16, made up of members of the African teaching staff and a number of senior students, was enlisted. Though only a few of them were Ashanti, most of them came from culturally related areas and all spoke Ashanti.

It is worth recording that the request for help from these girls was met with enthusiasm. The principal felt that the enquiry would make the girls aware of many things in the life of African women which their ordinary curriculum could not teach them; and the girls themselves welcomed the task as an opportunity of social service. I found, in discussions with them, that the subject of our enquiry was of the deepest interest to them. They had been taught some physiology and hygiene and this made it easy to explain to them fairly fully and frankly what kind of information was sought and what out object was. A questionnaire (See Appendix B) was drawn up in consultation with Mr. Kyei and other Ashanti advisors and the girls were thoroughly drilled in the details of it. They were then taken out by Mr. Kyei and myself on a house-to-house visit in the township and given some practice in interviewing the women. They were next divided into four groups, of four members each, and it was arranged that they should work in pairs so as to check one another. A map showing the location of every house in the township was prepared by Mr. Kyei, on

263

the basis of which a section of the township was allocated to each team of interviewers.

The field work was divided into two parts. First of all, on a selected day, a record was made of all the adult women who were normally resident in the township, an adult woman being defined as one who had reached or passed the age of menstruation. This list was compiled by visiting every house and interviewing every adult woman present. Information about absent women was given by those at home. We thus had a list as complete as the circumstances permitted of all women of child-bearing age and over who regarded Agogo as their home and would normally be resident there. It served as a most valuable check in the main enquiry. For this, the interviewers again visited every house in each of the sections allocated to each group. Every adult woman was interviewed and the information recorded on a separate form for each woman. Completed forms were turned in every day and were checked by Mr. Kyei. If he found discrepancies or inaccuracies, the faulty forms were corrected by a second interview on the following day. Only information personally given by the women whose reproductive histories were being taken was recorded and only this inform-ation is used in the present analysis. The field work, it is obvious, was laborious, and called for great patience and tact. It took just a fortnight to finish. As far as could be ascertained, no births during this fortnight escaped notice and no infant deaths occurred. This is a matter on which error is easy, however, as there is no public funeral for an infant. The census thus records the population dealt with as it was on the last day of the fortnight.

This census, which will be referred to as the fertility census, was carried out in October 1945. In December 1945 Miss Ady and her field staff made a socio-economic census of a one-in-three sample of Agogo households. This included all the men, women and children resident in the houses selected during the three or four days of the enquiry. The population covered in this census overlaps partly with that of the fertility census; but as it was made independently by a different group of interviewers at a different time, it affords a valuable check on some of the data of the Fertility Census.[1]

The accuracy achieved in the fertility census exceeded my expectations; but there are unavoidable snags in field studies of this kind which affect the reliability of the data. Some are of a general kind, others are due to the special social and cultural circumstances of Ashanti. On the other hand, certain Ashanti attitudes and customs helped to make our enquiries easier, and I shall discuss these first and turn to the difficulties later.

The main object of the fertility census was to obtain as full and accurate a record as possible of the reproductive history of the total female popu-lation of Agogo. Now Ashanti attach exceptional importance to having

[1] I have to thank Miss Ady for placing this material at my disposal.

offspring. To be childless is the greatest personal tragedy and humiliation for both men and women and the larger the family the prouder is the parent. In Southern Ashanti a public ceremony of congratulation is performed for a couple who have 10 living children. This attitude is as characteristic of the townsfolk as of the villagers and is as common among the educated minority as among the illiterate farmers.

It is not surprising, therefore, that family limitation is unknown in rural Ashanti. Even the widespread African custom which prohibits intercourse between the parents of a nursing child until it is able to walk is not practised in Ashanti. A woman is secluded for 40 days after childbirth and then given a further 40 days of convalescence. She then returns to her husband and normal sexual relations are resumed. Apart from special occasions when intercourse is forbidden for ritual reasons, the only regular prohibition of intercourse is during the wife's menstrual periods. Ashanti wives say they expect to have a pregnancy every two or three years. In the big towns a small number of sophisticated people are beginning to make use of European contraceptives, but this is mainly for sexual relations outside or before marriage. Some educated men talk of the need for family limitation so as to enable better provision to be made for the education and standard of living of children. But this is merely the aspiration of a very small minority, and in discussion these men admit that contraception is contrary to Ashanti ideals and sentiments. Denial of sexual satisfaction is an infringement of marital rights in Ashanti law and any other method of contraception would be regarded by a wife as a slur on her womanhood.[1]

This attitude extends also to abortion. The idea of an unwanted pregnancy in marriage is unheard of. An Ashanti country-woman would be horrified at the suggestion of an induced miscarriage. This applies even to an unmarried girl, provided she has celebrated her nubility ceremony. The only cases of induced abortion I heard of concerned married women impregnated in adultery, which is a very serious private wrong against the husband.[2] It was, and in rural areas still is, regarded as a very serious crime and sin for a girl to become pregnant before her nubility ceremony; but abortion would, I was told, never be resorted to in such a case (see below). Nor do the Ashanti practise infanticide. Twins are welcomed and

[1] This applies to all but a very small number of educated women in the towns. An educated Ashanti friend of mine decided to limit his family to three children. He therefore sent his wife to stay with her parents after the birth of their third child. At the end of a year, he was obliged to yield to her protests and to allow her to come back to him. He then proposed that they should try to limit their family by practising continence. Outraged and in distress, his wife accused him of making this suggestion as a pretext for seeking to divorce her. She ran to her mother's brother, who called a meeting of the elders of his own and the husband's families. The husband was reprimanded at this meeting and was obliged to promise never to repeat his offence.

[2] cf. R. S. Rattray, *Ashanti Law and Constitution*, p. 306. Abortion in these cases is said to be induced by means of native medicines.

honoured. Special ritual observances distinguish them and their mother. Girl twins become the wives of the chief of their mother's chiefdom and boys become his personal attendants. Deformed and abnormal children, such as dwarfs, hunchbacks and albinos, are also taken into the chief's service.[1]

In short, the ideal of every Ashanti is to have as many children as life permits. That is why impotence in men is derided. Like proven sterility, it is an irremediable ground for divorce, and an impotent or sterile chief is forthwith deposed. It is the same with women. Barrenness is ground for divorce and no expense is spared to find a remedy. A great deal of money is spent on imported patent medicines intended for treating disorders of menstruation but which many women believe to be cures for barrenness. Many native doctors claim to have medicines, mostly of a magical kind, for inducing pregnancy and successful practitioners soon become very wealthy. This is not so difficult as its sounds, as Ashanti women become anxious at the merest suspicion that their fecundity is impaired. A newly married girl starts worrying and seeks medicine if she does not conceive before the first year of her marriage is out, and a woman who is not pregnant again within two or three years of a birth does the same. Chance, therefore, ensures a fair proportion of successes to a fashionable native doctor, and suggestion and reassurance techniques may also play a part. One of the main reasons why men and women flock in such numbers to the so-called 'fetish' cults which abound in Ashanti, is because these cults offer magical protection against sterility and sexual disorders. Both medical officers and well-informed laymen state that venereal diseases, especially gonorrhea, are very widespread in Ashanti owing to the increasing laxity of sexual morality. The effect of these diseases on fecundity is not known to most Ashanti country folk, but they are regarded with disgust and apprehension because they are believed to cause sexual disorders.[2]

The high value attached to fertility is related to many features of Ashanti culture and social organization. Ashanti informants stress two reasons most of all. They point, first, to the importance of the matrilineal lineage, that is the group of men, women and children descended from a common ancestress, usually about ten generations back. As property and

---

[1] Ninth-born children were believed to be unlucky and were put to death, in the old days, in Northern Ashanti, and there may be a connexion between this old custom and the praise given to parents of 10 living children. But I was assured that this custom was never followed in Southern Ashanti.

[2] Statistical evidence to support the statements made above is nowhere available. I am relying on personal impressions and the opinions of local informants. I can state, from personal observation, that 'M & B 693' and other sulpha drugs have become known in the most remote Ashanti villages as a miraculous cure for gonorrhea. Indeed, Ashanti believe that these drugs will cure any disease and they gladly pay exorbitant prices for them. When first introduced, sulpha drugs could be bought over the counter in any patent medicine shop. Now that they cannot be obtained without a medical prescription, there is a profitable black market for them. There have been one or two scandals through the theft of large quantities of these drugs from Government hospitals by African employees.

266

rank are transmitted from generation to generation in the lineage, and as the influence of a lineage in public affairs is proportional to its numbers, the desire to increase its numbers is strong. This desire is further strengthened by the cult of the lineage ancestors, which can only be carried on as long as there are offspring to do so. Thus, it is the social dominance of the rule of matrilineal descent which is said to explain the welcome given by her brothers and uncles to every child born to a woman of a lineage. A father's motives are different, and this brings up the second reason commonly stressed. In the old days a man desired sons so that the worship of his *ntoro*, which is transmitted from father to child, should be perpetuated. Nowadays, it is often expressed in personal terms. A man feels that his children are himself reborn. They will care for him in his old age and will perpetuate his name.[1] If he holds public office, his children will support him out of affection and a sense of moral obligation.

This ardent desire for offspring is undoubtedly a big factor in the high level of fertility we found in Agogo. It also helped to make the task of the interviewers easier, as it seemed a very natural thing to the women of Agogo that we should be interested in their children. But the pride Ashanti have in their living children is counterbalanced by a reluctance, bordering on dread, to speak about dead children. Indeed, this applies to the dead in general. Though there is no religious prohibition against speaking of the dead in public or in the profane situations of daily life, Ashanti have a strong emotional inhibition against dwelling on the dead in discussion, especially with strangers. The death of a child is a terrible shock to its parents and their close kinsfolk. The fact that an infant who dies before it is able to walk is not given a funeral shows not indifference but anxiety to forget the painful occurrence as quickly as possible. Children and young people who die before reaching marriageable age receive only perfunctory funerals since they have never taken an adult part in the life of the community.[2] In Ashanti a person is an adult when he or she is ready for marriage. These attitudes cause Ashanti, even more than most peoples, to ignore their dead children and concentrate all attention on the living ones.[3] This was specially noticeable among the older women, whose information about dead offspring was no doubt also impaired by failing powers of

[1] The ideas and values are more fully discussed in Fortes, 'Kinship and Marriage among the Ashanti', loc. cit., where references to Rattray and other authorities are given.

[2] These observations refer only to pagan Ashanti, of course. But the attitudes described persist among Christians too. Thus, even among Christian Ashanti, the parents of a dead infant are given food immediately after the burial and put on white clothes in sign of affected rejoicing. The traditional belief is that a child who dies in early infancy is a spirit which has taken on human shape to mock its parents. Its departure must be welcomed, else it may return as a spirit child. If a child dies in childhood or early youth, it is thought of as an immature plant whose death is not an irreparable loss.

[3] But this is a common failing, and not only among Africans. R. R. Kuczynski, *Measurement of Population Growth*, p. 85, notes that in the British census of 1911 women tended to omit children who died young.

memory.[1] In the face of these impediments the results achieved by the interviewers are surprisingly good, and show how well they succeeded in winning the confidence of the women of Agogo. It seems certain, however, that estimates of mortality, especially in childhood, based on these data are lower than the true figures.

The information obtained about stillbirths (understood by the Ashanti to mean fully formed children born dead), and miscarriages (understood to mean involuntary abortions at any stage before the child is fully formed) is even less reliable.[2] Though a stillbirth or miscarriage is not a stigma, the woman who suffers it is commonly very upset, and does not like talking about it. It is, therefore, most unlikely that all cases of stillbirth and miscarriage were divulged to the interviewers. There are instances in the records of children who were declared to have died at various ages from a few hours to a few days, and some of these may actually have been stillbirths. Special efforts were made by the interviewers to get at the truth in such cases, but they were not always successful.

To counterbalance these difficulties, the Ashanti also have customary practices and attitudes that made for greater accuracy than is possible in some other pre-literate societies. The onset of menstruation is the most important event in an Ashanti girl's life. Pagan Ashanti in the rural areas celebrate this with a public ceremony of congratulation and purification. Among the Christians in Agogo the rite of confirmation has come to take the place of this ceremony. Whether they are pagan or Christian, parents make an effort to perform a daughter's nubility ceremony with the least possible delay after her first menses; in rural areas this is usually within six months or so. One reason is that a girl is expected to marry as soon as she becomes capable of child-bearing.[3] Thus the first menstruation ceremony is very often also a betrothal ceremony.

A stronger motive for not delaying the ceremony is fear of the girl's becoming pregnant before it takes place. As has been mentioned before, this is both a sin and a crime of exceptional gravity. The girl and her lover are expelled from the village until the child is born and heavy fines have to be paid by their families for the provision of sheep to sacrifice in order to purify the community of the defilement. The shame for the girl's parents is so great that, as Ashanti say, they would rather be dead than endure it. In the countryside, people are extremely sensitive to public criticism or gossip. This, coupled with the religious horror of pregnancy before the

[1] Many Ashanti, both literate and illiterate, nowadays keep a written record of important family events such as births, deaths and marriages, but this practice is of very recent growth.
[2] But this has been found to be the case in modern European societies, too. cf. Raymond Pearl, *The Natural History of Population*, 1939, pp. 88–9.
[3] Physique as well as the onset of menstruation is taken into account in deciding this. I failed to make sure of the point, but I have the impression that the nubility ceremony is delayed in the case of a girl whose menses begin at an unusually early age. The ceremony is described in R. S. Rattray, *Religion and Art in Ashanti*, Ch. VII.

nubility ceremony, is commonly recognized as the strongest sanction of chastity amongst pre-nubile Ashanti girls. After the nubility ceremony a girl may have a lover, if she is not married, without incurring disgrace, provided she does not break the laws of incest and exogamy, and behaves with decorum. It is only if she is promiscuous or prostitutes herself that she is despised. It is no shame for a nubile girl to have a child by a lover. The child belongs by birth to its matrilineal lineage and so escapes any stigma of illegitimacy. Moreover, Ashanti custom provides ways by which a man can acknowledge paternity of a love child, and fulfil the main responsibilities of fatherhood without marrying the mother and without suffering in reputation.[1]

The interest focused on the menarche is a sign of the great importance attached to sex life and marriage. In Ashanti, marriage is regarded as the normal state for every adult. Investigations in a number of rural areas show that very few men remain unmarried after the age of 25,[2] and even fewer women after the age of 20. Voluntary celibacy in either sex is considered abnormal. Enquiries at Agogo confirmed the view generally held in Ashanti country districts that unmarried men and women are either divorced or widowed, or else suffer from some sexual disability such as impotence, or are known to be sterile, or have some chronic disease which prevents sex life and procreation. Moreover the primary purpose of marriage is considered to be the production of children, and women in particular think of sexual relations chiefly as a means to procreation. That is why a childless marriage rarely lasts and an unmarried woman who bears a child incurs no disgrace.

Divorce is frequent in Southern Ashanti. An investigation of a sample of 262 men of all ages from nine scattered rural areas showed that 45 per cent of them had been divorced once or more. Table 30 below shows that 44 per cent of the Agogo women of our sample who had been married before the date of the census had had more than one husband, and in the majority of these cases plural marriage was due to divorce. As polygyny is permitted in Ashanti (and is surreptitiously practised even by many Christians) remarriage in the case of a young woman often takes place quickly after

[1] As has been mentioned before, it is notorious that traditional ideals of sex morality are being rapidly undermined in modern Ashanti. Promiscuity, prostitution and adultery are said to be widespread among girls and young women in the towns and to be spreading to the rural areas. In the opinion of many responsible people this is most common among girls who have been to school. There is undoubtedly a great deal of truth in these allegations, but it is impossible to find out precisely how widespread these immoral habits are. Ashanti attribute this state of affairs to the breakdown of parental authority and the decay of traditional religious beliefs. Christianity and schools are specially blamed on the grounds that they create contempt for the traditional nubility ceremony.

[2] Except in the case of a handful of clerks, teachers and other 'black-coated' workers in both towns and countryside, who are beginning to postpone marriage (but not adult sex life) for economic reasons. It is a common thing for a man in this position to have an illiterate country girl living with him as his mistress and housekeeper, and to recognize as his own any children born of this union.

a divorce. If she does not remarry she very often has a lover. Thus a woman does not necessarily stop bearing children because she is divorced, but it is possible that divorce may slow down her successive pregnancies and thus reduce their total number, as compared with a woman who has never been divorced. On the other hand, the sexual freedom allowed to unmarried women after they reach physiological maturity and the high esteem in which fertility is held, as well as the absence of disabilities for what we should call illegitimacy, contribute to make it normal for a woman to bear children throughout her span of fecundity.

These ideas and customs made it easier than was expected for the interviewer to record all the women of a household who had reached childbearing age, whether they were married or not. It also helped them to get definite statements on the interval that elapsed between the onset of menstruation and a woman's first pregnancy, as it is a matter about which the women show great concern; as has already been mentioned, a girl who thinks that her first pregnancy is being too long delayed after her marriage quickly runs to a native doctor. But there are sources of misinformation which make the figures less reliable than was hoped. The physical onset of menstruation is overshadowed by its social recognition in the nubility ceremony, and there is little doubt that a proportion of the women interviewed, in spite of careful explanation, reckoned the time to their first pregnancy from their nubility ceremony. On the other hand, Ashanti women usually take a pregnancy to be established only when two successive menstrual periods have passed without the catamenia occurring. The common opinion is that birth takes place in the tenth lunar month after conception. Yet it seems that some informants reckoned the period between their first menses and first pregnancy as including the time between conception and the recognition of the pregnancy. An error of from three to six months in the time stated may have been made by a proportion (not possible to estimate) of the women.

In Ashanti rural areas the domestic group may be either a conjugal family of husband, wife and children and some other dependents or a matrilineal group consisting, for example, of a woman, her sons and her daughters and their children. In Agogo, married women are apter to be found living in matrilineal domestic groups than with their husbands, the ratio being nearly 4:1 during the childbearing years. With very few exceptions, children under the age of 15 live with their mothers; but this does not mean that they live in their fathers' houses. In fact, only about half of them do so.[1] The routine care of young children is thus peculiarly the concern of the mother and her female maternal kin. An Ashanti father, though no less affectionate and devoted to his children than fathers elsewhere, is often not on the spot and may not even be sent for if minor troubles occur with the children. The restriction of our enquiries to the

[1] More detail is given in Fortes, 'Time and Social Structure', loc. cit.

women fitted in very well with these social habits and was an aid to accuracy. A mother and daughter, or a pair of sisters, would often help each other to settle a doubtful point.

A problem that occasionally arose deserves mention. The Ashanti have a classificatory kinship system, and sisters are especially closely identified. Thus it sometimes happened that a woman claimed as her own the children of a dead sister who were living under her care. Ashanti are very touchy about this sort of thing, and it would be regarded as an insult to both children and their proxy mother to query their relationship. The interviewers had been warned that this might happen and it speaks much for their tact that very few cases of this kind escaped detection. Wherever possible the children named were seen personally by the interviewers and this helped to clear up doubts about their true parentage as well as to make sure of their ages.

A major problem of demographic research in pre-literate societies is the determination of age.[1] The Ashanti Social Survey included a number of investigations in which classification of the population concerned by age groups was essential. It was necessary therefore to work out a reliable technique for ascertaining people's ages. We followed the usual ethnographic technique of referring to dateable events well known to everybody. But in Ashanti more precision is possible than in societies which have had less contact with the European world. In the traditional culture, chronological age is not reckoned for social purposes. States of individual maturation are distinguished by such overt physiological changes as the onset of menstruation and, with boys, the appearance of pubic and body hair. But the traditional culture does provide a means of reckoning short periods of time. A native year of 12 lunar months is counted and the alternation of rainy season and dry season, of planting and harvest, also serves to fix the memory of events. Periodical ceremonies play an important part in the Ashanti calendar, the main ones being the Adae ceremonies at intervals of 40 days and 20 days.[2] There are also the annual harvest festivals; and funeral ceremonies are spaced at intervals of 40, 80, and 360 days.

These customs and ceremonies enable illiterate Ashanti to date recent events with some precision. For long periods of time they refer to historical events, like the wars of the old days, the reigns of kings, the year of a local chief's installation or deposition, and such like. These ways of reckoning the course of time are, however, rapidly giving way to the European calendar. Even illiterate people in remote villages now usually date events by reference to anno Domini and the English months. This is due not only to the spread of literacy but even more to the changes in the economic and political structure of the country. The written record and the schedule

---

[1] cf. Charles and Forde, loc. cit.; Fortes, loc. cit., *Sociological Review*, Vol. XXV, 1943.
[2] For descriptions of these ceremonies see R. S. Rattray, *Religion and Art in Ashanti*, 1927, Ch. V–IX.

of activities and transactions tied to the European calendar have become matters of routine. Court cases, tax payments, loans, debts, and sales are everywhere recorded both by native administration clerks and by private individuals. Indeed, few men or women under 30 now know the traditional names of the lunar months. The ubiquitous public letter writer and the schoolboy or schoolgirl found in almost every home enable the illiterate to indulge, as much as the literate, what has become a passion for correspondence, petitions to authorities, and the keeping of a personal 'pass-book' in which all kinds of family events are entered. The birth of a child, the date of a daughter's nubility ceremony, the death of a relative and the cost of the funeral, and other events of this kind can often be precisely dated by an illiterate villager by reference to his 'pass-book'.

At the same time there has been an increasing recognition of age as a significant datum of social relations; when a child is sent to school its age must be stated. Baptism and confirmation draw the attention of Christians to age. Patients attending hospitals have to state their age. Government departments and private employers are beginning to take age into account in making clerical and technical appointments. Thus a European attitude to age is becoming widespread. One interesting sign of this is the definition now generally used by native authorities of adult males and females liable to tax payments. An adult male is one who is over 18 and an adult female a woman over 16. If, as often happens, the exact age of an adolescent cannot be ascertained, the clerk compiling the nominal roll of taxpayers falls back on the customary criteria. He records a girl under the heading '16 years of age and over' if she has reached the menarche.

But though these ideas and habits have become widespread they are not universal. Women, in particular, unless they have had some schooling, have less use for them than men. The majority of the older women and very many in the over-thirty age group are apt to be vague about their own ages and the ages of their children.

A schedule was therefore drawn up with the help of local elders, setting out a list of dated events well known to all the people of Agogo, and all statements of age were checked against it by the interviewers (see Appendix C). By enquiring from the mothers of most of the infants under one year old in the township, and by seeing the children for ourselves, we ascertained approximately the earliest age of cutting the first tooth (6 months), beginning to crawl (7 months) and beginning to walk (11 months), and these served as a guide for estimating ages up to one year.

The same table of dates and the same technique of estimating ages was used by the interviewers engaged on the fertility census and by Miss Ady's and Mr. Steel's field staff. As has been mentioned, Miss Ady's enquiry took place three months after the fertility census. The overlap between her sample and the fertility census thus affords a valuable check on the accuracy of the age estimates reached. Owing to the fact, previously mentioned, that Ashanti are often away from home for several days at a time, it was found that Miss Ady's sample included a number of women who were not at home during the fertility census and vice versa. In a random selection of approximately one-third of the women in Miss Ady's census, 91 were found who also appeared in the fertility census. Comparison of the two age estimates showed: A discrepancy of 0–1 year in 33 cases, 2–5 years in 32 cases, 6–7 years in 10 cases, 8–10 years in 9 cases, over 10 years in 7 cases.

Thus, in 36 per cent of these cases there was no significant discrepancy in the estimates, and in 35 per cent of cases it was less than five years—that is, for 71 per cent of these cases a distribution in quinquennial age groups would be approximately the same for both censuses. It is significant also that the large discrepancies of 10 years and more occur only with women estimated to be over 50 in both censuses, and that differences of 6–10 years are found mainly among women aged 35–50. The average discrepancy for the whole series is 4.4 years ±5.2 years. It should be added that internal evidence showed that the fertility census reached a higher degree of accuracy than Miss Ady's census.[1]

We may conclude, then, that a distribution of our population in 5-year age groups will have a reasonable degree of reliability for the women up to the age of about 50.

AGE COMPOSITION AND SOCIAL CHARACTERISTICS OF THE SAMPLE

The fertility census included a total of 1,017 women, these being all the women resident in the township during the fortnight of the census who were stated to be of marriageable age and over. Among them were 975 Ashanti women and 42 non-Ashanti women, mainly immigrants from the Northern Territories of the Gold Coast. As the latter constitute less than 5 per cent of the whole sample they have but little weight and are unlikely to bias the results significantly. For greater precision they will, however, be excluded from some of the later calculations.

The age composition of the sample is shown in Table 23.[2] A detailed consideration of this table is instructive as an example of the special problems met with in demographic field work in non-literate communities. The age distribution of women of childbearing age (15–49) shown in this table is not, however, directly comparable with similar distributions given in demographic studies of European and Oriental societies. It does not include all the women aged 15–19 who were resident in Agogo at the time.

---

[1] A woman with two living children aged 12 and 7 is more likely to be 32, as shown in the fertility census, than 26, as shown in the other census, and this probability becomes certainty when it is seen that her oldest child was preceded by one who died in infancy.

[2] Age groups throughout this paper are inclusive. Thus, the age group 15–19 years includes all the women who have passed their nineteenth birthday but have not yet reached their twentieth birthday, i.e., strictly speaking all women aged 15 years to 19 years 11 months.

The women of our sample had 163 living daughters stated to be aged 15–19, and of these, 146 were resident in the chiefdom, 134 being in the township and 12 on farms. Examination of the records gave the following results among women aged 15–19 years:

Recorded only among the sample of adults interviewed	57
Recorded among adults as well as among surviving offspring	58
Recorded among surviving offspring only	105
Total	220
Living outside township	29
Total in township	191

Thus, there were altogether 191 girls aged 15–19 in Agogo during the census. How is it then that 76 (i.e., 191–115) were not recorded among the adults as of marriageable age? It was found that 46 were stated to be 15 or 16 years old and the implication that they had not yet reached the menarche can be accepted. The remaining 30 aged 17–19 years included

TABLE 23.   Age Composition of Census Sample.

Age group	Ashanti	Non-Ashanti	Total	Per 1,000
15–19	113	2	115	113
20–24	164	6	170	167
25–29	174	12	186	182.8
30–34	90	3	93	91.4
35–39	93	9	102	100.3
40–44	52	3	55	54
45–49	68	2	70	68.8
50–54	57	1	58	57
55–59	42	1	43	42.3
60–64	43	2	45	44.2
65–69	25	0	25	24.6
70–74	27	0	27	26.5
75–79	11	0	11	10.8
80	16	1	17	16.7
Total	975	42	1 017	999.4

some who had apparently not menstruated yet, some who may have menstruated but had not yet had their nubility ceremony, and some who suffered from chronic illness or physiological defects which made them unmarriageable in Ashanti eyes. After the age of about 20 no Ashanti woman is willing to admit that she is not marriageable even if she has a chronic illness or is physiologically defective. Several cases of this kind came to notice during the census.

Two possibilities for correcting the age table previously given are thus implied. We can regard the total of 191 girls aged 15–19 as being the correct number. We would be assuming, then, that the age estimates for the 46 girls stated to be 15–16 years old are correct. But if the ages of these girls were overestimated by one year, they would properly belong to the 10–14 year age group. On this assumption, the correct total of girls aged 15–19 would be 145. The procedure used in estimating ages makes the second assumption highly probable, though there was no doubt also some compensating overestimation of the ages of 14–15 year olds. It is highly suggestive that not a single instance of a girl under 15 appears among the adult women, who were selected, it will be remembered, on the criterion of having reached or passed the menarche. Whatever the mean age of first menstruation may be among the Ashanti (this is considered later) it is unlikely that no girl under 15 had reached the menarche. Social and physiological criteria obviously biased the interviewers in regard to the 15–19 age group, though not to the extent that might have been expected. If it had been otherwise, the number of girls recorded among the offspring as aged 15–19 but not among the adult women would have been much smaller.

If the total of 191 girls aged 15–19 is accepted as correct, the amended figures would read as shown in Series A of Table 24. On the other hand, if the 46 girls apparently aged 15–16 are excluded, the amended table reads as shown in Series B. It is of interest to compare these distributions with that of the adult women of Miss Ady's sample, which are shown in Series C.

Comparing Series A and B, it appears that the trend of the two distributions is the same (see Figure 1). But there appear to be some appreciable discrepancies, especially in the proportions of the 15–19 year and the 45–49 year groups in the two samples. The two samples are, of course, not independent and the age estimates were made by the same technique. It is, therefore, not surprising to find substantial agreement between the two distributions. As to the discrepancies, these appear less significant when the women are grouped in 10-year age groups (see Figure 2). This suggests that the discrepancies are due mainly to the variations in the age estimates previously referred to. It is possible that Miss Ady's field staff, all of whom were men, simply followed the conventional attitude of regarding all girls who have not yet menstruated as 'children' and therefore placed a number of non-nubile 15–16 year olds among the 14 year olds. Or, it may be that my interviewers, being over-conscientious in following their instructions to include all women of childbearing age, became prone, as has already been suggested, to place some cases of 14–15 year olds among the 15–16 year olds.[1]

[1] There is circumstantial evidence in favour of this interpretation in the fact that the ratio of 10–14 year olds to 15–19 year olds in Miss Ady's census is approximately 10:6.5, whereas among the surviving female children of the fertility sample it is approximately 10:9. cf. Tables 21–26.

TABLE 24.   Age Distribution. Women of Childbearing Age and Over. (Series A. Census Sample, Hypothesis I; Series B. Census Sample, Hypothesis II; Series C. Census Sample, Miss Ady's Sample.)

Age group	Series A		Series B		Series C	
	Number	Per 1,000	Number	Per 1,000	Number	Per 1,000
15–19	191	175	145	138.5	52	137
20–24	170	156	170	162	62	163
25–29	186	170	186	178	53	140
30–34	93	85	93	89	43	113
35–39	102	93	102	97	32	84
40–44	55	50	55	53	25	66
45–49	70	64	70	67	36	95
50–54	58	53	58	55	19	50
55–59	43	39	43	41	11	29
60–64	45	41	45	43	13	34
65–69	25	23	25	24	7	18
70–74	27	25	27	26	14	37
75–79	11	10	11	10	6	16
80	17	16	17	16	6	16
Total	1 093		1 047		379	

The same bias might have caused the fertility census staff to underestimate the age of women who declared themselves to be still capable of bearing children, and this may be the reason for the divergence between the two samples in the 45–49 year group. It is all the more satisfactory that there is close agreement over the years of maximum child bearing, 20 to 44, between the two samples in the age distribution. This group represents just over 56 per cent of the total in both samples and the age range 15–49 includes 80.1 per cent of the women in the fertility census and 79.8 per cent of those in Miss Ady's sample.

If Series B in Table 24 is compared with Series C there is good agreement between the two estimates for the age groups 15–19 and 20–24, as well as in the estimates by 10-year groups for the age groups to 45. The relative values, per 1,000 women of childbearing age or over, run as follows:

TABLE 25.

Age Group	15–19	20–24	25–34	35–44	45–54	55–64	65–74	75 +
Series B	138	162	267	150	122	84	50	26
Series C	137	163	253	150	145	63	55	32

FIG. 1. Age Distribution of Women.

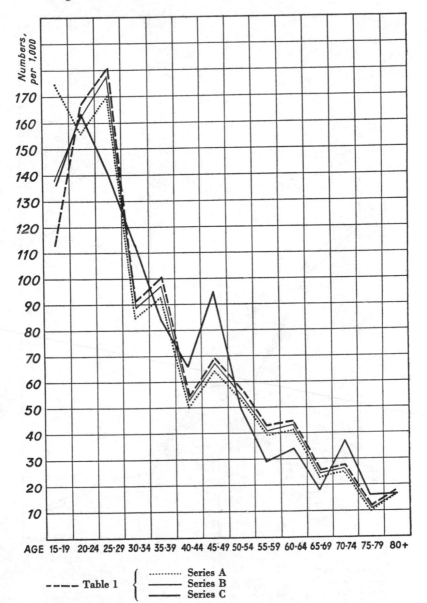

FIG. 2. Age Distribution of Women, 10-year groups.

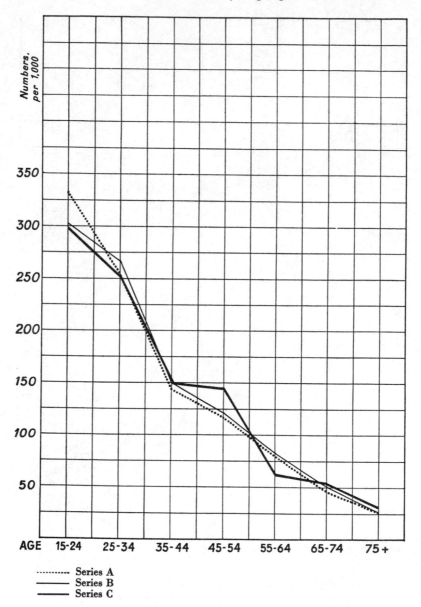

It seems justified therefore to conclude that Series B gives as good an approximation as the circumstances permit of the correct age distribution of women aged 15 and over, resident in Agogo at the time of the census.[1]

OCCUPATIONAL DISTRIBUTION

As has been indicated, our sample was very homogeneous in its social composition. Thus 902 (92.5 per cent) of the Ashanti women were born in Agogo. The occupational homogeneity of the sample comes out in Table 26.

TABLE 26. Occupational Distribution of Agogo Women by Age Groups.

Age groups	Farmer and housewife	Petty trader	Food hawker	Craft-worker	Priest-ess	Depend-ent	Unspeci-fied	Total
15–19	98	4	2	2	—	6	3	115
20–24	145	14	5	—	—	—	6	170
25–29	144	23	7	3	—	—	9	186
30–34	82	4	3	1	1	—	2	93
35–39	82	8	5	2	1	—	4	102
40–44	51	3	—	—	—	—	1	55
45–49	58	6	—	—	—	—	6	70
50–54	53	2	—	—	—	—	3	58
55–59	38	—	—	—	—	1	4	43
60–64	40	1	—	˙1	1	—	2	45
65–69	19	—	—	—	—	5	1	25
70–74	22	—	—	—	1	4	—	27
75–79	7	—	—	—	—	4	—	11
80	4	—	—	2	—	8	3	17
Total	843	65	22	11	4	28	44	1 017

[1] This distribution does not accurately represent the age distribution of all adult females alive at the time of the enquiry who regarded Agogo as their home by right of birth. The age groups under 25 and those over 50 are overweighted in proportion to those aged 25–49. This is due to the fact that among the women away on farms and living outside the chiefdom as temporary emigrants there was a disproportionate number from the age groups 25–49. For, as elsewhere in Ashanti, it is the men and women in the prime of life who carry the main burden of work on the cocoa farms and who also make up the main body of emigrants to the towns. There is confirmation for this if the tables given above are compared with the following age distribution based on a random sample from the whole of Ashanti which I have extracted from the 1948 census report, Table VIII, p. 36.

Distribution in Quinary Age Groups of Women Aged 15 Years and Over, Per 1,000 Total.

Age Group	15–19	19–24	25–29	30–34	35–39	40–44	45–49
Number	139	191	182	138	97	69	74

Age Group	50–54	55–59	60–64	65–69	70–74	75	
Number	41	25	19	10	8	7	

In comparison with this distribution the number of women over 50 in Agogo appears to be markedly excessive.

Nearly 83 per cent of the women declared themselves to be housewives and farmers, as is the general rule among Ashanti countrywomen. Their farming activities consist almost entirely of food growing and there are very few women in rural areas who do not grow some food for themselves. Thus most of the petty traders, food sellers and craftworkers of our sample were also food growers and housewives who engaged in the occupations stated mainly to augment their cash resources. The need for extra cash is greatest while a woman has young children dependent on her, and it is not surprising to find that women over 50 rarely engage in money-earning occupations. Ashanti women, moreover, maintain their own food farms as long as they are physically fit to do so. This is reflected in the very small proportion of women, almost all over 60, who were recorded as being dependent on their close kin for their livelihood. The handful of girls under 20 recorded as dependents should really be put among the 'farmers and housewives', but were described as dependents because they have no food gardens of their own and are still assisting their mothers in both farming and housework. This indeed applies to the majority of unmarried girls in the 15–19 year age group, except those who are chronically ill or infirm, but in strictly occupational terms they are rightly classified among the 'farmers and housewives'.

LITERACY AND RELIGION

Just over 90 per cent of the women stated that they were illiterate; those for whom information on this point was not obtained were also probably illiterate. The majority—nearly three-quarters—of these illiterate women were pagans, and about a quarter of them were Christians. Among the 4.8 per cent of the sample who claimed to be literate, four-fifths were Christians, as might have been expected. Indeed, the literacy of most of them went no further than being able to read the Bible and the Prayer Book in the vernacular and to write a simple letter in the vernacular. Table 27 summarizes these data, which offer further evidence of the social homogeneity of the sample. Christianity makes no appreciable difference to the habits and routines of daily life among the illiterate, especially as regards the care of children. It is only among women who have been to school that higher standards of domestic amenity than are usual in rural areas are sometimes found; but this depends also on their husbands' level of income, and the illiterate wife of a well-to-do storekeeper may have a more comfortable home than the educated wife of a young mission teacher. As there were only 20 women in our sample who had been to school at all, and most of them had not even completed the whole primary school course, their influence on the social composition of the sample is negligible.

It is worth noting, incidentally, that literacy is rarely turned to economic advantage by women in rural areas.[1]

It is of interest to enquire whether or not there is differentiation by age in respect to literacy and religion. Table 28 gives the relevant data.

TABLE 27. Literacy and Religion of Agogo Women.

Literacy	Religion				Total
	Pagan	Christian	Muslim	Unspecified	
Illiterate	669	233	7	10	919
Literate	8	40	—	1	49
Unspecified	29	11	3	6	49
Total	706	284	10	17	1 017

TABLE 28. Literacy and Religion of Agogo Women by Age Groups.

Age groups	Literacy			Religion			
	Illiterate	Literate	Unspeci-fied	Pagan	Christian	Muslim	Unspeci-fied
15–19	104	6	5	87	24	—	4
20–24	151	11	8	113	55	1	1
25–29	165	13	8	115	67	1	3
30–34	80	7	6	69	21	2	1
35–39	95	3	4	68	27	5	2
40–44	51	2	2	33	21	—	1
45–49	61	4	5	50	20	—	—
50–54	55	1	2	45	12	—	1
55–59	41	—	2	32	9	—	2
60–64	41	1	3	36	8	1	—
65–69	22	1	2	19	6	—	—
70	53	—	2	39	14	—	2
Total	919	49	49	706	284	10	17

Christian missions have been active in Agogo since 1893, and it might therefore be expected that their influence would be most marked among the women born and brought up in Agogo since that date. The following table tests this expectation, the women being classified in 10-year age groups, owing to the smallness of the sample.

[1] The introduction of literacy in the vernacular was due first to the missions. Schooling in the Western sense was not locally available to Agogo girls until the opening of a primary school in the township in the nineteen thirties.

281

	Age Group				
	15–24	25–34	35–44	45–54	55
Literates					
Observed Numbers	17	20	5	5	2
Expected Numbers	13.5	13.4	7.5	6.2	8.4
Christians					
Observed Numbers	79	88	48	32	37
Expected Numbers	79.5	78	43	32.5	46.9

χ^2 Literates $= 10.127$
χ^2 Christians $= 4.299$

The expected numbers are calculated on the assumption that there is no
correlation with age, in which case the numbers of literates and Christians
might be expected to be proportional to the incidence of each age group
in the total sample. According to Fisher's table[1] for P $= 0.05$, $\chi^2 = 9.488$
when n $= 4$. It appears therefore that literacy is correlated with age since
there is a significant difference between the observed and the expected
numbers, whereas Christians are found in approximately expected numbers
in each age group. These results confirm general impressions. As regards
literacy, the older women had no opportunity for schooling nor indeed
would there have been any incentive for them to go to school. But since
the late thirties it has become increasingly common for girls to go to school.
As regards Christianity, literacy is not a pre-requisite for membership of
a church. Conversion to Christianity occurs at all ages after childhood and
is a matter of personal choice. Children however nowadays often become
members of a church through the action of their parents, who have them
baptized in infancy. Thus, the number of Christians in the younger age
groups is in part conditioned by the number in the older age groups. But
many children also become Christians through attending school, irrespective
of their parents' religious beliefs. As girls have only recently started attending school in appreciable numbers at Agogo, this practice has not yet
markedly influenced the spread of Christianity among the younger women.
As a matter of fact, the leading women in the Christian community in
Agogo belong to the age groups over 50. They are women who were
converted in their girlhood, and most of them are illiterate.

As has been remarked, membership of a Christian church appears to
make no specific difference to ways of living in Agogo. It has no obvious

[1] R. A. Fisher, *Statistical Methods for Research Workers*, Table III.

influence on habits and customs connected with child-bearing and child-rearing. Preferred residence patterns are the same for Christians as for non-Christians. As women of all ages have an equal chance of being Christians, membership of Christian churches is not likely to introduce an age-correlated bias into our data. But literacy does influence ways of living and has an age-correlation, though the number of literate women is so small that any bias due to them will be negligible.

MARITAL CONDITIONS

The number of marriages each woman of our sample had entered into up to the time of the census is shown, in relation to their ages at the time of the census, in Table 30.

TABLE 30.   Women of Specified Ages by Number of Marriages.

Age Groups	Number of marriages										Total	Mean
	0	1	2	3	4	5	6	7	8	9		
15–19	38	71	5	1	—	—	—	—	—	—	115	0.75
20–24	2	126	28	13	1	—	—	—	—	—	170	1.32
25–29	6	112	50	14	2	1	1	—	—	—	186	1.44
30–34	—	41	40	12	—	—	—	—	—	—	93	1.69
35–39	1	50	30	16	3	1	—	1	—	—	102	1.72
40–44	—	21	18	9	7	—	—	—	—	—	55	2.03
45–49	1	24	25	14	3	2	—	—	1	—	70	2.09
50–54	1	22	15	14	5	1	—	—	—	—	58	2.06
55–59	—	21	11	6	4	1	—	—	—	—	43	1.9
60–64	—	21	12	7	4	—	—	—	—	1	45	2.02
65–69	—	9	9	5	1	—	1	—	—	—	25	2.08
70–74	—	11	8	5	2	—	—	—	—	1	27	2.18
75–79	—	4	—	5	1	1	—	—	—	—	11	2.56
80+	—	5	5	5	2	—	—	—	—	—	17	2.24
Total	49	538	256	126	35	7	2	1	1	2	1 017	

The table shows that only 49 women had not been married up to the time of the census, and the great majority of these fall into the 15–19 year age group. This bears out the Ashanti statement[1] that every girl reckons to be married before she is about 20, if she has no physiological defects. Even if as high a proportion as a quarter of the 15–19 year age group are fated not to marry, the inference would still be that under 2.5 per cent of

[1] Of course, it might also mean that the information given by the women was biased by this ideal. Some women who had never been married might have claimed that they had been, to save embarrassment.

Ashanti women fail to marry and thus have no opportunity of bearing children in wedlock. As has been indicated before, however, this does not mean that they will not have children at all. But a woman who bears a child before marriage very rarely remains unmarried throughout life. It is only those who are incapable of childbearing through early recognized disease or infirmity who remain unmarried.

Of the women who had been married, 55.6 per cent had had only one husband up to the time of the census. If the table is carefully studied it will be seen that plurality of marriages is correlated with age. There is in fact a positive correlation ($r = 0.31 \pm 0.018$) which, though not high, is significant, and thus confirms the impression formed by inspection of the table. This is in conformity with what is generally known about the instability of Ashanti marriage. The table suggests that rather more than half of all Agogo women who live to the end of their reproductive period get divorced and remarried during this period. Very few appear to make more than four marriages. Moreover, in each group there is a regular trend, the proportion of those who have made only one marriage being greater than those who have made two marriages, those with two marriages being greater than those who have married three times, etc. This is partly due to chance, since the possibility of remarriage is limited to the reproductive years and the chances of a woman making n marriages are greater than for her to make $n + 1$ marriages. But this trend also reflects social factors which work against excessive divorce and remarriage. The age factor itself works in this way. Up to the age of about 30 women are much readier to initiate or accept divorce with a view to remarriage than after that age, for they are still highly eligible for marriage and motherhood. After 35 as their childbearing capacity diminishes, their eligibility for remarriage diminishes, and even if they are divorced they might not remarry. Women of this category are included among those who claim to have been married only once. Women over 35 are also likely to have several children, some already adolescent. Children form a strong bond between husband and wife and this is a deterrent to rash divorce. But even where, as is very common, divorce occurs in spite of the existence of children of a union, the older woman's interests are so largely focused on her children and the household which she and they constitute that she has no wish to remarry. This is strengthened by the fact that she has also by the age of about 35 attained a considerable degree of economic independence and in any case looks to her children rather than her husband for support. This partly explains the rapid rise in the proportion of women without husbands in the age groups over 44. Furthermore, though divorce carries no stigma, constancy in marriage wins approval.

To sum up, all fit women in Agogo marry. They have a strong tendency to marry more than once, and this tendency is strongest during the first half of their reproductive life and is followed by a disinclination to remarry after divorce or widowhood when the menopause has been reached; but various restraining influences keep this tendency towards successive marriages within bounds, so that a substantial proportion of women—probably over 40 per cent—marry only once. This picture is found amongst both pagan and Christian women. The problem of divorce and remarriage is different for the men. If they are pagans they are free to have more than one wife at a time, and the Christian minority are for the most part not strictly monogamous either.

Though 95 per cent of the women of our sample claimed to have been married, not all of them had husbands at the time of the census. Those who claimed to have husbands, numbering 687 (67.5 per cent of the sample), were distributed by age as in Table 31.

TABLE 31. Women by Age Group and by Marital Status.

Age Distribution of women with husbands alive	A Number ever married	B Number married at time of census	B/A %	Divorced or widowed %
15–19	77	66	85	15
20–24	168	150	89	11
25–29	180	150	83	17
30–34	93	76	82	18
35–39	101	82	81	19
40–44	55	43	78	22
45–49	69	48	70	30
50–54	57	29	51	49
55–59	43	13	30	70
60–64	45	14	31	69
65	80	16	20	80
Total	968	687		

Though divorce means the cessation of sexual, domestic, and economic relations between the spouses, it does not, in the large number of cases[1] of wives who are living with their maternal kin, alter their conditions of residence; and for wives who are living with their husbands it is an easy and approved thing to return to their mothers' homes. Nor does divorce deprive a man of his rights over, and responsibilities for, his children. Thus, though the figures given in Table 31 represent the number of women in each age group who claimed to have husbands at the time of the census, it is possible that some of them were divorcees who did not admit this. Few Ashanti women conceal the fact that they are divorced if they are asked direct, but not many volunteer this information; and as there is nothing to indicate to an outsider that a woman is divorced it might have

[1] Probably up to 50 per cent. See Fortes, 'Time and Social Structure', loc. cit.

happened that our interviewers failed to make sure of this point in some cases.

If the table is taken at its face value, however, it confirms the ethnographic impression that the great majority (average, 83 per cent) of marriageable women have husbands throughout their reproductive life. The proportion, as might be expected, is highest in the first decade of the reproductive life, when sexual needs are strongest, and begins to fall as the reproductive period draws to a close. After that it falls very rapidly, as sexual needs diminish. Not only is it common for widows and divorcees after the menopause to remain unmarried, but even those with husbands often live apart from them with their own children and daughters' children. Still, the mean proportion of 17 per cent of reproductive women who are without husbands because of divorce or widowhood is considerable for such a community. I cannot tell what effect this has on the birth rate, as I have no data on how long women generally remain unmarried after divorce or widowhood.

TABLE 32. Distribution of Married Women Among Singly and Plurally Married Husbands.

Age groups	Husband's present number of wives							Not stated	Total
	1	2	3	4	5	6	7		
15–19	45	15	3	—	—	—	—	3	66
20–24	89	45	7	3	—	—	3	3	150
25–29	74	50	15	2	1	—	4	4	150
30–34	28	28	12	5	—	—	—	3	76
35–39	32	33	12	2	—	—	—	3	82
40–44	19	9	11	3	—	—	1	0	43
45–49	23	14	5	2	1	1	1	1	48
50–54	11	6	8	—	1	—	—	3	29
55–59	3	6	1	—	—	—	—	3	13
60–64	3	4	2	1	1	—	—	3	14
65–69	4	1	2	—	—	—	—	1	8
70–74	2	1	2	—	—	—	—	—	5
75–78	—	1	—	—	—	—	1	—	2
80	—	—	1	—	—	—	—	—	1
Total	333	213	81	18	4	1	10	27	687

Table 33 shows how the women who claimed to have husbands were distributed among monogynists and polygynists.[1] It will be seen that nearly half of these women were married monogamously and, of those married to polygynists, 65 per cent have husbands with only two wives.[2] Table 33

[1] Information obtained from the women.
[2] The 10 women married to men with seven or more wives are all wives of the chief.

TABLE 33. Women with Monogynous and with Polygynous Husbands by Age of Wife.

Age group of women	All married women	Monogynous husbands		Polygynous husbands		Not stated
		Number	Per cent	Number	Per cent	
15–19	63	45	71	18	29	
20–24	147	89	60	58	40	
25–29	146	74	51	72	49	
30–34	73	28	38	45	62	
35–39	79	32	40	47	60	
40–44	43	19	44	24	56	
45–49	47	23	50	24	50	
50–54	26	11	42	15	58	
55–60	10	3	30	7	70	
60	26	9	34	17	66	
Total		333		327		27

shows that there is also apparently a connexion between age and a tendency to be polygamously married.

There is a definite tendency for the proportion of women married to polygynists to increase with age up to the age of 40. It is of interest to compare this observation with the data of Table 30. It appears that the great majority (80 per cent) of women aged 15–24 had had only one marriage at the time of the census. In the next 10-year group the percentage of those with only one marriage drops to 56 per cent; in the final 10 years of the reproductive period it drops to 45.5 per cent; in the next 10 years it drops still further to 37 per cent and remains at approximately this level, being 42 per cent for women over 55. We have here two obviously parallel trends. As women grow older during the reproductive period they tend to make more marriages and tend also to be more commonly married to polygynists. An explanation for this must be sought in norms and practices of Ashanti marriage which lie outside our present scope. One factor is that there is a strong preference among young women to marry young men, especially if it is their first marriage; and young men are not as a rule able to have more than one wife. First marriage no doubt accounts for a considerable proportion of the monogamously married younger women. Another factor, at the other end of the age scale, is that husbands of women at the end of, or past, the childbearing years, are likely to take another and younger wife if circumstances permit, and if they are still vigorous. Again a divorced or widowed woman is less opposed to marrying a polygynist than a woman who has not been married before, and this attitude is stronger if the woman has growing children of the previous marriage and is living with her maternal kin. But there are various complications. Thus a number of the ostensibly monogamous marriages, especially among the older women, are really surviving unions of polygynists among whom are some who will not marry another wife for reasons of age, infirmity, or personal choice.

TABLE 34. Type of Marriage by Religion.

Husband	Wife			
	Pagan	Christian	Not stated	Total
Pagan	393	74	1	468
Christian	64	104	2	170
Not stated	27	7	15	49
Total	484	185	18	687

$Q = 0.47$

It is natural to ask how Christianity influences the conditions of marriage. As Table 34 shows, there appears to be a bias among Christian women in favour of marriage with Christian men. In fact, the coefficient of association (Q) between the religion of husband and the religion of wife is 0.79. But there is also a substantial amount of inter-marriage between pagans and Christians; 42 per cent of Christian women have pagan husbands, some of whom are polygynous, and the total number of marriages in which one spouse is Christian and the other pagan (138) exceeds that of the purely Christian marriages (104). Though the churches of all denominations prefer their adherents to marry only Christians—and preferably of the same denomination—this ideal is not in fact attained. Christians do not form an endogamous community in Ashanti. Roman Catholics are subject to suspension or even exclusion from church membership if they marry out of the faith, but in practice many who profess to be Catholics are married to pagans in accordance with Ashanti custom, and accept their exclusion from the sacraments with equanimity. Both practising and nominal members of Protestant churches are often married to pagans. I know several Protestant women who are devout and active church workers but are married to pagan or lapsed polygynists. The desire and need to marry usually overrides the regulations made by churches. As there are still many more pagans than Christians in Ashanti, and as marriage is still predominantly governed by traditional ideals, extensive inter-marriage between Christians and pagans is inevitable. Though most observant Christian parents prefer, and some insist, that their daughters should marry Christians, in my experience it is unusual for parents to object to an otherwise desirable marriage on religious grounds.

288

It seems that up to the present the numerical inferiority of Christians has limited their influence on the general conditions of marriage in Agogo, and this applies throughout rural Ashanti. The spread of Christianity is, however, closely bound up with the spread of schooling owing to the fact that almost all rural primary schools are under mission supervision. Though school education has not hitherto been a significant selective factor in rural marriage,[1] there are indications that it is becoming one. Girls who reach the higher primary school standards are showing reluctance to marry men who have had no schooling, and the younger educated men are showing a preference for marrying girls who have been to school. Christianity is, moreover, thought of as being an intrinsic feature of the European way of life which most of the younger people are avid to follow. Add to this the bias that does exist in Christian families in favour of marriage to Christians, and it becomes plausible to expect a tendency among younger Christian women to show a preference for Christian husbands. Active church members often say that this is so, and there is some evidence in support of their view in our data.

Table 35 shows the age distribution of (a) the Christian women married to pagan husbands, and (b) the Christian women married to Christian husbands. It will be seen that among the three youngest age groups (women aged 15–29) those married to Christians are more than twice as numerous as those with pagan husbands, whereas among the women over 30 there is no significant difference. This suggests that there has been a definite tendency during the last 15 years for Christian girls to marry Christian men in preference to pagans. This can be tested in another way. If it were simply a question of availability of husbands, the age distributions we are discussing should not differ significantly from the age distribution

TABLE 35. Age Distribution of Christian Wives by Religion of Husband.

Age groups	Christian wives with pagan husbands	Christian wives with Christian husbands
15–19	4	9
20–24	12	30
25–29	18	32
30–34	10	4
35–39	11	11
40–44	6	9
45–49	6	6
50–54	4	3
55	3	—
Total	74	104

[1] To a large extent because it has been almost wholly confined to boys in the past.

289

TABLE 36. Observed and Expected Age Distributions for Christian Marriages.

Age groups	Christian wives with pagan husbands		Christian wives with Christian husbands	
	Observed number	Expected number	Observed number	Expected number
15–24	16	20.6	39	28.9
25–34	28	22.9	36	32.2
35–44	17	12.6	20	17.6
45–54	10	8.3	7	11.7
55	3	9.6	2	13.5

χ^2 (a) = 8.57
χ^2 (b) = 16.08   P = 0.05

of all the Christian women in our sample, as shown in Tables 28 and 29. On the basis of these tables, and the age distributions given above, Table 36 emerges. By this test it would appear that the age distribution of Christian women married to pagan husbands does not differ significantly from that of Christian women in the population as a whole, whereas the age distribution of those married to Christian husbands does differ significantly; there is a bias in favour of the younger age groups in the latter distribution. These findings can be interpreted as confirming the views mentioned above. I estimate the number of literate men, that is, those able to read and write adequately in their vernacular or in English, to be at the most one in five of the total adult male population of Agogo. The majority of these men—about two-thirds, if the information given by their wives is correct—are or were at one time practising Christians. Roughly speaking, therefore, for every Christian and literate husband available for an Agogo woman there are four illiterate pagan husbands available. Of the 49 literate women of our sample, 40 of whom are Christians, 31 gave information as to the education of their husbands; and of these 20 stated they were married to literates. This is a small point, but it strengthens the argument that there is a tendency for literate and Christian girls to show a preference for marriage with literate and Christian men.

While, as has been mentioned, a marriage with a Christian man is not necessarily a monogynous marriage, there is evidence that monogyny is more common among marriages in which the husband is a Christian than in marriages with pagan husbands. This is shown in the following table:

TABLE 37.

Women married to pagan husbands:	467;	monogynous 196 (42 per cent)
Women married to Christian husbands:	168;	monogynous 112 (66 per cent)

We conclude that though Christianity and literacy have not given rise to widespread changes in Ashanti marriage, as this works in Agogo, a tendency for preferential, monogamous marriage among literate Christians is beginning to appear,[1] although its extent is still so small as to be most unlikely to affect current demographic trends.

THE INFLUENCE OF HUSBAND'S OCCUPATION AND RESIDENCE

Table 38 shows the relationship between the occupations of the married women of our sample and those of their husbands. It should be remembered that half of these women were wives of polygynists. Thus, the total number of husbands represented in the table is considerably less than the total number of marriages (687). For instance, of the 21 marriages with native political officers, eight are marriages of one man. The table must therefore be read as referring to the women, not to their husbands. Agogo is a rural area in which 70 per cent of the adult males are engaged in food and cocoa farming, and the great majority (probably 90 per cent) of the women also have food gardens. It must be expected, therefore, that the majority of our sample would be married to farmers and other primary producers. This is the case, though one might have expected the proportion to be higher than 58 per cent. It is surprising to find that as many as 10 per cent approximately are married to traders and nearly 14 per cent to artisans and craftsmen. The two somewhat specialized occupations found among the women are craftwork, mainly dressmaking, and petty trade, which is sometimes a full-time occupation. Both are often carried on in addition to the tasks of the housewife. But dressmaking calls for a special skill and is chiefly followed by girls who as well as possessing a sewing machine, have been to school, and the petty trader needs some working capital and also time to make her purchases of goods in the larger towns for resale locally. It is not so easy for a farmer's wife to find the means or the opportunities for these occupations as for the wife of a man whose work requires him to live permanently in the township. It is therefore not surprising to find that only about one in seven (about 15 per cent) of the women engaged in these two occupations are married to farmers and that about 70 per cent are married to men with what might be called urban occupations, such as traders, carpenters and clerks. The women married to civil servants, clerks, native administration officers, big traders and soldiers (109, i.e., about 16 per cent of the married women) generally have a higher standard of living than the majority of farmers' wives or the wives of petty traders. But in marriage, domestic life and child-rearing, most of them follow the customs of the rest of the community,

[1] Ashanti informants confirm that this is so as regards formal marriage. But it is well known that Christian men often have generally recognized, though legally invalid, quasi-marital associations with women other than their wives.

TABLE 38. Occupations of Husbands in Relation to Those of Married Women.

Occupations of wives	Occupation of husbands				
	Farmers and other primary producers	Big traders	Petty traders	Artisans and craftsmen	Labourers
Farmers and housewives	368	18	24	79	8
Craftworkers	—	—	1	2	—
Petty traders	7	3	16	5	—
Food hawkers	5	—	2	2	2
Priestesses	1	—	—	1	—
Dependents and aged	1	—	—	—	—
Unspecified	15	1	1	5	2
Totals	397	22	44	94	12
Per cent	57.7	3.2	6.4	13.7	1.8

though their children might have more and better food and clothing than the children of the ordinary illiterate housewife. It is of interest to consider from another angle the occupations of the husbands of the married women of our sample. Table 39 shows the relationship between the occupations of the husbands and the number of present wives the husbands have. The mode for all the occupational groups except those of the big traders and the native administration officers is marriage with monogynists, and in every case it represents approximately 50 per cent of the marriages in that group. But 86 per cent of the women married to big traders have polygynous husbands; and small though the sample of marriages in this group is, the divergence from the rest of the table is too striking to be without significance. Similarly, 81 per cent of the women married to native administration officers have polygynous husbands. These findings correspond with commonly accepted opinion in Ashanti. It is known that produce buyers and other big traders very often have more than one wife as they can afford to maintain a plural household; and chiefs and councillors are practically obliged to have more than one wife for the sake of prestige and in order to fulfil what is regarded as a duty to the State of having a large number of children. This gives rise to one of the hardest dilemmas faced by an observant Christian when he becomes a chief. Hitherto custom has won in most cases and Christian chiefs have usually acquiesced in the duty of plural marriage.

It is clear from the data we have been discussing that the social and economic changes going on in Ashanti today have not as yet brought about wide variations in the conditions of marriage or in the material circumstances of the Agogo wife and mother. The degree to which marriage

292

		Occupation of husbands				
Fetish priests	Soldiers	Native administrative officials	Civil servants and other literate workers	Miscellaneous	Unspecified	Total
8	25	19	21	8	9	587
—	—	—	3	1	—	7
—	4	1	6	1	2	45
1	3	—	2	—	—	17
—	—	—	—	—	—	2
—	—	1	—	—	—	2
1	—	—	2	—	—	27
10	32	21	34	10	11	687
1.5	4.7	3.1	5.0	1.6	1.5	100

is still governed by traditional norms and prejudices is well brought out in the tables which follow. Table 40 shows the relationship between the clans of 592 married women of our sample for whom the data are available, and those of their husbands. It is significant that only 46 of these women (just under 8 per cent) stated that their husbands were of the same clans

TABLE 39. Occupations of Husbands and Plural Marriage.

Occupation of husbands	Number of present wives						Total
	1	2	3	4	5+	Unspecified	
Farmers and other primary producers	187	132	43	10	6	19	397
Big traders	3	15	4	—	—	—	22
Petty traders	24	13	4	2	—	1	44
Artisans and craftsmen	51	23	16	—	1	3	94
Labourers	7	2	2	—	—	1	12
Fetish priests	2	2	—	5	—	1	10
Soldiers	26	6	—	—	—	—	32
Native administrative officers	4	3	7	—	7	—	21
Civil servants and other literate workers	17	12	4	—	—	1	34
Miscellaneous	7	2	—	—	—	1	10
Unspecified	5	3	1	1	1	—	11
Total	333	213	81	18	15	27	687

TABLE 40. Clans of Wives and Clans of Husbands (Ashanti Only).

Wife's clan	Husband's clan									Total
	Atwea	Asona	Aduana	Oyoko	Bretuo	Asa-kyeri	Asenie	Agona	Ekuana	
Atwea	—	2	1	—	—	—	1	—	1	5
Asona	—	11	75	22	13	14	15	7	6	163
Aduana	5	64	27	24	14	13	13	13	9	182
Oyoko	3	11	27	1	1	3	2	3	2	53
Bretuo	1	6	20	6	3	4	—	3	2	45
Asakyeri	—	13	16	1	1	—	1	2	3	37
Asenie	—	8	21	5	1	4	3	2	1	45
Agona	—	9	16	1	—	1	4	1	2	34
Ekuana	—	4	13	1	4	2	3	1	—	28
Total	9	128	216	61	37	41	42	32	26	592

as themselves. A check of the information suggested that some of them had given wrong information, but the majority were women of slave descent or belonging to attached lineages not of the authentic line of descent of their husbands' lineages. Several such attached lineages are found at Agogo, associated especially with the two largest and politically most powerful lineages, the Aduana and the Asona. The rule of clan exogamy is thus still strictly observed, even among Christians, in Agogo; and this applies to the whole of Ashanti.

Table 41 shows the tenacity of traditional attitudes in a different way.

TABLE 41.

Wife's birth-place	Husband's birth-place								Total
	Agogo	Ashanti else-where	Other Akan areas	Ga-Ewe	Nor-thern Terri-tories	Yoruba	Hausa	Un-speci-fied	
Agogo	488	82	14	4	9	—	—	6	603
Ashanti elsewhere	29	20	1	—	1	—	—	—	51
Other Akan areas	6	2	9	1	—	—	1	—	19
Ga-Ewe	—	—	—	—	—	—	—	—	—
Nothern Territories	1	—	—	—	6	—	—	—	7
Yoruba	—	—	—	—	—	1	—	—	1
Hausa	—	—	—	—	—	—	4	—	4
Unspecified	1	—	1	—	—	—	—	—	2
Total	525	104	25	5	16	1	5	6	687

The Ashanti, as we have remarked before, like marrying as near home as possible, partly because marriage outside one's own village or local community is incompatible with the preference of both men and women for living in their maternal households, rather than with their spouses. As this table shows, 80 per cent of the Agogo-born married women of our sample were married to men also born in the township and its environs; and if those married to Ashanti from elsewhere are added, we find that 95 per cent of these women are married to Ashanti men. This testimony to the Ashanti prejudice against marrying out of the local community—and its corollary the objection to marrying non-Ashanti—may seem exaggerated (for the Agogo women who have married out and have gone to live in their husband's villages are not adequately represented in the sample), but evidence from other enquiries suggests that this is not so. The marriages of the small number of non-Ashanti women[1] (5 per cent) in this sample show that the Ashanti prejudice against intertribal marriage is also shared by the other West African peoples represented in this sample. It should be added that 78 per cent of the husbands of the married women of our sample were living in the chiefdom of Agogo at the time of our enquiry. Reference has already been made to the local inbreeding that result from these marriage preferences.

SUMMARY

The social characteristics of the sample of women interviewed for the purpose of the present enquiry can be summarized as follows: Our sample is thoroughly representative of the total population of adult women who regarded Agogo as their home and would normally reside there. It is economically homogeneous in that about 90 per cent of the women in effect earned their living as housewives and food growers. It is also culturally homogeneous. The small incidence of literacy among them had not, at the time of the enquiry, appreciably influenced their mode of life, nor had the adherence of a considerable number of them to various Christian denominations. All the women over 20, with the exception of the few who were physiologically defective or infirm, had been married, the older ones generally more than once. This means that every woman would be bearing children throughout her reproductive years. In marriage, traditional custom and prejudice still prevailed at the time of the enquiry, with the result that there was a high degree of local endogamy. As a consequence of local endogamy over many generations the great majority of the Ashanti women of the sample were Agogo-born of Agogo-born parents. As well as being socially homogeneous, our sample was thus also ethnically homogeneous, apart from the small number of immigrant women.

[1] Almost all of them were immigrants whose husbands lived in Agogo for the purely economic reason that they earned their living there.

CHAPTER II

The Fertility of Agogo Women

The preceding discussion has made it clear that Agogo is a relatively homogeneous community in the social and economic sense. It also has a very high degree of ethnic uniformity, its population being very largely maintained by many generations of local endogamy. We now wish to ascertain what level of fertility is achieved in this community. But before we try to estimate reproduction rates, some of the limiting factors in reproductive performance must be discussed. Though the information provided by the fertility census is far from perfect, it is sufficient to give some broad indications.

AGE OF MENARCHE AND OF FIRST MARRIAGE

It is significant that no case was recorded of a girl who claimed to have reached the menarche and whose age was estimated to be under 15 years.[1] As has been previously suggested, it may of course be that the interviewers automatically placed girls who had begun to menstruate among the 15–16 year age group, since it is generally held among Ashanti that girls begin to menstruate at about 16. However, there is evidence in support of this popular opinion. There is the fact that a considerable number of 15 year old girls was recorded among the offspring of the women interviewed but did not themselves appear in the sample. This suggests that, in making their estimates of age, the interviewers tried to follow the

---

[1] Raymond Pearl, op. cit., pp. 46–50, reaches the conclusion that the average age of the menarche, as judged by a world wide sample, is approximately 15 years. No statistical data are available for the Gold Coast, but R. W. B. Ellis has shown (*British Medical Journal*, Jan. 1950, p. 85) that the mean age of the menarche among Nigerian girls from schools in Lagos was 14.22 years in one sample and 14.40 years in another. These means are significantly higher than the mean age of 13.73 years found in one sample of English girls and 13.6 years found in another sample for the onset of menstruation. Professor Ellis points out that the Lagos school girls included in his samples probably had better standards of nutrition and of general physical care than is common in rural areas of West Africa, and menstruation is therefore likely to commence at a somewhat earlier age among them than among rural girls.

instructions with care. Again, several fathers showed me personal diaries in which they had noted the dates of birth and of first menstruation of their daughters, and in every case the onset was in the sixteenth or seventeenth year. I checked this with a woman medical officer who had for some years been concerned with maternity and child welfare work in Ashanti and she was of the opinion that Ashanti girls seldom menstruate before 16 years.

As has been mentioned, it is still the custom for pagan girls in rural Ashanti to undergo a public nubility ceremony within about six months after the menarche. Confirmation takes the place of this for many Christian girls, though some of them also follow traditional custom in this matter. Marriage commonly takes place within a few months after this ceremony. This points to the conclusion that an Ashanti country girl's first marriage usually takes place in her seventeenth year.

INTERVAL BETWEEN PUBERTY AND FIRST PREGNANCY

The tremendous value attached to childbearing and the absence of birth control means that a first pregnancy is eagerly looked forward to by both spouses and their kinsfolk. Indeed, if it is too long delayed the marriage may be in danger of breaking up. It is of interest, therefore, to know the average length of the interval between commencement of cohabitation in marriage and first pregnancy. As pre-marital sexual freedom is, however, not uncommon among Ashanti girls of child-bearing age, and as pregnancy sometimes results, the question should rather be put in the form: what is the mean interval between the onset of menstruation and first pregnancy? Further interest also attaches to this question in view of the contention that there is a period of adolescent sterility in females between the onset of puberty and the establishment of reproductive capacity.[1] The results of our enquiry on this subject are given in Table 42; but as has already been mentioned, an error of three to six months is highly probable. According to Table 42, the mode is for the first pregnancy to start in the second year after the beginning of menstruation. The mean interval is 1.9 years (S.D., 1.7 years) for the whole group, including those who had not yet had a pregnancy. But the variation is considerable, the maximum interval admitted being nearly 8 years. These figures must be taken with great caution, but it does not seem unwarranted to infer that an interval of roughly two years between the onset of menstruation and the achievement of first pregnancy is typical; and this would imply perhaps a year of

[1] The evidence for and against this contention is analysed at length in M. F. Ashley Montagu, *Adolescent Sterility*, 1946 (published by Thomas, Springfield, Ill.). Montagu concludes that 'the evidence . . . indicates that there exists an absolute period of adolescent sterility in most females and that this period, in any given population, is extremely variable in duration' (op. cit. p. 117).

TABLE 42. Interval Between Menstruation and First Pregnancy.

Interval (years)	Age distribution of women, in five-year-groups					
	15–19	20–24	25–29	30–34	35–39	40–44
No pregnancy	64	26	27	9	4	2
Under 1	10	19	17	4	19	4
1–2	26	73	56	48	33	14
2–3	12	32	38	19	19	18
3–4	3	7	18	5	18	8
4–5	0	7	9	2	3	1
5–6	0	4	6	2	0	3
6–7	0	2	2	1	0	2
7–8	0	0	9	2	4	2
Not stated	0	0	4	1	2	1
Total	115	170	186	93	102	55

Note. This table includes all the women of our sample. Exclusion of the non-Ashanti women does not affect the results. Among the women of our sample were some who were in their first pregnancy; hence this table is not comparable with later tables that refer to

'adolescent sterility'. Inspection of the table shows, moreover, that the modal interval is constant for all age groups. This not only strengthens the inference that there is a period of adolescent sterility, but also suggests that this is related to physiological conditions that have not changed with changing social conditions during the past 40 years. It is apparent, also, why young married women and their husbands become worried if there is no pregnancy within two or three years after marriage.[1]

Ashanti themselves say that menstruation commences in the sixteenth year, that marriage usually follows within the following twelve months, and that a woman's first child will be born to her within the next two years.[2] Our data suggest that these judgments are correct. It seems safe

[1] If a period of adolescent sterility is normal among all human races it is obviously a datum of importance for the understanding of sex life and marriage among a people like the Ashanti where marriage takes place so soon after a girl reaches physiological maturity. I must, therefore, add that beside the sources of inaccuracy of information already mentioned, it is quite possible that some women either deliberately or unwittingly claimed to have had their first pregnancy in the second year of marriage just because this is considered to be usual. On the other hand, the fact that many women admitted to a lapse of a longer interval, and the fact that Ashanti women always watch for the signs of their first pregnancy with special care and anxiety, must have contributed to accuracy. Furthermore, a woman's first born (*piesie*) has a position of special respect among her children.
[2] cf. in this connexion, J. Clyde Mitchell, 'An Estimate of Fertility in some Yao Hamlets in Liwonde District, Southern Nyasaland', *Africa*, XIX, 4, 1949, pp. 293ff., Table II. According to these data, the median age of Yao women at the birth of the first child varies from 17.9 years for women under 30 to 20.6 years for women over 45. The lower estimate would put the beginning of first pregnancy at about the same age as among our Ashanti sample. The median age of first marriage among the Yao appears to be 16.9 years.

Age distribution of women, in five-year-groups								Total
45–49	50–54	55–59	60–64	65–69	70–74	75–79	80	
5	1	2	1	0	1	0	1	143
6	9	6	7	3	3	1	0	108
26	23	18	16	8	9	3	7	360
12	10	9	7	5	9	5	5	200
10	4	4	5	7	2	1	2	94
3	3	1	2	1	1	0	1	34
3	4	1	2	0	1	0	0	26
1	0	1	2	1	0	0	0	12
2	2	0	3	0	1	0	0	25
2	2	1	0	0	0	1	1	15
70	58	43	45	25	27	11	17	1 017

completed pregnancies. As in previous tables the women are grouped in accordance with their ages at the time of the investigation.

to say that the normal age of the menarche among the Ashanti is about 15.5 years, that first marriage takes place at about 16.5–17 years, and that the first pregnancy follows at about 17.6 to 18.

PREGNANCIES, STILLBIRTHS AND MISCARRIAGES

Miscarriages and stillbirths are said to be very common among African women on the Gold Coast. But it is difficult to obtain reliable information. A miscarriage or stillbirth is a very distressing occurrence to an Ashanti woman and information about such a misfortune is given with reluctance. Some pregnancies which were said to have resulted in live-born children who died shortly after birth may in fact have been stillbirths. The incidence of miscarriages and stillbirths shown in the following tables is, therefore, likely to be an underestimate.[1]

Table 43 shows that approximately 84 per cent of the women of the sample claimed to have had one or more pregnancies during their lifetime. There is a steady decline, correlated with age, in the proportion of women

[1] At the time of the outbreak of the war in 1939, Agogo women were beginning to attend the Basle Mission Hospital in appreciable numbers for ante-natal advice and the maternity ward was well patronized. In cases of difficult labour the mission doctors and sisters were also often called in. But the proportion of the total female population thus helped seems to have been small. The majority had no obstetric care other than that of the old women of the family at the time of delivery. A source of embarrassment in enquiring about neonatal mortality is the Ashanti belief that an infant which dies before it is eight days old is not really human, and hence is not given proper burial.

TABLE 43.   Women Classified Ever-pregnant or Never-pregnant by Age Groups.

	Age distribution of women by five-year age groups				
	15–19	20–24	25–29	30–34	35–39
All women	115	170	186	93	102
One or more pregnancies	44	141	156	82	98
Never pregnant					
Number	71	29	30	11	4
Per cent of all women	[61.7]	[17]	[16.1]	[11.8]	3.9

Note. Figures in brackets refer to age groups among whom some women may still be expected to bear children. Those not in brackets refer to age groups which have probably

in the age range 15–34 who had not had a pregnancy up to the time of the census; then there is a steep drop, showing an apparent incidence of about 4 per cent barrenness, throughout the stretch from 35 to 64. The age groups over 65 can be neglected as the numbers are so small. It is so unlikely that an Ashanti woman free from physical infirmity should reach the age of 35 without having had one pregnancy, if she is fertile, that any woman over that age who has never been pregnant can be taken to be barren. It would appear, then, that about 4 per cent of the women in our sample over the age of 35 are barren. The disparity between this figure and the nearly 12 per cent of apparent sterility in the 30–34 age group is striking, for it is not very likely that a fertile woman of 30 would never have been pregnant.[1] Ashanti themselves say that there has been a marked increase in sterility both among men and among women in the past twenty or thirty years, owing to the spread of venereal diseases. It may be that this is reflected in the large apparent incidence of sterility in the age groups under 34. Agogo was only accessible on foot until 1923; in that year the first lorry reached the township. Allowing two or three years for road traffic with the mining and commercial centre of Konongo to become established, we can conjecture as follows. The women who were married before 1926 would be at least 35 years old in 1945, whereas those who were

[1] Involuntary childlessness, to use the term preferred by the Royal Commission on Population, is difficult to investigate among an African people where it is regarded as a misfortune of an almost shameful kind. Comparable data from other African areas are so variable as to be hardly worth citing. For instance, a Belgian investigator reports sterility rates of 6 per cent, 13 per cent, and 40 per cent as the averages for the women of all ages of three Congo tribes, the variation within the tribe for which the average is lowest being from 2.4 per cent for women aged 25 to 35 years to 18 per cent for women aged 20–25 years. (L. Geurts, 'Etude Démographique des populations Bakwa Mputu', *Zaire*, IV. 1., 1950.) The Royal Commission on Population (*Papers*, Vol. IV, 1950, pp. 35 ff.) discusses data from various European countries and concludes that an average of between 5 per cent and 8 per cent of married women in Great Britain are likely to be involuntarily childless. It would appear from this that the average of about 4 per cent for the older Ashanti women is an underestimate.

Age distribution of women by five-year age groups							
40–44	45–49	50–54	55–59	60–64	65–69	70–74	70
55	70	58	43	45	25	27	28
53	65	57	41	44	25	26	27
2	5	1	2	1	0	1	1
3.6	4.7		3.4		1.9		3.6

or certainly passed the age at which there is still a chance of a pregnancy.

married after 1926 would be under 34. If the Ashanti critics of the morals of the present day are right—and what they say about the effect of venereal diseases is supported by qualified European observers as well—then it may well be that these diseases increased very rapidly, as often happens in Africa in like circumstances, with the opening of the road. As it is always the younger women, both those not yet married and those not yet securely settled in marriage, who are most vulnerable to these diseases, this might account for the discrepancy noted. But this is pure conjecture, advanced merely because no more satisfactory explanation can be offered.

Table 44 shows the distribution of pregnancies claimed by the women by age groups. Twin and triplet pregnancies are counted as single pregnancies. Though twins are specially honoured by the Ashanti, it was found to be impossible to determine with any accuracy the incidence of multiple pregnancies or live births among the women of Agogo. Twins are so closely identified in Ashanti custom that they are often spoken of as if they were one person. Thus, if one or both of a pair of twins died in earliest infancy, the interviewer was often given the impression that only a single live birth was involved; and time could not be afforded for checking details of this sort. The estimate of 15 twin and triplet pregnancies per 1,000 finally reached is perhaps too low.[1]

The table shows a steady rise in the mean number of pregnancies per mother in each age group from 15 to 49. After that age the means fluctuate but the average for all age groups over 50 is 6.8 pregnancies, and this is the same as the average for the age group 45–49. For the women of reproductive age (15–49 years) there is a high positive correlation (r = 0.64 — 0.02) between number of pregnancies and age. The corresponding correlation coefficient for the women over 50 is not significant. This confirms the view that the reproductive span among Ashanti women terminates at the age of 45–49, which gives a maximum span of 35 reproductive years

[1] But Pearl, op. cit., p. 60, gives figures ranging from 15.9 per 1,000 births for Denmark to 4 per 1,000 for Colombia.

TABLE 44. Number of Completed Pregnancies (Including Miscarriages and Stillbirths) to Women by Age at Census.

Number of pregnancies	Ages														Total
	15–19	20–24	25–29	30–34	35–39	40–44	45–49	50–54	55–59	60–64	65–69	70–74	75–79	80+	
1	30	47	28	8	7	5	3	2	1	1	0	1	0	0	133
2	11	52	35	6	11	6	4	6	2	5	0	2	0	0	140
3	3	33	37	11	8	3	2	3	1	2	2	3	1	0	109
4	—	6	28	18	12	5	6	7	2	6	2	0	2	4	98
5	—	2	17	17	11	3	8	3	3	6	0	2	2	0	79
6	—	1	10	11	14	6	7	4	5	5	5	4	2	2	76
7	—	—	1	8	11	1	11	10	4	4	3	2	1	4	60
8	—	—	—	2	10	5	7	7	4	3	7	1	0	2	48
9	—	—	—	1	4	9	4	6	1	4	3	4	2	2	40
10	—	—	—	—	6	9	4	5	11	8	2	2	0	0	47
11	—	—	—	—	1	1	6	3	3	0	1	1	1	1	18
12	—	—	—	—	—	—	1	1	3	0	0	1	0	0	6
13	—	—	—	—	—	—	0	0	1	0	0	0	0	1	2
14	—	—	—	—	—	—	1	0	0	0	0	0	0	0	1
15	—	—	—	—	—	—	0	0	0	0	0	1	0	0	1
17	—	—	—	—	—	—	1	0	0	0	0	0	0	0	1
Total pregnancies	61	290	473	357	519	326	441	365	322	269	179	174	69	114	3 959
Ever-pregnant women	44	141	156	82	98	53	65	57	41	44	25	26	11	16	859
Total women	115	170	186	93	102	55	70	58	43	45	25	27	11	17	1 017
Mean no. of pregnancies: per 'mother'	1.4	2.05	3.03	4.35	5.3	6.15	6.78	6.4	7.85	6.11 / 6.8[1]	7.16	6.7	6.27	7.12	
per woman	0.53	1.7	2.54	3.84	5.09	5.93	6.3	6.29	7.49	5.97 / 6.6[2]	7.16	6.41	6.27	6.7	

[1] Pregnancies per 'mother' 50 years and over: 6.8.

[2] Pregnancies per woman 50 years and over: 6.6.

between the ages of 15 and 50. The table also shows that childbearing continues throughout the reproductive span. The average of approximately seven pregnancies achieved by the end of the childbearing years may however be an underestimate, owing to inaccuracies in the number of stillbirths and miscarriages admitted.

But though the maximum reproductive span stretches from 15 to 50 years, this is obviously not the effective span of fertility. If the average number of pregnancies per woman (as against the rate per mother) is considered, it appears that effective fertility is only 0.53 completed pregnancies per woman in the 15–19 year age group. This may be related to 'adolescent sterility' or it may be due to the fact that marriage does not as a rule occur before the age of 16.5. At the other end of the age scale, the increase in the mean number of completed pregnancies of the 45–49 years age group over that of the 40–49 year group is less than 0.5 and there is no appreciable increase in the combined average for the age groups over 50. It seems reasonable, therefore, to conclude that fertility stops nearer the mid-point of the 45–49 year group than at 49.5 years. An effective fertility span of 31 years (16.5 to 47.5) is probably nearer the true span than the maximum of 35 reproductive years.[1]

An Ashanti married woman of childbearing age and in normal health hopes to have a pregnancy every third year and our records suggest that this is very commonly realized. A woman might therefore expect to have 10 pregnancies in her lifetime. Table 44 shows that 76 (8.8 per cent) of the mothers in our sample achieved 10 or more pregnancies. But there is a substantial difference between this figure and the average of approximately seven pregnancies for women who have passed through the child-bearing years. Part of the discrepancy may be due to suppression of still-births and miscarriages. But it may be that the fertility of Ashanti women is not at the same level all through the childbearing years, and of course individual differences in fecundity also affect the mean rate.[2] We do not know whether conditions of nutrition, hygiene and disease adversely influence reproductive performance in tropical Africa.

We come now to our data on miscarriages and stillbirths. Table 45 shows the incidence and frequency of miscarriages among the 138 women who admitted any. About 16 per cent of the women who had had one or more pregnancies admitted to miscarriages, a high figure by European standards.[3] As number of pregnancies is positively correlated with age during the childbearing years, it is not surprising to find that the percentage of mothers in each age group who have had miscarriages rises steadily with

---

[1] This is in agreement with Pearl's conclusion that the mean reproductive span of women is 31–32 years, op. cit., pp. 46–50.

[2] The Royal Commission on Population (*Papers*, Vol. I., p. 10) records that 30 per cent of the 'K' sample of women 'can be regarded as experiencing at least one sterile period in their reproductive life'.

[3] It is about double the incidence reported for Great Britain by the Royal Commission on Population (*Papers*, Vol. IV, par. 6).

TABLE 45. Number of Women Reporting Miscarriages and Number of Miscarriages by Age at Census.

	Ages of women					
	15–19	20–24	25–29	30–34	35–39	40–44
Number of miscarriages						
1	3	14	15	10	6	10
2	—	1	5	2	4	4
3	—	—	—	1	2	0
4–6	—	—	1	1	1	0
Women reporting miscarriages (a)	3	15	21	14	13	14
Total 'mothers' (b)	44	141	156	82	98	53
Per cent of 'mothers' miscarrying (a/b)	6.8	10.6	13.4	17.0	13.2	26.4
Number of miscarriages	3	16	30	22	24	18
Total pregnancies	61	290	473	357	519	326
Miscarriages per 1,000 mothers	68	113	192	268	245	340
Miscarriages per 1,000 pregnancies	49	55	63	61	46	55

TABLE 46. Number of Women Reporting Stillbirths and Number of Stillbirths by Age of Women at Census.

	Ages				
	15–19	20–24	25–29	30–34	35–39
Number of stillbirths					
1	2	8	6	5	3
2	—	—	—	1	1
3	—	—	—	—	1
4–7	—	—	—	—	—
(a) Women reporting stillbirths	2	8	6	6	5
(b) Total stillbirths	2	8	6	7	8
(c) Total 'mothers'	44	141	156	82	98
(d) Total pregnancies	61	290	473	357	519
Percent of mothers with stillbirths	4.5	5.6	3.9	7.3	5.1
Averages		4.8		6.2	
Stillbirths per 1,000 mothers (b/c)	45	56	39	85	81
Averages		48		83	
Stillbirths per 1,000 pregnancies (b/d)	33	28	13	19	15
Averages		21		17	

<table>
<tr><th colspan="9">Ages of women</th><th>Mean
all ages</th><th>Mean ages
50 and over</th></tr>
<tr><th>45–49</th><th>50–54</th><th>55–59</th><th>60–64</th><th>65–69</th><th>70–74</th><th>75–79</th><th>80+</th><th>Total</th><th></th><th></th></tr>
<tr><td>10</td><td>7</td><td>7</td><td>4</td><td>4</td><td>1</td><td>2</td><td>3</td><td>96</td><td></td><td></td></tr>
<tr><td>4</td><td>3</td><td>1</td><td>1</td><td>4</td><td>0</td><td>0</td><td>0</td><td>29</td><td></td><td></td></tr>
<tr><td>0</td><td>1</td><td>2</td><td>0</td><td>0</td><td>0</td><td>2</td><td>0</td><td>8</td><td></td><td></td></tr>
<tr><td>1</td><td>0</td><td>0</td><td>0</td><td>0</td><td>1</td><td>0</td><td>0</td><td>5</td><td></td><td></td></tr>
<tr><td>15</td><td>11</td><td>10</td><td>5</td><td>8</td><td>2</td><td>4</td><td>3</td><td>138</td><td></td><td></td></tr>
<tr><td>65</td><td>57</td><td>41</td><td>44</td><td>25</td><td>26</td><td>11</td><td>16</td><td>859</td><td></td><td></td></tr>
<tr><td>23.0</td><td>19.3</td><td>24.4</td><td>11.3</td><td>32.0</td><td>7.7</td><td>36.3</td><td>18.8</td><td></td><td>16.1</td><td>21.4</td></tr>
<tr><td>22</td><td>16</td><td>15</td><td>6</td><td>12</td><td>6</td><td>8</td><td>3</td><td>201</td><td></td><td></td></tr>
<tr><td>441</td><td>365</td><td>322</td><td>269</td><td>179</td><td>174</td><td>69</td><td>114</td><td>3 959</td><td></td><td></td></tr>
<tr><td>338</td><td>287</td><td>366</td><td>136</td><td>480</td><td>231</td><td>728</td><td>188</td><td></td><td>234</td><td>345</td></tr>
<tr><td>50</td><td>44</td><td>46</td><td>22</td><td>67</td><td>34</td><td>115</td><td>26</td><td></td><td>51</td><td>51</td></tr>
</table>

<table>
<tr><th colspan="9">Ages</th><th></th></tr>
<tr><th>40–44</th><th>45–49</th><th>50–54</th><th>55–59</th><th>60–64</th><th>65–69</th><th>70–74</th><th>75–79</th><th>80+</th><th>Total</th></tr>
<tr><td>2</td><td>4</td><td>3</td><td>3</td><td>4</td><td>0</td><td>2</td><td>1</td><td>1</td><td>44</td></tr>
<tr><td>1</td><td>2</td><td>1</td><td>3</td><td>0</td><td>1</td><td>0</td><td>0</td><td>0</td><td>10</td></tr>
<tr><td>2</td><td>0</td><td>0</td><td>2</td><td>0</td><td>0</td><td>0</td><td>0</td><td>0</td><td>5</td></tr>
<tr><td>—</td><td>1</td><td>0</td><td>0</td><td>0</td><td>0</td><td>1</td><td>1</td><td>0</td><td>3</td></tr>
<tr><td>5</td><td>7</td><td>4</td><td>8</td><td>4</td><td>1</td><td>3</td><td>2</td><td>1</td><td>62</td></tr>
<tr><td>10</td><td>12</td><td>5</td><td>15</td><td>4</td><td>2</td><td>7</td><td>8</td><td>1</td><td>95</td></tr>
<tr><td>53</td><td>65</td><td>57</td><td>41</td><td>44</td><td>25</td><td>26</td><td>11</td><td>16</td><td>859</td></tr>
<tr><td>326</td><td>441</td><td>365</td><td>322</td><td>269</td><td>179</td><td>174</td><td>69</td><td>114</td><td>3 959</td></tr>
<tr><td>9.4</td><td>10.7</td><td>7.0</td><td>19.5</td><td>9.0</td><td>4.0</td><td>11.5</td><td>18.0</td><td>6.3</td><td></td></tr>
<tr><td colspan="2">10.1</td><td></td><td></td><td></td><td>10.7</td><td></td><td></td><td></td><td></td></tr>
<tr><td>189</td><td>184</td><td>87</td><td>366</td><td>91</td><td>80</td><td>269</td><td>727</td><td>63</td><td>110</td></tr>
<tr><td colspan="2">187</td><td></td><td></td><td></td><td>240</td><td></td><td></td><td></td><td></td></tr>
<tr><td>30</td><td>27</td><td>13</td><td>46</td><td>15</td><td>11</td><td>40</td><td>116</td><td>9</td><td>24</td></tr>
<tr><td colspan="2">29</td><td></td><td></td><td></td><td>36</td><td></td><td></td><td></td><td></td></tr>
</table>

age till the menopause. The large increase in the proportion of miscarrying women in the last decade of the reproductive span may simply reflect the fact that they have been longer exposed to the risks than the younger women, but it may be that they are specially prone to miscarry by comparison with younger women. But it will be seen that whereas the incidence of miscarriages per 1,000 mothers increases with age, after the age of 20, the incidence per 1,000 pregnancies 'appears to remain constant or to diminish with age.[1] It seems therefore that the risks of miscarriage for each pregnancy are not correlated with age of mother but are due to conditions which affect all mothers equally, regardless of age, and indeed seem to affect the pregnancies of young women in the early stages of their reproductive history more strongly than those of the older women. The increase in the incidence of miscarriages with increasing age must be due simply to the longer exposure of the older women to the risks. This is a problem that calls for medical investigation.

The figures for stillbirths, given in Table 46, show the same general picture. But they are probably even less reliable than those for miscarriages. It is impossible to believe that they do not in reality exceed the rate for England and Wales in 1947.[2]

To sum up, it seems that approximately 75 per 1,000 of the pregnancies achieved by the women of the sample up till the time of the enquiry had been lost by miscarriage or stillbirth. But as this is certainly an underestimate, a loss of at least 100 per 1,000 pregnancies (10 per cent) can safely be assumed to have occurred in this way.[3]

In view of the fact that a woman often has more than one husband in the course of her life, it is of interest to see if this has any influence on fertility. Table 47 shows the distribution of the numbers of pregnancies claimed by the women of our sample in relation to the number of marriages made by them (including unions which were not legally formalized but which resulted in offspring). The 465 mothers who stated that they had had only one husband throughout their lives had 2,007 pregnancies, an average of 4.3 per woman; and the 394 mothers who said they had married more than once, or had had children by more than one man, had 1,952 pregancies, an average of 4.1 per woman. The difference is not significant. This confirms what was previously said to the effect that Agogo women,

[1] The proportions of women in each age group who had had pregnancies up to the time of the enquiry are approximately: 38 per cent in the 15–19 year group; 83 per cent in the 20–24 year old group; 84 per cent in the 25–29 year group. This suggests that women do not become fully exposed to the risks of childbearing till they enter the 20–24 year group.

[2] This is given as 24 per 1,000 in *Papers*, Vol. IV, par. 14, of the Royal Commission on Population.

[3] Even this is probably too low an estimate. R. D. Harding, 'A Note on some Vital Statistics of a Primitive Peasant Community in Sierra Leone', *Population Studies*, II, 3, 1948, p. 373, reports that miscarriages and stillbirths amounted to 22.9 per 100 live births in the small Kissi community he studied. Pearl, op. cit., p. 90, states that a reproductive wastage of around 20 per cent of legitimate pregnancies is usually allowed for.

TABLE 47. Pregnancies by Number of Marriages.

Number of pregnancies	Number of marriages										Total women	Total pregnancies
	Nil	1	2	3	4	5	6	7	8	9		
Nil	48	74	25	9	1	1	0	0	0	0	158	0
1	—	88	28	13	4	0	0	0	0	0	133	133
2	1	81	41	12	3	1	0	0	1	0	140	280
3	—	61	25	20	1	1	1	0	0	0	109	327
4	—	52	26	12	7	0	0	0	0	1	98	392
5	—	45	14	12	6	2	0	0	0	0	79	395
6	—	33	29	8	5	1	0	0	0	0	76	456
7	—	24	22	10	3	0	0	1	0	0	60	420
8	—	18	17	10	3	0	0	0	0	0	48	384
9	—	18	13	6	1	1	0	0	0	1	40	360
10	—	29	12	6	0	0	0	0	0	0	47	470
11	—	9	2	6	0	0	1	0	0	0	18	198
12	—	3	2	1	0	0	0	0	0	0	6	72
13–17	—	3	0	1	1	0	0	0	0	0	5	72
Total	49	538	256	126	35	7	2	1	1	2	1 017	3 959

in common with women in all rural areas of Ashanti, as a rule bear children throughout their reproductive life and that this is not determined by individual marital circumstances. As, however, there is a greater proportion of older women among the plurally married than among the once-married women,[1] we should expect the former to have had more pregnancies on the average.[2] Our observed result may be connected with the well known demographic fact that women under 40 generally have higher fertility rates than those over 40. Or it may be connected with social factors. A plurally married woman will have one or more intervals between husbands when absence of, or casual, sex relations may make her chances of conception less than those of a woman married to one husband all her life.

As we have already seen, there is a high correlation between age and the likelihood of a woman's being married to a polygamist. A woman who, at the age of 20, was monogamously married might very well be the wife of a polygamist at the age of 40, and might revert to monogamous status 10 years later as the surviving wife of a formerly polygamous

[1] There is naturally correlation between the number of marriages a woman has made during her life and her age, with a higher proportion of older women among those who have had several marriages than among those only once married. From Table 30 it can be seen that about 22 per cent of the once-married women are over 45 as compared with 41 per cent of the plurally married.
[2] Comparative African material is scarce. The best known to me is from the previously cited paper by M. L. Geurts, Zaire, 1950. From his Table 12 it appears that the average number of children born to a woman aged 45 and over is about the same (approximately four) whether she has been only once married or several times married.

husband. The question often raised as to whether monogamously married women are more or less fertile than the wives of polygamists is therefore obviously unanswerable for a community like Agogo, especially in view of the fact that women continue to bear children all through the child-bearing years.[1]

REPRODUCTION RATES

The discussion has hitherto been based on the total sample of 1,017 women. In what follows we shall confine ourselves to the data for the Ashanti women only. In fact, owing to the very small number of non-Ashanti women in the sample, this makes no difference to the estimates finally arrived at; but with data so subject to errors of fact it is a safeguard to have the maximum of ethnic and cultural homogeneity. For example, some of the non-Ashanti women belonged to tribes which, unlike the Ashanti, prohibit cohabitation between husband and wife throughout the lactation period, and this may last for three years. There are differences also in child-rearing customs which may have an effect on infant mortality.

In constructing the tables that follow the main difficulty has arisen over the dead children. It was impossible for the interviewers to ascertain the year of birth or of death of a dead child unless it was very recent; even then there were the difficulties due to Ashanti reluctance to talk about the dead. What the interviewers did was to find out the approximate age of the child at the time of its death. From this and other data the quinquennium in which the dead child was born can be determined. For living children, age to the nearest year was recorded, thus it was easy to derive the year of birth. All the offspring of each woman were recorded in order of birth. It was thus possible to make a very good guess at the year of birth of a dead child by interpolation between dates of birth of living children, an interval of three years being allowed between successive births. As has been mentioned, this corresponds to the views of Ashanti women themselves, and was also found by experience of handling the record sheets to fit the data where information was complete.[2]

To simplify the setting out of the tables the data are grouped in quinquennia, to which dates are attached as if retrospectively from 31 December 1945. Thus the actual twelve months from October 1944 to October 1945 are treated as if they made up a calendar year and the data referring to this period are classified as falling within the year 1945. Preceding and

---

[1] Culwick and Culwick, loc. cit., found no evidence of a difference in fertility between polygamous and monogamous marriage. As in Ashanti and indeed in most African societies for which the data are available, polygyny in the area they studied meant, in effect, an average of two wives per polygynist and the great majority (74 per cent) of the married women monogamously married at the time of their inquiry.

[2] A statistical check of this assumption would have involved such elaborate tabulations as hardly to be worth while for the kind of data we had.

TABLE 48. Female Live Births by Date of Birth and by Present Age of Mother, Ashanti Only.

Assumed date of birth	Present ages of children	Present age of mother															All ages
		15–19	20–24	25–29	30–34	35–39	40–44	45–49	50–54	55–59	60–64	65–69	70–74	75–79	80+	
1944–45	0–1	18	20	24	12	17	1	1	—	—	—	—	—	—	—	93
1941–44	1–4	12	70	65	29	18	13	4	—	—	—	—	—	—	—	211
1936–41	5–9		38	97	60	43	27	26	3	—	—	—	—	—	—	294
1931–36	10–14			31	53	63	25	23	14	4	—	—	—	—	—	213
1926–31	15–19				18	67	33	43	33	17	6	1	—	—	—	218
1921–26	20–24					22	36	51	35	25	22	2	4	—	—	197
1916–21	25–29						12	48	56	32	19	12	4	2	—	185
1911–16	30–34							15	42	41	29	15	17	1	3	163
1906–11	35–39								8	30	31	14	16	3	7	109
1901–06	40–44									6	22	12	12	7	10	69
1896–1901	45–49										7	13	20	4	11	55
1891–96	50–54											1	18	3	3	25
1886–91	55–59												1	2	8	11
1881–86	60–64														10	10
–81	65+															—
Not stated	Not stated	—	—	—	—	—	1	1	—	1	—	—	—	—	—	3
Total female live birth		30	128	217	172	230	148	212	191	156	136	70	92	22	52	1 856
Women in sample		113	164	174	90	93	52	68	57	42	43	25	27	11	16	
Mean female live birth per woman		0.26	0.78	1.24	1.91	2.47	2.84	3.12	3.35	3.73	3.16	2.8	3.39	2.0	3.25	

TABLE 49. Dead Female Children by Age at Death and by Date of Birth, Ashanti Only.

Age at death	Assumed date of birth																Not stated	Total
	1944–45	1941–44	1936–41	1931–36	1926–31	1921–26	1916–21	1911–16	1906–11	1901–06	1896–01	1891–96	1886–91	1881–86	1876–81			
0–1	8	25	25	12	34	30	30	34	17	13	3	1	1	—	—	0	233
1–4		6	15	22	18	13	13	18	6	6	9	4	1	1		0	132
5–9			4	4		2	3	6	3	1	1					0	24
10–14			—		5	3	5	6	6	1	1	1	1			0	29
15–19				—	4	3	5	5	3	4	3	4	3			0	34
20–24						2	2	2	3	5	1	1	1			0	17
25–29						—	3	4	2	2		1	1			0	13
30–34								1	5	—	1					1	8
35–39									1	4						1	6
40–44										2	2					0	4
45–49																1	1
50–54																0	0
55–59																0	0
60+														1		0	1
Not stated																	
Total	8	31	44	38	61	53	61	76	46	38	21	12	8	2	0	3	502

TABLE 50. Surviving Female Children by Date of Birth and by Present Age of Mother.

Assumed date of birth	Age	Present age of mother														Total
		15-19	20-24	25-29	30-34	35-39	40-44	45-49	50-54	55-59	60-64	65-69	70-74	75-79	80+	
1945	0-1	12	14	20	8	11	1	1	—	—	—	—	—	—	—	67
1944-45	1	5	4	3	3	3	—	—	—	—	—	—	—	—	—	18
1941-44	1-4	11	54	56	27	16	13	3	—	—	—	—	—	—	—	180
1936-41	5-9		32	84	52	34	23	22	3	—	—	—	—	—	—	250
1931-36	10-14			25	47	48	19	19	14	3	—	—	—	—	—	175
1926-31	15-19				12	52	23	30	23	12	—	—	—	—	—	157
1921-26	20-24					16	33	32	25	17	4	—	—	—	—	144
1916-21	25-29						9	33	36	20	15	1	—	—	—	124
1911-16	30-34							9	22	20	14	2	4	—	—	87
1906-11	35-39								2	18	15	10	10	1	6	63
1901-06	40-44									3	9	10	11	2	3	31
1896-1901	45-49										4	9	6	2	7	34
1891-96	50-54											10	10	3	1	13
1886-91	55-59											1	8	3	2	13
1881-86	60-64													1	8	3
-81	65+														8	8
Total female survivors		28	104	188	149	180	121	149	125	93	75	51	49	14	28	1 354
Women in sample		113	164	174	90	93	52	68	57	42	43	25	27	11	16	975
Female survivors: mean no. per woman		0.25	0.63	1.08	1.65	1.93	2.32	2.19	2.19	2.21	1.8	2.04	1.81	1.27	1.75	
Total survivors: M+F		47	209	345	270	344	220	232	280	165	133	106	80	27	52	2 510
Mean no. total survivors per woman		0.416	1.27	1.98	3.0	3.7	4.23	4.11	4.07	3.93	3.09	4.24	2.96	2.45	3.25	2.57

TABLE 51. Male Live Births by Date of Birth and by Present Age of Mother, Ashanti Only.

Assumed date of birth	Age	Present age of mother														Total
		15-19	20-24	25-29	30-34	35-39	40-44	45-49	50-54	55-59	60-64	65-69	70-74	75-79	80+	
1944-45	0-1	8	34	25	10	8	1	3	—							89
1941-44	1-4	16	69	65	32	33	8	7	—							230
1936-41	5-9		28	75	39	44	16	15	4							221
1931-36	10-14			28	52	58	30	37	11	5						221
1926-31	15-19				16	51	30	33	10	9	4	1				154
1921-26	20-24					18	38	44	33	19	11	3	1			167
1916-21	25-29						12	38	38	29	23	11	5	3	1	160
1911-16	30-34							16	41	38	21	16	8	4	3	147
1906-11	35-39								11	23	28	21	6	4	3	96
1901-06	40-44									9	29	24	16	12	10	100
1896-1901	45-49										3	13	21	6	10	53
1891-96	50-54											6	11	—	10	27
1886-91	55-59												2	4	9	15
1881-86	60-64														7	7
-81	65+															
Not stated		2	1	1	1	—	1	—	5	1	—	—	—	—	1	13
Total male live births		26	132	194	150	212	136	193	153	133	119	95	70	33	54	1 700
Total women in sample		113	164	174	90	93	52	68	57	42	43	25	27	11	16	
Mean male live births per woman		0.23	0.804	1.12	1.67	2.28	2.62	2.84	2.68	3.16	2.77	3.80	2.61	3.0	3.37	

TABLE 52. Dead Male Children by Age at Death and by Date of Birth. Ashanti Only.

Age at death	Assumed date of birth															Not stated	Total
	1944–45	1941–44	1936–41	1931–36	1926–31	1921–26	1916–21	1911–16	1906–11	1901–6	1896–1901	1891–96	1886–91	1881–86	1876–81		
0–1	10	35	24	36	27	22	21	28	18	14	5	2	3	2	—	2	249
1–4	—	10	15	14	12	14	11	12	12	16	5	4	—	1	—	2	128
5–9			3	3	2	4	5	2	4	6	4	—	1	—	—	1	35
10–14				2	3	2	4	4	5	4	4	—	—	—	—	1	29
15–19					4	5	4	2	3	2	3	2	1	—	—	1	27
20–24						4	4	4	3	4	1	1	—	2	—	2	25
25–29						1	2	7	3	1	3	1	3	—	—	1	22
30–34								5	2	1	2	3	—	—	—	0	13
35–39										2	2	1	—	—	—	1	6
40–44										1	—	—	—	—	—	0	1
45–49											2	3	—	—	—	1	6
50–54												1	—	—	—	0	1
55–59													1	—	—	0	1
60+															—	0	0
Not stated												1				0	1
Total	10	45	42	55	48	52	51	64	50	51	31	19	9	5	—	12	544

313

TABLE 53. Surviving Male Children by Date of Birth and by Present Age of Mother. Ashanti Only.

Assumed date of birth	Age	Age of mother														Total
		15–19	20–24	25–29	30–34	35–39	40–44	45–49	50–54	55–59	60–64	65–69	70–74	75–79	80+	
1945	0–1	8	25	16	9	6	1	1	—	—	—	—	—	—	—	66
1944–45	1	—	5	5	—	2	—	1	—	—	—	—	—	—	—	13
1941–44	1–4	11	53	53	28	30	6	4	—	—	—	—	—	—	—	185
1936–41	5–9		22	60	36	32	13	12	4	—	—	—	—	—	—	179
1931–36	10–14			23	40	45	23	20	11	4	—	—	—	—	—	166
1926–31	15–19				8	36	23	22	8	5	3	1	—	—	—	106
1921–26	20–24					13	28	33	23	10	5	2	1	—	—	115
1916–21	25–29						5	30	29	16	15	9	4	—	1	109
1911–16	30–34							8	25	20	9	13	5	2	1	83
1906–11	35–39								7	10	11	10	4	3	1	46
1901–6	40–44									6	15	11	8	4	5	49
1896–1901	45–49											7	8	2	5	22
1891–96	50–54											2	1	—	5	8
1886–91	55–59													2	4	6
1881–86	60–64														2	2
–81	65+															
Not stated										1						1
Total males		19	105	157	121	164	99	131	107	72	58	55	31	13	24	1 156
Women in sample		113	164	174	90	93	52	68	57	42	43	25	27	11	16	975

subsequent periods of twelve months are treated in the same way and the corresponding adjustment is made for quinquennial periods.

Children falling into the age group under five are divided into two groups, those aged twelve months and less, and those who had passed their first birthday but had not yet reached their fifth. In a small number of cases the age of the child was given as exactly twelve months, though other evidence indicated that some of them probably fell into the 0–1 year group and others into the 1–4 year group. However, the data have been tabulated as recorded.

THE SEX RATIO

Table 54 is derived from the totals shown in Tables 48–53. The age groups 0–1 year and 1–4 years have been kept separate in this table. If they are added together, the sex ratios prove to be 104.9 males per 100 females for live births and 99.6 males per 100 females for survivors, for the total age group 0–4. It would appear that the general tendency over the 50 years preceding our investigation was for female births markedly to exceed male births, and the excess of females seems to have been even greater among those who survived till 1945. Our data may be faulty in this matter, and suspicion is certainly aroused by the fact that the sex ratio among surviving

TABLE 54. Number of Males to 100 Females, Among Offspring Aged 0–49.

	Age group										
	0–1	1–4	5–9	10–14	15–19	20–24	25–29	30–34	35–39	40–44	45–49
Live births[1]	95.7	109	75.2	103.7	70.6	84.7	86.5	90.2	88.1	144.9	96.5
Survivors[2]	92.9	102.7	71.6	94.8	67.5	79.8	87.9	95.4	73	158	64.7

[1] 'Live births' refers to children born alive who have either survived to the age group in which they are recorded or would have been so recorded if they had survived to the date of the census.

[2] 'Survivors' refers to children alive at the time of the census.

children aged 0–4 years is approximately unity. But it is significant that the data are broadly consistent for all age groups, and there must be some reason for this, No satisfactory explanation can be suggested. If the Ashanti were like the Chinese and put to death or neglected infants of the sex opposite to that of their legally stressed descent line a plausible reason for the excess of female survivors could be offered.[1] But nothing of this sort occurs; and a mystical connexion between matrilineal descent and the preponderance of female births is hardly conceivable. An examination of the published tables of the 1948 census of the Gold Coast shows that discrepancies in the sex ratio of survivors in favour of one sex are common among all age groups in Ashanti. For Agogo the sex ratio for the enumerated[2] population is unity for the children under 1 year, 91 males to 100 females for the age group 1–16, and 97.4 males to 100 females for the age groups 16–45.[3] The excess of females is not so marked as in our data; but it is enough to confirm that such an excess was found among the living inhabitants of the township. It suggests, though it is not conclusive evidence of, a high gross reproduction rate.

FERTILITY RATIOS AND GROSS REPRODUCTION RATE

Tables 48 and 51 show that there were altogether 529 children of both sexes under the age of five among the surviving offspring of the Ashanti women of our sample. According to Table 23 the sample included 754 Ashanti women aged 15–49. These figures give a ratio of 701 children under 5 years per 1,000 women of childbearing age. If the age distribution of Series B in Table 24 is used, the number of women is 786 and the corresponding ratio is 673 children per 1,000 women. Mitchell[4] has calculated the correlation coefficient between child-woman ratios and gross reproduction rates for a number of countries. Using his equation for the regression line, we find that the child-woman ratios for Agogo correspond

---

[1] Dr. Ta Chen, 'Population in Modern China', *American Journal of Sociology*, Vol. 52, 1, Part 2, 1946, shows that the mortality of female children is higher than that of male children in Chinese rural areas. He attributes this to unconscious neglect of girl babies owing to the very high value attached to male offspring for the perpetuation of the family line. Similar findings are reported by G. W. Skinner, 'A Study in Miniature of Chinese Population', *Population Studies*, Vol. 5, 2, 1951. But no such differences in the care given to children of one sex, be it males in patrilineal societies or females in matrilineal societies, has been reported from any African people. Ashanti are as proud of sons as of daughters and give the same care to both.

[2] This is not, of course, unique. Differential mortality and such social factors as emigration of males and the effect of wars have led to an abnormally high proportion of women in the adult population of Great Britain during the past 100 years (cf. Royal Commission on Population, *Report*, 1949, p. 97). In India, on the other hand, there has long been a marked deficiency of females after the age of five. S. Chandrasekhar ('The Population Problems of India and Pakistan', *Science News*, 13, 1949, pp. 103ff.) explains this on the same lines as Dr. Ta Chen, that is, as due to the comparative neglect of girl children and also to the greater and earlier death rate among women as a result of early marriage and the strain of early and frequent child bearing. Among the Tallensi of the Gold Coast (Fortes, loc. cit., *Sociolog. Rev.*) I found a tendency for females to exceed males both among live births and among survivors.

[3] *Gold Coast Census Report*, 1950, Table 10, p. 70.

[4] Clyde Mitchell, loc. cit., *Africa*, p. 303.

to a gross reproduction rate lying between 2.86 and 2.34 for the ratio 701, and a rate between 2.75 and 2.23 for the ratio 673.

Another rough approximation can be obtained by a method that has been previously used with similar data.[1] We take the mean number of female live births born to women who have passed the menopause as a rough measure of the average gross reproduction rate in the community over the past 30 years. (The mean age difference between Agogo women who have passed the menopause and their living daughters is 30 years.) The menopause is reached among Agogo women between the ages of 45 and 50; the 221 women of our sample aged 50 and over had 719 live-born daughters. The average of 3.22 female live births probably represents the upper limit of the average gross reproduction rate of this community during the 30 years preceding our enquiry; for a proportion of the 221 women are probably selected by reason of their longevity and their completed families would tend toward the maximum. At any rate, a gross reproduction rate lying between 2.23 and 3.22 would put this community among the most fertile in the world, comparable for example with Poland in 1911.[2] A gross reproduction rate of about 3.0 would be consistent with the mean number of 6.22 live births of both sexes produced by these 221 women. Gross reproduction rates lying between 2 and 3 have been reported from other parts of Africa and from Oriental peasant communities.[3]

THE NET REPRODUCTION RATE

The total number of female children surviving to old women aged 50 years or over is 435. This yields an average of 1.97 children per woman, which may be taken to indicate the upper limit of the net reproduction rate, since some of the daughters will die before reaching maturity. From Table 50 it appears that 20 of the daughters were under 15 at the time of the census. If we deduct 10 (i.e., 25 per cent) of the daughters aged 15–19, to allow for those who might not have been of childbearing age at the time of the census, we are left with a total of 405 daughters of childbearing

[1] cf. Fortes, loc. cit., *Sociolog. Rev.*, In view of the great importance attached by the Royal Commission on Population to the size of the completed family (see *Report*, pp. 60 ff.) as an index of fertility, this method seems to have greater value than was previously supposed.

[2] cf. R. R. Kuczynski, 'The International Decline of Fertility', in L. Hogben, *Political Arithmetic*, 1938, at pp. 56–7.

[3] For Africa, cf. Mitchell, loc. cit., *Africa*; Fortes, loc. cit., *Sociolog. Rev.*; Charles and Forde, loc. cit.; for India, cf. D. Ghosh and Rama Varna, 'A Study in Indian Fertility', *Eugenics Rev.*, 31, 1940, who report a G.R.R. of 2.56 for Cochin. A survey of the literature shows that between six and seven live births is the commonest average number produced by women who complete the reproductive span in communities of this type. It should be added that birth and survival rates implying much lower gross reproduction rates have also been reported from Africa, notably from the Belgian Congo. The figures and the alleged causes are discussed in a number of recent papers in the *Bulletin du Centre d'Etudes des Problèmes Sociaux Indigènes*, Elisabethville.

age and over. The average number is 1.83 and this figure is probably nearer to the true replacement rate achieved by the women of Agogo in the 30 years before our investigation.

A more systematic attempt to arrive at a net reproduction rate for Agogo women has been made from the data given in Tables 48, 49, and 50 by Miss Sheila Mallett. The details of the calculations by which she has arrived at alternative estimates are given in Appendix A. The assumptions set out in her discussion of the reliability of the data are to a certain extent justified, as the analysis of the social background and composition of our sample shows. But as in all studies of the kind attempted in this paper, the major problem is the establishment of reliable death rates. Miss Mallett's calculations (Table 58) suggest that there was a fall in death rates in all age groups under 35 during the 30 years preceding our investigation. Administrative officers, medical officers and Ashanti themselves say that this has in fact been the case; but as there are no statistics of death rates for rural areas like Agogo it is impossible to test this opinion by reference to sources independent of the present enquiry. All we can say is that the death rates shown in Table 58, especially those for the first year of life, seem rather low for a community of the type to which Agogo belongs.[1] This is brought out in the death rates from a small selection of countries of comparable social development and roughly similar climatic conditions to those of Ashanti set out in Table 59. Again, the fertility rates (Tables 62 and 63) derived from the data of Tables 48, 49, and 50 are liable to error due to possible defects in the age estimates and age grouping of the women of the sample, and Miss Mallett's corrected fertility rates are calculated to bring the observed rates into line with what might be expected on the basis of the average rate for the women past childbearing. Using the four different estimates of the age-specific death rates previously arrived at in combination with, first, an 'optimistic' fertility rate, and, second, a 'pessimistic' fertility rate, Miss Mallett has calculated the series of net reproduction rates shown in Table 64 and at the foot of Table 65. On the basis of the observed fertility rates and the observed mortality rates over 15 years, the net reproduction rate works out at 2.214. If the higher mortality rate of the preceding 30 years is used, the net reproduction rate is 2.055. When the most optimistic fertility rate is combined with the most optimistic estimate of mortality rates the figure is 2.444; but this falls to 1.865 if the most pessimistic fertility and mortality rates are used.

---

[1] cf. what was said above about health conditions in rural Ashanti. It is notorious among medical officers in the Gold Coast that infants are specially vulnerable just after weaning when they are put on a diet made up mainly of starchy foods. They also become subject to intestinal parasites and other diseases that lead to malnutrition. cf. in this connexion, M. J. Colbourne, *et al.*, 'A Medical Survey in a Gold Coast Village', *Trans. Royal Soc. of Tropical Medicine and Hygiene*, 44, 3, 1950, 271–90. But the conditions described in this paper seem far worse than what was observed in the relatively prosperous area of Agogo.

From our foregoing discussion, and from general knowledge of death rates in such communities, it seems probable that a net reproduction rate of about 2.4 is too high an estimate. The very rough calculation made on the basis of the average number of daughters surviving to women past childbearing suggests a lower limit to the net reproduction rate of about 1.8, which is approximately the same as the lowest rate estimated by Miss Mallett. A death rate in the first year of life of less than 100 seems most unlikely in a community of this type. Taking everything into consideration, we may reasonably conclude that the best estimate of the net reproduction rate is the figure of 2.069, a figure which lies roughly midway between the estimates of 1.865 and 2.213 given by Miss Mallett at the end of Table 65. According to the 1948 census of the Gold Coast,[1] the average annual increase of the population between 1931 and 1948 in the Kumasi Administrative District, which includes Agogo, was 3.72 per cent. If allowance is made for the considerable influx of immigrants into this area, an estimated net reproduction rate of 2 would seem to be a reasonable one for the area.

CONCLUSIONS

One of the aims of this investigation was to test the possibility of using untrained volunteer interviewers for demographic enquiries in illiterate communities. The results show that volunteers who are well enough educated to understand the purpose of the investigation can, with suitable briefing and supervision, produce valuable and relatively accurate data. In the present investigation it is obvious that defects in the data are due mainly to socially and culturally motivated misunderstanding, concealment, or reticence on the part of the informants. These difficulties can only be got over by patient enquiry, through the medium of the native language, by field workers fully acquainted with the social and cultural conditions of the community.

Another aim was to see what influence the specific social and cultural conditions of contemporary rural life in Ashanti have on the trend of fertility. A net reproduction rate of the order of 2, though very high by prevailing European standards, is not extreme for settled tribal communities in Africa—rates of the same order are found in Oriental peasant societies. Such a rate means a doubling of the population in a generation. What are the social and cultural conditions which make this possible? In Agogo the most important are the extremely high valuation placed on offspring by the people, and the sexual and marital institutions which make it not only possible but desirable and praiseworthy for a woman to bear children all through her procreative years. Modern changes which do not radically alter these institutions and ideals will not lead to any serious

[1] *Gold Coast Census Report*, p. 31.

reduction in reproductive rates. As children are highly valued, not merely by their parents, but also by the elders of their lineage whose influence in local government affairs depends to some extent on their numbers, no big change in reproductive habits is likely to occur as long as the corporate organization of the lineage remains as important in Ashanti social life as it is today. An intensive study of demographic trends among urban Ashanti would be a valuable check on this hypothesis. Such an enquiry would show to what extent the lineage is breaking down in urban conditions and whether or not the emergence of a strong conjugal family is associated with a decline in the fertility of the women. Another factor that requires further study is the effect of education. The results will probably not be what might be expected by analogy with what happens in Europe or America. If, for example, education merely leads to a postponement of marriage for a few years, but not to changes in the ideals of parenthood, the effect on birth rates may be negligible. It is now generally recognized among demographers that the reproductive habits of a people depend as much upon the prevailing 'attitudes towards marriage and the family' and the ideals of parenthood[1] as upon legal and economic conditions. The smallscale study here attempted bears this out. It is, indeed, just because they show up much more clearly than broad studies based on nation-wide sampling the influence of cultural and social factors on demographic movements, that small scale studies of this kind are of special value.

If, as we have argued, Agogo is a representative rural community of the cocoa growing areas of Southern Ashanti, the high net reproduction rate indicated by this investigation has practical consequences of great importance. There is an obvious danger of a Malthusian situation developing in the Gold Coast where suitable land is increasingly occupied by a profitable cash crop like cocoa. This danger is, fortunately, recognized by the Government of the Gold Coast and energetic efforts are being made to stimulate a higher level of food production throughout the country.

[1] I quote from the admirable statement of the problem by Dr. Mark Abrams, *The Population of Great Britain*, 1945, p. 40.

320

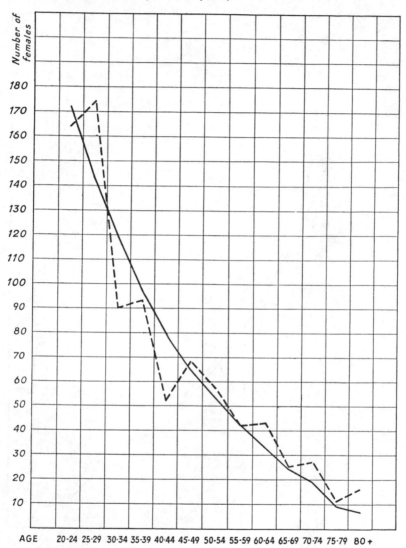

FIG. 3. Age Distributions (Net reproduction rate 2.443 [females]. Age difference mother/child, 30 years).

——— Estimated from optimistic death rate and optimistic fertility rate (467)
– – – – Actual distribution

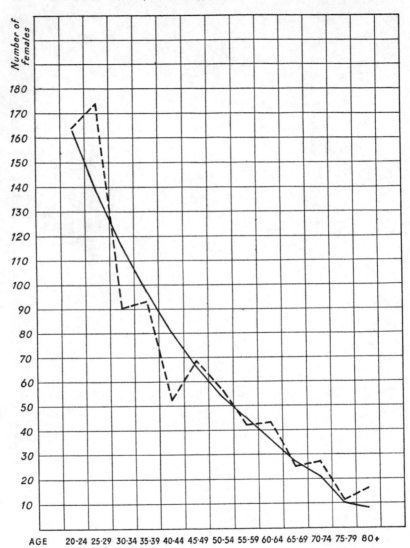

Fig. 4. Age Distributions (Net reproduction rate 2.213 [females]. Age difference mother/child, 30 years).

———— Estimated from optimistic death rate and pessimistic fertility rate (468)
– – – – Actual distribution

322

AGE 20-24 25-29 30-34 35-39 40-44 45-49 50-54 55-59 60-64 65-69 70-74 75-79 80+

——— Estimated from pessimistic death rate and optimistic fertility rate (469)
–––– Actual distribution

323

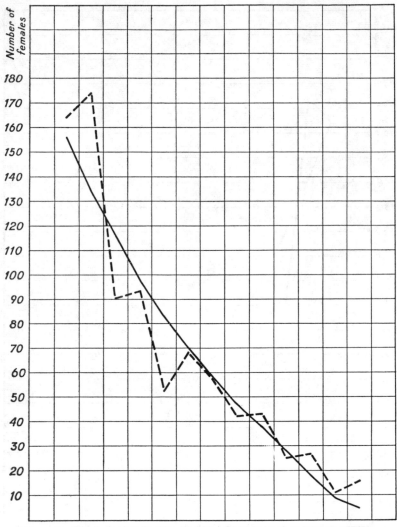

Fig. 6. Age Distributions (Net reproduction rate 1.865 [females]. Age difference mother/child 30 years).

——————— Estimated from pessimistic death rate and pessimistic fertility rate (bB × b) (470)
— — — Actual distribution

Estimation of the Net Reproduction Rate for Agogo, Ashanti

by

S HEILA M ALLETT, M.A., B. COMM.[1]

The data from which the estimations of the net reproduction rate were made are given in Tables 48, 49, 50 in the text, showing all live female births, dead female children and surviving female children, each table being subdivided into age-groups of mothers and children.

The nature of the data makes it impossible to calculate the net reproduction rate accurately and the results obtained in various stages of the calculation have been adjusted where comparison with other demographical statistics indicates that the data are producing unreliable figures.

The stages 'on which the estimations are based are the calculation of (a) the death rates for females by age-groups, (b) the fertility rates for females by age-groups, (c) the net reproduction rate.

All figures throughout relate to females only.

Calculation of the Death Rate

As the sample is not large enough to give reliable figures on the basis of each age-group, three five-year age-groups were added together. The method of estimation is shown in detail in Table 55, deaths at 0–1 years being subtracted from all live births, leaving the number of children surviving to age 1. The number of survivors divided by total births gives the survival factor, where one minus the survival factor is equal to the death rate for the age-group. The number of deaths at ages 1–4 is then subtracted from the number of survivors to age 1, leaving the number of children surviving to age 5. Then the number of survivors to age 4, divided by the survivors to age 1, gives the survival factor to age 4. One minus this survival factor divided by four gives the annual death rate for this age-group, and similarly all subsequent figures are divided by five to give the annual death rates.[2]

In each case the most recent group of figures is used for obtaining the death rate for the age-group, and the results are shown in Tables 56 and 57, whence it can be seen that the calculations can only be extended to the age-group 35–39, since the two later groups show a decreasing death rate

[1] Assistant in Statistical Research, Cambridge University.
[2] This procedure does not give either population death rates (m_x) or life table death rates (q_x) by single years [the editor].

for an increase in age which is obviously inconsistent with the facts. Table 58 gives a summary of the death rates obtained by taking different groups according to the above method. The calculation of the net reproduction rate necessitates the inclusion of death rates up to the ages 50–54, and guessed figures have been inserted in the table.

The guessed figures are based on comparisons with death rates for various other countries shown in Table 59, and these death rates, compared with the calculated death rates in the previous table, are used as a basis for compiling two hypothetical death rates, one optimistic and one pessimistic, shown in Table 60.

Table 61 shows the number of survivors to each age out of 1,000 births (i.e. survival factor to age 1 applied to 1,000 births, survival factor to age 5 applied to survivors to age 1, etc.), and the average number of females alive per year in each age-group (e.g. half the sum of those surviving at age 20 and those surviving at age 25, gives the average number alive per year in the age-group 20–24). Similar tables for the optimistic and pessimistic death rates (57 and 58) are shown in more detail in the Life Tables, 66 and 67.

Calculation of the Fertility Rates

Two estimations of the fertility rate were made, both based on the data for Agogo as set out in Table 48, 49, and 50 in the text.

The first was obtained by taking total female live births in an age-group and dividing by the number of women in the sample shown in Table 48. The differences between successive numbers gives the average number of live female births in each age-group, though only on the assumption that each woman has passed completely through the age-group (Table 62).

Consequently a second estimate was made. The first assumption in this was that the figures shown in Table 48 for the 15–19 age-group should be adjusted for those who are not married, and to take account of this, the fertility rate was reduced by two-thirds.[1] Assuming that the women are evenly spread throughout each age-group, then the fertility rate of the group when each woman has passed completely through it is equal to the average of the sums of pairs of fertility rates for successive age-groups, and the results are shown in column (2), Table 63. The peak in this distribution is seen to lie within the age-group 30–34, and since no country for which data are available has the peak later than the 25–29 age-group (see the *Demographic Year Book*, United Nations), the three groups 20–24, 25–29, 30–34 have been adjusted to the figures shown in column (3). The average number of female children shown here is 3.045, and in column (4) the figures have been raised to yield an average of 3.40 female live births per woman passing through the reproductive ages, this being the average number of female live births to women aged 50–64.[2]

[1] This is in keeping with the age distribution of the women of the sample established in Table 24, Series A.
[2] The actual total comes to 3.41, due to rounding off.

326

Calculation of the Net Reproduction Rate

The net reproduction rate is obtained by multiplying the average number of women alive per year in each age-group by the appropriate fertility rate for the age-group. The results are shown in Table 64, and give a possible range, on the assumptions set out above, of 1.865 to 2.444.

Reliability of the Data

As stated previously, the data on which the calculations are based are insufficient to give definite results, and the choice of a 'best estimate' depends to a great extent on a personal knowledge of conditions in Ashanti. The estimate of 3.40 female live births per woman is based on a sample of 142 women, and the variation shown between the 5-year age-groups above age 50 is quite considerable, so that the choice of a different average would give very different results.

A rough check of the estimates has been made, but on assumptions which are possibly invalid, though not altogether unjustified in the light of the information given in the text of this paper.

Assuming that there has been no change in (a) death rates, (b) age at marriage, (c) birth rates, (d) size of families, (e) differences of age between mother and daughter, and (f) no migration, calculations can be made to see whether the rates estimated give an age distribution similar to that prevailing in the sample. This also assumes that the sample is representative.

The average age difference between mother and child is approximately 30 years (based on mothers aged 50 and over). Using this figure and the net reproduction rate, an annual rate of increase of the female population can be obtained by using the formula $(1 + \text{annual rate of increase})^{30}$ is equal to the net reproduction rate.

Adjusting the figures of the average number of females alive in each age-group by the factor $(1 + \text{annual rate of increase})$ raised to the appropriate power for each age-group gives the expected age distribution for each set of figures based on the assumptions listed above. Converting this to a percentage of the groups aged 20 and above, and applying the percentages to the actual number of women in the sample, gives the results shown in Table 65, which are also shown in chart form.

These calculations have not been made for the Agogo death rates, since the rates for the older age-groups would have to be guessed and the optimistic and pessimistic death rates include the highest and the lowest net reproduction rates shown in Table 64.

Tables 66 and 67 show the expectation of life at different ages for the optimistic and pessimistic death rates respectively.

The number of years lived is obtained by taking the average number of females alive per year and multiplying it by the number of years within the age-group. The time left to live is obtained by summing the number of years lived, starting from the oldest age-group and adding the earlier ones successively. The expectation of life is equivalent to the number of years left to be lived by all females, divided by the number surviving to each age.

327

TABLE 55. Calculation of Death Rates.

	Born between the years		
	1931–45	1926–41	1921–36
(a) Births (Table 48)	811	725	628
(b) Deaths at 0–1 years (Table 49)	70	71	76
(c) Survivors to age 1 (a–b)	741	654	552
(d) Survival rate, age 0–1 (c÷a)	0.914	0.902	0.879
(e) Deaths at 1–4 years (Table 49)	—	55	53
(f) Survivors to age 4 (d–e)	—	599	499
(g) Survival rate, age 1–4 (f÷c)	—	0.916	0.904

Note. Figures in this table have been corrected to three decimal places but were taken to five decimal places for the detailed calculations.

TABLE 56. Female Survivors by Date of Birth.

Survivors up to age	Born between the years										
	1931–45	1926–41	1921–36	1916–31	1911–26	1906–21	1901–16	1896–1911	1891–1906	1886–1901	1881–96
0 (Live births)	811	725	628	600	545	457	341	233	149	91	46
1	741	654	552	506	451	376	277	200	132	86	44
4		599	499	462	407	339	247	179	113	72	38
9			493	457	396	327	237	174	111	71	38
14				444	382	310	224	166	108	68	36
19					369	297	212	156	97	58	29
24						290	202	147	90	55	27
29							194	143	87	53	25
34								137	86	52	25
39									82	52	25
44										50	25
49											25

1916–31	1911–26	1906–21	1901–16	1896–11	1891–1906	1886–1901	1881–96
600	545	457	341	233	149	91	46
94	94	81	64	33	17	5	2
506	451	376	277	200	132	86	44
0.843	0.828	0.823	0.812	0.858	0.886	0.945	0.957
44	44	37	30	21	19	14	6
462	407	339	247	179	113	72	38
0.913	0.902	0.902	0.892	0.895	0.856	0.837	0.864

TABLE 57. Survival Rates per 1,000 Females, Agogo Data.

Survival rate per thousand to age	Born between the years										
	1931–45	1926–41	1921–36	1916–31	1916–26	1906–21	1901–16	1896–1911	1891–1906	1886–1901	1881–96
1	914	902	879	843	828	823	812	858	886	945	957
4		916	904	913	902	902	892	895	856	837	864
9			988	989	973	965	960	972	982	986	1 000
14				972	965	948	945	954	973	958	947
19					966	958	946	940	898	853	806
24						976	953	942	928	948	931
29							960	973	967	964	926
34								958	989	981	1 000
39									953	1 000	1 000
44										962	1 000
49											1 000

TABLE 58. Death Rates for Agogo (death rates per 1,000 per year).

Age-group	Based on 15-year periods (0–1 based on 1931–45)	Based on 15-year periods (0–1 based on 1926–41)	Based on 30-year periods (0–1 based on 1916–45)
0–1	86	98	117
1–4	21	24	22
5–9	2.4	2.2	4.3
10–14	5.7	7.1	7.5
15–19	6.8	8.4	8.4
20–24	4.7	9.4	7.1
25–29	7.9	5.4	7.8
30–34	8.4	2.3	7.1
35–39	9.3		10 g
40–44	10 g		12 g
45–49	11 g		14 g
50–54	12 g		16 g

g = guessed figure.

TABLE 59. Age Specific Death Rates—Females (death rates per 1,000).[1]

Age-group	Ceuta and Melilla (N. Africa) 1940	Nicaragua 1940	Malaya 1947	Chile 1940	Singapore 1947	Venezuela 1945	Palestine (Muslims) 1944
0–1	150.1	83.5	159.3	230.4	127.1	90.2	108.5
1–4	24.5	22.1	24.8	32.1	16.1	21.7	38.3
5–9	4.7	4.6	8.3	2.7	2.8	5.0	3.6
10–14	3.7	1.9	4.1	3.5	1.8⎱	3.4	2.3
15–19	6.5	3.5	5.1	7.0	3.2⎰		2.5
20–24	4.9	6.3	8.2	9.4	4.2⎱	6.8	4.7
25–29	4.2	8.1	10.6	9.7	6.5⎰		7.6
30–34	4.2	8.6	11.7	9.6	6.6⎱	10.7	5.8
35–39	6.3	8.7	12.8	10.5	7.9⎰		6.5
40–44	8.3	10.2	14.1	11.2	9.6⎱	12.4	4.8
45–49	10.4	12.5	15.4	12.9	10.9⎰		6.2
50–54	10.2	12.3⎱	23.3	16.3	12.1⎱	20.0	5.8
55–59	11.9	15.2⎰		23.3⎱			9.3
60–64	17.7	21.4⎱		30.8			13.5
65–69	28.5	41.1⎰		49.3			24.3
70–75	⎱	49.7⎱	61.0	64.6⎱	30.3⎱	60.8	37.8
75–79	59.3	79.6⎰		100.1			119.7
80–84	⎰	98.8⎱		126.7			
85+		123.0⎰		244.8⎰			

[1] Source: *Demographic Year Book*, United Nations.

TABLE 60.   Estimated Death Rates for Females.

Age-group	Agogo (0–1 based on 1931–1945) A		Agogo (0–1 based on 1916–1945) B		Optimistic C		Pessimistic D	
	Death rate	Survival factor	Death rate	Survival factor	Death rate	Survival factor	Death rate	Survival factor
0–1	86	0.914	117	0.883	100	0.900	150	0.850
1–4	21	0.916	22	0.910	20	0.920	30	0.880
5–9	2.4	0.988	4.3	0.979	4	0.980	7	0.965
10–14	5.7	0.972	7.5	0.963	3	0.985	5	0.975
15–19	6.8	0.966	8.4	0.958	5	0.975	7	0.965
20–24	4.7	0.976	7.1	0.964	6	0.970	8	0.960
25–29	7.9	0.960	7.8	0.961	7	0.965	10	0.950
30–34	8.4	0.958	7.1	0.964	9	0.955	12	0.940
35–39	9.3	0.953	10 g	0.950	10	0.950	13	0.935
40–44	10 g	0.950	12 g	0.940	11	0.945	14	0.930
45–49	11 g	0.945	14 g	0.930	12	0.940	15	0.925
50–54	12 g	0.940	16 g	0.920	13	0.935	17	0.915
55–59					14	0.930	20	0.900
60–64					20	0.900	25	0.875
65–69					40	0.800	50	0.750
70–74					60	0.700	70	0.650
75–79					80	0.600	100	0.500
80–84					100	0.500	130	0.350
85+					140	0.860	250	0.750

Note. The survival factors are for the appropriate number of years within the interval, except for the age-group 85+ which is the yearly rate.   g = guessed figure.

TABLE 61.   Average Number of Females Alive per Year.

Survivors reaching age	Agogo A		Agogo B		Average number alive per year in age-group
	Survivors	Average number alive	Survivors	Average number alive	
0	1 000		1 000		0–1
1	914		883		1–4
5	837		804		5–9
10	827		787		10–14
15	803	789.5	758	742	15–19
20	776	766.5	726	713	20–24
25	757	742	700	686.5	25–29
30	727	711.5	673	661	30–34
35	696	679.5	649	633	35–39
40	663	646.5	617	598.5	40–44
45	630	612.5	580	559.5	45–49
50	595		539		

TABLE 62. Estimation of Fertility Rates, All Live Births.

Age-group	Average number per woman	Average number per woman per age group
15–19	0.26	0.26
20–24	0.78	0.52
25–29	1.24	0.46
30–34	1.91	0.67
35–39	2.47	0.56
40–44	2.84	0.37
45–49	3.12	0.28
		3.12

TABLE 63. Estimation of Fertility Rates (b), All Live Births.

Age-group	(1) Average number per woman per age-group	(2) Averages of successive groups	(3) Adjusted figures	(4) Corrected figures
15–19	0.17 (a)	0.345	0.345	0.39
20–24	0.52	0.490	0.500	0.56
25–29	0.46	0.565	0.670	0.75
30–34	0.67	0.615	0.500	0.56
35–39	0.56	0.465	0.465	0.52
40–44	0.37	0.325	0.325	0.36
45–49	0.28	0.240	0.240	0.27
50–54 (b)	0.20			
	3.32	3.045	3.045	3.41

(a) Assuming one-third of the age-group are (unmarried).
(b) Based on the average for women aged 50 to 74.

TABLE 64. Net Reproduction Rates, Calculations Based on Different Estimated Death Rates.

Age-group	Fertility rates		Agogo (based on 15 years) A			Agogo (based on 30 years) B			Optimistic C			Pessimistic D		
	(b)	(a)	(1)	(2)	(3)	(1)	(2)	(3)	(1)	(2)	(3)	(1)	(2)	(3)
15–19	0.39	0.26	789.5	308	205	742	289	193	789	308	205	692.5	270	180
20–24	0.56	0.52	766.5	429	399	713	399	371	767.5	430	399	665.5	373	346
25–29	0.76	0.46	742	557	341	686.5	515	316	743	557	342	635.5	477	282
30–34	0.56	0.67	711.5	398	477	661	370	443	713.5	400	478	600.5	336	402
35–39	0.52	0.56	679.5	353	381	633	329	354	679.5	353	381	563	293	315
40–44	0.36	0.37	646.5	233	239	598.5	215	221	644	232	238	525	189	194
45–49	0.27	0.28	612.5	165	172	559.5	151	157	607	164	170	487	131	136
	3.41	3.12		2 443	2 214		2 268	2 055		2 444	2 213		2 069	1 865
Annual rate of increase (%)				3.0	2.7		2.8	2.4		3.0	2.7		2.4	2.0

(b) Optimistic fertility rate.
(a) Pessimistic fertility rate.
(1) Average number of females alive per year.
(2) Average number of females alive per year x optimistic fertility rate.
(3) Average number of females alive per year x pessimistic fertility rate.

TABLE 65. Age Distributions of Agogo Women if Rates Had Been Constant.

Age-group	Actual distribution	Chart 1[1]	Chart 2[2]	Chart 3[3]	Chart 4[4]
20–24	164	172	163	167	156
25–29	174	143	138	142	134
30–34	90	119	116	119	116
35–39	93	97	97	99	98
40–44	52	79	80	82	83
45–49	68	65	66	67	70
50–54	57	53	54	55	58
55–59	42	42	45	44	47
60–64	43	33	36	35	38
65–69	25	24	27	25	28
70–74	27	19	21	16	18
75–79	11	9	10	8	9
80+	16	7	8	4	5

[1] Based on net reproduction rate 2.443 and optimistic death rate (C).
[2] Based on net reproduction rate 2.213 and optimistic death rate (C).
[3] Based on net reproduction rate 2.069 and pessimistic death rate (D).
[4] Based on net reproduction rate 1.865 and pessimistic death rate (D).

TABLE 66. Agogo Women: Life Table for Optimistic Death Rate (C).

Survivors reaching age	Number	Years lived	Average number alive per year	Time left	Expectation of life
0	1 000	950	950	50 788.5	50.8
1	900	3 456	864	49 838.5	55.4
5	828	4 097.5	819.5	46 382.5	56.0
10	811	4 025	805	42 285	52.1
15	799	3 945	789	38 260	47.9
20	779	3 837.5	767.5	34 315	44.1
25	756	3 715	743	30 477.5	40.3
30	730	3 567.5	713.5	26 762.5	36.7
35	697	3 397.5	679.5	23 195	33.3
40	662	3 220	644	19 797.5	29.9
45	626	3 035	607	16 577.5	26.5
50	588	2 845	569	13 542.5	23.0
55	550	2 655	531	10 697.5	19.5
60	512	2 432.5	486.5	8 042.5	15.7
65	461	2 075	415	5 610	12.2
70	369	1 567.5	313.5	3 535	9.6
75	258	1 032.5	206.5	1 967.5	7.6
80	155	582.5	116.5	935	6.0
85	78	252.5	50.5	352.5	4.5
90	23	75	15	100	4.3
95	7	22.5	4.5	25	3.6
100	2	2.5	0.5	2.5	1.3

TABLE 67. Agogo Women: Life Table for Pessimistic Death Rate (D).

Survivors reaching age	Number	Years lived	Average number alive per year	Time left	Expectation of life
0	1 000	925	925	41 811	41.8
1	850	3 196	799	40 886	48.1
5	748	3 675	735	37 690	50.4
10	722	3 565	713	34 015	47.1
15	704	3 462.5	692.5	30 450	43.3
20	679	3 327.5	665.5	26 987.5	39.7
25	652	3 177.5	635.5	23 660	36.3
30	619	3 002.5	600.5	20 482.5	23.1
35	582	2 815	563	17 480	30.0
40	544	2 625	525	14 665	27.0
45	506	2 435	487	12 040	23.8
50	468	2 240	448	9 605	20.5
55	428	2 032.5	406.6	7 365	17.2
60	385	1 805	361	5 332.5	13.9
65	337	1 475	295	3 527.5	10.5
70	253	1 042.5	208.5	2 052.5	8.1
75	164	615	123	1 010	6.1
80	82	277.5	55.5	395	4.8
85	29	90	18	117.5	4.1
90	7	22.5	4.5	27.5	3.9
95	2	5	1	5	2.5
100	0				

Questionnaire Used in the Enquiry

Village .... Date .... Compound no. .... Serial no. ....

Woman's name .... Occupations ....

Her abusua .... Birthplace .... Religion ....

Literacy .... Nationality............ Mother's compound no........

Own mother's name, if alive .... Own mother's serial no. ....

Own mother's residence if not same village ....

Number of marriages including present one ....

*Number of husbands with whom she has had children ....

Woman's age .... How long after puberty first pregnancy ....

Past childbearing or still childbearing ....

Present husband............... His abusua .... Birthplace ....

His occupations .... Present residence ....

Religion .... Literacy .... Nationality..........

Number of present wives ....

* Number of wives with whom he has had children including deceased wives ....

* Include unmarried lovers by whom children born, and note this on other side.

Husband no.	Pregnan-cies	Miscarri-ages	Stillborn	Live-born	Sex	If dead age at which died	If alive present age	Present residence	Remarks (note especially if love child)

A Guide to the Estimation of Ages

General

1874	Too-too bere
1875	Asafo-Adjaye revolt
1886–88	Mampong War
1890–93	Nkoranza War
1893	Basel Mission established at Agogo
1900	Yaa Asantewaa War
1905	Agogo burnt down
1906	Death of Nana Yaw Sapong (Juabenhene)
	Earthquake at Agogo
1908	Komfo Aninakwaa's death
1909	Aberewa Fetish abolished
1914	East African Campaign (Kameroo Sa)
1917	14 February, Agogo riot
1918	Influenza Epidemic
1919	Paper Money Introduced
1923	First Lorry reached Agogo
1924	Repatriation of Nana Prempeh I
1925	Visit of H.R.H. The Prince of Wales
1928	12 December—Foundation stone of the Basel Mission Hospital laid
1929	Opening of the Basel Mission Hospital
	Foundation stone of the Basel Mission Girls' School laid
1931	1 March—Opening of the Basel Mission Girls' School
1933	Enstoolment of Nana Kyei Mensah
	Foundation Stone of the Presbyterian Church laid
1935	Ashanti Confederacy
1936	Second Cocoa boom (£1. 5s. per load)
1937	Cocoa hold-up
1939	June—Earthquake
1939	September—Second World War

Agogo Chiefs

Kofi Amponsah	1867–95
Kwaku Kyei	1895–1901
Kofi Amponsa	1901–10
Konkonsew (First enstoolment)	1911–13
Kofi Aka (80 days)	1913
Kwabena Tano	1914–22
Kwasi Gyinaye (Amoako)	1923–26
Konkonsew (Second enstoolment)	1926–32
Kyei Mensah	1933

Teachers, Catechists and Agents

1.	Charles Meyer	1893–1900
2.	Joe Atiemo	31/12/1900–26/1/1901
3.	Sam Agyei	2/2/1901–26/1/1901
4.	George W. Okyere	31/1/1906–10/2/1911
5.	Theodore E. Dankyi	2/2/1913–23/4/1917
6.	W. G. Saka	1/6/1917–17/1/1921
7.	J. W. Twum	17/1/1921–31/1/1921
8.	W. J. Obeng	1/2/1921–25
9.	A. Labi	1925–19/1/1929
10.	Ata	1929 (died)
11.	E. E. Ntim	1929 (2 months)
12.	Kwakye	Sept. 1929–34
13.	S. R. Asihene	1935–37
14.	C. J. Oteng	1938 (1 year)
	Rev. Appiah	1939–40
	Birikorang	1941

Infants (Approximate Ages)

Cutting of first tooth	6 months
Crawling begins at	7 months
Walking	11 months

Some Aspects of the Relation of Social Conditions to Human Fertility in the Gold Coast

by
K. A. BUSIA

Purpose of Study

The purpose of the study was defined by Professor Lorimer in the following directive:

'To investigate the effect of certain "modern" conditions such as education, urban residence, or changes in standard of living on human fertility through their influence either on age at marriage or on family limitation within marriage or both. The study is directed in part to an investigation of *attitudes* relating to marriage and fertility because (a) these may help to explain changes in behaviour; (b) changes in attitudes may precede marked changes in actual behaviour; (c) it is difficult to obtain accurate measure of actual fertility in the study of small samples.'

He further suggested that information on background and attitudes should be sought from all persons in the populations under investigation aged 18 years and over, but that the enquiry concerning fertility be limited to women aged 25 years and over. He suggested that the following age-groups be used in the tabulation: (a) 18–24; (b) 25–29; (c) 30–34; (d) 35–39; (e) 40–47; (f) 48–59; (g) 60 and over.

Method

It was clear from the beginning that, in the absence of the necessary vital records, the investigation could not give exact fertility rates. To achieve this, it would have been necessary for a census of the entire population of each area studied to be taken, and compared with data from a similar census taken earlier or later. Such data were not available, and the time and staff available did not permit the entire population of any area to be included. All we set out to do, then, was to collect data that would give a general indication of the relation of some social conditions to variations and trends in human fertility.

To do this, it was thought best to use the mixed procedure of random and purposive sampling, i.e., stratified sampling. Towns were purposely selected to represent urban, small town or rural conditions, and within each town a systematic random sample was selected by each investigator.

The towns selected were within Ashanti and the 'Colony'. The Northern

Territories could not be included, as none of the students who conducted the investigation had sufficient time or knowledge of the local languages to be able to conduct a study in the North within the short period at their disposal during the Easter vacation when the investigations were carried out. (21 March–17 April 1952.)

The towns selected included Accra (Population: 135,926); Kumasi (78,483); Sekondi-Takoradi (44,557); Cape Coast (23,346) which were regarded as urban areas; Keta (Population: 11,380); Nsawam (11,273); Kororidua (17,806); Winneba (15,171) which were regarded as small towns; and villages with populations varying from 1,500 to 8,000, regarded as rural. These included Dawu, Peki, Aburi, Mampong, Akropong, Nyakrom, Anyinaso, Ayensini, Kwanyaku, and Abura-Dunkwa. The samples varied from 3 to 5 per cent of the total population in the case of the small and rural towns, and 1 per cent in the case of the large (urban) towns.

The investigators consisted of 21 men and five women college students. They all used the same interview questions divided into three parts, dealing respectively with background information, attitudes and fertility. Some of the interview forms were filled in by the students themselves, others by literate collaborators. Information was sought from both men and women. I have already sent copies of the questionnaires and instructions issued to the investigators.

I attempt in this report only a summary and interpretation of the more significant aspects of the information collected.

FERTILITY OF GOLD COAST WOMEN

Combining the figures for all the towns studied, we get the following for the different age groups:

TABLE 68.

Age-group of women	Children born per woman (including miscarriages and stillbirths)
18–24	1.8
25–29	2.9
30–34	4.3
35–39	5.6
40–47	6.6
48–59	7.2
60+	Sample too small

These averages are slightly higher than those given in the 1948 official census. The differences may be due to our inclusion of miscarriages and stillbirths, and the exclusion of the Northern Territories where, according

344

to the official census, the fertility rates were lower than in the 'Colony' and Ashanti.

For the three groups of towns, rural, small town and urban, the figures were:

TABLE 69.

Age group	Children born per woman		
	Rural	Small town	Urban
18–24	1.9	1.8	1.5
25–29	2.9	2.9	2.7
30–34	4.3	4.3	4.1
35–39	5.7	5.7	5.4
40–47	6.7	6.7	6.5
48–59	7.3	7.2	7.2
60+ (Sample too small)			

The answers to the question on divorces and remarriages showed that 30 per cent of the women got divorced and remarried during the reproductive period, but the effect of this, if any, on fertility could not be ascertained.

The differences in the mean averages of the number of children born per woman between the various age groups in rural and in urban areas were small, but tentative inferences could be drawn from them. The differences in the younger age groups as between rural and urban areas are beginning to reflect the later marriages in the urban areas. This trend might emerge to a greater degree in later studies. Such data as to age at first marriage as were collected showed that on the average both men and women marry earlier in the rural areas than in the urban areas. This trend towards late marriages was more marked amongst literate couples; but as in many cases in the rural areas the ages were unknown, or estimated, comparative figures might be misleading. On the average, the age of first marriages for girls in the rural towns was about 18, just over 21 for girls in the urban towns. The difference between men was more marked, being 20 for the rural areas, 27 for the urban towns.

EDUCATION

In order to ascertain whether education had any effect on fertility, the wives returned as having had school education were compared with those who had not:

345

TABLE 70.

Age group	Children born per woman		
	Illiterate	Primary	High school and college
18–24	2.1	1.9	0.9
25–29	3.1	2.9	1.9
30–34	4.5	4.4	3.6
35–39	5.9	5.7	4.9
40–47	6.9	6.7	6.2
48–59	7.3	7.2	7.0
60+ (Sample too small)			

Children are desired by literate and illiterate parents alike, and in the older age groups the differences in average births were small. The differences in the younger age groups reflected to a certain extent the effect of the delay in marriage resulting from schooling. The place of residence showed no significant difference in this regard. The returns on the frequency of child-lessness (figures given later) showed that it was higher among high school and college trained women than others, and their families tended to be smaller; but the high school and college group was a 'special population' sorted out from cases obtained in the general studies, and was a comparatively small sample (only 2.3 per cent of the total).

RELIGION

Whilst education showed a tendency to affect fertility through delayed marriages, religious affiliation did not seem responsible for any marked differences. For all the age groups, the average number of children born to the women—Muslim, Christian, or traditional believer—was about the same. It should be noted, however, that in all instances in which both husband and wife were literate, they were also returned as Christians, and the differences resulting from this correlation appear to be due to the effect of education; because as between Christians who were illiterate, and illiterates who were not Christians, there were no significant differences in fertility.

THE INCIDENCE OF POLYGYNY

The incidence of polygyny was nearly as high in the urban as in the rural areas:

346

TABLE 71.

Age group	Number of wives per married man		
	Urban	Small town	Rural
18–24	1.2	1.2	1.2
25–29	1.2	1.3	1.3
30–34	1.4	1.5	1.5
35–39	1.4	1.5	1.5
40–47	1.4	1.4	1.4
48–59	1.3	1.3	1.3
60+ (Sample too small)			

The inference that may be drawn is that town life has not yet made any significant difference to polygyny. In both rural and urban areas, polygynous husbands were either those who could afford to maintain more than one wife, or those whose occupation made the assistance of more than one wife an economic advantage as in farming, trading, or laundry. No significant difference in fertility appeared between women married monogamously, and those married to polygynists.

FREQUENCY OF CHILDLESSNESS

For the entire population studied (rural, small town, urban) the percentages of married couples returned as childless at the time of the investigation were:

TABLE 72.

Age group	Percentage
18–24	17
25–29	7.6
30–34	4.2
35–39	3.4
40–47	3.4
48–59	Sample too small

The information obtained was not sufficient for any reliable inferences to be drawn on the basis of residence; but, as has been stated, childlessness was higher among educated than among illiterate women. In the urban areas, 8 per cent of the cases of childlessness reported admitted that there

347

had been venereal disease. This is mentioned only for interest; the investigators were not in a position to establish any causal connexion between venereal disease and childlessness, that being an intricate medical problem. The incidence of venereal disease may be higher, since many were reluctant to give information on the point. It will be noted, however, that many of the wives returned as childless at the time of the investigation were within the reproductive span, some of them married under three years, and likely to have children before menopause.

ATTITUDES RELATING TO MARRIAGE AND FERTILITY

Of the total population interviewed, only 6 per cent considered that the best age for a man to marry was between 18 and 21, whilst 94 per cent thought the best age was 21 and over; on the other hand, 62 per cent thought that the best age for girls to marry was between 18 and 21, and only 38 per cent thought that girls should marry at 21 and over.

The opinion that girls should marry under 21 was expressed by the majority in all age groups interviewed. These opinions reflect the social fact, namely that girls do in fact marry much earlier than men. The differences at age of first marriage for men and for women show wider differences in the urban areas than in the rural. For a selected sample of 1,000 couples from the returns for the urban areas, the average age at first marriage was 21 for women, but 27 for men; and for a similar selection from the returns for rural areas, it was 18 for the girls and 20 for the boys; but it should again be emphasized that most ages have to be estimated, so these figures can be regarded as giving only an indication rather than an exact representation of the social situation.

As to the reasons for waiting until the age of marriage, suggested answers were given in the questionnaire and coded. The results were as in Table 73.

TABLE 73.

	Boys %	Girls %
Physical maturity	25	35
'Know one's mind' or 'Take time to find the right person'	12	12
Acquire work skills or complete schooling	15	15
'Acquire property' or 'Have job'	40	30
Help support parents or family before marriage	7	7
Have time to enjoy oneself before marriage	1	1

These distributions reflect the fact that, for men, the emphasis is on their acquiring property or securing a job before marriage; men in the rural

348

areas find employment quicker as farmers, while those in the urban areas are exposed to the insecurity of unemployment, and hence the later marriages. For women, the first consideration is that they should reach physical maturity before marriage, though acquiring property or having a job is a close second. The latter is a reflection of the insecurity felt by married women, namely, that on the death of their husbands, other relations may inherit and possibly throw out the wife and children; a situation which is prevalent owing to the system of inheritance by which the claims of matrilineal or patrilineal kin may supersede those of wives and children. The anxiety finds expression in the increasing practice of married women engaging in some gainful occupation, usually 'petty' trading in the large towns, and farming in the rural towns.

With regard to schooling, 30 per cent of those interviewed said they would want their sons to continue schooling till the end of the primary school stage, and 70 per cent said they would like them to have higher education; with regard to daughters, however, 45 per cent of those interviewed said girls should have schooling to the end of the primary school stage only, whilst 55 per cent thought girls should receive higher education. As a matter of fact, there are fewer girls at school than boys, and high school and college education for girls is a privilege which only a comparatively small number enjoy.

All the couples interviewed except 10 considered it wrong to attempt in any way to delay having children or to prevent having them, and thought the use of contraceptives wrong.

The investigation did in fact show that in general deliberate limitation was not practised within marriage. There were only three admissions of the practice—for economic or health reasons.

In conclusion, though a study of this type cannot be considered adequate for an exact appraisal of the effects of social conditions on human fertility, it does clearly indicate trends towards postponement of marriage among educated members of the Gold Coast Community, and amongst city dwellers as compared with those in rural areas. It also indicates a declining fertility, but this should be regarded as a tentative hypothesis until supported by further statistical studies.

Total population (all samples): 3,423
    Men   1,423
    Women   2,000

Age composition of sample (all interviewed):

Men and women	Total	Married women only (basis of fertility analysis)
(a) 18–24	365	146
(b) 25–29	631	350
(c) 30–34	610	383
(d) 35–39	525	359
(e) 40–47	663	378
(f) 48–59	507	314
(g) 60+	122	70

Residence of women in sample:
    Rural   800
    Small town   500
    Urban   700

Education—women:
    Illiterate   1,500
    Primary   450
    High school and college   50

Religion—women:
    Muslim   50
    Pagan   1,600
    Christian   350

PART FOUR

Report on Fertility Surveys in Buganda and Buhaya, 1952

by
AUDREY I. RICHARDS
and
PRISCILLA REINING

ORIGINS OF THE PROJECT

At the suggestion of Professor Frank Lorimer, who visited the Institute in December 1951 on behalf of the Social Science Division of Unesco, the East African Institute of Social Research undertook an intensive study of fertility in some selected area, or areas, in Buganda. Buganda is a political division of Uganda; its principal people are the Baganda (singular Muganda). According to the 1948 census, this is a ⟨egion of apparently low fertility, and it seemed important to investigate the validity of this finding and, if possible, to throw light on related conditions.[1] It was proposed to select for the study villages comprising one of the sample areas used in the 1948 census enquiry on fertility, in order that the results obtained by census methods might be checked with those obtained in a more intensive social survey.

A complementary proposal was subsequently received from Dr. Laurie, Director of the East African Medical Survey, which has its headquarters at Mwanza in Tanganyika Territory. Dr. Laurie proposed a joint medical and sociological survey, also to be directed largely towards the study of fertility, infant mortality and other demographic topics in the Bukoba area of Buhaya in Tanganyika, in order to check by means of an intensive village survey the results obtained from a series of 2,000 maternity histories previously collected in the same area. Bukoba is part of the Buhaya region, i.e., that inhabited chiefly by the Bahaya.

As a result of these suggestions, it was agreed:

To carry out two parallel social and demographic studies in Buganda and in Buhaya. These are both areas, according to the 1948 census, with low fertility rates compared with those of other parts of East Africa. Both

---

[1] The results of the 1948 census are as yet largely unpublished. Some summary results are presented in the UN Demographic Yearbook; other findings are described by C. J. Martin in 'Colonial Statistics', *J. of the Royal Statistical Society* A113 (3): 271–97, 1950, also in The East African Census, 1948. Planning and Enumeration, *Population Studies* 3 (3): 303–20, 1949. Census information on distribution by area and by tribal affiliation of the African population is presented by The East African Statistical Department: *African Population of Uganda Protectorate*, 1950. Some other (unpublished) items of information from the 1948 census have been provided by the Statistical Department.

the Baganda and the Bahaya are banana-eating peoples and there are other similarities in the two districts. Both are cash crop areas with a rather higher standard of living than in most other peasant societies in East Africa. Moreover, both were areas where the Institute had already had anthropologists working during the previous year, Mrs. Priscilla Reining in Buhaya and Dr. Audrey Richards in Buganda.

To combine the collection of data on fertility (obtained by means of maternity histories, marriage histories of men and women and household questionnaires) with a medical examination of the population in the two sample areas with special reference to venereal diseases and other factors likely to affect fertility rates. Dr. Hope Trant undertook this work on behalf of the Medical Survey in Bukoba and Dr. Ladkin, Provincial Medical Officer for Buganda, arranged for Dr. Hebe Welbourn to undertake this work in the Buganda village selected.[1]

To combine the fertility and medical surveys with the collection of social data, e.g., on the composition of households, clan, religious and occupational grouping and simple economic questions. Some of this information was required to throw light on a problem of special interest to the Unesco enquiry, as regards sociological factors affecting fertility rates. It was also valuable for two other purposes; as a cross-check on the information provided by maternity histories and medical examinations, and as a means of adding to information required by the Institute for other comparative sociological studies, including a study of the stability of marriage in several areas.

Later the provincial agricultural and veterinary officers in each area agreed to conduct short surveys which would give an idea of the agricultural resources of each of the sample areas and the extent to which cattle and other livestock were being kept by the villagers.

The following questionnaires were used:

A household questionnaire giving data on household composition (sex, age, and relationship to the head of household), district of birth, clan, lineage, religion, schooling, occupation of male members, land-ownership, livestock, production of cotton and coffee at last harvest, and marital histories of men and women respectively.

A maternity history, which was adopted from one already used by the Medical Survey in the enquiry referred to above. It contained data on age, marital status, total number of pregnancies, number of children alive, age-groups of children still living, age-groups of children at death, loss of children before birth, age of puberty, age at first pregnancy, etc.

A medical examination form as used by the Medical Survey in Buhaya. A simplified version of this form was used in Buganda.

[1] These studies are as yet unpublished and are, therefore, not quoted in the present paper.

Bukoba, in Tanganyika, is the home of the Bahaya, a tribe very similar in culture to the Baganda; it is reckoned as belonging to the same ethnic group, the Interlacustrian Bantu. A characteristic feature of their social structure is a very hierarchical system of government. The Bahaya practise mixed husbandry with bananas as the staple crop; their cash crop is coffee; they own more cattle than the Baganda. Like Buganda, Buhaya is a relatively wealthy area, owing to the high price obtained recently for coffee. By African standards the people are healthy and well-fed. They live along the western shore of Lake Victoria in well-watered country, with a relatively high density of population.

Bukoba was selected for the study because one of the Institute anthropologists was working there, and the East African Medical Survey had collected 2,000 maternity histories in the area. The officers in charge of the Survey had been led to question the validity of a common assumption that the high frequencies of sterility and infant mortality were due wholly to venereal disease. The Bahaya are supposed to be addicted to prostitution, and Bahaya women travel across Lake Victoria to urban centres like Kampala in Uganda. Neither for venereal infection nor prostitution rates were accurate figures available. V.D. rates for Buhaya are given in summary, i.e. 10 per cent.

Selection of the Sample Area

Two contiguous sample villages were selected in relation to the sample used in the 1948 census, i.e., Buhembe and Kyasha in the Nyakato district, of which Bukoba is the capital. Buhembe had a total *de jure* population of 552 persons, 267 males and 285 females, while Kyasha had a total of 293 persons, 131 males and 162 females—giving as total 845 persons, of whom 47 per cent were males. The number present in these villages at the time of the survey was 728 persons: 337 males and 391 females (46 per cent males).[1]

The villages lie a short distance from Bukoba, the principal town in the district. They resemble the villages in the Buganda sample area in size and many other respects. The Bukoba sample contained 227 huts. Social and economic data were obtained on 280 men over 16 years of age, and on 371 women and girls; 300 maternity forms were completed. In the medical investigation, which followed the sociological survey, 739 persons (adults and children) were examined: 394 males and 345 females.

More than half of all married men in the sample area are cultivators only; but 9.5 per cent were reported as unskilled labourers, and 32 per cent as skilled workers, such as mechanics, drivers, or carpenters in addition to

---

[1] On this and other topics, see *Comparative Tables* (*General*) at end of the Introduction.

the living they gained by cultivation. The villages are homogenous in character, with few migrants from other regions; in each village about 55 per cent of the inhabitants were born in the same village. The number of non-Haya inhabitants is very small. Only 1.7 per cent of the inhabitants of Kyasha were born outside Tanganyika, and 3.3 per cent in the case of Buhembe.

The households tended to be small. Among the 227 huts covered by the survey, 7.1 per cent contained only one person, 18.5 per cent two persons, 27.3 per cent three persons, and 18.5 per cent four persons, leaving only 29 per cent with five or more persons. Of these 227 huts, 21 were owned by women, in a few cases by women living alone, but usually by women with one or two dependent relatives.

The villagers in the sample area were mainly Catholic or pagan. Reported distribution: 43 per cent Catholic, 46 per cent pagan, 4 per cent Protestant, 4 per cent Muslim, 2 per cent unknown. Religious affiliation seemed to have little relation to the stability of marriage.

The educational standard of the adults was roughly gauged by questioning men and women as to the school they had attended, i.e., primary or secondary, and also by asking them to read a sentence out of a vernacular newspaper. The educational level of the women in the Buhaya sample was low by this method of reckoning, as 90.7 per cent were illiterate, while only 9.3 per cent had attended primary school or had taught themselves to read.

Survey Methods

The survey started in mid-July with a meeting attended by the local hereditary chief. In distinction from the approach used in the Buganda area, the investigator (Mrs. Reining) announced that she was interested in 'how the people live'—with no specific reference to fertility. The favourable response in the Buhembe meeting may have been due to this approach. The subject of fertility can rouse a good deal of emotion in African communities at the present time, and it is unwise to start a fertility survey with a direct address on the subject. It is also true that the Bahaya accept the orders of a chief more readily than the Baganda. In this case the chief had summoned the people to the meeting with his hereditary drum.

The social survey was kept distinct from the maternity investigation. Mrs. Reining worked for six weeks with two African clerical assistants on the collection of the economic and social data and also completed a number of genealogies on every household. The maternity forms were filled in separately by an educated African woman, Mrs Mulahangalwa, and a missionary with long experience in the area, Miss Amy Boeash.

The sociological study preceded the medical survey. Mrs. Reining rented a house in the area and she and two African assistants worked from house to house. She found it convenient to have the whole family gathered

356

together, since one member of the family jogged the memory of the other. Mrs. Reining trained her African assistants with great care until they were able to fill in the forms themselves. She accompanied one or the other, alternately, in the house-to-house visits.

During the medical survey, the doctors lived at a government secondary school nearby, and had a pathologist with them. The advantage of prolonged residence by the doctors in the area was very evident. Both in Buganda and Buhaya the people came hesitantly for medical examination on the first day and, after that, tended to come more rapidly. Part of the success of the medical examinations in the Bukoba area seems to have been due to the fact that the doctors were able to live on the spot.

Agricultural and veterinary surveys were made after the sociological and medical work had been completed.

Mrs. Reining took charge of the checking of the data from the sociological, medical, and maternity forms, so that all the information was cross-checked.

Validity of Evidence

In distinction from the Buganda survey, Mrs. Reining believes that none of the Bahaya were deliberately evasive. She thinks that such mistakes as were made were due to misunderstanding or failures of memory.

Age. The investigator compiled a calendar of dates in local history by which calculations of age could be made. She first took the stated age, and then obtained a calculated age by means of these dates and material from the collected genealogies. In the case of the medical examinations, the stated age was taken.

There was exact agreement in only 35 per cent of the cases between the stated age given to the doctors and the computed age reckoned by the sociologist. There was more agreement at the younger ages, and less agreement in the older age groups. At age 50 years and over, the average difference between the ages obtained by the two methods was as much as 10 years, and age 60 years and over, as much as 17 years.

The differences appear to have been due to the fact that the sociologist computed ages after having collected genealogies and obtained answers to questions on marriage and children. In the medical records there was a distinct tendency to group the population around certain ages, particularly 5, 12, 16, 25, 40, 50, and 60. There was also a tendency to depress ages. In the older age-groups the medical estimates were generally lower than those of the social unit. With the sociologist's method there is more differentiation, that is, less 'bunching', and the ages of the total population display a smoother curve. This is less important, however, in dealing with fairly broad age-groups.

357

Relationship and Clanship

There was no difficulty over this question. Relationships to head of household and clan were readily given although there was some reluctance to give the lineage.

Marriage. As in Buganda, this proved the most difficult information to obtain. In Buganda deliberate concealment of absent wives was common. In Buhaya there does not seem to have been much concealment of this kind, but women who married at 15 and subsequently contracted other unions, often found it almost impossible to remember the dates of the second and third unions. Questions were asked on this subject in the medical questionnaire, the maternity form and the sociological questionnaire. There was a serious lack of agreement between these three sets of data. The sociological data appear most accurate, judging by internal consistency and from the fact that the genealogies and the information from various members of one household formed a check on each other.

THE BUGANDA SURVEY

Selection of the Sample Area

It was intended to select a village in relation to the sample areas used in the 1948 census, and with attention to size and distance from the municipality of Kampala (the headquarters of the East African Institute of Social Research). The area chosen was in Busiro county, Sabagabo sub-county (gombolola), Sabagabo parish (muruka). By an unfortunate error it turned out that the selected sub-county was not to be the sample census sub-county, although it lies near one. The conditions in the two sub-counties are roughly similar except that Sabagabo, the district chosen, lies nearer the town.

The selected area contained 299 households, divided into three separate estates (Kisozi, Sumba and part of Namagoma). It lies 12 miles from Kampala, the largest industrial centre in Uganda, and a number of the male householders work there. The area is about two miles from King's College, Budo, a big secondary school.

A village in this position was chosen because it was thought that villagers rather closely in contact with town life might show changed attitudes towards childbearing and child-rearing, and that these might indicate future fertility trends. It was also expected that changed types of marriage might be found in such a village. An African nurse had been appointed as a health visitor to the area a year previous to the survey and Dr. Welbourn held a clinic at King's College once a fortnight.

Kisozi and Sumba are referred to as villages (mitalla) but both are really estates mainly owned by two large Baganda landowners. Kisozi, the larger of the two villages, lies near the main road to Masaka and has a primary school and a church. Sumba is more remote. The third estate was also the property of one landowner near Namagoma, another village which lies along the opposite side of the Masaka road. Kisozi had a total population of 661, Sumba 306, and Namagoma 154, making a total of 1,121 persons.

These estates must be reckoned as long settled areas. Busiro county is considered as the heart of Buganda, and as the district first occupied by the Baganda when they moved into this region. The father of the present landowner of Kisozi was allotted his land in 1900 and brought many of his own relatives to live on it, but cultivation must have taken place for 200 to 300 years before that. Thus, although the sample area falls in the rich elephant grass belt of South Uganda, there are signs of soil erosion and, like most areas within a 30-mile radius of Kampala, it is very closely settled. The average size of holding is 3 acres per household in Kisozi and Sumba and 5.1 acres in Namagoma, a more recently occupied area with more land available for cattle grazing. The average household lot here is well below the average for Buganda as a whole.

The staple food crop here, as elsewhere in Buganda, is the banana. About half the crop is eaten and half is used for beer. Food crops also include beans, sweet potatoes, cassava, and some groundnuts. The villagers in Kisozi grow cotton and coffee and also sell vegetables to King's College and Kampala. All cultivation is done with a hand hoe. There are 20 owners of cattle, although there is little ground available for communal grazing in such a densely settled area.

For these reasons the householders in the sample communities are either peasant cultivators who would be reckoned rather poor (in relation to those, for instance, in the Masaka or Kyagwe areas), or work in skilled or unskilled occupations in Kampala or Budo. Slightly less than half of the adult males in the three areas were employed in skilled or unskilled work, for instance, as carpenters, mechanics, domestic servants, brickmakers, masons, bricklayers or roadmakers, in Kampala, Budo or in the village itself. About 7 per cent of the men bicycle 12 miles each day to Kampala and return in the evening.

The occupants of the villages are mainly Baganda, but there is a high rate of immigrant settlement in most parts of Buganda. Slightly less than one-third (31.6 per cent) of the total population of the sample area was born there; and 8.8 per cent was born outside Uganda. The proportion of female householders appears high, i.e., 28 per cent, and also the number of households consisting of one person, i.e., 17.4 per cent. It appeared that men and women who had become used to living in the vicinity of Kampala tended to retire to villages of this type in their old age. There were also some retired African government officers and clerks. On the other hand, a considerable part of the *de jure* population of this area, 24 per cent of the males and 22 per cent of the females of all ages, were absent at the time of the survey.

The analysis of the religious affiliation shows that Sumba is mainly Catholic (34 per cent Roman Catholic, 25 per cent Protestant, 1 per cent Muslim); Kisozi is mainly Protestant (37 per cent Protestant, 24 per cent Roman Catholic, 3.3 per cent Muslim); and Namagoma mainly Muslim (38.3 per cent Muslim, 22.7 per cent Protestant, 18 per cent Roman Catholic). It was thought that this might affect marriage customs, but this did not prove to be the case.

The educational standards of the women in the sample villages were substantially higher than those in Buhaya. Here 35 per cent had attended a primary school or had taught themselves to read; and 2 per cent had attended a secondary school. The proportion of illiterates here was 63 per cent, as against 91 per cent in Buhaya. This figure of illiteracy may appear high for a village with its own school, but it is estimated that in 1950 only 30 per cent of the girls in Uganda attended school for more than one year. So the presence of a school does not necessarily bring a big increase in female literacy. However, literacy is rising; among girls between 16 and 29 years of age, 50 per cent were found to be literate. The findings of the study in this respect are similar to those for Mengo County as a whole, according to the 1948 census.

Survey Methods

The investigators were warned from the start that they would have special difficulties over the fertility aspects of the survey because the Baganda do not like to count their children. They fear that this will bring bad luck, and consider it bad manners to question a woman as to the actual number of her children. Medical experience in the area showed that the whole question of fertility has great emotional significance for the people. It is the current belief that the Baganda are less fertile than in the past and that their children die oftener. Women attending hospitals often complain of sterility and ask for treatment against barrenness, sometimes after they have been married only one or two years. The prophecies of difficulties in the survey proved well founded. The extent to which the survey was able to overcome these objections can be gauged from the section on reliability of evidence given below.

The survey was opened with a village meeting held in Kisozi on 31 July, which was addressed by Dr. Welbourn and Dr. Richards. The medical aspect of the enquiry proved more alarming than the sociological. There was considerable apprehension over the possible taking of blood samples, probably due to rumours circulating as to a blood transfusion unit which had been going round the country and about the work of a sleeping sickness unit. Co-operation on the clinical survey was poor, and the examination had to be limited to volunteers who felt they needed treatment rather than to the whole population as was possible in the Buhaya survey. Dr. Welbourn and Dr. Sembeguya examined 73 adults (25 men and 48 women). Dr. Welbourn also examined 101 school children (58 boys and 43 girls). Considerable emotion was displayed over the question of fertility. Speakers at the first meeting expressed concern over the falling birth rate and were irritated by the information that other tribes had higher reproduction rates.

The sociological aspects of the survey elicited little comment, perhaps because they were not fully understood. It is believed that the survey might have proceeded better if the general sociological queries had been asked first and the medical examination and maternity histories had been undertaken later and, as it were, incidentally. The Buhaya experience tends to support this suggestion.

Preliminary information was obtained by means of the tax registers which list males between the ages of 18 and about 60. This provided the basis of the list of households to be visited. But women do not pay tax and immigrants do not pay for two years. It was therefore necessary to divide the village into separate areas, each of which was under the control of a bailiff of the landowner in question (musigire), who led the investigators to each house in his charge.

Birth registers were also examined at the sub-county headquarters and were used to check information given as to the ages of the children in the sample. However, the registers were available only for the past two years, and were found to be very inaccurate.

The investigators then made a house-to-house investigation, generally in pairs (a man and a woman). The usual procedure was for the man to fill in the household questionnaire and the woman the maternity history. The information obtained separately from the male householder and his wife or other adult females in the house was then checked. Two hundred and fifty-nine men and 261 women were interviewed in this way. Two hundred and eighty-two maternity histories were also collected.

Once the forms had been filled in and checked, the information was checked again with the landowner's bailiff, and with the health visitor's records, the schoolmaster's records, and in some cases with neighbours.

Dr. Welbourn and Dr. Sembeguya started medical examinations at the end of September and made three separate visits to the village. In some cases the information obtained from women by Dr. Welbourn was also checked against that given on the maternity form.

A brief agricultural survey was carried out by Mr. D. J. Parsons in December, and a veterinary survey in April 1953.

Validity of Evidence

On the whole, the investigators were received with great patience by the villagers, in view of the length of the questionnaires used and the fact that the counting of children is an unpleasant and even painful operation for them. Complete refusals to answer questions were very rare, although it was sometimes necessary to visit a house three times in order to get co-operation. There were only four direct refusals, and these were by women who were individuals found difficult by the whole community, two of whom were said to be witches.

A more common form of refusal was a civil greeting, followed either by reluctance to give any information, or by quite obvious mis-statements. In the former case, the reason was usually general suspicion and fear of strangers, or active hostility to the purpose of the survey as it had been rumoured round the village. It was sometimes necessary to give explanations lasting up to an hour before a householder would co-operate. Where the hostility was more active, information changed from interview to interview, or frivolous answers were given. For instance, a man who had refused to give any information to the two first investigators, finally gave the names of two children to the third investigator, and later ran after the enquirer, fetched her back, and admitted to 10 children. He still concealed a second wife living in another village. Another was interviewed three times; the first time he said he had no children at all, the second time that he had three children, and it was finally learned that he had two small boys and three girls living in the house, and two married daughters and one married son in the village. A third informant of this type gave different information to two investigators, in the first of which he claimed to be a Munyoro of the Lugave clan but was later found to be a Muganda of the Mkima clan. He said he had never been married, but was found to have been married and to have several children.

In some cases, it appeared that younger people were reluctant to give accurate information in the absence of the head of the household. Thus, three young married girls gave false names and ages of themselves and their children, but smilingly gave the right answers when their elderly mother returned. Another woman, who was living in some kind of casual union with a man, described herself first of all as his daughter, and when asked if she had ever had children, replied without hesitation, 'I had seven children, but they all died of plague—in the same year'. She was proved never to have had a child.

A third variety of informant gave a friendly reception to the investigators and was reliable on some points but not on others. The validity of different types of evidence will be listed below.

Age. The fixing of age is invariably difficult among illiterate peoples, and some of those questioned were unable to hazard even a guess at their age. All ages given here were calculated in the first instance by means of a calendar of dates including the beginning and end of the reigns of different kings, dates in the two world wars, famines, and other local events. The probable age was then checked by the date of marriage given by a husband or wife, and in relation to the ages of living children. It is thought that the ages given here are accurate to within five years in the case of those under 30, but are less accurate above that age. There was a very fair correlation between the figures given to the medical and the sociological investigators respectively.

Fertility Data. There seemed to be little reluctance to give details of miscarriages, abortions or stillbirths, or—where dead children were admitted—to group them according to the age at death, except in the case of three old women who tearfully refused to give any details at all. The age at puberty was estimated by asking the age at which the breasts first formed and adding one year. The age of first pregnancy is probably only accurate within three or four years. Data on miscarriages are probably inaccurate in the case of older women, e.g., over 45; in the case of younger women, reasonably accurate information seems to have been furnished at the time of the medical examination, and the figures given here are corrected in the light of this check. It is probable that the figures as to sterility were accurate, since it is unlikely that a woman would describe herself as barren unless this was actually the case.

The most important mis-statements were with respect to the number of children, as was expected. The most common was the complete omission of sons and daughters who had grown up. Altogether, 30 men and women either omitted or refused to admit to grown-up children. Some of these apparently did not understand that grown men or women were to be counted as children. Some felt that children who were adults should answer for themselves, and one very co-operative informant who was the father of one of the survey helpers omitted two grown sons and three daughters who were absent because, he said, 'he was not used to counting them like that'. In most of these cases, the informants could have no hope of ultimately deceiving the investigators. For instance, a woman who said she had no grown children was discovered to have five married children living near her house. She explained that she thought the children could answer for themselves.

Seven informants omitted the names of young children living in their houses, and six others concealed the names of children of past marriages. The figures for numbers of children were corrected in the light of information given by neighbours, etc. The largest source of error is probably the under-reporting of children to men of the sample area by women living outside it. Only partial correction of such error was possible.

Marriage Data. Fourteen respondents are known to have concealed second marriages, and the actual error is probably very much higher, especially in the case of men. Marriages might be denied either because a Christian union had been followed by a customary one, or because one partner did not like to speak of a previous union in front of the present spouse. Second wives in other villages were usually concealed, and second wives living in the same house were sometimes described as sisters of the first wife. Information on unions of this sort was readily given by neighbours. An old man refused to mention the names of two dead wives, as well as four grown children, and was obviously pained and distressed by reference to the past.

Summary

In all, 11 per cent of the answers were found to be untrue on recheck; 10 per cent answered only partially; and 1.6 per cent only on the second, third or fourth visits. In every case, however, the picture was made as accurate as possible with the aid of additional information.

Any fertility survey is likely to be difficult in Buganda, but a fairly close approximation to the truth can be reached if sufficient time is taken over the enquiry. Where investigators live in the survey village, they are able to check the information with neighbours and those in authority, and also to become familiar with the people in question. It is thought that the medical survey would also have been more successful if the doctor had been able to give full time to this task. The difficulties encountered in this study were much greater than in some previous surveys—for example an immigrant labour survey carried out the previous year.

TABLE 74.   Size and Sex Composition of Sample Populations.

	Males		Females		Total
	Number	Per cent	Number	Per cent	
Buhaya sample					
Total population	398	47	447	53	845
Present population	337	46	391	54	728
Buganda sample					
Total population	556	49	565	51	1 121
Present population	430	49	439	51	869

Percentage of total males absent
  Buhaya sample: 15
  Buganda sample: 24
Percentage of total females absent
  Buhaya sample: 13
  Buganda sample: 22

Per Cent Distribution of Households by Size.[1]

	Buhaya	Buganda
Households of		
one	7.1	17.4
two	18.5	20.7
three	27.3	18.1
four	18.5	14.4
five	15.0	10.0
six or more	6.2	6.0
Total	100	100

[1] Data in Tables 75–79 relate to total population, present and absent.

T ABLE 76. Per Cent Distribution of Populations by Religious Affiliation.

	Total	R.C.	Pro-testant	Muslim	Other	Un-stated
Buhaya						
Kyasha	100	32.1	6.8	3.8	53.9	3.4
Buhembe	100	50.0	2.0	4.2	42.4	1.4
Total sample	100	43.8	3.7	4.0	46.4	2.1
Buganda						
Kisozi	100	24.2	37.0	3.3	2.1	33.4
Sumba	100	34.3	25.5	1.0	2.0	37.2
Namagoma	100	18.2	22.7	38.3	0.0	20.8
Total sample	100	26.1	31.9	7.5	1.8	32.7

T ABLE 77. Present Population by Place of Birth.

	Born in villages %	Born in colony %	Born outside colony %	Unstated %
Buhaya sample	54.9	42.0	2.7	0.4
Buganda sample	31.6	30.0	8.8	29.6

365

TABLE 78. Occupations of Married Men.

| | Married men | Cultivators | Distribution by occupation | | Unstated |
			Unskilled wage earners	Skilled wage earners	
Buhaya sample					
Number	190	98	18	61	13
Per cent	100	51.6	9.5	32.1	6.8
Buganda sample					
Number	289	137	40	92	27
Per cent	100	46.0	14.0	31.0	9.0

TABLE 79. Women by Age and by Literacy Status.

| Age group | Number of women | Per cent distribution | | |
		Illiterate	Primary schooling	Secondary schooling
Buhaya				
15–29	87	74	26	—
30–39	52	92	8	—
40–49	39	92	8	—
50–59	54	100	—	—
60–69	27	100	—	—
70+	44	100	—	—
All women	303	90.7	9.3	—
Buganda				
15–29	106	48	49	3
30–39	51	73	25	2
40–49	39	67	33	—
50–59	42	71	29	—
60–69	22	86	14	—
70+	11	83	17	—
All women	271	63	35	2

CHAPTER I

Social Conditions and Fertility

INTRODUCTION

The following types of sociological factor will be discussed in relation to fertility in the two areas:

Kinship and Political Structure as they may Affect the Desire for Children

It is obvious that some forms of social structure put a high premium on the production and rearing of children. These may be required for enlarging the kinship group or a political group based on descent, or to secure the passing on of land or other privileges. It is suggested that such societies encourage the remarriage of widows and widowers and the inheritance of wives, and to make very strict rules as regards succession and descent and the possession of children. These suggestions will be discussed with respect to the two areas.

The Institutions of Marriage [1]

Forms of marriage and family grouping may affect the fertility rate, such as the age at marriage, the stability of marriage, the existence of polygamy or monogamy, rules governing remarriage and views on extra-marital unions.

Restrictions on Childbearing

These may include tabooed periods, contraceptive practices, self-induced abortions and attitudes to childbearing; also for instance the prolonged absence of males in areas with a high rate of male emigration at certain seasons of the year.

Factors Affecting the Survival of Children

It seems likely that the survival rate of young children is influenced by

---

[1] Statistical information on marriage, from a preliminary tabulation of survey data, is presented in Comparative Tables, Series B, at the end of this section.

types of childbirth and child-rearing, the educational level of the parents and their standard of living, nutrition and the rate of infection, particularly of venereal disease.

Before proceeding with the consideration of social conditions, we should take account of the apparent variations of fertility among various districts in Uganda, as indicated by the 1948 fertility sample census data. These run as follows:[1]

Province	District	Average number of children ever-born, as reported by women aged 45+
Northern	Lango	7.0
	West Nile	4.6
	Modi	7.0
Western	Bunyoro	4.6
	Toro	5.2
	Ankole	3.6
	Kigezi	6.4
Eastern	Busoga	5.4
	Mbale	5.7
	Teso	5.1
Buganda	(All districts)	3.7
	Musaka	4.0
	Mubende	4.1
	Mengo[1]	3.2

[1] District including our Buganda sample area.

In the Bukoba district (chiefly Bahaya) of northern Tanganyika, 4.3 children ever-born were reported on the average by women aged 45 years or over.[1]

SOCIAL CONDITIONS IN RELATION TO FERTILITY IN BUHAYA: KINSHIP AND POLITICAL STRUCTURE

The particular aspects of the kinship structure of the Bahaya and Baganda which may be supposed to effect the fertility of their women or the survival of their children will now be discussed. Before doing so, it is necessary to emphasize the fact that they belong to one type of kinship structure rather than to two distinct ones. The Nilotic and Nilo-Hamitic inhabitants of Uganda, e.g., the Lugbara, Alur, Lango or Teso, have a characteristically segmentary type of descent system with strongly organized patrilineal clans, divided sometimes into sub-clans, and always into lineages of

[1] Unpublished data provided by East African Statistical Department.

various orders of magnitude such as maximal, major and minimal segments which remain structurally connected throughout time. In such societies a man, his sons and grandsons tend to form a corporate local group, under the rule of its geneological senior, and control over marriages and their resultant offspring is very close.

Among the Interlucustrian Bantu, including both the Bahaya and Baganda, the clans tend to be more dispersed, and the local lineage is rarely a corporate group. The institution of chieftainship also cuts across the segmentary kinship organization, and leads to different allegiances and often to greater mobility of individual families. Added to this, the Bahaya and Baganda happen to live on the fertile shores of Lake Victoria, which expose them to contact with the outside world. They have been more affected by contacts with European influences and development than the Nilotic peoples to the north.

Compared to the northern Uganda tribes, the two tribes under discussion appear to be very similar in kinship organization. Comparing these two types with one another, it will be seen that the Baganda now have a more individual type of family than the Bahaya.

According to Cory and Hartnoll, the Bahaya are organized in a series of patrilineal clans and lineages. At the time of the introduction of German rule at the beginning of this century, the clan system formed the base of the political system; rule was in the hands of various clan heads. Above these clan heads were chiefs who themselves belonged to one or two ruling dynasties, thus forming a series of semi-autonomous chiefdoms. From leadership in the village to that in the district and over each chiefdom itself, political authority was based on descent. The Bahaya are divided into a large number of clans which are in turn divided into subclans and lineages, but none of these are corporate local groups. The hierarchical political system, based on villages and aggregates of villages, cross-cuts the clan system.

The Haya child takes its father's clan and belongs to his lineage. Additional boys are welcome as building up the strength of the local lineage or, at a higher level, of the royal dynasties. Girls, by their marriages, form alliances with neighbouring lineages, or are given to nobles or chiefs as wives in token of respect.

The patrilineal kinsman formerly took charge of the marriage of both boys and girls within the lineage. Even nowadays Cory reports that the father chooses a spouse for his sons as well as for his daughters.[1] A father still sometimes exercises his right to 'give' his daughter to a man in marriage, though there are various arrangements by which a marriage by elopement can be regularized. Yet the normal pattern is for the father to arrange the marriage of his daughter as soon as she has reached puberty. The bridewealth collected for the girl is divided among quite a wide circle

[1] Cory and Hartnoll. *Customary Law of the Haya Tribe*, 1945.

of relatives on the father's and mother's side.[1] The family control over the girl's marriage has supernatural sanction because the ancestral spirits are believed to punish the union with sterility if the payment is not so divided. In the case of a boy, the money for the bridewealth is collected among the patrilineal relatives and is given jointly. So much is marriage a matter of family arrangement that a younger brother or sister is not allowed to marry before his or her elder.

Cory, writing in 1945, makes a great point of the factor of consent by the boy's or girl's family as constituting an essential element in the legality of marriage. The father and mother must each take the girl publicly on their laps to signify their approval. Even in the case of a girl's elopement she must tell some of her relatives of her plan before she leaves and in the case of a secret wedding, described by Cory,[2] when a girl is married privately in order to avoid witchcraft, she must take her father's sister to show that the patrilineage gives consent. A girl may also marry with her brother's consent if her father refuses.[3] The consent of the lineage is necessary in the case of a remarriage. Here, as in other parts of East Africa, a man's lineage secures control of the reproductive powers of the girl by means of passing bridewealth, in theory fixed now at one goat, two barkcloths, one hoe and two calabashes of beer;[4] but in our sample 61 per cent gave money and only 10 per cent cattle or goats.

The marriage payment gives control over the child to the man's lineage. The birth of a boy is particularly required. As a rather unusual feature in Bantu society, the widow who has not borne a son to her husband may not remarry legally, but can only live in an unrecognized union with another man. Otherwise she should be inherited by the heir of the dead man or one of his other brothers. In the case of divorce the bridewealth is retained if the woman who asks for a divorce has already borne a son. So great are the claims of the marriage tie and the payment of the bridewealth that the first child born to a woman who remarries after divorce belongs to her previous husband. This child is known as a *bisisi* child. Similarly, the child of a woman by someone other than her husband after the birth of a child is a *bisisi* child and is given to the lineage of her husband.

All these structural features suggest that the Bahaya look on their women as reproductive assets, which pass from the control of the father's lineage to that of the husband (and then often to subsequent husbands), and that an increase of children is very much desired. These traditional values apparently remain operative, although factors such as the increase in value of land owing to the introduction of coffee as a perennial crop, and the increasing pressure on land, tend to create a situation in which the number of children desired is somewhat less than formerly.

[1] op cit., p. 59.
[2] op. cit., para. 350.
[3] op. cit., para. 362.
[4] op. cit., para. 265.

There are various recognized types of marriage in Buhaya. These are:

Customary Marriage. To contract a marriage of this kind, a man must pass bridewealth (*makulu*). He must obtain the consent of the girl's parents and of his own, as has been stated, and he must go through a ceremonial with several stages, including the ritual giving of consent by the parents of both sides of the family, and a feast.

As is common where the family retain strong control over the marriage of both boy and girl, there are alternative forms of marriage by which elopement and similar irregular types of union can afterwards be regularized. Examples of such practice are: the *kulehega*, or elopement followed later by the passage of bridewealth but without a marriage ceremony; the *kushutula*, or abduction of a girl without her consent; the *kuteza* by which the father's consent is obtained by a conditional curse put by the bridegroom on the girl (this forces the father's hand, since he believes that his daughter will be barren unless the curse is removed by the bridegroom); and lastly the *kunayisa*, or secret transfer of the girl to the bridgroom by the father's sister. All these forms of union are recognized as legal.

Christian Marriage. In this case either the Catholic or the Protestant marriage service is carried out, usually along with the main elements of a customary marriage ceremony described above, plus the passage of bridewealth.

Concubinage. It is presumed that concubines are women who cannot contract a legal marriage after the death of their first husband because they do not want to be inherited by his lineage, and they have not borne sons (see above).

In the present survey, 82 per cent of marriages for women were customary, and 84 per cent of men, whereas only 14 per cent of women's marriages were Christian, and 12 per cent of men.

Separation and Divorce. In the course of the survey we followed a distinction made by the Bahaya themselves between a marriage terminated through change in residence only (separation) and a marriage terminated through change in residence and a return of bridewealth to the man's family (divorce). The word 'divorce', though not perfect, is used because the return of bridewealth is regarded in the courts as evidence of termination of the marriage contract and is tantamount to legal separation. A man, partner to a woman whose first marriage was terminated through change in residence and the return of bridewealth, may not be sued for adultery. The courts do not grant a divorce decree, *per se.* Among the Bahaya, a woman whose first (or previous) marriage has been terminated by what we are calling divorce, may enter into a second marriage in which consent of her parents is obtained and bridewealth exchanged. It should be added that only in exceptional cases can such a second marriage be celebrated in and recognized by the Christian churches.

371

Polygyny

In Buhaya, polygyny is, except for the firmest of Protestants or those living in the vicinity of a mission, considered a normally desirable state of affairs. In point of fact, with the land usuage—and, as a contributory factor, the difficulty of maintaining more than one household on the average size plot—true polygyny is relatively rare. Many men have been married more than once, but these marriages are usually consecutive rather than simultaneous. Occasionally, men marry a second wife while their first wife is still present. However, after a year or so, one of the wives is likely to leave. In other words, there is some overlapping of wives but not for any length of time. Again, some women own their own land, normally through inheritance, and these women are often married. They will sometimes leave their husbands if the newly inherited land is in a village distant from that of their husbands. They may contract a marriage with a man in the same or a nearby village. In the latter event, husband and wife visit back and forth but maintain two households. The husband in this case will have his own land, wife and household, plus the other wife and her land. If a man acquires a new (additional) piece of cultivated land (*kibanja*) he will often marry and establish another wife on this second plot. There is, then, a substantial gap between the attitude toward polygyny and the number of men who are able to maintain polygynous households. The successive marriages may satisfy this to a certain extent. With respect of fertility, the few true polygynous households appear to have at least the normal, if not more than the normal, number of children. An economic factor may enter here as well. A richer man with two or more cultivated plots and several wives is likely to be able to provide his wives with superior conditions of living and better diets.

Sororal polygyny is relatively rare among the Bahaya, though they are not against it if a woman is barren. She or her family bring a younger sister, or brother's daughter, or a father's brother's daughter, as a second wife to provide her husband with children. When this happens, the barren first wife stays in the household. In point of fact, the instances of this are very rare: only a few women who have not had children are actually co-wives with a younger sister. Similarly, the levirate, while quite possible as far as the Bahaya are concerned, occurs very rarely and even in these instances, a man will rarely take his brother's widow as his own wife.

Age at Marriage

The average age at marriage in the survey village has not yet been computed, but the impression from the maternity history interviewing was that girls at present are usually married between the ages of 15 and 18. The estimated average age at puberty was 13.6 years in the survey.[1] The

---

[1] Age at puberty was estimated by asking when breasts began to round, and adding one year. The validity of this procedure has not been tested, and is subject to serious doubt.

average age at first pregnancy among ever-pregnant women was 19.1 years. As regards women in the older age groups, some of them—those now 60 plus—explained that when there was a new chief, he often selected attractive young girls to become concubines. Parents of potential concubines, i.e., of girls considered attractive, would marry off their daughters earlier than they would otherwise, to prevent them being made concubines. Thus, a number of women said, 'I was married young', meaning before puberty. When this happened the girl was brought up in her father-in-law's house, but the consummation of the marriage was delayed until after puberty.

A man's first marriage is most often contracted when he is in his mid-twenties. His bride for first marriage will be a young woman several years his junior. In subsequent marriages, however, he will marry as young a woman as possible. If he contracts a marriage at 50, his new wife may be as much as 20 or 30 years his junior. The Bahaya believe that if a middle-aged man marries a young woman he will beget children, whereas if he marries a woman nearer his own age he will not. Attractiveness and personality aside, girls who come from average-to-prosperous families will marry bridegrooms near their own age at a first marriage, while those who come from poor-to-average families will be more likely to marry an older and possibly less desirable man. On the other hand, an older man is often richer and able to compete on that basis with younger men.

Emphasis on Virginity Prior to Marriage

Premarital pregnancies, as distinguished from extra-marital ones, are very rare. In the course of interviewing the 302 women in the Buhembe survey and in collecting genealogies among 287 women in Kishenge, one case only came to our attention. One case also occurred in the maternity clinic at Ndolage, a Swedish mission hospital. There is deep shame attached to a woman who becomes pregnant before marriage, the children of such a union have a special name, and unless the father of the child marries her, it is extremely unlikely that she (or her father for her) will be able to contract a favourable marriage. To say that there is no premarital promiscuity would be rash, but mothers or grandmothers keep an eye on adolescent daughters, brides are literally inspected by appointed members of the bridegroom's family before the wedding, and one can fairly safely take the marriage age of girls as indication of their entrance into the child-bearing period.

Stability of Marriage

Buhaya marriages, of whatever sort, can and should be legally registered—a great difference from the Buganda situation where, as will be seen, only Christian marriages are so registered. Divorce can be obtained in the African court with arbitration concerning the return of the bridewealth.

373

A majority of the married women in our sample had been married only once; but a substantial proportion (104 out of 339) had entered into a second marriage. Very few (14), however, had gone on to a third marriage. While we say that it is normal for a woman to be married only once, it is clearly not unusual for one to be married a second time. Second marriages are, however, by no means confined to the younger generation. Women whose first marriages were contracted in the nineteenth century were remarried following the death, separation or divorce (return of bridewealth) of their first spouse. Further, there seems to be a tendency for a first marriage to terminate after a few years, but to be followed by a more lasting second marriage.

The interval between these marriages is of especial interest for our purposes. Some women remarried the same year, but the modal pattern was remarriage in the year following the termination of the first marriage. The size of the group not yet remarried diminishes year by year up to 10 years, (figures given below). There is a small scatter beyond 10 years, including one woman who told us that she had remarried after an interval of 40 years, but the majority of women remarried in the period one through 10 years following the termination of their first marriage; the median is in the two-year class. All things considered, this interval probably does not affect conception rates. One might argue that, even if it were larger, it would still not do so, since the constraints put on a formerly married woman are much less than for a girl who has not been married. Negotiations for a second marriage are less rigorous than those for the first, and it seems possible that frequent cohabitation with some man will usually lead to marriage.

The figures for the interval between marriages are:

Intervals in years between marriages	0	1	2	3	4	5	6	7	8	9	10	11+
Number of women remarrying in each interval	15	34	21	16	9	6	4	4	3	4	1	7

According to Table 84, 35 per cent of the married women and 60 per cent of the married men in the Buhaya sample have remarried, and the number of unions contracted successively by the men is very large. In the present sample, 39 per cent of all the men questioned had contracted one union, 28 per cent two unions, 15 per cent three unions, 8 per cent four unions, 2 per cent five unions and 2 per cent six unions. The largest number by one man was nine marriages.

Extra-marital Intercourse

It is somewhat surprising, in the light of the material presented above, to learn that the Bahaya have a reputation for loose marriage morals.

374

The women are said to be unusually independent, and Buhaya prostitutes are said to travel far afield, e.g., to Buganda by lake steamer. It is one of the constant complaints of the African government authorities that they are not allowed to arrest women getting into boats, and the subject of prostitution is constantly discussed by both white and black in Bukoba.

Exact figures are impossible to obtain, and it is probable that these regular prostitutes are a very small proportion of the female population. It must be recognized, however, that the proportion of absentee women in the sample villages is high by African standards, e.g., 13 per cent absent women compared to 15 per cent absent men, and this might argue a degree of independent movement of women which is unusual.

The cause of this type of prostitution, if indeed it proves to be so common as reputed, is being investigated. The proportion of women to men is high. Under present conditions it is difficult for young men to get enough land to marry early; this may be another cause for the movement of women from their home villages. Cory suggests that the attitude toward adultery on the part of a woman is more lenient than that common among Bantu peoples. He suggests that divorce is only given in the case of adultery when the woman can be proved to have been unfaithful many times.[1] Our observations on the institution of *bisisi* children tends to confirm this suggestion.

Although some Bahaya women have extra-marital pregnancies, it is virtually impossible for them to have an illegitimate child in the European sense of the term. A child always has a pater. There is a strict and acknowledged distinction between physiological (genitor) and sociological (pater) paternity. Ideally, here as elsewhere, they coincide, but if they do not the pater entertains all rights over the child. A man acquires these overriding rights through the operation of *bisisi*, and children who enter a man's family in this fashion can be known as *bisisi* children. The term *bisisi* comes from the phrase *kuiya sisisi* which literally translated is 'to remove or cleanse from the condition of having had a child'. This refers to the first post-delivery intercourse and has ritual overtones for a man, establishing his inalienable right to the woman's next child. This right was initially established when the marriage was consummated and is reinstated, in a sense, after the birth of each successive child. A man does not automatically acquire a right to all his wife's progeny, although by implication in the ideal marriage this would be the case. The rights of genitor do not supersede those of the pater, no matter how separated in time or space. If a child is born years later and in a different country, it still belongs to the pater, or his family, and not to the genitor. In a literal application of the term all children born after their parents have had the right-establishing intercourse, are by virtue of that right, *bisisi* children. In practice, the term *bisisi* is applied only to a child whose genitor is not

[1] Cory, Hartnoll, op. cit., para. 424.

375

his pater, a child conceived by a man who is not the woman's first or prior husband.

In Buhaya, where a third of the women remarry after the termination of their first marriage, this means that the first child of each of these new marriages must be returned to the husband of the first marriage, or his family. This rule, that a child of a marriage shall not belong to the partners of that marriage, seems improper to Europeans and, through mission education, to some Bahaya. The most recent expression of this reaction is a ruling of the chief's council to the effect that the rights of a *bisisi* child shall not be acknowledged in the courts. Parenthetically it may be noted that the traditional rule figures in some of the numerous cases of litigation over land. A child, though not previously acknowledged, may after his pater's death claim—by virtue of the *bisisi* connexion—to be his heir to the land or to have a legitimate right to a share. Since land is so important and litigation so frequent, it is often difficult in the courts to weigh the respective rights of a man's own children as against those of a *bisisi* child. The ruling is designed to remove this problem.

If a woman is impregnated by a man other than her husband (for example while visiting her parents in their village), the fact of this extra-marital pregnancy does not necessarily terminate the marriage because the child is the husband's, regardless of physiological parentage, and will be reared in the husband's household in any event. Or, if a man is sterile, his wife may conceive a child which for all social purposes is his. Viewed in this fashion, the exercise of rights-over-children can be seen as a factor which may lead to marital stability.

However, most of the *bisisi* children of which we have knowledge through genealogies are the first-born children of second marriages. Not infrequently they are returned to a man who is not the genitor of other living children. Cause and effect here are perhaps somewhat delicate, since it seems quite possible that sterility or barrenness or the deaths of children born are important in assessing the break-up of a marriage. This leads, rather indirectly, into the very specialized use of the *bisisi* principle with respect to a man's need for heirs. All men want at least one heir and the Bahaya say that a man cannot die without heirs, meaning that one of his wives must at some time have a child which will be his even if it is engendered after his death. Short of marrying another wife in the hopes of an heir, and this is not always possible, a man can plan to have a *bisisi* child. He will go to a woman who has been delivered and is thus of proven fertility, and persuade her to give him *bisisi* rights. If she does—and it is her sole right to state which man has had access to her after delivery—the next child becomes his and, after it is weaned, will be sent or returned to him. This use of the *bisisi* principle means at least two things; it is a rather special form of adoption (there are no orphans in Buhaya) enabling a man to have children; and no woman, whatever the circumstances, is without a father for her child.

376

In point of fact, there are few instances in which a woman may give *bisisi* rights to a man other than her husband, and continue, particularly after the *bisisi* child has been sent away, to be married to her first husband. The *bisisi* father can be sued for adultery. However, if a woman has several children without having remarried, the first child goes to her former husband while the remaining children go to their respective *bisisi* fathers. Since the woman does not suffer the sanctions employed in European society against mothers of illegitimate children, the *bisisi* principle is said to lead to immoral behaviour and is associated by Christian missionaries with the presumed problem of prostitution.

The termination of marriages through separation or divorce often results from a quarrel or some cause of disagreement between husband and wife or members of their respective families. In this case, a woman may well regret the obligation to present her former husband with a child. The sanction for doing so is strong; that all later children are expected to die if she does not. Given the high frequency of second marriages and the high infant mortality, this happens in fact often enough to convince the majority of people that the children do die if the *bisisi* child is not returned. There are at least two Bahaya solutions to this problem. If a woman who knows that she plans to leave her husband is pregnant, and has planned her second marriage, she will give her husband-to-be rights after the birth of her first husband's child, thus obviating the first husband's *bisisi* rights. The next child belongs, in this case, to the pater-genitor, her second husband. Or she may abort her next pregnancy and since the pregnancy counts, whether or not it terminates in a living birth, the *bisisi* rights of the first husband are nullified. Two cases—but only two cases—of such practice were discovered in our sample.

The chief inferences to be drawn from this discussion are that women in Buhaya have no fear of extra-marital pregnancies, and ordinarily have no motivation to induce abortion in case of such pregnancy.

With respect to maternity histories and genealogies, the *bisisi* principle has very definite implications for the classification of children by parentage. It is perfectly possible for a man who has never been a genitor to be the pater of several children, or for a man who is not a pater to be the genitor of several children. Since a man will reply to a question involving his children in terms of his role as a pater, the inquiry needs to be conducted with some care. Similarly, a woman replying to a question on the number of her children will include in her enumeration those of her children for whom the husband is pater. Thus, if she has had, literally, three children by her first marriage and four by her second, she will state that she had four by her first and three by her second. If she has had only one child and that by her second marriage, she will state, if not specifically questioned, that it is the child of her first marriage. In our genealogical records of several hundred marriages, 47 children were especially reported as *bisisi*.

The Bahaya are very fond of children and deserve to have many. To ask
a woman how many children she would like is meaningless. The women
so questioned in the survey tended to answer 'as many as I can', or to
name an impossible number such as '50' or '100'. Very few thought
specifically in terms of 'I now have three children and would like two more'.
At the same time, they tend to count five or six living children as 'many'.
A woman with five children said, 'I have many children'.

Possessing real property in the form of land to be passed from one generation to the next, all men want at least one son to nominate as heir.
Since a man with many daughters is accounted happy and fortunate,
children of both sexes are equally desired. Hence, women who are barren
are pitied and a man who has died without heirs (obuchueke) will frequently
have this phrase as a referent included in his name; this is one of the first
things one says of such a man. However, the Bahaya have a saying that
a man is never heirless (omushaija tachueka), referring here again to a man's
inalienable right to his wife's offspring regardless of their physical parentage.

Households tend to be small, with an average of only 3.4 persons per
hut, owing largely to high infant mortality and the frequent breaking
up of families. A household which contains four or six children comes
to be regarded as one with 'many children'. While this kind of value
judgment is made with reference to a specific household, it is not translated into a standard—so that the majority of women think of four or
six as an 'ideal family' and one to which they would approximate if they
could.

With the Bahaya system of fixed cultivation, land planted with perennial
crops is at a premium. Unless a man is a fortunate heir or has considerable
capital, he is unable to expand the basic land owned and occupied. Cultivated plots are small (average size 1.5 acres) and productivity is already
relatively high. Therefore, an increase in family size does not lead to
increase in production. The case of the Bahaya is thus substantially
different from that of the Bantu relying on seasonal crops; where, other
things being equal, the larger the family unit, the more the labour available, and through the availability of labour the greater the potential food
production. With the Bahaya, production is relatively fixed, particularly
with respect to subsistence, and the larger the family the larger the consumption. Similarly a cultivated plot as a small-household-supporting unit
can in effect be bequeathed to only one heir and only very limited fragmentation is possible. However, these relations were not explicitly developed
by our informants.

The co-ordination of all this with the stated desire for children makes
the means of 'some' and 'many' rather uncertain. All Bahaya want

some children, and not to have them contravenes all ideas of family continuity.[1]

Nevertheless the Bahaya, like other Bantu peoples, practise some voluntary restriction on childbirth by the use of the tabooed period during the suckling of the first child. The Bahaya have a pragmatic attitude toward the common Bantu custom of abstention from intercourse while the woman is nursing a child. They do not want another pregnancy to intervene before the first child may be properly weaned, and this is the primary consideration affecting their abstention, rather than a ritually enforced abstract notion. After the birth of each child, there is a ritual intercourse which establishes or re-establishes (in all chiefdoms except Kiziba) a man's inalienable right to his wife's next child, a right which became his initially at the consummation of their marriage. This is called *kuiyabisisi*. The fact that it must be re-established after the birth of each child is one of the reasons for *bisisi* children, as already noted. The stated time for this is eight days after delivery of the child. However, one informant stated that if a man does not trust his wife, he will go to her almost immediately after delivery, but that if he does, he may wait several months or even a year—implying that the couple abstain from intercourse even for ritual purposes for a fairly lengthy period after the birth of each child.

If the couple have had several children and know that the wife does not normally conceive while she is nursing a child, they will, after the first ritual intercourse, follow their normal practice. If it is the first child, and they do not know how long it may be before the woman will conceive again, they must be more careful. If the young couple are living in a house with the man's parents, the parents will try to restrain the young couple, but, so my informants stated, not always successfully. The Bahaya have a local herb which they use to stimulate lactation if the mother's milk fails owing to a second pregnancy. Or, if the family have cattle, the first baby will be weaned onto cow's milk. Children are fed small amounts of solid food from six months and are weaned between a year and 18 months. Under the circumstances one might expect either a short interval between children or, at present, some knowledge of contraceptives. Neither of these appear to be the case.

The Bahaya, on all and sundry occasions, will reckon the interval

[1] At the same time the margin between 'some' and 'many' is not really large. Thus 'some' children are two or three, while 'many' are five or six. In this discussion I have been speaking of the great majority of peasant cultivators who form roughly 99 per cent of the population. However, the very top members of the ruling clan (the Bakama and *balangila*), have, even today in spite of the mission pressure, very large families. Most of the present Bakama are half-siblings of some fifty to eighty children. These large families of the Bakama (less large today) are not the result of very high fertility per woman but rather the result of the number of wives and concubines which a Mukama had. Their average conception rate, if memories are to be trusted with respect to the genealogies of the Bukama of this and the preceding generations, was low. Most wives of the Bakama had a single child or at most two.

between children at two years or more. It is true that one very rarely sees a mother with several small children; three children under six is a maximum, again indicating either that children are spaced by some means or other, or that infant mortality is high. (It will be seen from the tables that about one-fourth of all children in the sample area died under one year.) On the other hand, there is almost no evidence that the Bahaya use contraceptives.

However, the low frequency of true polygyny poses problems for the majority of monogamous households, and in this connexion we must again mention prostitution. The Bahaya are famed for their prostitutes, although most of the fame stems from the external ones—the number of Bahaya women who go as prostitutes to the larger East African towns is perhaps commonly exaggerated. The situation may be different as regards internal prostitution, but here one must be careful to distinguish casual contacts from active solicitation in which ability to pay is the prime factor. However, the belief that children should be spaced in a society where the solution of polygyny is rare may be conducive to local prostitution.

On the other hand the use of contraceptives in the modern sense is practically unknown and induced abortions are rare. In the course of interviewing Bahaya women and in discussing the matter with Bahaya informants and with medical officers and nursing sisters, very little specific information has come to my attention regarding either the use of contraceptives or the inducement of abortions. With the exception of one woman (out of some 300) interviewed by Dr. Joseph Mutahangalwa, all women denied knowledge of abortifacients. Miss Boeash, in consultation with her servant, a Muhaya woman, found several herbs which are considered to be abortifacients. Whether they are such in fact, and the extent of their use, remains obscure. There is no clinical record of induced abortions at Bukoba General Hospital, Kalema Maternity Clinic or Ndolage Hospital. There are records of women who have aborted, but these are believed to be spontaneous. A Muhaya midwife at Kalema has said that prostitutes will take large doses of magnesium sulphate to induce abortion, but no records of an actual case appear.

With regard to contraceptives, there is no record of any woman, or man, having enquired for these or information regarding these at any of the hospitals. This is countered by its opposite: a considerable number of women questioned said that they used medicine in an attempt to become pregnant. There are a number of cases of women coming to the hospitals to be treated for sterility. A few informants intensively questioned on this topic who might be expected to give a fairly realistic answer, say that they do not know of anyone using contraceptives. On the other hand, there are some prostitutes who have been in the large East African towns who may well know of their use, returning and bringing that knowledge. It seems quite probable that a knowledge of contraceptives would be welcomed by a couple who do not want the wife to become pregnant again until their child is weaned. One suspects that they would be used under these circumstances, but probably such usage is limited due to lack of sophistication. Contraceptives or induced abortions cannot, apparently, be considered as having any appreciable effect on present fertility rates.

SOCIAL CONDITIONS IN RELATION TO FERTILITY IN BUGANDA: KINSHIP AND POLITICAL STRUCTURE

As has been explained earlier, the traditional kinship structure of the Baganda is in many ways similar to that of the Bahaya. The people were divided into patrilineal clans and lineages with recognized clan heads and centres of origin. These clans were arranged in order of precedence which determined social status and the right to carry out certain court functions, and the kings themselves came from a royal dynasty. As in most societies of this type, there seems to have been a desire to build up the lineage of the house by the birth of children and to make alliances with important groups by judicious marriages. Girls could be given by their male relatives in marriage and boys were dependent on their patrilineal relatives for marriage payment.

But the political structure of Buganda was much more centralized than that of Buhaya. By the middle of the nineteenth century, Buganda was a kingdom acknowledging one king rather than a series of multiple kingdoms, and the authority of the king and the chiefs appointed by him came to be stronger than that of the clan heads. Children tended to be attached to chiefs for education and support rather than to senior relatives. The king acquired the power to give out land to his faithful subjects and these strips of land might be far away from the clan centre.

The arrival of the Europeans affected the kinship structure in three important ways. First, the adherents of the new religions, Catholicism, Protestantism and Mohammedanism, engaged in bitter and protracted fighting at the end of the nineteenth century and this led to a wide dispersal of people. Secondly, land which had formerly been held temporarily at the king's pleasure was given out by the British administration in freehold tenure to the chiefs then occupying it, and this led to further movement and the regrouping of relatives round the new landowners. Clan centres continued to be recognized and are so recognized today, but there was a wide dispersal of clan members over the country. The villages that have been settled longest probably have a history of little more than fifty years and the sample village is one of these. Individual homesteads rather than groupings of extended family homes became common. The lineages of the landowners tended to remain corporate bodies in relation to landownership and distribution, but the lineage ties of peasants tended to become looser and looser.

Thirdly, Christianity took immediate hold in this part of Uganda and made many changes in the kinship structure. It caused a big drop in the frequency of polygamous marriages, and some think that the present rate of polygamy is, if anything, higher than that which obtained in the early days of missionary work in the country. The inheritance of widows ceased and is practically never carried out now. Christian marriage was recognized legally but customary marriage was not so recognized. This made it difficult for a man to obtain a divorce in the case of a customary union.

Furthermore, the central authority of the Buganda Government enabled it to pass legislation of a very summary character which is still effective, such as, for instance, the rule giving the guardianship of children to the man, whatever the cause of divorce or desertion and whether the children are casually begotten or born in wedlock.[1]

It would be true to say that most Baganda still desire to have children and to build up their family. The legal position of the father is very strong on account of the Guardianship Law just described. He, or the members of his lineage, can always acquire possession of children, however casually begotten. Nevertheless, marriage appears to be a much more individual affair than in Buhaya. The bridewealth (*mutwalo*) is not divided among relatives in such regular ways, although the mother, the father's sister and the brother of the girl can claim presents at the marriage. The marriage payment itself tends to be provided by the individual efforts of the young man rather than by his whole family. Senior relatives in a wealthier or in a more old-fashioned family claim children begotten by a man belonging to the lineage whether in wedlock or not and feel a responsibility for them, but this responsibility is becoming more and more limited to the man himself and such of his own brothers as may agree to help him. It is perhaps significant that under present conditions the genitor always claims the child, not the pater. In other respects, too, the absence of a strong system of corporate lineages is even more complete in Buganda than it is in Buhaya.

THE INSTITUTION OF MARRIAGE

Marriage and other unions among the Baganda consists of three main types. These include:

Customary Marriage (*kiganda* marriage). This is the traditional form of marriage which is carried out with the consent of the parents or guardians of the girl, and usually those of the boy; with some form of ceremony carried out in public; and with the passage of goods, usually money, between the bridegroom's family and that of the bride, in the form of bridewealth and customary presents of different kinds.

Christian Marriage. Christian marriage is celebrated with a church

[1] Buganda Guardianship Law, 1904.

ceremony, and is usually followed by a new-style feast such as a tea party, and often by a customary feast as well. Some payment is usually made to the girl's parents, and the cost of a modern wedding (which includes white dress and veil for the bride, special clothes for the bridesmaids, special clothes for the bridegroom, the taking of a photograph, a wedding cake and the furnishing of a house with crockery and so forth) nearly always exceeds the cost of a customary marriage. The parents' consent is usually, although not necessarily, involved.

Muslim Marriage. Muslim marriage is celebrated with a Muslim ceremony followed by the customary feast, and bridewealth is passed. The consent of the girl's relatives is necessary. The wedding is now often as elaborate and expensive as a Christian wedding, since Muslim brides have adopted the white dress and white veil of the Christian wedding, the wedding cake, and the photograph.

Of these three forms of marriage, the Christian and the Muslim confer the highest social status, since they are generally associated with the biggest display of wealth. L. P. Mair, writing in 1940, associates Christian marriage with membership of the wealthy class. The *kiganda* marriage is less expensive and may be preferred on that account, and also because it is an easier union to break if necessary. Thus, men and women who reckon themselves Protestants, Catholics, or Muslims, may prefer to contract a customary marriage, and it will be seen that according to the survey data the majority of all unions were of this type.

Temporary Unions

These consist of the 'friend' relationship (*mukwano*). This is a tie which varies from a casual union of a few weeks or months to a more permanent tie, in which a man and woman may live like a married couple in one house for some years. Such a union is, however, clearly distinguished from marriage by the Baganda since it is contracted without the consent of the girl's relatives, and there is no ceremony or transfer of goods. It is probably for this reason that so many women in the Entebbe area are recorded in the 1948 census as being single although the childbirth rate in this area is no lower than in any other.

The *mukwano* union is common in the case of a young man who is too poor to marry, and who contracts a union for some years, often with an older and childless woman; or in the case of a man who falls in love with a second woman, but yet does not wish to leave his first wife. In suburban areas, young girls may be persuaded to leave home without their parents' consent on the promise of clothes, or other presents. Their union will then be referred to as a *mukwano* tie.

The *mukwano* union may lead to marriage in some cases, and there is often something of an element of trial about it. It can probably be distinguished from the entirely casual unions contracted by prostitutes or by those who are described as being 'free' (*bwerere*) or from those described as 'just wandering about' (*kutambula butambusi*). The proportion of these different types of unions is shown in the figures below:

TABLE 80.

	Number	Total	Percentage distribution				
			Christian	Muslim	Customary	Mukwano	Unstated
Women	333	100	30	8	45	13	4
Men	367	100	26	10	46	8	10

Polygamy and Monogamy

The Baganda formerly practised polygamy, although such unions are said to have been limited to the wealthy. Nowadays, polygamy is an accepted institution only in the case of Muslims and pagans, and those who admit that they are pagans form a very small group in Buganda today. It is true that a number of so-called Christians marry two women whether openly or not, but the expense of present-day housing makes it difficult for a man to provide a second wife with a house of her own, as used to be common in the past, and Baganda women resent sharing their home with a second wife unless she is a woman who is closely related. True polygamy, in the sense of a man living openly with two or more women with the legal status of wife, is therefore rare.

More common is the situation of the man who has his main wife in one village and a permanent liaison with a woman in another village. The man who brings a second wife into the same home risks the break-up of his marriage, although some polygamous unions seem to be peaceful, especially if two sisters are married to one man or if a relative of the first wife is brought in as a second wife because the first is barren. Fertility is probably affected in the case of a polygamous union, especially where the second wife lives in another village. The survey figures are on too small a scale to be convincing, but here the figure for live births for women married polygamously was 1.6 per head and for monogamously married women 2.0 per head.

The Age of Marriage

It appears that women formerly married just after puberty, and the estimated average age of puberty is 13.8 years according to the present survey. But the age of marriage for women is tending to rise and must be reckoned as between 16 and 20 nowadays. The girls in wealthier families

384

often stay at boarding schools until 17 or 18 years old, and there were one or two of these in the village. Even in peasant families some attend day schools up until 16 or 17. The average age at the first pregnancy was 18.5 years in the present sample.

The marriage age of men appears always to have been higher than that for women. Now a man legally comes of age in the sense of being able to bind himself by contract at 20 years (cf. the Coming of Age Law 1920). He has, however, to get money together in order to marry. As has been said, the marriage payment itself is not high in this area. One hundred to two hundred shillings are common figures for the *mutwalo* (or bridewealth) as against a figure of about 2,000 shillings—given for Acholi or Alur. Nevertheless the young man or his family are responsible for the cost of the wedding in most cases, and he must also provide a house. Figures given for an educated man's wedding are in the neighbourhood of £100, plus £50 to £100 for a very simple house. For a peasant it would not be uncommon to spend £30 on the wedding and £20 for the cheapest kind of thatched house. For these reasons, the marriage age of a young man is often between 25 and 30.

Pre-marital intercourse by girls was formerly strongly condemned, and is still considered very bad conduct in rural areas. A girl who was pregnant before marriage used to be isolated and made to eat by herself and this is still apparently sometimes done in rural areas. Special rites are performed when such a child is born because it is considered to be in a dangerous state. The girl's lover should participate in these rites, and her parents endeavour to induce him to marry her. Even in suburban areas, where pre-marital intercourse is regarded tolerantly, it is still considered difficult for a girl to make a Christian or customary marriage with a man of good family or to find a husband either in a Christian or a customary union if she has already had a child, and many such girls drift into a series of casual unions as a consequence.

The age of consent for a girl is fixed by Buganda law. By the Buganda Adultery and Fornication Law, a man can be given up to two years imprisonment for sleeping with an unmarried girl over 12 and under 15. If he abducts a girl under 20 without her parent's consent, he is liable to a fine of 20 shillings or two months' imprisonment.

Stability of Marriage

Under present conditions it is extremely rare for a Ganda marriage to be dissolved in court. The Protectorate High Court has ruled that an African Christian cannot contract a marriage according to Ganda custom. A man who contracts a customary union after a Christian monogamous marriage is technically liable to a charge of bigamy and five years' imprisonment, although such penalties do not appear to be exacted. The Protectorate Courts will grant divorce in the case of a Christian monogamous marriage, but it is only the High Court which can do so and this makes it a very unusual procedure for an ordinary African. Nor will the Churches bless a second union after a divorce. The Buganda courts cannot give divorce, unlike those of Bukoba where divorce takes place according to customary law, with the return of the bridewealth. A Muslim wishing to divorce his wife takes the case to a local malim who arranges the return of the bride-wealth (*mayala*).

Under such conditions a marriage according to Ganda law breaks up by one partner simply leaving the other. The community then waits to see if he or she will decide to return. During this time the deserted partner may continue to declare that he or she is still married and that the spouse has just gone to visit his or her people, while the village may consider the marriage as being permanently broken. After some time it will be clear to all that the couple are not going to come together again. These are the cases described as 'separation' in the tables given below. The point has some significance in relation to marital statistics since, in the absence of a clear-cut legal act by which marriage can be said to be at an end, infor-mants often differ on the exact marital status of a couple.

Common causes of the break-up of a marriage are quarrelling, infidelity on the part of the woman, or bringing in another wife on the part of the man. The sterility of a union may also lead to its dissolution.

Marriage among the Baganda is thought to be very unstable; the figures collected in the sample village show that, of completed unions, 18 per cent ended in separation in the case of women, and 30 per cent in the case of men. Even though these figures are likely to be too low rather than too high, they are very similar to those collected by Barnes in Nyasa-land.[1]

The marriage records from our sample give the following distributions. In the case of 293 women: 79 per cent with one union, 15 per cent with two unions, 1 per cent with three unions, 2 per cent unstated, 2 per cent unmarried. In the case of 279 men: 40 per cent with one union, 29 per cent with two unions, 7 per cent with three unions, 8 per cent unstated. The average length of the 229 first unions was 9.6 years.

Though there are many marriages in Buganda which would be reckoned as stable according to English standards, yet amongst those who separate, the length of union seems to be unusually short. For instance, 16 per cent of the separated women and 9 per cent of the separated men had remained with their spouses only one year before the separation.

It is difficult to verify the statement so frequently made by Baganda that marriage is much less stable than it was in the old days. It would require far larger numbers of older women in the sample in order to be able to establish the point. It is likely, however, that some factors have tended to have this effect: (a) the frequent absence of men doing work in the

[1] J. A. Barnes, 'Marriage in a Changing Society', *Rhodes-Livingstone Paper 20*, 1951.

towns; (b) easy communications by means of bus services; (c) the desire of women, and especially young women, for the clothing sold in the towns as an inducement to contract temporary liaisons with men who will dress them as they wish; (d) the concept of individual and, in fact, romantic love as presented in European films. Many young people now reject the traditional arranged marriage, with family approval on both sides. In fact, some of those living in casual liaisons without their parents' approval feel that they are behaving in a very advanced European fashion. This practice tends to be called 'going with a man just for love'. Religious affiliations apparently make very little difference to the stability of marriage, as will be seen from the following figures.

Men	Of 97 Christian marriages	31 per cent broke up.
	Of 38 Muslim marriages	45 per cent broke up.
	Of 20 Customary marriages	30 per cent broke up.
Women	Of 100 Christian marriages	20 per cent broke up.
	Of 26 Muslim marriages	8 per cent broke up.
	Of 193 Customary marriages	20 per cent broke up.

It also appears to make very little difference to the stability of marriage whether bridewealth has been passed or not, but it must be remembered that in Buganda the cost of the wedding, which can never be recovered, is usually higher than the amount of the bridewealth, which at any rate in the old days, could be recovered.

It is possible that unstable marriages and casual unions have an effect not only on fertility but also on the survival rate of children. There is some evidence that children of a broken marriage, here as elsewhere, tend to be less well looked after. By Buganda law, the child always belongs to the father or to his lineage, although a girl under 18 and a boy under 7 may remain with the mother to be cared for if both parties wish this to be done. However, it is sometimes difficult for a woman to remarry when she has children of a previous marriage with her, owing to the present-day cost of rearing children (see below). Such a woman may, therefore, leave her children with her mother or brother, or with her ex-husband or one of his female relatives. Where children are cared for by relatives other than the father there may be delay in the proper treatment of illness. To get to the hospital may mean a heavy expense. The cost of a car from Kisoze village to Kampala, for instance, is equal to about one month's unskilled wages. The guardian delays before incurring such a heavy outlay, or sends to ask for the father's permission. Doctors at Mulago hospital had the impression that a large proportion of children brought too late to the hospital were living not with their parents but with relatives.

Again, where the children of a broken marriage remain with the father and are cared for by a step-mother, it is said that the latter treats her step-children less well than her own children as regards food. Here again, it is those who buy food rather than grow it who begin to count expense in a way that would have been unusual in the old days. Women say that a step-mother will give her children the ordinary foods, but will not give them meat, milk and sugar or other foods which she has to buy with money. In the same way, a woman who keeps her children with her in their early years will find difficulty either if she remains alone or with her own relatives, or if she marries a new husband. The children are the financial responsibility of·their father. Their mother, if left alone, cannot find money for food, clothing or schooling. These are all results of the introduction of a money economy and of new standards of living that can only be satisfied by the payment of money.

ATTITUDES TO FAMILY INCREASE OR FAMILY LIMITATION IN BUGANDA

Restrictions on Childbearing

Baganda as a whole desire children intensely. Barren women are treated with pity, and in village areas often look depressed. It is said that many women employed in the towns as ayahs for European and Indian children originally left home since they failed to bear children, possibly after marrying more than one man. There is at least a suggestion in our data that women who lose many children tend to be deserted by their husbands, and cases of husbands taking a second wife because the first had failed to bear a child are relatively common. Medical practitioners in the Kampala area say that they are often approached by women who ask for help because they are 'barren', although in some cases these patients have only gone two or three years without having a child.

It might be thought that women would be less desirous of bearing children, since in the event of a broken marriage the children invariably belong to the husband or his family (cf. the Buganda Guardianship Law). This is so, even if the mother is a relatively educated woman such as a teacher or a hospital nurse and has cared for the upbringing of her son until the statutory age of 7 years. But such women seem, nevertheless, to want to bear children and to lavish great affection on them, although they accept the father's guardianship of the child. They say that it is an affair of money. Who else but the child's own father will pay for its school fees when it becomes older and who else will find the money to clothe it? Men also want children and their families are glad to have them, whether boys or girls. Peasants want the help of children in the house, but it seems likely that the possession of a large household is thought desirable in itself since in the old days it was a sign of wealth and high status. Childless couples sometimes exert traditional kinship rights which enable them to adopt the children of a brother or other near relative, and in such instances the actual parentage of the child is often concealed.

The question for those interested in fertility trends is, therefore, not whether the Baganda want children, since we have seen that both men and women do, and that the community as a whole is worried at the supposedly low fertility rate of Baganda of the present day. The point is rather whether the size of family desired is now smaller than it was and whether the people know any means of limiting its size, should they wish to do so.

It is clear that Baganda living in the towns are beginning to worry about the cost of very large families. The main cause of the changing attitudes of this very small minority is the rising standard of living and the need to pay school fees. Where an extra mouth merely means a slightly smaller share of food from the common dish, the 'cost' of an extra child does not seem to be counted. In fact, peasants find it difficult to give any figures of their family expenses in this way. But expenses which consist of school fees, clothing, bedding and crockery can be reckoned up, and are so reckoned, and it is these costs which are revolutionizing Ganda kinship ties, making step-parents unwilling to look after the children of a spouse by a previous match and brothers less willing to feed their brothers' children. It would probably be true to say that children are still wanted by the educated African, but not in such large numbers as before. Many of those mothers who managed to answer the question in the survey as to the number of children they wanted said automatically, '10'; but some of those who thought, said with much hesitation, 'four or five'.

In the family of an agricultural worker, with cash income of 800 to 1,000 shillings per year (half of which may be received from sale of cash crops, and half from work for wages), the estimated expenditure for each child would be about 100 shillings per year for a boy of 5 to 10 years, and perhaps 116 shillings for a 15-year old boy—to provide clothes, bedding, plate and tea cup, and purchased food (tea, sugar, and meat). In the family of an urban labourer with similar cash income, it can be estimated that the increased cost of food needing to be purchased might rise for boys at various ages, as follows: at 5 years, 173 shillings; at 10 years, 209 shillings; at 15 years, 219 shillings—exclusive of school fees, for children in school, at 30 to 50 shillings per child per year. Expenditures for children in upper economic classes, with greater allowance of clothes, use of a mattress and sheets, and higher standards for food (e.g., including milk) as well as more exclusive dependence on purchased foods are much higher. The expected expenditures at this level may rise to nearly 500 shillings for a 5-year old boy, over 500 shillings for a 10-year old boy, and over 700 shillings per year for a boy aged 15 years, plus school fees for children in school. As many parents in upper economic classes send children to boarding school at a cost of 400 to 500 shillings per year (partially offset by reduction of expense for food at home), the cost expenditure per child is often greater than the foregoing estimates. Such expenditures are beyond the means of primary school teachers and lower-class clerks, earning 1,200 to 2,600 shillings per year, but are sometimes borne by secondary school teachers and skilled artisans, earning 2,000 to 4,000 shillings per year, and by upper class clerks, business and professional workers, and cultivators of large farms.

Some methods of limiting the size of the family existed in the old days. Thus it was thought dangerous for a woman to resume intercourse with her husband whilst she was suckling a child, and this period lasted about two years as in other parts of Africa. It was also considered dangerous for either partner to contract an adulterous union during the time when the child was being suckled. This was called spoiling the child (*kusobyo mwana*), and was thought to result in various diseases such as weakness and spasmodic movements of the tongue. Various rites existed to protect the child from dangers of this sort. Nowadays the time of suckling tends to be shorter, and women attending baby clinics are instructed to give their children additional food after the sixth month. The average age of suckling in the sample area was about 12 months. Moreover, intercourse between husband and wife is now resumed more quickly and is said to be when the 'wife feels she is normal'. The decision apparently depends on the individual woman and periods from six to nine months are mentioned. A child is weaned at once if his mother becomes pregnant again. Hence, it seems that one restriction on conception is being removed by European influence.

The practice of *coitus interruptus* as with many African tribes was known before the arrival of Europeans in the area; it seems to have been practised by a man who had to keep taboos during the time his child was being suckled, and who had no second wife. It is said to be used nowadays in the case of casual unions.

However, the question 'how many children would you like to have' asked in the survey showed how unfamiliar was the notion of family limitation to most of the villagers. The question was frequently met by a refusal to answer, or it caused giggles or pained surprise. Questions addressed to the main hospitals in the area (Mulago, Mengo and Nsambya) showed that requests for knowledge of modern contraceptive methods are extremely rare, and only come from the most educated members of the community. The senior obstetrician of Mulago hospital, with a very large out-patient attendance, stated that she had only been asked four times for information as to birth control during the course of the past year, and in each case by educated Baganda. However, some Indian stores sell contraceptives. It is reported that contraceptives are used by some employed women in industrial concerns in Jinja (in a neighbouring province).

There seems to be little motive for self-induced abortion under urban conditions where illegitimacy confers so little stigma, but a young girl who conceives before marriage may feel that she has damaged her chances of making a good marriage by this act, and may try to produce an abortion. In rural areas an extra-marital pregnancy appears still to be frowned upon, and the motive for abortion may be greater. Two African abortificients have been reported and others probably exist. We have also been told that tying a cord or cloth tightly round the abdomen is a method

390

used, and that a woman living in a town knows that quinine injections may produce abortions, and may claim that she has a severe fever in order to obtain these. Nevertheless, self-induced abortions must be very rare in Buganda villages. The case of a pregnant woman recently brought to Mulago Hospital in a dying condition, due to an attempt to induce abortion by use of a native drug, appears to have been unprecedented.

We conclude that abortion, like contraception, can have had little influence on fertility in Buganda villages during previous decades, and that it remains a relatively negligible factor.

Factors Affecting the Survival Rate of Children

Stillbirth or infant mortality in primitive areas is often said to be due to conditions of childbirth in African huts. In Buganda, however, the rate of hospitalization is high. The sample village was near Kampala, and it has become a mark of status for a man to send his wife to the hospital for her confinement. It is also the custom for a man to display his wealth by supplying specially good food such as meat for his wife at the hospital and this she might not get at home. In the sample area, 56 out of 131 babies were born at the hospital and 75 at home. There is also a clinic at Budo nearby, where pregnant women wanting pre-natal advice are treated. It is likely, therefore, that stillbirths or deaths in childbirth occurred most frequently in the poorest section of the community, among those who could not afford motor transport to Kampala. The wife of a poor immigrant labourer in Kisozi, who had already lost two children in childbirth or directly after, was in trouble during the survey after giving birth to a baby. At last her husband collected or borrowed the money for a car, but by the time he had returned the woman showed a slight improvement. He immediately cancelled the car and the woman remained dangerously ill for some time. These points are worth mentioning because it is clear that there is little fear of hospitals in this area. With a rising standard of living or cheaper transport, it seems likely that more women might go to the hospital for the delivery of their children than in England at present.

The study yields some tentative evidence on the relation of standards of living on the survival of children. In spite of its proximity to Kampala, 63 per cent of the women in the village were illiterate and were probably rearing their children in much the same way as their parents had; 35 per cent had only had primary education or had taught themselves to read. In the present survey 30 per cent of 398 pregnancies of illiterate mothers resulted in pre-natal losses, or deaths prior to 15 years of age; only 18 per cent of 166 pregnancies of mothers who had primary education resulted in similar wastage. In a social survey of Jinja, in the neighbouring Province to Buganda, the Sofers found a lower death rate among infants of church marriages, which they attributed to the higher education of the parents.

Dr. Welbourn examined 101 school children (58 boys and 43 girls) during the course of the survey. This examination showed the children to be suffering from milk protein deficiency, very mild signs of vitamin A and riboflavin deficiency, small septic skin lesions and ringworm, and chronic respiratory infections. Dental caries were rare, but abnormal teeth and gingivitis were common. Blood slides were not taken for malaria or other infections, owing to the suspicion of the people.

With regard to the protein deficiency it was found that most of the villagers except those at the lowest level of poverty eat meat once a week, and the butcher in Kisozi gave it as his opinion that families bought one to two pounds of meat a week. There were 20 cattle owners in the area, but the herds were small and the yield per cow averaged one pint a day. Most of this milk was sold in Kampala and few children of cattle owners seemed to get more than a little milk in their tea, once or twice a day.

As to venereal infection, it was unfortunately impossible to persuade every adult in the village to be examined, as was done in the case of the Bukoba survey. Venereal disease is openly discussed by the Baganda and little stigma is attached to infection. All the women were asked if they had had syphilis or gonorrhea and 29 per cent reported that they had had one or the other of these diseases, but the figures are not reliable because the women tended to call an undiagnosed illness, especially those producing skin rashes, by the general name of *Kabotongo* or syphilis. On the other hand, some may have suppressed information on this subject.

CONCLUSIONS

It will have been seen that the salient differences in the kinship and marriage system of the Bahaya and the Baganda are the following:
1. Marriage and the family have a more individual character among the Baganda than among the Bahaya—though both would appear individual and informal institutions to the peoples of the West Nile with their strongly corporate lineages.

    The household is relatively small in each area. The joint homestead of a man and his married sons and their children hardly exists. The Baganda households tend to be smaller than those of the Bahaya.
2. The influence of Christianity is greater among the Baganda. Only 46 per cent of the unions reported by males and 45 per cent of those reported by females were customary marriages in Buganda, as compared with 84 per cent and 82 per cent among the Bahaya.
3. The present-day arrangements for divorce differ, since the Bahaya can obtain what amounts to legal separation from the African courts through recognition of return of bridewealth; the Baganda cannot easily get a legal divorce and rarely try to do so. Hence, the Bahaya tend to have a series of separate marriages, sometimes overlapping, while the Baganda marry once, usually with a great expenditure in ceremonials,

and then contract subsequent informal unions (usually in another village) concurrently with the main marriage or following it. Such subsequent unions are not reported as marriages in census returns.

This is seen by the figures in Table 84 which show that 40 per cent of Baganda men contracted one union, 29 per cent two unions and 7 per cent three, whereas 35 per cent Bahaya men contracted one union, 24 per cent two unions, 13 per cent four, 2 per cent five and 2 per cent six unions. Marriages, however, tend to last longer among the Bahaya women than the Baganda, e.g., 14.9 years for the first union, 12.9 for the second and 7.4 for the third, as compared with 9.6 for the first, 5.7 for the second and 1 year for the third among the Baganda women.

4. Baganda men have the right to claim the children which they have begotten in any type of union, whereas among the Bahaya the pater often has precedence over the genitor, and he can claim as his own the first child produced by his wife in a subsequent union with another man. In both systems women must surrender all or some of their children in the case of a broken marriage.

5. Both the Baganda and Bahaya desire children, although the rising cost of school fees and clothing among the Baganda and shortage of land among the Bahaya seem to be bringing in the notion of an optimum size family. Contraceptive practices are known only to a very small minority of educated people, and apparently only in Buganda.

TABLE 81.   Reported Conjugal Unions by Type.

Present ages	Reported by men: types						Reported by women: types					
	Chris-tian	Mus-lim	Custo-mary	Concu-binage	Not stated	All types	Chris-tian	Mus-lim	Custo-mary	Concu-binage	Not stated	All types
Buhaya												
15–19	2	—	2	—	—	4	16	—	15	—	—	31
20–24	8	—	8	—	—	16	9	—	19	1	—	29
25–29	9	—	8	1	—	18	13	—	41	1	1	56
30–34	12	1	21	—	—	34	9	—	32	5	1	47
35–39	4	—	41	—	—	45	8	—	52	4	—	64
40–44	2	—	35	1	—	38	3	—	32	—	—	35
45–49	1	1	35	1	—	38	2	—	21	2	1	26
50–54	6	1	57	2	—	66	2	—	45	—	1	48
55–59	3	2	52	1	2	60	1	—	28	2	—	31
60–64	2	—	28	1	1	32	2	1	29	—	—	32
65–69	2	—	23	—	—	25	—	—	19	—	1	20
70+	3	—	56	2	—	61	—	—	56	—	1	57
All ages:												
Number	54	5	366	9	3	437	65	1	389	15	6	476
Per cent	12	1.1	84	2	0.6	100	14	0.2	82	3	1.2	100
Buganda												
15–19	—	2	2	—	—	4	11	3	10	5	—	29
20–24	5	3	7	10	1	26	9	8	14	8	1	40
25–29	12	2	18	3	—	35	14	3	20	10	4	51
30–34	10	3	21	5	—	39	13	5	21	2	1	42
35–39	9	6	18	2	—	35	8	3	9	5	2	27
40–44	10	5	20	3	3	41	3	2	20	2	1	28
45–49	6	6	7	1	—	20	9	—	12	2	1	24
50–54	9	—	10	2	3	24	16	—	15	4	2	37
55–59	9	3	26	2	4	44	2	—	8	2	—	12
60–64	14	3	18	2	7	44	4	—	7	—	—	11
65–69	2	—	1	—	3	6	5	2	3	1	—	11
70+	7	2	15	—	8	32	5	—	10	1	2	18
Unknown	4	3	6	2	2	17	1	—	2	—	—	3
All ages:												
Number	97	38	169	32	31	367	100	26	151	42	14	333
Per cent	26	10	46	8	8	100	30	8	45	13	4	100

TABLE 82. Polygamous Unions.

	Number (reported by persons of all ages)	Per cent of all reported unions
Buhaya sample		
Men	Data not yet tabulated	
Women		
Buganda sample		
Men	23	8.4
Women	48	16.3

TABLE 83. Reported Conjugal Unions Ended by Separation, by Type of Union.

	Reported by men: types				Reported by women: types			
	Christian	Muslim	Customary or concubinage	All types	Christian	Muslim	Customary or concubinage	All types
A. Buganda sample								
(a) Number of unions	97	38	201	367	100	26	193	333
(b) Number of separations	30	17	62	109	20	2	39	61
Per cent of separations	31	45	30	30	20	8	20	18
(c) Number ended by death	—	—	—	32	—	—	—	48
Per cent ended by death	—	—	—	9	—	—	—	14
(d) Per cent of completed unions ended by separation[1]	—	—	—	77	—	—	—	53
B. Buhaya sample	Data to be tabulated							

[1] (c) / (b ± c), expressed as per cent.

TABLE 84. Persons by Number of Marriages (excluding concubinage).[1]

Present ages	Men									
	0	1	2	3	4	5	6	7	8	9
Buhaya										
15–19	17	4	—	—	—	—	—	—	—	—
20–24	6	12	1	—	—	—	—	—	—	—
25–29	1	13	2	—	—	—	—	—	—	—
30–34	3	9	11	1	—	—	—	—	—	—
35–39	1	6	10	6	—	—	—	—	—	—
40–44	—	8	4	3	4	—	—	—	—	—
45–49	—	6	2	2	2	—	1	1	—	—
50–54	—	8	13	4	5	—	—	—	—	—
55–59	—	6	5	7	3	1	1	—	—	—
60–64	—	3	6	4	—	1	—	—	—	—
65–69	—	1	1	3	2	1	—	—	—	—
70+	—	7	3	2	2	1	2	1	—	1
All ages										
Number	28	83	58	32	18	4	4	2	—	1
Per cent	12	35	24	13	8	2	2	1	—	—
Buganda										
15–19	10	2	1	—	—	—	—	—	—	—
20–24	6	18	4	—	—	—	—	—	—	—
25–29	5	20	6	1	—	1	—	—	—	—
30–34	1	9	9	4	—	—	—	—	—	—
35–39	4	15	6	1	—	—	—	—	—	—
40–44	3	13	12	—	1	—	—	—	—	—
45–49	1	2	6	2	—	—	—	—	—	—
50–54	3	5	8	1	—	—	—	—	—	—
55–59	1	4	12	4	1	—	—	—	—	—
60–64	—	11	8	3	2	—	—	—	—	—
65–69	1	2	—	—	1	—	—	—	—	—
70+	1	6	10	2	—	—	—	—	—	—
Not stated	—	5	1	2	1	—	—	—	—	—
All ages										
Number	36	112	83	20	6	1	—	—	—	—
Per cent	13	40	29	7	2	—	—	—	—	—

[1] Reported conjugal unions without specification of type are also excluded. The reports refer to Christian, Muslim, and customary marriages.

| | | Women | | | | | | | |
Not stated	All men	0	1	2	3	4	5	Not stated	All women
—	21	6	31	—	—	—	—	—	37
2	21	—	19	5	—	—	—	—	24
1	17	—	25	14	1	—	—	—	40
—	24	—	22	10	—	—	1	—	33
1	24	—	17	17	3	1	—	—	38
1	20	—	17	6	2	—	—	—	25
1	15	—	9	7	1	—	—	—	17
—	30	—	14	14	2	—	—	—	30
—	23	—	14	7	1	—	—	—	22
—	14	—	11	9	1	—	—	—	21
—	8	—	7	5	1	—	—	—	13
1	20	—	34	10	1	—	—	—	45
7	237	6	220	104	13	1	1	—	345
—	100	2	64	30	4	—	—	—	100
—	13	6	29	—	—	—	—	—	35
—	28	1	31	3	1	—	—	—	36
—	32	—	36	6	1	—	—	1	44
3	26	—	24	9	—	—	—	—	33
1	28	—	15	6	—	—	—	1	22
1	30	—	12	8	—	—	—	1	21
1	12	—	13	4	1	—	—	1	19
—	17	—	27	5	—	—	—	1	33
—	22	—	12	—	—	—	—	—	12
—	24	—	9	1	—	—	—	1	11
—	4	—	9	1	—	—	—	—	10
1	20	—	9	3	1	—	—	1	14
14	23	—	3	—	—	—	—	—	3
21	279	7	229	46	4	—	—	7	293
8	100	2	79	15	1	—	—	2	100

TABLE 85.   Summary of Table 84, Women Only, Aged 35 Years or Over.[1]

	Total number	Married once only	Married 2 or more times	Percent married once only
Buhaya sample	212	123	89	58.0
Buganda sample	138	109	29	78.9

[1] Excluding women by whom number of marriages was not stated.

TABLE 86.   Mean Lengths of Reported Conjugal Unions in Years.

Present ages	Reported by men					Reported by women		
	1st union	2nd union	3rd union	4th union	5th union	1st union	2nd union	3rd union
Buhaya								
15–19	1.6					1.9		
20–24	5.3	2.0				3.2	2.2	
25–29	3.5	3.6				6.6	3.7	
30–34	6.8	4.0				8.5	5.0	
35–39	10.4	7.8	2.2			12.8	3.7	4.5
40–44	10.1	7.9	6.1	3.0		18.5	8.8	1.7
45–49	15.3	7.8	7.8	7.6		19.5	15.5	
50–54	14.1	10.7	12.3	5.0		15.8	17	15
55–59	12.0	14.4	8.3	5.6	6.5	16.3	15.5	
60–64	19.6	13.3	7.0			23.8	12.7	
65–69	19.1	19.1	11.4	13.0		21.5	31.8	
70+	23.9	27	16.6	22.1	11.6	30.7	26	
All ages	11.8	10.6	9.7	9.3	9.5	14.9	12.9	7.4
Buganda								
15–19	0.8	1.0				1.3		
20–24	1.8	1.5				3.0	2.2	1.0
25–29	3.0	1.9	0.8			5.2	2.4	
30–34	5.1	2.5	3.5			7.6	2.2	
35–39	8.0	5.4	3.7	5	4	11.3	6.6	
40–44	9.0	4.1	12.0	14		15.8	6.9	
45–49	15.0	5.1	5.5			17.3	4.8	1.0
50–54	10.4	6.2				21.6	6.0	
55–59	14.0	12.5	4.8			10.3		
60–64	14.7	16.4	6.8	2	1	29.5		
65–69	40.5					24.2	31.0	
70+	23.8	23.7	15			18.0	34	
Unknown	6.8	1	4			3.5		
All ages	8.9	8.7	6.7	8.5	2.5	9.6	5.7	1.0

Preliminary Demographic Findings

It has unfortunately been impossible to complete a systematic analysis of the demographic data obtained in these surveys in time for publication in this report. It is especially unfortunate, in view of the nature of the problems with which we are confronted, that it has also been impossible as yet to carry through a joint analysis of the demographic data and the data obtained through medical examinations. The possibility of a precise comparison of data from such intensive surveys with data from the same areas was largely frustrated by the error in selection of the sample area in Buganda, mentioned above in the Introduction.

We can, therefore, at this time present only preliminary summary results. These however may be found highly significant in some respects. In some other respects, they merely tend to emphasize the need for reliable information on certain critical problems relating to fertility on which we are still sadly ignorant.

TABLE 87.   Average Number of Children Ever Born Per Woman by Age. Sample Population.

Ages	Buhaya sample			Buganda sample		
	Number of women	Number of live births	Live births per woman	Number of women	Number of live births	Live births per woman
15–19	33	15	0.45	35	11	0.31
20–24	21	25	1.19	31	28	0.90
25–34	52	110	2.11	69	120	1.74
35–44	52	116	2.23	40	95	2.38
45–59	71	235	3.31	64	187	2.92
60 +	71	290	4.08	33	106	3.21
All ages	300	791	2.63	272	547	2.01

TABLE 88.   Frequency of Childlessness Among Women Aged 35 Years and Over. Sample Population.

	Total women	Women with no live births	Per cent childless
Buhaya sample			
35–44	52	11	21.2
45–59	71	13	18.3
60+	71	5	7.0
35+	194	29	15.0
Buganda sample[1]			
35–44	41	16	39.0
45–59	66	21	31.8
60+	32	10	31.3
35+	139	47	33.8

[1] There is a discrepancy in these preliminary tabulations between numbers of women in the Buganda sample at ages 35 and over, as given in Tables 87 and 88.

TABLE 89.   Comparative Data on Fertility: 1952 Institute Surveys and 1948 Sample Census.[1]

	Average number of children ever born per woman		Childless women as percent of all women over 45
	Aged 15–44	Over 45	
Tanganyika—Bukoba district			
Survey findings:			
Buhaya sample	1.7	3.7	12.7
1948 census:			
Bukoba district	2.7[2]	4.3	—
All Tanganyika	2.6[2]	4.4	17
Uganda			
Survey findings:			
Buganda sample	1.5	3.0	31.6
1948 census:			
Mengo district	1.7[2]	3.2	—
All Buganda	2.1[2]	3.7	24.4
All Uganda	2.7[2]	4.8	18
Kenya			
1948 census	3.2[3]	5.3	12

[1] For references to 1948 census data, see note at beginning of Introduction, above.
[2] Values for women 'aged 16–45 years'.
[3] Values for women 'aged 14–45 years'.

TABLE 90.   Average Number of Children Ever-Born Per Conjugal Union, and Frequency of Childlessness, by Type of Marriage, Jinja.[1]

Type of union	Number of unions	Childless unions	Average number of live births per woman
Christian or Muslim marriage	76	16	2.2
Tribal marriage	309	104	1.6
Living together	24	15	—

[1] Unpublished survey data by Rhona Sofer. Jinja is an industrial town in eastern Uganda. The data refer to unions with classification by age of husband or wife (all wives aged 16 years or over).

TABLE 91.   Mean Age at First Pregnancy, Pregnancy Wastage, and Related Data.

	Buhaya sample	Buganda sample
Mean age at first pregnancy	19.1	18.5
Total reported pregnancies[1]	860	604
Total reported abortions[2]	35	51
Total reported stillbirths	19	15
Miscarriages per 100 pregnancies	4.1	8.4
Stillbirths per 100 pregnancies	2.2	2.5
Males per 100 live births	53.6	53.2
Twin pairs per 100 live births	5.6	—
Living children per woman		
Women aged 48 and over	2.03	1.77
Women, all ages	1.51	1.36
Live births per mother[3]		
Aged 60 and over	4.4	4.8
Aged 45–59	4.1	4.2
Aged 35–44	2.8	3.8

[1] Completed pregnancies only.
[2] Chiefly spontaneous abortions (i.e., miscarriages).
[3] Numbers of births from Table 87, relative to numbers of women minus childless women from Table 88.

TABLE 92.   Child Mortality Quotients (preliminary results).[1]

Age interval	Number living to beginning of age interval, exclusive of children within age interval at time of survey	Deaths within age interval	Mortality quotients
Buhaya sample:			
0–1	806[2]	221	0.274[3]
1–5	585	33	0.056
5–15	552	16	0.029
0–15	806	270	0.335
Buganda sample:			
0–1	538[2]	88	0.164[3]
1–5	450	35	0.078
5–15	415	27	0.065
0–15	538	150	0.279

[1] Preliminary results, subject to later verification. Tabulation, contrary to specifications in headings, appears to relate deaths at specified ages to total live births, including children living within stated age intervals in denominator of quotients. If so, correct quotients in all cases would be somewhat higher.

[2] Children living at age zero, i.e., live births.

[3] Corresponding infant mortality rates per 1,000 live births; 274 and 164, respectively.

The survey results agree with the results of the 1948 sample census in indicating a region in the vicinity of Lake Victoria where fertility is much lower than that found in some other parts of East Africa—and in many other non-European countries. At the same time, the intensive survey reveals the acute sensitivity of all such findings to possible sources of bias that often may be unsuspected, and suggests the importance of combining intensive studies in sample areas with any comprehensive census programme. The level of fertility found in the Buhaya sample, though appreciably above that in the Buganda sample, is well below that indicated by the census for the Bukoba district as a whole; but the sample relates only to a few villages near the lake. Before the extent of agreement or disagreement in the results can be appraised, it will be necessary to compare the survey findings with more detailed census information for particular localities. The findings of the Buganda survey more closely approximate to the census findings for sample areas in the Mengo district as a whole—being slightly lower with respect to average number of previous live births reported both by women of childbearing age and by older women.

The most startling demographic finding of the surveys is the apparently high incidence of childlessness in the Buganda sample (31.6 per cent among all women over 45 years of age, all of whom reported some marital experience). This is in line with the census finding that 24 per cent of the older women in all Buganda, where average fertility is well above that in the Mengo district, were childless. The information by sub-classes is weakened by the small size of the samples. However, both the survey and the census seem to show that sterility has been widely prevalent among the Baganda over a fairly long period. The age-specific data on childlessness in the Buhaya sample seem to tell a different story. Only a moderate proportion (7 per cent) of the Buhaya women over 60 years old were reported as childless, but the figure jumps to 18 per cent among those between 45 and 60 years of age; moreover, it seems unlikely that many of the childless women (21 per cent) at ages 35–44 years will ever bear a living child. The suggestion, then, is that there has been a quite pronounced increase of sterility in these villages in recent decades. It was found that about 10 per cent of all those given medical examinations in this area show evidence of present or previous venereal disease. It will be important to determine whether or not there is any definite relation in individual cases between this factor—or other medical findings—and the fertility records.

There is a suggestion of decline in average number of children per mother from the oldest cohorts (present ages: 60 years or over) to the younger cohort of completed fertility (present ages: 45–59 years) in both samples, but little confidence can be placed in this finding owing to the small size of the samples.

The evidence as to the general prevalence of early marriage (usually under 20 years of age) among women in both sample areas has been supplemented by evidence showing a rather high degree of instability in both areas with respect to personal marital relations, which for our purposes are more important than degree of formal stability of marriage as a legal institution. The information on social conditions relating to fertility, viewed in conjunction with the information on the frequency of childlessness, leads to the tentative conclusion that the factors responsible for low fertility in these regions must be largely physiological in character—though these physiological conditions may have been indirectly influenced by changing social conditions. But the nature of these physiological factors cannot be definitely determined on the basis of the information at present available.

PART FIVE

The Brazilian Birth Rate:
Its Economic and Social Factors

by
GIORGIO MORTARA
Technical Consultant to the National Council of Brazil

The Population of Brazil and its Development over the Last 100 Years

About the middle of the nineteenth century, when France already had 35 million inhabitants, Italy 24 million, and England and Wales 17 million, Brazil had scarcely 7 million. In 1950, Brazil, with its 52 million inhabitants, had a larger population than Italy, with 46 million, England and Wales, with 44 million, and France, with 42 million.[2]

This enormous increase in the population of Brazil is partly due to the influx of immigrants, but much more to the generally high birth rate. It is estimated that, between 1851 and 1950, immigrants exceeded emigrants by 3.5 million and that the increase in the number of births due to the presence of the immigrants was about the same, giving a total of some 7 million. The total increase in the population, however, was 45 million, so that the natural increase, apart from immigration, was 38 million or 84 per cent of the total. The very high excess of births over deaths was not due to a low death-rate, since even now the latter is between 18 and 20 per 1,000 inhabitants, and was much higher for most of the 100 years under consideration. On the other hand, the annual number of births is between 42 and 44 per 1,000 inhabitants, and was even higher in the past, which accounts for the net increase.

The demographers of the Brazilian Institute of Geography and Statistics have calculated that a generation, subject to a death-rate for each

Years	Average population (in thousands)	Years	Average population (in thousands)
1850	7 233	1910	22 216
1860	8 418	1920	27 404
1870	9 797	1930	33 568
1880	11 748	1940	41 114
1890	14 199	1950	52 071
1900	17 984		

At the end of 1952, Brazil had over 55 million inhabitants.

[1] Publications mentioned in the text are referred to by the name of the author or publisher, followed by the number given in the bibliography at the end.
[2] The following table shows the stages in the growth of the population of Brazil over this period of 100 years.

age-group equal to that observed for the corresponding group in Brazil during 1940, and with a fertility rate equal to that of the Brazilian population, would produce a generation nearly twice (1.8 to 1.9) as large. When a similar 'Boeckh co-efficient' was calculated for certain European countries just before the second world war, the figures obtained were in striking contrast—1.1 for Italy, 0.9 for France and 0.8 for England and Wales. The exceptionally high birth-rate in Brazil makes this study particularly interesting.

For the reader's convenience, we shall give a few preliminary particulars about the territorial distribution of the population of Brazil. The Brazilian Institute has divided the country into five main physical regions: north, north-east, east, south and west-centre. Each region is subdivided into several political units. These number 26, including 20 States, five Federal Territories (four frontier zones and one island) and one Federal District (the city of Rio de Janeiro, the capital). The population and area of each of these political units is shown in Table 93, the figures for the population at 1 September 1950 being estimated from the preliminary results of the census of 1 July 1950. (The Brazilian census is normally taken on 1 September but in 1950 was advanced by two months because of the impending political elections.)

The population of Brazil, which is slightly larger than that of Italy or of England and Wales, occupies a country with an area 28 times larger than that of the former and 56 times greater than that of the latter. The average population density—slightly more than six per square kilometre—is low, not only in comparison with the averages of 150 and 290, respectively, found in these two countries but also with that of 19 inhabitants per square kilometre found in the United States of America.

The distribution of the population over the country's land area is, however, very uneven. The north and west centre regions are still largely uninhabited, having a population density of one half, and less than one inhabitant per square km. respectively. Their net land area is 5,420,000 square km., which is greater than that of Europe (excluding the European part of the Soviet Union within the 1938 frontiers), and their total population less than 4 million as compared with over 400 million in Europe. They represent 64 per cent of the area of the country but only 7 per cent of the population.

The north-east region has a population density of 13 inhabitants per square km., the east, 15 and the south, 21. Even in these regions, where there are over 48 million inhabitants occupying a net surface area of 3,040,000 square km., there are great stretches of territory where the population density is very low, such as the States of Maranhão and Piauí, in the north-east (less than five) and parts of Bahia, in the east, and Paraná, in the south.

There is an exceptionally high population density in the Federal District of Rio de Janeiro itself, which, though relatively small, contains the most populous town in the country, but, of the states, only Rio de Janeiro has

TABLE 93. Brazil. Area and Population, by Physical Regions and Political Units.

Unit of the federation [1] physical region	Area in km[2]	Population at 1.9.50 no. of inhabitants	Population density no. of inhabitants per km[2]
T. Guaporé	254 163	37 176	0.15
T. Acre	153 170	115 311	0.75
S. Amazonas	1 595 818	527 204	0.33
T. Rio Branco	214 316	17 500	0.08
S. Pará	1 188 769	1 134 846	0.95
T. Amapá	133 796	38 105	0.28
North	*3 540 032*	*1 870 142*	*0.53*
S. Maranhão	332 239	1 589 193	4.78
S. Piauí	249 317	1 056 987	4.24
S. Ceará	153 245	2 716 552	17.73
S. Rio Grande do Norte	53 048	976 687	18.41
S. Paraíba	56 282	1 718 669	30.54
S. Pernambuco	97 016	3 406 616	35.11
S. Alagoas	28 531	1 098 709	38.51
T. Fernando de Noronha	26	643	24.73
North-East	*969 704*	*12 564 056*	*12.96*
S. Sergipe	21 057	645 581	30.66
S. Bahia	563 281	4 866 116	8.64
S. Minas Gerais	581 975	7 784 913	13.38
(Sierra dos Aimorés)[2]	10 137	160 928	15.88
S. Espírito Santo	40 882	864 890	21.16
S. Rio de Janeiro	41 666	2 309 918	55.44
Federal district	1 171	2 396 260	2 046.34
East	*1 260 169*	*19 028 606*	*15.10*
S. São Paulo	247 223	9 177 912	37.12
S. Paraná	200 731	2 134 462	10.63
S. Santa Catarina	93 849	1 567 112	16.70
S. Rio Grande do Sul	267 455	4 183 823	15.64
South	*809 258*	*17 063 309*	*21.09*
S. Mato Grosso	1 262 572	524 752	0.42
S. Goiás	622 463	1 226 097	1.97
West-Centre	*1 885 035*	*1 750 849*	*0.93*
Brazil	*8 464 198*	*52 276 962*	*6.18*

[1] S = State; T = Federal Territory.
[2] A contested zone between the states of Minas Gerais and Espírito Santo.

a density higher than 50 (55). Alagoas has a population density of 39, São Paulo 37, Pernambuco 35 and Paraíba 31. At the other extreme there are very low densities in Goiás (2), Pará (1), Mato Grosso (0.4) and Amazonas

(0.3). Amazonas and Mato Grosso are the two largest states in Brazil and have the lowest population density. In some of the Federal Territories, the population density is still lower than in Amazonas.

Not all the country is habitable. High mountains occupy only a little of the surface but there are enormous stretches of territory where the possibility of settlement is doubtful because of drought, periodic flooding or very irregular rainfall. There is no doubt, however, that Brazil could support a much larger population than it does at present.

Most of the present population is concentrated in the coastal strip from Ceará to the Rio Grande do Sul, nearly three-quarters of the total population being crowded into less than one-fifth of the total area of the country. Nearly all the large towns are on or near the Atlantic coast.

The great differences in area and population between the various states, shown in Table 93, must be borne in mind in interpreting the data concerning the birth rate in the various states given in the following sections of this study.

The tendency for population to concentrate increasingly in the towns and surrounding districts is already to be noted in Brazil, as can be seen from the information given in Table 94.

TABLE 94. Brazil. Distribution of the Population According to Type and Size of Place of Residence.

Locality	Population at 1 September 1950[1]	
	No. of inhabitants	Percentages of the tota
Urban settlements		
with more than 500,000 inhabitants	4 865 812	9.31
from 100,001 to 500,000 inhabitants	2 383 495	4.56
from 50,001 to 100,000 inhabitants	1 391 662	2.66
from 10,001 to 50,000 inhabitants	3 693 741	7.07
from 5,001 to 10,000 inhabitants	1 833 103	3.51
from 2,001 to 5,000 inhabitants	2 130 221	4.07
Small settlements and scattered dwellings	35 978 928	68.82
Total	52 276 962	100.00

[1] Estimated from the preliminary results of the census of 1 July 1950.

If we regard urban settlements with over 5,000 inhabitants as 'towns', in the sociological and demographic sense of the term,[1] we find that only 27

[1] From the administrative point of view, a centre of population in which the seat of a municipality is situated is always treated as a town ('cidade') and one in which the seat of a municipal district is situated as a village ('vila'). There are, however, 'cidades' with only a few hundred inhabitants and 'vilas' with several thousand.

410

per cent of the tota lpopulation lives in towns. Even if we extend the term to cover smaller settlements with a population of over 2,000, the proportion of town dwellers is scarcely 31 per cent. Only 14 per cent of the total population lives in large towns, in the traditional acceptance of the term, i.e. in urban settlements with over 100,000 inhabitants. The two main towns are Rio de Janeiro, the Federal capital, with 2,300,000 inhabitants in the town and its suburbs and 400,000 in the satellite centres, and São Paulo, the capital of the state of that name, with 2 million in the town and suburbs and 200,000 in the satellite centres.

Of the other large towns, the most populous are Recife, the capital of Pernambuco, with 520,000 inhabitants; Salvador, the capital of Bahia, with 390,000; Pôrto Alegre, the capital of the Rio Grande do Sul, with 380,000; Belo Horizonte, the capital of Minas Gerais, with 320,000; Belém, the capital of Pará, with 230,000; Fortaleza, the capital of Ceará, with 210,000; and Santos, the great port of São Paulo, with 200,000. There are five other towns (Niterói, Curitiba, Manaus, Maceío and Campinas) with over 100,000 inhabitants.

The population of Brazil consists of a great variety of ethnic and national components, much intermingled and partly fused together. When the Portuguese first arrived (in 1500), the native population of the country was small, and was reduced by massacres. At the same time, intermarriage occurred between natives and colonists, and is still continuing. A few remnants of the indigenous population now have a place in the country's economic and social life; others are already in contact with civilization; but there are still a few barbarian 'pockets', not included in the census returns; the number of individuals is liberally estimated at a few hundred thousand.

The slave trade brought a few million Africans, of varying origin, to Brazil over a period of 300 years. These Negroes have intermingled to some extent with the European and indigenous stocks—a process which was accelerated by the abolition of slavery in 1888.

During the first 350 years of colonization in Brazil, the Portuguese furnished the largest number of immigrants, though there were also considerable numbers from other countries. The Portuguese, however, constitute less than a third of the immigrants who have flocked to Brazil in the last 100 years (1,480,000 out of 4,800,000). The other major groups are the Italians (1,540,000), Spaniards (600,000), and Germans (230,000), while fairly large numbers have also come from certain parts of the old Austro-Hungarian and Russian Empires. There have been far fewer immigrants from Asian countries, the largest number coming from Japan (190,000). The Syrians and Lebanese, though fewer in numbers, have made a considerable contribution to the development of commerce. The number of immigrants from other American countries is relatively negligible.

At the beginning of the large-scale immigration movement, possibly a third of the country's population was white and, in 1872, when the first census was taken in Brazil, only 38 per cent of the inhabitants were classified as 'white' (a term, incidentally, which is fairly widely applied in Brazil, where there is no 'colour bar').

After the end of the slave trade, the increase in the black (African) and dark-skinned (indigenous and cross-breed) groups slowed down, in spite of their high birth rates, owing to the low standard of living, particularly among the former group, and consequent high death rate.

On the other hand, the white group, whose numbers were increased by immigrants and their descendants, grew more rapidly. In 1940 it represented nearly two-thirds of the total population, and it is possible that it has now reached that proportion. At the same time, it must be borne in mind that, as mentioned above, the percentages of whites calculated from the census figures are higher than those that would be shown by a strictly accurate and objective survey.

The foregoing brief particulars about the ethnic and national origins of the Brazilian people are enough to show how many different groups have been associated and partially fused in the formation of the population. The inter-mixture of immigrants and their descendants with the population of Portuguese origin, in which there are large numbers of cross-breeds, has been easier and quicker in the case of the Spanish and Italian groups than in that of the Slav and Germanic peoples, being hastened by similarities of language, religion, tradition and customs. The Japanese group is still almost self-contained, but this is explained by the fact that the Japanese are recent immigrants and by the ethnic and social differences which necessarily retard their assimilation.

The total number of citizens and ex-citizens of foreign countries living in Brazil in 1940 was rather under 1,410,000, including 380,000 Portuguese, 325,000 Italians, 161,000 Spaniards and 141,000 Japanese. The proportion of foreigners in the whole population, which was over 3 per cent in 1940, must now be down to about 2 per cent, their actual numbers having, decreased because the flow of new immigrants in the last few years has been too small to compensate for the number of deaths.

Attention may be drawn to certain features in the composition of the Brazilian population which either influence, or are influenced by, the birth rate. There is no great disparity between the sexes in the composition of the population. Among those born in the country, the larger number of male babies is more than offset by the higher mortality among males at all times of life. Among the immigrants, the men generally outnumber the women but, as has already been shown, the proportion of immigrants in the total population is nearly negligible.

The high birth and death rates, the speed with which the population has grown and the reduction in immigration have all had a part in determining the main features of age-distribution among the population; these are the high proportion of children and adolescents and the low proportion of old people. In 1940, out of every 1,000 head of population in Brazil, 425 were under the age of 15 (as compared with 309 in Italy in 1936, 247 in France in the same year, and 238 in England and Wales in 1931), 534 were between 15 and 59 (as compared with 579 in Italy, 606 in France, and 646 in England and Wales), and only 41 were aged 60 and over (as compared with 112 in Italy, 147 in France and 116 in England and Wales). So far as they are known, the results of the 1950 census in Brazil show that these features of age-distribution have not altered substantially since 1940.

The average number of economically non-productive persons—children and old people—dependent on each economically productive person is thus fairly high in Brazil, and, in order to alleviate the burden, children are often set to do manual work. This prevents some children and adolescents from attending school, or at least from attending regularly, and thus helps to slow down the spread of education, even at the primary level. In 1940, 57 per cent of the population aged 10 years and over were unable to read or write, and even today the figure is probably over 50 per cent.

The main economic activities are rural—agriculture, stock-rearing, exploitation of natural products.

Out of every 1,000 males aged 10 and over at the 1940 census, 567 were engaged in agricultural and pastoral work. The proportions of those engaged in other branches of extra-domestic activity were comparatively low: 77 per 1,000 in the processing industries, 52 in commerce and banking, 34 in social services and social work, 32 in transport and communications, 24 in the extraction industries, 16 in public administration, the law and public education, 12 in national defence and public safety, and 6 in the liberal professions, the Church, private education and private administrative posts. Of the remaining 180, 71 were students, 9 were engaged in domestic activities and 100 were inactive (mostly adolescents, old people, the sick and the infirm).

Only a small proportion of women are employed outside the home. In 1940, out of every 1,000 women aged 10 and over, 87 were engaged in agricultural and pastoral work, 31 in social services and social work, 20 in the processing industries and 17 in all other forms of extra-domestic activity. The majority—668 per 1,000—were engaged in domestic activities (632 in their own homes and 36 as paid domestic workers); 65 were students and 112 inactive.

Since 1940, the proportions of those employed in the processing industries, commerce and banking, and transport and communications must have increased[1] but rural occupations still predominate. We shall see that this is one of the main factors, and probably indeed the main factor, accounting for the high birth rate in Brazil.

[1] The full figures for the 1950 census on the employment classification of the population are not yet available, but the results already published by 14 of the 20 states suggest that the numbers engaged in the activities mentioned will be found to have increased.

CHAPTER I

The Level of the Birth Rate in Brazil

Studies of the birth rate in Brazil encounter an apparently insurmountable difficulty owing to the absence of reliable statistics of births. This is due to incomplete registrations of births, and also to omissions in the forwarding of records by the local offices to the central statistical office.[1]

The cumulative effect of these omissions is considerable. For the three years from 1939 to 1941 the records show a total of 2,741,855 births comprising 1,570,550 live births registered during the year of birth, 1,127,758 live births registered later than the year of birth (the exceptionally high number being the result of the amnesty granted to encourage registration in view of the 1940 census) and 93,547 still-born children.[2]

If the birth rate is calculated according to the number of live births registered during the year of birth, a rate of 12.29 per 1,000 inhabitants is obtained. Even if the live births registered later than the year of birth are included the rate does not exceed 21.40 per 1,000 inhabitants.

The improbability of these results is evident. In fact the number of children of less than five years enumerated in 1940 was 6,442,288; that is, an average of 1,288,458 for each yearly age group. If the latter figure is divided by the average population of Brazil during the five years preceding the census (39,230,000) this gives a ratio of 32.84 per 1,000, between the number of live births during the five years before 1 September 1940 and the average population during the same period:

It has been estimated that these surviving children represent about 78 per cent of the total number of live births.[3] Consequently the annual average birth rate can easily be calculated from the above figure as follows: 32.84 × 0.78 = 42.10 per 1,000.

---

[1] These omissions, unthinkable in a country with a well-developed administrative system, are very considerable, as can be seen from the statistics published by the central statistical administration. See Brazilian Institute of Geography and Statistics (BIGS) 2, 1939/40, pp. 105/6.

[2] See BIGS 9, p. 18.

[3] See BIGS 16 and the supplementary note to Section V.

The same calculation[1] for the 10 years preceding the census gives a slightly higher figure: 32.68 × 0.75 = 43.57 per 1,000.

The Brazilian birth rate, between 1930 and 1940 may therefore be estimated at between 42 and 44 per 1,000 inhabitants.[2]

The number of births has been determined not only for the whole of Brazil but also for each of the political units into which the federation is divided (States, Federal Territories and Federal Districts). It has thus been possible to determine that the percentage of live births registered during the year of birth and included in the official records represents only 28–30 per cent of the total for the country as a whole.

The percentages in the different political units vary from less than 5 per cent (States of Amazonas and Piauti, Territory of Acre) to between 60 and 70 per cent (State of São Paulo, Federal District).

The more recent statistics of birth registrations are no more reliable than those for previous years, and the 1950 census must be used to estimate the present birth rate. The analysis of the results of this census has not yet been completed, but the partial results available indicate that the birth rate is comparable with the year 1940.

Another important contribution to the calculation of the birth rate is furnished by the results of an enquiry into fertility carried out during the 1940 census. Adults included in the census were asked how many children they had had up to the date of the census, distinguishing live and stillbirths. The replies obtained have made it possible to calculate cumulative fertility rates (proportion of children born up to a given age to persons of that age at the time of the census). It is possible to deduce the curve of annual fertility rates from the curve of these cumulative rates, as a function of age, and this has been done for the female population.[3]

The enquiry into female fertility included 12.43 million women over 14 years of whom 7.26 million had given birth to 39.45 live children.

The following table gives the cumulative and age specific female fertility rates calculated from the results of this enquiry.[4]

If the age specific fertility rates are applied to the female population included in the 1940 census[5] a total estimate of 1,966,457 live births is obtained which corresponds to a birth rate of 47.69 per 1,000 inhabitants, a figure appreciably higher than the estimates obtained earlier. The difference

[1] This extension is advisable in view of the errors in the declaration of children's ages. See the supplementary note to Section V quoted above.
[2] The Brazilian birth rate may seem exceptionally high when compared with that of Western Europe. However, it should be recalled that the birth rate in Mexico and in several central American countries was between 40 and 48 per 1,000 inhabitants in the years around 1940.
[3] See BIGS 10 Section I, and Morata, 6, Section IV. A summary of the methods used in Brazil to calculate changes in the population from the census returns was given at the 26th Session of the International Statistical Institute (see Morata, 4), and a bibliography of their applications to the 27th Session (see Morata, 7).
[4] See BIGS 10, p. 19.
[5] See BIGS 10, pp. 25 and 26.

TABLE 95.

Age (x)	Number of live births per 1,000 women	
	Up to age x years	Between ages x and (x+1) years
14	—	6
15	6	12
16	18	35
17	53	74
18	127	128
19	255	169
20	424	205
21	629	236
22	865	262
23	1 127	283
24	1 410	299
25	1 709	310
26	2 019	316
27	2 335	311
28	2 646	305
29	2 951	298
30	3 249	290
31	3 539	281
32	3 820	271
33	4 091	260
34	4 351	248
35	4 599	235
36	4 834	221
37	5 055	206
38	5 261	191
39	5 452	175
40	5 627	159
41	5 786	143
42	5 929	126
43	6 055	109
44	6 164	92
45	6 256	75
46	6 331	57
47	6 388	39
48	6 427	21
49	6 448	3

Note. For 50 years the cumulative fertility rate is 6.451 per 1,000 women.

is due partly to the errors inherent in this kind of estimate, but the major influence is probably the difference between the periods under consideration.

The preceding calculations referred to the five or ten years immediately before the census. The present estimate is based on the statements of the women questioned in 1940, a proportion of whom had borne children a considerable number of years before that date. It is only necessary to compare the calculated figure of 16.27 million live births during the 10 years before the census with the figure of 39.45 million live births declared by the women questioned in 1940 to realize the importance of the less recent age groups in the total.

As the birth rate has declined, although only slowly, during the whole period during which these children were born[1] this fall appears to be the main cause of the low birth rate arrived at in the earlier calculations.

The female fertility rates estimated for Brazil are high when compared with most western countries, but seem quite credible when compared with the rates observed in Russia about 1900 and with some other Eastern European countries, as well as with those estimated in other Latin American States (Mexico, Peru, etc.)[2] On the other hand, it should be borne in mind that a population growth as rapid as that which took place in Brazil during the last 100 years could not have occurred in the absence of a very high birth rate. Consequently, it can be concluded that the birth rate in Brazil, around 1940, was between 42 and 44 per 1,000 inhabitants and that there is reason to believe that the present level is approximately the same.

Another method used to obtain an estimate of female fertility, when it is not possible to measure this directly, is that of comparing the number of children of less than five years with the number of women of child-bearing age (15 to 49 years), these figures being obtained from the census.

It is not possible to examine the bases and significance of this method here.[3] It is only necessary to recall that the relationship so defined depends not only upon the level of female fertility but also upon changes in the number and age structure of the female population of child-bearing age, migratory movements and mortality rates among young children during the five years before the census. Nevertheless, the major influence is, in general, that of female fertility and the relationship does provide an approximate index of the latter.

In the case of Brazil, as has already been pointed out, it is preferable to use the relationship between the number of children under 10 years and the number of women of child-bearing age. This relationship has been calculated for a number of countries[4] whose demographic situations differ

[1] See BIGS 15, p. 13.
[2] See BIGS 10, p. 29.
[3] For a detailed discussion see BIGS 16, and the note to Section V. The relation between this method and the one applied in the first paragraph of this section is apparent.
[4] See BIGS 8, no. 34, p. 5.

TABLE 96.

Country	Year	Children less than 10 years for each 100 women between 15 and 49 years
Philippines	1939	135.39
Turkey	1935	133.79
Peru	1940	128.33
Columbia	1938	121.34
Brazil	1940	121.33
India	1931	116.40
Mexico	1940	115.20
Venezuela	1941	112.93
Yugoslavia	1931	104.93
Japan	1940	102.04
Chile	1940	96.97
Rumania	1930	95.48
Poland	1931	92.15
Portugal	1940	83.65
Italy	1936	79.84
Spain	1940	71.71
Canada	1941	70.96
Australia	1933	68.45
France	1936	64.47
Sweden	1945	58.88
United States	1940	58.83
England and Wales	1931	56.41
Germany	1937	54.84
Switzerland	1941	52.48

greatly. As will be seen from Table 96, the results for Brazil, according to the 1940 census, are among the highest found.

It is not yet possible to calculate this relationship for Brazil for 1950 as the results of the census are not yet available. But the calculation for 14 states, the Territory of Acre and the Federal District gives 120.33 per 100 for 1950 compared with 119.98 in 1940. The stability of the figures does not necessarily imply a corresponding stability of female fertility. It is probable that the latter has fallen slightly but child mortality has also decreased and these two factors roughly cancel each other out. However, the figure obtained indicates that fertility remained at a high level in recent years.

The Birth Rate in the Different Natural and Political Regions

A high birthrate such as that found in Brazil cannot be the result of widely different levels in different areas of the country. It is only in zones of limited demographic importance that large deviations from the average are to be found. This is verified by the information available regarding the different regions of Brazil given in Table 97 below which shows: (a) Maximum and minimum limits of the birth rate as computed by the Brazilian Institute of Geography and Statistics from the results of the 1940 census;[1] (b) The average number of live births per 100 women over 15 years calculated from the results of the 1940 inquiry into fertility; (c) The relationship between the number of children less than 10 years old and the number of women between 15 and 49 according to the same census.

The information given in Table 97 on the population of the different regions makes it possible to estimate the relative importance of each region in the national average birth rate.

There is a considerable difference between the different regions in this respect. The influence on the national average is practically negligible for the Federal Territory of Acre (0.19 per cent) and varies considerably for the states between a minimum for the Mato Grosso (1.05 per cent) and a maximum for São Paulo (17.43 per cent). The Federal Territory, with its almost entirely urban population represents 4.28 per cent in the national average.

The birth rate is very high in the thinly populated territory of Acre, and very low in the more densely populated Federal District, compared with the national average. But the differences in the level of the birth rate in the states are not great and vary from a minimum of 39 per 1,000

[1] See BIGS 9, p. 11. In the birth-rate estimates of Table I these limits have been taken into account as well as the rate of child mortality obtained by the comparison of the number of surviving children at the time of the census with the total number of children born to the women questioned (see BIGS 12, pp. 59 and 64). For example, the estimated rate of 47 per 1,000 inhabitants in the State of Rio Grande do Norte, where child mortality is very high, has been taken as nearer the maximum of 50.02 than the minimum of 41.40, whereas the rate of 44 for the State of Paraná, where child mortality is fairly low, is nearer the minimum (42.41) and considerably below the maximum (51.24).

(Rio Grande do Sul) and a maximum of 48 per 1,000 (Paraíba). In all the states it is high and in 13 out of 20 is between 41 and 45 per 1,000 inhabitants.

The number of live births per 100 women aged 15 and over varies between

TABLE 97. Brazil 1940. Birth Rates and Fertility Rates According to the Different Regions.

Natural and political regions	Population as of 1/9/40	Birth rate per 1,000 inhabitants (1938–40)	Average number of live births per 1,000 women aged 15 and over (1940)	Number of children under 10 years per 1,000 women aged 15–49 (1940)
Acre	79 768	48	412	154
Amazonas	445 460	45	314	131
Pará	944 644	43	298	115
North	*1 469 872*	*44*	*309*	*122*
Maranhão	1 235 169	45	320	126
Piauí	817 601	46	337	134
Ceará	2 091 032	47	352	135
Rio Grande do Norte	768 018	47	385	121
Paraíba	1 422 282	48	379	125
Pernambuco	2 688 240	45	347	115
Alagoas	951 300	44	350	123
North-East	*9 973 642*	*46*	*352*	*124*
Sergipe	542 326	45	356	117
Bahia	3 918 112	43	324	119
Minas Gerais	6 736 416	42	344	129
Espírito Santo	750 107	47	362	143
Rio de Janeiro	1 847 857	41	340	126
Distrito Federal	1 764 141	28	224	71
East[1]	*15 625 953*	*41*	*326*	*119*
São Paulo	7 189 493	40	329	113
Paraná	1 236 276	44	341	132
Santa Catarina	1 178 340	44	344	145
Rio Grande do Sul	3 320 689	39	307	124
South	*12 924 798*	*40*	*326*	*115*
Mato Grosso	432 265	41	288	135
Goiás	826 414	44	318	134
West-Central	*1 258 679*	*42*	*298*	*135*
Brazil[1]	*41 252 944*	*42*	*330*	*121*

[1] 'East' and 'Brazil' include the region of the Serra dos Aimores (population 66,994) which is contested by the states of Minas Gerais and Espírito Santo but does not appear separately in the Table.

a minimum of 288 (Mato Grosso) and a maximum of 385 (Rio Grande do Norte). These figures are very high[1] and in 14 out of 20 states the figure is between 310 and 360. The ratio between the number of children aged less than 10 years and the number of women between 15 and 49 years is also high and varies between a minimum of 113 (São Paulo) and a maximum of 145 (Santa Catarina). In 17 of the 20 states it was between 115 and 135 per 100.

The position of the different states in the list in Table 97 is not the same according to the different indices. Nevertheless, the three relationships established in Table 97 indicate in each case a birth rate above the national average for the States of Piauí, Ceará, Rio Grande do Norte, Paraíba, Alagoas, Minas Gerais, Espírito Santo, Paraná, Santa Catarina and below average for the State of São Paulo.

It should be borne in mind that these three indices of the level of the birth rate have not the same significance in each case, as was pointed out above. Consequently, the differences between them should not be interpreted as being proof of a contradiction. For example, the estimated birth rate and the average number of live births by women over 15 years of age in the Rio Grande do Sul are considerably below the national average, whereas the relationship between the number of children under 10 years and the number of women between 15 and 49 years is a little higher than the average. The contradiction is only apparent, the high level of the latter index being the result of the fairly low level of infant mortality. The same explanation is valid for the Mato Grosso.

In Pernambuco, on the other hand, the estimated birth rate and the average number of live births for women over 15 are above the national average whereas the relationship between the number of children under 10 years and the number of women between 15 and 49 years is considerably below, probably because of the high child mortality rate.

Even if the discrepancies observed between the different series in Table 97 are due to unavoidable errors in the collection of data, and the calculation of estimates of this kind, they do not invalidate the general picture of the territorial distribution of the birth rate in Brazil which shows a high level in all parts of the country. No doubt physical differences exercise an influence but the results show that this is small compared with other factors.

If the data, for Pará, on the northern frontier, the Rio Grande do Sul, in the south, Maranhão, along the Atlantic coastline, Goiás, with its Mediterranean climate, the arid region of Ceará with an equatorial climate, or Santa Catarina, richly endowed with water and a temperate climate, are compared, the analogies are so striking that one is forced to recognize the predominance of non-physical over physical factors.

[1] In Peru, a country which also has a very high birth rate, the average number of live births per 100 women aged 15 and over was 329 according to the 1940 census or about the same as the average calculated for Brazil (330). Both these figures are below those calculated for 12 of the 20 states in Brazil.

The high birth rate in all parts of Brazil also leads to the conclusion that biological factors as well are of a secondary nature. In the north the native population is the most important element, in the north-east the Negro element is predominant whereas, in the south, the Europeans[1] are in a large majority. But these differences are not reflected in the birth rate figures. It is not possible to conclude from this that they are without influence but their action is hidden by that of other factors.

The same reasoning could lead to the conclusion that social factors also have very little influence but this conclusion would be premature. In fact, it is the action of several social factors over the whole country which explain both the high general level of the birth rate and the limitation of the number of births.

The existence of a high birth rate in all parts of the country has so far been stressed, as this is the dominant feature. However, regional differences also exist and an attempt is made in the following paragraphs of this section to analyse their importance and the factors which give rise to them.

A general picture of the influence of social factors on the birth rate is given in Table 98 where the states are arranged in descending order according to the average number of live births by women over 15 years of age (corrected by the standard population method).[2] Table 98 gives, for each state, the rural population and the inhabitants of small towns of less than 5,000 inhabitants as percentages of the total population, the percentage of the population aged 10 years and over who are unable to read and write, and the percentage of the female population between the ages of 20 and 29 who are, or who have been, married. The object of this classification is to bring out the influences of life in the town or country, of the level of education and of marriage, on the birth rate.

A rough indication of the correlation between female fertility and social conditions can be obtained by calculating the averages[3] for the first and last 10 of the 20 states, grouped according to the importance of the female fertility rate, in Table 98.

For the ten states with the highest fertility rates the average rural population is 88 per cent, for the other 10 states, with the lowest fertility rates, it is 82.7 per cent. The percentage of the population unable to read or write is 65.5 per cent in the first group of states and 59.7 per cent in the second. The respective percentages of women between 20 and 29 who are, or who have been, married are 63 per cent and 55.6 per cent. There is,

---

[1] According to the 1940 census the proportion of the white population to the total in the different states varied between 28.74 per cent and 30.96 per cent in the States of Bahia and Amazonas respectively, and 88.66 per cent and 94.44 per cent in the Rio Grande do Sul and Santa Catarina.

[2] See BIGS 16, and Section V for details of this correction.

[3] Unweighted arithmetic average.

State	Average number of live births per 100 women aged 15 and over [1]	Rural population as a percentage of total [2]	Illiterates over 10 years as percentage of total	Women between 20–29 married widowed or divorced as percentage of total female population between 20–29
Rio Grande do Norte	381	90	70	61
Espírito Santo	381	90	54	64
Paraíba	380	88	76	59
Paraná	354	86	51	72
Minas Gerais	353	88	62	66
Santa Catarina	353	90	44	67
Ceará	351	89	70	62
Piauí	346	92	78	66
Pernambuco	345	80	72	54
Alagoas	343	87	78	59
Sergipe	343	87	70	51
Amazonas	334	85	58	52
Rio de Janeiro	334	72	52	56
Goiás	329	96	74	66
São Paulo	329	64	42	70
Bahia	322	88	73	48
Maranhão	312	95	76	56
Rio Grande do Sul	307	77	39	58
Mato Grosso	304	83	54	53
Pará	294	80	54	46

[1] Corrected by standard population.
[2] Rural population and inhabitants of small towns with less than 5,000 inhabitants.

therefore, some evidence of the existence of a correlation but it is rather low and there are numerous and, sometimes, important exceptions.

However, it is preferable to single out the cases where the influence of the circumstances under consideration corresponds with international experience, rather than to stress examples where this influence is not discernable at first sight due to the predominance of other factors. For example, in the eight states with the highest fertility rates all have a very high percentage of rural populations and, in seven of them, the percentage of married women is high. Conversely, in the seven states with the lowest fertility rates, two (São Paulo and Rio Grande do Sul) have fairly low percentages of rural populations and five show low percentage figures for women who are, or who have been, married. The correlation between fertility and illiteracy is less marked, but in the north-eastern states, where fertility is high, there is a high level of illiteracy, whereas in São Paulo and the Rio Grande do Sul lower fertility rates and lower percentages of illiteracy are found.

The conclusion which can be drawn from an examination of Table 98 is that these different factors sometimes act together in the same direction, whereas elsewhere their action tends to be opposed so that they are without influence on the final result. It will be the object of the following sections to analyse in greater detail the action of the various factors present.

CHAPTER III

The Birth Rate in the
Different Ethnic Groups

In the 1940 census, the enquiry into female fertility included information regarding the colour of the person interviewed. The question was asked quite simply and no detailed criteria were laid down for the guidance of interviewers. It must, therefore, be concluded that the definition used followed the custom of the region. This lack of precision in the question regarding race and colour in the 1940 census enquiry is explained by the desire of the National Census Commission to avoid any formulae which could contribute to the strong current of neo-fascist racial propaganda in the country at the time of the census.

It should be recalled that the ethnical origins of the Brazilian population are extremely complex and varied. The wide range of colour groups makes it impossible to classify a large number of cases which fall between the two extremes of negro and white. However, Japanese immigration, being of more recent date, presents no difficulty in this respect. Persons of Japanese descent have been classified as 'yellow',[1] their intermarriage with other ethnic groups was of small importance in 1940.

A critical analysis of the results of the 1940 census[2] suggests that the definition 'white' was applied somewhat indiscriminately to a number of persons who, according to a more objective classification, would have been included in the group 'half-caste'. The same type of problem arises in the case of the 'negro' and 'half-caste' groups, though here the problem of the correct grouping to adopt is more complicated. There were cases where people who should have been grouped under 'half-caste' were put under 'negro', and, less frequently, the contrary, as is shown by a comparison of the results of the 1940 and 1950[3] censuses.

These imperfections in the census figures are more important for ethnological than for social studies, as the classification of half-castes as 'white' or 'negro' was in part a result of the social standing of the individual.

As regards the study of the birth rate in the different ethnic groups,

[1] The same term was applied to a few hundred individuals whose skin had become yellow as a result of illness, but these have been eliminated from the figures.
[2] See BIGS 14 and Section I.
[3] See BIGS 8, no. 35.

425

which forms the subject matter of the following paragraphs, the census figures[1] are quite adequate.

From the census figures of the total number of women (W) in each group, the number of women having given birth to live children (F) (referred to henceforth as 'fecund'), and the total number of children (C) the following relationships can be established:

$\dfrac{C}{W}$ – cumulative fertility rate, expressed per 100 women.

$\dfrac{F}{W}$ – fraction of the total number of women who have given birth to live children, expressed as a percentage.

$\dfrac{C}{F}$ – cumulative reproduction rate expressed per 100 women.

The equation
$$\frac{C}{W} = \frac{F}{W} \times \frac{C}{F}$$

means that the cumulative fertility rate varies as a function of the number of fecund women and the cumulative reproduction rate.

The following results, shown in Table 99, were obtained in 1940 for women aged 15 and over.

TABLE 99.

Age	Average number of live births per 100 women	Percentage of fecund women	Average number of live births per 100 fecund women
15–19	12.2	8.7	140.7
20–29	169.0	57.4	294.4
30–39	443.7	81.0	547.7
40–49	609.2	84.4	721.8
50–59	640.3	84.2	760.2
60+	643.3	83.7	768.9
15+	330.4	60.8	543.4

The averages of from six to seven children in column (1) and of seven to eight in column (2) for the number of children born to the two categories of women distinguished in Table 99 at the end of the reproduction period are an indication of the high level of female fertility in Brazil.

The percentage of women who have given birth to live children increases gradually up to the ages between 35 and 39 years and remains relatively stable thereafter. In the earliest age groups the influence of the marriage

[1] See BIGS 10 and 16.

426

institution is predominant and this aspect is dealt with in the next section.

For the moment the figures in Table 99 will be used for a comparison with the different colour groups given below in Table 100.

TABLE 100.   Female Fertility According to Colour and Age Groups.

Age	White	Half-caste	Negro	Yellow
Average number of live births per 100 women				
15–19	12.0	13.5	11.3	5.7
20–29	167.7	178.4	160.9	161.1
30–39	442.0	463.9	423.3	433.1
40–49	615.6	623.8	566.9	567.8
50–59	652.2	643.8	588.9	519.4
60+	661.5	643.6	580.7	456.1
Percentage of women having given birth to live children				
15–19	8.7	9.3	7.9	4.6
20–29	58.3	57.5	53.1	63.6
30–39	81.8	81.2	77.1	91.6
40–49	85.1	84.4	81.1	94.8
50–59	84.9	84.2	81.0	93.7
60+	84.5	83.6	80.7	90.8
Average number of live births for 100 fecund women				
15–19	138.5	145.3	142.8	125.1
20–29	287.6	310.1	303.1	253.2
30–39	540.3	571.6	548.8	472.8
40–49	723.1	739.0	698.8	599.2
50–59	768.2	764.5	727.0	554.4
60+	782.8	770.1	719.6	502.4

The numerical importance of the women in each group, compared with the total number over 15, should be borne in mind.

The percentages are as follows:[1] white 63 per cent, half-caste 21.15 per cent, negro 15.34 per cent, yellow 0.51 per cent.

It will be seen that the cumulative fertility rates for women in the white and half-caste groups differ only slightly. The rate for half-caste women is a little higher up to the age of 49 and that for white women beyond 49. This difference may be due to the introduction, very restricted as yet, of family limitation methods by younger people especially in the white colour group. This is, however, only an hypothesis, although one which seems to be justified by the experience of the large towns.

[1] In absolute figures: 7,521,526 white; 2,525,681 half-caste; 1,831,641 negro; 60,954 yellow. Total 11,939,810. For the age distribution see BIGS 10, p. 65.

The cumulative fertility rates for negro women are below those for the two other groups. The difference is most marked compared with half-castes up to 49 years, and with white women beyond that age, this being the possible consequence of the circumstances mentioned in the previous paragraph.

In the half-caste group, the number of fecund women as a percentage of the total number of women (F/W) is slightly lower in nearly every case than in the white group. On the other hand, the cumulative reproduction rate (C/F) is somewhat higher in the age groups below 49. The association of a higher percentage of fecund women in the white group among younger women with a lower cumulative reproduction ratio may also be interpreted as an indication of family limitation in these groups.

The most characteristic feature of the negro group is the lower percentage of women who have had children. This difference, compared with the other groups, is light in the later age groups (81 compared with 84 and 85). But it is greater for younger women and seems to indicate a certain disadvantage for negro women as regards marriage. The cumulative reproduction rate for negroes, though lower than in the half-caste group, is higher than the white group up to 39 years of age, beyond which it falls below. To some extent this may be explained by the high mortality rate among negroes, most of whom belong to the poorer classes. No doubt the proportion of widows in the reproduction age group is higher in the case of negroes than for the other two groups, though this difference is less marked in the case of half-castes.[1]

The 'yellow' group, although of small numerical importance, is extremely interesting for the demographer and sociologist. The cumulative fertility rates for women in this group are comparable with those in the other two groups (slightly higher than for negroes and a little below the white and half-caste groups) up to the age of 50, but considerably below beyond that age. The proportion of fecund women is exceptionally high in this group, most immigrants having arrived in the country as family units already formed. The cumulative reproduction rate is fairly high among the younger women who have spent most of their adult lives in Brazil, but low in the case of older women who were already nearing the end of the child-bearing period when they left Japan. This contrast illustrates the process of adaptation on the part of immigrants to conditions prevailing in the country of immigration.

To complete the general picture of the birth rate in the three main colour groups, the results of a recent study[2] on age-specific fertility rates are given in Table 101. These rates have been calculated from the cumulative rates obtained from the 1940 census and reproduced in Table 100.

---

[1] This fact also contributes, though to a limited extent, to the lower level of the cumulative reproduction ratio in this group compared with white women.
[2] See BIGS 16, Section V.

428

TABLE 101. Average Annual Number of Live Births per 100 Women According to Colour and Age.

Age	White	Half-caste	Negro	Total women[1]
15–19	8.0	8.8	7.8	8.1
20–24	25.4	27.2	24.4	25.6
25–29	30.6	32.4	30.2	30.8
30–34	27.8	27.0	25.4	27.1
35–39	21.2	20.2	19.2	20.7
40–44	14.4	11.0	8.4	12.7
45–49	4.6	3.4	2.6	4.1

[1] The total includes the 'yellow' group not shown separately, in the table.

Very interesting results have been obtained by combining the classification according to colour with the figures for the different regions. It has thus been possible to calculate the same ratios given in Tables 99 and 100 for each political unit of the Federation.[1] For the purposes of comparison these results have been standardized with reference to the female population for the whole country aged 15 and over.

Table 102 below gives the cumulative fertility rates and Table 103 the percentage of fecund women. In each case the figures refer to women aged 15 and over for each political unit and for the three main colour groups.[2] The rate before standardizations is also included in the tables, where the political units are arranged in descending order according to the standardized cumulative fertility rate.

In the complete study these results are analysed in great detail as the results obtained did not correspond with currently held views on the subject. For example, some writers had maintained that the birth rate was much higher among negroes due to their lower social standing and evolution. On the other hand, it had been suggested that the negro element was doomed to extinction due to the combined influence of a low birth rate and a high mortality. The results of the 1940 census, confirmed in 1950, show that these opinions were far from the truth, but for the moment only the main features of the results obtained will be mentioned.

The figures in Table 102 show that the standardization of the cumulative fertility rates does not alter the general picture of the relative positions of the three main colour groups. The average number of live births per 100 women is 333 for the white group in both cases and 334 : 340 and 316 :

[1] See BIGS 16, Section V.
[2] The 'yellow' group being concentrated for the most part in the State of São Paulo, it was considered advisable not to show this group separately as the calculations in the case of states are based on a small number of observations.

309 respectively for half-castes and negroes. The figure for half castes is slightly increased by the application of a standard correction and the figure for the negro group reduced, but the differences are small.

The advantage of the standard population method is to eliminate differences due to the age distribution in the various states. For example, the average number of live births per 100 white women is changed from 306 to 332 in the Mato Grosso and from 223 to 197 in the Federal District. The correction also has the effect of increasing the cumulative fertility rates for all the colour groups in the Territory of Acre and of reducing them in the Federal District.

If these two areas are excluded from the comparison it is found that the corrected average number of live births per 100 women over 15 years varies as follows: Between 290 (Pará) and 389 (Rio Grande do Norte, Paraíba) for the white group; between 278 (Mato Grosso) and 388 (Rio Grande do Norte) for half-castes; between 255 (Rio Grande do Sul) and 359 (Espírito Santo) for negroes.

An analysis of the territorial distribution of the cumulative fertility rates confirms the slight, but generalized, inferiority of the negro group, being less than the rates for half-castes and whites in 19 and 18 of the 20 states respectively. In 12 states the half-caste rate is below that for the whites but the average is higher.[1]

Table 102 shows that there is a very high degree of correlation between the territorial distributions of the fertility rates for the different colour groups. If Acre, where fertility is very high, and the Federal District, where it is very low, are included, the correlation index is very high. Even if they are excluded, coefficients of correlation of + 0.82, between the distribution by states of the corrected fertility rates for half-caste and white women, and of + 0.63 between negroes and white women, are obtained. Indices of the degree of dependence[2] are 0.64 and 0.47 respectively. The presence of a high degree of interdependence between the territorial distribution of the fertility of the different groups is thus established. An exhaustive documentation on this subject is given in the study quoted earlier, from which the details of Table 102 have been taken.

The role of ethnical factors is evidently quite secondary. Fertility among negroes is generally lower than among whites, but sometimes it is higher. For example, in the State of Rio de Janeiro, the cumulative standardized fertility rate for negro women reaches 349.4 while the rate for white women is 323.9. In six states, the standardized rate for negro women is higher than the general average for the female population (330.4), and in six states the standardized rate for white women is below the average.

[1] There is no contradiction between these two statements due to the relative importance of the weights of the different groups in the average.

[2] Calculated according to the author's formula, this index measures the proportion of common factors in the variations of two phenomena; in this case, the fertility of white and half-caste women, or whites and negroes.

TABLE 102. Average Number of Live Births per 100 Women Aged 15 and Over for the Three Main Colour Groups and for the Population as a Whole According to Political Regions.

Region	White		Half-caste		Negro		Total	
	C[1]	S	C	S	C	S	C	S
Acre	411.0	449.6	407.0	441.1	424.5	427.3	411.5	442.8
Rio Grande do Norte	391.2	388.5	385.7	388.4	360.1	339.8	384.5	381.2
Espírito Santo	364.8	385.8	364.5	386.3	347.2	359.2	361.6	381.0
Paraíba	386.1	388.8	379.1	384.7	350.8	338.4	378.8	379.9
Paraná	342.1	355.9	336.7	346.8	329.3	332.2	340.8	353.5
Minas Gerais	352.7	363.7	343.5	357.4	317.9	320.3	343.8	353.4
Santa Catarina	345.4	355.0	322.7	337.9	324.8	324.8	344.2	353.1
Ceará	356.2	358.8	355.4	358.6	339.5	329.3	352.0	351.4
Piauí	344.8	357.3	334.0	352.5	328.6	327.6	337.1	346.1
Pernambuco	357.1	355.2	347.2	351.3	315.7	302.6	347.4	345.2
Alagoas	353.7	349.8	351.8	349.3	329.2	306.4	349.5	342.8
Sergipe	367.6	356.2	350.6	345.2	334.8	307.3	355.5	342.6
Amazonas	311.6	328.4	312.4	337.9	331.8	332.5	313.8	334.4
Rio de Janeiro	332.8	323.9	347.5	348.1	355.7	349.4	340.4	333.6
Goiás	326.1	345.6	344.5	348.4	272.1	260.9	318.2	328.8
São Paulo	331.3	329.4	328.3	345.5	310.8	318.5	328.7	328.7
Bahia	333.0	330.4	326.8	331.7	306.5	291.3	324.3	322.4
Maranhão	327.9	323.1	309.6	308.7	314.8	296.6	319.6	311.9
Rio Grande do Sul	309.7	310.6	324.8	321.8	264.9	255.3	307.2	306.9
Mato Grosso	306.4	331.8	265.5	278.1	283.2	275.8	287.8	304.1
Pará	293.3	289.6	301.6	303.5	298.8	274.1	297.5	294.0
Distrito Federal	223.1	197.0	229.0	224.9	224.8	219.6	224.3	204.7
Brazil[2]	332.9	332.8	334.0	340.0	316.1	308.8	330.4	330.4

[1] C = crude figures, S = standardized figures.
[2] The total includes the 'yellow' group. 'Brazil' includes the region of the Serra dos Aimores.

It should be noted that the author considers 'ethnical factors' to be essentially biological in origin. The handicap for negro women as regards selection and marriage depends on social factors, in particular racial prejudice, and is not considered to be an ethnical factor. Table 103 gives some idea of the extent of this handicap. In the 20 states the standardized figures for women over 15 who have borne live children vary between: 57.5 per cent (Bahia) and 66.9 per cent (Paraná) for white women; 58.7 per cent (Pernambuco) and 68.6 per cent (Goiás) for half-castes; 51.8 per cent (Rio Grande do Sul) and 63.4 per cent (Maranhão) for negroes.

TABLE 103. Percentage of Women Over 15 Having Given Birth to Live Children According to Colour Groups and for the Total Population, Grouped According to Political Regions.

Region	White		Half-caste		Negro		Total	
	C[1]	S	C	S	C	S	C	S
Acre	69.0	70.9	69.0	71.2	68.2	68.4	68.8	70.5
Rio Grande do Norte	58.5	58.8	60.6	61.2	57.0	55.7	59.2	59.4
Espírito Santo	63.9	65.8	64.0	65.8	60.7	62.0	63.3	65.1
Paraíba	58.4	58.9	58.5	59.4	55.8	55.1	58.1	58.5
Paraná	65.7	66.9	65.2	66.3	61.9	62.6	65.5	66.6
Minas Gerais	62.2	63.1	61.8	63.2	58.2	58.7	61.3	62.2
Santa Catarina	64.7	65.9	63.4	65.4	60.1	60.5	64.4	65.6
Ceará	57.5	58.2	59.1	59.8	57.8	57.3	57.9	58.4
Piauí	63.0	64.0	62.3	63.9	63.2	62.8	62.9	63.6
Pernambuco	57.7	57.6	58.3	58.7	55.3	53.9	57.5	57.3
Alagoas	60.7	60.3	61.4	61.4	58.8	56.7	60.6	60.1
Sergipe	58.7	58.0	60.0	59.8	58.0	55.3	59.0	58.1
Amazonas	60.7	61.9	63.6	65.6	63.1	63.0	62.7	64.2
Rio de Janeiro	62.6	61.7	63.0	63.4	62.9	62.7	62.7	62.2
Goiás	61.7	63.3	68.7	68.6	56.2	54.8	61.5	62.3
São Paulo	63.5	63.2	61.1	62.3	57.9	58.6	63.1	62.9
Bahia	57.6	57.5	58.6	59.1	56.6	55.2	57.9	57.8
Maranhão	65.4	64.6	65.1	64.6	65.8	63.4	65.5	64.3
Rio Grande do Sul	60.6	60.8	64.8	64.5	52.7	51.8	60.2	60.3
Mato Grosso	60.8	62.8	58.8	59.8	57.6	56.6	59.7	61.0
Pará	61.8	60.7	63.8	63.3	62.2	59.1	62.7	61.7
Distrito Federal	56.7	52.4	54.3	53.1	50.9	49.6	55.5	52.2
Brazil[2]	61.5	61.5	60.4	61.0	58.3	57.6	60.8	60.8

[1] C = crude figures, S = standardized figures.
[2] The total includes the 'yellow' group. 'Brazil' includes the region of the Serra dos Aimores

The percentage of fecund women is lower among negroes than half-castes in 20 states and lower than among whites in 18.

The adoption of the standard-population method accentuates the inferiority of negro women in this respect compared with the other two groups. The crude and standardized figures are the same for the white group (61.5 per cent) and increases slightly for half-castes from 60.4 per cent to 61.0 per cent, while the percentage for negroes falls slightly from 58.3 per cent to 57.6 per cent.

The hypothesis that the negro woman is handicapped in marriage receives some support from Table 104.

TABLE 104. Ratio of the Percentage of Fecund Negro Women to Fecund White Women[1] is Compared with the Number of Negroes as a Percentage of the Total Population of the State.[2]

State	Percentage of negroes	Index of the proportion of fecund negro women
Piauí	31.94	98
Maranhão	27.56	98
Ceará	23.31	98
Rio de Janeiro	21.33	102
Bahia	20.14	96
Minas Gerais	19.28	93
Sergipe	18.71	95
Espírito Santo	17.25	94
Goiás	16.95	87
Pernambuco	15.51	94
Alagoas	13.83	94
Paraíba	13.68	94
Rio Grande do Norte	13.38	95
Pará	9.52	97
Mato Grosso	8.46	90
São Paulo	7.31	93
Amazonas	7.17	102
Rio Grande do Sul	6.65	85
Santa Catarina	5.21	92
Paraná	4.89	94

[1] Calculated from the standardized figures in Table 103.
[2] See BIGS 14, p. 33.

The relatively lower level of the proportion of fecund negro women is very slight in the north-east and eastern states, where this colour group is strongly represented. It is more marked in the southern states where the percentage of negroes is less. Also, it is not only the negro percentage of the population which is a determinate. The ethnic composition of the rest of the population also exercises an important, and sometimes preponderant influence. In the states of Rio Grande do Sul, Santa Catarina and Paraná, and to a less extent, in São Paulo, the Slav and Teutonic immigrants are important and have spread racial prejudices which could not have taken root in the States of Piauí, Maranhão, Ceará and others where whites of Portuguese origin or half-castes are predominant. The same is true of the States of Amazonas and Pará where the aboriginal element is important. In the two states the negro population is small numerically but the percentages of fecund negro and white women are roughly the same.

433

As regards the cumulative reproduction rates, Table 102 confirms the statement that there are no great differences between the three colour groups: for the whole country the average numbers of live births per 100 fecund women aged 15 and over which according to the crude rates, were 541 for white women, 553 for half-castes and 543 for negroes, become 542, 558 and 536 when the crude results are standardized, but the differences between the groups remain limited.

In 20 states the standardized rates vary between: 477 (Pará) and 661 (Rio Grande do Norte) for the white group; 465 (Mato Grosso) and 648 (Paraíba) for half-castes; 464 (Pará) and 614 (Paraíba) for negroes.

The cumulative reproduction rate for negroes is lower than for whites in 18 states and lower than the rate for half-castes in 15.

TABLE 105. Average Number of Live Births per 100 Fecund Women Over 15 in the Three Main Colour Groups According to Political Regions.

Region	White		Half-caste		Negro		Total	
	C[1]	S	C	S	C	S	C	S
Acre	595.8	634.1	589.9	619.5	622.8	624.7	597.7	628.1
Rio Grande do Norte	668.5	660.7	636.8	634.6	631.2	610.1	649.8	641.8
Espírito Santo	571.2	586.3	569.8	587.1	572.2	579.4	571.1	585.3
Paraíba	661.4	660.1	647.8	647.6	628.5	614.2	652.5	649.4
Paraná	520.4	532.0	516.3	523.1	531.9	530.7	520.0	530.8
Minas Gerais	567.4	576.4	556.4	565.5	546.3	545.7	561.1	568.2
Santa Catarina	533.8	538.7	508.6	516.7	540.8	536.9	534.1	538.3
Ceará	619.7	616.5	601.7	599.7	587.8	574.7	607.8	601.7
Piauí	547.2	558.3	535.9	551.6	520.0	521.7	535.7	544.2
Pernambuco	618.6	616.7	595.8	598.5	571.3	561.4	604.3	602.4
Alagoas	583.2	580.1	572.7	568.9	559.9	540.4	576.8	570.4
Sergipe	626.8	614.1	584.3	577.3	577.7	555.7	602.9	589.7
Amazonas	513.8	530.5	491.7	515.1	526.0	527.8	500.8	520.9
Rio de Janeiro	532.1	525.0	551.3	549.1	565.5	557.3	542.7	536.3
Goiás	528.2	546.0	501.5	507.9	484.4	476.1	517.5	527.8
São Paulo	521.3	521.2	537.6	554.6	536.5	543.5	521.1	522.6
Bahia	578.2	574.6	557.9	561.3	541.3	527.7	560.3	557.8
Maranhão	501.0	500.2	475.7	477.9	478.4	467.8	488.2	485.1
Rio Grande do Sul	511.0	510.9	501.1	498.9	502.9	492.9	510.0	509.0
Mato Grosso	503.8	528.3	452.5	465.1	491.5	487.3	482.0	498.5
Pará	474.7	477.1	472.6	479.5	480.3	463.8	474.3	476.5
Distrito Federal	393.3	376.0	421.5	423.5	441.8	442.7	403.8	392.1
Brazil[2]	541.4	541.5	552.7	557.5	542.5	536.1	543.4	543.4

[1] C = crude figures, S = standardized figures.
[2] The total includes the 'yellow' group. 'Brazil' includes the region of the Serra dos Aimores.

The absence of any consistent ethnical influence on these rates is demonstrated by the fact that in nine states the cumulative reproduction rate for negroes is higher than the national average whereas in nine other states the rate for white women is below the average. As has already been pointed out, the slightly lower rates for negro women may be due to the higher mortality rate.

An analysis of the preceding paragraph makes it possible to distinguish the influence of two factors on female fertility; the percentage of fecund women and the average number of children born to each.

For the country as a whole, Table 106 groups the rates obtained, by the application of the standard population method, for the three main colour groups.

TABLE 106.

Women aged 15 and over	White	Half-caste	Negro
Cumulative fertility rate	332.8	340.0	308.8
Percentage of women bearing children	61.5	61.0	57.6
Cumulative reproduction rate	541.5	557.5	536.1

The fertility of the white group is a little lower than for half-castes, in spite of the slightly higher percentage of women bearing children, due to the lower level of the cumulative reproduction rate.

The fertility of the white group is markedly higher than for the negro group, due essentially to the higher percentage of women bearing children. The cumulative reproduction rate is scarcely higher in the first group than in the second.

The fertility of the half-caste group is higher than for negroes, due either to the higher percentage of women bearing children or to the higher reproduction rate.

Nevertheless, the relatively small importance of these differences and the high level of fertility in all groups should be stressed, as well as the correlation between the territorial distribution of the fertility rates of these groups.

In eight of the 22 states the standardized cumulative fertility rates are higher than the national averages for the three groups. In three of these areas—Territory of Acre, States of Espírito Santo and Minas Gerais—the percentages of women bearing children as well as the cumulative reproduction rate are above the national averages for the three groups.

In two of these areas—Paraná and Piauí—the predominant factor is the percentage of women who have borne children, which is higher than the national averages for the three groups, while the cumulative reproduction rate is below the national averages for the three groups in Paraná and for the half-caste and negro groups in Piauí.

435

In the last three of these eight states (Rio Grande do Norte, Paraíba, and Ceará) the major factor is the reproduction rate which is higher than the averages for each group, while the percentage of women who have borne children is below the averages for the three groups in Paraíba and Ceará and for the white and negro groups in the Rio Grande do Norte.

At the other extreme are six states where the standardized cumulative fertility rates are below the national averages for the three groups. In only one of these states—the Federal District—are the two factors, percentage of women bearing children and cumulative reproduction rate, below the national averages in the three groups.

In one other state, Bahia, the influence of the percentage of fecund women, which is below the average, is predominant, whereas the cumulative reproduction ratio is higher for the white and negro groups.

In the other four states with a low fertility level—Maranhão, Rio Grande do Sul, Mato Grosso, and Pará—the cumulative reproduction ratio is decisive, being lower than the average for each of the three groups, whereas the percentages of fecund women are higher than the average for the three groups in Maranhão, for the half-caste and negro groups in Pará, the half-caste group in the Rio Grande do Sul and the white group in the Mato Grosso.

.There remain eight states whose position on the list according to fertility varies according to the groups. In six of them the standardized cumulative fertility rate is above the average for the total adult female population, but is below for one or more colour groups—half-caste in Santa Catarina, negro in Pernambuco, Alagoas and Sergipe, white in Rio de Janeiro, white and half-caste in Amazonas.

The percentages of fecund women are above the average for the three groups in Santa Catarina, Amazonas, Rio de Janeiro and São Paulo, lower in Pernambuco and Sergipe. The standardized reproduction ratios are higher than the national averages for the three groups in Pernambuco, Alagoas and Sergipe, lower in Amazonas.

These results confirm the previous findings regarding the existence of a fairly close correlation between territorial variations in fertility and the factors with an immediate bearing on its level—the percentage of fecund women and the reproduction rate—for the three main colour groups in Brazil.

The two areas at the extremes of the list of states, arranged according to the degree of fertility, merit some additional comments.

The Territory of Acre is a frontier region whose main economic activity is the exploitation of the natural resources of the territory. The population is small and widely dispersed over a large area. The number of adult women, aged 20 and over, was noticeably lower than the number of men at the time of the 1940 census (14,748 compared with 22,419). For this reason women tend to marry earlier, and this fact, together with the almost complete absence of racial prejudice, makes for a high level of fertility in all colour groups.

436

In the Federal District the population is high, and concentrated for the most part in urban areas. Conditions in the capital, as in all large cities, are not favourable to large families. The percentage of women who have borne children is low, as is the cumulative reproduction rate. The colour bar is not absolute but the existence of race prejudice no doubt contributes to the exceptionally low percentage of negro women who marry. However, fertility is also particularly low among white women where the obstacles to the growth of large families and the spread of family limitation are greatest.

The similarity between the reactions of the different colour groups to differing social conditions, such as exist in the Territory of Acre and the Federal District, is brought out in Table 107 by the comparison of indices for the different fecundity rates, based on the standardized rates, calculated with reference to the national average for each group.

TABLE 107.

Women over 15	White		Half-caste		Negro	
	Acre	F.D.	Acre	F.D.	Acre	F.D.
Index of cumulative fertility rate	135	59	130	66	138	71
Index of percentage of fecund woman	115	85	117	87	119	86
Index of cumulative reproduction rate	117	69	111	76	117	83

In the Territory of Acre the indices of fertility are from 30 to 38 per cent higher than the national averages in all groups. In the Federal District the rates vary from 29 to 41 per cent below, the strongest reaction to the conditions of town life coming from the white group.

The temptation to formulate more detailed hypotheses regarding the causes of local differences between the different colour groups must be resisted. The present state of demographic studies in Brazil does not warrant such attempts.

The information given by the 1940 census on the percentages of children under 10 and of women between 15 and 49 years provides an indirect method for the calculation of comparative fertility levels in the different colour groups, these results not always corresponding with the results of the enquiry into fertility used above. However, they in no way invalidate the general conclusions already arrived at.

In Table 108 below, the ratios between the number of children under 10 and the number of women between 15 and 49 are calculated for each colour group and political unit and arranged in descending order.

Acre is again at the head of the list with 154 children per 100 women and the Federal District at the bottom with a ratio of 71 per 100. The positions of the other states, however, are not identical with the list in

437

Table 102. This result was to be expected, given the different basis of calculation.

The greatest differences occur in the case of the Rio Grande do Norte and Pernambuco, the ratios in Table 108 being lower than the national averages, whereas those in Table 102 were higher. The reverse is true of Goiás, Maranhão, Rio Grande do Sul, and the Mato Grosso. The high child mortality rates in Pernambuco and the Rio Grande do Norte, and the low child mortality rates in the Rio Grande do Sul and the Mato Grosso, are at the origin of these differences. But this explanation is not valid in the case of Maranhão.

TABLE 108. Number of Children Under 10 per 100 Women Aged 15–49.

Political unit	White	Half-caste	Negro	Yellow	Total
Acre	156.82	153.13	143.70	...	153.88
Santa Catarina	145.87	122.27	128.60	...	144.83
Espírito Santo	146.31	146.26	126.61	...	142.80
Mato Grosso	139.19	133.84	116.45	168.70	135.31
Ceará	133.91	142.54	129.26	...	134.83
Goiás	140.64	132.42	110.87	...	134.46
Piauí	136.98	138.77	126.28	...	133.91
Paraná	133.97	124.14	113.96	155.13	132.43
Amazonas	123.80	135.88	115.96	...	130.68
Minas Gerais	131.84	131.69	115.51	143.61	128.52
Rio de Janeiro	123.81	133.51	125.78	...	126.03
Maranhão	129.57	129.75	115.80	...	125.78
Paraíba	125.88	128.21	115.78	...	125.21
Rio Grande do Sul	125.87	114.33	110.24	...	124.22
Alagoas	124.69	126.76	106.39	...	122.71
Rio Grande do Norte	119.83	125.91	106.98	...	120.67
Bahia	118.39	124.56	104.76	...	118.69
Sergipe	119.68	122.23	103.56	...	117.48
Pará	113.37	121.96	94.09	...	115.41
Pernambuco	117.06	116.84	103.03	...	114.75
São Paulo	113.44	116.79	100.53	143.15	113.42
Distrito Federal	71.41	79.52	60.85	...	71.48
Brazil[1]	122.22	125.51	110.98	143.01	121.33

[1] The total includes the 'yellow' group. 'Brazil' includes the region of the Serra dos Aimores.

Despite the differences which occur in particular instances, the figures in Table 108 on the whole confirm the conclusions arrived at regarding comparative fertility in the main colour groups; being highest among half-castes, closely followed by the white group, with the negro group considerably below the other two. The high ratio of children under 10 per

TABLE 109.   Number of Children Under 10 per 100 Women Aged 15–49.[1]

Political unit	White	Half-caste	Negro	Yellow	Total
Acre	148.13	164.74	122.22	...	157.48
Mato Grosso	141.39	147.48	125.38	158.30	142.11
Piauí	138.24	145.07	120.47		139.86
Ceará	136.93	141.81	127.74	...	138.18
Goiás	141.30	133.63	107.69	...	135.37
Espírito Santo	136.61	137.77	115.63	...	134.33
Rio Grande do Norte	130.01	136.64	116.68	...	131.45
Alagoas	129.88	133.22	101.03		129.35
Paraíba	130.72	129.44	115.49	...	128.45
Sergipe	135.41	125.92	108.43	...	128.04
Pará	117.14	132.19	96.45	...	125.69
Maranhão	127.77	128.71	107.69	...	125.01
Rio de Janeiro	118.01	128.72	119.60	157.14	120.68
Rio Grande do Sul	120.49	117.56	107.87	...	119.64
Pernambuco ‹	120.55	122.87	99.91	...	119.48
Distrito Federal	65.29	73.48	60.36	...	66.10
Total: 16 units	118.38	128.98	105.37	152.45	120.33

[1] Ratios calculated only where number of women exceeds 500.

100 women aged 15 to 49 in the yellow group is noteworthy, and is the result either of the favourable age structure or of the low level of infant mortality.

It was also possible to calculate the same ratio for 16 states[1] from the results now available for the year 1950. The respective positions of the Territory of Acre and of the Federal District are the same as before. Once again, in 12 of the 16 political units the half-caste group is superior to the white and, in all cases, except one, the negro group is lowest.[2]

The ratios obtained in Tables 108 and 109 are also influenced by the level of child mortality and, as this is higher in the half-caste group than in the white and highest of all among negroes, the true ratios, if the influence of child mortality is eliminated, are in fact closer together than the figures would suggest.

The range of variations in the ratios for each of the three groups, if the two extremes, Acre and the Federal Districts are omitted, was as follows in 1940: between 113.37 (Pará) and 146.31 (Espírito Santo) for white women; between 114.33 (Rio Grande do Sul) and 146.26 (Espírito Santo) for half-castes; between 94.09 (Pará) and 129.26 (Ceará) for negroes.

[1] The number of political units was increased from 22 in 1940 to 26 in 1950 by the creation of four new Federal Territories. These have been excluded from Table 109 as the results of the 1950 census, though available, show that their demographic importance is small.
[2] The high ratios obtained for the yellow colour group cannot be taken as representative until the results for the State of São Paulo are available.

In 1950, according to the results available, the ratios for white and negro women fell between the same limits as in 1940, the maximum for half-castes was a little higher (147.48 in the Mato Grosso).

The fall in child mortality probably explains the increase in the ratio in several states from 1940 to 1950. In others, particularly the Rio Grande do Sul, the fall in the birth rate has caused a corresponding decline. The variations between the two census years are, however, limited and the average does not exceed 5 per cent.

As regards the classification according to colour, the criteria adopted in 1950 were not entirely comparable with the earlier census and the numerical importance of certain groups has no doubt been influenced by this. Consequently, it is not possible to attribute all the divergences between the two census years to changes in the fecundity of the different groups.

In the Federal District, where differences between the two censuses are slight, the ratio between the number of children under 10 and women between 15 and 49 fell from 71.41 per 100 women in 1940 to 65.29 per 100 in 1950 in the white group, from 79.52 to 73.48 for half-castes and from 60.85 to 60.36 for negroes. As infant mortality fell considerably during this period[1] it would seem that there was a considerable reduction in fecundity, especially in the first two groups. However, this conclusion is not borne out by the birth-rate figures.[2]

In Table 110 below a comparison is made between the index numbers of the ratio between the number of children under 10 and the number of women between 15 and 49, based upon the respective national averages[3] for the Territory of Acre and the Federal District.

TABLE 110.

| Census year | Index for each colour group | | | | | |
| | White | | Half-caste | | Negro | |
	Acre	F.D.	Acre	F.D.	Acre	F.D.
1940	128	58	122	63	129	55
1950	125	55	128	57	116	57

The results confirm those given at the end of the preceding paragraph. Social factors are predominant compared with ethnical factors.

The lesson of this analysis of the birth rate in the different ethnic groups is that social factors are much more important than biological

[1] See BIGS 16, Section II.
[2] See BIGS 15, Section II.
[3] As the national averages for 1950 are not yet known, the average for the 16 states in Table 109 has been used.

influences. The differences observed between the rates measuring fecundity in the different groups depend essentially upon the relative position of each group from an economic, social and cultural point of view, on the one hand, and upon the territorial localization of the groups on the other. Also, this latter factor exercises its influence, as has been seen earlier, for the most part by its action on social, rather than on physical, conditions.

CHAPTER IV

The Birth Rate in the Various National Groups

As the time of large-scale immigration into Brazil is already far past, the proportion of adult foreign-born women, which was already low in 1940 (less than 5 per cent) is steadily decreasing. The study of the fertility of foreign women is therefore, quantitatively, of no great interest to the demographer, but cannot be overlooked by the sociologist, who is concerned with determining the influence of social factors on the birth rate. Each group of immigrants tends to preserve the customs of their original country or region in their new environment, and those customs are only gradually changed by a process of adaptation, which may be very slow or fairly rapid, under the influence of the different conditions and customs of the country of immigration.

The proportion of women bearing children is, generally speaking, relatively high among foreign immigrants to Brazil, partly because of the comparative scarcity of women in immigrant groups (in 1940, there were scarcely 77 women for every 100[1] men among the foreign-born persons[2] living in Brazil), which ʹmakes their marriage and child-bearing more probable, and partly because some of the immigrants come in as family units, thus introducing a larger number of married women and mothers.

The proportion of fecund women among the foreign-born women covered by the 1940 census was not quite 7 per cent in the 15–19 age-group, but was 62 per cent in the 20–29 group, and rose to 78 per cent for the 30–39 group, 85 per cent for the 40–49 group, 88 per cent for the 50–59 group and 90 per cent for the age-group 60 and over. These proportions are not very different from the corresponding averages for the whole of the female population. There is, however, a considerable difference in fertility between foreign-born women and those who are natives of Brazil, as can be seen from Table 111.[3]

[1] Absolute numbers: 790,375 men and 610,709 women.
[2] For the sake of brevity, citizens of foreign countries and ex-citizens of foreign countries who have become Brazilian by naturalization will be referred to as 'foreign-born' persons.
[3] The data given in this table and in Tables 112 and 113 are taken from the study by Ernani Timóteo de Barros, cited in the bibliography.

The absolute numbers of fecund foreign-born women were: 15–19, 1,970; 20–29, 46,528; 30–39, 89,066; 40–49, 103,668; 50–59, 101,847; 60 and over, 114,532; total, 457,611.

Table 111.

Age	Average number of live births, for every 100 fecund women, being natives of	
	foreign countries	Brazil
15–19	140.05	140.65
20–29	250.56	295.41
30–39	416.68	553.94
40–49	608.83	730.86
50–59	716.55	766.24
60+	748.65	772.55

The cumulative fertility rate for foreign-born women is considerably lower than that for Brazilian-born women in the age-groups from 29 to 49, while there is less difference in the age-groups 50 and over.[1]

The analysis of the main national groups of foreign-born women,[2] given in Table 112 will be of help in determining the factors responsible for the movement of cumulative fertility rates according to age.

TABLE 112. Average Number of Live Births, for Every 100 Fecund Women Aged 15 and Over, Classified According to Age Group and Country of Mother's Birth.

Age	Country of mother's birth						
	Brazil	Italy	Spain	Japan	Portugal	Germany	Other countries
15–19	140.65	177.48	147.97	123.65	143.03	129.91	139.86
20–29	295.41	270.51	285.69	264.55	233.91	212.63	241.11
30–39	553.94	457.94	515.97	480.38	357.62	284.59	398.22
40–49	730.86	724.09	726.36	605.84	520.00	350.11	549.92
50–59	766.24	852.87	758.27	553.91	606.39	436.95	631.26
60+	772.55	839.11	731.12	490.85	659.38	631.76	669.45

In the 15–19 age group, the proportion of live births for every 100 fecund foreign-born women varies considerably, from the minimum of 124 for the Japanese to the maximum of 177 for the Italians. The proportion among

[1] Some of the foreign-born women have had children before immigration to Brazil. I have already mentioned this fact in speaking of the older generations of Japanese women. Among women of European origin, however, most of the children have been born after the mother's immigration to Brazil.

[2] The absolute figures for fecund women, natives of the various foreign countries, are as follows: Italy, 130,101; Spain, 64,259; Japan, 35,609; Portugal, 98,983; Germany, 22,216; other countries, 106,443; total, 457,611.

the Spaniards and the Portuguese is also higher than that for the Brazilians (141). This is probably due to the early marriages which are common in Italy and the Iberian peninsula, but it must be noted that these proportions have been calculated from a very small group of foreign-born women,[1] so that they cannot be taken as definitely representative.

In the 20–29, 30–39, and 40–49 age groups, the cumulative fertility rates for all the national groups of foreign-born women are lower than for Brazilians. The differences are smallest in the case of the Spaniards and largest in that of the Germans. The fertility rate for Italian women is slightly lower than for Spanish.

The relative positions change in the 50–59 and 60 and over age-groups, where Italian women come first, with cumulative fertility rates considerably higher than those of the Brazilians (which themselves are very high) and of the Spaniards, which are slightly lower. German women still take the lowest place in the 50–59 age group, but their cumulative fertility rate rises sharply in the 60 and over age group, while that for Japanese women drops below those of all other groups.

In the case of the German women, attention must be drawn to the contrast between the older generations, who emigrated at a time when birth control was little practised in their country, and the younger generations, who reached maturity when the practice was rapidly spreading in Germany. Birth control seems to be the main factor accounting for the relatively low fertility rate in the age-groups from 20 to 59 among the German-born women.

The relatively low cumulative fertility rates (for Brazil) of Portuguese women in the age groups from 20 to 59 cannot be explained in the same way. Here the determining factor is probably the concentration of many of the Portuguese immigrants in the large towns,[2] where social conditions are not conducive to high fertility.

Among the younger generations of Italian women, birth control may have been practised to some extent, though not on a large scale. The same applies to a few sub-groups in the group of women born in 'other countries', which includes emigrants from countries with widely differing fertility rates (Austrians, Poles, Russians, Syrians, Lebanese, South Americans, etc.). Among the oldest generations, the cumulative fertility rate is very high for Italian women and also comparatively high for those from 'other countries'.

A single figure can be given to sum up those for different age groups shown in Table 112, for each country of origin, by the 'standard population' method, counting each national group as having the same proportional age-structure as was actually found in the whole group of fecund women

[1] Fecund women between the ages of 15 and 19: Italians, 151; Spaniards, 123; Portuguese, 337.

[2] Of the 380,325 natives of Portugal living in Brazil in 1940, over six-tenths (236,769) were concentrated in the Federal District and the Municipe de São Paulo.

of 15 and over, both Brazilian and foreign, at the 1940 census. The figures in the second column in Table 113 have been worked out by this means. The average cumulative fertility rates for women of 15 and over obtained by direct calculation, are given in the first column of the table.

TABLE 113. Average Number of Live Births, for Every 100 Fecund Women Aged 15 and Over, Classified According to the Mother's Country of Birth.

Country of birth	O[1]	C[1]
Brazil	540.13	548.18
Italy	780.28	531.34
Spain	644.09	529.20
Japan	465.72	441.41
Portugal	502.79	406.49
Germany	421.54	325.13
Other countries	491.02	429.17

[1] O = observed figures; C = corrected figures.

The corrected figures show that, upon the whole, female fertility among the Italians and the Spaniards is almost as high as among the Brazilians. The Japanese, Portuguese and women from 'other countries' have considerably lower fertility rates while the German rate is lower still.

Had we taken the rates calculated from the actual observed figures, the comparison would have been thrown out, because the immigrant women include higher proportions of mature and old women than are found among Brazilian women. The use of the 'standard population' method considerably reduces the rates representing the oldest immigration movements (particularly in the case of the Italians).

Unfortunately no data comparable with those given in Table 112 are available for Spanish, Japanese, Portuguese and German women living in their own countries. It seems probable, however, that the fertility rate of the Brazilian immigrants is higher than that of their countrywomen in their respective countries of origin.

This supposition seems to be borne out by the comparative data for Italian women (Table 114).

The fertility of Italian women in Brazil is higher than that of Italian women in Italy. The difference would be still greater if figures were available for Italy in 1940 (which would be lower than those for 1931) and for all fecund women (not only those who were or had been married).

It would seem that Brazilian conditions are conducive to the increase of fertility among immigrant women, although it should be noted that, in some of the regions of Italy from which large numbers of Brazilian immi-

TABLE 114.

| Age | Average number of live births for every 100 fecund women | |
	Natives of Italy, Brazil, 1940	Living in Italy, 1931 [1]
15–19	177	119
20–29	271	208
30–39	458	355
40–49	724	514
50+	845	609

[1] Proportion calculated for women who were or had been married.

grants have been drawn, the fertility rate is higher than the average for the country. It is possible that this is partly responsible for the difference noted above.

The fact that, even in the states which have been populated to a considerable extent by immigrants from European countries where birth control is practised, the birth rate is very high, bears out the supposition that immigrants tend to become adapted to Brazilian *mores* in the matter of reproduction. It is true that the large-scale immigrations from Germany, Italy and Austria took place before the spread of birth control in the countries of origin, but the fertility rate among these immigrants and their descendants in Brazil today is higher not only than that now observed in Germany, Italy and Austria, but also than the much higher rate noted during the last 20 or 25 years of the nineteenth century.

CHAPTER V

The Influence of the Marital Institution on the Birth Rate

The work of the sociologists has shown that the institution of marriage exercises a restraining influence on reproduction in societies where extra-marital relations are subject to social disapproval. This aspect of marriage is the one which will be examined more particularly here, although it is only one of the factors in a complex institution which has developed under the combined influence of very varied biological, psychological and social forces.

Today in Brazil the predominant attitude towards marriage is that inspired by the Catholic religion with whose doctrines in this regard the other religions generally agree. The sexual promiscuity practised by the slaves remained in force after their liberation in 1888, but only slight traces are to be found today. Consequently, the reproduction function is exercised essentially within the marriage institution, though numerous exceptions exist.

TABLE 115.

Age	Total number of women	Unmarried women			
		Total		Number having borne live children	
			%		%
12–14	1 548 020	1 541 670	99.59	388	0.02
15–19	2 286 293	1 957 928	85.64	27 528	1.20
20–24	1 977 508	950 634	48.07	103 111	5.21
25–29	1 707 064	497 467	29.14	128 177	7.51
30–34	1 281 173	280 361	21.88	98 710	7.70
35–39	1 154 010	212 617	18.42	91 046	7.89
40–44	946 182	160 900	17.01	69 338	7.33
45–49	705 963	106 079	15.03	46 045	6.52
50+	1 881 617	273 578	14.54	107 953	5.74
12+	13 487 830	5 981 234	44.35	672 296	4.98

Of a total of 10,058,193 women of child-bearing age between 15 and 49 years in 1940, 4,165,986 or 41.42 per cent were stated to be unmarried. Among these latter 563,955, or 5.61 per cent of all women, between 15 and 49, stated they had borne children. The remaining 35.81 per cent of unmarried women included, no doubt, a certain number who did not admit to having borne children or whose children were stillborn. Consequently, the percentage of 35.81 per cent unmarried women who had not borne children should no doubt be reduced slightly to take this into account. However, even if the figure of 30 per cent is taken as a maximum it remains true that a considerable number of women of child-bearing age remained childless, mostly because they had not found husbands.

Table 115 shows the number of unmarried women[1] in each age group and the number of these who had given birth to live children.

The difference between the two percentages in Table 115 gives the percentage of unmarried childless women in each age group at the time of the census, as follows:

TABLE 116.

Age	15–19	20–24	25–29	30–34	35–39	40–44	45–49	50+
Percentage	84.44	42.86	21.63	14.18	10.53	9.68	8.51	8.80

The whole of the reproduction period varies inversely to the age of the mother when the first child is borne.

Detailed comparisons of fecundity according to the marital status of women in different age groups are given in Tables 117, 118 and 119.[2]

The three tables correspond to the three measures of fecundity which have been developed in previous sections, calculated for each age group.

Table 117 gives number of live births per 100 women in each age group according to marital status. For the total of all women over 12 the ratio is 45 per 100 unmarried women, 467 per 100 married women, 388 per 100 women separated or divorced and 613 per 100 widows.

Among married women the ratio increases with age to the high level of 753 per 100 at the age of 50 and over.

Among widows the proportions increase in a like manner, but are much higher than among married women in the earlier age groups, probably because many young widows belong to the poorer classes of the population where women marry young and have many children. But beyond the 25–29 age group the number of children among widows, although very

[1] These figures are taken from BIGS 12, Section I.
[2] Space does not permit the inclusion of the absolute figures in each case. Of the 13,505,432 women aged 12 and over in 1940, 5,989,968 were unmarried, 6,167,973 married, 41,394 separated or divorced, 1,284,922 widowed and for the remaining 21,225 no details were given.

448

high, is less than in the corresponding groups of married women and reaches a limit of 679 per 100 at 50 years and over. The shorter duration of married life is the explanation for this difference.

The same is true, to an even greater extent, of women who are separated or divorced, but the figure for the last age group (50 and over) is nevertheless 573 per 100. It should be noted that this group is of small numerical importance in Brazil where divorce is not legally recognized and separation (*desquite*) rather infrequent.[1]

Among unmarried women the ratio of live births to the number of women in each age group is very low in the earlier groups, but increases with a surprising rapidity in the later periods to over 200 per 100 women between 35 and 39 years. This is due to the progressive reduction in the number of women in each age group who remain unmarried. Beyond 35 to 40 years this factor becomes less important and new births are infrequent. The ratio remains around 200 per 100 women and reaches a maximum of 222 per 100 at the age of 50 and over.

Tables 118 and 119 make it possible to distinguish two factors which exert a direct influence on the cumulative fertility rate. Table 118 shows the number of women who have borne children in each age group according

TABLE 117. Average Number of Live Births per 100 Women Aged 12 and Over, According to Marital Status, and Age Groups.

Age	Unmarried	Married	Separated and divorced	Widows	Total[1]
12–14	0.03	28.63	60.00	92.23	0.13
15–19	2.07	75.00	83.30	131.19	12.59
20–24	23.46	179.07	168.04	191.86	104.29
25–29	79.39	316.85	248.01	292.21	246.63
30–34	140.11	460.47	313.69	392.52	386.13
35–39	203.87	591.60	386.81	489.36	510.48
40–44	225.22	684.73	459.55	563.26	588.21
45–49	240.53	738.78	521.34	620.29	639.64
50–59	224.09	749.21	564.41	652.24	641.18
60–69	214.85	763.21	595.04	688.84	648.41
70–79	215.94	760.45	582.63	700.45	642.77
80+	245.30	720.21	581.68	702.46	625.10
Unknown	37.33	387.65	380.00	532.74	224.16
12+	45.29	467.09	387.92	612.57	293.31

[1] The total includes women whose marital status is unknown.

[1] The difficulty of obtaining a legal separation (cost, time, etc.) and the non-recognition of divorce mean that *de facto* separations are fairly frequent. So also are free unions.

TABLE 118.
TABLE 118. Percentage of Women Aged 12 and Over Having Borne Live Children, According to Marital Status and Age Groups.

Age	Unmarried	Married	Separated and divorced	Widows	Total[1]
12–14	0.03	20.39	35.00	43.69	0.09
15–19	1.41	51.95	54.38	65.48	8.66
20–24	10.85	79.07	77.17	81.70	46.26
25–29	25.77	88.72	81.47	87.26	70.27
30–34	33.21	91.50	83.45	89.59	79.02
35–39	42.82	92.52	84.77	91.58	83.22
40–44	43.09	92.34	86.15	92.02	83.85
45–49	43.41	92.55	87.24	92.73	85.14
50–59	40.12	91.69	88.39	92.13	84.22
60–69	38.24	91.32	85.37	91.75	84.05
70–79	37.82	91.12	83.64	91.35	83.57
80+	42.45	88.66	84.73	90.31	81.89
Unknown	9.23	69.92	78.00	83.52	39.81
12+	11.24	87.12	83.49	91.35	53.82

[1] The total includes women whose marital status is unknown.

TABLE 119. Average Number of Live Births per 100 Fecund Women, According to Marital Status.

Age	Unmarried	Married	Separated and divorced	Widows	Total[1]
12–14	137.63	140.37	171.43	211.11	142.29
15–19	147.00	144.36	153.19	200.34	145.38
20–24	216.25	226.47	217.75	234.83	225.42
25–29	308.10	357.15	304.43	334.87	350.96
30–34	397.94	503.25	375.92	438.14	488.65
35–39	476.09	639.40	456.31	534.36	613.42
40–44	522.63	741.56	533.44	612.10	701.47
45–49	554.13	798.23	597.57	668.93	751.29
50–59	558.52	817.10	638.54	707.94	761.29
60–69	561.89	835.80	697.12	750.76	771.43
70–79	570.99	834.57	696.62	766.76	769.18
80+	577.83	812.31	686.49	777.87	763.32
Unknown	404.47	554.39	487.18	637.88	563.11
12+	403.05	536.12	464.64	670.57	545.02

[1] The total includes women whose marital status is unknown.

to marital status. The rates for all women aged 12 and over in each marital group are strongly influenced by differences in the age structure. For example, the very low percentage of women who have borne children among unmarried women of all ages is partly due to the large numbers in the lower age groups. In the same way the high ratio among widows is partly explained by the predominance of the aged in this group.

Among married women the percentage who have borne children increases rapidly with age, being 79 per cent in the group 20 to 24 and over 90 per cent from 30 to 34 years onwards. At the age of 50 and over the percentage is 91.5 per cent.

Among widows the corresponding percentages are noticeably higher than for married women in the younger age groups and the possible cause for this has already been mentioned. In the 25–44 age group the percentage is lower and, beyond 45 years, slightly higher. At the age of 50 and over the percentage is 91.7 per cent.

The figures also indicate that the proportion of childless marriages at the end of the child-bearing period is less than one-tenth. Even in the separated or divorced category the percentage of women who have borne children reaches 87.3 per cent at the age of 50 and over.

Among unmarried women the percentage of women who have borne children increases rapidly with age up to 35 to 39 years either because of free unions or because of elimination from the group due to marriage. The average of 39.5 per cent for women over 50 is an indication of the extent of extra-marital unions among these women.

The cumulative reproduction rates in Table 118 furnish the details necessary for an analysis of the influences acting on fecundity.

The ratio between the number of live births and the number of women who have borne children increases with age among married women to 823 per 100 at 50 and over. This is as would be expected in a country where family limitation is little practised.

In the case of widows the ratio is higher than among married women in the lower age groups but falls below from 25 to 29 years onwards, the reasons for this being evident. For women in this category aged 50 and over the ratio is 740 per 100 women.

In the least important class numerically, women separated or divorced, the ratio changes in the same way as for married and unmarried women but is lower in all cases than for widows. For the whole group, after 50 years of age, it attains 657 per 100 women.

The changes in this ratio in the case of unmarried women could not easily have been estimated. In fact it is nearly 400 per 100 in the group between 30 and 34 years and exceeds 500 per 100 between 40 and 44 to attain the high level of 562 per 100 after the age of 50. The average of five to six children for each unmarried woman having borne children is proof of the fact that a great many of these women live, or have lived in free union for long periods. These unions, which are much more frequent in Brazil than in most Western European countries or in North America, but less frequent than in some other countries of South America,[1] include several different types of extra-marital association.

The most stable type is perhaps that consecrated from a religious point of view but not in law. However, the most prevalent form met with is the union which is intended as permanent by the two parties, or which becomes so in time, but which remains without legal sanction through inertia[2] or because of material, economic or judicial obstacles such as distance, previous marriage, cost etc.

In spite of the frequency of free unions the predominant factor in the field of reproduction remains the marriage institution. Only 673,102 or 9.28 per cent of the 7,255,207 women aged 12 or over, who said they had borne live children at the time of the 1940 census, were unmarried. Only 6.86 per cent of the 39,554,541 children borne to these same women, or 2,712,918 children, were declared by unmarried women. However, it is necessary to take account of two factors when evaluating these figures.

In the first place, it may be assumed that a number of women who were living, or who had lived, in free union, stated that they were married or widowed in order to conceal this fact. This was made possible because census officials were not authorized to request proof of marriage. Secondly, some women who had been married or who were widows, at the time of the census, had given birth to children outside of marriage.

The importance of extra-marital relations is thus greater than the figures would suggest, but even if it is estimated at 10 per cent the overall importance is slight. The marriage institution is a powerful influence which tends to limit reproduction in Brazil and is more important than any other factor.

The influence of marriage varies considerably, however, in different parts of the country. In the State of Maranhão, 69 per cent of unmarried women aged 30 and over had given birth to live children. In the State of São Paulo the percentage is 14 per cent or only one-fifth of this. Between these two extremes a wide variety of percentages is found.

The analysis in this instance follows the same plan as that adopted earlier. Three sets of figures relating to the different categories of marital status of women aged 12 and over[3] in the various regions of Brazil will be examined, as follows: average number of live births per 100 women (Table 120); percentage of women having given birth to live children (Table 121); average number of live births per 100 women having borne children (Table 122).

[1] See the details on 'Consensually married' women in UN, I, pp. 172–87.
[2] In some cases this is a remnant of the slave period when many unions among slaves were permanent although without legal or religious sanction.
[3] Twelve years was the age limit chosen for the Brazilian publications on fecundity (see BIGS 12). The results would not differ greatly if 15 years was adopted, except in the case of unmarried women.

TABLE 120. Average Number of Live Births per 100 Women Aged 12 and Over in the Natural and Political Regions of Brazil, Grouped According to Marital Status

Political and natural region	Un-married	Married	Separated and divorced	Widows	Total[1]
Acre	57.3	508.4	471.8	709.5	359.3
Amazonas	91.0	443.7	378.0	585.0	276.4
Pará	119.6	410.9	377.1	574.2	265.6
North	*109.8*	*427.2*	*384.8*	*583.6*	*272.9*
Maranhão	130.8	418.1	378.2	578.3	287.7
Piauí	44.1	456.4	330.5	605.7	296.8
Ceará	15.5	529.1	464.6	666.4	309.2
Rio Grande do Norte	29.4	571.1	541.4	706.5	340.1
Paraíba	24.4	575.5	483.0	704.0	335.5
Pernambuco	46.8	528.1	434.7	640.8	308.6
Alagoas	55.7	501.8	382.4	615.1	310.2
North-east	*48.0*	*517.9*	*441.2*	*645.0*	*311.7*
Sergipe	83.3	537.2	487.6	648.7	318.9
Bahia	88.2	497.7	461.0	638.1	289.4
Minas Gerais	13.8	481.3	417.2	622.1	303.3
Espírito Santo	30.7	503.8	463.7	681.2	314.8
Rio de Janeiro	81.5	467.6	417.1	626.2	300.5
Distrito Federal	37.4	301.1	271.7	464.7	208.9
East[2]	*51.3*	*464.2*	*367.6*	*601.8*	*288.4*
São Paulo	9.2	438.1	350.9	609.3	292.2
Paraná	21.6	449.2	395.9	613.4	300.6
Santa Catarina	24.1	470.7	461.2	645.6	301.7
Rio Grande do Sul	45.3	436.8	388.6	588.4	272.4
South	*22.3*	*441.7*	*375.6*	*607.0*	*288.6*
Mato Grosso	91.2	414.7	422.5	559.9	256.4
Goiás	49.8	435.3	385.4	596.0	287.4
West-central	*65.4*	*429.2*	*403.6*	*586.6*	*277.2*
Brazil[2]	*45.3*	*467.1*	*387.9*	*612.6*	*293.3*

[1] The total includes women whose marital status is unknown.
[2] 'East' and 'Brazil' include the region of the Serra dos Aimores.

453

TABLE 121. Percentage of Women Over 12 Years Who Have Borne Live Children in the Natural and Political Regions of Brazil.

Political and natural regions	Un-married	married	Separated and divorced	Widows	Total [1]
Acre	12.7	88.0	85.9	91.7	59.9
Amazonas	23.6	87.7	82.7	91.1	55.0
Pará	30.6	86.1	80.7	91.8	55.8
North	*28.2*	*86.7*	*81.8*	*91.6*	*55.8*
Maranhão	32.2	84.4	81.3	91.2	58.7
Piauí	11.9	86.0	81.6	92.4	55.3
Ceará	4.0	88.4	87.8	92.7	50.8
Rio Grande do Norte	7.3	88.0	86.9	92.0	52.3
Paraíba	5.9	88.6	86.6	92.0	51.3
Pernambuco	11.3	86.6	85.9	90.6	50.9
Alagoas	13.7	86.2	84.3	90.9	53.7
North-east	*11.9*	*87.1*	*85.8*	*91.5*	*52.6*
Sergipe	19.5	85.6	84.2	89.1	52.7
Bahia	20.4	86.8	85.7	90.7	51.5
Minas Gerais	4.1	87.8	85.8	92.2	53.8
Espírito Santo	7.9	90.4	87.7	94.5	55.0
Rio de Janeiro	17.8	88.5	85.9	92.6	55.2
Distrito Federal	11.3	80.1	77.6	86.1	51.0
East [2]	*12.4*	*86.8*	*82.5*	*90.8*	*53.1*
São Paulo	2.5	87.4	81.0	91.8	55.9
Paraná	6.0	88.4	86.2	93.3	57.7
Santa Catarina	6.7	90.0	89.5	94.5	56.4
Rio Grande do Sul	11.3	87.4	84.1	91.0	53.3
South	*5.8*	*87.7*	*83.2*	*91.9*	*55.4*
Mato Grosso	23.3	85.0	85.8	89.8	53.1
Goías	13.6	85.5	83.7	92.2	55.4
West central	*17.2*	*85.4*	*84.7*	*91.6*	*54.6*
Brazil [2]	*11.2*	*87.1*	*83.5*	*91.4*	*53.8*

[1] The total includes women whose marital status is unknown.
[2] 'East' and 'Brazil' include the region of the Serra dos Aimores.

TABLE 122. Average Number of Live Births per 100 Fecund Women Aged 12 and Over in the Natural and Political Regions of Brazil.

Political and natural regions	Un-married	Married	Separated or divorced	Widows	Total[1]
Acre	450.7	577.8	549.3	773.8	599.5
Amazonas	385.5	505.9	456.9	642.2	502.1
Pará	390.2	477.2	467.4	625.5	476.0
North	390.0	492.7	470.6	637.2	489.4
Maranhão	406.4	495.2	465.0	634.2	490.1
Piauí	369.3	530.9	405.3	655.8	537.1
Ceará	384.8	598.5	529.0	719.0	609.0
Rio Grande do Norte	404.0	649.0	622.8	767.6	650.8
Paraíba	412.4	649.4	557.7	765.3	654.0
Pernambuco	414.8	610.0	505.9	707.7	606.0
Alagoas	406.2	582.1	453.6	676.4	578.1
North-east	404.8	594.9	514.4	704.8	592.5
Sergipe	427.7	627.4	579.2	727.7	605.2
Bahia	432.7	573.2	538.2	703.8	562.5
Minas Gerais	338.7	548.1	486.4	674.6	563.3
Espírito Santo	389.9	557.1	528.7	720.9	572.3
Rio de Janeiro	458.5	528.3	485.4	676.6	544.0
Distrito Federal	332.3	375.9	350.0	539.9	409.6
East[2]	413.3	535.0	445.7	662.5	543.6
São Paulo	366.8	501.3	433.0	663.8	522.6
Paraná	362.8	508.2	459.0	657.7	521.2
Santa Catarina	360.0	522.8	515.5	683.0	534.9
Rio Grande do Sul	400.7	499.7	461.9	646.7	511.1
South	385.3	503.5	451.7	660.4	520.7
Mato Grosso	391.0	488.0	492.2	623.4	483.3
Goiás	367.2	509.1	460.7	646.7	518.6
West-central	379.3	502.9	476.4	640.8	507.3
Brazil[2]	403.1	536.1	464.6	670.6	545.0

[1] The total includes women whose marital status is unknown.
[2] 'East' and 'Brazil' include the region of the Serra dos Aimores.

The number of live births per 100 married women aged 12 and over is very high in all states, varying between 411 in Pará and 575 in Paraíba. In the Federal District it is much lower, only 301 per 100. The regional differences are considerable, from a minimum of 427 in the north to a maximum of 518 in the north-east.

The corresponding figure for women separated or divorced is generally lower and varies from 331 per 100 and 541 per 100 in Piauí and Rio Grande do Norte respectively to 272 per 100 in the Federal District. In the natural regions the lowest figure is found in the east (368) and the highest in the north-east (441).

In the case of widows, where the younger age groups are less important, the ratio is much higher than for married women. The minimum in the Mato Grosso (560) is only a little below the maximum, for married women, and the maximum, in the Rio Grande do Norte (706) is exceptionnally high. In the Federal District the figure is 465 per 100 widows. The regional distribution corresponds roughly with that for married women. The minimum is in the north (584) and the maximum (645) in the north-east.

The most considerable regional differences are found in the case of unmarried women. The maximum for the states is found in Maranhão (130.8 per 100) and the minimum in São Paulo (9.2 per 100). The ratios are above 80 per 100 in Pará, Mato Grosso, Amazonas, Bahia, Sergipe, and Rio de Janeiro. Lower figures are found in Ceará and Minas Gerais which are both below 20 per 100.

Table 123 indicates that all the states with high fertility rates for unmarried women correspond to states with a high non-white population.

TABLE 123.

State	Average number of live births per 100 women unmarried aged 12 and over (1940)	Percentage of non-white population (1940)
Maranhão	130.8	53.2
Pará	119.6	55.4
Mato Grosso	91.2	49.2
Amazonas	91.0	69.0
Bahia	88.2	71.3
Sergipe	83.3	53.3
Rio de Janeiro	81.5	40.1

It may be assumed that the high level of fertility among unmarried women in the first and last three of the states shown in this table is due, in part, to the traditions of the slave period. In the three remaining states the influence of the aboriginals is probably the reason for this phenomenon.

Nevertheless, in Ceará, despite a high proportion of non-white women

(47.3 per cent) the fecundity of unmarried women is relatively low and the same remark applies to Minas Gerais. In São Paulo, on the contrary, the fecundity of unmarried women is at a minimum and the percentage of non-whites low (15.1 per cent).

In the three states with the lowest percentages of non-whites (Santa Catarina 56 per cent, Rio Grande do Sul, 11.3 per cent, Paraná, 13.4 per cent) fecundity is not high among unmarried women. These southern states of Brazil have received many German and Austrian immigrants from regions where illegitimate births were not infrequent, whereas the Italian immigrants in São Paulo come from regions where illegitimacy was lower.

The figures in Table 120 indicate the wide differences to be found in the level of the cumulative fertility rate in different parts of the country, but the division into natural regions does bring out certain regularities. In the north and mid-west, where many inhabitants are of native origin, fertility rates are high. They are also high in the east and north-east, with a high proportion of negroes and half-castes. The lowest rates are to be found in the south among the populations of European origin.

Among women who were or had been married, geographical differences in the cumulative fertility rates depend rather upon differences in fecundity than upon the percentage of fecund women. This latter percentage does not show large variations in the different states, only the Federal District having a percentage considerably below the national average. The same is true for the natural regions, where the percentages vary only from 85.4 per cent in the mid-west to 87.7 per cent in the south for married women.

The cumulative reproduction rates for these groups, however, vary considerably. In the states, the ratio of live births per 100 fecund women aged 12 and over varies between 477 (Pará) and 649 (Paraíba and Rio Grande do Norte) for married women, between 623 (Mato Grosso) and 768 (Rio Grande do Sul) for widows, and between 405 (Piauı) and 623 (Rio Grande do Norte) for women separated or divorced. In the Federal District the ratios are lower for each category.

The differences may be due, to some extent, to differences in the age structure of each category. The details of the age structure for the two extremes mentioned above, Paraíba and Pará, are given in Table 124. It will be seen that the percentages of women in each age group are lower in Paraíba up to 40 years of age and higher from 40 onwards.

However, even if this factor is eliminated, the reproduction rates in Pará are still below those for Paraíba. It is not easy to account for this but, given the high absolute level in Pará, which only appears low when compared with the very high rate found in Paraíba, it is perhaps this latter rate which merits attention.

It is only possible to advance a series of hypotheses to explain the differences in the fecundity of married women in the states. Family limitation is an element which is appreciable only among certain groups in urban

TABLE 124.

Age	Percentage of different social groups of fecund married women in each age group		Number of live births for 100 fecund women	
	Paraíba	Pará	Paraíba	Pará
12–14	0.02	0.03	139.3	144.4
15–19	2.96	3.64	164.9	149.7
20–29	32.90	34.87	363.8	293.2
30–39	29.10	31.58	694.5	518.4
40–49	20.27	18.19	909.4	659.4
50–59	9.64	8.33	943.1	723.5
60–69	3.68	2.64	927.4	762.2
70–79	1.19	0.59	926.2	751.3
80+	0.24	0.13	925.6	723.3
12+	100.00	100.00	649.4	477.2

centres, particularly in São Paulo and Rio Grande do Sul. The average age at which women marry is also a contributory factor.

The influence on the reproduction rate of work undertaken by women outside their homes cannot be great, as only a small proportion of married women (15–20 per cent) take such work, for the most part in agriculture.

The special influences which exist in the Federal District form the subject matter of a later section.

If the territorial variations in fecundity among unmarried women are compared with those among married women, it is found that the major influence is the percentage of fecund women rather than differences in the reproduction rate. The latter varies only between 339 (Minas Gerais) and 459 (Rio de Janeiro) per 100 in the case of unmarried women, whereas the percentage of fecund women varies from 2.5 per cent in São Paulo to 32.2 per cent in Maranhão. The high general level of the reproduction rate in this category seems to confirm what was said earlier regarding the relative stability of free unions. However, there are very great regional variations in the percentages of unmarried women who have borne children, due to differences in attitudes towards extra-marital relations in different parts of the country. Table 125 illustrates this for the States of Maranhão and São Paulo.

The difference between the average percentages of unmarried mothers in the two states is also verified for each individual age group. As regards the geographical distribution of unmarried mothers, the figures vary from 28.2 per cent in the north to 5.8 per cent in the south. The influence of aboriginal and slave customs only partly explains these disparities.

The fact that procreation outside of marriage is to a considerable extent the result of unions which become quasi-permanent in fact, if not always

TABLE 125.

Age	Percentage of unmarried women having borne children in each age group		Number of fecund unmarried women as a percentage of total number of unmarried women	
	Maranhão	São Paulo	Maranhão	São Paulo
12–14	0.05	0.07	0.08	0.01
15–19	3.62	5.18	4.72	0.34
20–29	30.40	40.04	40.04	4.57
30–39	27.86	28.39	67.52	13.25
40–49	18.38	15.33	72.16	16.39
50–59	9.92	6.31	70.13	14.13
60–69	5.69	2.78	70.33	12.52
70–79	2.58	1.23	69.20	14.06
80+	1.52	0.67	67.78	17.19
12+	100.00	100.00	32.19	2.51

in intention, reinforces the opinion expressed earlier regarding the influence of marriage on the birth rate. From a sociological point of view many free unions may be considered as substitutes for marriage. This is confirmed by the fact that the percentage of unmarried women, who have not given birth to children, is roughly the same in Pará and São Paulo despite the fact that, in the former, the percentage of unmarried mothers is much higher than in the latter.

Even in the parts of Brazil where free unions are widespread the latter

TABLE 126.

State	Number of unmarried women as a percentage of married mothers [1]	Number of children born to unmarried mothers as a percentage of the number born to married mothers
Pará	30.61	25.10
Maranhão	27.65	22.92
Mato Grosso	23.03	18.62
Amazonas	22.08	16.95
Bahia	21.31	16.39
Santa Catarina	4.84	3.26
Paraná	3.89	2.71
Ceará	3.59	2.26
Minas Gerais	3.12	1.87
São Paulo	1.68	1.18

[1] Women stated to be married.

are only of secondary importance for the birth rate as a whole. This fact is illustrated in Table 126 which shows the number of unmarried women as a percentage of married mothers and the number of children born to unmarried mothers as a percentage of the number born to married mothers. In the country as a whole, 9.28 per cent of mothers were stated to be unmarried.

Despite the difficulty of obtaining accurate information on this subject, it may be concluded that the contribution of unmarried mothers to the birth rate is of secondary importance even in those regions where it is most frequent.

CHAPTER VI

Fecundity in Relation
to the Initial Childbearing Age

The criteria adopted in the Brazilian enquiry into fertility in 1940 were not the same in all respect as those adopted in other countries. Because of the existence of free-unions in many parts of the country it was decided to include all women, whether married or not. For the same reason, women who had given birth to children were asked the date of birth of their first child instead of the date of their marriage.

The results obtained regarding the age of women at the time of the birth of their first child and their ages in 1940 have been published in a series of special studies.[1] The average number of live births up to the age $x + n$ years by women who gave birth to their first child at the age of x years has also been calculated. Some of the results of this work are given in Table 127.

TABLE 127.

Years since birth of first child (n)	Average number of live births up to age ($x+n$) years per 100 women whose first child was borne at:				
	14 years	18 years	22.5 years	27 years	32 years
0	100	100	100	100	100
5	272	308	309	282	242
10	423	484	479	427	359
15	554	627	608	535	452
20	666	739	698	606	520
25	757	819	747	640	
30	828	866	758		
35	879	881			

Women who bore their first child before the age of 20, and who lived through the entire reproduction period, gave birth to an average of between eight and nine children. The average is still seven and eight for

[1] See BIGS 11.

461

women whose first child was borne between 20 and 25 years. The average falls rapidly beyond the age of 35, but from 30 to 35 years is still five children.

Mothers whose first child was borne when they were very young are able to contribute to procreation during a longer period than women who bear their first child later in life. The enquiry showed that they also contribute with a greater intensity. For example, women whose first child was borne at the age of 18 give birth to more children on an average, in the same period of years after the birth of the first child, than women who gave birth to their first child at 32 (527 per 100 women compared with 352 per 100, in 15 years).

The age 22.5 years in the above table is of particular interest as it is approximately the average age at which mothers give birth to their first child in Brazil.[1] The average of seven to eight live births for each mother whose first child was borne at that age, and who lives through the entire reproduction period, is very close to the averages in Table 99 for women aged 50 and over.

It has also been possible to calculate the age distribution, according to the age at which the first child was borne, of a generation of mothers, assuming mortality and the frequency of the first birth at different ages to be those found for Brazil.

In Table 128 the results are given for the calculation based on the age of mothers when their first child was borne.[2]

TABLE 128.

Age	Number of women of one generation whose first child was borne at the ages indicated	
	Absolute figures	Percentages
12–14	430	1.52
15–19	10 182	35.89
20–24	11 435	40.31
25–29	4 197	14.79
30–34	1 392	4.91
35–39	541	1.91
40–44	149	0.53
45+	40	0.14
Total	28 366	100.00

[1] This average has been calculated by two methods which give 22.8 and 22.3 years respectively (see BIGS 10, p. 48 and BIGS 11, p. 25).

[2] See BIGS 11, p. 25. Another method, whose results correspond approximately with those given in the table, is based on the number of women in each age group who said they had not borne live children.

It should be borne in mind that the 28,366 mothers are a fraction (58,4 per cent) of the 48,544 girls among the original 100,000 new-born babies. A number of the 48,544 babies[1] die before reaching the age of 14 and the number is thus reduced to 35,640 or 73.4 per cent at that age. This percentage is low due to the high death-rate as may be seen when it is compared with the same age group in the United States where 94.1 per cent of girl babies reach the age of 14.

Table 128 shows that, of these 35,640 girls aged 14, 28,366 or 85 per cent will give birth to live children. Among the remaining 7,274 women, 3,138 reach the age of 50, of whom the majority could have borne children if they had married.

Among the 28,366 women who become mothers, 10,612 or 21.8 per cent of the 48,544 girl babies, gave birth to their first child before the age of 20. Thus only 22 per cent approximately, of the total number of girls in a generation are able to bear children throughout the entire reproduction period. In fact, this figure is considerably reduced by mortality among wives and husbands.[2]

The 17,754 women (36.6 per cent of the 48,544 female births) whose first child is borne after the twentieth birthday contribute to a lesser extent to the procreation of the next generation.

Eighteen thousand four hundred and three of the 28,366 women reach the age of 50 and one-third of these survivors are widows.

[1] See BIGS 10, p. 49.
[2] It has been calculated that, if all the 28,366 women lived to the end of the reproduction period, they would give birth to 217,000 children compared with the calculated number of 195,500 when mortality is taken into account.

CHAPTER VII

The Influence of an Urban
or Rural Environment on the Birth Rate

The percentage of the Brazilian population living in urban conditions is quite small. In 1940, 21.5 per cent of the population were living in towns of over 5,000 inhabitants. In 1950, the percentage had increased to 27.2 per cent. Only in the States of Rio de Janeiro and São Paulo does the percentage of the urban population exceed 40 per cent and in 14 states it is less than 20 per cent. As a result the rural birth rate is predominant in most parts of the country. However, the situation in the urban districts is sufficiently distinct to merit special consideration.

TABLE 129. Total Population, Percentages Living in Urban, Suburban and Rural Areas and Percentages in Towns with 5,000 Inhabitants and Over, in 14 States.

State	Population on 1/7/50	Percentages			Percentages in towns with 5,000 inhabitants and over
		Urban	Suburban	Rural	
Rio Grande do Sul	4 164 821	24.39	9.75	65.86	26.36
Pernambuco	3 395 185	14.70	19.68	65.62	26.82
Ceará	2 695 450	11.79	13.42	74.79	14.65
Rio de Janeiro	2 297 194	40.53	6.98	52.49	40.31
Paraíba	1 713 259	18.34	8.32	73.34	16.69
Maranhão	1 583 248	10.47	6.85	82.68	9.06
Goiás	1 214 921	14.88	5.34	79.78	8.02
Pará	1 123 273	16.58	18.05	65.37	24.69
Alagoas	1 093 137	13.66	12.54	73.80	16.23
Piauí	1 045 696	8.03	8.28	83.69	9.49
Rio Grande do Norte	967 921	17.72	8.50	73.78	16.20
Espírito Santo	861 562	15.80	6.83	77.37	13.25
Sergipe	644 361	21.36	10.45	68.19	18.43
Mato Grosso	522 044	23.37	10.69	65.94	19.52
The 14 states as a whole	23 322 072	18.92	11.16	69.92	21.03

In the last census figures the sex and age distribution of the population was determined separately for each of the three types of administrative area; urban, suburban and rural. This distinction is not the same as would be applied in a demographic study of urban and rural conditions but although some villages were classed as towns for census purposes, the results may be used as a guide to the distribution of the population between town and country. The available results for the states from the 1950 census are given in Table 129 above. The figures for the total population indicate the weight given to each state in the national average. For the 14 states the percentage of the urban population is 18.9 per cent, that for suburban dwellers 11.2 per cent and the remaining 69.9 per cent of the population live in the country.

A more satisfactory guide to the percentage of the urban population is given in the last column of Table 129 which shows the percentage of the population living in towns with more than 5,000 inhabitants. For the 14 states in Table 129 the percentage is 21 per cent.

The information on the age and sex distribution of the population may be used to calculate the ratio between the number of children under 10 and the number of women between 15 and 49 years. This ratio, with the reserves mentioned earlier, may be taken as an index of female fecundity. Table 130 gives the results of this calculation for 14 states.

TABLE 130. Ratio Between the Number of Children Under 10 and Women Between 15 and 49 According to States and Administrative Areas.

State	Urban	Suburban	Rural
Rio Grande do Sul	74.43	109.95	143.41
Pernambuco	80.12	95.58	139.88
Ceará	95.30	108.19	153.37
Rio de Janeiro	93.75	123.96	145.75
Paraíba	90.23	108.08	143.33
Maranhão	86.07	104.78	132.93
Goiás	100.86	117.33	144.52
Pará	85.05	108.30	144.30
Alagoas	84.56	94.76	147.47
Piauí	87.59	112.67	149.64
Rio Grande do Norte	91.84	113.26	146.27
Espírito Santo	90.86	115.80	147.40
Sergipe	87.18	111.23	147.53
Nato Grosso	103.36	141.02	159.78
The 14 states as a whole	86.43	106.36	144.76

For the 14 states the ratio is only 86.4 per 100 women in urban areas, but this increases to 106.4 per 100 in suburban, and to 144.8 per 100 in rural areas. The variations in the ratio for urban and suburban areas are considerable between the different states. In rural areas, on the contrary, the differences are slight, the ratio being everywhere very high.

However, the birth rate is not the only factor which influences the level of this ratio. Child mortality, among others, must also be taken into account. It would be incorrect, for example, to conclude from Table 130 that the rural birth rate is about the same in Pernambuco and Rio Grande do Sul. In fact, infant mortality is high in the former and low in the latter. As a result, the birth rate is probably higher in Pernambuco than in Rio Grande do Sul.

A feature of Tables 129 and 130 is the lower ratio in urban compared with suburban areas, and in suburban compared with rural areas. The ratio for urban areas is from 30–48 per cent below that for rural districts in the 14 states for which details are available, and the maximum for urban areas is still below the minimum for the rural population.

The ratio between the number of children under 10 per 100 women aged 15–49 tends to vary inversely to the child mortality rate.[1] In some

TABLE 131.

State	Percentage of unmarried women between 20 and 29 (in 1940)
São Paulo:	
Capital (São Paulo)	41.42
Rest of state	27.10
Minas Gerais:	
Capital (Belo Horizonte)	51.63
Rest of state	32.76
Bahia:	
Capital (Salvador)	73.20
Rest of state	49.76
Rio Grande do Sul:	
Capital (Porto Alegre)	44.16
Rest of state	41.49
Pernambuco:	
Capital (Recife)	54.56
Rest of state	44.11
Pará:	
Capital (Belém)	58.52
Rest of state	52.83

[1] For a detailed exposition of these factors, see BIGS 16, pp. 107–9.

urban areas in Brazil the child mortality rate is higher than in the country. Nevertheless, this explanation of the low ratio of children to women between 15 and 49 in urban districts is only valid in a few states.

Migratory movements also exercise their influence on these ratios. As a result, women of childbearing age leave the countryside and swell the numbers in this category in urban districts. In large towns, in particular, considerable numbers of young unmarried women come from the country to take up domestic work for a few years before returning to the country. The importance of this factor is difficult to measure statistically as the figures in Table 131, which indicate a higher percentage of young unmarried women between 20 and 29 in large towns than in the rest of the state, may also be influenced by the later age at which women marry in large towns. However, the general nature of these considerations must be completed by a more detailed study of the populations of two large towns, Rio de Janeiro and São Paulo. This subject is dealt with in the following chapter.

The preceding tables also indicate that variations are not infrequent between the ratios found in urban and suburban areas. As regards the latter, this is due mainly to differences in the populations considered. In Pernambuco, where the ratio between the number of children under 10 and women between 15 and 49 is low, more than half the suburban population is concentrated around the centre of a single large town, Recife. The same is true for Alagoas where more than half the suburban population is concentrated in the suburbs of the State capital, Maceio. In the Mato Grosso, on the other hand, there are practically no large towns. The majority of the population classified as suburban is, in fact, rural, and this explains the high fertility ratio in this category. In the State of Rio de Janeiro the population classified as suburban is also mainly rural. However, the general conclusion of this analysis is that the social factors unfavourable to a high birth rate are particularly strong in large towns.

CHAPTER VIII

The Birth Rate in the Large Towns

In some large towns omissions in the registration of births are rare, and in others it has been possible to estimate the extent of omissions from the results of the census. The birth rate in seven large towns in Brazil has been calculated from the 1940 census and the figures are given in Table 132.

TABLE 132.

Town	Population 1940		Birth rate per 1,000 inhabitants (average 1938–40)
	Total [1]	Town [1]	
Rio de Janeiro	1 764 141	1 700 000	24.21 [2]
São Paulo	1 326 261	1 258 482	26.30
Recife	348 424	323 177	34.67
Salvador	290 443	290 443	31.38
Pôrto Alegre	272 232	259 246	26.85
Belo Horizonte	211 377	177 004	32.80
Belém	206 331	164 673	32.39

[1] The figures are for the population of the administrative district in which the town is situated. The urban and suburban population is given in the second column of the table.
[2] Average 1939–40.

When compared with the average birth rate of 42 to 33 for 1,000 inhabitants for the whole of the country, the rates in the above table are low. When compared with large towns in Western Europe and North America, however, they are high. The lowest rates are found in São Paulo and Rio de Janeiro whose demographic importance is much greater than the other five towns. The birth rate appears to have increased slightly in these two, as in other large towns in recent years, but is still far below the national average.

A rise in the birth rate was observed in many countries after the war, due in most cases to the fall which had taken place during the war. This explanation cannot be applied to Brazil, but a possible influence has been the movement of the population from rural districts to the large towns between 1941–50.

However, the most noticeable feature of the demographic situation in the large towns is the low level of the birth rate. According to the above table the birth rate in Rio de Janeiro (24.21) and São Paulo (26.30) in 1940 was from 39 to 44 per cent below the national average (43.00). The ratio between the number of children under 10 and women between 15 and 49 was 71.5 per 100 in São Paulo or 41–43 per cent below the national average (121.3).

An analysis of the causes of this phenomenon forms the subject matter of the following paragraphs.

In Table 133 cumulative age-specific fertility rates for Rio de Janeiro (Federal District) and São Paulo *(Municipe)* are compared with the corresponding rates for the whole country.[1]

TABLE 133. Percentage of Fecund Women Aged 15 and Over According to Age.

Age	Federal District	São Paulo	Brazil
15–19	9.1	6.0	12.2
20–24	67.2	56.3	103.0
25–29	146.8	136.6	245.3
30–34	221.0	219.7	385.1
35–39	286.3	305.2	508.8
40–44	338.4	388.3	587.2
45–49	384.8	466.1	638.7
50–59	412.3	535.2	640.2
60–69	462.6	596.9	647.6
70–79	476.9	590.3	642.0
80+	490.6	569.2	623.9
15+	224.3	245.1	330.4

In both Rio de Janeiro and São Paulo the fertility rates are below the national average by 32 per cent and 26 per cent respectively. The variations in the fertility rate according to age may be compared with the national average in Table 136 below, where it is expressed as a percentage of the national average.

The lowest percentages occur between the ages of 30 and 44 in Rio de Janeiro and 20 and 34 in São Paulo. In the later age groups the difference between these rates and the national average is reduced to 32 per cent in Rio de Janeiro and 12 per cent in São Paulo.

[1] See BIGS 17, p. 55.

The considerable difference between the cumulative fertility rates in the later age groups is probably due to the different rates of growth of the two towns. In 1940 the population of Rio de Janeiro was 155 per cent over that in 1900, and in São Paulo 453 per cent. Consequently, a larger percentage of the population of São Paulo had spent most of the reproduction period in a rural environment which was more favourable to a high birth rate. This phenomenon is less marked in the case of Rio de Janeiro but, nevertheless, in 1950, only 28 per cent of women over 50 were born in the Federal District.

Table 134 shows the influence on fertility of the number of fecund women as a percentage of the adult female population.

In most age groups, except the highest, in São Paulo the percentages are lower than the corresponding national averages.

TABLE 134.   Percentage of Fecund Women Aged 15 and Over According to Age.

Age	Federal District	São Paulo	Brazil
15–19	6.6	4.3	8.7
20–24	36.2	33.5	46.3
25–29	57.9	59.9	70.3
30–34	67.6	72.0	79.0
35–39	71.8	77.8	83.2
40–44	73.5	80.7	83.9
45–49	75.0	83.3	85.1
50–59	75.7	85.4	84.2
60–69	77.1	88.3	84.1
70–79	77.1	89.1	83.6
80+	75.1	87.9	81.9
15+	55.5	58.1	60.8

The percentages are only 9 per cent below the national average in Rio de Janeiro and 4 per cent below in São Paulo. However, the percentages are lowest in the younger age groups which contribute most to the number of births. In the group from 20–24 years, for example, the percentages are 36.2 per cent and 33.5 per cent in Rio de Janeiro and São Paulo respectively, compared with 46.3 per cent for the whole country.

In the later age groups the percentage of fecund women in Rio de Janeiro is still below the average, but in São Paulo, it is noticeably above, due to the presence of immigrants from rural areas.

Table 135 gives the comparative figures for the reproduction rate in the two cities and the national average.

TABLE 135. Average Number of Live Births per 100 Fecund Women According to Age.

Age	Federal District	São Paulo	Brazil
15–19	138.5	137.4	140.6
20–24	185.5	167.8	222.7
25–29	253.5	227.9	349.1
30–34	326.9	305.1	487.3
35–39	398.6	392.3	611.5
40–44	460.4	480.9	700.3
45–49	512.9	559.3	750.2
50–59	544.5	627.0	760.2
60–69	599.8	676.1	770.4
70–79	618.2	662.6	768.2
80+	653.0	647.9	761.9
15+	403.8	421.8	543.4

The rate is lower than the national average for all age groups in both towns by 22–26 per cent. The reproduction rates for the 15–19 age group, generally the poorer classes, are roughly the same as for the country as a whole. In the later groups the rates fall considerably below the national average, particularly between 25 and 49 years. Among older people the difference is less marked, owing to migration from the country and the more recent spread of family limitation.

The low rates in Rio de Janeiro and São Paulo can be partly explained by the later age at which women marry and bear children. It may be estimated that one-third of the difference between the rates in these towns and the national average is due to this. For the rest, the most important influence is, no doubt, the spread of family limitation practices.

The ratios in Tables 133, 134 and 135 are summarized in index form in Table 136. According to these figures, the lower fecundity of women in the two largest towns in Brazil is due, in the first place, to the low reproduction rate and, secondly, to the low percentage of fecund women.

In the 15–24 age group it is the second of these factors which is the most important. This is the result of the larger number of unmarried women and the later age at which women marry. The latter circumstance tends to lower the reproduction rate in the later age groups. In Rio de Janeiro, the low percentage of fecund women considerably reduces the cumulative fertility rate even beyond 24 years. In São Paulo, on the contrary, the percentage is above the national average from 24 onwards.[1]

The effect of family limitation methods is seen most clearly in the low level of the cumulative reproduction rate between 30 and 49. It is much less marked in the older groups.

[1] This is due to the low percentage of unmarried women in São Paulo compared with Rio de Janeiro. See BIGS 17, p. 62.

TABLE 136. Indices of Cumulative Fertility Rates, Percentage of Mothers and Cumulative Reproduction Rates According to Age (National Average: 100).

Age	Federal District			São Paulo		
	Fertility rate	Percentage of mothers	Reproduction	Fertility rate	Percentage of mothers	Reproduction
15–19	75	76	99	49	49	98
20–24	65	78	83	55	72	75
25–29	60	82	73	56	85	65
30–34	57	86	67	57	91	63
35–39	56	86	65	60	93	64
40–44	58	88	66	66	96	69
45–49	60	88	68	73	98	75
50–59	64	90	72	84	101	82
60–69	71	92	78	92	105	88
70–79	74	92	80	92	107	86
80+	79	92	86	91	107	85
15+	68	91	74	74	96	78

The later age at which women marry in these towns is seen in Table 137 derived from the declarations made by women in 1940 of their age when their first child was borne.

TABLE 137. Comparison of the Distribution of Women Aged 50 to 59 According to the Age at Which They Gave Birth to Their First Child.

Age when first child borne	Percentage of women aged 50–59	
	Federal District	Brazil
12–14	1.77	1.89
15–19	26.85	31.43
20–24	36.26	38.58
25–29	19.48	16.96
30–34	9.57	7.31
35–39	4.56	2.86
40–44	1.28	0.80
45+	0.23	0.17
12+	100.00	100.00

It will be observed that the percentage of women from 50 to 59 in 1940 who were aged less than 20 when their first child was borne was 28.6 per cent in Rio de Janeiro (Federal District) compared with 33.3 per cent for the whole country. The percentage aged 30 and over when their first child was borne was 15.6 per cent in Rio de Janeiro and 11.1 per cent in Brazil.

The average age of the mother at the birth of her first child was 23.9 for Rio de Janeiro, a year later than the average for the country as a whole. The later age at which women marry in the capital of Brazil is thus established.

The results of the 1940 census also make it possible to compare the distribution of the number of women who have borne children according to the number of children, in the Federal District (Rio de Janeiro) and Brazil as a whole.

This comparison is made in Table 138 where a series of age groups have been chosen to illustrate the comparative situation in the two groups at successive ages during the reproduction period.

TABLE 138. Distribution of the Number of Mothers in Different Age Groups According to the Number of Children.

Number of live births	Percentage of mothers having borne (x) live children at age of:									
	18–22		28–32		38–42		48+		13+	
	F.D.	Br.	F.D.	Br.	F.D.	Br.	F.D.	Br.	F.D.	Br.
1	58.73	47.79	28.09	12.29	18.41	7.41	12.49	6.55	24.03	14.58
2	28.49	31.08	25.74	14.65	18.36	8.15	13.04	6.83	20.25	13.73
3	9.05	13.87	16.76	15.02	14.92	8.41	11.90	7.01	14.15	11.76
4	2.47	4.95	11.70	15.35	12.18	9.04	10.94	7.73	10.55	10.41
5	0.75	1.53	7.68	13.95	9.60	9.36	9.62	8.03	7.90	9.06
6	0.23	0.49	4.92	11.31	7.58	9.78	8.61	8.45	6.15	8.09
7	0.18	0.18	2.60	7.60	5.41	9.37	7.10	7.80	4.47	6.72
8	0.08	0.07	1.31	4.70	4.44	9.46	6.44	8.78	3.57	6.17
9	0.01	0.03	0.66	2.50	3.14	7.96	5.20	7.78	2.65	4.91
10	0.01	0.01	0.29	1.38	2.36	7.11	4.42	8.05	2.09	4.39
11	—	—	0.11	0.63	1.43	4.74	3.01	5.94	1.34	3.01
12	—	—	0.06	0.33	0.92	3.68	2.69	5.80	1.10	2.61
13	—	—	0.03	0.15	0.52	2.10	1.54	3.53	0.62	1.55
14	—	—	0.02	0.07	0.35	1.41	1.18	2.78	0.46	1.14
15	—	—	0.02	0.03	0.18	0.88	0.66	1.87	0.25	0.74
16	—	—	0.00	0.02	0.09	0.51	0.45	1.21	0.17	0.46
17	—	—	0.00	0.01	0.04	0.26	0.20	0.62	0.07	0.24
18	—	—	0.01	0.01	0.03	0.17	0.19	0.52	0.07	0.19
19	—	—	—	0.00	0.02	0.09	0.09	0.26	0.03	0.09
20	—	—	—	0.00	0.01	0.06	0.08	0.21	0.03	0.07
21	—	—	—	—	0.01	0.03	0.05	0.09	0.02	0.03
22	—	—	—	—	0.00	0.01	0.03	0.06	0.01	0.02
23	—	—	—	—	0.00	0.01	0.02	0.03	0.01	0.01
24	—	—	—	—	0.00	0.00	0.03	0.03	0.01	0.01
25+	—	—	—	—	—	0.00	0.02	0.04	0.00	0.01
1+	100.00	100.00	100.00	100.00	100.00	100.00	100.00	100.00	100.00	100.00

In the 33–37 group,[1] 59.7 per cent had from one to three children, 33.1 per cent from four to seven and 7.2 per cent eight and over. The national percentages were 28.9 per cent, 45.1 per cent and 26 per cent.

In each of these groups, the number of children is lower in Rio de Janeiro than in Brazil as a whole. The lower average number of children born to mothers in the age group 28–42 would suggest the fairly widespread use of family limitation techniques.

Fertility tables have been calculated for Rio de Janeiro according to two hypotheses. The first assumes that the mortality rate is that actually found in the city, the second uses the mortality rate for the country as a

TABLE 139. Fertility Table for Female Population of the Federal District and Brazil.

Number of live births (x)	Number of women in a generation who have borne live children			
	Numbers		Percentage	
	Federal District	Brazil	Federal District	Brazil
1	4 061	2 431	16.33	8.57
2	3 893	2 482	15.66	8.75
3	3 200	2 445	12.87	8.62
4	2 726	2 443	10.96	8.61
5	2 272	2 433	9.14	8.58
6	1 942	2 387	7.81	8.42
7	1 538	2 308	6.18	8.14
8	1 343	2 209	5.40	7.79
9	1 058	2 043	4.26	7.20
10	881	1 827	3.54	6.44
11	589	1 553	2.37	5.47
12	513	1 234	2.06	4.35
13	293	876	1.18	3.09
14	221	617	0.89	2.18
15	124	412	0.50	1.45
16	82	255	0.33	0.90
17	37	153	0.15	0.54
18	35	98	0.14	0.35
19	17	60	0.06	0.21
20	15	39	0.06	0.14
21	9	23	0.04	0.08
22	5	15	0.02	0.05
23	3	9	0.01	0.03
24	5	6	0.02	0.02
25+	4	8	0.02	0.02
1+	24 866	28 366	100.00	100.00

[1] See BIGS 4, 178.

whole.[1] The second method has been used in the construction of Table 139 above.

Because of the lower percentage of women who have children in Rio de Janeiro (51.2 per cent compared with the national average 58.4 per cent) only 24,866 of the 48,544 girl babies of the first generation give birth to live children as against 28,366 in the country as a whole.

In Rio de Janeiro 65.0 per cent of mothers have from one to five children, compared with 43.1 per cent in Brazil as a whole, whereas the percentage

TABLE 140.   Female Fecundity According to Marital Status in the Federal District and Brazil (1940).

Age	Unmarried		Married		Widowed	
	F.D.	Brazil	F.D.	Brazil	F.D.	Brazil
Average number of live births per 100 women						
15–19	2	2	77	75	172	131
20–24	19	23	134	179	170	192
25–29	53	79	201	317	230	292
30–34	91	140	269	460	295	393
35–39	124	204	335	592	354	489
40–44	135	225	394	685	407	563
45–49	140	241	437	739	457	620
50–59	123	224	471	749	497	652
60+	99	219	517	761	549	694
Percentage of fecund women						
15–19	1.6	1.4	54.2	52.0	73.6	65.5
20–24	10.1	10.9	71.6	79.1	76.6	81.7
25–29	20.3	25.8	79.3	88.7	81.5	87.3
30–34	27.2	35.2	82.2	91.5	84.4	89.6
35–39	32.3	42.8	83.3	92.5	85.3	91.6
40–44	31.4	43.1	83.8	92.3	85.4	92.0
45–49	30.5	43.4	84.0	92.6	86.6	92.7
50–59	26.6	40.1	83.5	91.7	87.0	92.1
60+	20.2	38.7	84.4	91.2	86.8	91.4
Average number of live births per 100 fecund women						
15–19	145	147	142	144	234	200
20–24	190	216	188	226	221	235
25–29	262	308	254	357	283	335
30–34	334	398	328	503	350	438
35–39	384	476	402	639	415	534
40–44	431	523	471	742	477	612
45–49	460	554	520	798	527	669
50–59	463	559	564	817	571	708
60+	491	567	613	835	632	760

[1] See BIGS 16, pp. 25–31.

with six to ten children is 27.2 per cent in Rio de Janeiro compared with the national average of 38.0 per cent. The percentage of mothers with more than 10 children is even lower compared with the percentage for the country as a whole.

The lower birth rate in large towns is summarized in the statement, derived from Table 139, that the total·number of live births per generation of girls is 120,385 in Rio de Janeiro and 191,304 in the whole country. This difference indicates a deficiency of 37 per cent [1] in fecundity in the capital, or approximately the same percentage as in first paragraph of this chapter.

The fecundity of the female population of Rio de Janeiro has also been studied in relation to marital status. [2]

The results obtained from the 1940 census are given in Table 140. As regards married women, the average number of live births per 100 women is below the national average except in the youngest age group. This is partly due to the lower percentage of mothers among married women in Rio de Janeiro. In the age groups above 30 the percentage is about 83.5 per cent compared with 92 per cent for the country as a whole. The main reasons for this, illnesses apart, are the later age at which women marry and family limitation.

Social factors are particularly important in an analysis of the low reproduction rate among women in Rio de Janeiro. The rate is 17 per cent below the national average in the 20 to 24 age group, 29 per cent below from 25 to 29, 35 per cent below from 30 to 34 and 41 per cent below from 35 to 39. The rate is still 27 per cent below in the case of women aged 60 and over. The rate is particularly low in the middle age groups where family limitation is most widespread.

In the case of widows the percentage of mothers is generally lower than the national average, as is the number of live births per 100 widows, though the difference is less marked.

Fertility rates are low in most age groups among unmarried women. Free unions are less frequent and birth control methods are more widely used. However, the fairly high reproduction rate in this group indicates that in Rio de Janeiro, as in the rest of the country, many free unions are of a permanent character. This conclusion seems justified despite the possibility that the fathers of these children are not the same in each case.

The preceding paragraphs have confirmed that the birth rate in large towns in Brazil is lower than elsewhere in the country, even though the rate is high when compared with Western Europe and North America.

Fertility among women is reduced by the combined action of a high percentage of unmarried women, the later age at which women marry and, in general, the later age of mothers when their first child is borne. The influence of family restriction is more limited in its action on the birth rate.

[1] The corresponding values of the 'net reproduction rate' are 1.20 (Rio de Janeiro) and 1.91 (Brazil).
[2] See BIGS 12, Section V.

476

The lower reproduction rate among mothers is also a factor which reduces the number of births and, in this respect, the later age at which women marry and the spread of family limitation are particularly important.

It has not been possible to establish fertility rates in the different sectors of large towns in Brazil due to omissions in the registration of births. However, the 1940 census provides some information on this subject for the administrative districts of Rio de Janeiro. These results of the 1940 census are given in Table 141 below.

TABLE 141. Federal District 1940. Fertility Among Women by Administrative Areas.[1]

District	Women aged 12+		Number of live births	Average number of live births per 100 women	Percentage of mothers	Average number of live births per 100 mothers
	Total	Number having given birth to live children				
I II[2] III	62 811	32 083	106 282	169	51.1	331
IV	140 042	60 996	198 180	142	43.6	325
V	113 086	52 176	187 876	166	46.1	360
VI	85 348	43 815	167 691	196	51.3	383
VII	211 039	119 797	500 356	237	56.8	418
VIII	51 496	29 232	136 213	265	56.8	466
Islands	7 067	3 994	16 903	239	56.5	423
Total	670 889	342 093	1 313 501	196	51.0	384

[1] Figures taken from BIGS 3, Regional Series, Part XVI.
[2] II includes the islands but these have been shown separately.

The numbers of the administrative districts correspond roughly to the distance from the centre of the town. Numbers I to III include the city and the business and administrative centres (9 square kilometers). The IVth district (61 sq.km.) is mainly residential, in the Vth (71 sq.km.) and the VIth (29 sq.km.) are the middle and working class areas. The VIIth district is much larger (388 sq.km.) and contains the working class quarters as well as some suburban and rural areas. The VIIIth is entirely suburban and rural. The population of the islands in the Bay of Guanabara (35 sq.km.) is mainly working class. It should be borne in mind that there is no clear cut division in Rio de Janeiro between poor and wealthy districts. Even in the rich cosmopolitan quarters in the IVth district very poor inhabitants are to be found.

However, if it can be assumed that the wealthy classes comprise the majority of the population of the IVth district, and that the VIIth is mainly the poorer quarter, it is found that the percentage of fecund women in the wealthy district (43.6 per cent) is considerably below that found in the poorer (56.8 per cent). The reproduction rate is also lower in the first group (325 compared with 418). This phenomenon is due to the causes already mentioned, although the figures may not provide a correct basis for comparison due to the presence of numerous unmarried domestic servants in the wealthy district. However, this factor may not be important as the reproduction rate is also lower among men.

In the Vth district, poorer than the IVth, the percentage of fecund women is 46.1 per cent and the reproduction rate 360. These rates are higher again in the VIth and VIIth districts. Fertility in the first three districts is low, due mainly to the low reproduction rate. They may be considered as mainly wealthy districts. On the islands the rates are comparable with those found in the VIIth, working class district.

The results of this section regarding fertility in the various districts of Rio de Janeiro are confirmed by the study of fertility among men, which forms the subject matter of the next section.

CHAPTER IX

Male Fertility in Relation to Economic Activity and Professional Status

In a country like Brazil, where the majority of women do not work outside their homes,[1] it is not possible to distinguish between the various social classes from the replies given to interviewers at the time of the census. Only the husband's occupation makes it possible to determine the social class to which each woman belongs. Consequently, the analysis of fertility in the various social groups has been based upon the replies of men regarding the size of their families and their social status.

The results presented in this section have been taken from the work of the Brazilian Institute of Geography and Statistics[2] based on the results of the 1940 census. The same criteria as for women were applied in the determination of the various rates and these are given in the tables below. In Table 142 the male population between 20 and 79[3] is grouped according to the branch of economic activity. In Tables 143, 144 and 145 the fertility rates, percentage of fathers[4] and reproduction rates respectively are given for the male population according to age.

The list of occupations in Table 142 brings out the larger number of men employed in agriculture and similar activities (62.44 per cent of the total). The percentage in industry is fairly small (9.58 per cent in transformation industries, 2.9 per cent in extractive industries). It does not exceed 12 per cent even if certain groups included under services are added to the total. Commercial occupations of all kinds employ 6.65 per cent, transport and communications 4.41 per cent and social services 4.07 per cent. The percentages employed in the other occupations listed in Table 142 are also very small. This characteristic of the occupational distribution of the male population in Brazil must be borne in mind when drawing conclusions from the rates in Tables 142, 143 and 144 regarding male fertility in the various occupational groups. The age distribution in the different groups is also a factor which influences the different measures of fertility among males.

---

[1] This is the result of the high level of fertility among Brazilian women.
[2] See BIGS 13, Section V and BIGS 17, Section I.
[3] Men aged less than 20 and 80 and over have been omitted due to their small numerical importance and the difficulty of classification according to professions.
[4] 'Fathers' include all men who stated that they were fathers of live children.

TABLE 142. Brazil 1940. Fertility Among Males According to Occupation.

Occupation	Number of men aged 20–79	Average number of live births per 100 men aged 20–79	Percentage of males aged 20–79, fathers of live children	Average number of live births per 100 fathers
Agriculture	5 939 984	390	67.26	579
Extraction industries	275 963	262	55.52	471
Transformation industries	911 566	264	59.10	447
Commerce	588 645	267	59.65	447
Real estate, finance, etc.	43 558	192	53.24	360
Transport and communications	419 589	268	63.19	424
Administration, justice, teaching	215 292	296	64.23	461
National defence and police	149 912	146	43.35	337
Liberal professions	73 844	196	50.52	389
Social services	386 757	243	55.79	436
Domestic activities and students	110 739	155	32.98	470
Not employed	396 519	300	49.86	601
Total	9 512 368	340	63.26	538

TABLE 143. Brazil 1940. Average Number of Live Births per 100 Men Aged 20–79 According to Occupation.

Occupation	Age					
	20–29	30–39	40–49	50–59	60–69	70–79
Agriculture	83	366	623	749	789	821
Extractive industries	65	262	444	554	594	622
Transformation industries	60	259	455	565	635	672
Commerce	54	241	417	521	596	636
Real Estate, finance, etc.	34	173	306	424	540	601
Transport and communications	76	268	435	528	580	651
Administration, justice, teaching	58	239	426	545	630	667
National defence and police	39	219	362	471	543	571
Liberal professions	33	151	295	381	416	459
Social services	55	230	401	500	562	610
Domestic activities and students	27	207	366	443	501	551
Not employed	27	157	319	458	568	646
Total	72	316	547	668	720	748

TABLE 144. Brazil 1940. Percentage of Males, Fathers of Live Children, According to Age and Occupation.

Occupation	Age					
	20–29	30–39	40–49	50–59	60–69	70–79
Agriculture	36.40	79.56	87.66	89.26	89.71	89.80
Extractive industries	29.51	65.77	76.58	81.29	80.81	81.24
Transformation industries	29.86	71.46	81.75	84.92	85.96	85.89
Commerce	26.89	68.89	79.85	82.09	83.63	84.30
Real estate, finance, etc.	20.82	64.42	75.96	80.00	81.10	83.03
Transport and communications	36.27	73.12	81.00	82.49	82.80	83.59
Administration, justice, teaching	29.65	70.18	81.95	84.49	85.82	87.11
National defence and police	20.70	69.63	78.96	82.13	82.79	79.28
Liberal professions	20.12	55.51	69.43	70.91	65.80	65.36
Social services	27.16	65.57	76.55	79.42	81.52	80.39
Domestic activities and students	11.69	53.48	66.31	70.65	72.34	76.28
Not employed	12.53	42.68	59.43	71.67	79.34	82.95
Total	32.63	74.72	84.08	86.25	86.96	86.98

TABLE 145. Brazil 1940. Average Number of Live Births per 100 Fathers Aged 20–79 According to Occupation and Age Group.

Occupation	Age					
	20–29	30–39	40–49	50–59	60–69	70–79
Agriculture	229	460	711	839	879	914
Extractive industries	221	399	580	682	736	765
Transformation industries	202	362	556	666	739	783
Commerce	200	349	522	635	713	755
Real estate, finance, etc.	162	269	403	531	665	724
Transport and communications	211	366	537	640	700	779
Administration, justice, teaching	196	340	520	646	734	766
National defence and police	187	315	459	573	656	720
Liberal professions	166	272	425	538	632	702
Social services	202	350	523	630	689	758
Domestic activities and students	233	388	551	628	692	723
Not employed	214	368	536	638	716	778
Total	221	423	651	775	828	860

481

It is for this reason that the figures have been grouped according to 10-year age groups.

The male fertility rate for men aged between 20 and 79 is 340 per 100 males.[1] Only in agriculture is the rate higher than the average (390), either because of the high percentage of fathers of live children in this group (67.3 per cent compared with the average 63.3 per cent)[1] or because of the high reproduction rate among males in agriculture (579 per 100 compared with the average of 538).[1]

The high level of male fertility in agriculture is seen when the rates in that branch of activity are compared with industrial and commercial occupations. The influence of the age structure on these rates may be eliminated by a classification according to 10-year age groups. The figures for the two occupational groups, industry and commerce, are then expressed as indices with the corresponding rates in agriculture as a base. The low relative level in the first two groups is then seen to diminish in the later age groups. This is due to the later age at which men marry in industrial and commercial occupations compared with agriculture,[2] and, also, to the fact that, among older men, the differences between occupations are less marked.

In all age groups the percentage of fathers is lower in industry and commerce than in agriculture. Table 146 compares the various indices for each 10-year age group in these three occupations.

If the reproduction rate is considered the same situation is found. The average agricultural family is much larger in all age groups.

TABLE 146.

Age	Percentage of fathers of live children in:			Indices (per cent in agriculture: 100)	
	agriculture	industry	commerce	industry	commerce
20–29	83	60	54	72	65
30–39	366	259	241	71	66
40–49	623	455	417	73	67
50–59	749	565	521	75	70
60–69	789	635	596	80	76
70–79	821	672	636	82	77

[1] These figures do not differ greatly from those obtained earlier for women. See Table 99.
[2] Fertility is generally higher in the years immediately after marriage. This tends to swell the number of births in later groups when the age at which men marry is itself later. However, the effect on the cumulative rates is generally slight.

TABLE 147.

Age	Average number of live births per 100 fathers in:			Indices (agriculture): 100	
	agriculture	industry	commerce		
20–29	36.4	29.9	26.9	82	74
30–39	79.6	71.5	68.9	90	87
40–49	87.7	81.8	79.9	93	91
50–59	89.3	84.9	82.1	95	92
60–69	89.7	86.0	83.6	96	93
70–79	89.8	85.9	84.3	96	94

The reproduction rates in industry and commerce are 88 per cent and 87 per cent respectively of the comparable rate in agriculture for men aged 20 to 29. The percentages fall to 79 per cent and 76 per cent respectively in the following age group 30–39. The fairly high level in the younger groups is due to the fact that a large proportion among the poorer classes between those ages tend to marry at an early age.

The results of this comparison between industry and commerce on the one hand, and agriculture on the other, confirm the conclusions of the previous sections regarding the higher level of the birth rate in the country-side. The rates found among men in other urban manual occupational groups follow the same general pattern as for the two major categories.

The method of occupational classification adopted by the 1940 census does not permit the separation of non-manual and manual workers in each occupational group. However, if the workers in the liberal professions and commercial activities, other than distribution, may be taken as representative of the non-manual workers, it is found that the measures of fertility are considerably lower than in the groups where manual workers are in a majority. In the liberal professions and commercial activities of a financial character the percentages of men, fathers of live children, are only 50.5 per cent and 53.2 per cent respectively. The reproduction rates are also low, 389 and 360 per 100. The low percentage of fathers in the lower professional age groups is no doubt explained by the longer period of training necessary. In the later age groups the number of clergy included in this category reduces the percentages. These percentages are higher in the case of commercial activities. The rates found in administrative occupations merit special mention, as the indices of fertility are roughly the same as in other urban occupations of a manual character. It should be recalled that the standard of life of many employees in this group is low and that their duties are often of a very humble nature.

In the private sector of the economy it has been possible to distinguish the employers, employees (manual and non-manual), artisans and other

TABLE 148. Brazil 1940. Fertility Among Males Employed in Agriculture and Transformation Industries According to Professional Status and Age Group.

Age	Agriculture and associated activities				Transformation industries			
	Employers	Employees	Independent workers	Family workers	Employers	Employees	Independent workers	Family workers
Average number of live births per 100 men								
20–29	156	85	121	6	91	57	90	7
30–39	424	349	391	62	258	248	309	79
40–49	688	584	648	138	419	440	512	156
50–59	824	692	776	299	541	545	625	161
60–69	896	715	817	561	673	606	682	579
70–79	923	731	851	684	740	621	722	538
Percentage of fathers								
20–29	62.84	37.44	52.32	3.31	45.79	28.63	40.55	4.09
30–39	86.37	77.31	84.10	18.45	78.04	70.30	75.75	27.20
40–49	90.79	85.18	89.88	25.64	85.56	80.93	83.72	32.22
50–59	91.66	86.10	91.14	47.89	88.72	84.26	86.13	24.32
60–69	92.60	85.54	91.72	76.12	89.57	85.05	87.14	74.42
70–79	92.26	85.45	91.63	83.45	91.19	83.85	87.67	71.43
Average number of live births per 100 fathers								
20–29	249	227	232	181	199	198	223	168
30–39	491	451	465	337	330	352	408	290
40–49	758	686	722	538	490	543	611	483
50–59	899	804	851	624	609	647	726	663
60–69	968	836	891	737	751	713	783	778
70–79	1 000	855	929	820	812	741	824	753

independent workers, and the members of the families of this last group who, for the most part, do not receive a separate remuneration.

The details for each of these categories have been grouped according to age to avoid difficulties due to the widely different age structures.[1]

A comparison of the various measures of fertility in the major occupational groups is given in Tables 148, 149 and 150.

According to the first section of Table 148, the fertility rate for men in agricultural and related activities [2] is highest, at all ages, among employers,

[1] For example, in agricultural activities the percentage in the age group 20–29 as a percentage of the total in agriculture, are 14 per cent employers, 27 per cent independents, 40 per cent employees and 87 per cent family members.

[2] The absolute figures for each category are as follows: employers 230,267; employees 2,256,849; independents 2,947,151; family members 492,768.

TABLE 149. Brazil 1940. Fertility Among Males Employed in Commerce and Services According to Professional Status and Age Group.

Age	Commerce				Social services			
	Employers	Employees	Independent workers	Family workers	Employers	Employees	Independent workers	Family workers
Average number of live births per 100 men								
20–29	80	36	90	6	83	42	74	7
30–39	237	183	287	73	218	195	264	59
40–49	390	337	464	115	354	352	440	94
50–59	495	435	563	362	431	449	540	407
60–69	589	499	633	548	580	500	596	588
70–79	657	532	664	781	634	526	642	733
Percentage of fathers								
20–29	40.44	19.92	40.61	3.90	41.45	22.19	34.82	4.19
30–39	72.96	61.05	74.43	27.77	70.90	60.48	69.97	21.71
40–49	81.29	74.71	82.31	31.43	78.88	72.93	79.00	27.78
50–59	83.62	77.67	83.74	77.36	82.01	76.01	81.39	70.37
60–69	86.88	78.95	84.78	83.33	84.82	80.32	82.41	70.83
70–79	86.69	79.11	85.45	90.48	86.36	75.50	82.11	83.33
Average number of live births per 100 fathers								
20–29	197	180	221	164	200	189	214	169
30–39	324	299	386	262	308	322	377	274
40–49	480	452	563	367	448	483	557	340
50–59	591	560	673	468	528	590	663	579
60–69	677	632	747	658	683	622	723	829
70–79	758	672	777	863	735	697	781	880

followed by independent workers, and employees. The 'family members' group in agriculture consists mainly of young unmarried men in the lower age groups and fertility rates are consequently low.

The percentage of fathers is also highest among employers in each age group. The percentage of fathers among independent workers is much lower in the younger age groups but the difference is greatly reduced for older men. The percentage of fathers among employees is generally lower than for independent workers.

The last section of Table 148 measures the influence of the reproduction rate on fecundity. Here again the employers group has the highest rates followed by the independents and employees. It is apparent that the later age at which men marry in the independents group, compared with employers, and among employees, compared with both groups, helps reduce the average family size.

TABLE 150. Brazil 1940. Fertility Among Males Employed in Transport and Communications and Extractive Industries According to Professional Status and Age Group.

Age	Transport and communications				Extractive industries			
	Employers	Employees	Independent	Family workers	Employers	Employees	Independent workers	Family workers
Average number of live births per 100 men								
20–29	109	73	102	14	67	57	77	5
30–39	305	261	295	160	257	254	270	36
40–49	452	424	481	476	441	436	449	103
50–59	556	516	577	533	578	566	551	300
60–69	607	564	636	543	689	596	593	436
70–79	660	641	676	—	766	584	627	458
Percentage of fathers								
20–29	49.13	35.05	45.54	6.51	31.21	26.34	34.56	2.64
30–39	78.08	72.29	76.84	43.93	62.55	63.19	67.93	11.54
40–49	86.40	80.33	83.61	57.14	75.75	72.27	78.64	31.58
50–59	86.29	82.01	84.38	88.89	80.68	81.01	81.57	50.00
60–69	84.03	81.79	86.64	71.43	85.40	80.27	80.94	71.79
70–79	80.00	82.16	87.35	—	87.14	77.33	82.07	66.67
Average number of live births per 100 fathers								
20–29	222	208	224	208	216	216	224	185
30–39	391	361	384	364	410	402	397	312
40–49	523	527	576	833	583	603	571	326
50–59	644	629	684	600	717	699	675	600
60–69	722	690	734	760	807	743	733	607
70–79	825	780	774	—	879	755	763	688

Note. The small numbers in these groups do not permit the calculation of percentages.

Index numbers have been calculated for employees in agriculture with reference to the corresponding rates for independent workers. These groups are the two most important numerically: 50 per cent of men between 20 and 79 are independent workers and 38 per cent employees.

In the younger age groups, the level of fertility is lower than for independent workers, due mainly to the lower percentage of fathers among men in these groups which, in turn, is the result of the later age at which employees marry. In the later age groups, the percentage of fathers is still below the percentage for independent workers and the cumulative reproduction rate is lower still, due once again to the age at which men marry in this group.

In conclusion it may be said that the economically independent classes in agricultural occupations are more prolific than the employed workers. The main reasons for this are the later age at which men marry in these

TABLE 151.

Age	Indices of measures of fertility among employees in agriculture (independent workers: 100)		
	Cumulative fertility rate	Percentage of fathers	Cumulative reproduction rate
20–29	70	72	98
30–39	89	92	97
40–49	90	96	95
50–59	89	95	94
60–69	88	93	94
70–79	86	93	92

groups and the later age at which the first child is borne among employed workers.

As regards the transformation industries [1] in Table 148, the situation is a little different.

In each age group the fertility rate is higher among independent workers than among employees, due, either, to the higher percentage of fathers among men in the first group or to a higher reproduction rate which itself depends upon the age at which the first child is born. Among employers, the percentage of fathers is higher in each age group, than in the case of independent workers, yet the reproduction rate is lower between the ages of 30 and 69. This ratio even falls below that for employees in the group 40–59. The explanation appears to be the spread of family limitation among the younger generations of employers as, among older men from 50–79, the reproduction rate is roughly the same as for independent workers.

The lower level of fertility in urban occupations compared with agriculture may also be seen from a comparison of the two groups in Table 148. The corresponding rates in industry compared with agriculture are given in Table 152 in the form of index numbers.

The fertility rate in transformation industries is low compared with agriculture, particularly in the ages from 20 to 29. The difference between the two occupations decreases in the higher age groups due either to movement from the country to industrial employment, or to the absence of family limitation among the older generations. It will be noticed that the fertility rate among employers in industry remains well below the rate for employers in agriculture at all ages. The difference is the least marked in the case of independent workers.

The situation in the other occupational groups given in Tables 149 and 150 may be summarized more rapidly as the major characteristics have already been dealt with.

[1] The absolute figures are: employers 29,015 (3 per cent), employees 715,852 (79 per cent), independent workers 160,784 (18 per cent), family members 4,391 (less than 0.5 per cent).

487

TABLE 152.

Age	Indices of fertility rates among professional groups in industry (agriculture: 100)		
	Employers	Employees	Independent workers
20–29	58	67	74
30–39	61	71	79
40–49	61	75	79
50–59	66	79	81
60–69	75	85	83
70–79	80	85	85

Fertility is, in general, lower among men employed in commerce[1] and services[2] than in the case of industry. The fertility rate for 100 men in commercial occupations is highest for independent workers. Fertility in the employers groups is lower, especially between the ages of 30 and 59. The percentages of fathers among employers and independent workers in this group are roughly equivalent, but the reproduction rate is considerably lower in the case of employers. This is the same situation as was found in the transformation industries and is, no doubt, due to the same causes.

The fertility rates among employees are lower in each case than among employers and independent workers. It should be recalled that most employers and employees in this occupational group live in towns of large size whereas many independent workers are found in villages in semi-rural conditions.

In the transport and communications occupations[3] the fertility rate is generally higher in the younger age groups, compared with industry, due to the influence of rural elements. It is lower in the older groups where urban workers predominate. The cumulative fertility rate for independent workers aged 40 to 79 is higher than for employers, but the difference is slight. The lower level of the reproduction rate for employers between these ages probably indicates the influence of family limitation.

The fertility rates for employees are lower at all ages due to the later age at which men marry and have children in this group.

In the extractive industries (Table 150) the most important groups numerically are the independent workers and employees.[4] There are no

[1] Absolute figures are: employers 51,863 (9 per cent), employees 248,035 (42 per cent), independents 281,982 (48 per cent), family members 5,550 (1 per cent).
[2] Absolute figures are: employers 15,912 (4 per cent), employees 179,731 (47 per cent), independents 187,369 (49 per cent), family members 1,731 (0.4 per cent).
[3] Absolute figures: employers 3,061 (0.7 per cent), employees 343,302 (82 per cent), independents 71,035 (17 per cent), family members 1,343 (0.3 per cent).
[4] Absolute numbers: employers 3,891 (1 per cent), employees 88,767 (32 per cent), independents 175,101 (64 per cent), family members 7,374 (3 per cent).

marked differences in fertility between the two groups. The conditions of work for the independent workers in this industry tend to neutralize the influence of circumstances which, in other groups, increase fertility among independent workers compared with employees. The percentage of fathers is lower among employees between the ages of 20 and 49 but the reproduction rate is higher. The differences in fertility between employers and independent workers are not marked except in the higher age groups.

The analysis of fecundity among males in various economic groups in the same occupation has brought out the relationship between high fertility, on the one hand, and the degree of stability and the standard of life on the other. This result does not correspond with experience in many other countries where family limitation is widely practised by all social groups, particularly among the wealthier classes of the population. However, the situation in Brazil, when considered objectively, might be thought to be more 'normal'; those who can more easily support large families have the most children.

However, even in Brazil, the spread of family limitation among the wealthier urban classes tends to counteract the influence of a high birth rate among the employers and independents, as the results of the enquiry into fertility among males in Rio de Janeiro indicate.[1]

The results of this enquiry are summarized in Table 153 below where they are compared with the average figures for the country as a whole.

TABLE 153. Comparative Fertility Among Males in the Federal District and in Brazil, According to Age.

Age	Average number of live births per 100 males		Percentage of fathers		Average number of live births per 100 males	
	F.D.	Brazil	F.D.	Brazil	F.D.	Brazil
20–29	38	72	20.9	32.6	180	221
30–39	163	316	58.9	74.7	278	423
40–49	281	547	70.4	84.1	399	651
50–59	362	668	74.1	86.3	489	775
60–69	426	720	75.8	87.0	562	828
70–79	481	748	76.9	87.0	626	860
20–79	183	340	50.9	63.3	359	538

The fertility rate per 100 males is much lower for all age groups in the Federal District due to the lower percentage of men who have children and the lower reproduction rate per 100 fathers.

The number of fathers as a percentage of the male population is lower for all groups in Rio de Janeiro, although the difference tends to diminish

See Alceu Carvalho in BIGS 17, Section I.

in the later age groups. The movement towards the cities is an important factor in this respect. The male migrant is much freer to move if he is unmarried.

The reproduction rate in Rio de Janeiro is also consistently below the national average at all ages. The fact that the difference is less in the higher age groups no doubt indicates the absence of birth control among the older immigrants from rural areas.

The previous analysis of fertility in the various occupational groups suggests immediately that one of the reasons for the lower fertility in Rio de Janeiro is the absence of agriculture from the occupational distribution. Nevertheless, it is not possible to determine to what extent the high fertility rates found in agriculture are the result of the profession or the fact that it is an occupation which is exercised in rural areas.

Table 154 compares male fertility in the main occupational groups in Rio de Janeiro and in Brazil.

TABLE 154. Comparative Male Fertility According to Occupation in Rio de Janeiro and Brazil.

Occupation	Average number of live births per 100 males aged 20–79		Percentage of fathers in male population		Average number of children per 100 fathers	
	F.D.	Brazil	F.D.	Brazil	F.D.	Brazil
Agriculture	287	390	57.9	67.3	496	579
Extractive industries	272	262	61.9	55.5	439	471
Transformation industries	190	264	52.8	59.1	361	447
Commerce	156	267	49.6	59.7	315	447
Real estate, finance, etc.	146	192	50.1	53.2	291	360
Transport and communications	200	268	57.1	63.2	349	424
Administration, justice, teaching	220	296	59.7	64.2	368	461
National defence and police	133	146	43.8	43.4	303	337
Liberal professions	150	196	47.5	50.5	317	389
Social services	170	243	49.6	55.8	342	436
Domestic activities and students	91	155	26.2	33.0	346	470
Not employed	226	300	47.5	49.9	476	601
Total	183	340	50.9	63.3	359	538

It will be observed from this table that the fertility rate among males is lower in Rio de Janeiro in all occupational groups except the extractive industries, which are not important in the Federal District. In eight occupational groups the fertility rate is at least 25 per cent below the national average for the group. These results seem to confirm the importance of the influence of an urban or rural environment on the birth rate, irrespective of the occupational group. Also according to Table 154, the low cumulative fertility rate depends upon the lower percentage of men who have children (except in extractive industries and national defence)[1] and upon the low level of the reproduction rate.

It may, therefore, be concluded that the conditions of life in towns (higher degree of celibacy, later age of parents when the first child is born and family limitation) all contribute to lower fertility in all classes of the population.

There remains, however, the question of the age structure in the various occupational groups, which has already been referred to and which may tend to influence the cumulative measures of fertility. In order to eliminate the age factor, men in the major urban occupational groups[2] have been divided according to 10-year age groups. These figures are given in Table 155 and the corresponding indices in Table 156.

TABLE 155. Federal District. Fertility Among Males According to Age and Occupation.

Age	Transformation industries	Commerce	Transport and communications	Services	Liberal professions	Real estate, stock market, etc.	Public administration	National defence
Average number of live births per 100 males								
20–29	46	32	52	38	26	28	48	35
30–39	183	139	176	152	108	129	183	176
40–49	311	241	296	262	214	222	308	289
50–59	395	315	370	339	285	313	387	374
60–69	444	396	421	398	370	415	435	439
70–79	499	414	426	481	393	494	468	397
Percentage of fathers								
20–29	24.5	19.2	28.3	21.8	17.3	18.1	26.4	20.0
30–39	62.0	56.8	61.9	55.6	50.0	58.9	64.9	65.1
40–49	73.6	69.3	72.9	67.7	65.5	70.7	75.0	72.5
50–59	76.4	73.0	75.3	72.5	69.9	75.3	78.3	78.1
60–69	77.9	75.7	74.9	74.1	70.5	75.9	78.3	80.5
70–79	78.7	73.3	75.3	74.9	68.7	78.2	76.8	65.2
Average number of live births per 100 fathers								
20–29	186	164	184	177	151	153	181	175
30–39	295	245	284	274	216	219	282	270
40–49	423	347	405	387	326	314	410	399
50–59	517	431	491	467	407	415	494	479
60–69	570	524	563	538	525	547	556	546
70–79	634	565	566	642	573	632	609	609

[1] This is the result of the age structure in this group.
[2] 83.66 per cent of men between 20 and 79 in the Federal District.

TABLE 156. Federal District. Indices of Fertility Among Males According to Age and Occupation.

Age	Trans-formation indus-tries	Com-merce	Transport and com-muni-cations	Services	Liberal pro-fessions	Real estate, etc.	Public adminis-tration	National defence
Indices of live births per 100 men								
20–29	77	59	68	69	79	82	83	90
30–39	71	58	66	66	72	75	77	80
40–49	68	58	68	65	73	73	72	80
50–59	70	60	70	68	75	74	71	79
60–69	70	66	73	71	89	77	69	81
70–79	74	65	65	79	86	82	70	70
Indices of percentage of fathers								
20–29	82	71	78	80	86	87	89	97
30–39	87	82	85	85	90	91	92	94
40–49	90	87	90	88	94	93	91	92
50–59	90	89	91	91	99	94	93	95
60–69	91	91	90	91	1.07	94	91	97
70–79	92	87	90	93	1.05	94	88	82
Indices of live births per 100 fathers								
20–29	92	82	87	88	91	94	92	94
30–39	81	70	78	78	79	81	83	86
40–49	76	66	75	74	77	78	79	87
50–59	78	68	77	74	76	78	76	84
60–69	77	73	80	78	83	82	76	83
70–79	81	75	73	85	82	87	80	85

The maximum age-specific fertility rates are found in the transformation industries for all age groups, from 30 to 79, as a result of the high reproduction rate in this occupation, although the percentage of men who become fathers is not as high as in other occupations. The high fertility rates in the public administration group are also noteworthy and confirm the conclusion already arrived at as regards this group. In the transport and communications group, where manual workers are in a majority, fertility rates are a little below the two groups mentioned above, except between 20 and 29 where the percentage of men who become fathers is higher than for any other occupation. The higher cumulative fertility rate among men in this occupational group compared with those working in industry, which was found in Table 154, is therefore the result of the more favourable age structure in the former.

In the services group, the fertility rates for each age group are lower than in the occupations mentioned above, the percentage of fathers and the reproduction rate both being lower. Fertility in the national defence group is comparable with that found among manual workers. In the lower age groups the large number of young conscripts tends to reduce the cumulative fertility rate for the group as a whole.

In the liberal professions and commercial activities of a financial character, fertility rates are considerably below those found in the other groups, particularly between the ages of 20 and 49.

When the different measures of fertility in the Federal District are compared with those for the country as a whole it is found that the results correspond with those already established earlier for Brazil.

Agricultural workers are numerically unimportant in the Federal District. The most important occupational groups are the transformation industries, commerce, services and transport and communications.[1] These groups all have a fairly high level of fertility, although considerably below that found in agriculture. It is in the liberal professions and financial activities that the level of fertility is noticeably lower than in the other occupational groups.

In Table 156 the rates in Table 155 are expressed as a percentage of the corresponding averages for the country as a whole. The cumulative fertility rates found in Rio de Janeiro are lower than the national averages. The difference varies from 23 to 32 per cent below in the transformation industries, 30 to 37 per cent below for the transports and communications group and 11 per cent to 28 per cent in the liberal professions. The influence of the factors already discussed which tend to reduce fertility in large towns, is apparent in all classes of the population.

The generally low level of the percentage of men who become fathers is the result of the later age at which men marry and of the higher percentage of unmarried men.

The reproduction rate indices in the third section of Table 156 are low because of the later age at which men marry and the spread of family limitation. The latter factor probably explains the low reproduction rates in the middle, rather than in the younger, age groups. Family limitation is generally adopted later in life, after the birth of the first children.

The major causes of the lower level of the birth rate in urban areas remain the later age at which men marry, partly due to the apprenticeship period necessary in many professions, and the larger proportion of men who do not marry, partly due to the migration of unmarried men to the towns. Family limitation, though by no means a negligible factor, is of secondary importance.[2]

The analysis of fertility among men in the various occupational groups

[1] 63.2 per cent of the male population are employed in these occupations.
[2] It is argued that family limitation is still extremely infrequent in Brazil due to the conflict between such practices and religious beliefs. As regards anti-conceptual methods, this may be so, but the frequency of abortions, particularly in the poorer classes, must also be taken into account.

493

may be completed by a consideration of fertility in the administrative areas of the Federal District.[1]

Table 157 below has been constructed in the same way as Table 154 in the previous section regarding female fertility. The remarks concerning the character of the different districts of the city also apply to Table 157.

TABLE 157. Federal District 1940. Male Fertility According to Administrative Districts.

District	Men aged 20–79		Number of live births	Average number of live births per 100 men	Percentage of fathers	Average number o live births per 100 fathers
	Total	Number of fathers				
I, II, III	89 513	34 651	109 314	122	38.7	315
IV	92 833	42 760	127 726	138	46.1	299
V	73 737	37 945	125 267	170	51.5	330
VI	63 531	33 341	117 282	185	52.5	352
VII	160 392	93 831	370 444	231	58.5	395
VIII	43 719	23 991	107 383	246	54.9	448
F. D.	523 725	266 519	957 416	183	50.9	359

The various measures of fertility increase on passing from the wealthy district (IV) to the middle-class districts (V and VI) and the poor district (VII). This result confirms the conclusion of the previous section regarding female fertility in the various administrative districts of Rio de Janeiro. The indices for men and women are given in Table 158 for two districts representing the extreme limits of wealth and poverty.

TABLE 158. Fertility Indices.

		District IV (wealthy)	District VII (poor)
Live births per 100	women aged 12+	142	237
	men between 20 and 79	138	231
Percentage of parents	women aged 12+	43.6	56.8
	men between 20 and 79	46.1	58.5
Live births per 100 parents	women aged 12+	325	418
	men between 20 and 79	299	395

It must be concluded that the lower level of fertility among the wealthier social groups is due to the higher percentage of unmarried persons, the later age at which people marry, and the lower level of the reproduction

[1] Figures taken from the archives of the National Census Service 1940 and ratios calculated by the BIGS.

494

rate, this latter factor being itself the result of the later age at marriage and family limitation.

The influence of differences in the age structure between the various districts is illustrated in Table 159 where the population in each district is divided into 10-year age groups.

TABLE 159. Federal District 1940. Male Fertility in the Administrative Districts According to Age.

Age	District					
	I, II, III	IV	V	VI	VII	VIII
Average number of live births per 100 men						
20–29	23	27	33	37	52	46
30–39	105	116	143	161	213	250
40–49	190	200	247	282	354	429
50–59	260	279	341	369	434	517
60–69	318	357	424	460	475	558
70–79	350	457	460	510	511	622
Percentage of fathers						
20–29	13.6	16.5	19.5	21.9	27.5	22.9
30–39	43.2	51.8	58.9	60.7	68.4	70.2
40–49	56.3	64.8	71.1	72.9	77.2	81.3
50–59	62.2	70.9	76.2	75.7	78.7	82.1
60–69	64.4	73.6	78.3	78.7	78.8	81.9
70–79	65.1	80.8	76.3	78.9	76.9	84.6
Average number of live births per 100 fathers						
20–29	171	165	167	170	189	199
30–39	243	225	243	265	312	356
40–49	338	308	347	387	459	528
50–59	418	393	448	488	551	630
60–69	494	485	541	585	603	681
70–79	537	566	603	646	665	735

However, the importance of the age structure is slight and does not change the general conclusions derived from Table 157 regarding the higher level of fertility in the poorer districts.

In district VIII, which is suburban and rural in character, all the fertility indices are at a maximum except in the case of the 30–39 age group, where the percentage of fathers is lower than in VII. But this may be due to accidental features such as the presence of military establishments in district VIII. Nevertheless, the indices in the district VIII are still considerably below those for the country as a whole, as is seen from Table 160.

495

TABLE 160.

Age	Average number of live births per 100 men aged 20–79		Percentage of fathers		Average number of live births per 100 fathers aged 20–79	
	F.D. Zone VIII	Brazil	F.D. Zone VIII	Brazil	F.D. Zone VIII	Brazil
20–29	46	72	22.9	32.6	199	221
30–39	250	316	70.2	74.7	356	423
40–49	429	547	81.3	84.1	528	651
50–59	517	668	82.1	86.3	630	775
60–69	558	720	81.9	87.0	681	828
70–79	622	748	84.6	87.0	735	860
20–79	246	340	54.9	63.3	448	538

The inhabitants of district VIII seem to participate more actively in the social and economic activities of the town, although their place of residence is outside the topographical limits of the town proper.

Summary and Conclusions

The analysis in the first section of this study brought out the importance of the high Brazilian birth rate for the growth of the population. The population increased during the 100 years from 1850 to 1950, from 7 to 52 million. Only a small part of this increase of 45 million can be attributed to the influence of immigration. In fact net immigration during the period 1850 to 1950 was only approximately 3.5 million and the increase in the population due to births among immigrants was about the same figure. Consequently, 38 million of the 45 million increase since 1850 was due to the excess of births over deaths, exclusive of immigration.

This very considerable increase was made possible by the high birth rate which today is still between 42 and 44 per 1,000 inhabitants and exceeds the death rate by 24 per 1,000. The high birth rate is a characteristic of the Brazilian population in all the natural and political regions of the country with the exception of the Federal District whose urban population, concentrated in a single large town, is a special case.

A high birth rate is also general among the three main colour groups in the Brazilian population. The fecundity of negro women, however, is slightly lower than for the other groups owing to the smaller percentage of mothers among negroes, the result perhaps of handicaps for the negro woman in marriage. The differences observed in the level of female fecundity in all colour groups in various regions of Brazil are essentially the result of social forces, the influence of physical or biological factors being of secondary importance. The existance of a high positive correlation between fertility in the three main colour groups in all parts of the country leads to the conclusion that the social forces at work in each case tend to act together and with the same intensity in the determination of fertility in the three colour groups.

Female fertility among immigrants tends to retain the pattern of the country of origin. However, the Brazilian environment exercises a strong influence, as can be seen from the higher birth rate found even among first generation immigrants. The general uniformity and high level of the birth rate in regions with extremely mixed populations indicate that national differences are soon absorbed in the general environment of the country.

497

The marriage institution is the most important of the social factors influencing the birth rate. This conclusion is not invalidated by the number of free unions and of illegitimate births found in some regions, particularly where the customs of the slave period have survived. The fact that extra-marital relations are subject to social disapproval means that marriage acts as a restraining factor on the level of female fecundity, either by preventing a number of women from contributing to the growth of the population, or by delaying the age at which the first child is born. The effective child bearing period is thus reduced by approximately eight years.

The average family size is very high in all parts of Brazil, except in the Federal District where it is low compared with the rest of the country. The age-specific reproduction rates do not, as a rule, indicate the wide-spread use of family limitation methods and it may be assumed that these are little used as yet in Brazil. The reproduction rate is also high in the case of free unions, though below the rate for married women. This seems to indicate that many extra-marital associations are of a fairly permanent nature.

The age distribution of mothers when their first child is borne indicates that the average age of the mother is from 22 to 23 years and that only a little over one-third of mothers give birth to their first child before their twentieth birthday. This fact illustrates, once again, the influence of marriage on the birth rate.

The action of social factors which tend to reduce the level of the birth rate is particularly marked in urban, compared with rural, areas. In rural areas it is very high in all states; among the urban population it is con-siderably lower and varies greatly according to the region concerned.

In the case of the capital, Rio de Janeiro, and of São Paulo which have been studied in greater detail as representative of the large towns and also because of the more adequate information available, the birth rate is low compared with the rest of Brazil, but is nevertheless high compared with other large towns in Europe and North America. The statistical information available indicates that the three immediate causes of the low birth rate in large towns are the high percentage of unmarried women, the later age at which the first child is borne, and the lower level of the reproduction rate.

The importance of family limitation techniques cannot be inferred directly from the statistical evidence available. However, the variations in the age-specific reproduction rate and evidence of a qualitative nature lead to the hypothesis that birth control methods are little used as yet even among the wealthier social groups, but that abortion is more widespread, particularly among the poorer classes. Nevertheless, the factors which limit the average size of families are more important in the wealthier groups, as the study of male and female fertility in the different districts of Rio de Janeiro indicates.

The difference between the birth rate in the town and in the country is seen also in the very high level of fertility among men engaged in agriculture and allied pursuits. Male fertility is well below the level found in agriculture in all the urban manual occupations and even lower in the professional groups.

In each occupational group, male fertility varies according to the professional status of the individual. In rural occupations, fertility is highest among the employers and independent workers. Even in urban occupations, the fertility of these two groups is generally higher than among employees. The greater stability and economic well-being of the employer and independent groups compared with employees, facilitate parenthood at a comparatively early age and reduce the economic obstacles which tend to limit the size of families. In many cases a large family is even an asset, from an economic point of view, in these groups. The relatively low level of fertility among persons classified as 'family members' is the result of the generally impermanent character of the group.

The analysis of male fertility in Rio de Janeiro shows that the rates are low when compared with the country as a whole in the different occupational groups, even when the occupation is essentially urban in character. The low birth rate, general among urban populations, is therefore particularly marked in the case of the Brazilian capital.

The conclusions of this study on the Brazilian birth rate are relatively simpler than would be the case in a country where family limitation is widespread. Indeed, recent studies of the influence of social and economic factors on the birth rate tend to concentrate on this aspect of the problem. It is not possible to consider family limitation as an important element in the determination of the level of the birth rate in Brazil. It may only be inferred that these methods have begun to make their influence felt, particularly in a few large cities, the methods used being essentially birth control techniques in the case of wealthier groups and abortion among the poorer classes.

The teachings of the church on this question oppose a very effective barrier against the spread of birth control techniques and reinforce the natural reluctance to adopt artificial methods. However, the various moral, religious and legal obstacles in the way of the adoption of birth control techniques have been powerless to prevent an increase in the number of deliberate abortions.

The strongest factor limiting the birth rate in Brazil remains the institution of marriage. A certain degree of economic independence and security are the indispensable adjuncts of marriage. As a result, a man tends to complete his training, or apprenticeship, and even to work at his profession for some time, before he thinks of marrying. The longer period of training necessary for the intellectual compared with the manual worker, the urban compared with the rural worker, contributes to delay marriage among the more educated and wealthier classes, particularly in the towns.

In a country like Brazil, the problems of food and clothing, which must be resolved by town dwellers, are less important for large groups of the population due to the abundance of uncultivated land in the countryside. There are also profound differences between the psychology of the inhabitants of the towns and those who live in rural areas. In the towns there are many rival claims on the use of income which enter into competition with the desire to have children, claims which are absent in the countryside. In a not inconsiderable number of cases, town life effectively prevents marriage, as the high percentage of unmarried men and women in the towns indicates, though the migration of young unmarried men to the town may increase these percentages unduly.

The later age at which people marry reduces the period during which they can have children and this reflects itself in the smaller average size of families. Even where the obstacles to marriage are avoided by recourse to free unions, the influence on the birth rate must be slight as, in Brazil, the majority of such unions are of a semi-permanent character. Consequently, they present the same material problems as in the case of married couples. In the wealthier and economically independent groups, the economic obstacles are less important and this fact contributes to raise the birth rate above that found among employees. It is not possible, however, to detect any positive correlation between the birth rate and the distribution of incomes and property. Nevertheless, the most striking feature of the birth rate is its high uniform level in all parts of the country which indicates that all such influences are of secondary importance when compared with the general conditions making for a high birth rate in Brazil.

The most notable variations in the level of the birth rate in Brazil concern the differences between town and country and between those engaged in agriculture and other occupations. These differences are not related to income or property variations, but are the result of a series of circumstances which are only partly economic in character. The same reasoning may be applied to the differences in fertility in the different urban social groups. The high level of the Brazilian birth rate cannot be considered the result of economic factors. On the contrary, it is essentially the result of biological influences and demonstrates that the restraining influence exercised by economic and social factors is fairly weak, except in so far as they act through the marriage institution.

The conclusions derived from a study of the birth rate in Brazil could be applied perhaps to other countries whose demographic situation is similar and where birth control methods have not yet become the principal factor acting on the birth rate.

The most unusual feature of the Brazilian demographic situation is perhaps the fact that, despite the close association of Brazil with Western civilization, the predominant influence on the birth rate is biological and social factors only of secondary importance. It is for this reason that the enquiry into fertility in 1940 may be considered of very great demographic importance as the first enquiry of its kind in a country where the birth rate has not yet begun to decline. The principal merit for the realization of that project resides with the members of the National Census Commission and, in particular, with its late chairman, Professor José Carneiro Felippe, thanks to whose tenacity the difficult undertaking was brought to a successful conclusion. May one of his devoted collaborators be allowed to render hommage here to the memory of this eminent scholar and administrator too soon lost to us.

Publications of the Brazilian Institute of Geography and Statistics [BIGS] *of Rio de Janeiro*

1. *Recenseamento geral do Brasil* (1 September 1940). National series 5 volumes; Regional series 32 volumes.
2. *Anuário estatístico do Brasil* (yearly).
3. *Censo demográfico* (1 July 1950). Seleção dos principais dados (A booklet for each unit of the Federation).
4. 'Análises de resultados do censo demográfico.' Studies published by the Technical Section of the National Census Service (1940) between 1943 and 1948. A list of these studies and summaries of the main conclusions may be found in the *Revista Brasileira de Estatística*, no. 38, 1949.
5. *Aplicações do censo demográfico para a reconstrução do movimento da população.* (See notes in 4 above.)
6. *Estudos complementares das análises do censo demográfico.* Studies published by BIGS from 1950 onwards.
7. *Estudos complementares das aplicações do censo demográfico.* (See notes in 6 above.)
8. *Estudos demograficos.* Studies based on the 1950 census and published from 1951 onwards.
9. *Estimativas da taxa de natalidade paro o Brasil, as Unidades da Federação e as principais capitais*, vol. 4 of the series *Estudos de estatística teórica e aplicada; estatistica demográfica.* (Referred to below by the abbreviation E.D.) 1948.
10. *Estudos sôbre a fecundidade e a prolificidade da mulher no Brasil, no conjunto da população e nos diversos grupos de côr.* E.D., vol. 5, 1949.
11. *A prolificidade da mulher segundo a idade inicial da atividade reprodutora no Brasil.* E.D., vol. 6, 1949.
12. *Estudos sôbre a fecundidade da mulher no Brasil, segundo o estado conjugal.* E.D., vol. 9, 1949.
13. *Pesquisas sôbre a natalidade no Brasil.* E.D., vol. 10, 1950.
14. *Estudos sôbre a composição da população do Brasil segundo a côr.* E.D., vol. 11, 1950.

15. *Pesquisas sôbre o desenvolvimento da população do Brasil.* E.D., vol. 13, 1951.
16. *Estudos sôbre a natalidade e a mortalidade no Brasil.* E.D., vol. 14, 1952.
17. *Estudos sôbre a natalidade em algunas grandes cidades do Brasil.* E.D., vol. 15, 1952.

Works by Professor Giorgio Mortara

1. 'Lezioni di Statistica metodologica.' *Giornale degli Economisti.* Rome, 1922.
2. 'Estudos sôbre a utilização do censo demográfico para a reconstrução das estatísticas do movimento da população do Brasil.' A series of eight studies published in the *Revista Brasileira de Estatística*, nos. 1–7 and 9. Rio de Janeiro 1940–42.
3. 'Quelques possibilités de reconstruction du mouvement d'une population à l'aide des recensements démographiques.' *Revue de l'Institut International de Statistique*, nos.1/2, La Haye 1941.
4. 'Sur les méthodes appliquées pour la reconstitution du mouvement de la population du Brésil à l'aide des recensements.' *Bulletin de l'Institut International de Statistique*, vol. XXXII, 2nd section, Berne, 1950.
5. 'Nota sôbre as possibilidades de aproveitamento dos resultados de censo demográfico para a determinação da fecundidade total da mulher brasileira.' *Revista Brasileira de Estatística*, no. 13, Rio de Janeiro, 1943.
6. 'Methods of Using Census Statistics for the Calculation of Life Tables and other Demographic Measures with applications to the Population of Brazil.' United Nations, *Population Studies*, no. 7, New York, 1949.
7. *Contributions of the Brazilian Institute of Geography and Statistics to Population Studies.* Paper read before the 27th Session of the International Statistical Institute. Published by BIGS, Rio de Janeiro, 1951.

Brazilian Demographic Studies

Alceu Carvalho. *A fecundidade masculina no Districto Federal, segundo a idade, a atividade principal e a posição na ocupação.* E.D., 15.
Ernani Timóteo de Barros. 'A prolificidade das mulheres naturais do exterior, conforme o censo demográfico de 1-IX-1940.' *Revista Brasileira de Estatística*, no. 35, Rio de Janeiro, 1948.

United Nations Publications

1. *Demographic Yearbook, 1949–50.* New York, 1950.
2. *Demographic Yearbook, 1951.* New York, 1951.

[1] In view of the specific nature of the subjects treated, citations to parts II–V are limited to names of authors of other studies cited here. For list of subjects treated in Parts II–V see Table of Contents.

506

Indianapolis Study, 36 ff.
Individualism, 201, 213, 227.
Industrialization, 207–8, 212, 217, 230.
Infanticide, *see* Anti-natal practices.
Inheritance, *see* Land.
Institut National d'Etudes Démographiques, 35n.
Institut International de Statistique, 44n.
Instituto Brazileiro de Geografia e Estatistica, 32, 52–3, 237.
Ireland, 166n, 172–5.
Islam, 99, 186–7. *See also* Arabs; Muslims.

Japan
social organization, 153–5, 158, 162–4.
transitions, 231–6.
Jesus, 189–90.
Jews, 184, 186, 189, 192n.

Kalahari Desert, 102.
Kanaka, 135–6.
Kazakhs, 94 ff.
Kentucky highlands, 223.
Kidder, N. R., 137n.
Kimball, S. T., 173n, 176.
Kinship systems, 58 ff.
absence of formal structure, 142.
agnatic, *see* patrilineal.
cognatic, 62 ff., 82, 201.
categories, 68.
dual, 65.
ecology of, 63, 66, 85, 102, 155.
matrilineal, 69 ff., 78, 119.
patrilineal, 64, 81 ff., 98–100, 110, 120, 126, 131.
population size, 95.
relation to family, 59.
religion, influence on, 152.
rope pattern, 112.
transformation in agrarian life, 151 ff.
unilinear, 63 ff., 81, 90–3, 199 ff.
west European, 154–5.
Kiser, C. V., 36 ff., 192.
Kollmorgan, W. M., 184n.
Krader, L., 94 ff., 152n.
Krige, E. J., 88n.
Kroeber, A. L., 81.
Kuczynski, R. R., 26n, 28, 34, 168, 177n, 218n, 267n.

Kulp, D. H., 157n.
Kyei, T. E., 254, 260–1, 262, 263.

Labour migrations, 131, 138, 140, 163.
Lactation, *see* Nursing mother.
Ladkin, 354.
Land holdings in pre-industrial Europe, 158–9, 164 ff.
dispossession in England, 214–15.
modes of inheritance, 165–6, 171–2, 212, 231.
Lang, O., 157 ff.
Laurie, 353.
League of Nations, 137.
Leaky, L., 89.
Leclercq, J., 195n.
Levasseur, E., 213n.
Levirate, 96.
Lewis-Faning, E., 24n, 37 ff., 206n.
Lineage, 64.
Literati, 151.
Loftus, P. J., 33.
Lesu, 110.
Lorimer, F., 25n, 31n, 97–8, 145n, 181n, 228–30, 343, 353.
Lowie, R. H., 63n, 102.
Lozi, 82 ff., 102.

Macomber, D., 23n.
Maine, H., 64n, 96, 155.
Mair, 383.
Malaya, 154n, 178–9.
fertility indices, 25–7.
Malinowsky, B., 80.
Mallet, S., 254, 318, 319.
Malthus, T., 116, 172n, 175.
Mantoux, P., 215n.
Maori, 67–8, 114, 136, 144.
Marginal areas, 92, 101, 199.
Marriage
age and frequency, 26n, 30, 36–7, 43–4, 132, 158, 160, 211, 227–8.
age as related to fertility, 23 ff., 41 ff., 54–6, 77, 89, 171, 174, 233, 238.
as arrangement between kin groups, 82, 159.
economic obstacles, 171.
informal conjugal relations, 194, 237–8, 242.

507